Consumer Credit Law and Practice
– A Guide

Consumer Credit Law and Practice
– A Guide

Fifth Edition

Dennis Rosenthal, of Gray's Inn, Barrister
Henderson Chambers

Contributor
Graham Haxton-Bernard Head of Legal and
Regulatory Affairs, Consumer Credit Trade Association

Bloomsbury Professional

Bloomsbury Professional

An imprint of Bloomsbury Publishing Plc

Bloomsbury Professional Ltd	Bloomsbury Publishing Plc
41–43 Boltro Road	50 Bedford Square
Haywards Heath	London
RH16 1BJ	WC1B 3DP
UK	UK

www.bloomsbury.com
BLOOMSBURY and the Diana logo are trademarks of
Bloomsbury Publishing Plc

While every care has been taken to ensure the accuracy of this work, no responsibility for loss or damage occasioned to any person acting or refraining from action as a result of any statement in it can be accepted by the authors, editors or publishers.

British Library Cataloguing-in-Publication Data

A catalogue record for this book is available from the British Library.

ISBN: HB   978 1 78451 836 3
ePDF 978 1 78451 835 6
ePub 978 1 78451 837 0

Typeset by Phoenix Photosetting, Chatham, Kent
Printed and bound by CPI Group (UK) Ltd, Croydon, CR0 4YY

To find out more about our authors and books, visit www.bloomsburyprofessional.com. Here you will find extracts, author information, details of forthcoming events and the option to sign up for our newsletters.

Foreword

A new edition of Dennis Rosenthal's *Consumer Credit Law and Practice –
A Guide* is always an event to be welcomed by the busy practitioner. Dennis is
widely acknowledged to be one of the country's leading experts on consumer
credit, a field made ever more complex by the promulgations of the Financial
Conduct Authority with its bewildering range of high-level standards, prudential
standards, business standards (COBS, ICOBS, MCOB, BCOBS, etc.), specialist sourcebooks, particularly CONC (Consumer Credit Sourcebook), rules and
guides. The full permissions form runs to 55 pages containing dozens of questions and requiring business plans, staff organisational structures, details of IT
systems, to mention only a few. The process takes six months or longer and
authorisations have to be examined and determined by hundreds of staff at a cost
of tens of millions of pounds to ensure suitability of applications for permissions.
The June 2016 data bulletin shows that 32,733 applications fell to be determined,
out of which a mere 53, or 0.16% of the total, were refused. What a pity that the
FCA chose not to follow the sensible practice of the Office of Fair Trading in
granting licences where nothing adverse was known at the time of application,
thus enabling the vast sums saved to be invested in stronger enforcement. Those
were the days!

In all this welter of regulation, there is a great need for a work which reduces
the mass of case law and regulation covered in encyclopaedic works into a clear,
concise and readable form which steers a way through the labyrinth. This is just
such a book and is one of the many strengths that has been responsible for its
popularity among those who have to deal with the law and practice of consumer
credit. In this new edition, to which Graham Haxton-Bernard, Head of Legal and
Regulatory Affairs at the Consumer Credit Trade Association, has contributed
five useful chapters on the FCA regime, the work is brought fully up to date and
retains all the clarity and conciseness of previous editions. It is to be warmly
welcomed.

Roy Goode
Oxford
5 December 2017

Preface

From the time of the first edition of this book in 1994 until now, consumer credit law has developed beyond all recognition. Originally, consumer credit law was restricted to the Consumer Credit Act 1974 ('CCA 1974') and regulations made under that Act. Compliance was supervised by a relatively benign Office of Fair Trading, whose writ rarely extended beyond warnings in respect of adherence to the law and extensive guidance issued by it. Businesses generally operated within the boundaries of the law and OFT guidance. This contrasts with the current position where the law and practice of consumer credit falls under the pro-active control and supervision of the Financial Conduct Authority, which is tasked with enforcing extensive laws and regulations, as well as rules and guidance made by it. Compliance has become a full-time activity of firms, with the scope of consumer credit regulation extending from CCA 1974 and those regulations under that Act which are still in force, to the Financial Services and Markets Act 2000 ('FSMA'), the Financial Services and Markets Act 2000 (Regulated Activities) Order 2001 ('RAO') and other relevant regulations, together with rules and guidance issued by the FCA in the FCA Handbook.

Recent notable landmarks include: various EU Directives relating to alternative dispute resolution, supervision of credit institutions and consumer credit agreements for residential immovable property; the transfer of licensing from the OFT under CCA 1974 to authorisation and permission by the FCA under FSMA; and substitution of substantial parts of CCA 1974 and regulation under that Act by FSMA, RAO and the FCA Handbook, notably the Consumer Credit sourcebook (CONC) and the Mortgages and Home Finance Conduct of Business sourcebook (MCOB). At the same time, there have been developments in the case law and legislative enactments in ancillary areas such as data protection, anti-money laundering and payment services.

Whilst it is trite to state that law and practice evolve at a fast rate, nowhere is this more evident than in the field of consumer credit. This presents the problem of presenting a crystallised picture as at a particular time, so that it serves both to reflect the current situation and to act as a standard for comparison with a view to the future. It is hoped that, in addition to meeting that objective, the text provides a readable, comprehensive and practical up-to-date guide to the law and practice of consumer credit, consumer hire and ancillary credit businesses.

Readers will be assisted by the inclusion of Chapters 30 to 34 on FCA requirements and procedures relating to authorisation and permission, treating customers fairly, supervision and reporting, and alternative dispute resolution. These have been clearly and thoughtfully contributed by Graham Haxton-Bernard, Head of Legal and Regulatory Affairs at the Consumer Credit Trade Association, whose expertise in consumer credit law and practice extends over many decades.

I wish to thank the publishers, Bloomsbury Professional, and in particular Andy Hill and Peter Smith, for their encouragement and assistance in bringing this edition to fruition.

The law is stated as at 30 November 2017.

Dennis Rosenthal
London
30 November 2017

Contents

Foreword   *v*
Preface   *vii*
Table of statutes   *xix*
Table of statutory instruments   *xxvii*
Table of cases   *xxxiii*

Chapter 1:   Consumer credit law in context   1

1.1   The European Union setting   1
1.2   The Consumer Credit Act 1974   2
1.3   The two consumer credit regimes   3
1.4   Transfer of the consumer credit regime from the OFT to
         the FCA   4
1.5   Consumer credit as a relationship issue   5

**Chapter 2:   The general structure of the regulation of
                 consumer credit agreements and consumer
                 hire agreements**   7

2.1   The starting point: the Mortgage Credit Directive 2014   7
2.2   Unsecured credit agreements: scope of the Consumer
         Credit Directive 2008   10
2.3   Unsecured credit agreements: determining which regulatory
         regime applies   11
2.4   Principal changes effected by the Consumer Credit
         Directive 2008   13
2.5   Residential renovation agreements   14
2.6   Consumer buy-to-let mortgages   14
2.7   Exempt agreements   15

Chapter 3:   Consumer credit and consumer hire   17

3.1   The meaning of 'credit'   17
3.2   The meaning of 'consumer' and 'individual'   21
3.3   The meaning of 'creditor' or 'lender'   23
3.4   The meaning of 'debtor' or 'borrower'   24

3.5	The meaning of 'consumer credit agreement' and 'regulated credit agreement'	25
3.6	The meaning of 'owner' or 'lessor'	25
3.7	The meaning of 'hirer' or 'lessee'	26
3.8	The meaning of 'hire' or 'lease'	26
3.9	The meaning of 'consumer hire agreement'	27
3.10	Credit hire	28
3.11	Capacity of the parties	28

Chapter 4: Types of credit and credit agreements   31

4.1	Consumer credit agreement	31
4.2	Running-account credit and fixed-sum credit	32
4.3	Restricted-use credit and unrestricted-use credit	34
4.4	Debtor-creditor/borrower-lender credit and debtor-creditor-supplier/borrower-lender-supplier credit	37
4.5	Cancellable agreements	40
4.6	Credit-token agreements	42
4.7	Specific consumer credit agreements	43
4.8	Loans secured by land mortgages	57

Chapter 5: Hire agreements   63

5.1	Meaning of a hire agreement	63
5.2	Types of consumer hire agreement	64
5.3	General characteristics of contracts for the hire of goods	66
5.4	Specific consumer hire agreements	69
5.5	Structure of an equipment lease	75

Chapter 6: Exempt agreements   77

6.1	Introduction and distinction between a 'regulated agreement' and an 'exempt agreement'	77
6.2	Exempt credit agreements	77
6.3	Types of exempt credit agreement	78
6.4	Exempt consumer hire agreements	92
6.5	Agreements excluded from certain provisions of CCA 1974, Part V	94
6.6	Partly regulated agreement	98

Chapter 7: Multiple agreements; modifying agreements; novation, variation and assignment of agreements   99

7.1	The multiple agreement	99
7.2	Multiple agreements in practice	103
7.3	Modifying agreement	106
7.4	Modifying agreements in practice	108

7.5	Novation	109
7.6	Variation	110
7.7	Assignment	112

Chapter 8: **The regulated agreement, pre-contract information and disclosure** 115

8.1	Background	115
8.2	Elements of a contract	116
8.3	Form and content of a regulated agreement	117
8.4	The regulated agreement and pre-contract disclosure of information	121
8.5	Pre-contract disclosure and adequate explanations (CONC 4.2)	125
8.6	Signature and copies of the agreement	129
8.7	Statutory information required by the regulations	137
8.8	Contents of the agreement copy	146

Chapter 9: **Contract terms** 147

9.1	Overview	147
9.2	The shape of a regulated agreement	147
9.3	Contract terms	151
9.4	Default	161
9.5	Variation clauses	163
9.6	Set off	165
9.7	Consolidation	165
9.8	'Entire agreement clause'	165
9.9	Assignability	166

Chapter 10: **Duties of creditor or owner and rights of debtor or hirer, prior to and during the lifetime of a regulated agreement** 169

10.1	Pre-contract information under the FCA Consumer Credit sourcebook (CONC)	169
10.2	Creditworthiness assessment	171
10.3	Other relevant disclosure requirements	172
10.4	Entitlement to copies of the agreement and to documents	172
10.5	Right of withdrawal from a consumer credit agreement	174
10.6	Right to cancel a regulated agreement	177
10.7	Right of withdrawal under s 58	178
10.8	Entitlement to information	179
10.9	Early payment by the debtor	180
10.10	Rebate on early settlement	181
10.11	Protected goods	183
10.12	Debtor's right to appropriate payments	185
10.13	Time orders	185
10.14	Prohibition on contracting out	186

Chapter 11:   Post-contract information   187

11.1   Background   187
11.2   Annual statements of account under fixed-sum credit agreements   188
11.3   Statements of account under running-account credit agreements   189
11.4   Notice of sums in arrears   190
11.5   Default notices   192
11.6   Notice of default sums   193
11.7   Notice of interest on judgment debts   195
11.8   Information sheets for arrears and default notices   195
11.9   Provisions applicable to various notices   196
11.10   Provisions applicable to specific agreement types   198
11.11   Post-contractual business practices   199

Chapter 12:   Linked transactions   201

12.1   Meaning of a 'linked transaction'   201
12.2   Duplication of treatment of a 'linked transaction'   202
12.3   Legal aspects of a linked transaction   202
12.4   Exempt linked transactions   203
12.5   Unfair relationships and linked transactions   205
12.6   Distinguishing 'linked transactions' from other connected
            agreements   205

Chapter 13:   Credit brokers   207

13.1   Meaning of 'credit broking'   207
13.2   Meaning of 'effecting an introduction'   209
13.3   Credit broking business   211
13.4   Financial promotions and communications   213
13.5   Credit broking and unfair relationships between creditor
            and debtor   214
13.6   Credit broker as agent   215
13.7   Consequences of carrying on unauthorised credit broking
            business   219
13.8   Credit brokers' charges   220
13.9   Credit broker and fiduciary relationship   221
13.10   Other regulated activities of credit brokers   223
13.11   Disclosure of details of a credit intermediary   224

Chapter 14:   Agency   225

14.1   Agency at common law   225
14.2   Contracts (Rights of Third Parties) Act 1999   226
14.3   Relationship between the dealer or retailer and the finance
            company   226
14.4   Agency under the Consumer Credit Act 1974   227
14.5   Agency under the Financial Services and Markets Act 2000
            ('FSMA')   231

Chapter 15: The supplier and related supplies 233

15.1 The supplier under the Consumer Credit Act 1974 233
15.2 Dealer agreements 234
15.3 Extended warranties 235
15.4 Insurance and the regulated agreement 236
15.5 Payment protection insurance ('PPI') 237
15.6 Card protection cover 238
15.7 Providers of maintenance services 239
15.8 Distance contracts and off-premises contracts 239
15.9 Timeshare agreements 240

Chapter 16: Ancillary credit businesses 243

16.1 Meaning of 'ancillary credit business' 243
16.2 Debt adjusting, debt counselling, debt collecting and debt
administration 243
16.3 Provision of credit information services 248
16.4 Providing credit references 249
16.5 Credit reference agency 249
16.6 Exclusions 254
16.7 Debt management 254
16.8 Ancillary credit business and unfair relationships 255
16.9 Claims management companies 255

Chapter 17: Credit cards and other payment cards 257

17.1 Structure of credit card transactions 257
17.2 Legal characterisation of payment by credit card 260
17.3 Liability for theft, loss or misuse of a credit card 260
17.4 Aspects of the regulatory regime 262
17.5 Types of credit card and credit card user 268
17.6 Other payment cards 270

Chapter 18: Security (including mortgages) 273

18.1 Types of security 273
18.2 Form and content of security documents 273
18.3 Precautions when taking security 287
18.4 Unfair relationships and security 289
18.5 General observations 290

Chapter 19: The total charge for credit and APR 291

19.1 Relevance of the total charge for credit 291
19.2 Evolution of the TCC Regulations 292
19.3 The APR 292
19.4 MCOB: TCC, APR and APRC 301
19.5 Reflections on the TCC and the APR 301

Chapter 20: Advertising and promoting credit and hire facilities and ancillary credit business 303

20.1	Background	303
20.2	The regulatory landscape	304
20.3	Consumer Credit Act 1974	304
20.4	Financial Services and Markets Act 2000	305
20.5	Financial Services and Markets Act 2000 (Financial Promotion) Order 2005 ('Financial Promotion Order')	306
20.6	The FCA Handbook	306
20.7	Breach of financial promotion provisions	313
20.8	Consumer Protection from Unfair Trading Regulations 2008 ('CPRs')	314
20.9	Other statutory controls	317
20.10	Non-statutory controls	318

Chapter 21: Credit marketing and responsible lending 319

21.1	Entitlement to credit	319
21.2	Credit grantors	321
21.3	Responsible lending	323
21.4	Credit scoring	326
21.5	Customer's entitlement to pre-contract information	327
21.6	Conducting business off trade premises	330
21.7	Circulars to minors	330
21.8	Unsolicited credit-tokens	331
21.9	Codes of practice	332
21.10	Distance selling and distance marketing	333
21.11	Plain English	334
21.12	Other statutory controls	334
21.13	The common law	335

Chapter 22: Discrete consumer credit agreements 337

22.1	High-cost short-term credit agreement	337
22.2	P2P agreement	339
22.3	Agreement secured by bill of sale or 'goods mortgage'	341
22.4	Student loans	341
22.5	Overdrafts on current account	342
22.6	Residential renovation agreement	346
22.7	Buy-to-let finance	347

Chapter 23: Electronic communications 349

23.1	Entering into the regulated agreement online	349
23.2	Electronic (EC Directive) Regulations 2002	350
23.3	Distance contract	351
23.4	Post-contract information	351

23.5   Electronic signature   352
23.6   Online services   353
23.7   'Durable medium'   353
23.8   FCA Handbook   354

Chapter 24:   Unfair relationships   355

24.1   The statutory provisions   355
24.2   Interpretation and application of the provisions   356
24.3   The burden of proof   363
24.4   Reflections on the unfair relationships provisions   363

**Chapter 25:   Enforcement, dispute resolution and
                damages claims**   369

25.1   Meaning of 'enforcement'   369
25.2   Enforcing a term of the agreement   371
25.3   Enforcement following default   371
25.4   Termination of agreement in non-default cases   373
25.5   Notice on surety   373
25.6   Recovery of possession of goods or land   373
25.7   Retaking 'protected goods'   374
25.8   Equitable relief   375
25.9   Consequence of failure to comply with the statutory notice
        requirements   375
25.10   Where formal notice is not required   376
25.11   Land mortgages   376
25.12   Judicial control   376
25.13   Enforcement orders in case of infringement   377
25.14   Time orders   377
25.15   Financial relief for hirer   379
25.16   Claims for delivery of goods under a hire-purchase agreement/
        conditional sale agreement   379
25.17   Distress for rent by landlord of debtor or hirer   379
25.18   Additional powers of the court   380
25.19   A note on procedure   381
25.20   Consequences of death of the debtor or hirer   381
25.21   Sureties   381
25.22   Financial Ombudsman Service   382
25.23   Enforcement by the Financial Conduct Authority   384
25.24   Action for damages   385

**Chapter 26:   Fraud, money laundering, criminal offences
                and civil penalties**   387

26.1   Fraud: the extent of the problem   387
26.2   Fraud: the law   387
26.3   Fraud prevention   389

26.4   Money laundering   391
26.5   CCA 1974 and FCA: offences and civil penalties and data
        subject's rights   392

Chapter 27:   Data protection   397

27.1   Background   397
27.2   EU Data Protection Regulation   397
27.3   GDPR: Principal definitions   399
27.4   GDPR: Processing personal data   400
27.5   GDPR: Some innovative provisions   401
27.6   GDPR: Transfer of personal data   401
27.7   Consent clauses   401
27.8   Associated records   402
27.9   Notification/registration   403
27.10   Freedom of Information Act 2000   403
27.11   Other rights of individuals   403
27.12   Codes of practice   404
27.13   Other confidentiality safeguards   405
27.14   The new Data Protection Act   405

Chapter 28:   Funding and outsourcing   407

28.1   Introduction   407
28.2   Methods of financing   407
28.3   Outsourcing   411

Chapter 29:   Miscellaneous accounting and tax aspects   415

29.1   Accounting for leases   415
29.2   Sale and leaseback transactions   417
29.3   Leasing and taxation   417
29.4   Capital allowances   418
29.5   'Funding lease' and 'long funding lease'   419
29.6   Value added tax   419

Chapter 30:   FCA authorisation and permission   423

30.1   Introduction   423
30.2   The 'general prohibition'   425
30.3   Principals and appointed representatives: an alternative to
        authorisation   426
30.4   Applying for permission   428
30.5   Threshold conditions   430
30.6   FCA approach to authorisation   431
30.7   The application procedure   433

Chapter 31:   FCA 'Authorised Persons' regime   437

31.1   Introduction   437
31.2   The statutory framework for approval   438

31.3	Controlled functions	439
31.4	Fitness and propriety of approved persons (FIT)	441
31.5	Statements of Principle and Code of Practice for Approved Persons (APER)	442
31.6	The Senior Managers and Certification Regime (SM&CR)	444

Chapter 32: FCA 'Treating Customers Fairly' regime 447

32.1	Introduction and history	447
32.2	The FCA's approach	448
32.3	Treating customers fairly and today's consumer credit market	449
32.4	Fair treatment of customers	449
32.5	'Culture'	451
32.6	Management information	452
32.7	Conclusion	453

Chapter 33: FCA supervision and regulatory reporting 455

33.1	Introduction	455
33.2	The statutory framework	456
33.3	The Supervision Manual (SUP)	456
33.4	The FCA's approach to supervision (SUP 1A.3.2)	457
33.5	Conduct classification: 'fixed portfolio' and 'flexible portfolio' firms	457
33.6	The FCA's three-pillar supervision model	458
33.7	Tools of supervision	459
33.8	Reports by 'skilled persons'	459
33.9	Consumer credit 'regulatory reporting'	460
33.10	Reporting requirements	461

Chapter 34: Alternative dispute resolution 465

34.1	Introduction and background	465
34.2	The Consumer Credit Act 2006 ('the 2006 Act') and the Financial Ombudsman Service ('FOS')	466
34.3	FCA regulation	467
34.4	The Ombudsman Scheme provided by the Financial Ombudsman Service (FOS)	471

Chapter 35: The European Community perspective 475

35.1	The road to European Community harmonisation	475
35.2	The Mortgages Directive	479
35.3	Credit institutions and the European passport	480
35.4	Authorisation and consumer credit EEA firms	481
35.5	The effect of Brexit	481
35.6	Unfair contract terms	481
35.7	Injunctions Directive	482
35.8	Applicable law and jurisdiction	482

Chapter 36:   Concluding reflections   485

36.1   Introduction   485
36.2   The EU heritage   485
36.3   Laws versus rules   486
36.4   CCA 1974 versus FSMA   486
36.5   Mortgages and goods mortgages   487
36.6   The culture of regulation   487
36.7   The new direction   487

Index   489

Table of statutes

[All references are to paragraph number]

A

Administration of Justice Act 1970
s 40.. 25.3.1
Administration of Justice (Scotland) Act
1972
s 4.. 11.7

B

Bills of Sale Act 1878 .... 4.7.2.2, 18.2.2,
18.2.5.1, 18.2.5.2,
22.3, 36.5
Bills of Sale Act 1890 .... 4.7.2.2, 18.2.2,
18.2.5.1, 18.2.5.2
Bills of Sale Act 1891 .... 4.7.2.2, 18.2.2,
18.2.5.1, 18.2.5.2
Bills of Sales Act (1878) Amendment) Act
1882 .... 18.2.5.1, 22.3, 36.5
s 10.. 18.2.5.1
Bribery Act 2010.................................. 26.2.1
s 1, 2, 7.. 26.2.1
Building Societies Act 1986..................... 6.3.3

C

Capital Allowances Act 2001 .... 5.4, 5.4.2,
29.4, 29.5
s 11.. 29.4
Pt 2 Ch 2 (ss 15–20)............................ 29.4
s 15, 33A.. 29.4
56, 67, 69, 70................................ 29.4
70A–70F.. 29.5
70G 5.4.1, 29.5
70H, 70I.. 29.5
70J 5.4.1, 29.5
70K–70M.. 29.5
70N 5.4.1, 29.5
70O–70YJ.. 29.5
71(1), (2).. 5.4.6
83, 91, 102, 173............................. 29.4
219.. 5.4.1
(1).. 5.4.1
228A–228M...................................... 29.2.1
Civil Jurisdiction and Judgments Act
1982.. 35.8.2
Sch 1.. 35.8.2
Companies Act 2006.............................. 13.4
s 860, 861, 870.................................. 18.2.2

Companies Act 2006 – *contd*
s 874... 4.7.2.2, 18.2.2
993 .... 26.2.1
Compensation Act 2006
Pt 2 (ss 4–15) 16.9
Computer Misuse Act 1990
s 1–3A.. 26.2.1
Consumer Credit Act 1974.......... 1.1, 1.2, 1.3, 1.4,
1.5, 2.2, 2.3, 2.3.1,
2.3.2, 2.3.4, 3.1, 3.2,
3.3, 3.4, 3.6, 3.9, 3.10,
3.11, 4.1, 4.2.2, 4.2.4,
4.3, 4.4, 4.4.2, 4.4.3,
4.5, 4.7.1, 4.7.2.1,
4.7.2.3, 4.7.3.1, 4.7.4.2,
4.7.4.8, 4.8.4, 4.8.5,
5.1, 5.2, 5.4.7, 6.1, 6.2,
6.6, 7.1, 7.2, 7.3, 7.4, 7.6,
7.7, 8.3.1, 8.3.2, 8.6.6,
8.7.2, 8.7.2.3, 8.7.4.3,
8.8, 9.1, 10.1.1, 10.1.2,
10.4, 10.6, 10.12, 10.14,
11.3, 11.4, 11.6, 11.9.5,
12.1, 12.2, 12.3, 13.2,
13.6.2, 13.7, 14.2, 14.4,
15.1, 15.5, 15.9, 16.1, 16.5,
16.8, 17.4.4, 17.6.2, 18.1,
18.2.3.1, 18.2.12, 18.5,
19.3.3, 20.1, 20.2, 20.8,
21.2.5, 21.4, 21.5, 21.5.2,
22.4, 22.5.1, 22.6, 23.1,
25.1, 25.3.1, 25.13, 25.17,
25.18, 25.19, 25.23, 26.5.1,
26.5.2, 26.5.3, 26.5.4, 27.11,
30.1, 30.4.1, 32.1, 34.1,
34.2, 35.1.3, 35.8.1,
35.8.2, 36.1, 36.3, 36.4
Pt II (ss 8–20)................................... 7.1
s 8(1) 3.5, 4.1
(3) 3.5, 4.1, 6.1, 8.3.1
9(4) 3.1, 4.3, 19.1
10.. 4.7.4.2
(1)(a), (b) 4.2.1
(2) 4.2.2, 7.3
(3) 4.2.2
11(1) 4.3

Consumer Credit Act 1974 – *contd*

s 11(1)(b) 4.4.2
        (c) 4.3
        (2), (3) 4.3
    12 .... 4.4, 4.4.2, 12.3
        (a) 13.6.2
        (b) 13.2, 13.6.2, 17.4.4
        (c) 4.4.2, 13.2,
                                            13.6.2, 17.4.4
    13 .... 4.4, 4.4.1
        (b) 3.1, 17.4.4
        (c) 4.4.2, 17.4.4
    14 .... 17.6.1
        (1) 4.6, 4.7.4.7,
                                            17.6.1, 21.8
        (b) 17.6.2
        (2) 4.6
        (3) 17.6.2
    15 .... 5.1, 5.2
        (1) 3.9, 7.2
        (2) 3.9, 5.2, 6.1, 8.3.1
    16A 1.2
    16B 1.2, 3.2
    17 .... 6.5.3
        (1) 35.1.2
        (b) 5.2
        (3) 6.5.3
    18 .... 3.10, 4.2.4, 7.1
        (1)(a), (b) 7.1
        (2) 7.1
    19 .... 15.5
        (1) 4.4.3, 12.1
        (a) 12.4
        (b) 12.3
        (2) 4.4.3, 12.1
        (3) 12.3, 12.4
    Pt III (ss 21–41A) 30.1
    s 25 .... 34.2
        (2) 11.3
        (2B) 24.4
    39 .... 1.2
        (1) 13.3.1
    39A–39C 1.2
    40 .... 6.5.1
    Pt IV (ss 43–54) 20.3
    s 43–45 .... 20.1
    46 .... 20.1, 20.7, 20.8
    47 .... 20.1
    48 .... 20.3, 21.6
    49 .... 20.3, 21.6
        (1), (2) 4.4.3
    50 .... 3.11, 20.3, 21.7
    51 .... 4.6, 17.4.1, 21.8
        (1), (2) 4.7.4.7
    51A 17.4.2
    52 .... 21.5.2
    Pt V (ss 55–74) 4.7.4.2, 5.2, 5.3.4,
                            6.5, 6.5.1, 6.5.2, 6.5.3,
                            6.5.4, 22.5.1, 22.5.2
    s 55 .... 6.5.2, 6.5.3, 6.5.4,
                            8.4.2, 8.5, 22.5.2
        (1) 2.4.1
    55A 2.4.1, 8.1.1,
                            10.1.2, 22.5.2

Consumer Credit Act 1974 – *contd*

s 55B 2.4.1, 10.2, 22.5.2
    55C 2.4.1, 6.5.2, 6.5.4,
                            10.4, 21.5.4, 22.5.2
        (4) 22.6
        (c) 2.5
    56 .... 4.5, 5.2, 5.3.3, 6.5.1,
                            6.5.2, 6.5.3, 6.5.4, 13.6.2,
                            14.4.1, 15.9, 22.5.2
        (1) 4.4.3, 5.2, 21.5.1
        (b) 13.6.2, 14.4.1, 24.2.1
        (c) 13.5, 13.6.2,
                            14.4.1, 24.2.1
        (2) 13.5, 13.6.2, 14.4.1
        (3) 14.4.1
        (4) 13.6.2, 14.4.1
    57 .... 3.4, 3.6, 3.7
        (1) 12.3
        (3) 14.4.4
    58 .... 3.4, 3.6, 3.7, 7.3, 8.3.1,
                            8.4.1, 8.4.2, 8.4.4, 8.4.5,
                            8.6.8, 10.1.1, 10.7
        (1) 4.8.3, 8.3.1,
                            8.7.3.2, 8.7.4.2, 8.8
        (2) 4.8.3, 8.3.1,
                            8.6.8, 10.7
    59 .... 3.4, 3.6, 3.7
    60 .... 6.5.2, 6.5.4,
                            8.3.1, 22.5.2
        (1) 6.5.5, 8.3.1, 8.7.2
        (2) 8.7.2
        (3), (4) 6.5.5, 8.7.2
        (5) 6.5.5, 8.7.2, 22.6
        (c) 2.5
    61 .... 2.4.1, 4.7.3.1, 6.5.2,
                            6.5.4, 8.3.1,
                            8.6.8, 22.5.2
        (1) 7.2, 8.3.1, 8.3.2
        (a) 4.7.2.2, 8.3.2
        (b) 5.4.4, 8.8, 9.3.2.3
        (c) 23.1
        (2) 8.6.8, 10.7
        (3) 4.8.3, 8.6.8, 10.7
        (4) 3.11, 8.3.2, 8.6.1
    61A 2.4.1, 6.5.2, 6.5.4,
                            8.6.1, 8.6.2, 8.6.4,
                            8.6.6, 22.5.2, 22.6
        (1)–(3) 10.4
        (6) 8.6.4
        (6A) 2.5, 8.6.4
    61B 2.4.1, 6.5.2, 22.5.2
    62 .... 8.6.3, 10.1.1, 10.4
    63 .... 8.6.4
        (1) 10.4
        (2) 10.4, 23.1
        (b) 10.4
        (3) 10.6, 23.1
        (4) 8.6.7, 10.4
        (5) 8.6.1
        (6) 8.6.1, 8.6.4
        (b)(ii) 8.6.4
    64 .... 8.3.1, 10.6
        (1) 8.3.1, 10.4
        (a) 8.6.7

Consumer Credit Act 1974 – *contd*

s 64(1)(b)................................. 8.6.7, 10.6, 23.1
(2) 10.4, 23.1
(5) 8.3.1
65............................... 4.7.2.2, 4.7.3.1, 6.3.1,
6.3.6.1, 8.6.8, 25.1
(1) 4.3, 8.3.1, 25.1
(2) 25.1
66(2) 4.7.4.8
66A................................. 2.4.1, 4.5, 6.5.2,
6.5.4, 8.6.6, 8.6.7,
10.5, 12.6, 22.5.2
(2) 86.2
(5) 23.1
(13) 12.6
(14) 22.6
(a).. 2.5
67................................... 4.5, 5.2, 5.3.3,
8.6.7, 13.6.1, 14.4.4
(1)(a), (b) 4.5
(2) 4.5, 8.6.7
68.. 10.6
(1) 8.6.7
69.................................... 4.4.3, 12.3, 24.1
(1) 10.6
(2) 10.6, 12.3
(4) 10.6
(6) 14.4.4
(7) 23.1
(b).. 10.6
70.. 4.4.3
71.. 4.4.3
(4) 14.4.4
72.................................... 4.4.3, 10.5, 12.3
(6) 14.4.4
73.................................... 4.4.3, 14.4.4
74.. 4.4.3
(1)(a)................................ 4.7.3.1, 5.2, 6.5.1
(b)................................ 4.7.4.2, 6.5.2
(c)... 6.5.4
(d)... 6.5.3
(1A) 6.5.1
(1B)–(1D) 2.2, 4.7.4.2,
6.5.2, 22.5.2
(1E).. 6.5.2
(2) 6.5.3
(3) 4.7.4.2, 22.5.1
(4) 4.7.4.2
74A... 22.5.3
(2) 22.5.3.1
74B... 22.5.3
75.......................... 2.4.1, 3.8, 4.4.2, 4.4.3,
4.7.4.5, 15.1, 15.9, 17.2,
17.4.4, 17.4.5, 24.4,
35.1.3, 35.8.1
(1), (2)................................ 17.4.4
(3) 17.4.4
(b).. 17.4.4
75A..................................... 2.4.1, 4.4.3, 12.6,
17.2, 17.4.5, 22.6
(1) 15.1, 17.4.4
(2) 15.1, 17.4.4
(3) 17.4.4
(5) 2.1.6, 17.4.4

Consumer Credit Act 1974 – *contd*

s 75A(6) 17.4.4
(b).. 2.5
76.. 25.1, 25.2
(1) 25.2, 25.16, 25.21
(2), (3), (6).. 25.2
77.. 10.4
(1) 10.8, 25.1
77A................................ 7.7, 10.8, 11.2,
11.9.6, 11.10.2
(3) 11.9.3
77B.. 7.7, 10.8
(9).. 22.6
(c).. 2.5
78.................................... 4.7.4.8, 7.7,
8.8, 10.4, 10.8
(1) 10.8
(4) 11.3, 11.9.6
(7) 6.5.3
78A.. 7.6, 10.8
(1)–(6).. 4.7.4.8
79.. 10.4
(1) 10.8
81(1), (2)................................ 7.2, 10.12
82.. 7.3, 7.6
(1) 7.4, 7.6, 9.5.1
(1A)–(1E) 7.6, 9.5.1
(2) 7.3, 7.4, 8.7.5.1
(2A) 7.3, 7.4
(2B) 7.3
(3) 7.3
(b).. 7.3
(4) 7.3
(5), (5A)....................................... 7.3, 7.4
(6), (6A), (6B), (8)........................... 7.3
82A... 2.4.1, 9.9
83.................................... 4.7.4.8, 14.4.5, 17.3
84.................................... 4.7.4.8, 14.4.5
(1)–(3).. 4.7.4.8
(3A)–(3C)... 4.7.4.8
(4) 4.7.4.8, 17.3
(5) 17.3
85.. 8.6.7
(3) 6.5.3
86.. 25.20
86A.. 1.2
86B.................................... 1.2, 7.7, 11.4
(2)(a), (b)... 11.4
(4), (6)... 11.4
(7) 11.9.3
86C.................................... 1.2, 7.7, 11.4
(3), (4)... 11.4
(5).. 11.9.3
86D.................................... 1.2, 7.7, 11.4
86E... 1.2, 7.7
(3)–(5)... 11.6
86F(2).. 11.6
87.................................... 7.7, 25.1, 25.3.1
(1) 11.5, 25.1, 25.3.1, 25.21
(2) 11.5, 25.2, 25.3.1
88(1)... 11.5
(2) 11.5, 25.3.1, 25.9
(4A) 11.5, 25.3.1
(5) 11.5

Consumer Credit Act 1974 – *contd*

s 90... 4.7.2.3, 7.3,
                                          10.11, 18.2.5.1
  (1)... 10.11, 25.7
  (2)–(4)... 10.11
91... 25.7
92(1), (2)... 25.6
93... 9.4.1
94... 2.4.1, 4.7.4.4,
                                          8.7.3.2, 10.10.1
  (1)–(3)............................... 10.9, 10.10.1
  (4)(c)... 10.9
95A... 2.4.1, 10.10.1
  (3)(c)... 10.10.1
96... 12.3
  (1)... 12.4
97... 10.9, 10.10.4
  (1)... 10.8
97A... 10.10.4
98(1)............................... 25.4, 25.16, 25.21
  (2)(a), (b)... 25.4
  (4)... 25.4
99... 4.7.2.3, 7.2,
                                          10.10.1, 35.1.3
  (1)... 14.4.4
100... 4.7.2.3, 7.2, 7.3,
                                          10.10.1, 18.2.5.1
101(1)............................... 5.3.3, 14.4.4
  (2), (3)... 5.3.3
  (7)... 3.2, 3.9
     (a)–(c)... 5.3.3
  (8), (8A)... 5.3.3
102(1)... 14.4.4
103... 10.9
  (1)... 10.8
105............................... 12.1, 18.2, 18.2.1
  (5), (7)... 18.2.1
  (9)... 18.1, 18.2
106............................... 12.1, 18.2.1
107............................... 12.1, 18.2.14
  (1)... 10.8
  (4)... 18.2.14
108............................... 12.1, 18.2.14
  (1)... 10.8
109............................... 12.1, 18.2.14
  (1)... 10.8
110............................... 12.1, 18.2.14
  (1)... 10.8
111............................... 12.1, 18.2.14,
                                          25.5, 25.21
112... 12.1
113............................... 12.1, 18.5
  (8)... 12.1
114–120............................... 12.1, 18.2.12
121............................... 12.1, 18.2.12, 20.6.3
  (1), (2)... 18.2.12
122............................... 12.1, 18.2.12, 25.13
123... 12.1
  (1), (3)... 18.2.13
124... 12.1
  (1), (2)... 18.2.13
126............................... 18.2.3.3, 25.6, 25.11
127... 4.7.3.1, 6.3.1,
                                          6.3.6.1, 25.13

Consumer Credit Act 1974 – *contd*

s 127(1)....................... 7.1, 8.3.1, 8.3.2, 8.7.3.1,
                                          8.7.3.2, 25.1, 25.13
  (2)............................... 8.3.1, 8.3.2, 25.13
  (3)... 1.2, 3.1, 7.2,
                                          8.3.2, 8.7.3.2
  (4), (5)... 1.2, 8.3.2
129... 25.14
  (1)... 10.13
  (ba)... 25.14
  (2)... 10.13
129A... 1.2, 10.13
  (1), (2)... 25.14
129B–130... 1.2
130A... 1.2, 25.18
  (1)–(3)... 11.7
  (4)... 11.9.3
  (5), (7)... 11.7
131... 25.18
132... 25.15
133... 25.16
134(1)... 25.3.1
135... 25.18
136... 25.14, 25.18
140A... 1.2, 3.8, 6.3, 6.3.1,
                                          6.3.6.1, 8.3.2, 9.3.3.5,
                                          10.8, 12.5, 13.5, 13.8,
                                          14.4.2, 14.4.3, 16.8,
                                          18.4, 24.1, 24.2.1,
                                          24.2.2, 25.19, 32.1
  (1)............................... 18.4, 24.1, 24.4
     (a)....................... 9.3.3.5, 24.2.2, 24.4
     (b)... 24.4
     (c)... 13.5, 14.4.3,
                                          24.2.2, 24.4
  (2)............................... 24.1, 24.2.1, 24.4
  (3), (4)... 24.1
140B... 1.2, 3.8, 6.1, 6.3.1,
                                          6.3.6.1, 12.5, 13.8,
                                          16.8, 18.4, 24.1, 24.4
  (9)............................... 24.1, 24.2.1, 24.3
140C... 1.2, 3.8, 6.1 6.3.1,
                                          6.3.6.1, 13.8, 18.4, 24.1
  (1)... 12.5, 18.4
  (2)... 3.3, 3.4, 3.6
     (a), (b)... 24.1
  (4)............................... 24.1, 24.2.1, 24.4
     (b)... 12.5
     (c)... 18.4
  (5)... 12.5
  (6)... 18.4
140D... 1.2, 24.1, 24.2.1
141... 25.12
142... 25.13
  (1)... 25.18
Pt X (ss 145–160A)... 13.1.1
s 145... 13.3.1
  (1)... 13.1.1, 16.1
  (2), (3)... 13.1.1
  (5)... 16.2.1
  (6)... 16.2.2
  (7)... 16.2.3
  (7A)... 16.2.4
  (7B)... 16.3

Consumer Credit Act 1974 – *contd*

s 145(8) 16.5
151–154 .... 20.3
155 .... 13.8, 20.3
   (2), (2A), (4) 13.8
156 .... 20.3
157 .... 16.5
   (A1), (1) 21.5.1, 27.11
158 .... 16.5, 21.5.1
   (1) 27.11
   (4A), (5) 21.5.1
159 .... 16.5, 21.5.1, 27.11
   (1) 21.5.1
160 .... 16.5
   (1) 16.5
160A 13.1.1
168(1) 26.5.4
170 .... 11.3, 26.5.4
   (1) 21.6, 26.5.4
   (2) 11.3
171(4) 17.3
172 .... 10.8, 11.3, 11.9.4
   (2) 10.9, 11.9.4
   (3) 11.9.4
173 .... 13.6.2, 14.4.6, 18.2.12
   (1), (2) 10.14
   (3) 25.6, 25.7,
                           25.11, 25.15
175 .... 14.4.4
176 .... 9.5.1, 10.5
   (1) 11.2
176A 8.6.6, 10.5, 11.9.2,
                           23.1, 23.4
   (1) 4.7.4.8, 8.6.5,
                       10.4, 10.6, 23.1
   (2) 23.1
177 .... 18.2.1
184 .... 5.3.3
185 .... 8.8
   (1) 11.9.5
     (a) 8.6.1
   (2), (2A), (2C), (2D) 11.9.6
187(3A) 17.4.4
187A 11.5
189 .... 4.7.4.8, 7.3, 17.4.5
   (1) 1.2, 2.2, 2.5, 3.2, 3.3,
             3.4, 3.6, 3.7, 4.1, 4.5,
            4.7.2.1, 4.7.3.1, 4.7.4.2,
            4.7.4.7, 4.8.1, 4.8.5,
            5.2, 6.1, 6.5.1, 7.7, 8.3.1,
            8.6.5, 10.4, 10.11, 11.2,
            11.9.2, 13.3.1, 16.1,
            17.4.5, 18.1, 18.2.12,
            19.3.3, 20.1, 22.5.1,
            22.6, 23.1, 23.4, 24.1, 24.4
   (2) 4.7.3.1, 6.5.1, 16.1
   (4) 5.4.4, 8.3.2,
             8.8, 18.1, 18.2
189B(2) 3.3
   (3) 3.4
Sch 1 .... 26.5.1
Consumer Credit Act 2006 .... 1.2, 3.2, 4.2.2,
            5.3.3, 9.1, 11.1, 11.4,
            11.6, 11.7, 34.1, 34.2

Consumer Credit Act 2006 – *contd*

s 1(1) 1.2
2(1) 1.2
3, 4 .... 1.2
6 .... 11.2
8 .... 1.2
9 .... 1.2, 11.4
10–12 .... 1.2
13 .... 1.2, 11.6
14–21 .... 1.2
19–21 .... 24.1
22 .... 1.2, 24.1
   (1) 1.2
24–28 .... 1.2
29 .... 1.2
   (2) 34.2
   (2A)(b)(ii) 34.2
30–54 .... 1.2
59, 60 .... 1.2, 34.2
61 .... 34.2
Sch 3 .... 11.4
   para 2 .... 11.2
     6(2) 11.4
     7 .... 11.4
     (2) 11.4
     9(1), (2) 11.6
Consumer Protection Act 1987 .... 3.2, 13.6.2,
            15.1, 20.9
s 21 .... 26.5.4
   46(2) 15.1
Consumer Rights Act 2015 .... 3.2, 4.7.2.1,
            4.7.2.3, 5.1, 5.3.1,
            5.3.2, 8.1.2, 8.3.2,
            9.1, 9.3.2.3, 9.3.2.4,
            9.3.3.1, 9.3.3.3, 9.3.3.4,
            9.6, 9.7, 9.8, 9.9,
            21.11, 25.23, 32.1, 36.2
s 2 .... 9.3.1
   (2) 5.1
   (3) 4.7.2.3, 5.1
   (8) 5.1
Pt 1 Ch 2 (ss 3–32) 9.3.2.1
s 3 .... 9.3.2.1
   5(1) 9.3.1
   (3) 4.7.2.1
7 .... 4.7.2.1
9–17 .... 4.7.2.3, 5.3.1, 9.3.2.1
18 .... 9.3.2.1
19–27 .... 9.3.2.1
28 .... 4.7.2.3, 9.3.2.1
   (3) 9.3.1
29 .... 4.7.2.3, 9.3.2.1
31 .... 4.7.2.3, 9.3.2.1
   (1), (2) 4.7.2.3, 9.3.3.1
   (3)–(7) 4.7.2.3
32 .... 9.3.2.2
Pt 1 Ch 3 (ss 33–47) 9.3.2.2
s 34–46 .... 9.3.2.2
47 .... 9.3.2.2, 9.3.3.1
Pt 1 Ch 4 (ss 48–57) 9.3.2.2
s 49 .... 9.3.2.2
50 .... 9.3.2.2, 9.3.3.1
51 .... 9.3.2.2
52 .... 9.3.2.2

Consumer Rights Act 2015 – *contd*
s 52(2), (3)... 9.3.1
53–56.. 9.3.2.2
57.. 9.3.2.2
(1)–(4).. 9.3.3.1
Pt 2 (ss 61–76) 9.3.3.3, 9.3.3.5,
24.4, 35.6
s 61 .... 9.3.3.2, 9.3.3.3
(1)(b).. 9.8
62 .... 9.3.3.3, 24.4
63 .... 7.6, 9.3.3.3
64 .... 9.3.3.3, 9.3.3.5, 21.11
(3) 8.3.2, 8.4.5
65, 67 .... 9.3.3.3
68 .... 21.11
(1) 8.3.2, 8.4.5
71 .... 9.3.3.3
Sch 1
para 2, 38.. 9.3.2.3
Sch 2 .... 9.3.3.2, 35.6
Pt 1 (paras 1–20).............................. 9.3.3.3
para 2... 9.6
11....................................... 7.6, 9.5.1
17... 9.8
19...................................... 9.9, 17.4.5
20... 9.6
Pt 2 (paras 21–25)........................... 4.7.2.3,
7.6, 18.2.2
para 22, 23................................... 7.6
Sch 3.. 35.6
Sch 4.. 35.6
Contracts (Applicable Law) Act 1990 ..... 35.8.1,
35.8.2
Contracts (Rights of Third Parties) Act
1999...................................... 14.2, 15.1
County Courts Act 1984
s 74... 11.7
Credit Unions Act 1979 .... 21.2.2
s 1A.. 21.2.2
Criminal Finances Act 2017..................... 26.2.2
Criminal Justice Act 1987
s 12.. 26.2.1
Criminal Law Act 1977
s 1 .... 26.2.1

D
Data Protection Act 1984......................... 27.9
Data Protection Act 1998.............. 9.1, 16.5, 21.4,
21.5.1, 27.1,
27.8, 27.11, 27.14
s 7....................................... 16.5, 21.5.1
(1), (2)... 27.11
9.. 16.5
12, 13... 21.4
Sch 1... 16.5
Pt I.. 16.5

E
Education Act 2011
s 76... 22.4
Electronic Communications Act 2000 ..... 8.3.2,
9.1
s 7.. 23.5
Employment Protection Act 1975........... 21.4

Employment Protection (Consolidation)
Act 1978... 21.4
Enterprise Act 2002................................. 11.10.1,
11.10.2, 15.5
Pt 8 (ss 210–236) 20.8.3, 32.4, 35.7
Equality Act 2010 .... 21.4
European Communities Act 1972........... 35.8.2

F
Factors Act 1889
s 9.. 4.7.2.3
Fair Trading Act 1973 .... 15.3, 21.4, 32.1
Family Law Reform Act 1969
s 1... 21.7
Finance Act 2004 .... 29.2.1
Finance Act 2006 .... 29.5
Financial Services Act 2012..................... 1.4
s 107... 1.4
115(2) 1.4
Financial Services and Markets Act
2000............................... 1.5, 2.1.4, 3.2, 4.1,
4.8.4, 6.1, 6.2, 7.4,
9.1, 13.8, 13.10, 14.5,
15.3, 15.4, 17.1, 17.6.1,
18.2.3.1, 20.2, 20.4, 20.5,
20.6.1, 21.2.2, 25.23,
26.5.3, 30.3, 31.1, 31.6,
33.1, 33.9, 36.1, 36.4
Pt IA Ch I (ss 1A–1T)..................... 32.3, 33.2
s 1B–1E.. 32.3
1G... 3.2
1K... 33.2
1L.. 32.3, 33.2
3B... 33.2
(1)(d)... 33.2
19... 13.7, 20.4,
30.1, 30.2
(1) 20.7
(b)... 30.3
21 .... 20.4, 20.5, 20.6.2
(1) 20.4, 20.7
(2) 20.7
(8), (9)... 20.4
(10) 20.5
(13) 20.6.2
22... 6.5.1, 16.2,
25.22.1, 30.2, 33.10
23... 20.4
(1) 13.7, 30.2
26... 13.7, 30.2
26A, 27 .... 30.2
31 .... 30.1, 30.2
(1)(b), (c)... 35.3
39 .... 13.10, 30.3
(1) 30.3
Pt IV (ss 40–55) 35.3
Pt IVA (ss 55A–55Z4)............... 7.7, 30.1, 30.2,
30.4, 30.4.2, 30.5,
31.1, 33.3, 33.10.4
s 55A 30.1
55B 30.5
55C 30.5
55H 30.4.2
55J 30.5

Financial Services and Markets Act
2000 – *contd*
s 55U–55W 30.7
Pt V (ss 56–71I) 31.2
s 56 .... 31.2
  (6) 25.24
59 .... 13.10, 30.1, 31.2, 31.3
  (1) 25.24
  (2) 25.24, 31.2
60 .... 31.2
  (2) 31.2
61 .... 31.2
  (1) 31.2, 31.4
  (2) 31.2, 31.4
63 .... 31.2
64A 31.2, 31.5
  (1)(a) 31.5, 31.5.1
66 .... 25.23, 31.2
  (1) 31.2
Pt IXA (ss 137A–141A) 14.5
s 137C(1)(a)(ii) 22.1.1
  (b) 22.1.1
137O 30.5
138D 20.6.3, 20.7, 25.24
  (2) 13.7, 25.24
  (3), (4) 25.24
139A 33.2
166, 166A 33.8
206, 206A 25.23
Pt XVI (ss 225–234B) 25.22.1, 34.4.1
s 225 .... 34.4.1
226 .... 34.4.4
  (2)(b), (c) 34.3.1
226A 1.2, 34.2
228(2) 34.4.4
  (5), (6) 34.4.4
231 .... 34.4.2
234 .... 34.4.3
234A 1.2
285(2), (3) 30.2
312A(2) 30.2
401 .... 25.23
404 .... 15.5
404E 3.2
417(1) 30.2
425 .... 3.2
Sch 3 .... 35.3, 35.4
  Pt II (paras 12–18) 35.4
    para 12, 13 .... 35.4
    19 .... 35.3
Sch 6 .... 30.5, 30.6.1
  para 2C, 2D, 2F 30.6.1
Sch 17 .... 25.22.1, 34.3.1,
                        34.4.3, 34.4.4
  Pt III (paras 12–16) 34.4.4
Financial Services (Banking Reform) Act
2013 .... 31.6
Forgery and Counterfeiting Act 1981 ...... 26.2.1
Fraud Act 2006 .... 26.2.1
s 2–4, 9, 11 .... 26.2.1
Freedom of Information Act 2000 .... 27.10
s 2 .... 27.10
  (3) 27.10
Sch 1 .... 27.10

H
Higher Education Act 2004
s 43, 50 .... 22.4
Higher Education and Research Act
2017 .... 21.2.5, 22.4
Hire Purchase Act 1964 .... 3.1
  Pt III (ss 27–29) 18.2.5.2
  s 27–29 .... 4.7.2.3
Hire-Purchase Act 1965 .... 3.1
Housing Act 1985
s 156(4) 6.3.3
  447(2)(a) 6.3.3
Housing Act 1996
s 17 .... 6.3.3
Human Rights Act 1998 .... 27.8
  Sch 1 .... 8.3.2

I
Improvement of Land Act 1899
s 7 .... 6.3.3
Industrial and Provident Societies Act
1965 .... 21.2.2
Insolvency Act 1986 .... 18.2.6
s 344 .... 18.2.5.2
Interpretation Act 1978 .... 30.2

L
Landlord and Tenant Act 1954 .... 6.3.1
Law of Property Act 1925
s 136 .... 18.2.4, 18.2.10
Law of Property (Miscellaneous Pro-
visions) Act 1989 .... 18.2.1, 18.2.2
Local Government Act 2003 .... 3.11
Local Government and Housing Act
1989 .... 3.11

M
Malicious Communications Act 1988 ...... 25.3.1
Misrepresentation Act 1967 .... 20.7, 20.9
Moneylenders Act 1900 .... 3.1
Moneylenders Act 1927 .... 3.1

P
Pawnbrokers Act 1872 .... 18.2.12
Pawnbrokers Act 1922 .... 18.2.12
Pawnbrokers Act 1960 .... 18.2.12
Police and Justice Act 2006 .... 26.2.1
Policies of Assurance Act 1867 .... 18.2.10
Prices Act 1974 .... 21.12
Prices Act 1975 .... 21.12
Proceeds of Crime Act 2002 .... 26.2.2
Property Misdescriptions Act 1991 .... 20.9
Protection of Depositors Act 1963
s 2(1) 20.1

R
Race Relations Act 1976 .... 21.4

S
Sale of Goods Act 1979 .... 4.7.2.3, 9.3.2.3
s 12, 13 .... 4.7.2.3, 9.3.2.3
14 .... 4.7.2.3, 9.3.2.3
  (3) 13.6.2
15 .... 9.3.2.3

Sale of Goods Act 1979 – *contd*
s 15A 4.7.2.3, 9.3.2.3
   21, 24, 25 .... 4.7.2.3
   61(1) 10.6
Senior Courts Act 1981
   s 51 .... 25.18
Sex Discrimination Act 1975 .... 21.4
Statute of Frauds (1677)
   s 4 .... 18.2.1
Supply of Goods and Services Act 1982 .. 5.3.2,
                                          9.1, 9.3.2.3
   s 2–5 .... 9.3.2.3
   5A 9.3.2.3
   7–10 .... 5.3.2, 9.3.2.3
   10A 5.3.2
   11 .... 9.3.2.3
   Pt IA (ss 11A–11L) 9.3.2.3
   s 13–15 .... 9.3.2.3
Supply of Goods (Implied Terms) Act
   1973 .... 4.7.2.3, 9.1, 9.3.2.3
   s 8, 9 .... 4.7.2.3, 9.3.2.3
   10 .... 4.7.2.3, 9.3.2.3
   (3) 13.6.2
   11 .... 9.3.2.3
   15 .... 4.7.2.1

T

Teaching and Higher Education Act
   1998 .... 21.2.5
   Pt II (ss 22–31) 22.4
   s 22 .... 22.4
Theft Act 1968
   s 17, 24A 26.2.1
Timeshare Act 1992 .... 8.7.3.2, 15.9
Torts (Interference with Goods) Act
   1977 .... 25.16, 25.18

Trade Descriptions Act 1968 .... 26.5.4
Tribunals, Courts and Enforcement Act
   2007 .... 25.1
   Sch 12
   para 60 .... 25.17

U

Unfair Contract Terms Act 1977 .... 3.2, 4.7.2.3,
                                          9.1, 9.3.2.4,
                                          9.3.3.2, 20.9,
                                        24.4, 32.1, 35.6f
   s 2 .... 9.3.3.2
   6 .... 4.7.2.3, 9.3.2.3, 9.3.3.2
   7 .... 9.3.2.3
   (3A) 9.3.2.3
   11, 13 .... 9.3.3.2
   20, 21 .... 9.3.2.3
   Sch 2 .... 9.3.3.2

V

Value Added Tax Act 1983
   s 2(1), (2) 15.6
   17(1) 15.6
   Sch 6
   Group 2 .... 15.6
Value Added Tax Act 1994
   s 31 .... 29.6.1
   Sch 9
   Pt II
   Group 5 .... 29.6.1
      item 1, 2 .... 29.6.4
      3 .... 29.6.3,
                                          29.6.4, 29.6.5
      4 .... 29.6.3, 29.6.4
      5 .... 29.6.4, 29.6.6
      6 .... 29.6.4

Table of statutory instruments

[All references are to paragraph number]

A

Alternative Dispute Resolution for Consumer Disputes (Amendment) (No 2) Regulations 2015, SI 2015/1972....... 25.22.3

Alternative Dispute Resolution for Consumer Disputes (Amendment) Regulations 2015, SI 2015/1392...... 25.22.3, 34.3.5

Alternative Dispute Resolution for Consumer Disputes (Competent Authorities and Information) Regulations 2015, SI 2015/542........ 25.22.3, 34.3.5

B

Banking Coordination (Second Council Directive) Regulations 1992, SI 1992/3218................. 35.3

Business Contract Terms (Assignment of Receivables) Regulations 2017 (draft) 28.2.5

Business Protection from Misleading Marketing Regulations 2008, SI 2008/1276

reg 6..................... 20.9

C

Cancellation of Contracts made in the Consumer's Home or Place of Work etc Regulations 2008, SI 2008/1816: 8.5, 10.6

Civil Procedure Rules 1998, SI 1998/3132.................. 35.8.2

r 7.9 .... 25.19

PD 7 .... 35.8.2

PD 7B.............. 25.7, 25.13, 25.14, 25.16, 25.19

Pt 16 .... 25.16

r 24.2 .... 25.19

31.16 .... 25.19

Pt 55 .... 25.11

Compensation (Claims Management Services) (Amendment) Regulations 2008, SI 2008/1441 .... 16.9

Compensation (Claims Management Services) (Amendment) Regulations 2014, SI 2014/3239 .... 16.9

Compensation (Claims Management Services) (Amendment) Regulations 2015, SI 2015/42 .... 16.9

Compensation (Claims Management Services) Regulations 2006, SI 2006/3322................ 16.9

Consumer Contracts (Information, Cancellation and Additional Charges) Regulations 2013, SI 2013/3134.................... 15.8.1, 21.10.1

reg 4...................... 15.8.1

5......................... 15.8.1, 21.10.1

6(1)...................... 15.8.1

Consumer Credit Act 1974 (Electronic Communications) Order 2004, SI 2004/3236.................. 9.1

Consumer Credit Act 2006 (Commencement No 2 and Transitional Provisions and Savings) Order 2007, SI 2007/123

art 3(2).................... 24.1

Sch 2...................... 24.1

Sch 3

para 1.................. 24.1

14(2)................ 24.1

Consumer Credit Act 2006 (Commencement No 4 and Transitional Provisions) Order 2008, SI 2008/831.................... 1.2

art 4 .... 7.4

Consumer Credit (Advertisements) Regulations 1989, SI 1989/1125.............. 26.5.4

reg 7(c)................... 20.7

Consumer Credit (Agreements) Regulations 1983, SI 1983/1553 .... 2,2, 2.3, 2.3.2, 2.3.4, 3.10, 4.2.4, 4.4.3, 4.7.2.2, 4.7.3.2, 4.7.4.8, 7.1, 7.4, 7.6, 8.1.2, 8.2, 8.3.1, 8.3.2, 8.4.3, 8.4.4, 8.7.3.1, 8.7.3.2, 8.7.4.1, 8.7.5.2, 8.7.5.3, 8.7.6, 9.2.1, 9.2.2, 9.5.1, 17.4.3, 18.2, 19.1, 23.1, 23.3

reg 2(2), (4) 8.7.3.2

(7)(b) 8.7.5.2

Consumer Credit (Agreements) Regulations 1983, SI 1983/1553 – *contd*

reg 2(8)	7.1, 7.2
3(2)	8.7.4.3
(4)	8.7.4.2
(6)	8.7.5.3
5	7.4, 8.7.5.2
6(1)	8.7.3.1
(2)	8.3.2
(a)	23.1
(3)(a)	3.11, 8.6.1
(c)	8.6.1
(5)	8.3.2, 23.1
7	7.5
(3)	8.7.5.2
(4)	8.7.5.2, 8.7.5.3
(10)	8.7.5.3
8	8.4.3
Sch 1	4.7.1, 8.7.3.2, 8.7.5.2
para 1	4.2.4, 6.6, 18.2
2	19.3.2
11	8.7.4.3
13, 14A	8.7.3.2
19	7.6
20	18.2
22–24	8.7.3.2
Sch 2	8.7.3.2, 8.7.5.2
para 3	18.2
Pt I	
form 2, 3	8.7.3.2
17	4.7.4.8
Sch 3	8.7.4.2, 8.7.4.3
para 1, 2	18.2
9	18.2
Sch 4	8.7.4.2, 8.7.5.3
para 3	18.2
Sch 5	8.7.3.2
Sch 6	8.3.2, 8.7.3.1, 19.3.2
para 5	8.7.3.2
Sch 7	17.4.3, 19.3.2
para 1	19.3.2
1A	19.1
Sch 8	8.7.5.3
Pt I	7.4, 8.7.5.2
Pt II	7.4

Consumer Credit (Agreements) Regulations 2010, SI 2010/1014 .... 1.3, 2.2, 2.3.1, 2.4.1, 4.2.4, 4.4.3, 4.7.2.2, 4.7.3.2, 4.7.4.2, 4.7.4.8, 5.4.7, 7.1, 7.4, 8.1.2, 8.2, 8.3.2, 8.4.1, 8.4.2, 8.6.6, 8.7.3.1, 8.7.3.3, 8.7.5.2, 9.2.2, 9.5.1, 13.11, 17.4.3, 18.1, 18.2.12, 23.1, 36.2

reg 1(2)	19.1
(3)	23.3
2	8.4.1
(2)	2.2
3	9.2.2
(1)	8.7.3.3
(3)	8.3.2, 23.1
(6)	7.2
(8)	7.1

Consumer Credit (Agreements) Regulations 2010, SI 2010/1014 – *contd*

reg 4	8.7.3.1
(1)	8.3.2, 8.7.3.1
(3)(a)	3.11, 8.6.1
(c)	8.6.1
(5)	23.1
5	7.4
(1)	7.4
8	2.2, 4.7.4.2, 8.4.1, 8.4.2, 8.7.6
Sch 1	4.2.4, 4.7.1, 8.4.1, 8.4.2, 8.7.3.3, 13.11
para 1	6.6
(5)	18.2
23	18.1
26, 27	8.7.3.3
Sch 2	8.4.1
Sch 3	8.4.2
Sch 4	17.4.3, 19.3.2
para 2	19.1

Consumer Credit (Amendment) Regulations 2010, SI 2010/1969 .... 2.3.1

reg 24	8.4.4

Consumer Credit (Amendment) Regulations 2011, SI 2011/11 .... 2.3.1

Consumer Credit (Cancellation Notices and Copies of Documents) Regulations 1983, SI 1983/1557 .... 2.3.2, 2.3.3, 2.3.4, 8.3.1, 8.4.1, 8.4.5, 8.8

reg 2(1)	23.1
3(1)	8.8
(2)(b)	8.8
5	8.8
10	18.2.14
11	8.8, 10.4
Schedule	8.6.7, 10.4
Pt V	8.8

Consumer Credit (Conduct of Business) (Credit References) (Amendment) Regulations 2000, SI 2000/291 .... 21.5.1

Consumer Credit (Conduct of Business) (Credit References) Regulations 1977, SI 1977/330 .... 21.5.1

Consumer Credit (Content of Quotations) and Consumer Credit (Advertisements) (Amendment) Regulations 1999, SI 1999/2725 ...... 10.1.1

Consumer Credit (Credit Reference Agency) Regulations 1977, SI 1977/329 .... 27.11

Consumer Credit (Further Increase of Monetary Amounts) Order 1998, SI 1998/997 .... 4.7.4.8

art 3	5.3.3

Consumer Credit (Quotations) Regulations 1989, SI 1989/1126 ...... 21.5.2

Consumer Credit (Quotations) (Revocation) Regulations 1997, SI 1997/211: 21.5.2

Consumer Credit (Credit Reference Agency) Regulations 2000, SI 2000/290 .... 16.5

reg 7	16.5

Consumer Credit (Credit-Token Agreements) Regulations 1983, SI 1983/
1555.. 4.7.4.8, 17.3
Consumer Credit (Disclosure of
Information) Regulations 2004,
SI 2004/1481.......................... 2.2, 2.3, 2.3.2,
2.3.4, 8.1.2, 8.4.2,
8.4.4, 8.7.1, 21.5.3, 23.3
reg 1(2)... 23.3, 23.7
2.. 8.4.4
(3).. 23.3, 23.7
3(1A)... 16.5
4(d)(iv)... 23.7
Consumer Credit (Disclosure of
Information) Regulations 2010,
SI 2010/1013............... 1.3, 2.2, 2.3.1, 2.4.1,
8.1.2, 8.4.1, 8.4.2, 8.4.4,
8.7.1, 13.11, 19.2, 19.3.1,
19.3.5, 21.5.3, 22.5.4, 23.3
reg 1(2)... 23.3
2.. 8.4.2
3(1)... 8.4.2
(2)... 8.6.2, 8.6.4
8.. 22.5.4
(1)... 21.5.3
(2)... 23.3
10.. 22.5.4
11.. 22.5.4
(1)... 21.5.3
Sch 1..................................... 8.7.1, 13.11, 16.5
para 2.. 18.1
Sch 2... 13.11, 19.3.5
Sch 3... 16.5, 22.5.4
Consumer Credit (EU Directive) Regulations 2010, SI 2010/1010.......... 2.2, 2.3.1,
9.1, 10.1.2
reg 2.. 4.7.4.2
17(1), (3)...................................... 4.7.4.2
39.. 4.7.4.2
48.. 7.6
Consumer Credit (Early Settlement)
Regulations 2004, SI 2004/1483...... 2.3.3,
10.10.1, 10.10.2
reg 2(1A), (3)..................................... 10.10.1
3(2)... 10.10.3
4, 4A, 5, 6..................................... 10.10.2
Consumer Credit (Enforcement,
Default and Termination Notices)
Regulations 1983, SI 1983/1561...... 2.3.3,
11.5, 25.2
reg 2(1)... 25.2
(4A).................................... 11.5, 11.9.2,
23.4, 25.2, 25.3.1
Sch 1... 25.2
Consumer Credit (Guarantees and
Indemnities) Regulations 1983,
SI 1983/1556............................... 18.2, 18.2.1
Consumer Credit (Information
Requirements and Duration of
Licences and Charges) Regulations
2007, SI 2007/1167........................ 2.3.3, 7.1,
11.3, 11.4, 11.5, 11.6,
11.7, 11.9.1, 11.10.2
reg 2.. 11.9.1, 11.0.2

Consumer Credit (Information
Requirements and Duration of
Licences and Charges) Regulations
2007, SI 2007/1167 – *contd*
reg 12.. 11.2, 11.10.2
(3)... 11.10.2
13–18.. 11.3
19.. 11.4
(1)(e)... 11.4
(2)(a)... 11.4
(d)... 11.9.1
(3)... 11.4
20–23.. 11.4, 11.9.1
24.. 11.4
(1)(e)... 11.4
25.. 11.4
28–32.. 11.6
33(3)(c)... 11.5
34.. 11.7
36, 37... 11.2, 11.9.2
38.. 11.9.2
39.. 11.2, 11.9.2
40.. 11.2, 11.9.2
41.. 11.4, 11.9.4
46–50.. 11.2
Sch 1
Pt 1 (paras 1–3A)......................... 11.2
Pt 2 (para 4)................................ 11.2
Sch 5... 11.7
Consumer Credit (Linked Transactions)
(Exemptions) Regulations 1983,
SI 1983/1560.......................... 8.6.7, 10.6
reg 2(1)... 15.4
(2)(a)... 15.4
Consumer Credit (Notice of Cancellation
Rights) (Exemptions) Regulations
1983, SI 1983/1558......................... 8.6.7
Consumer Credit (Notice of Variation of
Agreements) Regulations 1977, SI
1977/328........................... 4.7.4.8, 7.6, 9.5.1
reg 2, 3... 7.6, 9.5.1
48.. 9.5.1
Consumer Credit (Payments Arising
on Death) Regulations 1983,
SI 1983/1554............................... 6.5.4
Consumer Credit (Pawn-Receipts)
Regulations 1983, SI 1983/1566...... 18.2.12
Consumer Credit (Prescribed Periods for
Giving Information) Regulations
1983, SI 1983/1569......................... 10.8
Consumer Credit (Running-Account
Credit Information) Regulations
1983, SI 1983/1570
reg 2, 3... 11.3
Schedule.. 11.3
Consumer Credit (Settlement Information)
Regulation 1983, SI 1983/1564:....... 10.9
reg 2.. 10.10.4
3.. 10.9
Schedule 10.10.4
Consumer Credit (Total Charge for Credit,
Agreements and Advertisements)
(Amendment) Regulations 1999, SI
1999/3177 .... 19.1

Consumer Credit (Total Charge for
Credit) (Amendment) Regulations
2012, SI 2012/1745 .... 19.2
Consumer Credit (Total Charge
for Credit) Regulations 1980,
SI 1980/51 .... 19.2, 26.5.2
reg 1A... 19.2
7... 19.1
Consumer Credit (Total Charge for
Credit) Regulations 2010, SI 2010/
1011.. 19.2
reg 3... 19.2
Consumer Protection (Distance Selling)
Regulations 2000, SI 2000/2334...... 3.2,
4.7.4.8, 9.1
Consumer Protection from Unfair
Trading Regulations 2008, SI 2008/
1277.................................... 8.5, 9.1, 9.3.3.3,
10.3, 13.6.2, 20.2,
20.7, 20.8, 21.12, 32.1
reg 2(1)–(6) 20.8.1
3.. 20.8.2
(2)... 20.8.2
(3)... 24.4
(4)(a)–(c) 20.8.3
5(2)–(4) 20.8.3
6(1), (2) 20.8.3
7(1), (2) 20.8.3
8, 18... 20.8.3
Sch 1.. 20.8.3
Control of Hiring and Hire-Purchase
and Credit Sale Agreements (Revocation) Order 1982, SI 1982/1034 ... 3.8
County Court (Interest on Judgment
Debts) Order 1991, SI 1991/1184.... 25.18
art 2(3)... 9.4.1

D

Data Protection (Subject Access) (Fees
and Miscellaneous Provisions)
Regulations 2000, SI 2000/191 .... 27.11

E

Education (Student Loans) (Repayment)
(Amendment) Regulations 2013, SI
2013/607 .... 22.4
Education (Student Loans) (Repayment)
Regulations 2009, SI 2009/470 .... 21.2.5,
22.4
Electronic Commerce (EC Directive)
Regulations 2002, SI 2002/2013...... 8.5,
10.3, 20.9, 23.2
reg 2(1)... 23.2
6, 9.. 23.2
Electronic Identification and Trust
Services for Electronic Transactions
Regulations 2016, SI 2016/696........ 23.5
Electronic Money Regulations 2011, SI
2011/99 .... 9.1, 17.6.1, 25.22.1
reg 2(1)... 17.6.1

F

Financial Services Act 2012 (Consumer
Credit) Order 2013, SI 2013/1882.. 1.4, 26.5.3

Financial Services and Markets Act
2000 (Appointed Representative)
Regulations 2001, SI 2001/1217...... 13.10,
30.3
Financial Services and Markets Act 2000
(Consequential Amendments and
Repeals) Order 2001, SI 2001/3649. 35.3
Financial Services and Markets Act 2000
(Consequential Amendments) Order
2005, SI 2005/2967 .... 7.3, 7.4
Financial Services and Markets Act 2000
(Consequential Amendments) Order
2008, SI 2008/733 .... 7.3
Financial Services and Markets Act
2000 (Exemption) Order 2001, SI
2001/1201 .... 30.2
Financial Services and Markets Act 2000
(Financial Promotion) Order 2005,
SI 2005/1529 .... 20.2, 20.5, 20.7
art 6(a), (d) 20.6.2
17 .... 20.6.2
46A, 48, 50A, 72F 20.5
Sch 1
para 1–9.. 20.5
10.................................... 18.2.3.3, 20.5
(2).. 20.6.1
11–27... 20.5
Sch 5.. 20.5
Financial Services and Markets Act 2000
(Regulated Activities) (Amendment)
(No 2) Order 2013, SI 2013/1881.... 1.4, 4.6,
6.2, 13.1.1,
19.2, 22.5.3
Pt 3 (arts 10–12)................................ 34.3.1
art 10 .... 34.3.1
(19)... 30.6.1
20(15)... 17.4.1, 21.8
Pt 6 (arts 21–27)................................ 19.2
art 56–59 .... 30.4.1
Financial Services and Markets Act 2000
(Regulated Activities) Order 2001,
SI 2001/544 .... 1.3, 1.4, 1.5, 2.3,
3.1, 3.3, 3.4, 3.9, 4.1,
4.8.2, 6.1, 6.2, 6.3, 9.1,
13.1.1, 13.10, 15.3,
17.5.6, 17.6.1, 18.2.3.1,
18.2.3.2, 36.4
Pt II (arts 4–9L)............................ 30.2, 33.10
art 25A, 25C 13.1.3
Pt VIA (arts 36A–36G) 16.1
art 36A 13.1.3, 13.2,
13.7, 16.2.5, 16.3
(1)... 13.1.1
(c) 13.7
(2), (3)... 13.1.2
(4)... 13.1.1
36B.. 16.2.5
36E.................................... 13.1.3, 13.8
36H 16.2.3, 16.2.4, 16.3,
16.4, 21.2.3, 22.2.1, 22.2.2
(3)(e)–(h)..................................... 16.3
(4)–(6) 21.2.3
Pt VIIB (arts 39D–39M) 16.1
art 39D 16.2.1, 16.3

Financial Services and Markets Act 2000
(Regulated Activities) Order 2001,
SI 2001/544 – *contd*
art 39D(1), (2) 16.2.5
  39E.. 16.2.2, 16.3
    (1), (2)...................................... 16.2.5
  39F 16.2.3, 16.3
    (1), (2)...................................... 16.2.5
  39G 16.2.4, 16.3
    (1), (2)...................................... 16.2.5
  39H 16.2.5
  39I–39K, 39KA 16.2.6
  39L... 16.2.6
Pt II XIVA (arts 60B–60M) 3.5, 4.1,
                                              6.1, 13.8
art 60B................................... 3.5, 16.3, 22.7.2
    (3).. 3.2, 4.1, 6.2
  60C....................... 3.2, 3.5, 6.2, 6.3, 6.3.1,
                          6.4.2, 13.1.1, 14.4.2
    (2)...................................... 6.3.1, 7.3
    (3)......................... 6.3.1, 14.4.2, 35.1.3
      (b) 3.2
    (4)...................................... 6.3.1
    (5), (6) 6.3.1, 8.4.1,
                                          8.4.3, 14.4.2
    (7), (8) 6.3.1
  60D 3.5, 6.2, 6.3,
                                          6.3.2, 7.3, 13.1.1
    (1)–(4) 6.3.2
  60E..
                          3.3, 3.5, 4.4.3, 6.2,
                          6.3, 6.3.3, 13.1.1
    (1) 6.3.3
    (2) 6.3.3, 6.3.7
    (3), (4)................................ 6.3.3
    (5) 6.3.3, 6.3.7
    (6)–(10).............................. 6.3.3
  60F...................... 3.5, 6.2,, 6.3, 6.3.4
    (1), (2).............................. 6.3.4
    (3) 4.7.4.6,
                                          6.3.4, 17.5.6
    (4) 6.3.4, 6.3.7
    (5)–(8)............................... 6.3.4
  60G 3.5, 6.2, 6.3,
                                          6.3.5, 13.1.1
    (1)–(8)............................... 6.3.5
  60H 3.5, 6.2, 6.3,
                          6.3.6, 13.1.1, 35.1.3
    (1).................................... 6.3.7
  60HA.................................. 6.3, 6.3.3,
                          6.3.4, 6.3.6, 6.3.7
  60I, 60J, 60JA, 60JB, 60K 6.3, 6.3.8
  60L................................ 13.1.1, 18.1, 22.2.1
    (1) 3.1, 3.2, 4.1
  60LA 3.2
  60LB 3.5, 4.1
  60M....................................... 9.4.1
Pt II XIVB (arts 60N–60S) 5.2
art 60N 16.3
    (3)................................... 3.9, 5.2, 6.4
  60O 3.2, 6.4, 6.4.1,
                                          6.4.2, 13.1.1
    (1)–(3) 6.4.2
  60P 6.4, 6.4.1, 6.4.3

Financial Services and Markets Act 2000
(Regulated Activities) Order 2001,
SI 2001/544 – *contd*
art 60Q 6.4, 6.4.1,
                                          6.4.4, 13.1.1
  60R.................................... 6.4.1, 6.4.5
  61 .... 20.6.1
    (2) 18.2.3.2
    (3)................................... 2.1.1, 18.2.3.1,
                                          18.2.3.2
      (a) 2.1.1, 18.2.3.1,
                                          22.7.2
    (4)................................... 18.2.3.2
    (c) 18.2.3.1
    (5)................................... 18.2.3.2
  61A(1)............................. 2.1.1, 4.8.2, 6.3.1,
                          18.2.3.1, 18.2.3.2
    (2)................................... 2.1.1, 4.8.2,
                          18.2.3.1, 18.2.3.2
    (3)................................... 4.8.2, 18.2.3.2
      (a) 4.8.2
    (4)................................... 4.8.2, 18.2.3.2
    (5)................................... 18.2.3.2
    (6)................................... 2.1.1, 13.1.3
  62 .... 16.3
  63B(3)................................ 18.2.3.1
  63F(3)................................ 18.2.3.1
  63J(3)................................. 18.2.3.1
  72A 6.4.5, 16.2.6, 16.6
  72B(2)................................ 15.3
  72G 6.4.5, 16.2.6, 16.6
  72H 16.2.6, 16.6
  72I 22.7.1
  74A 17.6.1
Pt IIIA (arts 89A–89E).................... 16.1, 16.3,
                                          16.4, 33.10
art 89A 16.3, 16.6
    (1), (2).............................. 16.3
  89B................................... 16.3, 16.4,
                                          16.5, 16.6
    (1)–(3) 16.4
  89C................................... 16.6
  89D 16.6
Financial Services and Markets Act 2000
(Rights of Action) Regulations
2001, SI 2001/2256
art 3.. 25.24
Financial Services and Markets Act 2000
(Threshold Conditions) Order 2013,
SI 2013/555 .... 30.5
Financial Services and Markets Act 2000
(Variation of Threshold Conditions)
Order 2001, SI 2001/2507................ 30.5
Financial Services (Distance Marketing)
Regulations 2004, SI 2004/2095... 4.5, 4.7.4.8,
                          8.4.2, 8.4.5, 8.5,
                          8.6.7, 8.7.3.2, 8.7.4.3,
                          9.1, 10.3, 10.6, 15.8.2,
                          21.5.3, 21.10.2, 23.3, 23.7
reg 2(1)............................ 8.6.7, 15.8.2, 23.7
  7... 15.8.2
  8(1)...................................... 23.7
  10.. 8.6.7
    (1), (2), (5)........................ 10.6

Financial Services (Distance Marketing)
  Regulations 2004, SI 2004/2095 – *contd*
  reg 11(1)(d) 15.8.2
      (g) 8.6.7
  12... 15.8.2
Further Education Loans Regulations
  2012, SI 2012/1818 .... 21.2.5, 22.4

H

Hire-Purchase and Credit Sale Agreements (Control) Order 1976, SI 1976/
  1135... 3.8
Housing (Northern Ireland) Order 1981,
  NISI 1981/156 art 154(1)(a) 6.3.3

I

Insolvency Rules 1986, SI 1986/1925
  r 4.90 .... 18.2.6

J

Judgments   Enforcement   (Northern
  Ireland Consequential Amendments)
  Order 1981, SI 1981/234
  art 127 .... 11.7

M

Money Laundering Regulations 2007, SI
  2007/2157 .... 26.4
Money Laundering, Terrorist Financing
  and Transfer of Funds (Information
  on the Payer) Regulations 2017,
  SI 2017/692 .... 26.4
  reg 40, 41.. 26.4
Mortgage Credit Directive Order 2015,
  SI 2015/910 .... 1.3, 2.1.1, 2.1.2,
                              2.1.4, 2.3, 2.3.1,
                              2.5, 4.8.5, 18.2.2,
                              18.2.3.1, 35.2, 36.5
  Pt 3 (arts 3A–26) 2.6, 22.7.3
  art 4 .... 22.7.1
    (1)................................... 3.2, 22.7.2, 22.7.3
  Sch 1
    Pt 1 (paras 1, 2) 2.5

P

Payment Services Regulations 2009, SI
  2009/209 .... 4.7.4.8, 25.22.1
  reg 52.................................. 4.6, 17.4.1
  58(1)(b) 4.6, 17.4.1, 21.8
  59, 61, 62.. 4.7.4.8
  126.. 4.7.4.8
  Sch 6
    para 3.. 4.7.4.8

Payment Services Regulations 2017,
  SI 2017/752 .... 4.6, 4.7.4.8,
                              13.1.2, 17.6.1
  reg 2.. 13.1.2
  64, 76... 13.1.2
  Sch 1.. 13.1.2
Property Misdescriptions (Specified
  Matters) Order 1992, SI 1992/2834.. 20.9

R

Representation of the People (England
  and Wales) (Amendment) Regu-
  lations 2002, SI 2002/1871 .... 27.13.2
Rules of the Supreme Court 1965, SI 1965/
  1776
  Order 29
  r 4 .... 25.8

S

Stop Now Orders (EC Directive) Regulations 2001, SI 2001/1422 .... 35.7
Supply of Extended Warranties on
  Domestic Electrical Goods Order
  2005, SI 2005/37............................ 15.3
  art 8 .... 15.3

T

Timeshare, Holiday Products, Resale
  and Exchange Regulations 2010, SI
  2010/2960 .... 10.6, 15.9
Timeshare Regulations 1997, SI 1997/
  1081.. 15.9
Transfer of Funds (Information on the
  Payer) Regulations 2007, SI 2007/
  3298.. 26.4

U

Unfair Terms in Consumer Contracts
  Regulations 1994, SI 1994/3159...... 21.11,
                                          35.6
Unfair Terms in Consumer Contracts
  Regulations 1999, SI 1999/2083...... 3.2,
                              9.3.3.3, 9.3.3.4,
                              9.4.1, 11.6,
                              21.11, 35.6
  reg 5(5)... 8.4.5
  Sch 2... 9.3.3.4
  para 1(i)... 8.4.5
  (n)... 9.8

V

Value Added Tax Regulations 1995, SI
  1995/2518 .... 29.6.1, 29.6.7

Table of cases

[All references are to paragraph number]

A

Alliance and Leicester Building Society v Babbs [1999] GCCR 1657 .... 21.7
American Express Services Europe Ltd v Brandon [2011] EWCA Civ 1187, [2012] 1 All ER
    (Comm) 415, [2012] ECC 2, [2011] CTLC 177, [2011] GCCR 11353, CA.................... 25.3.1, 25.9
Anglo-Auto Finance Co Ltd v James [1963] 3 All ER 566, CA 9.3.2.4
Apex Supply Co Ltd, Re [1942] Ch 108, Ch D 9.3.2.4
Asda Stores Ltd v Mastercard Inc [2017] EWHC 93 (Comm), [2017] UKCLR 283, [2017]
    4 CMLR 32 .... 17.1, 17.5.1
Ashbroom Facilities v Bodley [1992] CCLR 31 .... 25.14
Axton v GE Money Mortgages Ltd [2015] GCCR 13105, [2015] EWHC 1343 (QB),
    [2015] ECC 29, [2015] CTLC 117 .... 24.2.1, 25.19

B

BICC Plc v Burndy Corp [1985] Ch 232, [1985] 2 WLR 132, [1985] 1 All ER 417,
    [1985] RPC 273, (1984) 81 LSG 3011, (1984) 128 SJ 750, CA 25.8
Bank of Credit and Commerce International SA (In Liquidation) (No 8), Re [1998] AC 214,
    [1997] 3 WLR 909, [1997] 4 All ER 568, [1998] Lloyd's Rep Bank 48, [1997] BCC 965,
    [1998] 1 BCLC 68, [1998] BPIR 211, (1997) 94(44) LSG 35, (1997) 147 NLJ 1653, (1997)
    141 SJLB 229, HL 18.2.7
Bank of Ireland (UK) plc v Dermot McLaughlin [2014] GCCR 12167...................................... 18.4
Bank of Scotland v Euclidian (No 1) Ltd [2007] EWHC 1732 (Comm), [2008] Lloyd's Rep
    IR 182, [2007] CTLC 151, (2007) 157 NLJ 1083 .... 4.5, 8.3.1, 10.6
Barber v NWS Bank plc [1996] 1 All ER 906, [1996] 1 WLR 641, CA 4.7.2.3
Barclays Bank plc v O'Brien [1994] 1 AC 180, [1993] 3 WLR 786, [1993] 4 All ER 417, HL .. 18.3
Barclays Bank plc v Taylor [1989] 1 WLR 1066, [1989] 3 All ER 563, [1989] Fin LR 304,
    (1990) 87(4) LSG 66, (1989) 133 SJ 1372, CA... 27.13.1
Barnes v Black Horse Ltd [2011] EWHC 1416 (QB), [2011] 2 All ER (Comm) 1130,
    [2011] GCCR 11301, QBD.. 24.2.2
Barton, Thompson & Co Ltd v Stapling Machine Co [1966] Ch 499, [1966] 2 WLR 1429, [1966]
    2 All ER 222, (1966) 110 SJ 313, Ch D 10.11
Bassano v Toft [2014] EWHC 377 (QB), [2014] ECC 14, [2014] CTLC 117, [2014] Bus LR D9,
    [2014] GCCR 12015 .... 6.5.1
Bentinck Ltd v Cromwell Engineering Co [1971] 1 QB 324, [1970] 3 WLR 1113, [1971] 1 All
    ER 33, [1971] RTR 7, (1970) 114 SJ 823... 25.6, 25.7
Bevin v Datum Finance Limited [2011] EWHC 3542 (Ch) 24.3
Black v Sumitomo Corpn [2001] EWCA Civ 1819, [2002] 1 WLR 1562, [2003] 3 All ER 643,
    [2002] 1 Lloyd's Rep 693, [2002] CPLR 148.. 25.19
Black Horse Ltd v Langford [2007] EWHC 907 (QB), [2007] All ER (D) 214, [2007] GCCR 6001,
    QB... 13.6.2, 14.3, 14.4.1
Black Horse Ltd v Speak [2010] EWHC 1866 (QB), [2010] CTLC 211, [2010] GCCR 10251,
    DR.. 3.1
Brandon v American Express Services Ltd *see* American Express Services v Brandon
Branwhite v Worcester Works Finance Ltd [1969] 1 AC 552, [1968] 3 All ER 104,
    [1999] RPC 397, HL.................. 5.2, 5.3.3, 10.11, 13.6.1, 14.3, 14.4.2
Bridge v Campbell Discount Co Ltd [1962] AC 600, [1962] 2 WLR 439, [1962] 1 All ER 385,
    (1962) 106 SJ 94, HL 4.7.2.3, 10.10.5

Bristol & West Building Society v Mothew (t/a Stapley & Co) [1998] Ch 1, [1997] 2 WLR 436, [1996] 4 All ER 698, [1997] PNLR 11, (1998) 75 P & CR 241, [1996] EG 136 (CS), (1996) 146 NLJ 1273, (1996) 140 SJLB 206, [1996] NPC 126 .... 14.1

British Eagle International Airlines Ltd v Compagnie Nationale Air France [1975] 1 WLR 758, [1975] 2 All ER 390, HL 18.2.6

Britax GmbH v Comrs of Inland Revenue *see* Lloyds UDT Finance Ltd v Chartered Finance Trust Holdings plc

Brookes v Retail Credit Cards Ltd (1985) 150 JP 131, [1986] CCLR 5, [1986] Fin LR 86, [1986] Crim LR 327, (1986) 150 JPN 15, DC 13.2

Brookman v Welcome Financial Services Ltd [2015] GCRR 13267 .... 24.2.1

Brophy v HFC Bank [2011] EWCA Civ 67, [2011] Bus LR 1004, [2011] ECC 14, [2011] CTLC 28, [2011] GCCR 11051, CA 8.3.2

Burrell v Helical (Bramshott Place) Ltd [2015] EWHC 3727 (Ch), [2017] ECC 3, [2016] HLR 18, [2016] CTLC 1, [2016] 1 P & CR DG21 .... 3.1

Butterworth v Kingsway Motors Ltd [1954] 1 WLR 1286, [1954] 2 All ER 694, (1954) 98 SJ 717, Assizes 4.7.2.3

C

C & E Comrs v Diners Club Ltd [1989] 1 WLR 1196, [1989] 2 All ER 385, [1989] STC 407, [1999] GCCR 1213, CA 17.1, 29.6.1

C & E Comrs v Mercedes-Benz Financial Services UK Ltd (unreported, 4 October 2017) 29.6.3

CIBC Mortgages plc v Pitt [1994] 1 AC 200, [1993] 3 WLR 802, [1993] 4 All ER 433, [1994] 1 FLR 17, [1994] 1 FCR 374, (1994) 26 HLR 90, (1994) 13 Tr LR 180, [1994] CCLR 68, [1993] Fam Law 79, [1993] EG 174 (CS), (1993) 143 NLJ 1514, (1993) 137 SJLB 240, [1993] NPC 136, HL 18.3

Car and Universal Finance Co Ltd v Caldwell [1965] 1 QB 525, [1964] 2 WLR 600, [1964] 1 All ER 290, CA 13.6.1

Card Protection Plan Ltd v Comrs of Customs and Excise [2001] UKHL 4, [2002] 1 AC 202, [2001] 2 WLR 329, [2001] 2 All ER 143, HL 15.6

Carey v HSBC Bank Plc [2009] EWHC 3417 (QB), [2010] Bus LR 1142, [2009] CTLC 103, (2010) 154(2) SJLB 28, [2009] GCCR 9951, QBD 8.8, 10.8, 25.18

Cedar Holdings Ltd v Jenkins [1988] CCLR 34 .... 25.18

Cedar Holdings Ltd v Thompson [1993] CCLR 7 .... 25.14

Charge Card Services Ltd (No 2), Re [1987] Ch 150, [1986] 3 WLR 697, [1986] 3 All ER 289, (1986) 2 BCC 99373, [1987] BCLC 17, [1987] PCC 36, [1987] ECC 91, [1987] Fin LR 1, (1986) 83 LSG 3424, (1986) 130 SJ 801, [2000] GCCR 1231, Ch D ... 4.2.2, 17.1, 17.2, 18.2.6, 18.2.7

Chartered Trust plc v Pitcher [1988] RTR 72, [1987] LS Gaz 1147, (1987) 131 SJ 503, CA ... 25.7, 25.15

Christie Owen & Davis plc v King, 1998 SCLR 786, 1998 GWD 22-1103, Ct of Sess 13.2

Christofi v Barclays Bank plc 2000] 1 WLR 937, [1999] 4 All ER 437, [1999] 2 All ER (Comm) 417, [1999] Lloyd's Rep Bank 469, [2000] 1 FLR 163, [1999] BPIR 855, [2000] Fam Law 161, (1999) 96(29) LSG 29, CA 27.13.1

Citibank International plc v Schleider [2001] GCCR 2281 .... 12.3

Clark v Ardington Electrical Services [2001] EWCA Civ 585, [2002] GCCR 4691, CA 5.2, 5.4.8, 6.3.4.1

Clayton's Case. See Devaynes v Noble

Clixby v Poutney (Inspector of Taxes) [1968] Ch 719, [1968] 2 WLR 865, [1968] 1 All ER 802, 44 TC 575, (1967) 46 ATC 398, [1967] TR 383, 117 NLJ 1343, (1968 112 SJ 16 .... 14.4.3

Close Asset Finance v Care Graphics Machinery Ltd [2000] CCLR 43, 97(12) LSG 42, [2000] GCCR 2617, QBD 4.7.2.1

Colesworthy v Collman Services Ltd [1993] CCLR 4 .... 10.6

Commercial First Business Ltd v Pickup & Vernon [2016] GCCR 14171 .... 13.9

Conroy v Kenny [1999] 1 WLR 1340, [1999] Lloyd's Rep Bank 43, [1999] CCLR 35, (1999) 96(7) LSG 36, [1999] All ER (D)146, CA 6.3.1, 13.3.1

Content Services Ltd v Bundesarbeitskammer (C-49/11) [2012] 2 All ER (Comm) 1019, [2012] 3 CMLR 34, ECJ 23.7

Cornelius v Phillips [1918] AC 199, (1917) 87 LJ KB 246, HL 6.3.1, 13.3.1

Coventry City Council v Lazarus [1999] GCCR 1909 .... 26.5.4

Currys Ltd v Jessop [1999] GCCR 3407 .... 20.7

D

Deutsche Bank (Suisse) SA v Khan [2013] EWHC 482 (Comm) 24.2.2

Devaynes v Noble (1816)1 Mer 572 .... 4.2.2

Dimond v Lovell [2000] QB 216, [1999] 3 WLR 561, [1999] 3 All ER 1, [2001] GCCR 2303, CA 3.1, 5.1, 5.4.8, 7.2, 8.3.2

Dimond v Lovell [2002] 1 AC 384, [2000] 2 WLR 1121, [2000] 2 All ER 897, [2001] GCCR 2751,
HL 3.10, 6.3.4.1, 8.7.3.1
Director General of Fair Trading v First National Bank plc [2001] UKHL 52, [2002] 1 AC 481,
[2001] 3 WLR 1297, [2002] 1 All ER 97, [2001] GCCR 3075, HL 9.3.3.4, 9.4.1, 24.4, 25.14,
25.18
Dixon v Clarke (1848) 5 CB 365 .... 10.11
Dudley Metropolitan Borough v Colorvision plc [1999] GCCR 2135 .... 20.7
Durant v Financial Services Authority (Disclosure) [2003] EWCA Civ 1746, [2004] FSR 28 .... 27.14

E
Elliott v Director General of Fair Trading [1980] 1 WLR 977, [1980] ICR 629, (1980) 124 SJ 463,
QBD 4.7.4.7, 17.4.1, 21.8

F
Financings Ltd v Baldock [1963] 2 QB 104, [1963] 2 WLR 359, [1963] 1 All ER 443, (1963)
107 SJ 15, CA 9.3.2.4, 25.3.1
Footman Bower & Co Ltd, Re [1961] Ch 443, [1961] 2 WLR 667, [1961] 2 All ER 161, (1961)
105 SJ 282, Ch D 4.2.2
Forthright Finance Ltd v Ingate (Carlyle Finance Ltd third party) [1997] 4 All ER 99,
[1997] CCLR 95, [1999] GCCR 2213, CA 4.7.2.1, 13.6.2, 14.4.1
Forward Trust plc v Whymark [1990] 2 QB 670, [1989] 3 WLR 1229, [1989] 3 All ER 915,
[1999] GCCLC 1363, CA 9.4.1, 10.10.2

G
GE Capital Bank Ltd v Rushton [2005] EWCA Civ 1556, [2006] 1 WLR 899, [2006] 3 All
ER 865, [2005] GCCR 5541, CA 6.3.1
Gaspet Ltd (formerly Saga Petroleum (UK)) v Elliss (Inspector of Taxes) [1985] 1 WLR 1214,
[1985] STC 572, (1985) 82 LSG 2742, 60 TC 91, (1985) 129 SJ 623 .... 14.4.3
Goker v NWS Bank plc [1990] CCLR 34, QBD 25.6
Goshawk Dedicated (No 2) Ltd v Governor and Company of Bank of Scotland [2005] EWHC 2906
(Ch), [2006] 2 All ER 610, [2005] GCCR 5431 .... 4.5, 8.3.1, 8.6.7, 10.6, 12.4
Governor and Co of the Bank of Scotland v Alfred Truman [2005] EWHC 583 (QB),
[2005] GCCR 5491 .... 4.4.2
Governor and Co of the Bank of Scotland v Euclidian (No 1) Ltd [2007] All ER (D) 330 .... 8.6.7, 12.4
Graves v Capital Homes Ltd [2014] EWCA Civ 1297, [2014] CTLC 233, [2015] 1 P & CR
DG17, [2014] GCCR 12047 .... 24.2.2

H
Hare v Schurek [1999] GCCR 1669, CA 6.5.1
Harrison v Black Horse Ltd [2011] EWCA Civ 1128, [2012] ECC 7, [2012] Lloyd's Rep IR 521,
[2011] CTLC 105, (2011) 155(39) SJLB 31, [2011] GCCR 11327, CA 24.4
Hazell v Hammersmith and Fulham London Borough Council [1991] 2 WLR 372, HL 28.2.6.2
Heath v Southern Pacific Mortgage Ltd. See Southern Pacific Mortgage Ltd v Heath
Helby v Matthews [1895] AC 471, [1895–99] All ER Rep 821, HL 4.7.2.1
Hicks v Walker [1984] Crim LR 495, (1984) 148 JP 636, [1999] GCCR 721 .... 13.2, 13.7
Hitchens v General Guarantee Corpn Ltd [2001] EWCA Civ 359 .... 4.7.2.3
Holman v Co-operative Wholesale Society Ltd [2001] GCCR 2777 .... 20.7
Home Insulation v Wadsley (1989) 153 JP 92, [1988] CCLR 25, DC 10.10.4
Hudson v Shogun *see* Shogun Finance Ltd v Hudson
Humberclyde Finance Ltd v Thompson [1999] ECCR 2141, CA 19.3.3
Hunter v Lex Vehicle Finance Ltd [2005] EWHC 223 (Ch), [2005] BPIR 586, Ch D 25.7
Hurstanger Ltd v Wilson [2007] EWCA Civ 299, [2007] 1 WLR 2351, [2007] 4 All ER 1118,
[2007] 2 All ER (Comm) 1037, [2008] Bus LR 216, [2007] CTLC 59, (2007) 104(16) LSG 23,
(2007) 157 NLJ 555, (2007) 151 SJLB 467, [2007] NPC 41, [2007] GCCR 5951, CA 8.3.2,
8.7.3.2, 13.9, 14.1

J
JD Williams & Co v McCauley Parsons & Jones [1999] GCCR 1375, CA 5.3.3, 13.6.1
JP Morgan Chase Bank, National Association v Northern Rock (Asset Management) plc
[2014] EWHC 291 (Ch), [2014] 1 WLR 2197, [2015] ECC 5, [2014] CTLC 33 .... 11.2, 11.4, 11.9.4
Jarrett v Barclays Bank plc; Jones v First National Bank plc; Peacock v First National Bank plc
[1999] QB 1, [1999] GCCR 2151, CA 15.9, 35.8.1
Jenkins v Lombard North Central plc [1984] 1 WLR 307, [1984] 1 All ER 828, [1999]
GCCR 623 .... 20.7

Johnson v Diprose [1893] 1 QB 512, CA 18.2.5.1
Jones v Link Financial Ltd [2012] EWHC 2402 (QB), [2013] 1 All ER (Comm) 572,
    [2012] ECC 23, [2012] CTLC 54, [2012] GCCR 11413, QBD 7.7

K

Kassam v Chartered Trust Plc [1998] RTR 220, [1998] CCLR 54, [1999] GCCR 2245, CA 25.7
Ketley v Gilbert [2001] 1 WLR 986, [2001] RTR 22, [2001] GCCR 2951, CA 6.3.4.1
Khodari v Tamimi [2008] EWHC 3065 (QB), [2008] CTLC 269, [2008] GCCR 8561, QBD 24.2.2
King v Daltray [2003] EWCA Civ 808, CA 6.3.4.1
Kneale v Barclays Bank Plc (t/a Barclaycard) [2010] EWHC 1900 (Comm), [2010] CTLC 233,
    QBD 25.19
Koksal (t/a Arcis Management Consultancy) v Financial Conduct Authority [2016] UKUT 478
    (TCC), [2016] CTLC 201, [2016] GCCR 14059 & 14117 .... 25.23

L

Lease Management Services v Purnell Secretarial Services Ltd (Canon (South West) Ltd, third
    party) [1994] CCLR 127, CA 9.3.4.1, 21.13
Lloyds Bowmaker Leasing Ltd v John R MacDonald [1999] GCCR 3443 (Sheriff's Court) 13.6.2
Lloyds UDT Finance Ltd v Chartered Finance Trust Holdings plc [2002] EWCA Civ 806,
    [2002] STC 956, [2002] UKHRR 929, 74 TC 662, [2002] BTC 247, [2002] STI 853 .... 5.1
Log Book Loans Ltd v The Office of Fair Trading; Nine Regions Ltd (trading as Log Book
    Loans) v Office of Fair Trading [2010] UKFTT 643, [2010] GCCR 1050, GRC 18.2.5.1, 20.1
Lombard North Central plc v Butterworth [1987] QB 527, [1987] 2 WLR 7, [1987] 1 All
    ER 267, CA 9.3.2.4, 25.3.1
Lombard Tricity Finance Ltd v Paton [1989] 1 All ER 918, CA 7.6
Lomard North Central plc v Stobart [1990] CCLR 53, CA 10.9
London North Securities Ltd v Meadows [2005] EWCA Civ 956, [2005] GCCR 5381, CA 3.1, 4.3,
                                                                                            8.7.3.1

M

Maurice Binks (Turf Accountants) Ltd v Huss 1971] 1 WLR 52, [1971] 1 All ER 104, (1970)
    114 SJ 930, QBD 20.7
McGinn v Grangewood Securities Ltd [2002] EWCA Civ 522, [2002] GCCR 4761, CA 3.1, 4.3, 8.7.3.1
McGuffick v Royal Bank of Scotland Plc [2009] EWHC 2386 (Comm), [2010] 1 All ER 634,
    [2010] 1 All ER (Comm) 48, [2010] Bus LR 1108, [2010] ECC 11, [2009] GCCR 9551,
    QBD 25.1
McMillan Williams v Range [2004] EWCA Civ 294, [2004] 1 WLR 1858, [2004] GCCR 5041,
    CA 3.1
McMullon v Secure the Bridge Ltd [2015] EWCA Civ 884, [2015] GCCR 13159 .... 24.2.2
McWilliam v Norton Finance (UK) Ltd (in liquidation) [2015] EWCA Civ 186,
    [2015] GCCR 13027, [2015] 1 All ER (Comm) 1026, [2015] 2 BCLC 730, [2015] PNLR 22,
    [2015] CTLC 60 .... 13.8, 13.9, 14.1
Maple Leaf Macro Volatility Master Fund v Rouvroy [2009] EWHC 257 (Comm), [2009] 2 All
    ER (Comm) 287, [2009] 1 Lloyd's Rep 475 .... 24.2.2
Mercantile Credit Co Ltd v Hamblin [1965] 2 QB 242, [1964] 3 WLR 798, [1964] 3 All ER 592,
    CA 13.6.1, 14.3
Metsoja v H Norman Pitt & Co Ltd [1999] GCCR 1339 .... 20.7
Monde Petroleum SA v WesternZagros Ltd [2016] EWHC 1472 (Comm), [2017] 1 All ER
    (Comm) 1009, [2016] 2 Lloyd's Rep 229, 167 Con LR 15 .... 9.3.3.4
Moorgate Mercantile Leasing v Isobel Gell and Ugolini Dispensers (UK) Ltd [1988] CCLR 1,
    CC 13.6.1, 13.6.2
Moorgate Services Ltd v Kabir [1999] GCCR 1947, CA 4.5
Multiservice Bookbinding Ltd v Marden [1979] Ch 84, [1978] 2 WLR 535, [1978] 2 All ER 489,
    (1978) 35 P & CR 201, (1978) 122 SJ 210, Ch D 24.4
Mutual Finance v Davidson (No 2) [1963] 1 WLR 134, [1963] 1 All ER 133, CA 7.2
Mynshul Asset Finance v Clarke (t/a Peacock Hotel) [1992] CLY 487, CC 13.6.1

N

NRAM plc v McAdam [2014] EWHC 4174 (Comm), [2015] 2 All ER 340, [2015] 1 All
    ER (Comm) 1239, [2015] Bus LR 443, [2015] ECC 11, [2014] CTLC 244; *revs'd*
    [2015] EWCA Civ 751, [2016] 3 All ER 665, [2016] 2 All ER (Comm) 333, [2016] Bus
    LR 232, [2015] ECC 30, [2015] CTLC 169 .... 11.2
National Employers Mutual General Insurance Association v Jones [1990] 1 AC 24, [1988]
    2 WLR 952, [1988] 2 All ER 425, HL 4.7.2.3

National Guardian Mortgage Corporation v Wilkes [1993] CCLR 1 .... 25.13
National Home Loans Corpn plc v Hannah [1999] GCCR 2071 .... 7.1
National Westminster Bank plc v Story and Pallister [2000] GCCR 2381, CA 7.1
National Westminster Bank v Devon County Council and Devon County Council v Abbey
    National plc [1999] GCCR 1685 .... 26.5.2
Nejad v City Index Ltd [2001] GCCR 2461, [2000] CCLR 7, CA 3.1
Nelmes v NRAM plc [2016] EWCA Civ 491, [2016] CTLC 106, [2016] GCCR 14081 .... 13.9, 14.1,
    24.2.2
Nissan Finance UK Ltd v Lockhart [1999] GCCR 1649, CA 8.3.2
North Central Wagon Finance Co Ltd v Brailsford [1962] 1 WLR 1288, [1962] 1 All ER 502,
    (1962) 106 SJ 878, Assizes 4.7.2.2
Northgran Finance Ltd v Ashley [1963] 1 QB 476, [1962] 3 WLR 1360, [1962] 3 All ER 973,
    (1962) 106 SJ 877, CA... 13.6.2

O

OT Computers, Re [2004] 1 All ER (Comm) 320, [2003] GCCR 4951 .... 15.1
Office of Fair Trading v Abbey National plc [2009] UKSC 6, [2010] 1 AC 696, [2009]
    3 WLR 1215, [2010] 1 All ER 667, [2010] 2 All ER (Comm) 945, [2010] 1 Lloyd's Rep 281,
    [2010] 1 CMLR 44, [2010] Eu LR 309, (2009) 159 NLJ 1702, (2009) 153(45) SJLB 28,
    [2009] GCCR 9851, SC... 4.7.4.2, 4.7.4.5, 9.3.3.4
Office of Fair Trading v Ashbourne Management Services Ltd [2011] EWHC 1237 (Ch),
    [2011] ECC 31, [2011] CTLC 237, [2011] GCCR 11201, Ch D 3.1, 9.3.3.3
Office of Fair Trading v Lloyds TSB Bank [2007] UKHL 48, [2007] 3 WLR 733, [2008] 1 All
    ER 205, [2007] GCCR 6101, HL... 4.3, 4.4.2, 17.4.4, 35.8.1
Office of Fair Trading v Lloyds TSB Bank plc [2004] GCCR 5061 .... 4.4.2
Office of Fair Trading v Lloyds TSB Bank plc [2006] EWCA Civ 268, [2007] QB 1, [2006]
    3 WLR 452, [2006] 2 All ER 821, [2006] GCCR 5701, CA..................................... 4.4.2, 17.1, 17.2
On Demand Information plc (in administrative receivership) v Michael Gerson (Finance Credit)
    plc [2002] UKHL 13, [2003] 1 AC 368, [2002] 2 WLR 919, [2002] 2 All ER 949, [2002] All
    ER (D) 116 (Apr), [2003] GCCR 4651, HL 25.8

P

PDHL Ltd v Financial Conduct Authority [2016] UKUT 130 (TCC), [2016] GCCR 14001,
    14013 & 14045 .... 25.23
Padden v Bevan Ashford Solicitors [2011] EWCA Civ 1616, [2012] 1 WLR 1759, [2012] 2 All
    ER 718, [2012] 2 Costs LO 223, [2012] 2 FCR 264, [2012] PNLR 14, CA................... 6.3.6.1, 18.3
Paragon Finance plc v Nash and Staunton [2002] 1 WLR 685, [2002] 2 All ER 248, [2001] 2 All
    ER (Comm) 1025, [2001] GCCR 3073D, CA.. 9.3.2.3, 9.5.1
Paragon Mortgages Ltd v McEwan-Peters [2011] EWHC 2491 (Comm), [2011] GCCR 11367,
    QBD 24.2.2
Pattini v First Leicester Buses Ltd [2011] GCCR 11387 .... 5.4.8
Phoenix Recoveries (UK) Ltd SARL v Kotecha [2011] EWCA Civ 105, [2011] GCCR 1101,
    [2011] ECC 13, [2011] CTLC 94 .... 8.8
Photoprint v Forward Trust Group (1993) 12 Tr LR 146 .... 9.3.3.2
Plevin v Paragon Personal Finance Ltd [2014] UKSC 61, [2014] 1 WLR 4222, [2015] 1 All
    ER 625, [2015] 1 All ER (Comm) 1007, [2014] Bus LR 1257, [2015] ECC 2, [2015]
    Lloyd's Rep IR 247, [2014] GCCR 12085 .... 7.1, 13.5, 13.8, 14.4.2, 14.4.3,
    17.4.5, 24.2.1
Powell v Lloyds Bowmaker Ltd [1999] GCCR 3523 (Sheriff's Court) 13.6.2
Primback Ltd v Comrs of Customs & Excise [1996] STC 757, [1996] 3 CMLR 589,
    [1996] CCLR 81, CA.. 29.6.3
Purnell Secretarial Services Ltd v Lease Management Services Ltd [1999] GCCR 1841, CA 5.3.3

R

R v Chapman [2015] EWCA Crim 539, [2015] QB 883, [2015] 3 WLR 726, [2016] 1 All
    ER 1065, [2015] 2 Cr App R 10, [2015] Crim LR 633, [2015] GCCR 13181 .... 26.5.4
R v Curr [1999] GCCR 533, CA 26.5.4
R v Delmayne (Anthony) [1970] 2 QB 170, [1969] 3 WLR 300, [1969] 2 All ER 980, (1969) 53
    Cr App R 392, (1969) 133 JP 458, (1969) 113 SJ 605, CA.. 20.1
R v Kettering Magistrates' Court, ex p MRB Insurance Brokers Ltd; sub nom R v Kettering
    Justices, ex p MRB Insurance Brokers Ltd [2000] 2 All ER (Comm) 353, (2000) 164 JP 585,
    [2000] CCLR 51, (2000) 164 JPN 762, (2000) 97(20) LSG 43, [2000] GCCR 2701, DC ... 20.7,
    26.5.4
R v Marshall (1989) 90 Cr App Rep 73, [1999] GCCR 1345, CA.. 13.3.1

R v Modupe [1999] GCCR 1595, CA 8.3.2
R v Priestly [1999] GCCR 641, CA.. 26.5.4
R (on the application of the British Bankers Association) v Financial Services Authority
    [2011] EWHC 999 (Admin), [2011] GCCR 11251, [2011] Bus LR 1531, [2011] ACD 71,
    (2011) 108 (18) LSG 20.. 15.5
R (on the application of Cherwell District Council) v First Secretary of State [2004] EWCA Civ
    1420, [2005] 1 WLR 1128, [2005] 1 P & CR 22, [2005] 1 PLR 11, [2005] JPL 768, [2004]
    45 EG 125 (CS), (2004) 101 (45) LSG 32, (2004) 148 SJLB 1284, [2004] NPC 159......... 14.4.3
R (on the application of Robertson) v City of Wakefield Metropolitan District Council
    [2001] EWHC Admin 915, [2002] QB 1052, [2002] 2 WLR 889, [2002] BLGR 286,
    [2002] ACD 40, (2002) 99 (2) LSG 28, (2001) 145 SJLB 267, [2001] All ER (D) 243 ...... 27.13.2
R (on the application of S) v Social Security Comr [2009] EWHC 2221 (Admin),
    [2010] PTSR 1785, (2009) 12 CCL Rep 654, (2009) 153 (34) SJLB 29 .... 14.4.3
R & B Customs Brokers Co Ltd v United Dominions Trust Ltd [1999] GCCR 1195, CA.......... 13.6.2
Rahman v HSBC Bank Plc [2012] EWHC 11, Ch D 24.2.2
Rankine v American Express Services Europe Ltd [2008] CTLC 195, [2009] CCLR 3,
    [2008] GCCR 7701, QBD... 25.1, 25.13, 25.18
Read's Trustee in Bankruptcy v Smith [1951] Ch 439, [1951] 1 All ER 406, (1951) 95 SJ 156,
    Ch D 10.11
Robertson v Canadian Imperial Bank of Commerce [1994] 1 WLR 1493, [1995] 1 All ER 824,
    [1995] ECC 338, (1994) 91(41) LSG 39, (1994) 138 SJLB 211, PC (St Vincent and
    Grenadines) 27.13.1, 27.13.2
Rochdale Metropolitan Borough Council v Dixon [2011] EWCA Civ 1173, [2012] PTSR 1336,
    [2012] HLR 6, [2012] BLGR 251, [2011] 43 EG 105 (CS).. 14.4.3
Roller Group Ltd and Roller Finance Ltd v Sumner [1995] CCLR 1 .... 20.7
Royal Bank of Scotland plc v Etridge (No 2) [2001] UKHL 44, [2002] 2 AC 773, [2001]
    3 WLR 1021, [2001] 4 All ER 449, [2001] GCCR 3105, HL............................... 6.3.6.1, 18.3

S
Santander UK plc v Harrison & Harrison [2013] EWHC 199 (QB), [2013] Bus LR 501,
    [2013] ECC 13, [2013] CTLC 69, [2013] GCCR 11700.. 3.1, 7.7
Scotland v British Credit Trust Ltd [2014] EWCA Civ 790, [2015] 1 All ER 708, [2015] 1 All
    ER (Comm) 401, [2014] Bus LR 1079, [2015] CTLC 25, [2014] GCCR 12141 .... 13.5, 24.2.1
Seddon v Tekin Seddon, Dowsett v Clifford, Beasly v PPP/Columbus Healthcare [2001]
    GCCR 2865 (Oxford County Court)... 6.3.4.1
Shogun Finance Ltd v Hudson [2003] UKHL 62, [2004] 1 AC 919, [2003] 3 WLR 1371, [2004]
    1 All ER 215, [2004] 1 All ER (Comm) 332, [2004] 1 Lloyd's Rep 532, [2004] RTR 12,
    (2003) 100 (46) LSG 25, (2003) 153 NLJ 1790, (2003) 147 SJLB 1368......................... 4.7.2.3, 14.3
Southern Pacific Mortgage Ltd v Heath; sub nom Heath v Southern Pacific Mortgage Ltd
    [2009] EWCA Civ 1135, [2010] Ch 254, [2010] 2 WLR 1081, [2010] Bus LR 616, [2010]
    1 All ER 748, [2010] 1 All ER (Comm) 839, [2010] 1 EGLR 55, [2010] 6 EG 116, [2009]
    45 EG 104 (CS), (2009) 159 NLJ 1581, [2009] NPC 124, [2009] GCCR 9051, CA........... 7.1
Southern Pacific Personal Loans Ltd v Walker [2010] UKSC 32, [2010] 1 WLR 1819, [2010]
    4 All ER 277, [2011] 1 All ER (Comm) 164, [2010] Bus LR 1396, [2010] CTLC 150,
    (2010) 160 NLJ 1011, (2010) 154(27) SJLB 28, [2010] GCCR 10151, SC 3.1, 19.1
Sovereign Leasing plc v Ali; Sovereign Leasing plc v Martindale [1992] CCLR 1, QBD 25.12
Sternlight v Barclays Bank Plc [2010] EWHC 1865 (QB), [2010] CTLC 115, QBD 19.3.2
Stevenson v Beverley Bentinck [1976] 1 WLR 483, [1976] 2 All ER 606, [1976] RTR 543, 19
    Man Law 2, (1976) 120 SJ 197, CA 4.7.2.3, 6.3.1
Stevens v Equity Syndicate Management Ltd [2015] EWCA Civ 93, [2015] 4 All ER 458,
    [2015] RTR 24, [2015] Lloyd's Rep IR 503, [2015] GCCR 13001 .... 5.4.8
Stoneleigh Finance Ltd v Phillips [1965] 2 QB 537, [1965] 2 WLR 508, [1965] 1 All ER 513,
    [1999] GCCR 259, CA 5.5
Sutherland Professional Funding Ltd v Bakewells [2013] EWHC 2685 (QB), [2014] CTLC 1,
    [2013] GCCR 11756 .... 4.4.2, 4.4.3, 4.5, 15.1

T
TRM Copy Centres (UK) Ltd v Lanwall Services Ltd [2007] EWHC 1738 (QB), [2007] All
    ER(D) 287, [2007] CTLC 207; *aff'd* [200] EWCA Civ 382, [2008] 4 All ER 608, [2008]
    2 All ER (Comm) 1021, [2008] Bus LR 1231, [2008] CTLC 181; *aff'd* [2009] UKHL 35,
    [2009] 1 WLR 1375, [2009] 4 All ER 33, [2010] All ER (Comm) 1098, [2009] Bus
    LR 1069, [2009] 2 Lloyd's Rep 332, (2009) 153 (24) SJLB 31 .... 3.9, 5.1, 5.2
Tesco Supermarkets Ltd v Nattrass [1971] 1 QB 133, [1970] 3 WLR 572, [1970] 3 All ER 357,
    68 LGR 722, (1970) 114 SJ 664, QBD.. 26.5.4

Tournier v National Provincial and Union Bank of England [1924] 1 KB 461, CA 27.13.1
Townson v FCE Bank plc (t/a/ Ford Credit) [2016] GCCR 14155.. 24.2.1
Transag Haulage Ltd v Leyland DAF Finance plc and Lease Plan UK Ltd [1994] BCC 356,
    [1994] 2 BCLC 88, [1999] GCCR 1819, Ch D 10.11, 25.8

U
UDT v Whitfield [1987] CCLR 60 .... 13.6.2
United Dominions Trust Ltd v Kirkwood [1966] 2 QB 431, [1966] 2 WLR 1083, [1966] 1 All
    ER 968, CA 4.7.4.2
United Overseas Bank v Jiwani [1976] 1 WLR 964, [1977] 1 All ER 733, (1976) 120 SJ 329,
    QBD 11.3, 11.9.4

V
Volkswagen Financial Services (UK) Ltd v Ramage [2007] CTLC 119, [2007] GCCR 6181 ..... 10.10.5

W
Wadham Stringer Finance Ltd v Meany [1981] 1 WLR 39, [1980] 3 All ER 789, [1980] Com
    LR 7, [1981] RTR 152, (1980) 124 SJ 807, [1999] CCR 551, QBD.................................... 4.7.2.3
Watchtower Investments Ltd v Payne [2001] EWCA Civ 1159, [2001] 35 LS Gaz R 32, CA..... 3.1, 4.3,
                                                                                                                      8.7.3.1
Wilson v First County Trust Ltd (No 1) [2001] QB 407, [2001] 2 WLR 302, [2001] HRLR 7,
    (2001) 98(3) LSG 42, (2000) 144 SJLB 288, [2001] GCCR 2901, CA 19.1
Wilson v First County Trust Ltd (No 2) [2003] UKHL 40, [2004] 1 AC 816, [2003] 3 WLR 568,
    [2003] 4 All ER 97, [2003] GCCR 4931, HL................................. 3.1, 8.3.2, 18.2.12, 24.4
Wilson v Robertsons (London) Ltd [2005] GCCR 5301 .... 3.1, 18.2.12
Wood v Capital Bridging Finance Ltd [2015] EWCA Civ 451, [2015] ECC 17, [2015] CTLC 155,
    [2015] GCCR 13013 .... 10.14
Woodchester Equipment (Leasing) Ltd v British Association of Canned and Preserved Foods
    Importers and Distributors Ltd [1999] GCCR 1923, CA.. 5.3.3, 13.6.1, 14.3
Woodchester Lease Management Services Ltd v Swain & Co [1999] 1 WLR 263, [1998] All ER
    (D) 339, [1999] ECCR 2255, CA 25.3.1
Woodchester Leasing Equipment Ltd v R M Clayton and D M Clayton (t/a Sudbury Sports)
    (October 1993, unreported) Sudbury County Court [1994] CCLR 87 .... 13.6.1, 13.6.2

Y
Yates & Lorenzelli v Nemo Personal Finance [2010] GCCR 10351... 7.1
Yeoman Credit Ltd v Waragowski [1961] 1 WLR 1124, [1961] 3 All ER 145, CA 9.3.2.4, 25.3.1

Z
Zoan v Rouamba [2000] 1 WLR 1509, [2000] 2 All ER 620, [2001] GCCR 2581, CA 6.3.4.1

Chapter 1

Consumer credit law in context

1.1 THE EUROPEAN UNION SETTING

The United Kingdom originally set the tone and pace for consumer credit law reform in the European Union, heralded by the Report of the Committee on Consumer Credit, known as the Crowther Report,[1] which led to the passing of the Consumer Credit Act 1974. The European Parliament and Council, with the objective of achieving full harmonisation in the European Union, superimposed its own position on consumer credit in the European Union, including the United Kingdom, by Council Directive 87/102/EEC and Directive 2008/48/EC of the European Parliament and of the Council.[2] The 2008 Directive is a full harmonisation Directive which applies to all EU Member States, twenty-seven in number at the time the Directive was made.

In the words of the Directive: 'Full harmonisation is necessary in order to ensure that all customers in the Community enjoy a high and equivalent level of protection of their interests and to create a genuine internal market. Member States should therefore not be allowed to maintain or introduce national provisions other than those laid down in this Directive. However, such restriction should only apply where there are provisions harmonised in this Directive. Where no such harmonised provisions exist, Member states should remain free to maintain or introduce national legislation'.[3] It still remains to be seen whether the Directive's objective of full harmonisation is achieved and whether this promotes cross-border credit.

As the Directive applies to consumer credit agreements for credit up to a prescribed limit and UK consumer credit law applies irrespective of any credit limit, there are now two regimes which apply to consumer credit agreements in the UK, one relating to consumer credit agreements within the scope of the Directive and the other to consumer credit agreements outside its scope.[4] It will become clear in the course of time whether the UK's dual consumer credit regime is workable and whether it achieves the purpose of protecting the consumer, whilst at the same time ensuring an adequate supply of credit.

Whilst regulated credit agreements secured on land were already subject to the Consumer Credit Act 1974 as early as that Act's enactment, they were only brought within the consumer credit regime in the EU by the so-called Mortgages Directive,[5] which was implemented in the UK by the Mortgage Credit Directive Order 2015.[6] The Mortgages Directive applies to:

(a) credit agreements which are secured either by a mortgage or by another comparable security commonly used in a Member State on residential immovable property or secured by a right related to residential immovable property; and

(b) credit agreements the purpose of which is to acquire or retain property rights in land or in an existing or projected building.

A brief consideration of the development of consumer credit law in the UK since 1974 will assist to place the subject in its context.

1 Established under the chairmanship of Lord Crowther, March 1971 (Cmnd 4596).
2 Directive 2008/48/EC of the European Parliament and of the Council of 23 April 2008 on credit agreements for consumers and repealing Council Directive 87/102/EEC.
3 Ibid., Recital (9).
4 See further **Chapter 2**.
5 Directive 2014/17/EU of the European Parliament and of the Council of 4 February 2014 on credit agreements for consumers relating to residential immovable property and amending Directives 2008/48/EC and 2013/36/EU and Regulation (EU) No 1093/2010.
6 SI 2015/910.

1.2   THE CONSUMER CREDIT ACT 1974

The Consumer Credit Act 1974 was exceptionally slow in its implementation, coming into force between 1975 and 1985. The Act was the bedrock of an extensive regime of secondary legislation which added flesh to the statutory framework. The principal regulations, in their subsequent amended form, substantially continue to apply to consumer credit agreements outside the scope of the Directive and to all consumer hire agreements. They include regulations governing the form and contents of consumer credit agreements and consumer hire agreements, copy agreements and early settlement.

Consumer credit law, being an evolving social, economic and highly politicised subject, was unsurprisingly the focus of the need for change in the government's White Paper on the Consumer Credit Market in the 21st Century[1] which set out its vision 'to create an efficient, fair and free market where consumers are empowered to make fully informed decisions and lenders are able to compete'. The White Paper identified problems in the consumer credit market which the proposed reforms were aimed to address. The problems identified fell under the following heads:

• informational problems pre-purchase;

• undue surprises post-purchase;

• unfair practices;

• illegal money lenders; and

• over-indebtedness.

New consumer credit regulations were made in 2004 relating to pre-contract disclosure, formalities for consumer credit and hire agreements, early settlement, advertisements, electronic communications and default.

Following extensive debate in both Houses of Parliament, during which the government resolutely stuck to its own proposals without conceding to any significant proposals for amendment, a new Consumer Credit Act 2006[2] was passed in March 2006. Its provisions were brought into force on various dates between June 2006 and October 2008. The Act amended the Consumer Credit Act 1974 in certain novel and radical respects, most significantly by the removal of a credit ceiling for consumer credit agreements and of the total rental amount for consumer hire agreements, with the result that today all such agreements, unless otherwise exempt, are regulated by the Consumer Credit Act 1974.[3]

The Act also introduced other radical changes. They include a new definition of 'individual'[4] which, compared to the previous definition that included a partnership of an unlimited number, restricts 'individual' to a partnership of two or three persons not all of whom are bodies corporate. The Act repealed section 127(3) to (5) (in respect of agreements made after 6 April 2007), which had previously rendered certain non-compliant regulated agreements automatically and irredeemably unenforceable,[5] and substituted sections 140A to 140D relating to unfair relationships between creditors and debtors for the previous ineffective extortionate credit bargain provisions.[6] Two new exemptions were introduced, namely an exemption relating to high net worth debtors and hirers, and an exemption relating to businesses;[7] procedural requirements were prescribed to deal with arrears, default sums (a new concept) and interest on judgment debts;[8] and extensive licensing provisions added to those already in existence, including the new licensable categories of debt administration and providing credit information services.[9] The Act empowered the Office of Fair Trading to impose civil penalties for failure to comply with a requirement imposed on the licensee by the OFT[10] and extended the jurisdiction of the Financial Ombudsman Service to cover consumer credit agreements and consumer hire agreements.[11]

1 Cm 6040 December 2003.
2 The Act's provisions are discussed in more detail in the following chapters, in the context in which the provisions apply.
3 The ceiling was then £25,000 which was removed by s 2(1) of the Consumer Credit Act 2006, implemented by the Consumer Credit Act 2006 (Commencement No 4 and Transitional Provisions) Order 2008, SI 2008/831, with effect from 6 April 2008.
4 CCA 2006, s 1(1) (CCA 1974, s 189(1)).
5 Ibid., s 15, read with Sch 3, para 11.
6 Ibid., ss 19 to 22(1) (CCA 1974, ss 140A to 140D).
7 Ibid., ss 3 and 4 (CCA 1974, ss 16A and 16B).
8 Ibid., ss 8 to 18 (CCA 1974, ss 86A to 86E and 129A to 130A).
9 Ibid., ss 24 to 51 (incorporated in various sections of CCA 1974).
10 Ibid., ss 52 to 54 (incorporated in CCA 1974, ss 39 to 39C).
11 Ibid., ss 59 and 60 (incorporated in Financial Services and Markets Act 2000, ss 226A and 234A).

1.3 THE TWO CONSUMER CREDIT REGIMES

The confluence of the 2008 Directive with the Consumer Credit Act 1974 (as amended) on consumer credit agreements, has resulted in two distinct consumer credit regimes in the UK, as shown below.

The following agreements fall within the scope of the 2008 Directive, that is, within the scope of the Information Regulations 2010 and the Agreements Regulations 2010:

(a)   consumer credit agreements for credit up to £60,260 (equating to €75,000 in April 2008) (other than a residential renovation agreement), which are not secured by a land mortgage and are not wholly or predominantly for the purposes of a business carried on or intended to be carried on by the debtor; and

(b)   overdraft agreements within the above description.

Agreements that fall outside the scope of the Directive but continue to be governed by the Consumer Credit Act 1974 are:

(a)   consumer credit agreements for credit exceeding £60,260;

(b)   consumer credit agreements for credit in any amount, secured on land and which are not otherwise governed by the Mortgages Directive or the Mortgage Credit Directive Order 2015;

(c)   all consumer hire agreements; and

(d)   consumer credit agreements for credit not exceeding £25,000, and consumer hire agreements requiring the hirer to make payments not exceeding £25,000, entered into by the debtor or hirer respectively, wholly or predominantly for the purposes of a business carried on or intended to be carried on by the debtor or hirer. (This is the only purpose for which the £25,000 financial ceiling has been retained.)

If pre-contract information is disclosed in compliance, or purported compliance, with the Information Regulations 2010, the Agreements Regulations 2010 apply to those agreements.

Exemptions, namely from the above regimes, are set out in the Financial Services and Markets Act 2000 (Regulated Activities) Order 2001 ('RAO'),[1] Chapters 14, 14A and 15.

1   SI 2001/544.

1.4   TRANSFER OF THE CONSUMER CREDIT REGIME FROM THE OFT TO THE FCA

HM Treasury and the Department for Business, Innovation and Skills published a Consultation Paper in December 2010 on 'A new approach to financial regulation: on reforming the consumer credit regime'. The Paper considered the merits of transferring responsibility for regulation of consumer credit from the Office of Fair Trading ('OFT') to a proposed new regulator for financial services. The responses suggested that there would be support for a single regulator for credit and other financial services and a rule book providing an appropriate degree of certainty and capable of being updated without the need for legislation.

The subsequent Financial Services Act 2012 (referred to below as 'the Act') amended the Financial Services and Markets Act 2000 ('FSMA'), including by replacing the Financial Services Authority with the Financial Conduct Authority ('FCA'). The FCA is charged with the following objectives: the consumer protection objective; the integrity objective; and the competition objective. The FCA's general functions are: making rules under the Act; preparing and issuing codes under the Act; giving general guidance under the Act; and determining the general policy and principles by reference to which the FCA performs particular functions under the Act.

The empowering legislation for the transfer of consumer credit regulation from the OFT to the FCA is contained in sections 107 and 115(2) of the Act[1] read with the Financial Services Act 2012 (Consumer Credit) Order 2013.[2]

In October 2013 the FCA consulted on 'Detailed proposals for the FCA regime for consumer credit',[3] together with a draft of the Consumer Credit sourcebook ('CONC'). CONC came into force on 1 April 2014. The underlying regulatory provisions for CONC are to be found in the Financial Services and Markets Act 2000 (Regulated Activities) Order 2001, as amended ('RAO').[4]

As a result of the transfer, much of consumer credit law and regulation which was originally contained in the Consumer Credit Act 1974 and regulations under that Act is to be found in FSMA, RAO and CONC.

1 Implemented by the Financial Services Act 2012 (Consumer Credit) Order 2013, SI 2013/1882.
2 SI 2013/1882.
3 CP 13/10.
4 SI 2001/544 as amended, principally by SI 2013/1881.

1.5 CONSUMER CREDIT AS A RELATIONSHIP ISSUE

Underlying consumer credit as a customer relationship issue are the Principles for Business, especially Principle 6, in the FCA Handbook, PRIN,[1] which underlie the conduct of all financial services business.

1 Integrity	A firm must conduct its business with integrity.
2 Skill, care and diligence	A firm must conduct its business with due skill, care and diligence.
3 Management and control	A firm must take reasonable care to organise and control its affairs responsibly and effectively, with adequate risk management systems.
4 Financial prudence	A firm must maintain adequate financial resources.
5 Market conduct	A firm must observe proper standards of market conduct.
6 Customers' interests	A firm must pay due regard to the interests of its customers and treat them fairly.
7 Communications with clients	A firm must pay due regard to the information needs of its clients, and communicate information to them in a way which is clear, fair and not misleading.
8 Conflicts of interest	A firm must manage conflicts of interest fairly, both between itself and its customers and between a customer and another client.

9 Customers: relationships of trust	A firm must take reasonable care to ensure the suitability of its advice and discretionary decisions for any customer who is entitled to rely upon its judgment.
10 Clients' assets	A firm must arrange adequate protection for clients' assets when it is responsible for them.
11 Relations with regulators	A firm must deal with its regulators in an open and cooperative way, and must disclose to the appropriate regulator appropriately anything relating to the firm of which that regulator would reasonably expect notice.

1 PRIN 2.1.1R.

A note on interpretation and usage in this text

In this text:

- 'CCA 1974' means the Consumer Credit Act 1974;

- 'Consumer Credit Directive' means Directive 2008/48/EC of the European Parliament and of the Council of 23 April 2008 on credit agreements for consumers and repealing Council Directive 87/102/EEC;

- 'FSMA' means the Financial Services and Markets Act 2000;

- 'RAO' means the Financial Services and Markets Act 2000 (Regulated Activities) Order 2001, SI 2001/544; and

- 'Mortgage Directive' or 'MCD' means Directive 2014/17/EU of the European Parliament and of the Council of 4 February 2014 on credit agreements for consumers relating to residential immovable property and amending Directives 2008/48/EC and 2013/36/EU and Regulation (EU) 1093/2010.

All references to Acts and regulations are to their amended form where they have been amended.

Chapter 2

The general structure of the regulation of consumer credit agreements and consumer hire agreements

2.1 THE STARTING POINT: THE MORTGAGE CREDIT DIRECTIVE 2014[1]

2.1.1 Scope of the Directive

The useful starting point, in considering the structure of regulation that applies to consumer credit agreements, is the significant date of 21 March 2016, when the Mortgage Credit Directive of 2014, which applies to consumer credit agreements secured on land ('the Mortgages Directive'), came into force in the UK in the form of the Mortgage Credit Directive Order 2015.[2] This marked the final divide between a consumer credit agreement secured on land and all other consumer credit agreements. The Directive has no impact on consumer hire agreements.

The Mortgages Directive applies to:[3]

(a) credit agreements which are secured either by a mortgage or by another comparable security commonly used in a Member State on residential immovable property or secured by a right related to residential immovable property; and

(b) credit agreements the purpose of which is to acquire or retain property rights in land or in an existing or projected building.

A 'credit agreement' is described by reference (and hence confined) to the grant, or promise of the grant, of credit to a consumer. A consumer is defined as a natural person who, in transactions covered by Consumer Credit Directive 2008, is acting for purposes which are outside his trade, business or profession.[4] This is a rather infelicitous combination of definitions by means of disparate Directives. However, the overriding distinction between a consumer and a non-consumer is made clear in Recital (12) of the Mortgages Directive, which states:

> 'The definition of consumer should cover natural persons who are acting outside their trade, business or profession. However, in the case of dual purpose

contracts, where the contract is concluded for purposes partly within and partly outside the person's trade, business or profession and the trade, business or professional purpose is so limited as not to be predominant in the overall context of the contract, that person should also be considered as a consumer.'

The Mortgages Directive specifically excludes certain credit agreements from its scope[5] and, in the case of other specified agreements,[6] permits Member States to determine whether or not the Directive should apply to them.

A credit agreement falling within the scope of the Mortgages Directive is described in the UK regulatory regime as a regulated mortgage contract or as an MCD regulated mortgage contract, namely a regulated mortgage contract entered into on or after 21 March 2016, under which the borrower is a consumer and which is not an exempt MCD regulated mortgage contract.

Subject to the exceptions listed below, a regulated mortgage contract[7] is a contract which, at the time it is entered into, meets the following conditions:

(a)   a lender provides credit to an individual or to trustees (the 'borrower'); and

(b)   the obligation of the borrower to repay is secured by a mortgage on land in the EEA, at least 40% of which is used, or is intended to be used, in the case of credit provided to an individual, as or in connection with a dwelling; or (in the case of credit provided to a trustee who is not an individual), as or in connection with a dwelling by an individual who is a beneficiary of the trust, or by a related person.

The following mortgage contracts are not regulated mortgage contracts:[8]

(a)   a regulated home purchase plan;

(b)   a limited payment second charge bridging loan;

(c)   a second charge business loan;

(d)   an investment property loan;

(e)   an exempt consumer buy-to-let mortgage contract;

(f)   an exempt equitable mortgage bridging loan;

(g)   an exempt housing authority loan; and

(h)   a limited interest second charge credit union loan where the borrower receives timely information on the main features, risks and costs of the contract at the pre-contractual stage and any advertising of the contract is fair, clear and not misleading.[9]

An MCD regulated mortgage contract is a regulated mortgage contract entered into on or after 21 March 2016, under which the borrower is a consumer and which is not an exempt MCD regulated mortgage contract, that is:

(a)   an MCD exempt bridging loan;

(b)   an MCD exempt credit union loan;

(c)   an MCD exempt overdraft loan; or

(d)   an MCD exempt lifetime mortgage.[10]

1 Directive 2014/17/EU of the European Parliament and of the Council of 4 February 2014 on credit agreements for consumers relating to residential immovable property and amending Directives 2008/48/EC and 2013/36/EU and Regulation (EU) 1093/2010 ('the Mortgages Directive').
2 SI 2015/910.
3 Mortgages Directive, Article 3(1)(a) and (b).
4 Article 4(1) and (3).
5 Article 3(2).
6 Article 3(3).
7 Financial Services and Markets Act 2000 (Regulated Activities) Order 2001, SI 2001/544 ('RAO'), art 61(3).
8 RAO arts 61(3)(a), 61A(1) and (2).
9 For the meaning of these terms, see RAO art 61A(6).
10 For the meaning of these terms, see the FCA Handbook, Glossary.

2.1.2 The Mortgage Credit Directive Order 2015[1]

The Mortgage Credit Directive Order 2015 implements the Mortgages Directive, for all practical purposes, with effect from 21 March 2016. The Order applies broadly to regulated mortgage contracts, credit agreements to which the Mortgages Directive applies, and consumer buy-to-let mortgages.

The Order effects the transfer of second (and later) charge mortgage lending from the previous scope of the consumer credit regime to the scope of the consumer mortgage regime.

1 SI 2015/910.

2.1.3 Application of the FCA sourcebook – MCOB

The Financial Conduct Authority ('FCA') Handbook applies to all firms or authorised persons. The Mortgages and Home Finance: Conduct of Business sourcebook ('MCOB') applies to every authorised person that carries on a home finance activity or communicates or approves a financial promotion of qualifying credit, of a home purchase plan, of a home reversion plan or of a regulated sale and rent back agreement.[1] Carrying on a home finance activity includes administering a regulated mortgage contract, home purchase plan, home reversion plan or regulated sale and rent back agreement.

Where MCOB applies, the prescribed European Standardised Information Sheet ('ESIS') and Instructions to Complete the ESIS, as set out in MCOB[2] and originally introduced by the Mortgages Directive,[3] must be used.

MCOB covers the range of lenders' activities, such as entering into a home finance activity (which includes entering into a regulated mortgage contract), business standards, financial promotions, communications with customers, advising and selling standards, disclosure to customers, responsible lending, arrears and repossessions, record-keeping and notifications.

1 MCOB 1.2, and see the definitions of these various expressions in the FCA Handbook, Glossary.
2 MCOB 5A.5.2R and 5.3R and MCOB 5A Annex 1 and Annex 2 respectively.
3 Mortgages Directive, Annex II, Part A and Part B respectively.

2.1.4   Form and content of consumer credit agreements within the scope of the Mortgage Credit Directive Order 2015

These agreements are governed by the Financial Services and Markets Act 2000 and by the FCA Handbook and sourcebook MCOB, notably the European Standardised Information Sheet ('ESIS') and Instructions to Complete the ESIS, as set out in MCOB.[1]

The total charge for credit (and APRC) is calculated in accordance with MCOB 10A.1, 10A.2 and 10A.3.

1   MCOB 5A.5.2R and 5.3R and MCOB 5A Annex 1 and Annex 2 respectively.

2.2   UNSECURED CREDIT AGREEMENTS: SCOPE OF THE CONSUMER CREDIT DIRECTIVE 2008[1]

The Consumer Credit Directive 2008 was implemented in the United Kingdom by the Consumer Credit (EU Directive) Regulations 2010, SI 2010/1010 and related regulations, in March 2010 and came fully into force on 1 February 2011.

The Directive governs a consumer credit agreement which provides for credit up to £60,260 and is not secured on land.[2] This includes an authorised non-business overdraft agreement. The Directive does not apply to a credit agreement entered into by the debtor wholly or predominantly for the purpose of a business carried on, or intended to be carried on, by the debtor.

Where a credit agreement would not otherwise have fallen within the scope of the Directive but pre-contractual information has been disclosed in compliance (or in purported compliance) with the Consumer Credit (Disclosure of Information) Regulations 2010[3] (which apply to agreements within the scope of the Directive), the Consumer Credit (Agreements) Regulations 2010[4] also apply to the credit agreement rather than the Consumer Credit (Agreements) Regulations 1983.[5] In other words, the agreement is then deemed to fall within the scope of the Directive.

Subject to various exemptions, consumer credit agreements outside the scope of the Directive which are not secured on land continue to be regulated by the Consumer Credit Act 1974 ('CCA 1974') and regulations under the Act that govern such agreements, namely the Consumer Credit (Disclosure of Information) Regulations 2004[6] and the Consumer Credit (Agreements) Regulations 1983. The Directive relates solely to consumer credit agreements so that consumer hire agreements fall outside its purview and continue to be regulated by CCA 1974 and the Regulations of 1983 and 2004 referred to above.

The Directive applies solely to credit for consumers. The Directive defines a 'consumer' as meaning a natural person who, in transactions covered by the Directive, is acting for purposes which are outside his trade, business or profession. However, Parliament extended the application of the Directive so as to apply also to partnerships of two or three persons not all of whom are bodies corporate and to an unincorporated body of persons which does not consist entirely of bodies corporate and is not a partnership[7] (the definition of an 'individual' in CCA 1974) and to authorised overdraft agreements.[8]

1   Directive 2008/48/EC of the European Parliament and of the Council of 23 April 2008 on credit agreements for consumers and repealing Council Directive 87/102/EEC.

2 An exception is a s 58 agreement which purports to comply with the new Agreements Regulations 2010.
3 Consumer Credit (Disclosure of Information) Regulations 2010, SI 2010/1013.
4 Consumer Credit (Agreements) Regulations 2010, SI 2010/1014, reg 2(2).
5 SI 1983/1553.
6 SI 2004/1481.
7 CCA 1974, s 189(1).
8 Ibid., s 74(1B), (1C), (1D) and the Consumer Credit (Agreements) Regulations 2010, reg 8.

2.3 UNSECURED CREDIT AGREEMENTS: DETERMINING WHICH REGULATORY REGIME APPLIES

CCA 1974, the Financial Services and Markets Act 2000 (Regulated Activities) Order 2001, SI 2001/544 ('RAO'), the Consumer Credit Directive 2008, the FCA Handbook and CONC govern consumer credit agreements for credit up to £60,260 not secured on land. The Directive does not apply to a credit agreement entered into by the debtor wholly or predominantly for the purpose of a business carried on, or intended to be carried on, by the debtor.

The above, save for the Consumer Credit Directive 2008, also govern consumer credit agreements for credit exceeding £60,260.

The consumer credit regime embodied in the Disclosure of Information Regulations 2004, the Agreements Regulations 1983 and CONC continues to apply to consumer credit agreements outside the scope of the Consumer Credit Directive 2008 which are not secured on land, as well as to all consumer hire agreements.

2.3.1 Form and content of consumer credit agreements within the scope of the Consumer Credit Directive 2008

These agreements are governed by the CCA 1974, as amended (including by the Consumer Credit (EU Directive) Regulations 2010, the Mortgage Credit Directive Order 2015), and by the following principal regulations:

- Consumer Credit (EU Directive) Regulations 2010, SI 2010/1010

- Consumer Credit (Disclosure of Information) Regulations 2010, SI 2010/1013

- Consumer Credit (Agreements) Regulations 2010, SI 2010/1014.

The above regulations are subject to the following principal amending regulations:

- Consumer Credit (Amendment) Regulations 2010, SI 2010/1969

- Consumer Credit (Amendment) Regulations 2011, SI 2011/11.

The total charge for credit (and APR) is calculated in accordance with the FCA Handbook: Consumer Credit sourcebook ('CONC'), CONC App 1.1 or 1.2, as appropriate.

2.3.2   Form and content of consumer credit agreements outside the scope of the Consumer Credit Directive 2008

These agreements are governed by CCA 1974, as amended, and by the following principal regulations:

- Consumer Credit (Disclosure of Information) Regulations 2004, SI 2004/1481

- Consumer Credit (Agreements) Regulations 1983, SI 1983/1553

- Consumer Credit (Cancellation Notices and Copies of Documents) Regulations 1983, SI 1983/1557.

The total charge for credit (and APR) is calculated in accordance with CONC App 1.1 or 1.2, as appropriate.

2.3.3   Provisions applying both to agreements within, and agreements outside, the scope of the Consumer Credit Directive 2008

Certain of the following provisions apply equally to both sets of consumer credit agreements:

- Consumer Credit (Cancellation Notices and Copies of Documents) Regulations 1983, SI 1983/1557

- Consumer Credit (Early Settlement) Regulations 2004, SI 2004/1483

- Consumer Credit (Information Requirements and Duration of Licences and Charges) Regulations 2007, SI 2007/1167

- Consumer Credit (Enforcement, Default and Termination Notices) Regulations 1983, SI 1983/1561

- The FCA Handbook and sourcebook CONC.

2.3.4   Form and content of consumer hire agreements

These agreements are governed by the Consumer Credit Act 1974, as amended, and by the following principal regulations:

- Consumer Credit (Disclosure of Information) Regulations 2004, SI 2004/1481

- Consumer Credit (Agreements) Regulations 1983, SI 1983/1553

- Consumer Credit (Cancellation Notices and Copies of Documents) Regulations 1983, SI 1983/1557.

2.4   PRINCIPAL CHANGES EFFECTED BY THE CONSUMER CREDIT DIRECTIVE 2008

2.4.1   Agreements within the scope of the Directive

The Directive introduced major changes affecting the making and content of consumer credit agreements within its scope and the rights and obligations of the parties in respect of such agreements, as briefly summarised below.

(a)   Pre-contractual information[1]

The debtor must be given pre-contractual information in prescribed form. This will generally be by way of the Standard European Consumer Credit Information (SECCI). In the case of an authorised non-business overdraft agreement, the corresponding information is in the form of European Consumer Credit Information (ECCI). The Consumer Credit (Disclosure of Information) Regulations 2010 set out the forms of SECCI and ECCI in the schedules to the regulations.

(b)   Pre-contractual explanations[2]

The creditor must supply the debtor with an adequate explanation of pre-scribed matters to enable the debtor to decide whether the agreement is suited to his needs and to his financial situation.

(c)   Assessment of the debtor's creditworthiness[3]

Before making the agreement or significantly increasing the amount of credit, the creditor must assess the debtor's creditworthiness.

(d)   Form and content of credit agreement and copy requirements[4]

Credit agreements must comply with the Consumer Credit (Agreements) Regulations 2010 and copy agreements must accord with the provisions of ss 61A, 61B and 55C (on the debtor's request).

(e)   Debtor's right of withdrawal[5]

The debtor has the right to withdraw from the credit agreement within 14 days from the date of the agreement, without having to give a reason.

(f)   Creditor's liability under a so-called 'linked credit agreement'[6]

The creditor is liable for the supplier's breach of contract under a linked credit agreement. This is the corollary to s 75.

(g)   Assignment[7]

An assignee of a creditor's rights under a regulated consumer credit agreement must arrange for notice of the assignment to be given to the debtor as soon as reasonably possible; or if, after the assignment, the arrangements for servicing the credit under the agreement do not change so far as the debtor is concerned, notice of the assignment must be given on or before the first occasion that they do change.

This requirement does not apply to agreements secured on land.

(h)   Early repayment by the debtor and compensation for early repayment[8]

   The debtor has the right to discharge his indebtedness under the agreement early in whole or in part at any time, subject to the creditor's entitlement to compensation in specified circumstances.

1 CCA 1974, s 55(1).
2 Ibid., s 55A.
3 Ibid., s 55B.
4 Ibid., ss 55C, 61, 61A and 61B.
5 Ibid., s 66A.
6 Ibid., s 75A.
7 Ibid., s 82A.
8 Ibid., ss 94 and 95A.

2.4.2   Agreements outside the scope of the Directive

Some of the above rights and obligations have been extended by the UK Parliament to apply to consumer credit agreements outside the scope of the Consumer Credit Directive 2008. They include an obligation on the creditor to assess the debtor's creditworthiness (where the agreement is not secured on land), the right of withdrawal in respect of credit agreements for business purposes where the credit amount does not exceed £25,000, the early repayment provisions, the linked credit agreement provisions, notice of assignment, and the obligation to inform a prospective debtor of a decision to decline credit where the decision was reached on the basis of information obtained from a credit reference agency, together with details of the agency.

2.5   RESIDENTIAL RENOVATION AGREEMENTS

The notion of a residential renovation agreement was introduced by the Mortgage Credit Directive Order 2015.[1] A residential renovation agreement is a consumer credit agreement which is unsecured and the purpose of which is the renovation of a residential property whether or not involving a total amount of credit exceeding £60,260.[2] The agreement is subject to unique provisions in CCA 1974, namely in sections 55C(4)(c), 60(5)(c), 61A(6A), 66A(14)(a), 75A(6)(b) and 77B(9)(c).

1 SI 2015/910, Sch 1, Pt.1
2 CCA 1974, s 189(1). See art 2(2a) of the Consumer Credit Directive 2008 inserted by art 46 of the Mortgage Credit Directive 2015.

2.6   CONSUMER BUY-TO-LET MORTGAGES

Whilst not directly relevant to this chapter, it should be mentioned that a new regulatory regime that applies to consumer buy-to-let mortgages was established by Part 3 of the Mortgage Credit Directive Order 2015.[1]

1 SI 2015/910.

2.7 EXEMPT AGREEMENTS

The reader is alerted to the existence of exempt agreements, namely agreements which are not regulated by the regimes applying to regulated mortgage contracts and regulated consumer credit/ consumer hire agreements. These agreements are discussed in **Chapter 6.**

Chapter 3

Consumer credit and consumer hire

3.1 THE MEANING OF 'CREDIT'

The Committee on Consumer Credit Law under the chairmanship of Lord Crowther in the period 1968 to 1971 examined the law as it then was. It laid the foundations for consumer credit and consumer hire law in the form of the Consumer Credit Act 1974 ('CCA 1974').

The Crowther Committee deserves credit for breaking the mould of the traditional legal analysis, which considered loans, the subject of the Moneylenders Acts 1900 to 1927, as conceptually different to credit sale, conditional sale and hire-purchase. The distinction between these various forms of facility is formal rather than functional: 'to the customer it is a matter of indifference whether he pays for a motorcar by credit sale or purchase-money loan. The law may distinguish between deferment of the price and the grant of a loan but in commercial terms the distinction is meaningless'.[1]

Viewed from the vantage point of CCA 1974 and the regulations made under it, the conceptual divide between the law which pre-dated, and that which followed, CCA 1974 is revolutionary. Indeed, so far was the functional as opposed to the formal approach adopted that, to a large extent, the distinctions between hire-purchase, credit sale, conditional sale and instalment sale agreements have been reduced by their common features being subsumed in the creation of a debtor-creditor-supplier agreement, or the more recently renamed borrower-lender-supplier agreement. This three-party, or so-called connected loan agreement, contrasts with a debtor-creditor or borrower-lender, or unconnected, loan agreement. CCA 1974 repealed the Moneylenders Acts 1900 to 1927, the bulk of the Hire-Purchase Act 1964 and the entire Hire-Purchase Act 1965. Accordingly, the legal framework of CCA 1974 was based upon the 'recognition that the extension of credit in a sale or hire-purchase transaction is in reality a loan and that the reservation of title under a hire-purchase or conditional sale agreement or finance lease is in reality a chattel mortgage securing a loan'.[2]

Not surprisingly, therefore, the concept of credit is couched in wide and all-embracing terms. In common parlance 'credit' means the right granted by a creditor to a debtor to defer payment of a debt. 'Credit' has been defined as a sum of money or equivalent purchasing power, as at a shop, available for a person's use; the sum of money that a bank makes available to a client in excess of any deposit and the practice of permitting a borrower to receive goods or services before payment.[3] In *Dimond v Lovell*[4] the Court of Appeal approved an earlier judicial definition of credit as a sum which, in the absence of agreement, would be immediately payable. Citing Professor Goode in *Consumer Credit Legislation* (now called *Consumer Credit Law and Practice*), the court said that the ingredients of credit are: (a) the supply of a benefit; (b) attracting a contractual duty of payment; (c) in money; (d) the duty to pay being contractually deferred; (e) for a significant period of time after payment has been earned; (f) such deferment being granted by way of financial accommodation.[5] Thus, deferment of a payment which would otherwise be due is the essence of credit.[6]

The CCA 1974 defines 'credit' as 'including a cash loan, and any other form of financial accommodation'.[7] Essentially the same definition is adopted by the Financial Services and Markets Act 2000 (Regulated Activities) Order 2001, SI 2001/544 ('RAO').[8] The breadth of the definition is indicative of the legislature's objective of bringing within the compass of the regulated regime not only loans but every form of agreement involving credit. It sweeps within its framework the lending of money, the honouring of trading cheques, payments to suppliers by use of credit-tokens and deferment of payment otherwise due. By way of an example of the latter, it was held in *Santander UK Plc v Harrison*[9] that the effect of a capitalisation agreement was to provide the borrowers with credit as, before the agreement was made, the amount of arrears was immediately due and payable, whereas payment was deferred by the agreement and that constituted the provision of credit.

Payments for ongoing services where the payment is made as and when the service is supplied or access to facilities provided, does not constitute credit. In *The Office of Fair Trading v Ashbourne Management Services Ltd*,[10] Kitchin J (as he then was) drew a distinction between the following classes of case: 'the first comprises cases in which a liability or obligation to pay is incurred or, but for the payment terms, would have been incurred at the outset, and is discharged in instalments; the second comprises cases in which payment falls due in stages as the contract is performed. In the first class of case credit is provided but in the second it is not'.

The Consumer Credit Directive 2008, whilst not defining 'credit', defines a 'credit agreement' in not dissimilar terms to the definition in CCA 1974 as 'an agreement whereby a creditor grants or promises to grant a consumer credit in the form of a deferred payment, loan or other similar financial accommodation, except for agreements for the provision on a continuing basis of services or for the supply of goods of the same kind, where the consumer pays for such services or goods for the duration of their provision by means of instalments'.[11] The exception seems superfluous and has presumably been inserted for the avoidance of doubt.

It must be said that the definition of 'credit' in the CCA 1974 is not as precise and unambiguous as one might have wished. Thus, were it not for the distinction that the Act makes between credit agreements and hire agreements, it is arguable that 'financial accommodation' might have encompassed hire. After all, in the halcyon days when finance leases were a tax efficient alternative to purchasing equipment, they might have been considered a type of financial accommodation. Likewise, pre-payment schemes for school fees or funeral expenses could be promoted on the basis of financially accommodating the payer. However, the expression 'financial accommodation' must be construed in its context, namely, 'a cash loan and any other form of financial accommodation'. In other words, it is of the same genus as a cash loan. Within the context of the Act as a whole, it clearly refers to an accommodation in respect of the advance of a sum of money or its equivalent in goods or services.

The limits of 'financial accommodation' must be drawn at arrangements for the pre-payment of goods or services where the goods or services are not allocated or provided until payment has been effected. In other words, no credit is involved where payment by instalments is not referable or attributable to the grant of credit. In *McMillan Williams v Range*[12] the court stated that where payment is made in advance of services to be rendered, that does not involve the notion of giving credit. As it was impossible to say at the time when the contract was made whether Miss Range would be the debtor or the creditor, at the time when the calculation (of salary paid in anticipation of earnings due) came to be made the agreement was not a credit agreement.

In *McMillan Williams v Range* the facts were that there was an arrangement between a Ms Range, an assistant solicitor and the solicitor's firm, McMillan Williams, whereby her salary was paid in anticipation of her earnings reaching a certain level at a certain date, subject to an agreement to repay any overpayment made to her. When the agreement was terminated the firm claimed repayment from Ms Range of the excess amount paid to her and she contended that the contract was an unenforceable regulated credit agreement. The Appeal Court held that the nature of the agreement had to be determined at the date of the agreement. As it was uncertain at the time when the contract was made whether there would be a surplus or shortfall when the calculation came to be made, the contract did not involve credit.

In *Nejad v City Index Ltd*[13] it was uncertain whether arrangements between the parties would give rise to a debt at all. The court held that there was no credit merely because the arrangements postponed any obligation to pay until such time as the future possible indebtedness had crystallised. The case involved placing bets on the movements of various financial indexes. To place bets the customer was required to open either a 'deposit account', paying in a specified amount as a pre-condition of participation or a 'credit account', based on an assessment of his creditworthiness. In respect of a claim on the credit account, it was alleged that the credit account was an unenforceable contract as it did not comply with the requirements of the CCA 1974. The court rejected the submission, stating that the contract was not one for the grant of credit but simply a contract pursuant to which, if the relevant stock exchange index was above or below a specified figure on a specified date, or on early closing of the contract in accordance with City Index's terms and conditions, the customer would pay or receive the appropriate amount of money. There may never be any indebtedness by the customer to City Index and, whether there would, depended on the movement of the relevant index. Until the closing of the relevant contract between the customer and City Index, it could not be said that there was a debt at all. Accordingly it could not be found that the effect of the agreement in providing what was called a 'credit allocation' to Mr Nejad was to grant him any credit in respect of what would be an indebtedness payable at an earlier date.

In *Burrell v Helical (Bramshott Place) Limited*,[14] it was held that, in determining whether a lease involved the provision of credit, the test to be applied is the construction of the lease provisions and not the commercial purpose or economic consequences of the lease. The question is whether there was an obligation at the commencement of the lease to pay a debt which was then deferred.

An important aspect of the definition of 'credit' is that an item entering into the total charge for credit is not to be treated as credit, even though time is allowed for its payment.[15] This is a critical foundation stone of CCA 1974 and is to be given its plain, literal meaning.

The fact that a charge is payable over a period of time, with interest accruing on it, does not convert the charge into an amount of credit within the meaning of the Act. As stated by Lord Clarke, delivering the judgment of the court in *Southern Pacific Securities 05-2 Plc v Walker*:[16] 'The problem is that section 9(4) provides that an item entering into the total charge for credit shall not be treated as credit. It follows that if an item is part of the total charge for credit, it cannot form part of the amount of credit, even if it would otherwise be regarded as credit'. The court recognised that this conclusion was also supported by the authorities, including *Wilson v First County Trust Ltd*.[17] In the latter a document fee of £250 was added to the loan amount of £5,000 and the credit amount stated as £5,250, with the result that one of the prescribed terms, namely the amount of credit, was misstated and the agreement was irredeemably unenforceable by virtue of s 127(3) of the Act, since repealed.

In *Wilson v Robertsons (London) Ltd*[18] it was successfully argued for Mrs Wilson (the same claimant as in the above case) that a document fee included in the credit amount of a series of pawn agreements had the effect of rendering the agreements unenforceable, even though no time was allowed for payment of the fee.

The conceptual clash between 'charges' and 'credit' has been the subject of various cases, briefly discussed below.

In *Watchtower Investments Ltd v Payne*[19] the question was whether the payment by Watchtower of arrears under a prior mortgage, made contemporaneously with the completion of a consumer credit agreement, constituted the financing of an amount of credit or of a charge for the credit. After a detailed analysis of the law, Gibson LJ, delivering the principal judgment of the Court of Appeal, held that refinancing of arrears was not payment of a charge but amounted to the grant of credit. Whilst this decision appears undoubtedly correct, in *McGinn v Grangewood Securities Ltd*[20] the Court of Appeal held that the facts were distinguishable from those in *Watchtower*. Thus, whilst in *Watchtower* it was a purpose of the new loan that part of the credit was used for repaying arrears under an existing loan, in *McGinn* it was a condition of the grant of the new loan that the arrears under an existing loan be discharged. The Court held that the condition rendered the amount of arrears part of the charges for credit and not part of the credit.

It is respectfully submitted that *McGinn* was wrongly decided. The CCA 1974 expressly recognises, as a form of debtor-creditor credit, restricted-use credit to refinance any existing indebtedness of the debtor's, whether to the creditor or another person.[21]

In the subsequent case of *London North Securities Ltd v Meadows*[22] the court adopted an intermediate approach. Whilst finding that the credit agreement made it a requirement that all prior arrears be cleared off and that the loan amount was increased to cater for this, the court also found on the facts that the borrowers had, by signing the documents, agreed that the arrears should be paid off and that the loan would provide the sums necessary for this purpose. On that basis payment of the arrears was one of the objective purposes of the transaction so that the arrears amount formed part of the credit and not the total charge for credit. In the writer's view, for the reasons stated above, there was no need to conduct this analysis in order to arrive at the judge's conclusion.

In *Black Horse Limited v Speak*[23] the court found that, as there was no requirement for the debtor to take payment protection insurance with the principal loan, the premium for the insurance was truly credit and not part of the total charge for credit.

1 Crowther Report Command 4596, para 6.2.38.
2 Ibid., para 1.3.7.
3 The Collins English Dictionary.
4 *Dimond v Lovell* [2001] GCCR 2303 at 2316, CA.
5 At para [56].
6 See *Goode: Consumer Credit Law and Practice* (LexisNexis Butterworths), IC [24.7].
7 CCA 1974, s 9(1).
8 RAO art 60L(1).
9 [2013] GCCR 11700, [2013] EWHC 199 (QB).
10 [2011] GCCR 11201 at para 95, [2011] EWHC 1237 (Ch).
11 Directive 2008/48/EC, Article 3(c).
12 [2004] GCCR 5041, CA.
13 [2001] GCCR 2461, CA.
14 [2015] EWHC 3727 (Ch).
15 CCA 1974, s 9(4).
16 [2010] GCCR 10151 (HL) at 10155.
17 [2003] GCCR 4931 (HL).
18 *Wilson v Robertsons (London) Ltd* [2005] GCCR 5301.
19 [2001] EWCA Civ 1159, (2001) 35 LS Gaz R 32, Times, 22 August.
20 [2002] GCCR 4761, [2002] EWCA Civ 522, CA.
21 CCA 1974, s 13(b).
22 [2005] GCCR 5381, [2005] EWCA Civ 956, CA.
23 [2010] GCCR 10251, [2010] EWHC 1866 (QB).

3.2 THE MEANING OF 'CONSUMER' AND 'INDIVIDUAL'

The second conclusion of the Crowther Committee was that the law ought to distinguish between consumer and commercial transactions. The Moneylenders Acts, for example, applied to all loans regardless of whether they were loans to individuals or to companies. The Committee was of the view that the purpose of the loan was an inadequate test, being too vague and subjective. It preferred the approach of excluding bodies corporate from the protection afforded to consumers and of setting a financial limit above which consumers were not entitled to statutory protection.

The long title to the CCA 1974 describes it as an Act 'to establish for the protection of consumers a new system, administered by the Director General of Fair Trading, of licensing and other control of traders concerned with the provision of credit for the supply of goods on hire or hire-purchase, and their transactions, in place of enactments regulating moneylenders, pawn-brokers and hire-purchase traders and their transactions; and for related matters'. The legislation is for the protection of the 'consumer' which, oddly, the Act does not define.

In reality, the legislation is for the protection of 'individuals', whether or not they are consumers per se, provided the credit or hire is not wholly or predominantly for the purposes of a business of the debtor or hirer. CCA 1974 defines 'individual' as including (a) a partnership consisting of two or three persons not all of whom are bodies corporate; and (b) an unincorporated body of persons which does not consist entirely of bodies corporate and is not a partnership.[1] In contrast, the RAO refers to 'an individual or relevant recipient of credit' and defines 'relevant recipient of credit' in the terms of (a) and (b) above.[2] A limited liability partnership or 'LLP' is a body corporate.[3]

Originally, the weakness of the regulatory regime was its failure to adopt what it sought to avoid, namely to apply 'the purpose of the loan test' in distinguishing between consumer and commercial credit, at least to the extent that this was practicable. As a result, consumer credit embraced both business loans to partnerships and commercial loans to individuals. However, Parliament had no difficulty in distinguishing between non-business and business, or between consumer and non-consumer, transactions e.g. the Unfair Contract Terms Act 1977, the Consumer Protection Act 1987, the CCA 1974 itself in s 101(7) and the Advertisements Regulations made under the Act. The European Parliament[4] similarly distinguished between a consumer and a non-consumer in Directives implemented as the Unfair Terms in Consumer Contracts Regulations 1999[5] and the Consumer Protection (Distance Selling) Regulations 2000.[6] Currently and, it must be said, somewhat surprisingly, 'consumer' is defined inconsistently in UK enactments; for example, as an individual acting for purposes that are wholly or mainly outside that individual's trade, business, craft or profession,[7] and as a person acting for purposes which are outside that person's trade, business or profession.[8] The Consumer Credit Directive 2008 defines 'consumer' similarly, as a natural person who, in transactions covered by the Directive, is acting for purposes which are outside his trade, business or profession.[9] Contrasting definitions of 'consumer' for purposes of other legislation are to be found, for example, in the Financial Services and Markets Act 2000.[10]

In 1988 the government, in its Deregulation Initiative, proposed the removal of lending and hiring to businesses from the scope of the Act.[11] A while later, in 1993, the Office of Fair Trading issued a Consultation Document on the Treatment of Business Consumers under the CCA 1974. This was followed by extensive consultations with the industry and trade associations. Then, in 1994, the Director General of Fair Trading issued a Consultation Document entitled 'Consumer Credit Deregulation'[12] recommending that the government's proposal should be implemented save that licensing should continue to cover all lending and hire to individuals, including sole traders, partnerships and unincorporated bodies. The Department of Trade and Industry conducted its own consultations by publishing a Consultation Document on 'Deregulation of United Kingdom Consumer Credit Legislation' in 1995 and a further consultation entitled 'Deregulation of Lending and Hiring to Unincorporated Businesses' in 1996. Notwithstanding extensive consultation and overwhelming support for the Deregulation Initiative, the House of Commons Deregulation Committee, which had itself sought the views of various organisations and bodies, surprisingly concluded that it did not believe that the Department of Trade and Industry had adequately addressed the concerns of consumer protection raised by a significant number of respondents. It voted against the proposal for the deregulation of lending and hiring to businesses and thereby killed off the Deregulation Initiative and eight years of lobbying for change.[13]

Lending and hire for business purposes (where the credit amount or rentals payable exceeds £25,000) was finally excluded from regulation (save in respect of the provisions relating to unfair relationships between creditor and debtor) by the Consumer Credit Act 2006, with effect from 6 April 2008,[14] some 20 years after the proposal was first mooted. This exemption is now contained in RAO arts 60C and 60O, relating to exempt consumer credit and consumer hire agreements respectively.

1 CCA 1974, s 189(1).
2 RAO art 60B(3) definition of 'credit agreement' and art 60L(1) definition of 'relevant recipient of credit'.
3 Limited Liability Partnerships Act 2000, s 1(2).
4 Council Directive 87/102/EEC of 22 December 1986.
5 SI 1999/2083.
6 Directive 87/102/EEC similarly defines 'consumer' in Article 3(a) as a natural person who, in [credit] transactions covered by the Directive, is acting for purposes which are outside his trade, business or profession.
7 Consumer Rights Act 2015.
8 Mortgage Credit Directive Order 2015, SI 2015/910 art 4(1); and note RAO art 60C(3)(b).
9 Article 3(a).
10 For example, sections 1G, 404E and 425 and RAO art 60LA.
11 'Releasing Enterprise' Cm 512, November 1988, p 24.
12 A Review by the Director General of Fair Trading of the Scope and Operation of the Consumer Credit Act 1974 (June 1994).
13 See 'Consumer Credit' (published by the CCTA), vol 52 (May 1997).
14 CCA 1974, s 16B.

3.3 THE MEANING OF 'CREDITOR' OR 'LENDER'

A 'creditor' (except in relation to a green deal plan: see instead s 189B(2)) is defined as the person providing credit under a consumer credit agreement or the person to whom his rights and duties under the agreement have passed by assignment or operation of law and, in relation to a prospective consumer credit agreement, includes the prospective creditor.[1] The Consumer Credit Directive 2008 defines 'creditor' as meaning a natural or legal person who grants or promises to grant credit in the course of his trade, business or profession.[2] By contrast, a person may be a creditor under UK law (with all the consequences attached to it in respect of a consumer credit agreement) even though he does not grant credit in the course of any trade, business or profession. The expression 'creditor' is replaced by 'lender' in the RAO and the FCA Handbook and is subject to the criticism set out at **3.4** below.

The CCA 1974 does not define a 'prospective consumer credit agreement' or a 'prospective creditor' but these should be construed in the context of sections 57, 58 and 59 which deal with prospective regulated agreements.

There are no restrictions on the natural or legal persons, or group of persons, which might constitute a creditor except that, in the case of a legal person, it must have the legal capacity and power to lend, i.e. the lending must be *intra vires*. Thus, a creditor may be an individual, a registered company, a partnership, a building society, a mutual society, an association, a charity, a local authority, a trade union, a credit union and the like. The only impact which the consumer credit regime and the RAO have on the foregoing is that they provide for certain types of creditor to be able to enter into exempt agreements. The reader is referred to **Chapter 6** for a full discussion of exempt agreements.

The types of body that are permitted to enter into exempt agreements relating to the purchase of land are the following: an authorised person with permission to effect contracts of insurance; a friendly society; an organisation of employers or organisation of workers; a charity; a land improvement company; a body corporate named or specifically referred to in any public general Act or in, or in an Order made under, a relevant housing provision; a building society; an authorised person with permission to accept deposits; and a local authority.[3] The reader is referred to **7.7** on the question of the assignability of a creditor's rights and duties under the agreement.

1   CCA 1974, s 189(1), and see also s 140C(2).
2   Article 3(b).
3   RAO art 60E, and note the qualifications referred to in that article.

3.4   THE MEANING OF 'DEBTOR' OR 'BORROWER'

A 'debtor' (except in relation to a green deal plan: see instead s 189B(3)) is defined as the individual receiving credit under a consumer credit agreement or the person to whom his rights and duties under the agreement have passed by assignment or operation of law, and, in relation to a prospective consumer credit agreement, includes a prospective debtor.[1] The CCA 1974 does not define a 'prospective consumer credit agreement' or a 'prospective debtor' but these should be construed in the context of sections 57, 58 and 59 which deal with prospective regulated agreements.

The reader is referred to **7.7** on the assignability of a debtor's rights and duties under the agreement.

The expression 'debtor' is replaced by 'borrower' (and 'creditor' by 'lender') in the RAO and the FCA Handbook, rather unnecessarily and confusingly. Whilst it is, of course, true that, at the outset of a credit agreement, the individual is a borrower and the credit grantor is a lender, no sooner has the credit been advanced to the individual, he is a debtor and the lender is a creditor, so that to replace well-established terminology and expressions in CCA 1974 with new descriptions seems a vain and pointless exercise (and which, notwithstanding the change of terminology, does not serve to reduce the appearance of the nation's total debt!).

1   CCA 1974, s 189(1), and see also s 140C(2).

3.5 THE MEANING OF 'CONSUMER CREDIT AGREEMENT' AND 'REGULATED CREDIT AGREEMENT'

A consumer credit agreement is an agreement between an individual ('the debtor') and any other person ('the creditor') by which the creditor provides the debtor with credit of any amount.[1]

A consumer credit agreement is a regulated credit agreement if it:

(a)   is a regulated credit agreement for the purposes of Chapter 14A of Part 2 of the Regulated Activities Order; and

(b)   is not an agreement of the type described in Article 3(1)(b) of Directive 2014/17/EU of the European Parliament and of the Council of 4 February 2014 on credit agreements for consumers relating to residential immovable property.[2]

Chapter 14A of Part 2 of the RAO aforesaid defines a regulated credit agreement as any credit agreement which is not an exempt agreement [under articles 60C to 60H], and a credit agreement:

(a)   in relation to an agreement other than a green deal plan, as an agreement between an individual or relevant recipient of credit ('A') and any other person ('B') under which B provides A with credit of any amount;

(b)   in relation to a green deal plan, has the meaning given by article 60LB.[3]

1   CCA 1974, s 8(1).
2   Ibid., s 8(3).
3   RAO art 60B.

3.6 THE MEANING OF 'OWNER' OR 'LESSOR'

The definition of 'owner', which is the term used in CCA 1974, is analogous to that of 'creditor'. An owner is a person who bails or, in Scotland, hires out goods under a consumer hire agreement, or the person to whom his rights and duties under the agreement have passed by assignment or operation of law. In relation to a prospective consumer hire agreement, 'owner' includes the prospective bailor or person from whom the goods are to be hired.[1] The Act does not define 'prospective consumer hire agreements' nor 'prospective bailor' and these terms must be read in the context of ss 57, 58 and 59 of the CCA 1974. As to the assignability of the owner's rights and duties, the reader is referred to **7.7**.

Whilst the legislation employs the term 'owner', it should be pointed out that 'owner' and 'lessor', as likewise 'hirer' or 'lessee', bear identical meanings respectively.

As in the case of a 'creditor', any natural or legal person can constitute an owner under a hire agreement. However, the owner must, of course, have the authority and power to enter into a hire agreement.

1   CCA 1974, s 189(1), and see also s 140C(2).

3.7   THE MEANING OF 'HIRER' OR 'LESSEE'

The term 'hirer' is defined in analogous terms to 'debtor'. A 'hirer' is an individual to whom goods are bailed or, in Scotland, hired under a consumer hire agreement, or the person to whom his rights and duties under the agreement have passed by assignment or operation of law and, in relation to a prospective consumer hire agreement, includes the prospective hirer.[1] Once again, the expressions 'prospective consumer hire agreement' and 'prospective hirer' are not defined and must be read in the context of the CCA 1974, ss 57, 58 and 59.

1   CCA 1974, s 189(1)..

3.8   THE MEANING OF 'HIRE' OR 'LEASE'

Hire is a form of bailment under which the hirer or bailee receives possession of the chattels or goods and the right to use them in return for payment by the hirer of rent to the bailor or owner and undertakings by the hirer to exercise reasonable care of, and to protect, the goods. At the end of the hire the hirer is obliged to return the goods to the bailor.

The Crowther Report drew attention to the need to bring hire agreements within the regulated fold. Consistent with its approach, the Committee maintained that 'a transaction which is in form a lease may achieve much the same result as an outright sale, as when the lease is for the full working life of the equipment at rentals totalling a sum equivalent to what would be charged for a sale on credit'.[1]

It is remarkable that, in contrast to the opprobrium which credit, money lending and usury have attracted over the centuries and the supervision to which they have become subject, hire has, for long, remained unregulated and, in more recent times, has only become lightly regulated.

Terms control, which related to monetary control rather than to affording protection to the hirer, applied to hire as well as to hire-purchase and instalment sale agreements. Terms control covered matters such as minimum down-payments and maximum periods of repayment.[2]

The light treatment of consumer hire is illustrated in various ways. Thus, there is no yardstick for hiring charges comparable to the annual percentage rate of charge in relation to credit agreements; no liability is imputed on the owner corresponding to the creditor's liability under CCA 1974, s 75; there are no equivalent provisions to the unfair relationships between creditors and debtors under CCA 1974, ss140A to 140C; there is no limit on the level of default charges which may be levied under a hire agreement; and hire is generally more lightly treated than credit in the FCA Handbook and the sourcebook CONC.

1   Crowther Report, Command 4596, para 5.2.7.
2   The Orders applying terms control were first introduced in 1939 and culminated in the final Control of Hiring Order 1977 (as amended) and the Hire-Purchase and Credit Sale Agreements (Control) Order 1976 (as amended). They were revoked by the Control of Hiring and Hire-Purchase and Credit Sale Agreements (Revocation) Order 1982, SI 1982/1034.

3.9 THE MEANING OF 'CONSUMER HIRE AGREEMENT'

A consumer hire agreement is an agreement made by a person with an individual (as defined at **3.2** above), the hirer, for bailment or, in Scotland, the hiring of goods to the hirer, which is not a hire-purchase agreement, and is capable of subsisting for more than three months.[1] A corresponding definition is contained in RAO.[2] A regulated consumer hire agreement is a consumer hire agreement which is not an exempt agreement.[3]

In *TRM Copy Centres (UK) Ltd v Lanwall Services Ltd*[4] the court rightly rejected the argument that an agreement which did not stipulate payment for the hire of equipment but required payment to be made only if and when the photocopier was used, constituted a hire agreement. The court commented that under a hire agreement the hirer pays for the hire of the goods which come into his possession even if he does not use them at all. As Professor Goode states (and this was cited with approval by the court), it is abundantly clear that the statutory provisions of CCA 1974 are concerned solely with bailment by way of hire, that is bailment under which the person receiving possession of the goods or equipment is to pay for their use during the period of his lawful possession.[5] The decision was upheld on appeal[6] to the House of Lords where Lord Hope stated that it is the fact that the hiring is in consideration of an ascertained hire or rent which the hirer agrees to pay that marks this kind of contract out from others under which the temporary use or possession of a thing is given to another.[7] If the incorporation of payments other than hire rentals results in the hire agreement being a multiple agreement, consideration must be given to whether the agreement is a unitary multiple agreement or an agreement in parts. However, it is submitted that all payments envisaged by the Agreements Regulations as being capable of being incorporated in a regulated hire agreement militate against the agreement being a multiple agreement by virtue of the inclusion of those payments.

Value added tax is payable on rentals so that they are rentals to be construed as inclusive of value added tax.

In contrast to consumer credit, a distinction has always existed, for very limited purposes, between consumer hire and hire for business purposes in relation to the hirer's right to terminate the hire agreement. Thus, the hirer is given an automatic right to terminate a hire agreement which has run for 18 months unless, in general terms, the hire agreement is for the purpose of the hirer's business and the goods are selected by the hirer and acquired by the owner at the hirer's request from a person who is not the owner's associate or the goods are hired for the hirer's business of sub-hire.[8] This distinction has been retained even though it has essentially lost its significance by virtue of the exemption of consumer hire agreements for business use. Its relevance now is limited to agreements for total rentals not exceeding £25,000, which remain regulated consumer hire agreements.

1 CCA 1974, s 15(1).
2 Article 60N(3).
3 CCA 1974, s 15(2); RAO art 60N(3).
4 [2007] All ER (D) 287.
5 *Goode: Consumer Credit Law and Practice* IC [23.75].
6 [2008] All ER (D) 235.
7 [2009] GCCR 9401, HL at 9405.
8 CCA 1974, s 101(7).

3.10   CREDIT HIRE

A new form of credit and hire agreement, namely so-called 'credit hire', was formulated by the court in *Dimond v Lovell*.[1] The House of Lords, in upholding the decision of the Court of Appeal, held that a car hire agreement under which hire charges are not payable until after conclusion of the hirer's claim against a third party for damage to the hirer's car, is also a consumer credit agreement, as it involves deferment of the hire charges beyond the time they would otherwise be payable. The court's finding is more palatable under the general law of credit than within the scheme of the CCA 1974. Does the decision mean, for example, that a consumer hire agreement may be combined in one agreement with a credit agreement? CCA 1974, s 18 and the Consumer Credit (Agreements) Regulations 1983 would suggest otherwise. Does it mean that a consumer hire agreement is incapable of being modified by a regulated modifying agreement to postpone the date of the final rental payment as this would give rise to the need for a consumer credit agreement? In any event, why should a 'postponed' final rental be given a different status than an 'advance rental'? In practice, following the above judgment, credit hire is dealt with by a combination of a regulated hire agreement and an exempt credit agreement, the latter by reference to the number of repayments, the period of repayment and the absence of interest and any charge.[2]

1 [2001] GCCR 2751, HL.
2 See the discussion and trenchant criticism in *Goode: Consumer Credit Law and Practice* at [24.48] to [24.64].

3.11   CAPACITY OF THE PARTIES

The creditor or owner must, of course, have legal capacity to enter into the relevant agreement. Generally speaking, this will be manifest from the company's or limited liability partnership's constitution, the partnership deed in the case of a partnership, the constitution, trust deed or rules of an association or charity, together with the Part 4A permission granted by the FCA authorising the lender or owner to carry on the business of entering into the agreement.

It will be remembered that, for the purposes of CCA 1974, an individual is a natural person, a partnership of two or three persons or an unincorporated body of persons not consisting entirely of bodies corporate. Under general principles of contract law most individuals will have capacity to enter into consumer credit agreements and consumer hire agreements.

A minor may enter into a consumer credit agreement or a consumer hire agreement although the agreement will be unenforceable against him unless the goods which are the subject of the agreement are necessaries supplied to the minor and the contract is beneficial to him. The lender can then recover the amount spent under the equitable principle of subrogation.[1] The CCA 1974 protects minors by making it an offence for a person, with a view to financial gain, to send to a minor any document inviting him to borrow money, to obtain goods on credit or hire, to obtain services on credit or to apply for information or advice on borrowing money or otherwise obtaining credit or hiring goods.[2]

Leasing by local authorities is restricted by the Local Government and Housing Act 1989 and the Local Government Act 2003. Finance leases, in contrast with operating leases, entered into by local authorities fall within the scope of credit arrangements and are subject to a monetary limit on expenditure.

Where the debtor or hirer is a partnership or an unincorporated body of persons, one person may sign the regulated agreement on behalf of such debtor or hirer.[3]

1 *Goode: Consumer Credit Law and Practice* (LexisNexis Butterworths), at [11.12], and see *Chitty on Contracts* (32nd edn, 2015) at 9-023.
2 CCA 1974, s 50.
3 CCA 1974, s 61(4) and Consumer Credit (Agreements) Regulations 1983, SI 1983/1553, reg 6(3)(a); Consumer Credit (Agreements) Regulations 2010, SI 2010/1014, reg 4(3)(a).

Chapter 4

Types of credit and credit agreements

4.1 CONSUMER CREDIT AGREEMENT

With the transfer of the consumer credit regime from governance by the CCA 1974 regime to that jointly of CCA 1974 and the Financial Services and Markets Act 2000, established terminology was jettisoned or commingled with new terminology. Thus, CCA 1974 refers to, and defines, a consumer credit agreement as an agreement between an individual ('the debtor') and any other person ('the creditor') by which the creditor provides the debtor with credit of any amount.[1] In contrast, in the new regime, such agreement is defined as a 'credit agreement' albeit in similar terms as, in relation to an agreement other than a green deal plan, an agreement between an individual or relevant recipient of credit ('A') and any other person ('B') under which B provides A with credit of any amount.[2] 'Credit' includes a cash loan, and any other form of financial accommodation.[3]

'Individual' in CCA 1974 encompasses the meaning of 'relevant recipient of credit' in the Financial Services and Markets Act 2000 (Regulated Activities) Order 2001, SI 2001/544 ('RAO').[4] 'Individual' is defined as including, apart from a natural person, a partnership consisting of two or three persons not all of whom are bodies corporate and an unincorporated body of persons which does not consist entirely of bodies corporate and is not a partnership.[5]

A consumer credit agreement is a regulated credit agreement within the meaning of CCA 1974 if it:

(a) is a regulated credit agreement for the purposes of Chapter 14A of Part 2 of the RAO; and

(b) is not an agreement of the type described in Article 3(1)(b) of Directive 2014/17/EU of the European Parliament and of the Council of 4 February 2014 on credit agreements for consumers relating to residential immovable property.[6]

A 'regulated credit agreement' is any credit agreement which is not an exempt agreement.[7] An 'exempt agreement' is a credit agreement which is an exempt agreement under RAO articles 60C to 60H.

1 CCA 1974, s 8(1). Prior to 6 April 2008 a consumer credit agreement was subject to a financial ceiling which was then £25,000.

2 RAO Chapter 14A of Part 2; and see definition of a green deal plan in RAO art 60LB.
3 CCA 1974, s 9(1). Compare to Consumer Credit Directive 2008 which defines a 'credit agreement' as 'an agreement whereby a creditor grants or promises to grant a consumer credit in the form of a deferred payment, loan or other similar financial accommodation, except for agreements for the provision on a continuing basis of services or for the supply of goods of the same kind, where the consumer pays for such services or goods for the duration of their provision by means of instalments' (Article 3(c)).
4 CCA 1974, s 189(1); RAO art 60L(1).
5 Ibid., s 189(1).
6 Ibid., s 8(3).
7 RAO art 60B(3).

4.2 RUNNING-ACCOUNT CREDIT AND FIXED-SUM CREDIT

4.2.1 The distinction between running-account credit and fixed-sum credit

Running-account, or revolving, credit is a facility under a consumer credit agreement whereby the debtor is enabled to receive from time to time (whether in his own person, or by another person) from the creditor or a third party, cash, goods and services (or any of them) to an amount or value such that, taking into account payments made by or to the credit of the debtor, the credit limit (if any) is not at any time exceeded.[1] Examples include bank overdrafts and credit card accounts, whether secured on land or otherwise, or unsecured.

Fixed-sum credit is defined as any other facility under a consumer credit agreement whereby the debtor is enabled to receive credit, whether in one amount or by instalments.[2] The definition of fixed-sum credit is rather infelicitous as it is only defined by reference to, and in contrast with, running-account credit. Not only is this strange from the point of view of fixed-sum credit being the more common form of credit but it means that one cannot adopt the statutory definition of fixed-sum credit without first defining running-account credit. One would have thought that it was sufficiently simple to define fixed-sum credit, independently of running-account credit, as a sum of money, certain in amount, which the creditor makes available for borrowing by the debtor in one or more tranches.

1 CCA 1974, s 10(1)(a).
2 Ibid., s 10(1)(b).

4.2.2 Features of running-account credit

The common features of a running-account credit account or agreement are a credit limit, the ability continually to pay into the account and to replenish the available credit and the fact that the account usually operates indefinitely until termination by one of the parties. 'Credit limit' is defined as, in respect of any period, the maximum debit balance which under the agreement is allowed to stand on the account during the period, disregarding any term of the agreement allowing that maximum to be exceeded merely temporarily.[1]

The notion of a credit limit (see **4.2.1** above) is not essential to a running-account credit agreement. It was of significance when the Consumer Credit Act applied to credit agreements which did not exceed a specified financial limit. This was the position until 6 April 2008 when the Consumer Credit Act 2006 removed the financial limit of £25,000 which then applied to consumer credit agreements and consumer hire agreements. With the removal of the financial limit, the only relevance of the anti-avoidance provisions of s 10(3) in their reference to an agreement not exceeding the credit limit, is to consumer credit agreements for business use where the creditor provides the debtor with credit not exceeding £25,000. A credit agreement will be assumed not to exceed £25,000 if the credit limit does not exceed that amount or, whether or not there is a credit limit (and if there is, notwithstanding that it exceeds the specified amount), if the debtor is not enabled to draw an amount which exceeds the specified amount or, if the agreement provides that if it so exceeds that amount, the rate of the total charge for credit increases or any other condition favouring the creditor or his associate comes into operation or if, at the time the agreement is made, it is probable, having regard to the terms of the agreement and any other relevant considerations, that the debit balance will not at any time exceed £25,000. In all those cases the running-account credit agreement for business use will be presumed to be a regulated running-account credit agreement. It is a rather odd preservation of what is otherwise an otiose s 10(3), especially as running-account credit for business use is hardly the order of the day in the financing of business requirements.

The characteristics of running-account are also recognised at common law. As early as 1816, in *Clayton's Case*,[2] the court defined the agreement in question as a banking account 'where all the sums paid in form one blended fund, the parts of which have no longer any distinct existence'. This passage was also cited in *Re Footman Bower & Co Ltd*[3] where the court described a current account as one where the debtor–creditor relationship of the parties is recorded in one entire account into which all liabilities and payments are carried in order of date, as a course of dealing extending over a considerable period and where the true nature of the debtor's liability is a single and undivided debt for the amount of the balance due on the account, without regard to the several items which as a matter of history contribute to the balance. More recently in *Re Charge Card Services Ltd (No 2)*,[4] the court described a running-account agreement by reference to the reciprocal obligations giving rise to credits and debits in a single running account and a single liability to pay the ultimate balance found due on taking the account.

1 CCA 1974, s 10(2).
2 *Devaynes v Noble* (1816) 1 Mer 572.
3 [1961] 2 All ER 161 at 165, Ch D.
4 *Re Charge Card Services Ltd (No 2)* [1986] 3 All ER 289 at 307, Ch D.

4.2.3   Features of fixed-sum credit

The most common form of fixed-sum credit is a single fixed-sum loan advance, although fixed-sum credit also includes a progress, or draw-down, loan under which the borrower is entitled to draw down the credit amount in tranches.

Fixed-sum credit extends beyond a loan agreement and includes credit sale, hire-purchase and conditional sale agreements. The underlying principle in treating these identically is the classification of the outstanding amount of the loan, or the purchase price or hire-purchase price, as the case may be, as credit and as an ascertained or fixed amount of credit.

4.2.4   Relevance of the distinction between a fixed-sum credit agreement and a running-account credit agreement

The relevance of the distinction between fixed-sum credit and running-account credit, in so far as CCA 1974 is concerned, is the fact that they are separate and distinct categories of credit for the purposes of the regulatory regime, subject to different requirements as to the form and content of the regulated credit agreement and give rise to different rights and obligations on the part of the parties. The distinction is also relevant to the issue of multiple agreements and whether fixed-sum credit agreements and running-account credit agreements can be combined in one form of agreement, which it is submitted they cannot.[1]

The regulations distinguish between the obligations of a creditor under a fixed-sum credit agreement and a running-account credit agreement. Distinctions are to be found in the periodicity of the issue of statements of account, the event upon which a notice of sums in arrears must be issued, the contents of statements and notices, and whether specific statutory notices may be incorporated in other notices or statements.[2]

It is interesting to note that both the Consumer Credit (Agreements) Regulations 1983 and the Consumer Credit (Agreements) Regulations 2010 provide for the identification of certain types of credit agreement in the statutory heading to the agreement. The specific headings accommodated are: hire purchase agreement, conditional sale agreement, fixed sum loan agreement, credit card agreement and certain headings for modifying agreements. Notable omissions are fixed-sum credit agreement (which may take the form of financial accommodation rather than a loan which would generally be identified as an advance of money), credit sale agreement and running-account or revolving credit agreement.[3]

1 See CCA 1974, s 18.
2 See **11.2** and **11.3**.
3 SI 1983/1553, Sch 1, para 1; SI 2010/1014, Sch 1.

4.3   RESTRICTED-USE CREDIT AND UNRESTRICTED-USE CREDIT

This distinction is the invention of the draftsman of CCA 1974. It is born out of the more important distinction drawn by the legislation between a debtor-creditor-supplier/borrower-lender-supplier agreement and a debtor-creditor/borrower-lender agreement, discussed at **4.4** below. As the description implies, restricted-use credit is credit whose purpose is prescribed or whose use is monitored by the creditor.

A restricted-use credit agreement is a regulated consumer credit agreement to finance a transaction between the debtor and the creditor or between the debtor and a person other than the creditor (e.g. the supplier) or to re-finance any existing indebtedness of the debtor, whether to the creditor or any other person; an unrestricted-use credit agreement is any other agreement.[1]

If the credit is in fact provided in such a way as to leave the debtor free to use it as he chooses, even though such use would contravene the agreement, the agreement is an unrestricted-use credit agreement.[2]

The distinction between restricted-use and unrestricted-use credit was considered in *Office of Fair Trading v Lloyds TSB Bank plc*[3] in relation to four-party structured credit card agreements. As described in this case, a four-party structure is one where there is interposed between the card issuer and the supplier, the merchant acquirer acting as an independent party. It involves an agreement between the merchant acquirer and the supplier, under which the supplier undertakes to honour the card and the merchant acquirer undertakes to pay the supplier, and an agreement between the merchant acquirer and the card issuer, under which the merchant acquirer agrees to pay the supplier and the card issuer undertakes to reimburse the merchant acquirer. There is, however, no direct contractual link between the card issuer and the supplier.[4] It was argued before the Court of Appeal that where credit is advanced in relation to transactions entered into under a four-party structure, this is unrestricted-use credit because the card issuer has not itself made any arrangements with the supplier. In such cases the arrangements have been made by the merchant acquirer. The court rejected this contention on the grounds that it cannot make any difference who made the arrangements with the suppliers. From the point of view of the cardholder, the card can only be used to buy goods or services from suppliers who have agreed to accept cards carrying the mark or logo in question. The fact that the number of places at which these cards can be presented is very extensive cannot disguise the fact that, in contrast to cash, they can only be used at places where the relevant sign is displayed. The decision was upheld by the House of Lords.[5]

It is imperative to distinguish between credit and charges, as any item constituting charges cannot form part of the credit amount, even though time is allowed for its payment.[6] Misstatement of the amount of credit will produce an improperly executed regulated agreement which is enforceable against the debtor only on an order of the court.[7]

Some confusion has arisen when determining whether a sum owing by a borrower to a creditor which is refinanced under a subsequent credit agreement constitutes part of the credit or part of the total charge for credit under the subsequent agreement. In *Watchtower Investments Ltd v Payne*[8] it was held that where part of an advance is to be used to discharge an earlier debt owed to another creditor, it is not part of the cost for credit but part of the credit itself. The court found that it was one of the debtor's purposes in applying for the loan to Watchtower Investments to discharge existing arrears owing to a building society. The court held that payment of the arrears did not form part of the charges because it was not of the nature of a charge for credit, but was part of the credit itself. The court stated that a line can and must be drawn between what constitutes charges and what constitutes credit, the former being payment exacted for the provision of services or the grant or use of facilities relating to the subject matter of the credit agreement, whereas the latter constitutes, for example, the purchase of land or goods under the agreement or amounts under some other agreement relating solely to what is to be provided under that other agreement and unrelated to what is being provided under the credit agreement.[9] It went on to state that it is necessary to consider all the circumstances, including the documents relating to the agreement, in order to ascertain objectively the purpose of the borrowing. The purpose of the court's consideration is to arrive at what in reality is the true cost to the debtor of the credit provided. On the facts, it found that payment of the arrears was a purpose of the debtor and, accordingly, that the sum in question was part of the credit and not part of the charges.

A different conclusion on the facts was reached in *McGinn v Grangewood Securities Ltd*[10] where the court held that a sum advanced under a credit agreement, which was used to repay the debtor's arrears under an existing agreement, constituted part of the total charge for credit and not the credit amount. The court held that it was not part of the debtor's purpose that the sum of arrears should be borrowed from *Grangewood Securities* in order to clear her arrears under her existing mortgage but that the sole purpose of the loan was to borrow money in order to extend and refurbish her house. On the other hand the obligation to discharge the arrears was an obligation to incur a charge payable under the transaction and was therefore part of the true cost of the credit and not part of the credit. In *Lombard North Securities Ltd v Meadows*[11] it was held that the facts of that case were more akin to those in *Watchtower Investments* than *Grangewood Securities*. The court found that payment of the arrears was one of the objective purposes of the transaction and that, accordingly, the sum which was in fact paid for the arrears was part of the credit and not part of the total charge for credit.

With respect, it appears difficult to reconcile the line of thinking of the courts with the definition of a restricted-use credit agreement in CCA 1974, s 11(1) (c), namely an agreement to refinance any existing indebtedness of the debtor's, whether to the creditor or another person. Arrears under an existing agreement are surely part of the debtor's indebtedness under that agreement and if those arrears are to be refinanced, whether as a condition of the grant of new credit and entering into a new credit agreement or otherwise, appears irrelevant. The distinction is, of course, important for the purposes of establishing whether the agreement is an improperly executed regulated agreement and whether it complies with the requirements of the various Agreements Regulations, and the prescribed terms of the agreement. In order to avoid any unnecessary confusion or risk, a creditor would be well advised to ensure at the outset that the refinancing of any existing indebtedness is part of the purpose of the loan.

1   CCA 1974, s 11(1) and (2).
2   Ibid., s 11(3).
3   [2006] GCCR 5701 at 5719–5720, CA.
4   At 5704–5705.
5   [2007] GCCR 6101, HL.
6   CCA 1974, s 9(4).
7   Ibid., s 65(1).
8   [2001] GCCR 3055, CA.
9   At 3069.
10 [2002] GCCR 4761, CA.
11 [2005] GCCR 5381, CA at para 35; see also **3.1**.

4.4 DEBTOR-CREDITOR/BORROWER-LENDER CREDIT AND DEBTOR-CREDITOR-SUPPLIER/BORROWER-LENDER-SUPPLIER CREDIT

A debtor-creditor agreement (synonymous with a borrower-lender agreement) and a debtor-creditor-supplier agreement (synonymous with a borrower-lender-supplier agreement) are descriptive of different types of credit agreements under CCA 1974.[1] One might, however, isolate the credit element from the agreement for the credit. On this basis, debtor-creditor-supplier (d-c-s) credit or supplier-connected credit is credit extended by the supplier or dealer to his customer (the debtor) to finance a transaction between himself and the debtor or credit extended by the creditor to the debtor pursuant to, or in contemplation of, arrangements made by the creditor with the supplier. The latter is commonplace in relation to the finance of motor vehicles, home improvements, furniture and equipment. A bank or other lender will have entered into arrangements with a dealer or supplier to assist with the financing of purchases. Often the dealer will have entered into arrangements with more than one source of finance.

In contrast, debtor-creditor credit is unrelated to any supply by the creditor or to any arrangements between the creditor and any supplier. It arises where the creditor advances a loan to a debtor or where a supplier simply introduces a customer to one or other creditor with whom it has no particular arrangements. The credit is debtor-creditor or unconnected-supplier credit. The distinction between debtor-creditor-supplier and debtor-creditor credit applies also to running-account credit. An overdraft facility on a bank account is debtor-creditor credit whereas an account for a Barclaycard, MasterCard or dedicated in-store card is for debtor-creditor-supplier credit unless it merely involves a cash advance.

Originally a purpose, but not the sole purpose, of categorising credit agreements was to prevent evasion of CCA 1974 by a creditor grouping together or aggregating disparate credit agreements and the credit limits or credit amounts under the agreements, thereby exceeding the financial limit and avoiding regulation. Since the abolition of the financial limit, the distinction between debtor-creditor and debtor-creditor-supplier agreements primarily serves the purpose of distinguishing between the different consequences of such agreements. However, it remains relevant to consumer credit agreements for business use where the £25,000 financial limit on regulated agreements continues to apply.

1 CCA 1974, ss 13 and 12 respectively.

4.4.1 Debtor-creditor/borrower-lender agreement

A debtor-creditor ('d-c')/borrower-lender agreement is a regulated consumer credit agreement for any of the following:

(a) restricted-use credit to finance a transaction between a debtor and a supplier (other than the creditor) not made under pre-existing arrangements or in contemplation of future arrangements between the creditor and the supplier;

(b) restricted-use credit to re-finance any existing indebtedness of the debtor, whether to the creditor or any other person; or

(c)   unrestricted-use credit which is not to be used to finance a transaction of the type referred to in (a) above.[1]

Examples of debtor-creditor agreements are bank loans, overdraft facilities, mortgage loans unconnected with a house-builder or property developer and cash advances from an Automated Teller Machine ('ATM').

1 CCA 1974, s 13.

4.4.2   Debtor-creditor-supplier/borrower-lender-supplier agreement

A debtor-creditor-supplier ('d-c-s')/borrower-lender-supplier agreement is a supplier-connected loan, being one of the following:

(a)   A restricted-use credit agreement to finance a transaction between the debtor and the creditor, whether forming part of that agreement or not. Examples are hire-purchase and instalment sale agreements, where the supplier is itself the creditor or a third party, and revolving credit agreements provided by a retailer for its customers.

(b)   A restricted-use credit agreement to finance a transaction between the debtor and a person (the supplier) other than the creditor, which is made by the creditor under pre-existing arrangements or in contemplation of future arrangements between himself and the supplier. Typically this relates to loan facilities agreed between a creditor and supplier for use by the supplier's customers.

(c)   An unrestricted-use credit agreement made by the creditor under pre-existing arrangements between himself and a person (the supplier) other than the debtor in the knowledge that the credit is to be used to finance a transaction between the debtor and the supplier. It is immaterial whether or not the debtor uses the credit for its intended purpose.[1]

It is unfortunate that the terms 'supplier' and 'pre-existing arrangements', which are central to various provisions of the Act, for example the meaning of debtor-creditor-supplier agreement and the application of CCA 1974, s 75, are not defined with any precision. The expression 'supplier' is merely defined in parenthesis in CCA 1974, ss 11(1)(b), 12(c) and 13(c). Indeed, the FCA Handbook definition of 'supplier' is no more explicit.[2] The identity and significance of the supplier in relation to a solicitor's fee funding arrangement was the subject of *Sutherland Professional Funding Ltd v Bakewells and others*[3] and is dealt with in at **4.4.3**.

'Pre-existing arrangements' is defined in CCA 1974, s 187 by reference to 'arrangements', but 'arrangements' is not defined. In *Governor and Co of Bank of Scotland v Alfred Truman*,[4] in deciding whether a party to a transaction was a supplier within the meaning of the Act, the court referred to the judgment of Gloster J in *Office of Fair Trading v Lloyds TSB Bank plc*[5] to the effect that 'arrangements' should be understood and construed in their ordinary popular sense and that there was evidence of a deliberate intention on the part of the draftsman to use broad loose language. It followed that a restricted construction would be contrary to the scheme of that part of the Act. This was endorsed by the Court of Appeal, which opined that '[T]he word "arrangements" is capable of carrying a broad meaning and a statute which elsewhere displays a high degree of precision in its choice of language must have been deliberately chosen by Parliament with a view to embracing a wide range of different commercial structures having substantially the same effect'.[6] The view of the courts is that the Crowther Committee and Parliament, when enacting the 1974 Act, did not know how the credit card market would develop but that the language of 'arrangements' used in the Act is capable of embracing the modern relationships between card issuers and suppliers under networks like VISA and MasterCard. Furthermore, the House of Lords has confirmed that there is nothing in the language of s 75 to exclude foreign transactions from the scope of debtor-creditor-supplier agreements.[7]

It is submitted that, where a finance company finances insurance premiums payable by a borrower and the borrower is introduced to the finance company by the insurance broker which sells the insurance to him, the supplier under the agreement is generally the insurer and not the broker. If there are no pre-existing or contemplated arrangements between the broker and the finance company, the credit agreement is a debtor-creditor agreement and not a debtor-creditor-supplier agreement.

1   CCA 1974, s 12.
2   See the Glossary.
3   [2013] GCCR 11756.
4   [2005] GCCR 5491 at para 95.
5   *Office of Fair Trading v Lloyds TSB Bank plc* [2004] GCCR 5061.
6   *Office of Fair Trading v Lloyds TSB Bank plc* [2006] GCCR 5701, CA, at 5722 para [64].
7   *Office of Fair Trading v Lloyds TSB Bank plc* [2007] GCCR 6101, HL.

4.4.3   Significance of the distinction between a debtor-creditor/ borrower-lender (d-c) agreement and a debtor-creditor-supplier/borrower-lender-supplier (d-c-s) agreement

The principal differences between a debtor-creditor ('d-c') and a debtor-creditor-supplier ('d-c-s') agreement are the following:

(a)   the creditor in a d-c-s agreement is liable for any misrepresentation or breach of contract by the supplier;[1]

(b)   the creditor in a d-c-s agreement incurs liability in respect of antecedent negotiations conducted by a credit broker or supplier in relation to the agreement;[2]

(c)   various consequences attach to linked transactions where the principal agreement is a d-c-s agreement, including the fact that if the d-c-s agreement is cancelled this will generally also undo the linked transaction;[3]

(d)   it is an offence to canvass debtor-creditor agreements off trade premises or to solicit a debtor to enter into a d-c agreement off trade premises by making oral representations to the debtor or any other individual during a visit carried out for such purpose unless it was preceded by the debtor's signed written request made on a previous occasion;[4]

(e)   there are differences in the prescribed contractual provisions and statutory notices as between d-c and d-c-s agreements.[5] The significance of this was highlighted in *Sutherland Professional Funding Ltd v Bakewells and others*[6] where the court stated:

'In my judgment the items identified as being *"our disbursements"* in the Conditional Fee Agreements and client care letters were payments that Bakewells were obliged to discharge on behalf of their client as an incident of the contract of retainer between Bakewells and their client. Since the client was obliged to reimburse Bakewells and that obligation was financed by the CCA loan agreements to that extent the transaction being financed was the transaction between the debtor and Bakewells, being the contract of retainer between them, and SPFS had a pre-existing arrangement with Bakewells. In those circumstances, in my judgment Bakewells was to be regarded as *"the supplier"* and the CCA loan agreement a DCS agreement. In those circumstances it was accepted that the relevant notices did not appear in the CCA loan agreements and that in those circumstances the agreements were irredeemably unenforceable.';

(f)   d-c and d-c-s agreements are treated differently in relation to exempt agreements;[7] and

(g)   d-c and d-c-s agreements are treated differently under various other sections of CCA 1974 and regulations made under the Act.[8]

1   See CCA 1974, ss 75 and 75A, and **17.4.4**.
2   CCA 1974, s 56(1).
3   Ibid., s 19(1) and (2).
4   Ibid., s 49(1) and (2).
5   See the Consumer Credit (Agreements) Regulations 1983, SI 1983/1553, and Consumer Credit (Agreements) Regulations 2010, SI 2010/1014, each including Schedules.
6   [2013] GCCR 11756 at 11769, para [35].
7   RAO art 60E ff, and see **Chapter 6**.
8   See CCA 1974, ss 69–74.

4.5   CANCELLABLE AGREEMENTS

A cancellable agreement is the generic description given to any regulated agreement which is cancellable under CCA 1974 by the debtor or hirer, within a stipulated period of the agreement being made. The Act defines 'cancellable agreement' as a regulated agreement which, by virtue of s 67, may be cancelled by the debtor or hirer.[1] Only regulated consumer credit agreements outside the scope of the Consumer Credit Directive 2008 and outside the scope of CCA 1974, s 66A (Right of withdrawal) can be cancellable agreements. A debtor's right to cancel a regulated consumer credit agreement has been overridden and replaced in respect of consumer credit agreements within the scope of the Consumer Credit Directive by the debtor's right to withdraw from the credit agreement.[2]

Regulated agreements are cancellable where negotiations preceding the credit agreement, described as antecedent negotiations, included oral representations made by the negotiator in the presence of the debtor or hirer.[3] These exclude telephone conversations on the grounds that they are not made in the debtor's or hirer's presence.

'Antecedent negotiations' are negotiations with the debtor or hirer, conducted by the creditor or owner in relation to the making of any regulated agreement or by a credit broker in relation to goods sold or proposed to be sold to the creditor before forming the subject matter of a debtor-creditor-supplier agreement, or conducted by the supplier in relation to a transaction financed or proposed to be financed by a debtor-creditor-supplier agreement, involving a supplier other than the creditor. 'Negotiator' means the person by whom negotiations are so conducted with the debtor or hirer.[4]

The meaning of 'representation' in the context of oral representations made in the presence of the debtor (or hirer) in CCA 1974, s 67 was considered in *Moorgate Services Ltd v Kabir*.[5] The Court of Appeal construed the word 'representation', defined in CCA 1974, s 189(1), as including any condition or warranty, and any other statement or undertaking, whether oral or in writing. It went on to state that the statement must be one of fact or opinion or an undertaking as to the future which is capable of inducing the proposed borrower to enter into the agreement. It need not be shown that it in fact induced the borrower to enter into the agreement. There was no need to enquire into the circumstances of the case to establish whether the particular borrower was likely to have been induced by the statement in question. Nor need it have been intended by the negotiator to induce the agreement. It sufficed if the statement was one which by its nature was capable of inducing an agreement.

If the agreement is signed by the debtor (or hirer) on the trade premises of any of the creditor (or owner), negotiator or a party to a linked transaction (but not on the premises of the debtor (or owner)) the agreement is not cancellable.[6] In addition, as a separate regime applies to agreements secured on land and to agreements for the purchase of land or for a bridging loan in connection with the purchase of land, such agreements are never cancellable.[7]

A regulated agreement may be cancellable under other legislation. Under the Financial Services (Distance Marketing) Regulations 2004 a contract is cancellable if it is a so-called 'distance contract'. Essentially this is a contract entered into exclusively through use of one or more means of distance communication, namely without the simultaneous physical presence of the supplier and the consumer or an intermediary of the supplier and the consumer.[8]

A cancellable regulated credit agreement must set out the debtor's rights of cancellation. Where the agreement is not cancellable, the agreement must contain a statement that the debtor has no right to cancel the agreement under the Consumer Credit Act 1974 or the Financial Services (Distance Marketing) Regulations 2004.

The importance of setting out the customer's cancellation rights in the agreement was underlined by the court in *Goshawk Dedicated (No 2) Ltd v Governor and Company of the Bank of Scotland*.[9] This case truly set the hawk among the pigeons in respect of the consequence of an incorrect statutory 'Note' to the prescribed 'Your Right to Cancel' notice, which the court stated would render the agreement unenforceable under s 127(4) (since repealed). The case was followed in *Bank of Scotland v Euclidean (No 1)*[10] and also *Sutherland Professional Funding Ltd v Bakewells.*[11]

As mentioned above, as a result of amendments effected to CCA 1974 pursuant to the Consumer Credit Directive 2008, the right of cancellation only applies to consumer credit agreements outside the scope of the Directive and to consumer hire agreements, other agreements being subject to the debtor's right of withdrawal.

1 CCA 1974, s 189(1).
2 Ibid., ss 66A and 67(2); see **10.5**.
3 Ibid., s 67.
4 Ibid., s 56.
5 [1999] GCCR 1947, CA.
6 CCA 1974, s 67(1)(b).
7 Ibid., s 67(1)(a).
8 SI 2004/2095.
9 [2005] GCCR 5431 (Ch).
10 [2007] EWHC 1732 (Comm).
11 [2013] GCCR 11756, [2013] EWHC 2685 (QB).

4.6   CREDIT-TOKEN AGREEMENTS

A credit-token agreement is a regulated agreement for the provision of credit in connection with the use of a credit-token.[1] A credit-token agreement usually takes the form of a running-account credit agreement.

A credit-token is a document or thing, of whatever kind or description, against the production of which a creditor or a third party will supply cash, goods or services on credit or pay a third party for such supply.[2]

The issue of unsolicited credit-tokens, originally under CCA 1974, s 51, which was repealed save for a limited purpose,[3] is now addressed in the FCA Handbook, CONC 2.9.2, as follows:

(1)   A firm must not give a person a credit token if he has not asked for it.

(2)   A request in (1) must be in a document signed by the person making the request, unless the credit-token agreement is a small borrower-lender-supplier agreement.

(3)   Paragraph (1) does not apply to the giving of a credit token to a person:

    (a)   for use under a credit-token agreement already made; or

    (b)   in renewal or replacement of a credit token previously accepted by that person under a credit-token agreement which continues in force, whether or not varied.

1 CCA 1974, s 14(2).
2 Ibid., s 14(1).
3 Section 51 was repealed by art 20(15) of the Financial Services and Markets Act 2000 (Regulated Activities) (Amendment) (No 2) Order 2013, SI 2013/1881. However, s 51 is saved for the purposes of reg 52 of the Payment Services Regulations 2009, SI 2009/209, the effect being that the section continues to apply in relation to a regulated credit agreement in place of reg 58(1)(b) of

the Payment Services Regulations. However, it appears that the saving of s 51 was not preserved by the Payment Services Regulations 2017, SI 2017/752, so it is only the Rule in CONC which now applies.

4.7   SPECIFIC CONSUMER CREDIT AGREEMENTS

4.7.1   Agreement types recognised by the Agreements Regulations

The two sets of Consumer Credit (Agreements) Regulations[1] identify the following specific types of credit agreement regulated by CCA 1974: a hire-purchase agreement, a conditional sale agreement, a fixed-sum loan agreement, a credit card agreement and an agreement modifying a regulated credit agreement. All other regulated credit agreements are subsumed under a prescribed generic description of a credit agreement regulated by CCA 1974. Further descriptions are to be added where the agreement is combined with a pawn receipt, where the document embodies a partly regulated credit agreement, or where the agreement is secured on land.

1 Consumer Credit (Agreements) Regulations 1983, SI 1983/1553, Sch 1 and Consumer Credit (Agreements) Regulations 2010, SI 2010/1014, Sch 1.

4.7.2   Conditional sale, credit sale and hire-purchase agreements

4.7.2.1   Definitions

Instalment sale agreements, under which the buyer pays the price by instalments, comprise two types of agreement, namely a conditional sale agreement and a credit sale agreement.

A conditional sale agreement is an agreement for the sale of goods or land under which the price or part of it is payable by instalments and the owner retains ownership of the goods or land (notwithstanding that the buyer may be in possession of the goods or land) until the conditions specified in the contract (for the payment of instalments or otherwise) are met.[1]

A credit sale agreement is an agreement for the sale of goods or land under which the purchase price or part of it is payable by instalments and property in the goods or land passes to the buyer immediately, although payment of the purchase price is deferred. Whilst land might be the subject of a credit sale agreement, it is somewhat surprising that, in contrast to a conditional sale agreement, a credit sale agreement is defined in CCA 1974 by reference only to the sale of goods.[2]

A hire-purchase agreement is an agreement under which goods are bailed (or, in Scotland, hired) in return for periodical payments by the bailee (or hirer) and property in the goods passes to that person if the terms of the agreement are complied with and one or more of the following occurs:

(i)   the exercise of an option to purchase by that person,

(ii)   the doing of any other specified act by any party to the agreement,

(iii) the happening of any other specified event.[3]

The Consumer Rights Act 2015 adopts an essentially similar definition with a slight alteration of wording.[4]

The hirer under a hire-purchase agreement merely has an option to buy and is not contractually committed to buy. Under the regulated consumer credit regime a hire-purchase agreement is classified as a consumer credit agreement rather than a consumer hire agreement. This follows from CCA 1974's functional analytical approach, a hire-purchase agreement being construed as a type of secured sale agreement. Hence the reference in the requisite financial particulars relating to a hire-purchase agreement of 'the total amount payable' and 'the amount of credit'. However, it is in truth a hybrid agreement displaying certain characteristics of a hire agreement, as evidenced by the statutory definition's reference to 'hire' and 'bailment'. As described by Professor Goode, it is 'a hybrid form of contract. It is neither a simple bailment nor a contract of sale but combines the element of both: of bailment, because it prescribes terms for the use of the goods irrespective of whether the hirer ultimately decides to purchase them; of sale, because of the right given to the hirer to acquire title.'[5]

In practice the distinction between a conditional sale agreement and a hire-purchase agreement can be a fine one. An agreement was found to be one of hire purchase in the leading and very first case on hire purchase, *Helby v Matthews*,[6] where the court found that the terms of the contract 'did not, upon its execution, bind him [the appellant] to buy [the piano], but left him free to do so or not as he pleased, and nothing happened after the contract was made to impose that obligation.' By contrast, it was held in *Forthright Finance Ltd v Carlysle Finance Ltd*[7] that an agreement which provides that on payment of all instalments, property in the goods will pass to the hirer, unless 'the hirer' has before that time told 'the owner' that such is not the case, was a conditional sale agreement., The hirer is deemed to have exercised the option to purchase and title in the goods passes to the hirer, even though the hirer is given the option to terminate the agreement at an earlier stage. In *Close Asset Finance v Care Graphics Machinery Ltd*,[8] the agreement contained a standard option to purchase clause, for a nominal amount. It was held that the fact that the option to purchase could be exercised for a nominal amount did not detract from the finding that the contract was a hire-purchase agreement. In the words of the court, the law does not go into the question of whether the consideration in the contract is sufficient; the option to purchase was not a bogus option, it was an absolutely genuine one. The parties were free to structure their agreements as they wished and in this case had chosen to structure the agreement as a hire-purchase agreement.

In each of *Forthright Finance* and *Close Asset Finance* the issue was whether a purchaser of the goods in question had acquired title to the goods by virtue of purchasing in good faith and without notice of any rights of the original seller in respect of the goods, pursuant to the Sale of Goods Act 1979, s 25 ('buyer in possession after sale').

---

1 See CCA 1974, s 189(1), Supply of Goods (Implied Terms) Act 1973, s 15 and Consumer Rights Act 2015, s 5(3), where it is described as a conditional sales contract.

2 Ibid.
3 Ibid., s 189(1).
4 CRA 2015, s 7.
5 Goode, *Hire Purchase Law and Practice* (2nd edn, LexisNexis Butterworths), p 33.
6 [1895] AC 471, [1895–99] All ER Rep 821, HL at 825.
7 *Forthright Finance Ltd v Carlyle Finance Ltd* [1997] 4 All ER 90, [1999] GCCR 2213, CA.
8 [2000] GCCR 2617, [2000] CCLR 43.

4.7.2.2　Structural features of the agreements

In the case of smaller value transactions the customer usually contracts for the goods or services directly with the supplier. The latter then supplies them on instalment credit or hire-purchase terms to the customer. The original supplier is also the creditor. The supplier might then discount the agreements with a finance company or bank, thereby replenishing his supply of funds to finance further consumer transactions.

In larger transactions the customer will identify and select the goods or services as well as their supplier. The supplier then arranges for their financing by a finance company, often one with which the supplier has entered into arrangements. The supplier will then invoice the finance company which will acquire the goods and enter into a conditional sale, credit sale or hire-purchase agreement in respect of them with the customer introduced by the supplier.

The customer might purchase goods from the supplier and sell them to a finance company before buying them back on conditional sale, credit sale or hire-purchase terms. The risk involved in this route is that it may be construed as a disguised secured loan transaction. In the case of a company purchaser, this might render it void for want of registration as a charge under the Companies Act 2006, s 874. Where the purchaser is an individual the risk is twofold. First, the transaction might be construed as a disguised bill of sale and void for want of compliance with and registration under the Bills of Sale Acts.[1] Second, if construed as a disguised loan it may be unenforceable on account of failure to comply with the appropriate Agreements Regulations.[2] The problems are overcome by ensuring that the transactions are in fact genuine, that the finance house has bought the goods in good faith and that the entire transaction is properly documented.

The finance company might require the supplier to grant warranties in respect of the goods. These would normally preserve the seller's implied warranties on a sale and include warranties that the goods are new, not the subject of a previous transaction with the same customer, so as to avoid the possibility of fraud, and that the customer has selected and is satisfied with the goods. The supplier might also enter into a re-purchase agreement with the finance company under which it undertakes to buy back the goods at a predetermined price (e.g. their residual value) if the agreement between the customer and the finance company is terminated, whether on expiry of the agreement or by virtue of early settlement or the customer's breach of the agreement.

1 Bills of Sale Acts 1878–1891; *North Central Wagon Finance Co Ltd v Brailsford* [1962] 1 All ER 502.
2 CCA 1974, ss 61(1)(a), 65 and Consumer Credit (Agreements) Regulations 1983, SI 1983/1553 or Consumer Credit (Agreements) Regulations 2010, SI 2010/ 1014.

4.7.2.3   *Characteristics of an instalment sale agreement and a hire-purchase agreement*

INSTALMENT SALE AGREEMENT

In an instalment sale agreement the buyer is committed to purchasing whilst in a hire-purchase agreement he retains the option to do so. An instalment sale agreement has all the incidents of a sale agreement.

Parts of the Consumer Rights Act 2015 apply to a contract for a trader that supplies goods, digital content or a service to a consumer. A 'consumer' is defined as an individual acting for purposes that are wholly or mainly outside that individual's trade, business, craft or profession.[1] The Act proceeds to deal with each such supply, chapter 2 addressing contracts for the supply of goods, including statutory rights under a goods contract, the consumer's rights and remedies and passing of risk. The Act sets out the implied terms or, as described, 'statutory rights' in consumer contracts, which are expanded upon in detail, relating to the following:

(a)   goods to be of satisfactory quality (s 9);

(b)   goods to be fit for particular purpose (s 10);

(c)   goods to be as described (s 11);

(d)   other pre-contract information included in contract (s 12);

(e)   goods to match a sample (s 13);

(f)   goods to match a sample seen or examined (s 14);

(g)   installation as part of the conformity of the goods with the contract (s 15);

(h)   goods not conforming to contract if digital content does not conform (s 16):

(i)   trader must have the right to sell or transfer the goods when ownership of the goods is to be transferred or, in a contract for the hire of goods, to transfer possession of the goods (s 17);

(j)   delivery of goods (s 28); and

(k)   passing of risk (s 29).

A term of a contract is not binding on the consumer to the extent that it would exclude or restrict the trader's liability arising under any of the above provisions.[2]

Provisions that apply in transactions with non-consumers are set out in the Sale of Goods Act 1979. They include the following implied terms on the part of the seller: that he has the right to sell the goods; that the goods are free from any undisclosed charge or encumbrance or known to the buyer; that the buyer will enjoy quiet possession of the goods, except insofar as it may be disturbed by the owner or other encumbrancer disclosed or known to the buyer; that the goods will correspond with their description and, if sold by sample, with that sample. Where goods are sold in the course of a business, there is also an implied term that the goods are of satisfactory quality. Goods are of satisfactory quality if they meet the standard that a reasonable person would regard as satisfactory, taking account of any description of the goods, the price (if relevant) and all other relevant circumstances. Where the buyer expressly or by implication discloses any particular purpose for which he is buying the goods, there is an implied term that they are reasonably fit for that purpose.[3]

Where the buyer would have the right to reject the goods by reason of a breach on the part of the seller of an implied term, as above, but the breach is so slight that it would be unreasonable for him to reject them, the breach is not to be treated as a breach of condition but may be treated as a breach of warranty.[4]

In *Barber v NWS Bank plc*[5] the seller of a motor vehicle under a conditional sale agreement was not the owner of the vehicle, which was the subject of a prior finance agreement in the name of a third party with monies outstanding to that party. The purchaser under the conditional sale agreement, on discovering this fact, rescinded the agreement on the grounds of total failure of consideration and demanded the return of all instalments paid. The court found in favour of the purchaser on the grounds that an implied condition (now a term) that the seller had a right to sell the goods under the then applicable Sale of Goods Act 1979, s 12, had been breached as the seller did not have title to the car either at the date of the agreement or at any time thereafter prior to the buyer's letter of rescission.

In the event of termination by the seller by reason of the buyer's breach, the buyer is usually liable for payment of the entire outstanding balance of the total purchase price less a discount attributable to the seller's receipt of accelerated payment. However, CCA 1974 stipulates differently in certain situations.[6]

In the event of the buyer's wrongful disposal of goods before he has paid the full purchase price, the 'nemo dat' rule will generally prevent title in the goods passing to their new purchaser. This rule provides that where goods are sold by a person who is not their owner and who does not sell them under the express, implied or apparent authority, or with the consent, of the owner, the buyer acquires no better title to the goods than the seller had. The Sale of Goods Act 1979[7] provides that, subject to its provisions, where goods are sold by a person who is not their owner, and who does not sell them under the authority or with the consent of the owner, the buyer acquires no better title to the goods than the seller had, unless the owner of the goods is by his conduct precluded from denying the seller's authority to sell. Nothing in the Act affects:

(a) the provisions of the Factors Acts or any enactment enabling the apparent owner of goods to dispose of them as if he were their true owner; or

(b) the validity of any contract of sale under any special common law or statutory power of sale or under the order of a court of competent jurisdiction.

There are several exceptions to the 'nemo dat' rule, notably dispositions by mercantile agents, dispositions by sellers and buyers of goods under the Factors Act 1889 and dispositions by a seller in possession after sale or by a buyer in possession after a sale of the goods.[8]

HIRE-PURCHASE AGREEMENT

At common law a hirer under a hire-purchase agreement is entitled to terminate the agreement at any time but he will be liable to pay the owner damages for early termination and to return the goods to the owner. Where the amount or method of calculation of damages is stipulated at the outset in the agreement, it may not exceed a genuine pre-estimate of the likely damages or loss which the owner would suffer in such event.[9]

The terms implied in hire-purchase agreements with consumers are as set out above under the Consumer Rights Act 2015. In the case of non-consumer agreements, they are contained in the Supply of Goods (Implied Terms) Act 1973 and are similar to those implied in sale agreements. There are statutory implied terms that the creditor will have a right to sell the goods at the time when the property is to pass; that the goods are free, and will remain free, when the property is to pass, from any charge or encumbrance not disclosed or known to the hirer before the agreement is made; and that the hirer's quiet possession of the goods will remain undisturbed by the creditor or any third person, except of course if the hirer breaches the agreement. This Act also imports into the hire-purchase agreement certain implied terms relating to the goods, namely that they are of satisfactory quality, fit for their purpose, and correspond with their description and with any sample.[10]

In *Butterworth v Kingsway Motors Ltd*[11] a hire-purchase agreement was entered into between the owner of a motor vehicle and a hirer, who was given the option of purchasing the vehicle. Until the option had been exercised the vehicle was to remain the property of the owner. Before all instalments had been paid, the hirer, not realising that she was acting unlawfully, purported to sell the vehicle to another, who in turn, acting in good faith, sold the vehicle to yet another person. None of the purported sellers had title to the vehicle at the times when the sales were made. The hirer subsequently paid all instalments and exercised the option to purchase, as a result of which title in the vehicle passed to her and served to feed the previously defective titles of the subsequent buyers. It was held that there was no failure of consideration, although the seller of the vehicle did not have title at the time of the sale, as the seller subsequently acquired title by virtue of the hirer under the hire purchase agreement exercising her option to acquire the vehicle, so that the title so acquired went to feed the previously defective titles of the subsequent buyers and enured to their benefit. However, if claims are made before the option to purchase is exercised, the seller may be in breach of the statutory warranty of the right to sell the goods.

In contrast to the position in a sale agreement, an innocent third party cannot acquire good title from a hirer under the Factors Act 1889, s 9 or the Sale of Goods Act 1979, s 25. However, by virtue of ss 27 to 29 of the Hire-Purchase Act 1964, where a motor vehicle is sold to a private purchaser who buys in good faith and without notice of the seller's defective title (and is oblivious of the fact that the vehicle is the subject of a hire-purchase or conditional sale agreement), the purchaser acquires good title from the hirer under a hire-purchase agreement or the buyer under a conditional sale agreement. This applies equally to a private purchaser from a trade seller.[12] However, it does not extend to a private purchaser buying a motor vehicle from a rogue who had obtained it fraudulently by signing a hire purchase agreement with a forged signature. In such circumstances it was held in *Shogun Finance Ltd v Hudson*[13] that the rogue was not the 'debtor' within the meaning of s 27 of the Hire Purchase Act 1964. The seller was liable in conversion to the true owner.

THE CUSTOMER'S TERMINATION RIGHTS

In both a regulated hire-purchase agreement and a regulated conditional sale agreement, save in exceptional circumstances, the hirer or debtor respectively has the right to terminate the agreement at any time before the final payment falls due.[14] Once the hirer or debtor has paid at least one-third of the total amount payable under the agreement, the owner or creditor may not take back the goods against his wishes without a court order, the goods being identified as 'protected goods'.[15] Upon termination, the debtor or hirer is liable for the return of the goods, payment of any installation charges and payment of one-half of the total amount payable under the agreement.[16] If the hirer under a hire-purchase agreement or the buyer under a conditional sale agreement commits a repudiatory breach of the agreement and the owner or creditor terminates the agreement (as he is entitled to do), it is debatable whether he will be entitled to recover more than he would have been entitled to had the customer terminated the agreement. It appears that, provided the owner or creditor has served the requisite notice under CCA 1974 and the debtor has not terminated the agreement before the due date for payment under the notice has arisen, the debtor is liable for payment of the full outstanding balance under the agreement. The rule against penalties would then not apply.[17] This conclusion would also accord with the literal meaning of s 99 of the CCA 1974.

EXCLUSIONS AND UNFAIR CONTRACT TERMS

Exclusions and unfair contract terms are governed by the Unfair Contract Terms Act 1977 and the Consumer Rights Act 2015, s 31, Part 2 and Schedule 2.

1   CRA 2015, s 2(3).
2   Ibid., s 31(1)–(7).
3   Sale of Goods Act 1979, ss 12, 13 and 14.
4   Ibid, s 15A.
5   [1996] 1 All ER 906, CA.
6   See below.
7   Sale of Goods Act 1979, s 21.
8   Ibid., ss 24 and 25 and Factors Act 1889, s 9. See also *National Employers Mutual General Insurance Association v Jones* [1988] 2 All ER 425, HL.
9   *Bridge v Campbell Discount Co Ltd* [1962] 1 All ER 385.
10 Supply of Goods (Implied Terms) Act 1973, ss 8, 9 and 10. Exclusions and unfair contract terms are governed by Unfair Contract Terms Act 1977, s 6 and Consumer Rights Act 2015, s 31, Pt 2 and Sch 2.
11 [1954] 2 All ER 694.
12 See the application of these sections in *Stevenson v Beverley Bentinck Ltd* [1976] 2 All ER 606 and *Hichens v General Guarantee Corpn Ltd* [2001] EWCA Civ 359, (2001) Times, 13 March.
13 [2003] GCCR 4971, HL.
14 CCA 1974, s 99.
15 Ibid., s 90.
16 Ibid., s 100.
17 See *Goode: Consumer Credit Law and Practice* (LexisNexis Butterworths), at 1C [36.203], citing the decision of Woolf J (as he then was) in *Wadham Stringer Finance Ltd v Meany* [1999] CCR 551.

4.7.3   Fixed-sum loan agreements

4.7.3.1   Definition

A fixed-sum loan agreement is an agreement under which an ascertained sum is advanced by the lender to the borrower for a specified period, either for a specified or an unspecified purpose, in return for the repayment of such sum together with interest and any other charges. The loan may relate to the supply of goods or services by a third party. When it is part of a tripartite arrangement or agreement it will fall into the category of a connected loan or a debtor-creditor-supplier/ borrower-lender-supplier agreement. In other cases, namely unconnected loans, it is characterised as a debtor-creditor/borrower-lender agreement. The most common form of fixed-sum loan agreement is that which is colloquially known as a personal loan agreement.

An agreement is for fixed-sum credit notwithstanding that the borrower may draw down the loan amount in tranches, e.g. on presentation of an architect's certificate or at the borrower's discretion, as in the case of a school fee payments plan.

Fixed-sum loan agreements include bridging loans, high-cost short-term credit agreements, residential renovation agreements and cheque or voucher agreements.

A residential renovation agreement is a consumer credit agreement entered into on or after 21 March 2016 which is unsecured and the purpose of which is the renovation of residential property, as described in Article 2(2a) of Directive 2008/48/EC of the European Parliament and of the Council of 23 April 2008 on credit agreements for consumers.[1]

Under a cheque or voucher agreement the purchaser purchases a series of cheques or vouchers, on credit, to be used at identified stores or suppliers and agrees to repay the credit over an agreed period of time.

As 'credit' is defined in CCA 1974 as including any form of financial accommodation, any agreement under which one party is indebted to the other, and is granted a period of time in which to make payment, will involve the grant of credit. If the debtor is an individual, the agreement will be a consumer credit agreement and a regulated agreement if it does not qualify as an exempt agreement. It is important to recognise this fact in practice as, if the agreement does not comply with the requirements of a regulated agreement, it will be unenforceable without an order of the court and potentially irredeemably unenforceable.[2] The need to comply is often obscured by the mistaken belief that credit agreements entered into on a one-off basis, as opposed to being entered into as part of a lending business, need not comply. However, the latter is to confuse the dispensation in respect of a non-commercial agreement (an agreement not made by the creditor in the course of a business carried on by him)[3] with the application of the consumer credit regime to even a single regulated agreement. Specifically with regard to the need for a lender to be authorised, the Act states that a person is not to be treated as carrying on a particular type of business (and hence is not required to be authorised by the FCA) merely because occasionally he enters into transactions belonging to a business of that type.[4]

1   CCA 1974, s 189(1).
2   Ibid., especially ss 61, 65 and 127.
3   Ibid., s 74(1)(a).
4   Ibid., s 189(2).

4.7.3.2 Common characteristics of a fixed-sum loan agreement

The Agreements Regulations[1] prescribe the information and financial particulars for fixed-sum credit agreements. This includes, in the case of a debtor-creditor-supplier/borrower-lender-supplier agreement for fixed-sum credit, a list or other description of the goods, services, things or land to be financed by the agreement and the amount of credit to be provided under the agreement. In contrast with a running-account credit agreement, the creditor under a fixed-sum credit agreement must grant the debtor a rebate of charges on early settlement of the agreement (at least equal to the statutory rebate) where the agreement levies credit charges in respect of the period after the settlement date of the agreement.

The utility of running-account credit agreements, and in particular credit-token agreements, has to a large extent resulted in their replacing fixed-sum loan agreements and credit sale, conditional sale and hire-purchase agreements, in relation to retail purchases in the small to medium ticket price range. This is predominantly due to the fact that running-account credit agreements can accommodate more than one transaction without requiring a fresh agreement to be entered into on each occasion, a feature which is particularly appealing to the marketing departments of lending institutions.

Most mortgages entered into by consumers take the form of fixed-sum credit agreements secured by a mortgage on the borrower's residential property. Mortgages are dealt with at **4.8** below and in **Chapter 18**.

1 Consumer Credit (Agreements) Regulations 1983, SI 1983/1553; Consumer Credit (Agreements) Regulations 2010, SI 2010/1014.

4.7.4 Running-account or revolving credit agreements

4.7.4.1 Agreement types

Running-account or revolving credit agreements include agreements for overdrafts, credit card accounts such as budget accounts, option accounts and charge card accounts.

4.7.4.2 Open-end agreement and overdraft agreement

The Consumer Credit Directive 2008 and implementing regulations introduced the inelegantly described open-end agreement into the scope of the Consumer Credit regime.[1] CCA 1974 defines 'open-end' in relation to a consumer credit agreement, as meaning 'of no fixed duration'.[2] Whilst this would generally take the form of a running-account agreement, it does not necessarily equate to a running-account credit, as defined in CCA 1974, s 10, which makes no mention of the duration, fixed or otherwise, of such agreement. A fixed-sum credit agreement might also be an open-end agreement. The concepts and treatment of an open-end agreement and a running-account agreement in the Act and regulations have been somewhat blurred.

As a result of the incorporation of overdraft agreements into the consumer credit regime, and the extension by government of regulation to overdrafts for business purposes, two new concepts have found their way into CCA 1974, namely an 'authorised non-business overdraft agreement' and an 'authorised business overdraft agreement'. They are defined as follows:[3]

(i) an 'authorised non-business overdraft agreement' means a debtor-creditor/borrower-lender agreement which provides authorisation in advance for the debtor/borrower to overdraw on a current account where:

   (a) the credit must be repaid on demand or within three months, and

   (b) the agreement is not entered into by the debtor/borrower wholly or predominantly for the purposes of the debtor's/borrower's business

(ii) an 'authorised business overdraft agreement' means a debtor-creditor/borrower-lender agreement which provides authorisation in advance for the debtor/borrower to overdraw on a current account, where the agreement is entered into by the debtor/borrower wholly or predominantly for the purposes of the debtor's/borrower's business).

Previously, by virtue of their exclusion from Part V of CCA 1974, overdraft agreements were not subject to the formalities applying to consumer credit agreements, provided that certain information was notified to the Office of Fair Trading.[4] As a result of the Consumer Credit Directive 2008 an authorised non-business overdraft agreement has been brought within the ambit (though subject to certain limitations) of CCA 1974 and the Agreements Regulations 2010.[5] Furthermore, the government extended the application of CCA 1974 and the Agreements Regulations 2010 to an authorised business overdraft agreement, even though credit for business purposes is outside the scope of the Directive.[6] The result is the inclusion in CCA 1974 of new subsections 74(1B), (1C), and (1D).

In practice an overdraft facility is a loan facility in conjunction with a current account, usually but not necessarily a bank current account, ordinarily but not necessarily repayable on demand. Bank accounts were previously largely operated by means of cheques but are now increasingly accessed by bank cards, debit cards and ATM cards. Differential interest rates are generally applied to the amount overdrawn, or the balance in debit on the account, depending on whether or not the overdraft has been previously authorised by the bank.[7] A bank customer has no entitlement to an overdraft and any transaction which would result in his account being overdrawn may, in the absence of authorisation, be lawfully dishonoured by the bank.

The expression 'current account' was the subject of judicial consideration in the case of *United Dominions Trust Ltd v Kirkwood*,[8] where the court described it as a running-account maintained for the bank's customer which records payments into and withdrawals from the account and which possesses the following features: the customer may from time to time make payments into and effect withdrawals from the account; the bank must undertake to pay cheques drawn on itself in favour of third parties up to the amount standing to the credit of the customer on the account, debiting the account with such payments; and the bank must undertake to collect cheques for the customer and credit the proceeds to the account.

The FCA may make a determination to exclude agreements for overdrafts from certain provisions of Part V of CCA 1974 (relating to form and formalities) on certain conditions.[9]

1 SI 2010/1010, regs 2, 39; date in force 30 April 2010.
2 CCA 1974, s 189(1).
3 Ibid., s 189(1).
4 Ibid., s 74(1)(b). The obligation formerly under s 74(3), to notify the OFT of agreements under s 74(1)(b), was repealed by SI 2010/1010, regs 2, 17(1) and (3) with effect from 1 February 2011.
5 Ibid., s 74(1C) and (1D); SI 2010/1014, reg 8.
6 Ibid., s 74(1B); SI 2010/1014, reg 8.
7 See *Office of Fair Trading v Abbey National plc* [2009] GCCR 9851, HL.
8 [1966] 1 All ER 968, CA.
9 CCA 1974, s 74(3). The writer believes that the cross-reference should be to s 74(1C). Prior to the transfer of the consumer credit regime to the FCA, the OFT stipulated the following conditions in its General Determination applicable to overdraft agreements: that the creditor shall have informed the OFT in writing of its general intention to enter into such agreements, that the debtor is informed at the time, or before the agreement is concluded, of any applicable credit limit, the annual rate of interest and charges applicable from time to time, the conditions under which these may be amended and of the procedure for terminating the agreement, and the creditor must undertake to inform the debtor in writing within seven days of the interest rate and charges arising where the debtor overdraws on his current account. In view of the Agreements Regulations 2010 applying to overdraft agreements, these conditions will inevitably have been met.

4.7.4.3   Budget account agreement

A budget account is a running-account credit agreement with a credit limit which is a multiple of the account holder's periodical payment, usually a monthly payment. The credit limit is commonly 24 times the monthly payment. This is the notional period over which any outstanding balance would be expected to be repaid. Monthly instalments and credit limits are variable, primarily at the instance of the account holder though the creditor may decline such request. Interest is charged on the outstanding balance, ordinarily on a daily basis and debited to the account at monthly intervals. Budget accounts have largely been overtaken by option accounts.

4.7.4.4   Option account agreement

An option account is a running-account credit agreement with a credit limit selected by the account holder and which requires the account holder to make a regular monthly payment, in a minimum sum usually equal to the greater of a fixed amount or, more usually, a specified percentage of the monthly outstanding balance. The account holder also has the option of repaying the account balance in full at any time. This latter aspect is an intrinsic right of any debtor under a regulated consumer credit agreement.[1]

1 CCA 1974, s 94.

4.7.4.5   Characteristics of budget and option account agreements

Budget and option accounts share various common features. These include monthly instalments, which are variable; interest charged on the outstanding balance, usually on a daily basis and debited monthly; the account holder is usually given a limited interest-free period if he repays the full outstanding balance by the due payment date, except in the case of cash withdrawals when interest runs from the date of withdrawal; the interest rate is usually variable; each account is normally operated by means of a credit card; each type of account will usually permit balance transfers from similar accounts with other creditors.

Budget and option accounts are invariably debtor-creditor-supplier/borrower-lender-supplier agreements. They may take the form of a store card, in which event they can only be utilised within specified retail outlets with whom the credit card provider has entered into an arrangement for their acceptance. Alternatively, they may take the form of generic cards, utilisable at any outlet accepting such card. If the card issuer is also a member of the Visa or MasterCard organisation and the cards are issued with the Visa or MasterCard symbol, the card can be used wherever that symbol is displayed. The generic card will also usually be a debtor-creditor-supplier/borrower-lender-supplier agreement by virtue of the creditor having entered into arrangements, directly or indirectly, with the supplier for the acceptance of the card. In so far as the credit card can be used to obtain cash advances, the credit agreement is also a debtor-creditor agreement.

In *Office of Fair Trading v Abbey National plc*[1] the House of Lords effectively recognised the worldwide utility of accounts under the VISA, MasterCard and similar rules, by their interpretation of s 75 of CCA 1974 to apply in respect of purchases from all outlets anywhere in the world which subscribed to those rules.

1 [2009] GCCR 9851, HL.

4.7.4.6 Charge card agreement

A charge card agreement is an agreement for the provision of credit under a running-account credit-token agreement, namely a revolving credit agreement operated by means of a credit card, under which the entire outstanding balance is payable in full at regular intervals, usually monthly against receipt of a monthly statement. It is a credit agreement and in so far as it is a debtor-creditor-supplier/borrower-lender-supplier agreement, it is an exempt agreement if it requires repayment of the entire debit balance, by means of one payment in relation to specified periods not exceeding three months, and the credit is provided without interest or other significant charges.[1] It is submitted that the reference to charges is to charges for credit and not to default charges or charges for enforcing the agreement.

The exemption does not apply to a charge card which is a debtor-creditor agreement, for example a charge card agreement under which cash advances can be obtained, with the result that such agreement will need to take the form of a regulated consumer credit agreement.

1 RAO art 60F(3).

4.7.4.7 Credit-token agreement

A credit-token agreement (or credit card agreement) is a regulated agreement for the provision of credit in connection with the use of a credit-token.[1] It is the generic description given to such agreements which are invariably in running-account credit form.

A credit-token is a card, cheque, voucher, coupon, stamp, form, booklet or other document or thing given to an individual by a person carrying on a consumer credit business who undertakes that, on the production of it to him (whether or not some other action is also required), he will supply any of cash, goods and services on credit or, on production of it to a third party (whether or not any other action is required), where the third party supplies any of the foregoing, he will reimburse such party in return for payment to him by the debtor.[2]

In *Elliott v Director General of Fair Trading*[3] the defendant, T Elliott & Sons Ltd, had sent to selected members of the public an envelope containing certain materials. One insert contained a statement: 'Your Elliott credit card account valid for immediate use. With your card in your hand, walk into any Elliott shop: give us your signature, show us simple identification, such as a cheque card and walk out of the shop with your purchase and all the credit you need. Please remember to sign your card as soon as you receive it. It is perfectly secure; it cannot be used by anyone until we have their signature in the shop'. A further item was a mock credit card which contained provision for a signature and statements, in summary, as follows: 'This credit card is valid for immediate use; the sole requirement is your signature and means of identification; credit is immediately available if you have a bank account; sign the card as soon as you receive it; it is perfectly secure because it can only be used when a signature has been accepted at an Elliott shop'.

A prosecution was instituted by the Director General of Fair Trading on the grounds that the documents, including the mock card, had been sent to individuals in contravention of CCA 1974, s 51(1) which renders it an offence to give a person a credit-token if he has not asked for it and the request, by virtue of s 51(2), must be in a document signed by the person making it.

The issue turned on the meaning of the word 'undertakes' in the definition of a credit-token as, notwithstanding what the documentation stated, the production of the card did not entitle the customer to the supply of goods on credit but only enabled him to apply for a credit card and despite the wording on the card, the card was not valid for immediate use, even if the customer had a bank account. The court gave short shrift to the defence, holding that 'undertakes' does not involve the necessity for any contractual agreement or possibility of contractual agreement. The court stated that one looks at the card and asks whether, on the face or on the back of that card, the defendant company is undertaking that on the production of the card, cash, goods and services (or any of them) will be supplied on credit, to which the court found that the answer was 'yes'. The fact that none of the statements was true did not absolve the card from being what it purported to be, namely a credit-token card.

It follows that, if production of some document, whether or not some additional action is required, will result in the supply of, cash, goods or services on credit, the document will constitute a credit-token.

However, 'production' of the document is a requirement, so that notifying the customer by a document, e.g. a customer letter, of his entitlement to the credit, will not constitute a credit-token if there is no requirement that the document be produced in order to obtain the credit. A credit agreement which is pre-signed by the creditor and is sent to a customer guaranteeing him credit on his signing and returning the agreement, or presenting the credit agreement to another, is not a credit-token as it is not within the genus or class of documents identified as a credit-token and, moreover, is itself the credit agreement under or in respect of which any relevant credit-token agreement would be operated. If this were not the case, every document comprising a credit agreement, even if not signed by the creditor in advance, would constitute a credit-token if it had not previously been requested by the borrower in writing.

The second limb of the definition of a credit-token refers to a document constituting a credit-token where, on its production to a third party, the third party supplies any cash, goods and services, the person carrying on a consumer credit business will pay the third party for them in return for payment to him by the individual. This second limb of the definition does not specifically require the person carrying on the consumer credit business to grant credit to the individual although, in practice, by virtue of the intervention of the person carrying on a consumer credit business, credit will invariably be granted to the individual.

1 CCA 1974, s 189(1).
2 Ibid., s 14(1).
3 [1980] 1 WLR 977.

4.7.4.8   Some characteristics of running-account and credit-token agreements[1]

A running-account or revolving credit agreement is inchoate or in suspense until such time as an amount of credit has been drawn down. However, acceptance of a credit-token might take place prior to, and independently of, utilisation of the credit facility. The debtor accepts a credit-token when it is signed or a receipt for it is signed or it is first used, either by the debtor himself or by a person who, pursuant to the agreement, is authorised by him to use it.[2]

The debtor's liability for misuse of the credit-token is limited by the CCA 1974 (and regulations under it) currently to the sum of £50, save where the person misusing the card acted as the debtor's agent or otherwise used the card or, it is submitted, obtained the card details and any personal identification number, with the debtor's consent.[3] It is submitted that reference to when the card is first used is to be interpreted as meaning when the card is first used to obtain credit and not when it is used for some other purpose, such as a customer identification form or for credit scoring or credit assessment purposes when applying for credit.

A debtor is not liable for any use made of the card after he duly reported its loss or theft to the creditor or that it was, for any other reason, liable to misuse.[4] A debtor, or 'payment service user' is not liable for any 'unauthorised or incorrectly executed payment transaction' provided he notifies the 'payment service provider' without undue delay.[5] These provisions of the Payment Services Regulations 2009 supersede those of s 84(3A) to (3C) of CCA 1974. The latter were inserted by the Consumer Protection (Distance Selling) Regulations 2000 and the Financial Services (Distance Marketing) Regulations 2004, but have since been repealed. The Payment Services Regulations 2009 have since been revoked and replaced by the Payment Services Regulations 2017.[6]

A credit-token agreement issued under the Agreements Regulations 1983, but not under the Agreements Regulations 2010, must contain the statutory form relating to the theft, loss or misuse of a credit-token.[7]

Pursuant to s 84(4) of CCA 1974, a credit-token agreement must also contain specified particulars of the name, address and telephone number of the person to whom notice of any loss, theft or liability to misuse of the credit-token, must be given.[8] Indeed, in the absence of the latter, the debtor does not incur any liability whatsoever following the loss or theft of the card.[9] It would appear, however, that there is no requirement to insert such terms in a credit-token agreement subject to the Agreements Regulations 2010, as these regulations emanate from the Consumer Credit Directive which, being a maximum harmonisation Directive, does not require its inclusion. The absurd result is that a creditor does not acquire any rights against the debtor under s 84(1) and (2) in the case of the omission (and arguably the impermissible inclusion) of information required by s 84(4) in a credit-token agreement. The vast majority of credit-token agreements will, of course, be subject to a credit limit below £60,260. A debtor under a running-account credit agreement is entitled to receive regular statements, showing the state of his account, at periodical intervals and, where there has been a movement in his account, at the end of the period during which there has been such movement (e.g. a credit or debit to the account). Where the statement includes a demand for payment it must be furnished within one month of the end of the period to which it relates. In other cases the period for the furnishing of statements varies from six to twelve months.[10]

A notice of variation of a regulated agreement must set out particulars and be served on the debtor before the variation takes effect. The previous requirement to give at least seven days' prior notice was regrettably removed in consequence of the Consumer Credit Directive 2008.

Special provision is made where the variation is of the rate of interest payable under the agreement and the interest is charged by reference to the daily outstanding balance. In that case notice of the variation may be given by publication in three national daily newspapers and by displaying the notice at the creditor's premises.[11] Notice of variation of interest rates and information flowing from such change must be given to the debtor in writing before the variation can take effect.[12]

1 See the illuminating discussion in *Goode: Consumer Credit Law and Practice* (LexisNexis Butterworths), IC [25.22] following.
2 CCA 1974, s 66(2).
3 Ibid., ss 83 and 84 and SI 1998/997.
4 Ibid., s 84(3).
5 Payment Services Regulations 2009, SI 2009/209, regs 59, 61 and 62; reg 126, Sch 6, para 3.
6 SI 2017/752.
7 Consumer Credit (Agreements) Regulations 1983, SI 1983/1553, Sch 2, Pt I, Form 17.
8 Consumer Credit (Credit-Token Agreements) Regulations 1983, SI 1983/1555.
9 CCA 1974, s 84(4).
10 Ibid., s 78 and Consumer Credit (Running-Account Credit Information) Regulations 1983, SI 1983/1570.
11 Consumer Credit (Notice of Variation of Agreements) Regulations 1977, SI 1977/328.
12 CCA 1974, s 78A(1) to (6). Section 189 defines 'give' as 'deliver or send by an appropriate method' and 'appropriate method' as post or transmission in the form of an electronic communication in accordance with s 176A(1).

4.8 LOANS SECURED BY LAND MORTGAGES

4.8.1 The Mortgage Credit Directive

Directive 2014/17/EU of the European Parliament and of the Council of 4 February 2014 on credit agreements for consumers relating to residential immovable property was implemented in the United Kingdom by the Mortgage

Credit Directive Order 2015, SI 2015/910, and came fully into force on 21 March 2016.

Pursuant to Article 3(1) the Mortgage Credit Directive applies to:

(a)   credit agreements which are secured either by a mortgage or by another comparable security commonly used in a Member State on residential immovable property or secured by a right related to residential immovable property; and

(b)   credit agreements the purpose of which is to acquire or retain property rights in land or in an existing or projected building.

A 'credit agreement' is defined as an agreement whereby a creditor grants or promises to grant, to a consumer, a credit falling within the scope of Article 3 of the Directive (above) in the form of a deferred payment, loan or other similar financial accommodation (Article 4(3)).

A 'consumer' is a consumer as defined in Article 3(a) of Directive 2008/48/EC (Article 4(1)). This defines 'consumer' as a natural person who, in transactions covered by this Directive, is acting for purposes which are outside his trade, business or profession.

For UK purposes, it is to be assumed that 'consumer' includes (a) a partnership of two or three persons not all of whom are bodies corporate, and (b) an unincorporated body of persons which does not consist entirely of bodies corporate and is not a partnership (see the definition of 'individual' in Consumer Credit Act 1974, s 189(1)).

Article 3(2) provides that the Directive shall not apply to certain specified credit agreements. Article 3(3) provides that Member States may decide not to apply the Directive to specified credit agreements.

4.8.2   Regulated mortgage contracts

Pursuant to the Financial Services and Markets Act 2000 (Regulated Activities) Order 2001:[1]

(a)   a contract is a 'regulated mortgage contract' if, at the time it is entered into, the following conditions are met:

(i)   the contract is one under which a person ('the lender') provides credit to an individual or to trustees ('the borrower');

(ii)   the contract provides for the obligation of the borrower to repay to be secured by a mortgage on land in the EEA;

(iii)   at least 40% of that land is used, or is intended to be used:

(aa) in the case of credit provided to an individual, as or in connection with a dwelling; or

(bb) in the case of credit provided to a trustee which is not an individual, as or in connection with a dwelling by an individual who is a beneficiary of the trust, or by a related person;

but such a contract is not a regulated mortgage contract if it [falls within article 61A(1) or (2)]. These exemptions are set out at **6.3.2**.

'Credit' includes a cash loan, and any other form of financial accommodation.

For the purposes of paragraph (3)(a):[2]

(a) 'mortgage' includes a charge and (in Scotland) a heritable security;

(b) the area of any land which comprises a building or other structure containing two or more storeys is to be taken to be the aggregate of the floor areas of each of those storeys;

(c) 'related person', in relation to the borrower or (in the case of credit provided to trustees) a beneficiary of the trust, means:

(i) that person's spouse or civil partner;

(ii) a person (whether or not of the opposite sex) whose relationship with that person has the characteristics of the relationship between husband and wife; or

(iii) that person's parent, brother, sister, child, grandparent or grandchild.

1 RAO art 61(3).
2 Article 61(4).

4.8.3 Land mortgages outside the scope of the Mortgage Credit Directive

In the case of a prospective regulated agreement to be secured on land, before sending the debtor the unexecuted agreement for his signature, the creditor must give the debtor an advance copy of the agreement containing a notice indicating the debtor's right to withdraw from the prospective agreement, accompanied by a copy of the proposed mortgage deed and any other document referred to in the unexecuted agreement. This so-called 'advance copy procedure' does not apply to a restricted-use credit agreement to finance the purchase of the mortgaged land or an agreement for a bridging loan in connection with the purchase of the mortgaged land or other land, for the reason that these transactions usually need to be concluded speedily.[1]

Where the advance copy procedure applies, the agreement for execution by the borrower must be posted to him not less than seven days after the advance copy was given to him. The borrower is then given a further seven days after the day on which the unexecuted agreement is sent for his signature, to consider whether or not he wishes to proceed with the agreement. This interval is known as 'the consideration period', during which the creditor must refrain from approaching the debtor, whether in person, by telephone or letter or in any other way except in response to a specific request made by the borrower after the beginning of the consideration period.[2] It also means that, except in response to such a request, the creditor may not send a surveyor or insurance broker to the debtor. Should the consideration period be broken by the creditor's communication, the creditor will have to recommence the procedure with fresh advance copy documents.

1 CCA 1974, s 58(1) and (2).
2 Ibid., s 61(2).

4.8.4   Mortgage types

There are essentially two types of mortgage, a repayment mortgage and an interest-only mortgage. Under a repayment mortgage, monthly instalments comprise both interest and capital, the capital portion representing a repayment of part of the original advance. Under an interest-only mortgage, the monthly instalments are of interest only and the capital, namely the original advance, is repaid in one lump sum ordinarily at the end of the mortgage term. Borrowers under interest-only mortgages are usually advised to enter into an endowment policy or some other investment in order to ensure that they will have available funds to repay the mortgage advance when the mortgage term expires.

There are various sub-sets of mortgage within the foregoing broad categories. Originally these acquired their nomenclature in a marketing context but with the passing of time the descriptions have acquired a distinct meaning.

Most mortgages are variable rate mortgages, meaning that the interest rate is variable in accordance with the terms of the mortgage. A discounted rate mortgage is a mortgage under which for an initial period of a stated number of years, usually a period not exceeding two years, interest is charged at a discount to the lender's standard variable mortgage interest rate. A fixed-rate mortgage is one under which, for an initial period, interest is charged at a fixed rate. A capped rate mortgage is one under which the lender's interest rate is capped, again during an initial period, so that although the interest rate is variable it cannot rise above that level. A tracker mortgage is like a variable rate mortgage except that the payments are linked to a rate, usually that set by the Bank of England, which the mortgage tracks by a certain percentage over that rate. An offset mortgage links the mortgagor's current and savings account balances to his mortgage and serves the purpose of reducing the chargeable interest on the mortgage by charging interest only on the net balance on the accounts. A flexible mortgage is one which permits the borrower to make repayments in excess of the monthly instalments, to take so-called 'payment holidays', during which no monthly instalments need be paid, although interest continues to accrue on the outstanding balance, and sometimes to draw down capital which has previously been repaid. A cashback mortgage is one under which the borrower receives a lump sum in cash on taking out the mortgage, which is not repayable to the mortgagee, and which the borrower might utilise for any purpose, including as part payment of the deposit on the mortgaged property.

Mortgages securing consumer credit agreements are regulated either by CCA 1974 and regulations under that Act or by the Financial Services and Markets Act 2000 ('FSMA') and regulations under that Act and, in each case, by the FCA Handbook, notably MCOB, the Mortgages and Home Finance: Conduct of Business Sourcebook.

The reader is also referred to **Chapter 18** and, in particular, **18.2.3**.

4.8.5   Residential renovation agreements

The Mortgage Credit Directive Order 2015[1] introduces the new concept of a 'residential renovation agreement,' which is defined in CCA 1974 (s 189(1)) as a consumer credit agreement: (i) which is unsecured; and (ii) the purpose of which is the renovation of residential property as described in Article 2(2)(a) of Directive 2008/48/EC of the European Parliament and of the Council of 23 April 2008 on credit agreements for consumers. Article 2(2a) of the Directive, as amended by the Mortgages Directive (Art 46), (and hence CCA 1974) applies to unsecured credit agreements the purpose of which is the renovation of residential property, whether involving a total amount of credit up to or exceeding €75,000 (equating to £60,260). However, it appears from Article 2(2)(a) of the 2008 Directive that the expression 'unsecured credit agreements' was intended to refer to credit agreements that are 'not secured either by a mortgage or by another comparable security commonly used in a Member State on immovable property or secured by a right related to immovable property'. But the reference to 'unsecured' in paragraph (a) of the definition of 'residential renovation agreement' above is wider and excludes any security whatsoever, 'security' being defined in CCA 1974, s 189(1). Accordingly, it is submitted that the provisions of CCA 1974 that apply to a residential renovation agreement can be avoided simply by the agreement being made subject to any security, such as a guarantee.

1 SI 2015/910.

Chapter 5

Hire agreements

5.1 MEANING OF A HIRE AGREEMENT

A hire agreement is a contract of bailment without any element of sale. The hirer receives both possession and use of the goods hired in return for rental paid to the lessor or owner and the hirer is obliged to return the goods at the end of the agreed term.[1]

Palmer on Bailment defines hire by reference to *Lloyds UDT Finance Ltd v Chartered Finance Trust Holdings plc*[2] where Sir Andrew Morritt V.C., citing the *Shorter Oxford English Dictionary*, states: 'The normal meaning of hire is … to obtain from another the temporary use of a chattel for a stipulated payment … the concept involves obtaining the right to possession of the chattel for the period of hire to the exclusion of the [owner]'.[3] After stating that decisions on the legal elements of hire have largely affirmed this analysis, the learned author expounds on four qualities that distinguish contracts of hire, namely:

(i)   the transfer of both the possession of a chattel and the right to possession of it, to a person who voluntarily receives it;

(ii)   an authority in the bailee to use it for his benefit;

(iii)   an advantage or reward accruing to the bailor in return for this possession and use; and

(iv)   a promise by the hirer to deliver up the chattel to the lessor (or at his instruction) at a stated or determinable time.[4]

The Consumer Rights Act 2015 provides that a contract is for the hire of goods if, under it, the trader [as defined in s 2(2)] of the Act] gives or agrees to give the consumer [as defined in s 2(3) of the Act] possession of the goods [as defined in s 2(8)of the Act] with the right to use them, subject to the terms of the contract, for a period determined in accordance with the contract. But a contract is not for the hire of goods if it is a hire-purchase agreement.[5] In passing, this definition of a hire contract appears deficient when compared with a so-called 'location agreement', mentioned below.

In *TRM Copy Centres (UK) Ltd v Lanwall Services Ltd*,[6] Lord Hope distinguished a hire agreement from a so-called location agreement, whereby the holder of a photocopier paid its owner a rate per photocopy less a commission, stating that 'for present purposes it is sufficient to note that it is the fact that the hiring is in consideration of an ascertained hire or rent which the hirer agrees to pay that marks this kind of contract out from others under which the temporary use or possession of a thing is given to another'.

The CCA 1974 defines a consumer hire agreement as an agreement made by a person with an individual (the 'hirer') for the bailment or (in Scotland) the hiring of goods to the hirer, being an agreement which is not a hire-purchase agreement and is capable of subsisting for more than three months.[7] However simple the definition of hire agreement may appear to be, it gave rise to substantial dispute in *Dimond v Lovell*,[8] where the court was concerned with whether the agreement in question was an exempt hire agreement or a regulated credit agreement; if the latter, as it did not contain the prescribed terms of a regulated hire agreement, the agreement was unenforceable. The Court of Appeal held that the fact that the respondent's obligation to pay for the car hire was to be deferred until her damages claim had been concluded meant that the agreement allowed her credit and should therefore have taken the form of a regulated credit agreement. As it did not, the agreement was not properly executed and was unenforceable. The court held that the agreement would also have been a regulated consumer hire agreement if it had been capable of lasting for more than three months. The argument that a contract for the bailment of goods to a hirer could not be both a consumer credit agreement and a consumer hire agreement was rejected. Surprisingly, these issues were not argued on appeal to the House of Lords.

Dimond v Lovell has been followed by a long line of cases in which the lower courts have sought to distinguish the cases before them, on the facts, from those in the House of Lords decision or to raise the unargued issues.[9]

1   9(1) *Halsbury's Laws* (4th edn), para 52.
2   [2001] STC 1653, on appeal *Britax GmbH v Commissioners of the Inland Revenue* [2002] EWCA Civ 806.
3   *Palmer on Bailment* (3rd edn, Sweet & Maxwell, 2009), para 21-004.
4   Loc. cit.
5   Section 6.
6   [2009] UKHL 35 at [9], [2009] GCCR 9401, HL. See also **5.2** below.
7   CCA 1974, s 15.
8   [1999] 3 All ER 1, [2001] GCCR 2303, CA; affirmed [2000] 2 All ER 897, [2001] GCCR 2751, HL.
9   See **5.4.8** below.

5.2   TYPES OF CONSUMER HIRE AGREEMENT

In contrast to the position in relation to credit agreements where there are various types of consumer credit agreements, there is in fact only one form of consumer hire agreement. As already mentioned, a consumer hire agreement is an agreement made by a person with an individual (which includes a partnership or two or three persons or an unincorporated body of persons not consisting entirely of bodies corporate) for the bailment or hiring of goods, which is capable of subsisting for more than three months.[1] A hire-purchase agreement is classified as a credit and not a hire agreement.[2]

In *TRM Copy Centres (UK) v Lanwall Services*[3] the court rejected the argument that a so-called location agreement, which stipulated payment for photocopying services but not a regular rental payment, constituted a regulated hire agreement. The decision was upheld by the Court of Appeal,[4] Thomas LJ stating that s 15 of CCA 1974 was concerned solely with bailment by way of hire, that a hire agreement could involve reward or recompense other than payment of money but that payment of commission by the owner of photocopying machines to the retailer based on use of the machine was not tantamount to bailment by way of hire by the retailer. The House of Lords[5] likewise upheld the original decision, Lord Hope stating that it is the fact that the hiring is in consideration of an ascertained hire or rent which the hirer agrees to pay that marks this kind of contract (i.e. a hire agreement) out from others under which the temporary use or possession of a thing is given to another.

The requirement that the hire agreement must be capable of subsisting for more than three months relates to the period of hire and not the time for payment of hire charges.[6]

A consumer hire agreement is a regulated agreement within the meaning of CCA 1974 if it is a regulated consumer hire agreement for the purposes of Chapter 14B of Part 2 of the Financial Services and Markets Act 2000 (Regulated Activities) Order 2001, SI 2001/544 ('RAO').[7] A regulated consumer hire agreement is a consumer hire agreement which is not an exempt agreement.[8] Exempt agreements are dealt with in **Chapter 6**.

A non-commercial hire agreement is one which is not made by the owner in the course of a business carried on by him. It is a regulated agreement but exempt from certain provisions of Part V of CCA 1974.[9] There are two instances of confused drafting in relation to hire agreements. The first relates to small agreements, being those which do not require the hirer to make payments exceeding £50.[10] As with small credit agreements, these were meant to be excluded from certain provisions of CCA 1974 but their minor status appears to have resulted in their being overlooked. Likewise, it was intended that the cancellation provisions that apply to regulated consumer credit agreements should also apply to regulated consumer hire agreements; but, by virtue of a drafting error, hire agreements are only cancellable if they were preceded by antecedent negotiations conducted by the owner or by the owner's authorised agent.[11]

---

1 CCA 1974, s 15.
2 Ibid.
3 [2007] All ER (D) 287, [2007] GCCR 6151.
4 *TRM Copy Centres (UK) Limited v Lanwall Services Limited* [2008] EWCA Civ 382, [2008] GCCR 7501.
5 [2009] GCCR 9401 at 9405, para 9.
6 *Clark v Ardington Electrical Services* [2003] GCCR 4691, CA.
7 CCA 1974, s 15(2).
8 RAO art 60N(3).
9 CCA 1974, ss 74(1)(a) and 189(1).
10 Ibid., s 17(1)(b).
11 Ibid., s 67 read with s 56 and the definition of 'negotiator' in s 56(1); see further **5.3** below and *Branwhite v Worcester Works Finance Ltd* [1969] 1 AC 552, [1968] 3 All ER 104, HL.

5.3   GENERAL CHARACTERISTICS OF CONTRACTS FOR THE HIRE OF GOODS

5.3.1   Hire of goods to consumers

A hire agreement with a consumer falls within the scope of the Consumer Rights Act 2015 and gives rise to the hirer's statutory rights regarding the following:

(a)   goods to be of satisfactory quality (s 9);

(b)   goods to be fit for particular purpose (s 10);

(c)   goods to be as described (s 11);

(d)   other pre-contract information included in contract (s 12);

(e)   goods to match a sample (s 13);

(f)   goods to match a model seen or examined (s 14);

(g)   installation as part of conformity of the goods with the contract (s 15);

(h)   goods not conforming with the contract if digital content does not conform (s 16); and

(i)   trader to have the right to supply the goods etc (s 17).

5.3.2   Hire of goods other than to consumers

A hire agreement outside the scope of the Consumer Rights Act 2015 is subject to the Supply of Goods and Services Act 1982, which imports certain implied terms into the hire agreement.[1] These include an implied condition on the part of the lessor or owner that he has a right to transfer possession of the goods by way of hire, and in an agreement for hire (as opposed to a hire agreement), that he will have such right at the time of hire.

There is an implied warranty that the hirer will enjoy quiet possession of the goods for the period of hire, except so far as possession may be disturbed by the owner or other person entitled to the benefit of any charge or encumbrance disclosed or known to the hirer before the contract is made.

In the case of a contract for the hire of goods by description, there is an implied condition that the goods will correspond with their description and in a contract for the hire of goods by reference to a sample as well as a description, that the bulk of the goods will correspond with the sample as well as their description. Where goods are hired by the lessor or owner in the course of a business, there is an implied condition that they are of satisfactory quality. Goods are of satisfactory quality if they meet the standard that a reasonable person would regard as satisfactory, taking account of any description of the goods, the price (if relevant) and all other relevant circumstances. Finally, where goods are transferred in the course of a business there is an implied term that the goods are in conformity with any particular purpose required and disclosed by the hirer.

Where the hirer would have the right to treat the contract as repudiated by reason of a breach of contract by the owner or bailor of an implied term, but the breach is so slight that it would be unreasonable for him to do so, the breach is not to be treated as a breach of condition but may be treated as a breach of warranty.[2]

1 Supply of Goods and Services Act 1982, ss 7, 8, 9 and 10.
2 Ibid., s 10A.

5.3.3   Unique aspects of a regulated consumer hire agreement

A unique aspect of a regulated hire agreement is the right conferred upon the hirer to terminate the agreement 18 months after entering into the agreement, unless the agreement is for a shorter period.[1] The rationale for this is that the hirer should not be bound by a lengthy agreement. However, as a result of industry pressure, this benefit does not apply to rental agreements requiring the hirer to make rental payments in any year exceeding £1,500 (a sum which is variable by Order but has remained unchanged since 1998).[2] This right of termination also does not apply to the common type of lease (e.g. of equipment or motor vehicles) where the goods are hired to the hirer for the purpose of a business carried on by him, or where the hirer holds himself out as requiring the goods for such purpose, and the goods are selected by the hirer and acquired by the owner for the purposes of the agreement, at the hirer's request, from a person other than the owner's associate.[3]

The standard regulated hire agreement, falling within such parameters, will usually contain declarations or acknowledgements by the hirer to such effect.

A hirer is also not entitled to terminate a lease after 18 months where he requires the goods or holds himself out as requiring them for the purpose of sub-hire or of hiring them to other persons in the course of a business carried on by him.[4]

The Financial Conduct Authority ('FCA') is empowered to exempt agreements from the above termination provisions, upon the application of an owner intending to enter into hire agreements, if it appears that it would be in the interests of hirers to exempt such agreements.[5] Whilst such applications have been granted, they are relatively rare. Applicants generally have to prove that without the certainty of a long-term hire agreement they could not offer agreements to hirers for the goods in question on terms likely to be acceptable to hirers. They also have to show why the offer of hire agreements by independent leasing companies alone is unsatisfactory, e.g. the need of the supplier company to maintain and service the goods as part of the hire arrangement or by reason of economies of scale underlying the operation.

A more recent section, introduced by CCA 2006,[6] makes provision for exemption from s 101 of CCA 1974, if it appears to the FCA that it would be in the interests of hirers to exempt consumer hire agreements falling within a specified description. The FCA is empowered to exempt such agreements.

Whilst at first sight it is difficult to reconcile the continuance of s 101 with the exemption of hire agreements for the hirer's business purposes, it continues to apply:

(a)   where the hire agreement for business purposes does not require the hirer to make rental payments exceeding £25,000; or

(b) where the hire agreement, albeit for business purposes, is not wholly or predominantly for business purposes.

As already mentioned, hire agreements are cancellable in more limited circumstances than those in which credit agreements are cancellable owing to the more restricted definition of 'negotiator' in respect of hire agreements than credit agreements. Thus, a regulated hire agreement may only be cancelled by the hirer if the antecedent negotiations included oral representations made in the presence of the hirer by an individual acting as or on behalf of the negotiator where the 'negotiator' is the owner.[7] By a drafting error a leasing transaction concluded by a dealer was omitted from the scope of the cancellation provisions of CCA 1974, s 67. This section refers to oral representations made in the presence of the hirer (or debtor) by an individual acting as or on behalf of the negotiator. 'Negotiator' is defined in CCA 1974, s 56 but, owing to an oversight, the definition omits from the meaning of 'negotiator' a credit broker involved in antecedent negotiations with the hirer prior to the hirer entering into the hire agreement. The supplier who conducts antecedent negotiations in relation to a hire agreement is likewise not included within the meaning of a 'negotiator'.

As a result of this lacuna in the law, various attempts have been made to find that a dealer is liable as agent of the owner. However, following *Branwhite v Worcester Works Finance Ltd*,[8] the courts have held that a dealer through whom business is introduced to a finance house is not in general to be treated as the agent of a finance house, including in respect of representations made by the dealer relating to the goods or the transaction. *Branwhite* related to hire-purchase transactions but the reasoning applies with equal force to leasing and rental agreements entered into with a leasing company on the introduction of a dealer. So it was held by the Court of Appeal in *JD Williams & Co v McCauley Parsons & Jones*[9] and *Woodchester Equipment (Leasing) Ltd v British Association of Canned and Preserved Foods Importers and Distributors Ltd*.[10] In both cases the owner was not held to be bound by fraudulent misrepresentations made by the supplier.

The position is otherwise where the finance company holds itself out as the dealer or where, on the facts, the dealer is the agent of the owner, as where the dealer is authorised to sign for the owner or authorised to commit the owner to the terms of the agreement.

A leasing company may also incur liability as the deemed agent of the supplier. Thus, in *Purnell Secretarial Services v Lease Management Services*,[11] Purnell agreed to lease a photocopier from a leasing company which traded under the name of the supplier. Purnell thought it was dealing with the supplier. The court held that the leasing company was estopped from denying such capacity and its apparent authority to make representations on behalf of the supplier.

A regulated hire agreement may be secured, including on land, in which latter event the advance copy of agreement, and withdrawal and consideration provisions applying to credit agreements, discussed earlier, would apply.

1 CCA 1974, s 101(1)–(3).
2 Ibid., s 101(7)(a); SI 1998/997, art 3.
3 Ibid., s 101(7)(b), and see the meaning of 'associate' in s 184.
4 Ibid., s 101(7)(c).
5 Ibid., s 101(8).
6 Ibid., s 101(8A).

7   Ibid., ss 67 and 56 and see **5.2** above.
8   [1969] 1 AC 552, [1968] 3 All ER 104, HL.
9   [1999] GCCR 1375, CA.
10 [1999] GCCR 1923, CA.
11 [1999] GCCR 1841, CA.

5.3.4   Reflections on the regulation of consumer hire agreements

Consumer hire agreements are subject to lighter regulation than that which applies to consumer credit agreements. Thus:

(a)   There is no means of comparing rental charges under consumer hire agreements with the APR which applies to credit agreements. This leaves the hire market open to some rapacious lessors, without remedy for vulnerable hirers. Various examples have highlighted this, including rentals for electrical and 'white' goods, hire charges imposed by credit hire companies and schools signing up for the hire of computer equipment at extortionate rentals.

(b)   There are no provisions applicable to consumer hire agreements comparable to the unfair relationships provisions that apply to consumer credit agreements.

(c)   There is no limit on default charges payable under consumer hire agreements in contrast with the position under regulated consumer credit agreements.

(d)   There is no requirement for the issue of regular statements, indeed not even an annual statement, to the hirer.

(e)   A consumer hire agreement is cancellable in only very limited circumstances, compared to the position with consumer credit agreements.

(f)   Although Part V of CCA 1974 is headed 'Entry into Credit or Hire Agreements', many of its provisions only apply to credit agreements, including the requirements for pre-contractual explanations and assessment of creditworthiness.

(g)   The right to terminate a hire agreement at the end of 18 months is largely nugatory, as it ceases to apply if the rentals in any year exceed £1,500, a limit not raised since 1998.

(h)   Consumer hire agreements are generally treated less restrictively than consumer credit agreements in the CONC sourcebook of the FCA Handbook, e.g. pre-contractual explanations in CONC 4.2.5.

5.4   SPECIFIC CONSUMER HIRE AGREEMENTS

It should be mentioned at the outset that the various consumer hire agreements described in this section are legally identical but functionally different. It should also be pointed out that there is no legal distinction between the expressions 'lease' and 'hire' and that, in this text, the term 'hire' is used in preference to 'bailment'.

Various types of lease have received statutory recognition for tax purposes in the Capital Allowances Act 2001. They include 'long funding lease', 'funding lease' and 'finance lease'. For the purposes of a consumer hire agreement, we are principally concerned with the types of lease identified below.

5.4.1   Finance lease

A finance lease is essentially a financial operation under which goods (usually comprising medium to high cost equipment) are leased under a lease whose minimum or primary term equates to the major part of the equipment's useful life and the rentals are structured to secure payment to the lessor, over the minimum period of the lease, of a sum equal to the capital cost of the leased equipment plus the desired return on capital. The latter will take into account corporation tax, any first year allowances, writing-down allowances and available grants. A finance lease is one that transfers substantially all the risks and rewards of ownership of an asset to the lessee.[1] For capital allowances purposes, a finance lease has been defined as any arrangement which provides for plant or machinery to be leased or otherwise made available by a person ('the lessor') to another person ('the lessee') and which under generally applied accounting practices falls or would fall to be treated in the accounts of the lessor, or a person connected with him, as a finance lease or a loan or is comprised in an arrangement to be so treated.[2] A presumption arises in tax and accounting practice that a lease is a finance lease when the present value of the minimum lease payments, including any initial payment, amounts to substantially all (normally at least 90%) of the fair value of the leased asset.[3]

The statutory finance lease test in s 70N of the Capital Allowances Act 2001 provides as follows:

'(1) A lease meets the finance lease test in the case of any person if the lease is one which, under generally accepted accounting practice, falls (or would fall) to be treated as a finance lease or a loan in the accounts–

(a) of that person, or

(b) where that person is the lessor, of any person connected with him.

(2) In this section 'accounts', in relation to a company, includes any accounts which–

(a) relate to two or more companies of which that company is one, and

(b) are drawn up in accordance with generally accepted accounting practice.

(3) Where for any period–

(a) a person is not within the charge to income tax or corporation tax by reason of not being resident in the United Kingdom, and

(b) accounts are not prepared in accordance with international accounting standards or UK generally accepted accounting practice,

any question relating to generally accepted accounting practice is to be determined for the purposes of this section by reference to generally accepted accounting practice with respect to accounts prepared in accordance with international accounting standards.'

Under a finance lease, the lessee will usually select the equipment and then negotiate the purchase terms with the supplier. The lessor provides the finance to meet the purchase price and either purchases the equipment from the supplier and leases it on to the lessee, or arranges to acquire it from the ultimate lessee by way of sale by the latter to the lessor and the lease-back of the equipment to the lessee. The payment terms are scheduled to meet the specific cash flow requirements of the lessee in terms of amounts and payment frequency. Indeed, the different rentals and frequency intervals can create quite a kaleidoscopic range of rental patterns. Frequently a balloon (or substantial residual rental) payment is provided for at the end of the primary or minimum rental period or, in the case of the hire of agricultural equipment, a balloon payment is due following each harvest season. Following the primary period the hirer is generally permitted to continue the agreement into a secondary period, commonly at a nominal or peppercorn rent, usually payable annually. Once the lessor has recovered his desired capital and return on the equipment in the primary period, he tends to cease to be concerned with the condition, whereabouts or fate of the leased equipment, although he remains its owner.

A finance lease will usually permit the lessor to increase the rentals if there is a change in tax structure, corporation tax, writing down allowances or other variable factors. This flows from the fact that by such a lease the lessor is aiming to recover a pre-determined return on his capital.

A finance lease will often be structured so as to leave a residual value in the equipment at the end of the primary period. The balloon rental would ordinarily equate to the residual value. The lessee might be given the right, either under the lease or in a side letter agency agreement, to sell the leased equipment at the end of the lease to an independent buyer in an arm's length transaction and to receive up to 90% of the net proceeds of sale.

More recent embellishments of finance leases are the provision of services, maintenance and the upgrading of the leased equipment at regular intervals. In a regulated finance lease these additional benefits are provided either free of charge, in other words the rentals would include the additional benefits, or against the receipt of periodical cash payments as consideration for them, paid to the lessor as agent for their provider.

As compared to an operating lease, where the rentals are generally charged on a straight-line basis over the lease term, a finance lease is recorded in the balance sheet of the lessee as an asset and an obligation to pay future rentals in an amount equal to the present value of future rentals. Rentals are apportioned between the finance charge and a reduction of the outstanding obligation for future amounts payable. The total finance charge is allocated to accounting periods during the lease term to produce a constant periodic rate of charge and the leased equipment is depreciated over the shorter of the lease term and its useful life. Corresponding entries will be made in the lessor's accounts.

1 Statement of Standard Accounting Practice No 21 (SSAP 21, para 15); International Accounting Standards Committee's Standard on Accounting for Leases (IAS 17); International Financial Reporting Standards (IFRS 17); Capital Allowances Act 2001, ss 70G, 70J and 70N and 219.
2 Capital Allowances Act 2001, s 219(1).
3 See note 1 above.

5.4.2   Operating lease

In the case of an operating lease the lessor lets the goods on hire to the hirer for a period related to the hirer's requirements and unrelated to the useful or working life of the goods or the lessor's need to recover his capital outlay and profits. An operating lease may be for as short a period as one day or for a minimum period of several years. The lessor will usually rely on the residual value of the goods to recover the balance of his investment and to earn any additional profit. The residual value is the value of the goods at the expiry of the lease term and is represented by the rental value of the goods under any extended or new lease or the net proceeds of the sale of the goods. In short-term leases the lessor will often assume responsibility for the maintenance, repair and insurance of the goods, whilst in longer-term leases the obligation will generally be passed on to the hirer. Goods commonly hired under operating leases include motor vehicles, building equipment, television sets, vending machines, photocopiers and small office equipment.

Under an operating lease the lessor may agree to provide a miscellanea of additional benefits such as ingredients for machines, paper for photocopiers, detergents for dishwashers, a chauffeur for a motor vehicle or an operator for a crane.

Operating leases are used where it is desired that the lease equipment should not appear as an asset in the lessee's balance sheet, or where rules prevent leasing unless some of the risks or rewards of ownership are assumed by the lessor, or where writing down allowances available to lessors who enter into finance leases are restricted by the Capital Allowances Act 2001 or the lessor is taxable on the excess of accountancy rental earnings over the normal rent.[1]

It is common for the lessor and supplier to enter into an agreement for the resale of the equipment on expiry of the lease so as to capitalise on any residual value in the equipment. This is especially so in the case of specialist equipment or equipment manufactured to the specific requirements of the hirer as the supplier will be more acquainted with the marketplace and hence better able to dispose of the equipment.

1 See SSAP 21.

5.4.3   Contract hire

This is the name given by the leasing industry to short-term operating leases, especially of motor vehicles and in particular the leasing by finance companies of fleets of motor vehicles. Contract hire agreements are for fixed hire periods, usually of 24 or 36 months, at the end of which the vehicle is returned to the owner and a new lease entered into in respect of another vehicle. The owner will usually assume the obligation of insuring, maintaining and repairing the vehicle, the cost of which will be borne by the hirer. The lessor of a fleet of vehicles will generally undertake to provide a replacement vehicle if, for any reason, the hired vehicle becomes unusable or to cover ancillary benefits such as AA and RAC membership fees, motor vehicle licence fees and recovery and breakdown service charges. A common feature of motor vehicle contract hire agreements is the imposition of an obligation on the hirer to pay an excess mileage charge at the end of the hire period if the vehicle has exceeded the stated anticipated mileage. This is to compensate the lessor for the additional depreciation of the vehicle.

5.4.4 Master lease

A master lease, as its name implies, is the document which sets out all the terms of the agreement save for the terms that apply to the specific transaction which will fall under the general umbrella of the master agreement. The particular terms relating to the specific transaction will be set out in a schedule to the master agreement. The master agreement will therefore be an inchoate agreement, signed by the parties at the outset of their relationship and the unique terms that apply to a specific agreement will usually be set out in a schedule and signed by the parties each time a transaction is entered into. The schedule will import the terms of the master agreement into the schedule and hence into each individual transaction. The benefit of a master agreement is that it establishes a relationship and basic terms of trading between the parties at the outset and enables them to enter into more than one transaction by completing several schedules. Master leases are commonly used in leasing transactions where the lessee intends entering into more than one lease with the lessor, e.g. in relation to a fleet of vehicles.

As a regulated hire agreement must contain all the terms of the agreement other than implied terms, care must be taken in relation to a master lease agreement where the leases will be regulated consumer hire agreements, to ensure that each schedule does in fact contain all the terms of the agreement. This is achieved by each schedule being drafted as a separate regulated hire agreement which embodies the master lease agreement by specifically referring to it in the schedule.[1]

1 CCA 1974, ss 61(1)(b) and 189(4).

5.4.5 Business finance lease

The Finance & Leasing Association's Business Finance Code[1] applies to the provision of asset finance to businesses by members of the Finance & Leasing Association (FLA). The Code contains Commitments which FLA members agree to be bound by and a checklist for business finance customers.

1 2016 and revised periodically.

5.4.6 Software lease

'Software' is not a term of art. It can be used to refer to diverse items such as the programming part of data processing, the range of services necessary to support the hardware, such as the information loaded into the machine and the directions given to the machine, or it can be taken to refer to support and consultancy services.

Computer programs are not normally sold, but licensed to the user, though the hard copy itself may be sold to the customer on a chip, tape, or disk. In this way the use of the program and the number of terminals on which it can be employed are controlled, variations are limited and the copyright protected. Although somewhat a legal fiction, it is increasingly commonplace for software to be leased. As regards capital allowances, the position is governed by s 71(1) and (2) of the Capital Allowances Act 2001 which provides that if a person carrying on a qualifying activity incurs capital expenditure in acquiring, for the purpose of that activity, the right to use or otherwise deal with computer software, it is to be treated as plant. This means that expenditure on software can qualify for plant and machinery allowances.

The Inland Revenue had issued a guidance note on their interpretation of the previous law.[1] The term 'computer software' is not defined for capital allowance purposes but the Revenue consider that the term covers both programs and data, such as books stored in digital form.

Simply calling a software agreement a lease does not necessarily convert it into a lease, as against a licence. A software lessor's ultimate concern is to protect his investment. For this he needs to be satisfied that he can grant to, or procure for, the lessee the necessary rights to enable the lessee to use the software and the lessor must be able to recover its value if the lease is terminated prematurely. The lessor must be in the position of either the ultimate licensor or sub-licensor of the software, with the right to assign the benefit of the licence to a purchaser from him. Interposing the lessor between the software owner, copyright holder or licensor and the lessee has the advantage of giving the lessor control over the hired equipment and software. It results in the lessor incurring express and implied obligations and liability to the lessee or licensee when otherwise the obligations and liability would be those of the software owner directly. In practice commercial considerations play a dominant role and often the software is merely listed as an item of leased equipment together with the hardware, in a lease of the whole. Where, however, the lessor does not possess the right to use or otherwise deal with the computer software, he is not in a position to bundle it in this way and the software user will need to license the software directly from the software provider.

1 Revenue Interpretation 56 (RI56).

5.4.7   Lease upgrade

It is common practice for suppliers and lessors of equipment to encourage lessees to upgrade the equipment subject to the lease, particularly in the case of office furniture and equipment. Often the lessee will be offered an inducement by way of reduced rentals or a higher 'part-exchange' value for the existing equipment to induce him to take on the new equipment.

Any agreement involving an upgrade of existing equipment must, in the case of a regulated hire agreement, comply with the requirements of a modifying agreement, in accordance with the CCA 1974 and the Agreements Regulations under the Act. An upgrade may involve in part a refinancing agreement and in part a new rental agreement. A modifying agreement is not a cancellable agreement unless it is entered into within the cancellation period applicable to the original agreement.

5.4.8 Credit hire

The law on credit hire evolved from the leading case of *Dimond v Lovell*[1] in the context of deferred payment car hire schemes. It usually takes the form of a combined regulated consumer hire agreement and an exempt consumer credit agreement. Recent cases have generally related to the more limited issue of the rate of hire charge to which the lessor was entitled. In *Clark v Ardington Electrical Services*[2] the Court of Appeal applied the principle that the wrongdoer must take his victim as he finds him and that the victim is entitled to the full benefit of the car repair scheme, subject to the obligation to mitigate his loss where reasonable. The court opined that the claimant was *prima facie* entitled to the cost of hiring a replacement car, whether or not the charge is at the top of the range of car hire rates.

In *Pattini v First Leicester Buses Ltd*,[3] involving a combined appeal, the Court of Appeal rejected the earlier notion of a spot rate in favour of a basic hire rate. The court held that, where the hirer is not impecunious, calculation of the basic hire rate involves a fact-finding exercise to ascertain the rate for the model of the car hired, with a discount applied where the repairs would take a considerable time to effect. The meaning of a 'basic hire rate' was enunciated by the Court of Appeal in *Stevens v Equity Syndicate Management Ltd*,[4] where Kitchin LJ stated that the search must be 'for the lowest reasonable rate quoted by a mainstream supplier for the basic hire of a vehicle of the kind in issue to a reasonable person In the position of the claimant. This, it seems to me, is a proportionate way to arrive at a reasonable approximation to the BHR [basic hire rate]'.[5]

1 See **5.1**, footnote 8 above.
2 [2002] EWCA Civ 510, [2003] GCCR 4691, CA.
3 [2011] GCCR 11387, CA.
4 [2015] EWCA Civ 93, [2015] GCCR 13001.
5 Ibid at para [39].

5.5 STRUCTURE OF AN EQUIPMENT LEASE

An 'equipment lease' is not a term of art and may take the form of a finance lease or an operating lease. It has certain characteristic features. The lessee will select the goods from the supplier, satisfy himself that they are suitable for his purpose and either lease them directly from the supplier or from a lessor introduced by the supplier. Often the lessor's identity is immaterial to the lessee who will be mainly concerned with the financial terms of the lease. Indeed, it has become increasingly common for lessees to sign standard form lease agreements with unnamed lessors, leaving it to the supplier to find a lessor with whom he has arranged for the supply of leasing facilities to his customers. It is submitted that until the lessor's identity is disclosed to the lessee in the agreement, one of the essentials of a lease is missing, with the result that it is not a binding agreement and the lessee would be entitled to withdraw from it before it has been accepted.

Frequently a customer, after being invoiced by the supplier, decides that it would be beneficial to lease the equipment. Two approaches might then be adopted. The preferable one is for the original invoice to be cancelled so that the supplier can invoice the proposed lessor directly and enter into the equipment lease with the lessee. The alternative is for the proposed lessee to forward the invoice to his proposed lessor, who will settle it directly with the supplier, and then enter into a lease agreement with the lessee. The original purchase by the lessee will then be deemed to have been effected by the customer as agent for an undisclosed principal, the lessor.

Where the proposed lessee has been in possession of (and has possibly used) the equipment for some period, he might enter into a sale and lease-back from the proposed lessor. The courts will scrutinise such transactions to ensure that the transfer of ownership was genuinely intended as a sale and does not amount to a disguised loan secured by a mortgage, with the possible consequence of the mortgage being an unregistered mortgage or constituting an unregistered bill of sale.[1]

To crystallise the relationship between supplier and lessor, the lessor will usually require the supplier to provide him with various warranties, indemnities and representations. These include warranties relating to the supplier's business, including compliance with the law and the holding of a valid credit broker's licence; warranties relating to the goods, including that their ownership will pass to the lessor; a warranty in respect of the goods' quality and condition and that they were selected by and meet the requirements of the lessee; a warranty that the lease was accurately and fully completed before signature and appropriate copies handed to the lessee after execution; and in respect of the lessee, a warranty that he requested the goods for business purposes and that the supplier did not give any warranties or make any representations to the lessee other than those contained in the agreement. Frequently the supplier will enter into a re-purchase agreement with the lessor, undertaking to re-purchase the equipment in the amount of its residual value on expiry of the lease agreement.

1 Compare *Stoneleigh Finance v Phillips* [1965] 2 QB 537, [1999] GCCR 259, CA.

Chapter 6

Exempt agreements

6.1 INTRODUCTION AND DISTINCTION BETWEEN A 'REGULATED AGREEMENT' AND AN 'EXEMPT AGREEMENT'

This chapter is concerned with exempt credit agreements and exempt hire agreements, which are dealt with in that order. An exempt agreement is an agreement which is not regulated by the Consumer Credit Act 1974 ('CCA 1974'), the Financial Services and Markets Act 2000 ('FSMA'), and regulations made under each of those Acts, except that an exempt credit agreement is subject to the unfair relationships provisions of sections 140A to 140C of CCA 1974.

The various categories of exempt agreements, and in particular exempt credit agreements, are subject to a web of complex and intricate regulations, notably the Financial Services and Markets Act 2000 (Regulated Activities) Order 2001, SI 2001/544 ('RAO').

A 'regulated agreement' is defined in CCA 1974 as a consumer credit agreement which is a regulated agreement within the meaning of s 8(3) of CCA 1974 or a consumer hire agreement which is a regulated agreement within the meaning of s 15(2) of CCA 1974.[1]

A consumer credit agreement is a regulated credit agreement within the meaning of CCA 1974 if it:

(a) is a regulated credit agreement for the purposes of Chapter 14A of Part 2 of the Regulated Activities Order; and

(b) if entered into on or after 21 March 2016, is not an agreement of the type described in Article 3(1)(b) of Directive 2014/17/EU of the European Parliament and of the Council of 4 February 2014 on credit agreements for consumers relating to residential immovable property.[2]

1 CCA 1974, s 189(1).
2 Ibid., s 8(3). For a discussion of 'credit agreement' and 'consumer hire agreement', see **Chapter 3**.

6.2 EXEMPT CREDIT AGREEMENTS

Originally, CCA 1974 and regulations under that Act governed exempt agreements. This changed over time as the consumer credit regime increasingly fell under the control of the FSMA, and the RAO, culminating in the whole regime relating to exempt agreements falling under their scope with effect from 1 April 2014,[1] when the FCA replaced the OFT, which was abolished.

A credit agreement is an exempt agreement if it falls under articles 60C to 60H of the RAO.[2] There are various types of exempt agreement dependent upon the type of creditor, the type of agreement and the type of debtor.

1 Principally under SI 2013/1881.
2 RAO art 60B(3).

6.3   TYPES OF EXEMPT CREDIT AGREEMENT

The various types of exempt credit agreement are detailed below under their respective headings and the provisions of the RAO, which have been slightly transliterated to assist with their comprehension. The types of exempt agreement are:

(1)   exemption relating to the nature of the agreement (RAO art 60C);

(2)   exemption relating to the purchase of land for non-residential purposes (RAO art 60D);

(3)   exemption relating to the nature of the lender (RAO art 60E);

(4)   exemption relating to number of repayments to be made (RAO art 60F);

(5)   exemption relating to the total charge for credit (RAO art 60G);

(6)   exemption relating to the nature of the borrower (RAO art 60H);

(7)   exempt agreements: exemptions not permitted under the Mortgages Directive (RAO art 60HA); and

(8)   other miscellaneous exclusions (RAO arts 60I to 60K).

6.3.1   Exemption relating to the nature of the agreement (RAO art 60C)

The notable exemption in this category is a credit agreement for a borrower's business purposes.

This category of exempt credit agreement covers the following agreements:

(1)   A credit agreement which is a regulated mortgage contract or a regulated home purchase plan.[1]

(2)   A credit agreement for credit exceeding £25,000, entered into by the borrower wholly or predominantly for the purpose of a business carried on, or intended to be carried on, by the borrower.[2]

If the agreement includes a declaration which:

(a)   is made by the borrower,

(b)　provides that the agreement is entered into by the borrower wholly or predominantly for the purposes of a business carried on, or intended to be carried on, by the borrower, and

(c)　complies with rules made by the FCA, the agreement is to be presumed to have been entered into by the borrower wholly or predominantly for the purposes specified above, unless, when the agreement is entered into:

(i)　the lender (or, if there is more than one lender, any of the lenders), or

(ii)　any person who has acted on behalf of the lender (or, if there is more than one lender, any of the lenders) in connection with the entering into of the agreement,

knows or has reasonable cause to suspect that the agreement is not entered into by the borrower wholly or predominantly for the purposes of a business carried on, or intended to be carried on, by the borrower.[3]

The FCA rules relating to a declaration for these purposes are set out in CONC App 1.4.5R and 1.4.8R.

Generally speaking, 'business' has a wide meaning. It must be construed independently of s 189(2) which states that a person is not to be treated as carrying on a particular type of business merely because occasionally he enters into transactions belonging to a business of that type. Each agreement must be considered on its merits, rather than as one of a series of transactions or as a transaction in the course of a business. As the test is whether the agreement itself is entered into wholly or predominantly for the purposes of a business, it does not suffice that the agreement is entered into in the course of a business or partly for business[4] and partly for investment purposes, e.g. buy-to-let mortgages, if it is not entered into predominantly for business purposes. It is clear that, to qualify for exemption, the agreement need not be entered into by the debtor or hirer exclusively for business purposes.

It is submitted that the test as to whether an agreement is entered into by the debtor or hirer for business purposes is a question of fact, to be decided upon the basis of all the circumstances and, once decided that it is for this purpose, the issue is whether it is entered into wholly or predominantly for the debtor's or hirer's business purposes. Whilst 'business' normally connotes the objective of profit or gain, it does not necessarily do so, as in the case of an unincorporated charity entering into a credit agreement, as debtor, for the purpose of the charity's business.[5] 'Business' might also encompass a single transaction. As stated by Moore-Bick LJ in *GE Capital Bank Ltd v Rushton*: 'Although the word "business" may often denote a degree of repetition and continuity, it need not always do so, as Kennedy LJ observed in *Conroy v Kenny*'.[6]

If the requirements relating to the business exemption are not complied with, the credit agreement or hire agreement is improperly executed and enforceable only on an order of the court.[7]

Notwithstanding the exempt status of these credit agreements, they remain subject to the unfair relationships provisions that apply as between creditors and debtors, pursuant to ss 140A to 140C of CCA 1974.

(3)   A credit agreement for credit of £25,000 or less entered into by the borrower wholly or predominantly for the purpose of a business carried on, or intended to be carried on, by the borrower and which is a green deal plan made in relation to a property that is not a domestic property.[8]

(4)   A credit agreement made in connection with trade in goods or services, between the United Kingdom and a country outside the UK, or within a country outside the UK, or between countries outside the UK, and in each case the credit is provided to the borrower in the course of a business carried on by the borrower.[9]

The reader is also referred to the FCA Handbook, PERG sourcebook at 2.7.19C.

1 See RAO arts 60C(2) and 61A(1). See also **Chapter 18** of this text.
2 RAO art 60C(3).
3 Ibid., art 60C(5) and (6).
4 Contrast this with *Stevenson v Beverley Bentinck Ltd* [1976] 2 All ER 606, CA.
5 For further examples of the scope of the meaning of 'business', see *Stroud's Judicial Dictionary of Words and Phrases*, vol 1, and particularly the cases cited in relation to the Landlord and Tenant Act 1954.
6 [2006] GCCR 5541, CA, at 5549; *Conroy v Kenny* [1999] 1 WLR 1340, CA; and see also *Cornelius v Phillips* [1918] AC 199.
7 CCA 1974, s 65; and see ibid., s 127.
8 RAO art 60C(4) and (7).
9 Ibid., art 60C(8).

6.3.2   Exemption relating to the purchase of land for non-residential purposes (RAO art 60D)

This exemption typically covers buy-to-let mortgages.
    The relevant provision reads as follows:[1]

'(1)   A credit agreement is an exempt agreement if, at the time it is entered into, any sums due under it are secured by a legal or equitable mortgage on land and the condition in paragraph (2) below is satisfied.

(2)   The condition is that less than 40% of the land is used, or is intended to be used, as or in connection with a dwelling–

(a)   by the borrower or a related person of the borrower, or

(b)   in the case of credit provided to trustees, by an individual who is a beneficiary of the trust or a related person of a beneficiary.

(3)   For the purposes of paragraph (2) above–

(a)   the area of any land which comprises a building or other structure containing two or more storeys is to be taken to be the aggregate of the floor areas of each of those stories;

(b)   "related person" in relation to a person ("B") who is the borrower or (in the case of credit provided to trustees) a beneficiary of the trust, means:

(i) B's spouse or civil partner,

(ii) a person (whether or not of the opposite sex) whose relationship with B has the characteristics of the relationship between husband and wife, or

(iii) B's parent, brother, sister, child, grandparent or grandchild.

(4) This article does not apply to an agreement of the type described in Article 3(1)(b) of the Mortgages Directive that is entered into on or after 21 March 2016 [namely, a credit agreement the purpose of which is to acquire or retain property rights in land or in an existing or projected building] and does not meet the conditions in paragraphs (i) to (iii) of art 61(3)(a) [namely, regulated mortgage contracts].' (See further **Chapter 18.**)

The reader is also referred to the FCA Handbook, PERG sourcebook at 2.7.19E.

1 RAO art 60D(1) to (4).

6.3.3 Exemption relating to the nature of the lender (RAO art 60E)

This exemption relates to a credit agreement for the purchase of land and applies to banks, building societies, local authorities and other specified lenders.

The detailed provisions are as follows:[1]

'(1) A credit agreement is an exempt agreement in the cases listed below.

(2) Subject to article 60HA [see **6.3.7** below], a relevant credit agreement relating to the purchase of land (as defined in paragraph (7) below) is an exempt agreement if the lender is–

(a) specified, or of a description specified, in rules made by the FCA under paragraph (3) below, or

(b) a local authority.

(3) The FCA may make rules (see paragraph (11) below) specifying any of the lenders mentioned below for the purposes of paragraph (2) above. It should be noted that, as mentioned in paragraph (4) below, FCA rules may specifically identify the lenders or circumscribe the class of lenders. The classes of lender comprise–

(a) an authorised person with permission to effect or carry out contracts of insurance;

(b) a friendly society;

(c) an organisation of employers or organisation of workers;

(d) a charity;

(e) an improvement company (as defined in section 7 of the Improvement of Land Act 1899);

(f) a body corporate named or specifically referred to in any public general Act;

(g) a body corporate named or specifically referred to in, or in an order made under, a relevant housing provision;

(h)   a building society (within the meaning of the Building Societies Act 1986);

(i)   an authorised person with permission to accept deposits.

(4) Rules under paragraph (3) above may–

(a)   specify a particular person or class of persons;

(b)   be limited so as to apply only to agreements or classes of agreement specified in the rules.

(5) Subject to article 60HA [see **6.3.7** below], a relevant credit agreement is an exempt agreement if it is–

(a)   secured by a legal or equitable mortgage on land,

(b)   that land is used or is intended to be used as or in connection with a dwelling, and

(c)   the lender is a housing authority.

(6) A credit agreement is an exempt agreement if–

(a)   the lender is an investment firm or a credit institution, and

(b)   the agreement is entered into for the purpose of allowing the borrower to carry out a transaction relating to one or more financial instruments.

(7) Definitions

For the definition of "housing authority" see sub-articles 7(a) to (c) and articles 7A and 7B.

"Relevant credit agreement relating to the purchase of land" means–

(a)   a borrower-lender-supplier agreement financing:

(i)   the purchase of land, or

(ii)   provision of dwellings on land,

and secured by a legal or equitable mortgage on that land,

(b)   a borrower-lender agreement secured by a legal or equitable mortgage on land, or

(c)   a borrower-lender-supplier agreement financing a transaction which is a linked transaction in relation to–

(i)   an agreement falling within sub-paragraph (a), or

(ii)   an agreement falling within sub-paragraph (b) financing–

(aa) the purchase of land,

(bb) the provision of dwellings on land,

and secured by a legal or equitable mortgage on the land referred to in sub-paragraph (a) or the land referred to in paragraph (ii);

"Relevant housing provision" means any of the following–

(a)   section 156(4) or 447(2)(a) of the Housing Act 1985,

(b)   section 156(4) of that Act as it has effect by virtue of section 17 of the Housing Act 1996 (the right to acquire), or

(c)   article 154(1)(a) of the Housing (Northern Ireland) Order 1981.

(8) For the purposes of the definition of "relevant credit agreement relating to the purchase of land", a transaction is, unless paragraph (9) applies, a "linked transaction" in relation to a credit agreement ("the principal agreement") if–

(a) it is (or will be) entered into by the borrower under the principal agreement or by a relative of the borrower,

(b) it does not relate to the provision of security,

(c) it does not form part of the principal agreement, and

(d) one of the following conditions is satisfied–

   (i) the transaction is entered into in compliance with a term of the principal agreement;

   (ii) the principal agreement is a borrower-lender-supplier agreement and the transaction is financed, or to be financed, by the principal agreement;

   (iii) the following conditions are met–

      (aa) the other party is a person to whom paragraph (10) applies,

      (bb) the other party initiated the transaction by suggesting it to the borrower or the relative of the borrower, and

      (cc) the borrower or the relative of the borrower enters into the transaction to induce the lender to enter into the principal agreement or for another purpose related to the principal agreement or to a transaction financed or to be financed by the principal agreement.

(9) This paragraph applies if the transaction is–

(a) a contract of insurance,

(b) a contract which contains a guarantee of goods, or

(c) a transaction which comprises, or is effected under–

   (i) an agreement for the operation of an account (including any savings account) for the deposit of money, or

   (ii) an agreement for the operation of a current account, under which the customer ("C") may, by means of cheques or similar orders payable to C or to any other person, obtain or have the use of money held or made available by the person with whom the account is kept.

(10) The persons to whom this paragraph applies are–

(a) the lender;

(b) the lender's associate;

(c) a person who, in the negotiation of the transaction, is represented by a person who carries on an activity of the kind specified by article 36A (credit broking) by way of business who is or was also a negotiator in negotiations for the principal agreement;

(d) a person who, at the time the transaction is initiated, knows that the principal agreement has been made or contemplates that it might be made.'

The rules made by the FCA in relation to the above are to be found in the FCA Handbook, CONC sourcebook, at Appendix 1.3.1R to 1.3.4R.

1 RAO art 60E(1) to (10).

6.3.4 Exemption relating to number of repayments to be made (RAO art 60F)

This exemption is known as 'the limited payments exemption'. The exemption applies to a credit agreement where the number of payments to be made by the borrower is limited in accordance with the requirements set out below. The exemption is particularly helpful for retail traders and suppliers.

The highlighted passages below are only intended to assist the reader with the identification of the principal characteristics of the different types of agreement.

The relevant provision reads as follows:[1]

'(1) A credit agreement is an exempt agreement in the cases below.

(2) A credit agreement is an exempt agreement if–

(a) the agreement is a borrower-lender-supplier agreement for fixed-sum credit, other than a green deal plan,

(b) the number of payments to be made by the borrower is not more than 12,

(c) those payments are required to be made within a period of 12 months or less (beginning on the date of the agreement),

(d) the credit is–

   (i)   secured on land, or

   (ii) provided without interest or other ... charges, and

(e) paragraph (7) below does not apply to the agreement.

(3) A credit agreement is an exempt agreement if–

(a) the agreement is a borrower-lender-supplier agreement for running-account credit,

(b) the borrower is to make payments in relation to specified periods which, unless the agreement is secured on land, must be of three months or less,

(c) the number of payments to be made by the borrower in repayment of the whole amount of credit provided in each such period is not more than one,

(d) the credit is–

   (i)   secured on land, or

   (ii) provided without interest or other significant charges, and

(e) paragraph (7) below does not apply to the agreement.

(4) Subject to article 60HA [see **6.3.7** below], a credit agreement is an exempt agreement if–

(a) the agreement is a borrower-lender-supplier agreement financing the purchase of land,

(b) the number of payments to be made by the borrower is not more than four, and

(c) the credit is–

   (i)   secured on land, or

   (ii) provided without interest or other charges.

(5) A credit agreement is an exempt agreement if–

(a) the agreement is a borrower-lender-supplier agreement for fixed-sum credit,

(b) the credit is to finance a premium under a contract of insurance relating to land or anything on land,

(c) the lender is the lender under a credit agreement secured by a legal or equitable mortgage on that land,

(d) the credit is to be repaid within the period (which must be 12 months or less) to which the premium relates,

(e) in the case of an agreement secured on land, there is no charge forming part of the total charge for credit under the agreement other than interest at a rate not exceeding the rate of interest from time to time payable under the agreement mentioned at sub-paragraph (c),

(f) in the case of an agreement which is not secured on land, the credit is provided without interest or other charges, and

(g) the number of payments to be made by the borrower is not more than 12.

(6) A credit agreement is an exempt agreement if–

(a) the agreement is a borrower-lender-supplier agreement for fixed-sum credit,

(b) the lender is the lender under a credit agreement secured by a legal or equitable mortgage on land,

(c) the agreement is to finance a premium under a contract of whole life insurance which provides, in the event of the death of the person on whose life the contract is effected before the credit referred to in sub-paragraph (b) has been repaid, for payment of a sum not exceeding the amount sufficient to meet the amount which, immediately after that credit has been advanced, would be payable to the lender in respect of that credit (including interest from time to time payable under that agreement),

(d) in the case of an agreement secured on land, there is no charge forming part of the total charge for credit under the agreement other than interest at a rate not exceeding the rate of interest from time to time payable under the agreement mentioned at sub-paragraph (b),

(e) in the case of an agreement which is not secured on land, the credit is provided without interest or other charges, and

(f) the number of payments to be made by the borrower is not more than 12.

(7) This paragraph applies to–

(a) agreements financing the purchase of land;

(b) agreements which are conditional sale agreements or hire-purchase agreements;

(c) agreements secured by a pledge (other than a pledge of documents of title or of bearer bonds).

(8) Definitions

"Payment" means any payment which comprises or includes:

(a) the repayment of capital, or

(b)   the payment of interest or any other charge which forms part of the total charge for credit.'

The reader is also referred to the FCA Handbook, PERG sourcebook at 2.7.19G.

1 RAO art 60F(1) to (8).

6.3.4.1   Interpretation by the courts

An advance payment, deposit or down payment is not included in the maximum number of instalments and may therefore be required to be paid in addition to the credit instalments.

The courts adopt a strict approach to the interpretation of the period of the agreement and the due date for final payment, in considering whether this falls within the required 12-month period.

In *Dimond v Lovell*[1] the House of Lords held that a hire agreement under which the hire charge was not payable until some future event, occurring after the conclusion of the period of hire, was also a credit agreement. As it contained provision for payment with no limit on the duration of the 'credit', save that it was payable on conclusion of the claim for damages, the agreement was potentially repayable outside the 12-month period. It was conceded by counsel (without argument) that the agreement was not an exempt agreement.

If the terms of the agreement are such that no payment is capable of being made outside the period of 12 months beginning with the date of the agreement, it will be an enforceable exempt agreement. *Seddon v Tekin*[2] dealt with three actions where similar or identical issues arose. The claimants had entered into broadly similar hire agreements under a 'credit repair facility' for a substitute vehicle under which charges were payable at the commencement of the hire and otherwise on demand, unless a credit hire agreement had been concluded. Credit hire agreements were concluded for a period of 51 weeks in two of the cases and 26 weeks in the other case. In concluding that they were exempt agreements, the County Court held that the hypothetical reasonable person would consider that the payment fell due in full at the end of the stated period and that therefore the agreements were valid exempt agreements. This was one of a series of similar cases decided by no less than six other circuit judges.

Similar types of agreement were considered by the Court of Appeal. In *Clark v Ardington Electrical Services*[3] the court held that a credit agreement which stipulated a liability to pay at the end of the credit period, namely after 26 or 51 weeks beginning with the date of the agreement, referred to the legal obligation to make payment at that time and, accordingly, the agreement was an exempt agreement.

In contrast with the above, the Court of Appeal in *Ketley v Gilbert*[4] found that an agreement where payment was to be made on the expiry of 12 months, starting with the date of the agreement, permitted payment to be made outside the statutory period for an exempt agreement. As it did not meet the requirements for an exempt agreement, it was unenforceable for want of compliance with the requirements of a regulated credit agreement.

The commencement of the period of 12 months is the date of the agreement. So it was held in *Zoan v Rouamba*[5] where the court stated that, where the period within which an act is to be done is expressed to be a period beginning with a specified day, it has been held with equal consistency over the past 40 years or so that the legislature (or the relevant rule-making body, as the case may be) has shown a clear intention that the specified day must be included in the period. As the agreement had to be construed as providing for a period of deferment of payment one day longer than that prescribed, it was not an exempt agreement and therefore unenforceable.

1 *Dimond v Lovell* [2001] GCCR 2751, HL.
2 *Seddon v Tekin, Dowsett v Clifford, Beasly v PPP/Columbus Healthcare* [2001] GCCR 2865 (Oxford County Court).
3 *Clark v Ardington Electrical Services* [2002] GCCR 4691.
4 *Ketley v Gilbert* [2001] GCCR 2951, CA; *King v Daltray; Thew v Cole* [2003] All ER (D) 280.
5 *Zoan v Rouamba* [2001] GCCR 2581, CA at 2589.

6.3.5   Exemption relating to the total charge for credit (RAO art 60G)

This is also known as 'the low cost credit exemption'.

The highlighted passages below are merely intended to assist the reader with the identification of the principal characteristics of the different types of agreement.

The relevant provision reads:[1]

'(1)   A credit agreement is an exempt agreement in the following cases.

(2)   A credit agreement is an exempt agreement if–

(a)   it is a borrower-lender agreement, …

(b)   the lender is a credit union and the rate of the total charge for credit does not exceed 42.6 per cent, and

(c)   paragraph (2A) applies to the agreement.

(2A)   This paragraph applies to the agreement if–

(a)   the agreement is not of a type described in Article 3(1) of the mortgages directive; …

(b)   the agreement is of such a type and–

(i)   the agreement is of a kind to which the mortgages directive does not apply by virtue of Article 3(2) of that directive,

(ii)   the agreement is a bridging loan within the meaning of Article 4(23) of the mortgages directive, or

(iii)   in relation to the agreement–

(aa) the borrower receives timely information on the main features, risks and costs of the agreement at the pre-contractual stage, and

(bb) any advertising of the agreement is fair, clear and not misleading; or

(c)   the agreement was entered into before 21 March 2016.

(3) Subject to paragraph (8), a credit agreement is an exempt agreement if–

(a) it is a borrower-lender agreement,

(b) it is an agreement of a kind offered to a particular class of individual or relevant recipient of credit and not offered to the public generally,

(c) it provides that the only charge included in the total charge for credit is interest,

(d) interest under the agreement may not at any time be more than the sum of one per cent and the highest of the base rates published by the banks specified in paragraph (7) on the date 28 days before the date on which the interest is charged, and

(e) paragraph (5) does not apply to the agreement.

(4) Subject to paragraph (8), a credit agreement is an exempt agreement if–

(a) it is a borrower-lender agreement,

(b) it is an agreement of a kind offered to a particular class of individual or relevant recipient of credit and not offered to the public generally,

(c) it does not provide for or permit an increase in the rate or amount of any item which is included in the total charge for credit,

(d) the total charge for credit under the agreement is not more than the sum of one per cent and the highest of the base rates published by the banks specified in paragraph (7) on the date 28 days before the date on which the charge is imposed, and

(e) paragraph (5) does not apply to the agreement.

(5) This paragraph applies to an agreement if–

(a) the total amount to be repaid by the borrower to discharge the borrower's indebtedness may vary according to a formula which is specified in the agreement and which has effect by reference to movements in the level of any index or other factor, or

(b) the agreement–

(i) is not–

(aa) secured on land, or

(bb) offered by a lender to a borrower as an incident of the borrower's employment with the lender or with an undertaking in the same group as the lender; and

(ii) does not meet the general interest test.

(6) For the purposes of paragraphs (5) and (8), an agreement meets the general interest test if–

(a) the agreement is offered under an enactment with a general interest purpose, and

(b) the terms on which the credit is provided are more favourable to the borrower than those prevailing on the market, either because the rate of interest is lower than that prevailing on the market, or because the rate of interest is no higher than that prevailing on the market but the other terms on which credit is provided are more favourable to the borrower.

(7) The banks specified in this paragraph are–

(a) the Bank of England;

(b) Bank of Scotland;

(c) Barclays Bank plc;

(d) Clydesdale Bank plc;

(e) Co-operative Bank Public Limited Company;

(f) Coutts & Co;

(g) National Westminster Bank Public Limited Company;

(h) the Royal Bank of Scotland plc.

(8) A credit agreement of a type described in Article 3(1) of the mortgages directive which is entered into on or after 21 March 2016 is an exempt agreement pursuant to paragraph (3) or (4) only if–

(a) the agreement meets the general interest test;

(b) the borrower receives timely information on the main features, risks and costs of the agreement at the pre-contractual stage; and

(c) any advertising of the agreement is fair, clear and not misleading.'

The reader is also referred to the FCA Handbook, PERG sourcebook at 2.7.19I.

1 RAO art 60G(1) to (8).

6.3.5.1   Meaning of certain terms

The *Concise Oxford Dictionary* defines 'class' as 'a group of persons or things having some characteristic in common'. This would probably be too wide a definition for present purposes and, whilst the further qualifying expression of 'not offered to the public generally' appears to restrict the parameters of 'class' to a group which cannot be described as the public generally, even if they share some characteristic in common, as a result of the further restriction to the agreement having to be offered under an enactment with a general interest purpose, members of a club or association, shareholders of a company and other 'ring-fenced' classes of persons who share some common characteristics and cannot properly be described as 'the public generally' are unlikely to fall within this exemption. Rather, the exemption is likely to apply to loans to students, to persons under social housing schemes and borrowers under business promotion schemes (where the agreement is not otherwise exempt), assuming an appropriate enactment in each case.

6.3.6   Exemption relating to the nature of the borrower (RAO art 60H)

This exemption is the so-called 'the high net worth individual' exemption. The relevant provision reads:

(1) Subject to article 60HA [see **6.3.7** below], a credit agreement is an exempt agreement if–

(a)   the borrower is an individual,

(b)   the agreement is either–

    (i)   secured on land, or

    (ii) for credit which exceeds £60,260 and, if entered into on or after 21 March 2016, is for a purpose other than–

        (aa) the renovation of residential property, or

        (bb) to acquire or retain property rights in land or in an existing or projected building,

(c)   the agreement includes a declaration made by the borrower which provides that the borrower agrees to forgo the protection and remedies that would be available to the borrower if the agreement were a regulated credit agreement and which complies with rules made by the FCA for the purposes of this paragraph,

(d)   a statement has been made in relation to the income or assets of the borrower which complies with rules made by the FCA for the purposes of this paragraph,

(e)   the connection between the statement and the agreement complies with any rules made by the FCA for the purposes of this paragraph (including as to the period of time between the making of the statement and the agreement being entered into), and

(f)   a copy of the statement was provided to the lender before the agreement was entered into.

(2) Where a credit agreement would be an exempt agreement pursuant to this article but for paragraph (1)(b)(ii)(bb) or article 60HA, the FCA may treat the agreement as an exempt agreement except for the purpose of the application of the requirements of the mortgages directive.'

The reader is also referred to the FCA Handbook, PERG sourcebook at 2.7.19J.

6.3.6.1   *The FCA rules referred to are those set out in CONC App 1.4*

They prescribe a Declaration by the borrower, a Statement of assets/income of the borrower signed by the borrower or by a member of a qualifying body, such as the Institute of Chartered Accountants in England and Wales, and a procedure relating to the completion and provision of the same.

When advice is given to a high net worth individual as regards the consequences of making the declaration, a solicitor would be well advised to take note of the decisions in *Royal Bank of Scotland plc v Etridge (No 2)*[1] and *Padden v Bevan Ashford Solicitors*[2] lest an individual allege that he was unduly influenced by his co-debtor or co-hirer into signing the declaration or that he was not properly advised.

If the provisions relating to high net worth individuals are not complied with, the result is that the credit agreement or hire agreement is improperly executed and enforceable only on an order of the court.[3]

Notwithstanding their exempt status, the agreements are circumscribed in an important respect, namely by the unfair relationships provisions that apply to agreements between creditors and debtors, pursuant to ss 140A to 140C of CCA 1974.

1 [2001] GCCR 3105, HL.
2 [2011] EWCA Civ 1616, CA.
3 CCA 1974, s 65; and see ibid., s 127.

6.3.7 Exempt agreements: exemptions not permitted under the Mortgages Directive (RAO art 60HA)

'(1) A credit agreement entered into on or after 21 March 2016 is not an exempt agreement pursuant to article 60E (2) or (5), 60F(4) or 60H(1) if–

(a) the agreement is of a type described in Article 3(1) of the mortgages directive, and

(b) paragraph (2) does not apply.

(2) This paragraph applies if–

(a) the agreement is of a kind to which the mortgages directive does not apply by virtue of Article 3(2) of that directive;

(b) the agreement is a bridging loan within the meaning of Article 4(23) of that directive; or

(c) the agreement is a restricted public loan in respect of which–

(i) the borrower receives timely information on the main features, risks and costs at the pre-contractual stage; and

(ii) any advertising is fair, clear and not misleading.

(3) In paragraph (2)(c) "restricted public loan" means a credit agreement that is–

(a) offered to a particular class of borrower and not offered to the public generally;

(b) offered under an enactment with a general interest purpose; and

(c) provided on terms which are more favourable to the borrower than those prevailing on the market, because it meets one of the following conditions–

(i) it is interest free;

(ii) the rate of interest is lower than that prevailing on the market; or

(iii) the rate of interest is no higher than that prevailing on the market but the other terms on which credit is provided are more favourable to the borrower.'

6.3.8 Other miscellaneous exclusions (RAO arts 60I to 60K)

Credit agreements relating to any of the following are excluded from regulated credit agreements:

(a) subject to the stated qualifications, an agreement by an unauthorised person, entered into with an authorised person with permission, for the latter to carry on a lender's rights and duties under a regulated agreement;[1]

(b) activities carried on by a person who is an EEA authorised payment institution, or an authorised electronic money institution, exercising passport rights in the UK in accordance with Article 16(3) of the Payment Services Directive, as applied by Article 6 of the Electronic Money Directive in the case of an electronic money institution;[2] and

(c) agreements relating to information society services, local authorities and registered buy-to-let mortgage firms.[3]

1 RAO arts 60I and 60J.
2 Ibid., arts 60JA and 60JB.
3 Ibid., art 60K.

6.4   EXEMPT CONSUMER HIRE AGREEMENTS

A consumer hire agreement is an exempt agreement if it falls under articles 60O to 60Q of the RAO.[1] A regulated consumer hire agreement is a consumer hire agreement which is not an exempt agreement.[2]

1 RAO art 60N(3).
2 Ibid.

6.4.1   Types of exempt consumer hire agreement

The various types of exempt consumer hire agreement are detailed below under their respective headings and the provisions of the RAO, which have been slightly transliterated to assist with their comprehension. The types of exempt agreement are:

(1) exemption relating to the nature of the agreement (RAO art 60O);

(2) exemption relating to the supply of essential services (RAO art 60P);

(3) exemption relating to the nature of the hirer (RAO art 60Q); and

(4) other exclusions (RAO art 60R).

6.4.2   Exemption relating to the nature of the agreement (RAO art 60O)

A consumer hire agreement is an exempt agreement if:

(a) the hirer is required by the agreement to make payments exceeding £25,000, and

(b) the agreement is entered into by the hirer wholly or predominantly for the purposes of a business carried on, or intended to be carried on, by the hirer.

If an agreement includes a declaration which:

(a) is made by the hirer,

(b) provides that the agreement is entered into by the hirer wholly or predominantly for the purposes of a business carried on, or intended to be carried on, by the hirer, and

(c) complies with rules made by the FCA for the purposes of RAO art 60O,

the agreement is to be presumed to have been entered into by the hirer wholly or predominantly for such purpose, unless the owner (or, if there is more than one owner, any of the owners), or any person who has acted on behalf of the owner (or, if there is more than one owner, any of the owners), in connection with the entering into of the agreement, knows or has reasonable cause to suspect that the agreement is not entered into by the hirer wholly or predominantly for the purposes of a business carried on, or intended to be carried on, by the hirer.[1]

This exemption mirrors the corresponding exemption relating to consumer credit agreements in RAO art 60C (see **6.3.1**(2) above).

The reader is also referred to the FCA Handbook, PERG sourcebook at 2.7.19M and 2.7.19N.

1 RAO art 60O(1), (2) and (3).

6.4.3   Exemption relating to the supply of essential services (RAO art 60P)

A consumer hire agreement is an exempt agreement if:

(a) the owner is a body corporate which is authorised by or under an enactment to supply gas, electricity or water, and

(b) the subject of the agreement is a meter or metering equipment which is used (or is to be used) in connection with the supply of gas, electricity or water.

The reader is also referred to the FCA Handbook, PERG sourcebook at 2.7.19O and 2.7.19P.

6.4.4   Exemption relating to the nature of the hirer (RAO art 60Q)

A consumer hire agreement is an exempt agreement if:

(a) the hirer is an individual,

(b) the agreement includes a declaration made by the hirer which provides that the hirer agrees to forgo the protection and remedies that would be available to the hirer if the agreement were a regulated consumer hire agreement and which complies with rules made by the FCA for the purposes of this paragraph, namely in CONC App 1.4,

(c) a statement has been made in relation to the income or assets of the hirer which complies with rules made by the FCA for the purposes of this paragraph, namely in CONC App 1.4,

(d) the connection between the statement and the agreement complies with any rules made by the FCA for the purposes of this paragraph, namely in CONC App 1.4 (including as to the period of time between the making of the statement and the agreement being entered into), and

(e) a copy of the statement was provided to the owner before the agreement was entered into.

This exemption mirrors the corresponding exemption relating to consumer credit agreements in RAO art. 60H. The reader is referred to the FCA Handbook, CONC App.1.4, PERG 2.7.19P and **6.3.6** above.

6.4.5 Other exclusions (RAO art 60R)

Other exclusions relate to any activity consisting of the provision of an information society service from an EEA state other than the United Kingdom[1] and any activity which is carried on by a local authority.[2]

1 See RAO art 72A.
2 See ibid., art 72G.

6.5 AGREEMENTS EXCLUDED FROM CERTAIN PROVISIONS OF CCA 1974, PART V

Certain consumer credit and consumer hire agreements, whilst not exempt agreements, are exempt from the application of certain of the provisions of Part V of CCA 1974. These agreements, and the relevant provisions of Part V which do apply, are set out below.

6.5.1 Non-commercial agreement[1]

These are consumer credit agreements or consumer hire agreements not made by the creditor or owner in the course of a business carried on by him.[2] Other than s 56, which relates to antecedent negotiations, Part V of CCA 1974 does not apply to non-commercial agreements.[3] Moreover, under section 22 of FSMA (relating to regulated activities), for an activity to be a regulated activity, it must be carried on 'by way of business'.

In *Bassano v Toft*[4] the court, citing *Hare v Schurek*,[5] stated:

> 'The same principle was applied to the Consumer Credit Act licensing provisions by the Court of Appeal in *Hare v Schurek* [1993] CCLR 47; (1993) GCCR 1669. Section 40 in its then form rendered regulated agreements by unlicensed creditors unenforceable unless they were "non-commercial agreements" which bore the definition then, as now, in section 189(1) as meaning "a consumer credit

agreement not made by the creditor or owner in the course of a business carried on by him". The Court held that if the transaction between the parties was "one off" or "of a type only occasionally entered into by the applicant in the course of his motor trade business" or "unique or a manifestation of occasional transactions" it did not fall within the licensing requirements because it was not made in the course of a business. This conclusion was supported by s 189(2) which provides "A person is not to be treated as carrying on a particular type of business merely because occasionally he enters into transactions belonging to a business of that type." Mann LJ observed that such a conclusion was consonant with the purpose of the Act which is to regulate those who carry on particular forms of business as a trade or profession. See also *Goode: Consumer Credit Law & Practice* Issue 41 para 23.141 which in my view correctly summarises the position and how the judgment of Mann LJ in *Hare v Schurek* is to be interpreted. An occasional or one off consumer credit transaction does not require the creditor to be licensed because it is not carried out in the course of *any* business, whether consumer credit business or any other business.'

1 CCA 1974, ss 74(1)(a) and 189(1).
2 See further at **10.5**.
3 CCA 1974, s 74(1A).
4 [2014] GCCR 12015, [2014] EWHC 377 (QB) at para [33].
5 [1993] GCCR 1669.

6.5.2   Debtor-creditor agreement enabling the debtor to overdraw on a current account[1]

Debtor-creditor agreements for overdrafts on current accounts are exempt from the certain provisions relating to the form and formalities which apply to regulated agreements. The agreements are divisible into the following sub-categories:

(a)   an authorised business overdraft agreement;

(b)   an authorised non-business overdraft agreement, i.e. for credit which is repayable on demand or within three months;

(c)   an agreement that would be an authorised non-business overdraft agreement but for the fact that it is not repayable on demand or within three months;

(d)   a debtor-creditor agreement enabling the debtor to overdraw on a current account but not falling within any of the above (a), (b) or (c).

The following provisions of Part V of CCA 1974 apply to agreements described at (a) above:[2]

(a)   section 56 (antecedent negotiations);

(b)   section 60 (regulations on form and content of agreements);

(c)   section 61B (duty to supply copy of overdraft agreement).

The following provisions of Part V of CCA 1974 apply to agreements described at (b) above:[3]

(a)   section 55 (regulations on disclosure of information);

(b)   section 55C (copy of draft consumer credit agreement);

(c)   section 56 (antecedent negotiations);

(d)   section 60 (regulations on form and content of agreements);

(e)   section 61B (duty to supply copy of overdraft agreement).

The following provisions of Part V of CCA 1974 apply to agreements described at (c) above:[4]

(a)   section 55 (regulations on disclosure of information);

(b)   section 55C (copy of draft consumer credit agreement);

(c)   section 56 (antecedent negotiations);

(d)   section 60 (regulations on form and content of agreements);

(e)   section 61 (signing of agreement);

(f)   section 61A (duty to supply copy of executed agreement);

(g)   section 66A (withdrawal from consumer credit agreement).

An agreement described at (d) above is subject to section 56 (antecedent negotiations).[5]

1 CCA 1974, s 74(1)(b).
2 Ibid., s 74(1B).
3 Ibid., s 74(1C).
4 Ibid., s 74(1D).
5 Ibid., s 74(1E).

6.5.3   Small debtor-creditor-supplier agreement for restricted-use credit[1]

These are regulated consumer credit agreements for credit not exceeding £50 or regulated consumer hire agreements which do not require the hirer to make payments exceeding £50. The agreement may be unsecured or secured by a guarantee or indemnity only. If it is secured by a pledge, pawn or other security, it is no longer considered a small agreement. The small sum exemption does not apply to hire-purchase or conditional sale agreements. Examples of small agreements are small sum credit sale, cheque trading or credit card agreements.

Subject to certain exceptions, Part V of CCA 1974 does not apply to a small debtor-creditor-supplier agreement for restricted-use credit.[2] The exceptions are s 55, s 56 relating to antecedent negotiations, and s 66A relating to withdrawal from a consumer credit agreement.[3] The Act contains an anti-avoidance provision which applies in relation to a series of small credit agreements.[4]

1 CCA 1974, s 17, and see the exemptions under ss 74(2), 78(7) and 85(3).
2 Ibid., s 74(1)(d) read with s 74(2).
3 Ibid., s 74(2).
4 Ibid., s 17(3).

6.5.4   Agreements to finance payments connected with the death of a person

Certain provisions of Part V of CCA 1974 do not apply to a debtor-creditor agreement to finance specified payments arising on, or connected with, the death of a person,[1] namely certain payments of tax and court fees.[2]

The following provisions of Part V apply to these agreements:

(a)   section 55 (regulations on disclosure of information);

(b)   section 55C (copy of draft consumer credit agreement);

(c)   section 56 (antecedent negotiations);

(d)   section 60 (regulations on form and content of agreements);

(e)   section 61 (signing of agreement);

(f)   section 61A (duty to supply copy of executed agreement); and

(g)   section 66A (withdrawal from consumer credit agreement).

1   CCA 1974, s 74(1)(c).
2   See the Consumer Credit (Payments Arising on Death) Regulations 1983, SI 1983/1554.

6.5.5   Exemption at the discretion of the Financial Conduct Authority

On an application made to it by a person carrying on a consumer credit business or a consumer hire business, the FCA is empowered to vary or waive any of the requirements as to the form and content of regulated agreements where it appears to the FCA impractical for the applicant to comply with any requirement of the regulations under s 60(1) of CCA 1974 in a particular case. The FCA must be satisfied that the exercise of its power will not prejudice the interests of debtors or hirers. An application may only be made if it relates to one of the following:

(a)   a consumer credit agreement secured on land;

(b)   a consumer credit agreement under which a person takes an article in pawn;

(c)   a consumer credit agreement under which the creditor provides the debtor with credit which exceeds £60,260 and which is not a residential renovation agreement;

(d)   a consumer credit agreement entered into by the debtor wholly or predominantly for the purposes of a business carried on, or intended to be carried on, by him; or

(e)   a consumer hire agreement.

1   CCA 1974, s 60(3) to (5).

6.6   PARTLY REGULATED AGREEMENT

There is no definition of a partly regulated agreement in the CCA 1974. However, the Agreements Regulations[1] recognise such a type of agreement, which they describe as a document which embodies an agreement of which at least one part is a credit agreement not regulated by the CCA 1974.

1 Consumer Credit (Agreements) Regulations 1983, SI 1983/1553, Sch 1, para 1 and Consumer Credit (Agreements) Regulations 2010, SI 2010/1014, Sch 1, para 1.

Chapter 7

Multiple agreements; modifying agreements; novation, variation and assignment of agreements

7.1 THE MULTIPLE AGREEMENT

Undoubtedly one of the most complex provisions of CCA 1974 is section 18 which creates the concept of a multiple agreement. The underlying rationale of the section was to prevent several credit agreements or hire agreements being combined so as to exceed the financial limit which then applied to such agreements and thereby to bypass the provisions which would apply to them if they were separate agreements. In other words, it was an anti-avoidance measure.

At first blush, the removal of the financial limit which applied to consumer credit agreements and consumer hire agreements removed the need for this provision. However, on reflection, the section serves to preserve the information provisions which apply under the rigid regulatory regime. Infringement of the section is now less likely to be driven by the desire to avoid the consequences of a regulated agreement than to be attributable to non-compliance for reasons of presentation or business efficacy. As the rationale of the provision is now solely to ensure that different categories of agreement are treated appropriately, it is hoped that the courts will give due recognition to the altered situation when exercising their discretionary enforcement powers under s 127(1).

Section 18 refers to categories of an agreement and to parts of an agreement. 'Category of agreement' is not defined and the only indication as to its meaning is the reference in s 18(1)(a) to categories of agreement mentioned in CCA 1974 and categories of agreement not so mentioned. In truth, however, this adds little clarity. The drafting is rendered even more complex by a subsection[1] which refers to 'two or more categories of agreement so mentioned', which might be construed as meaning categories of agreement mentioned in the Act or, more likely, all categories previously referred to, namely those mentioned in the Act and those not mentioned in the Act.

A possible meaning of 'category of agreement mentioned in the Act' is each and every type of agreement identified in the CCA 1974, and especially in Part II of CCA 1974, read with the Consumer Credit (Agreements) Regulations 1983 and the Consumer Credit (Agreements) Regulations 2010.[2] This would, therefore, include the following: a consumer credit agreement, a consumer hire agreement, a consumer credit agreement for running-account credit, a consumer credit agreement for fixed-sum credit or a fixed-sum loan agreement, a credit card agreement, a restricted-use credit agreement, an unrestricted-use credit agreement, a debtor-creditor-supplier agreement, a debtor-creditor agreement, a small agreement, a cancellable (and by contrast a non-cancellable) agreement, an authorised non-business overdraft agreement and an authorised business overdraft agreement. In addition CCA 1974 mentions, and defines in s 189, the following types of general agreement: conditional sale agreement, credit-sale agreement and hire-purchase agreement. Other types of agreement created by the Act are a modifying agreement, a multiple agreement (itself a creature of s 18), a regulated agreement, an exempt agreement and an unregulated agreement. Types of agreement recognised by statutory instrument under the Act are an agreement to aggregate and a home credit loan agreement.[3] It would appear that, provided some distinction can be drawn between one type of agreement and another, the agreements will fall into different categories of agreement.

Once having established that an agreement involves more than one category of agreement, one turns to s 18 to consider how that section applies to the agreement. In *National Home Loans Corpn plc v Hannah*,[4] a County Court decision, the court stated that whatever else s 18 was about, it seems clear that in referring to categories it refers to disparate ones and that any other interpretation would give rise to absurdities.

In *National Westminster Bank plc v Story and Pallister*,[5] the Court of Appeal, after opining that the main purpose of s 18 was to prevent frustration of the CCA 1974's protection to borrowers by the artificial combination of two or more agreements in one, and without being required to comment on the meaning of 'category', stated that it was inclined, influenced in part by the positioning of the provision in Part II of the CCA 1974, to construe the word 'category' in the more narrow sense. That is, it applies to different categories within Part II of the CCA 1974 rather than as between every type of agreement for which the Act, in its various parts, provides its own legal regime. On that approach, the court added, restricted-use and unrestricted-use agreements were separate categories of agreement.

An analysis of s 18 does not end with the differentiation of categories of agreement as the section distinguishes between an agreement which falls within two or more categories of agreement and an agreement in parts, each part of which falls within another category of agreement. If an agreement falls within more than one category and those categories are not disparate categories so that they can be combined within one agreement, the agreement can be drafted as a single multiple unitary agreement, i.e. as a single agreement with the same provisions applying to each category of agreement comprised in that agreement. If, on the other hand, the agreement is in parts or the agreement is one within two or more categories which cannot be combined within one unitary agreement, e.g. a conditional sale agreement in respect of a motor vehicle together with a personal loan agreement for fixed-sum credit to finance a caravan, each must be drafted as a separate agreement.

In *National Westminster Bank plc v Story and Pallister* the court referred with approval to the Office of Fair Trading's discussion paper on multiple agreements and the suggestion that an agreement is not an agreement in parts if the categories are so interwoven that they cannot be separated without affecting the nature of the agreement as a whole. The court was inclined to the view that the word 'part' includes, but is not restricted to, a facility that is different as to some of its terms from another facility granted under the same agreement or one that can stand on its own as a separate contract or bargain. However, the court was prepared to give 'part' a wider meaning so as to include a facility provided under an agreement by which it could be operated independently of another facility under the same agreement. In other words, it would suffice for an agreement to be in parts for its terms to differ as between the different parts or for a part to be capable of operating as a free-standing agreement, even if it does not in fact do so under the terms of the agreement. In relation to the agreement before it, the court came to the conclusion that the agreement needed to be construed as a whole, without distinguishing the purpose or terms of one loan from those of another.

In the Court of Appeal in *Southern Pacific Mortgage Ltd v Heath*,[6] Lloyd LJ stated: 'The starting point is that it is from the terms of the agreement that one must find out whether the agreement is one under which there are two or more parts, in different categories, or whether it, or part of it, falls into two or more categories. It is not correct to start from the proposition that more than one disparate category is concerned, and to conclude from this that the agreement must fall into two or more parts'. With respect, this is an oversimplification and would permit the distinction drawn by s 18 of the Act between different categories of agreement to be wholly overridden by the simple device of drafting the agreement in such a way as to ignore any distinction between categories of credit. That would undermine the very purpose of the provision.

Yates & Lorenzelli v Nemo Personal Finance[7] concerned a loan agreement which consolidated existing debts and, in addition, financed a payment protection insurance premium and a broker's fee. The Manchester County Court found that the PPI element was a separate part of the agreement, the agreement being for two specific purposes which were different and that, under s 18, it was a multiple agreement in parts. With respect, this reasoning was rightly rejected by Recorder Yip QC in the Manchester County Court in the case of *Plevin v Paragon Personal Finance Limited and LL Processing (UK) Limited (In Liquidation)*,[8] where she stated:[9]

'I have weighed the factors advanced on each side in the balance. To do so it is necessary to go to the terms of the agreement itself. The terms treat the loan being advanced as a single loan with a single interest rate and single monthly repayments, and on one single set of terms. The principal loan is over the limit for a regulated agreement. It is not the case that two separate sums both falling within the limit are being separated out in order to avoid the provisions for regulated agreements. The PPI loan could not and would not exist in isolation from the main loan. It was taken out as an adjunct to the principal loan. Without the principal loan, the PPI loan would not exist. As against those points, there are said to be different legal consequences and different legal rights created between the creditor and debtor when the two loans are compared. In particular, the PPI element and the loan for it can be terminated on notice whereas the main loan cannot. I have considered the reasoning of HHJ Platts in the case of *Yates* to which I have already referred in which he found that the PPI element was a separate agreement and as such was a regulated agreement. Nevertheless, my analysis in this case differs. Although I agree that the PPI loan was separate in that the main loan could have been taken without it and to that extent the PPI was "separate and additional", the same argument does not work in reverse for the reasons articulated by Mr Wilson. Without the main loan, the PPI loan would not have existed. It could not stand alone. In my judgment, once the offer of PPI was accepted by the Claimant, it was subsumed into the main loan, becoming part of it. The capital advanced for the PPI was amalgamated with the capital for the main loan and interest was charged and repayments taken on the basis of the total sum. The fact that the loan comprised a restricted-use and unrestricted use element did not of itself place the Agreement within section 18(2) of the Act. Certainly, the agreement as a whole falls within more than one category but that does not make it an agreement that is to be dissected into different parts. I adopt the reasoning set out by Professor Goode at paragraph 25.107 and helpfully set out for me at paragraph 57 of Mr Wilson's Skeleton Argument. I will not repeat the passage here but having considered it carefully I accept the submissions made at paragraph 58 of Mr Wilson's Skeleton Argument. I also accept Mr Wilson's arguments that the fundamental purpose of section 18 is anti-avoidance and that avoidance of the regulations did not lie behind the treatment of the principle loan and the PPI loan as one agreement.'

Where an agreement is in parts, s 18(2) treats each part as a separate agreement in the relevant category in question, so that each part must comply with the requirements of CCA 1974 and, of course, the regulations under the Act. The particulars common to each part need not be set out more than once. Where the agreements are of a completely different type, such as a credit and hire agreement, they cannot be combined as parts within one agreement and must, of necessity, be set out in separate agreements.

The Agreements Regulations[10] contain some interesting glosses on the subject of multiple agreements, including in relation to the heading to the agreement and the statements of protection and remedies available under CCA 1974. They also make provision for a form of agreement which embodies an agreement of which at least one part is a credit agreement not regulated by the Act.

In one respect the Agreements Regulations expressly countenance and accommodate a multiple agreement. This is where a document embodies a debtor-creditor-supplier agreement or a debtor-creditor agreement and also contains the option of a debtor-creditor-supplier agreement to finance a premium under a contract for payment protection insurance (i.e. covering one or more of accident, sickness, unemployment or death) or a contract of shortfall insurance or a contract relating to the guarantee of goods.[11]

1 CCA 1974, s 18(1)(b).
2 SI 1983/1553 and SI 2010/1014.
3 SI 2007/1167.
4 [1999] GCCR 2071, at 2078.
5 [2000] GCCR 2381, CA.
6 [2009] GCCR 9051, [2009] EWCA Civ 1135, at para 41.
7 [2010] GCCR 10351.
8 [2012] GCCR 11469.
9 Ibid., para 38.
10 Loc. cit.
11 SI 1983/1553, reg 2(8); SI 2010/1014, reg 3(6).

7.2 MULTIPLE AGREEMENTS IN PRACTICE

Having regard to the complications and complexities to which a multiple agreement gives rise, one is justified in asking why creditors and owners do not take measures to avoid them. The answer, of course, lies in the practical necessity of combining categories of agreement in a single unitary agreement or parts of an agreement in a single document. The draftsman sometimes has the choice of drafting an agreement which comprises more than one category, as an agreement in parts, setting out the distinctive particulars applying to each part, or as a single unitary agreement, without distinguishing the 'parts'. By way of example of the latter, a credit agreement combining restricted-use credit and unrestricted-use credit might be drafted in this manner. This is commonly the case with credit card agreements which combine the facilities of purchases, cash advances and balance transfers.

Where different provisions apply to different credit amounts or different credit uses, the agreement must, of necessity, take the form of an agreement in parts. The general type of revolving credit or credit card agreement will give rise to an agreement in parts if different interest rates (and APRs) apply to one or more of cash advances, balance transfers and transactions (purchases of goods and services). This is not always recognised, especially as regards a statement of the credit limit. Reliance appears to be placed upon an implied term that the credit limit is reduced in relation to certain facilities to the extent that the credit has been utilised in relation to other facilities. Payments and outstanding balances in respect of such agreements should be appropriately apportioned. Where a payment is insufficient to discharge the total sum due in respect of all the parts, the borrower has the right of appropriation. This right was originally contained in CCA 1974 and inexplicably removed from primary legislation to be restated as a rule in the FCA Handbook CONC sourcebook, where it reads:[1]

'(1) Where a firm is entitled to payments from the same customer in respect of two or more regulated agreements, the firm must allow the customer, on making any payment in respect of those agreements which is not sufficient to discharge the total amount then due under all the agreements, to appropriate the sum paid by him:

(a) in or towards the satisfaction of the sum due under any one of the agreements; or

(b) in or towards the satisfaction of the sums due under any two or more of the agreements in such proportions as the customer thinks fit.

(2) If the customer fails to make any such appropriation where one or more of the agreements is:

(a) a hire-purchase agreement or conditional sale agreement; or

(b) a consumer hire agreement; or

(c) an agreement in relation to which any security is provided;

the firm must appropriate the payment towards satisfaction of the sums due under the agreements in the proportions which those sums bear to one another.'

The provisions in the Agreements Regulations[2] which expressly recognise and provide for multiple agreements by combining 'the principal agreement' and 'the subsidiary agreement' in one form of credit agreement, have largely been rendered nugatory by the Competition Commission prohibiting the sale of payment protection insurance at the point of sale of credit facilities.[3]

In the case of mortgages, including all-monies mortgages, the mortgagee must take care to ensure that further advances, other than the original, are treated appropriately. Thus, assuming the mortgage is not a regulated mortgage agreement but a mortgage governed by the CCA regime, it may be the case that the original agreement secured by land mortgage is a regulated credit agreement and a subsequent further advance by the mortgagee is a separate regulated credit agreement in its own right. Some regulated agreements secured by a land mortgage permit the borrower to draw down loan amounts from time to time. If the agreement constitutes a single bargain on uniform terms it can take the form of a unitary agreement which may or may not be a multiple agreement. If what is offered is a single facility on a single set of terms, the fact that the facility may be used for different purposes in different categories, e.g. unrestricted-use and restricted-use credit for debtor-creditor credit and debtor-creditor-supplier credit, does not change the unitary character of the agreement. The position would be otherwise were the agreement to contain separate sets of terms for the different categories of agreement.

It may sometimes necessary to have regard to commercial considerations in deciding whether an agreement is a sham and has been artificially constructed so as to avoid the consequences of the law or whether in fact it truly reflects the true transaction of the parties. One example where this might arise is in the area of conditional sale and hire-purchase agreements. The Act confers certain rights on the hirer or buyer under such agreements, namely protection in relation to the goods once one-third or more of the total price of the goods has been paid and limits the liability of the customer under such agreements should the customer terminate the agreement.[4] Certain items, such as motor car insurance, do not lend themselves to being sold on hire-purchase or conditional sale terms and the question then arises as to whether they can be combined with a motor vehicle sold on hire-purchase or conditional sale terms.

This was the subject of *Mutual Finance v Davidson (No 2)*[5] where the hire-purchase agreement was drafted outside the then Hire-Purchase Acts of 1938 and 1954 and the hire-purchase agreement showed a single cash price relating to the motor vehicle and the motor vehicle insurance premium. The Court of Appeal held that the insurance premium was a legitimate component of the price and constituted part of the added value of the car. In other words, the buyer had agreed to purchase an insured vehicle under the hire-purchase agreement. The insurance premium was held to be a genuine part of the hire-purchase price of the vehicle which was worth more to the hirer by virtue of the insurance and there was nothing unnatural in the price increase. Another example mentioned by the court was a 'CIF' sale of goods contract where the price is expressed as a single sum although it covers the three elements of cost, insurance and freight. On the basis of such reasoning, a lump sum cash price for a three-year warranty and repair contract for the vehicle could likewise be included in the hire-purchase price of the vehicle. In contrast, a three-year warranty and repair contract payable by instalments would not be capable of being so combined.

Another example where market practice would countenance a combination of elements is a full repairing hire agreement under which the owner undertakes to effect repairs during the period of the agreement. The owner's undertaking to repair is an obligation assumed by it under the agreement. It would not be correct to isolate the hire element from the covenant to repair and appropriate payments to each, unless the agreement itself does so.

An unpleasant surprise may await the draftsman of an agreement which the parties, or at least the party proposing it, construed as an agreement of one kind but is subsequently found to be a combination of agreements of different kinds. Such was the case in *Dimond v Lovell*.[6] The court found the agreement to be a 'credit hire agreement' as it combined both a hire agreement and a credit agreement in circumstances where the lessor allowed the hirer credit on the hire charges until such time as a claim for damages had been concluded in relation to a vehicle involved in a road traffic accident. The Court of Appeal held that the hire agreement was also a consumer credit agreement since it provided for deferment of payment of the hire charges for a period extending beyond the end of the hire. As the agreement was not properly executed as a regulated consumer credit agreement, it was an improperly executed agreement under s 61(1) of CCA 1974 and accordingly unenforceable under s 127(3) of the Act, which has since been repealed. The decision was upheld by the House of Lords where Lord Hoffmann stated:[7]

> 'Finally on this issue I should mention that it was submitted to the Court of Appeal that a contract for the bailment of goods to a hirer (such as the bailment of the car to Mrs Dimond) could not be a consumer credit agreement. It was either a consumer hire agreement if it satisfied the requirements of s 15(1) of the Act or it was altogether unregulated. The argument, based upon a passage by Professor Goode (Consumer Credit Legislation 1999 Vol 1, para 456.5, pp 215–215), was rejected by the Court of Appeal ... and not pursued before your Lordships.'

Interestingly, this comment appears in the learned Lord's speech after he indicated that he experienced difficulty with the analysis of a multiple agreement in parts, saying:

> 'The difficulty I have with this argument is that it seems to sever the provisions that create the debt (hiring the car) from the provisions that allow credit for payment of the debt. Whatever a multiple agreement may be, one cannot divide up a contract in that way. The creation of the debt and the terms in which it is payable must form parts of the same agreement.'

With respect, this is how CCA 1974 might have dealt with multiple agreements, but does not. The court having found that the agreement involved both hire and credit, CCA 1974 does create a bifurcation between the two. Had the court found (which it did not) that only a hiring was involved, with a postponement of the event for payment of the hire rental, the above dictum would have correctly reflected the situation.

As the categories of credit and hire are disparate categories, one way of drafting this agreement within the original framework, was by way of two agreements, a hire agreement and a credit agreement, each complying with the requirements applying to that agreement. An alternative approach would be to extend the period of hire until such time as the claim for damages had been concluded but provide that the hirer may pay such hire charges and end the hire agreement at any earlier time, thereby avoiding the deferment of payment and any notion of credit arising. Another approach is to ensure that the credit aspect falls within the framework of an exempt credit agreement.

1 CONC 6.4.2R, previously contained in s 81(1) and (2) of CCA 1974.
2 SI 1983/1553, reg 2(8); SI 2010/1014, reg 3(6).
3 Order of 24 March 2011 which came into effect in April 2012.
4 CCA 1974, ss 99 and 100.
5 [1963] 1 WLR 134, [1963] 1 All ER 133, [1999] GCCR 163, CA.
6 [2001] GCCR 2303.
7 [2001] GCCR 2751, at 2761.

7.3   MODIFYING AGREEMENT

Another strange creature of statute is the modifying agreement, created by CCA 1974, s 82. This is an agreement which varies or supplements an earlier agreement, not necessarily a regulated agreement. The modifying agreement is treated as revoking the earlier agreement and containing provisions reproducing the combined effect of the two agreements.[1] If, therefore, the new modified agreement fails for any reason, as it has revoked the earlier agreement, both agreements fail. Likewise, if the earlier agreement was supported by a guarantee, as the modifying agreement revokes the earlier agreement, the guarantee is likewise ended. Obligations outstanding in relation to the earlier agreement are treated as outstanding instead in relation to the modifying agreement.[2]

If the earlier agreement is a regulated agreement but the modifying agreement is not then, unless the modifying agreement is for running-account credit or an exempt agreement, the modifying agreement is treated as a regulated agreement.[3] Originally this provision was mainly of relevance to the situation where the modifying agreement exceeded the financial limit, latterly £25,000, which then applied to a regulated agreement. Since the abolition of the financial limit, it appears that the likely relevance of this provision is where the modifying agreement would, but for this provision, have been an exempt agreement.

Earlier exempt agreements are excepted from the provisions relating to modifying agreements.[4] The proviso relating to a modifying agreement for running-account credit is of no real significance as it does not add to what the CCA 1974 otherwise provides in s 82(4) read with s 10(2). Moreover, it would not be possible for a modifying agreement, which is a running-account credit agreement, to vary a fixed-sum credit agreement.

The provisions relating to modifying agreements are not triggered if, as a result of the debtor's earlier discharge of part of his indebtedness under the earlier agreement, the modifying agreement varies the amount of the repayment to be made under the earlier agreement or the duration of the agreement.[5]

A modifying agreement is not a cancellable agreement unless it is entered into within the cooling-off period of an earlier cancellable agreement.[6] It follows that even if the modifying agreement is entered into in circumstances where ordinarily a regulated agreement would be cancellable, the modifying agreement is not cancellable. A modifying agreement which is an exempt agreement is not a cancellable agreement even if it is entered into within the cooling-off period of an earlier cancellable agreement.[7]

If the modifying agreement is entered into within the withdrawal period of the earlier agreement, the modifying agreement is itself subject to the debtor's right of withdrawal under s 66A, but is otherwise not subject to the right of withdrawal.[8]

A modifying agreement which varies or supplements an agreement which is secured on land, must itself comply with the advance copy procedure of CCA 1974, s 58.

Where it is possible to enter into a fresh regulated agreement, modifying agreements are best avoided as they involve the unique consequence of revoking the original agreement, which could have unexpected and unwanted consequences from the point of view of the creditor or owner. In practice, confusion might also be caused by the presumption that obligations outstanding in relation to the earlier agreement are treated as outstanding in relation to the modifying agreement.[9]

The various consequences of entering into a modifying agreement which are set out in s 82(2) are qualified by the words 'for the purposes of the Act' so that, it would appear, the order of priority of mortgages, i.e. a regulated loan secured by a mortgage, would not be affected by the subsequent modification of that agreement. Hence, in circumstances where a regulated agreement (not constituting a regulated mortgage contract under the FCA regime) was secured by a first mortgage on land and the borrower entered into subsequent mortgages with other mortgagees, the variation of the terms of the original regulated agreement by the modifying agreement would not affect the priority of the original mortgage, which will retain its status as a first charge on the property. However, it appears that the situation is different in relation to guarantees and indemnities so that a guarantee or indemnity given in respect of a regulated agreement where the agreement is subsequently varied by a modifying agreement will be extinguished by the modifying agreement, which will have revoked the earlier agreement, unless the guarantee or indemnity was expressed to extend to the regulated agreement as modified by any subsequent agreement.

Additional complications might arise where a regulated agreement is varied by successive modifying agreements.

The notion of the revocation of the original agreement and its substitution, as it were, by the modifying agreement might serve indirectly to extend the time before which goods under a hire-purchase or conditional sale agreement become protected goods under CCA 1974, s 90 and increase the liability of the hirer or debtor respectively under such an agreement for payment of at least one-half of the total price under s 100. This would not be the case, however, if the goods had become protected goods or the hirer had already paid half of the total price before the modifying agreement was entered into. A further consequence is the extension of the limitation period in respect of any claims which might be brought by the customer against a creditor under a credit agreement or a lessor under a hire agreement where the agreement has been modified by a modifying agreement. Finally, a modifying agreement might have the unintended result of the modified agreement being a multiple agreement and, indeed, a multiple agreement in parts.

It is to be noted that CCA 1974, s 189 no longer defines an 'exempt agreement', but that it is now defined in s 82(8) for the purposes of s 82. An exempt agreement is an agreement which is a regulated mortgage contract, a regulated home purchase plan or an agreement relating to the purchase of land for non-residential purposes, as described in SI 2001/544 ('RAO'), arts 60C(2) and 60D respectively.

1 CCA 1974, s 82(2).
2 Ibid., s 82(2).
3 Ibid., s 82(3).
4 Ibid., ss 82(2A), (3)(b) and (5A) inserted by the Financial Services and Markets Act 2000 (Consequential Amendments) Order 2005, SI 2005/2967, and the Financial Services and Markets Act 2000 (Consequential Amendments) Order 2008, SI 2008/733.
5 Ibid., s 82(2B).
6 Ibid., s 82(5) and (6).
7 Ibid., s 82(5A).
8 Ibid., s 82(6A) and (6B).
9 Ibid., s 82(2).

7.4   MODIFYING AGREEMENTS IN PRACTICE

Although it is suggested above that modifying agreements should be avoided, there are circumstances where their utilisation is practical, and sometimes unavoidable. Modifying agreements might be used for rescheduling payments, extending the term of an agreement, replacing or upgrading equipment, providing for a further advance and inserting additional agreement provisions. The Agreements Regulations themselves envisage circumstances in which modifying agreements might be used.[1] Thus, they provide directly, or indirectly in the case of the Agreements Regulations 2010, for a modifying agreement of a credit agreement where:[2]

(a)   goods, services, land or other things, specified in the earlier agreement, are varied or supplemented or where the cash price of the same is varied;

(b)   the advance payment to be made under the earlier agreement is modified;

(c)   the charge included in the total charge for credit or the credit amount in the case of a fixed-sum credit agreement is varied or supplemented;

(d)   the credit limit under an earlier agreement for running-account credit is varied;

(e)   the repayment provisions of an earlier agreement are varied;

(f)   any provision for security provided by the debtor in relation to an earlier agreement is varied or additional security is provided; and

(g)   any charges on default are varied.

The Agreements Regulations envisage the following circumstances where a modifying agreement might vary a hire agreement:[3]

(a)   where goods to be hired under an earlier agreement are varied or supplemented;

(b)   where any provision of an earlier agreement relating to an advance, hire or other payment is varied;

(c) where any of the provisions of the earlier agreement relating to hire or repayments are varied or supplemented;

(d) where the hire period is varied;

(e) where security provided by the hirer under the earlier agreement is varied; and

(f) where the default charges are varied.

A further advance in relation to a mortgage may give rise to a modifying agreement. For example, a further advance under an existing credit agreement which varies that agreement because it is not within the original facility and requires to be agreed between the debtor and creditor may give rise to a modifying agreement within CCA 1974, s 82(2).

The Financial Services and Markets Act 2000 (Consequential Amendments) Order 2005[4] introduced CCA 1974, s 82(2A) and s 82(5A) which exempt regulated mortgage contracts and regulated home purchase plans from s 82 of CCA 1974 from the provisions applying to modifying agreements under s 82(2) and s 82(5), but not variations under s 82(1), of the Act. Thus the variation of a regulated agreement under a power of variation under that earlier agreement could potentially be governed by both CCA 1974 and the Financial Services and Markets Act 2000.

The removal of the financial limit on consumer credit agreements has no effect where an agreement varies or supplements an agreement made before 6 April 2008 for credit exceeding £25,000 and either does not itself provide for further credit or is an exempt agreement under CCA 1974.[5]

1 SI 1983/1553, reg 7; SI 2010/1014, reg 5.
2 SI 1983/1553, Sch 8, Part I; SI 2010/1014, reg 5(1).
3 SI 1983/1553, Sch 8, Part II.
4 SI 2005/2967.
5 SI 2008/831, art 4.

7.5 NOVATION

A contract is novated where another party is substituted for one of the original parties to the agreement, so that all rights and duties of one party to the agreement are assumed by another. In other words, novation takes place where two contracting parties agree that a third, who also agrees, shall stand in the relation of either of them to the other. A new agreement comes into existence which requires the consent of all parties to it. It is the necessity for consent that distinguishes novation from assignment.[1]

For purposes of the consumer credit regime, it is important to recognise that a modifying agreement cannot be used to effect the novation of an agreement. For example, the transfer of equity in a property securing a regulated loan agreement, say from two spouses to only one of them, unless effected by means of the release of one of the parties, involves a change of parties to the agreement and cannot be dealt with by way of a modifying agreement. Likewise, if parties to an agreement agree to the substitution of new goods for the original goods under the agreement, not by way of remedy of defective goods or their replacement under an insurance policy as a result of any insurable risk having arisen, this must be dealt with by way of a new agreement. It cannot be effected by means of a modifying agreement as the subject matter of the original agreement will no longer be in existence.[2] However, the corollary is equally relevant. If the Agreements Regulations envisage the relevance and application of a modifying agreement in particular circumstances, then prima facie the modification is not tantamount to a novation.[3]

1 See *Chitty on Contracts: General Principles of Contract* (32nd edn, Sweet & Maxwell, 2015) at 19.087.
2 See the discussion in *Goode: Consumer Credit Law and Practice* (LexisNexis Butterworths), at para 1C [35.12].
3 See SI 1983/1553, reg 7.

7.6   VARIATION

It is always possible at common law to vary agreements. Not unexpectedly, the possibility of varying a regulated agreement is also recognised by CCA 1974. Section 82 provides that where, under a power contained in a regulated agreement, the creditor or owner varies the agreement, the variation shall not take effect before notice of it is given to the debtor or hirer in the prescribed manner.[1] However, this restriction does not apply to the variation of a range of interest rates and other charges under agreements specified in s 82(1A) to (1E). Regard should be had to the duty to give information to a debtor on a change of interest rate in accordance with s 78A.

The variation envisaged by s 82 is a unilateral variation, one which does not require the agreement of the parties, and which it is possible to effect unilaterally.

The mode of variation is governed by regulations made under CCA 1974.[2] These require notice of the variation of any regulated agreement to set out particulars of the variation and to be served on the debtor or hirer before the variation takes effect. Prior to 1 February 2010 at least seven days' prior notice had to be given of any variation.[3] However, there is provision for an exceptional mode of service of notice where the variation is of the rate of interest payable under a regulated consumer credit agreement secured on land, and the amount of the payments of interest charged under the agreement is determined, both before and after the variation takes effect, by reference to the amount of the balance outstanding established as at daily intervals. Basically this would apply to running-account credit agreements. Where those conditions exist, not less than seven days' prior notice of variation may be given by publication in at least three national daily newspapers or, if it is not reasonably practicable so to publish, in the London Gazette or other appropriate gazette. In each such case, if reasonably practicable so to do, the notice of variation must also be prominently displayed at premises open to the public where the agreement to which the variation relates is maintained.[4]

In the case of a regulated credit agreement under the Agreements Regulations 1983 but not under the Agreements Regulations 2010, where the rate or amount of any item included in the total charge for credit may be varied, the agreement must state the circumstances in which the variation may occur and the time at which it may occur.[5] The Regulations do not restrict the creditor's power to vary and the requirements are satisfied by a statement that the rate is subject to variation by the creditor from time to time.[6]

Part 2 of, and Schedule 2 to, the Consumer Rights Act 2015 substantially limit the unilateral right of a creditor under a credit agreement, and an owner under a hire agreement, to vary the agreement. Prima facie a term which has the object or effect of enabling a trader (including a creditor or owner) to alter the terms of the contract unilaterally without a valid reason which is specified in the contract, may be regarded as unfair.[7] An exception is made in relation to a contract by which the supplier of financial services reserves the right to alter the rate of interest or the amount of other charges payable by the consumer, without notice, where there is a valid reason, provided that the supplier is required to inform the consumer at the earliest opportunity and the latter is free to dissolve the contract immediately.[8] A further exception, to cancellation without reasonable notice, is where the supplier of financial services reserves the right to alter unilaterally the conditions of a contract of indeterminate duration, provided that he is required to inform the consumer with reasonable notice and the consumer is free to dissolve the contract.[9]

It is common for agreements to contain widely expressed variation clauses permitting the creditor or owner to vary the agreement in a host of specified, or indeed unspecified, circumstances. It will sometimes be open to question whether or not such power, or the exercise of such power, extends beyond the creditor's or owner's rights under the agreement or constitutes an unfair contract term. As noted above, the unilateral power of variation is subject to various legal limitations. It will often equally be open to question whether the purported variation in fact amounts to a new agreement or a modifying agreement. This will be the case where the variation is dependent upon the agreement of both parties and involves a consideration passing from the promisee to the promisor.

Frequently in the case of credit card accounts, the creditor will issue an entirely new set of terms and conditions. Regardless of whether the terms are capable of variation, this requires the creditor to set out the particulars of the variation and would normally take the form of a notice setting out the variations accompanied by a set of the new terms. Whilst the relevant regulations only require prior notice, if the creditor is a subscriber to the FLA Lending Code, it must give its customers at least 30 days' notice before increasing the credit limit or the interest rate, with the right for the customer to reject the same and, in the case of an increased interest rate, to close the account. Subscribers to the Code include banks, building societies and finance sections of traders.

No variation of an agreement is involved in circumstances where the event is referable to an ascertainable yardstick which operates independently of the agreement. An example is an agreement with interest at 2% above the Bank of England Base Rate from time to time in force. No notice of variation in respect of the altered interest rate need be given under CCA 1974 although notice may still be required under one or other Code of Practice or governing set of Guidelines which applies to the loan. The altered interest rate will in any event be notified to the borrower (albeit retrospectively) in statements issued by the creditor in respect of the agreement.

Variation of an agreement is to be distinguished from the grant of a concession, indulgence or waiver by the creditor or owner to, or in respect of, the other party to the agreement. This amounts to the unilateral withholding by one party of its entitlement to enforce the agreement or any of its rights under the agreement, without entering into a contract with, or receiving consideration for so doing from, the other party. A concession or indulgence might be granted in order to alleviate hardship which the other party to the contract would otherwise suffer. The party granting the concession or indulgence would usually reserve the right strictly to enforce the terms of the agreement at any future time. In order to avoid a dispute that the concession amounted to a contractual variation of the agreement, it should be granted without consideration in return for the concession and its terms recorded in writing.

1 CCA 1974, s 82(1).
2 Consumer Credit (Notice of Variation of Agreements) Regulations 1977, SI 1977/328. See especially reg 2.
3 Amendment effected by SI 2010/1010, reg 48.
4 SI 1977/328, reg 3.
5 Consumer Credit (Agreements) Regulations 1983, SI 1983/1553, Sch 1, para 19.
6 *Lombard Tricity Finance Ltd v Paton* [1989] 1 All ER 918, CA.
7 CRA 2015, s 63 read with Sch 2, Part 1, para 11.
8 Ibid., Sch 2, Part 2, para 22.
9 Ibid., para 23.

7.7 ASSIGNMENT

The assignability of a regulated agreement is the subject of debate. CCA 1974 defines 'creditor' as the person providing credit under a consumer credit agreement or the person to whom his rights and duties under the agreement have passed by assignment or operation of law.[1] 'Owner', 'debtor' and 'hirer' likewise include the persons to whom their respective rights and duties under the agreement have passed by assignment or operation of law. The inclusion of the phrase 'and duties' in the definition has caused some controversy. Professor Goode has described it as a drafting error since, as a matter of contract law, an assignment transfers rights but does not relieve the assignor of his duties to the contracting party. The draftsman of the Act recognises this criticism and maintains that, notwithstanding any assignment, the original creditor should continue to be treated as such until such time, if any, as his duties pass by operation of law to a person who also possesses the rights. Professor Guest, on the other hand, suggests that the meaning of 'creditor' depends upon the policy underlying the particular provision of the Act. In his view, the creditor's or owner's statutory duties to the debtor or hirer respectively will pass by assignment provided that the debtor or hirer receives notice of the assignment.[2] It is submitted that Parliament may have intended to extend the meaning of 'creditor' to include persons to whom the creditor's statutory duties (in addition to rights) have passed, if only to prevent the assignee evading duties imposed upon the creditor under the Act and in order to facilitate assignments. Clearly, if the agreement does not permit assignment, this restriction would override any interpretation to the contrary which might be suggested by the Act.

The various interpretations of the definition of 'creditor' were considered by Hamblen J in *Jones v Link Financial Ltd*,[3] citing Goode, Guest and the writer's submission above. Essentially accepting Guest's analysis, the court held that the legal (as opposed to the equitable) assignee stands in the shoes of the assignor, adding: 'The enforcement of the assignor's rights under the regulated credit agreement was subject to performance of the statutory duties laid down in the 1974 Act, and the legal assignee's rights are similarly so subject'.

In *Santander UK Plc v Harrison & Harrison*,[4] Males J referred to the above case and stated *obiter*:

> '... I should not be taken to accept the borrowers' submission that in the case of a legal assignment only the assignee can serve the default notice required under section 87 of the Act. I would accept, in respectful agreement with the analysis of Hamblen J in *Jones v Link Financial Ltd* [2012] EWHC 2402 (QB), that when notice of a legal assignment has been given, it is the assignee to whom the debtor is thenceforth liable for the debt and that the assignee can only enforce the debt if the applicable statutory duties laid down in the Act have been per-formed. However, I would at least wish to leave open whether such an assignee would be able to rely on notices served or information provided by the assignor. Moreover, in a case such as the present (but unlike *Jones v Link Financial Ltd*) where it is the assignor who remains entitled to enforce the mortgage as the legal holder of the registered charge, there would appear to be every reason why the assignor should also be the person to serve any default notice.'

The writer submits that the definitions of 'debtor' and 'hirer' and amendments of CCA 1974, inserted by the Consumer Credit Act 2006, underline the unique application of the Act to assignments of consumer credit agreements and con-sumer hire agreements. The following should be noted in this regard:

(a) 'Debtor' and 'hirer' are defined to so as include 'the person to whom his rights and duties under the agreement have passed by assignment or opera-tion of law'.[5]

(b) 'Consumer credit business' means any business carried on by a person so far as it comprises or relates to the provision of credit by him, or oth-erwise his being a creditor under regulated consumer credit agreements. 'Consumer hire business' means any business being carried on by a person so far as it comprises or relates to the hiring of goods by him or otherwise his being an owner under regulated consumer hire agreements.[6] 'Creditor' or 'owner' have the meanings referred to above and include their respective assigns.

(c) With regard to unfair relationships, references to 'creditor' or 'debtor' include references to the person to whom his (i.e. the creditor's or debtor's) rights and duties under the agreement have passed by assignment or opera-tion of law.[7]

(d) An assignee must be authorised in circumstances where the creditor, owner or provider of an ancillary credit business is required to be authorised. It is submitted that a legal assignee will therefore not be required to be author-ised for the purposes of debt-adjusting, debt-counselling or debt-collecting in relation to a debt arising under the assigned agreement.[8]

(e) Obligations of the creditor, unless carried out by the creditor as assignor, must be carried out by the assignee. This applies, for example, to the duty to issue statements[9] and statutory notices of sums in arrears, notices of default sums and default notices.[10] The debtor/hirer is entitled to plead against an assignee any defences available against the creditor/owner.

What is striking is the reiteration of the phrase, 'the person to whom his rights and duties under the agreement have passed by assignment or operation of law', even in relation to the debtor's rights and duties, when the latter clearly cannot be transferred without the creditor's consent. This reinforces the writer's above submission that the various references to 'duties' is to statutory duties which are collateral to the exercise of the creditor's or owner's 'rights'.

The formalities relating to the notice of assignment are now governed by CONC and are as follows:[11]

'(1) Where rights of a lender under a regulated credit agreement are assigned to a firm, that firm must arrange for notice of the assignment to be given to the customer:

(a)   as soon as reasonably possible; or

(b)   if, after the assignment, the arrangements for servicing the credit under the agreement do not change as far as the customer is concerned, on or before the first occasion they do.

(2) Paragraph (1) does not apply to an agreement secured on land.

(3) A firm may assign the rights of a lender under a regulated credit agreement to a third party only if:

(a)   the third party is a firm; or

(b)   where the third party does not require authorisation, the firm has an agreement with the third party which requires the third party to arrange for a notice of assignment in accordance with (1).'

1 CCA 1974, s 189(1).
2 *Goode: Consumer Credit Law and Practice* (LexisNexis Butterworths), para I23.31; Bennion, *Consumer Credit Control* (Sweet & Maxwell), para 1-920; Guest, *Encyclopaedia of Consumer Credit Law*, para 2–190.
3 [2012] GCCR 11413, [2012] EWHC 2402 (QB) at paras 29 to 31.
4 [2013] GCCR 11700, [2013] EWHC 199 (QB) at para [47].
5 CCA 1974, s 189(1).
6 Ibid., s 189(1).
7 Ibid., s 189(1).
8 See FSMA, Part 4A.
9 See CCA 1974, ss 77A, 77B and 78.
10 Ibid., ss 86B to 87.
11 CONC 6.5.2R.

Chapter 8

The regulated agreement, pre-contract information and disclosure

8.1 BACKGROUND

8.1.1 FCA Handbook: the Consumer Credit Sourcebook (CONC)

CONC amply provides for mandatory pre-contractual information to be given to debtors and hirers in place of the repealed provisions of CCA 1974, section 55A. The extensive subject matter is covered by CONC Rules under the following heads:

- CONC 4.1 Content of quotations;

- CONC 4.2 Pre-contract disclosure and adequate explanations;

- CONC 4.3 Pre-contractual requirements and adequate explanations: P2P agreements;

- CONC 4.4 Pre-contractual requirements: credit brokers;

- CONC 4.5 Commissions;

- CONC 4.6 Pre-contract disclosure: continuous payment authorities;

- CONC 4.7 Information to be provided on entering a current account agreement; and

- CONC 4.8 Pre-contract: unfair business practices: consumer credit lending.

8.1.2 Consumer credit legislation

It is easy to lose sight of the wood for the trees when first considering the content of a regulated agreement by overlooking the fact that the regulated aspects are merely the overlay to the underlying consumer transaction. This is understandable, having regard to the very detailed and prescriptive approach of the legislature to the content and form of the face, or front, of a regulated agreement.

The original legislative approach, especially to the form of pre-contract information, may in fact have been misconceived. The White Paper entitled 'The Consumer Credit Market in the 21st Century' states:[1]

> 'Although the existing legislative provisions require credit agreements to be documented in a prescribed format, there remains confusion among consumers about the information they receive from lenders, due to a lack of clarity. Research indicates that 39% of borrowers only read the main information on the front page of a credit agreement before signing, and are therefore unaware of clauses that may be to their detriment.'

The White Paper continues:[2]

> 'One of the reasons consumers do not read their credit agreements in detail is due to the way in which the information is presented, and the terminology used. The Government intends to revise the format of agreements to make them clearer and more transparent. This will include a requirement to state key financial particulars in addition to [the following] key information ... This is in response to our finding that 81% of borrowers said that they would welcome more information on their rights.
>
> In addition, the key financial information will be required to be presented together as a whole and with appropriate prominence ...'

This criticism is alleviated today by virtue of the pre-contract requirements of CONC and the Consumer Credit (Agreements) Regulations 2010, which implemented Directive 2008/48/EC,[3] as well as the unfair contract terms provisions and requirement for transparency in the Consumer Rights Act 2015, although based on pre-existing UK legislation.

It is to be noted that the above Directive and Agreements Regulations 2010 only apply to consumer credit agreements, so that consumer hire agreements remain subject to the Consumer Credit (Agreements) Regulations 1983.

There was originally no requirement to give the debtor or hirer prescribed pre-contract information. This was changed by the Consumer Credit (Disclosure of Information) Regulations 2004[4] which required the supply of truncated pre-contract information, essentially in the form of a copy of the financial and related particulars of the agreement, in respect of consumer credit agreements and consumer hire agreements falling within the scope of those regulations. Subsequently, pursuant to the EU Directive, the Consumer Credit (Disclosure of Information) Regulations 2010,[5] a more comprehensive outline of specific terms of the agreement must be supplied to a proposed debtor under a consumer credit agreement which falls within the scope of the latter regulations. The Regulations of 2004 continue to apply to pre-contract disclosure in respect of consumer hire agreements.

1 DTI, Con 6040, dated December 2003, para 2.18.
2 Ibid., paras 2.25 and 2.27.
3 Directive of the European Parliament and of the Council on credit agreements for consumers.
4 SI 2004/1481.
5 SI 2010/1013.

8.2 ELEMENTS OF A CONTRACT

Before turning to the form and content of a regulated agreement, it is worthwhile setting out the elements of a valid contract. They are the following: first, there must be two or more parties to the contract; second, those parties must be in agreement, i.e. there must be consensus on specific matters (often referred to in the older authorities as 'consensus ad idem'); third, those parties must intend to create legal relations in the sense that the promises by each side must be enforceable contractual promises; fourth, the promise by each party must be supported by consideration or by some other factor which the law considers sufficient.[1]

In the sphere of consumer credit and hire, the subject matter of the agreement must be identifiable and evident from the contractual terms. Thus, whilst the Consumer Credit (Agreements) Regulations 1983 and the Consumer Credit (Agreements) Regulations 2010 require statutory headings and information to be contained in the agreement, it does not necessarily follow that complying with these requirements would result in the setting out of all of the essential terms of the contract. A hire-purchase agreement must incorporate the hirer's option to purchase or to terminate the agreement, a conditional sale agreement implies retention of title until full payment of the purchase price, a credit agreement infers the passing of title at the outset and a hire agreement imports the notion of the hire of goods. If, notwithstanding the heading and contents of the agreement, it does not contain the essential provisions relating to an agreement of that type, no agreement may in fact have come into existence or the agreement may be void, at common law.

1 9(1) *Halsbury's Laws* (4th edn, LexisNexis Butterworths), para 603.

8.3 FORM AND CONTENT OF A REGULATED AGREEMENT

8.3.1 Form and content

The form and content of a regulated agreement are prescribed by CCA 1974, the sets of Agreements Regulations and the Copy Document Regulations.[1] In fact the requirements relating to the form and content of documents embodying regulated agreements are not set out in the Act itself but in regulations made by the Treasury under s 60. Section 61 sets out the minimum requirements in order for a regulated agreement to be 'properly executed'. If the agreement is improperly executed it is enforceable against the debtor or hirer on order of the court only.[2] In arriving at a decision as to whether to grant an enforcement order the court will have regard to its discretionary powers under s 127(1) and (2).

The minimum requirements of a regulated agreement are set out in s 61(1). A regulated agreement is not properly executed unless:

(a) a document in the prescribed form, itself containing all the prescribed terms and conforming to regulations under s 60(1), is signed in the prescribed manner both by the debtor or hirer and by or on behalf of the creditor or owner;

(b)   the document embodies all the terms of the agreement, other than implied terms; and

(c)   the document is, when presented or sent to the debtor or hirer for signature, in a state that all its terms are readily legible.

Additionally, where the agreement is a prospective regulated agreement which is to be secured on land, the agreement is not properly executed unless the requirements of CCA 1974, s 58(1) are adhered to. It is necessary for the debtor or hirer to be given an advance copy of the unexecuted agreement which contains a notice in the prescribed form indicating the right of the debtor or hirer to withdraw from the prospective agreement.

Section 58(1) only applies to a regulated agreement (as defined in s 189(1), by reference to ss 8(3) and 15(2)) and therefore specifically excludes an agreement to acquire property rights in land, or in an existing or projected building, which relates to residential immovable property. In addition, the following are expressly excluded:[3]

(a)   a restricted-use credit agreement to finance the purchase of the mortgaged land, or

(b)   an agreement for a bridging loan in connection with the purchase of the mortgaged land or other land.

These exclusions are based on the need to expedite completion of the contract in question.

If the agreement is a cancellable agreement, it is not properly executed if it does not contain a notice in the prescribed form indicating the right of the debtor or hirer to cancel the agreement, how and when that right is exercisable and the name and address of the person to whom notice of cancellation may be given.[4]

1   Agreements: CCA 1974, ss 60 and 61 and the Consumer Credit (Agreements) Regulations 1983, SI 1983/1533; Copy Agreements: CCA 1974, ss 58 and 64 and the Consumer Credit (Cancellation Notices and Copies of Documents) Regulations 1983, SI 1983/1557.
2   CCA 1974, s 65(1).
3   Ibid., s 58(2).
4   Ibid., s 64(1) and (5). See *Goshawk Dedicated (No 2) Ltd v Governor and Company of Bank of Scotland* [2005] GCCR 5431 (Ch), [2005] EWHC 2906 (Ch) and *Governor and Company of Bank of Scotland v Euclidean (No 1) Ltd* [2007] GCCR 6051, [2007] EWHC 1732 (Comm).

8.3.2   Elements of s 61(1)

We turn next to consider the elements of s 61(1):

(a)   *A document in the prescribed form*: The sets of Agreements Regulations set out the form and content of regulated consumer credit agreements, consumer hire agreements and modifying agreements.

(b)   *Prescribed terms*: These are specified in Schedule 6 to the Consumer Credit (Agreements) Regulations 1983 and in regulation 4(1) of the Consumer Credit (Agreements) Regulations 2010. They were originally the minimum terms which a regulated consumer credit, consumer hire or modifying agreement had to contain if the agreement was not to be regarded as improperly executed, for the purposes of s 61(1)(a).

Agreements entered into before 6 April 2007 were automatically unenforceable if they failed to contain the prescribed terms. This result was held to be compatible with the European Convention on Human Rights as set out in Schedule 1 to the Human Rights Act 1998.[1] However, s 127(3) to (5) has now been repealed in respect of agreements entered into after 6 April 2007,[2] with the result that the prescribed terms have been placed on the same plane as all other information required by s 61(1)(a), as no specific reference to prescribed terms is made in s 127(1) or (2), with the result that the prescribed terms have lost their previous heightened significance.

The current position contrasts strikingly with the legal position prevailing at the time in *Dimond v Lovell*.[3] In that case the hire agreement was for a maximum period of 28 days and, if truly a hire agreement, was outside the purview of the CCA 1974 as it was incapable of subsisting for more than three months. However, as payment of the hire charges was deferred until such time as a claim for damages had been concluded, which time was beyond the conclusion of the hire agreement, the Court of Appeal held that the provision for payment constituted a deferment of that payment, that the letting of the car on hire was the provision of services, that the services had been supplied on credit and that, as the agreement did not contain the prescribed terms of a credit agreement, it was unenforceable. The argument that the deferment did not amount to credit within the meaning of the Act was not put before the House of Lords which therefore restricted itself to the wording of the agreement. In view of references to 'credit facility' and the like, the Court concluded that the agreement was a credit agreement and not a hire agreement. The omission of the prescribed terms of Schedule 6 to the Agreements Regulations 1983 meant that the agreement was unenforceable by virtue of s 127(3).

Following the repeal of s 127(3), in the absence of any special significance attaching to implied terms, a court would need to consider the factors set out in s 127(1) and in s 140A (relating to unfair relationships in cases where the agreement in question is a credit agreement), in deciding whether to grant an enforcement order. It is submitted that the hirer in *Dimond v Lovell* was not prejudiced to any significant extent by the contravention in question and the prevailing practice did not involve any appreciable degree of culpability – the two tests of section 127(1). Nor does it appear that the agreement gave rise to unfair relationships between creditor and debtor, so that it is suggested that the court's finding would be different under the revised law.

A recent example where the court exercised its discretion under s 127(1) and (2) is *Hurstanger Ltd v Wilson*. The court awarded compensation to the debtor rather than rescission, having regard to all the circumstances of the case.[4]

Once a judge has exercised his discretion, the Court of Appeal will not interfere with such discretion unless it can be shown that the trial judge failed to exercise it on the right principles.[5]

The fact that an agreement is not enforceable without an order of the court, does not mean that it does not create liabilities. Thus, in *R v Modupe* the Court of Appeal upheld the appellant's conviction on various charges of false accounting, evasion of liability by deception and theft under the Theft Act 1978, notwithstanding the fact that the agreement was an improperly executed regulated agreement, enforceable against the appellant only on an order of the court. The court opined that the fact that the agreement was not enforceable without an order of the court did not mean that it did not give rise to an existing liability.[6]

(c) *Signed in the prescribed manner by the debtor or hirer and by or on behalf of the creditor or owner*: The debtor or hirer must himself or herself sign the agreement. In *HSBC Bank plc v Brophy*[7] the court held that there was compliance with the requirement that the agreement must be signed, where an application for a credit card agreement was signed by the debtor, followed by signature of the agreement on behalf of the creditor.

The agreement may not be signed by an agent or attorney on behalf of the debtor or hirer, except where the debtor or hirer is a partnership or an unincorporated body of persons, in which case it may be signed by a person by or on behalf of the debtor or hirer.[8] The Consumer Credit (Agreements) Regulations 1983 (but not the Consumer Credit (Agreements) Regulations 2010) prescribe statutory signature boxes for the debtor or hirer. There is no equivalent signature box for the creditor or owner. Significantly, the agreement must be signed by both parties to the agreement, a requirement which is often overlooked in respect of the creditor's signature to running-account credit agreements, with the result that the agreements are not properly executed.

Where an agreement is intended to be concluded by the use of an electronic communication (within the meaning of the Electronic Communications Act 2000), the signature box may contain 'information about the process or means of providing, communicating or verifying the signature to be made by the debtor or hirer'.[9]

(d) *The document embodies all the terms of the agreement other than implied terms*: A document embodies a provision if it is set out either in the document itself or in another document referred to in it.[10]

(e) *The document is, when presented or sent to the debtor or hirer for signature, in a state that all its terms are readily legible*: There is no further amplification of this requirement in CCA 1974. However, the Agreements Regulations and the Copy Document Regulations require the relevant documents to be easily legible and of a colour which is readily distinguishable from the background medium upon which the information is displayed.[11] The Agreements Regulations 1983 also require the lettering of the terms to be of equal prominence, except for headings, trade names and names of parties to the agreement.[12]

There are no prescribed print or font sizes and it appears that 'readily legible' in the Act and 'easily legible' in the Regulations have the same meaning, especially as they are used interchangeably. The Consumer Rights Act 2015 requires the terms of a consumer contract to be transparent, namely expressed in plain and intelligible language and legible.[13]

The reader is also referred to **Chapter 9** on contract terms.

1 See *Wilson v First County Trust Ltd (No 2)* [2003] GCCR 4931, HL.
2 SI 2007/123 (C.6).
3 [1999] 3 All ER 1, [1999] GCCR 2303, CA; affirmed [2000] 2 All ER 897, HL.
4 [2007] GCCR 5951, [2007] EWCA Civ 299.
5 *Nissan Finance UK Ltd v Lockhart* [1999] GCCR 1649, CA.
6 [1999] GCCR 1595, CA.
7 [2011] GCCR 11051, [2011] EWCA Civ 67.
8 CCA 1974, s 61(4).
9 Agreements Regulations, reg 6(5).
10 CCA 1974, s 189(4).
11 Agreements Regulations 1983, reg 6(2); Agreements Regulations 2010, reg 3(3); Copy Document Regulations, reg 2(1).
12 Ibid.
13 CRA 2015, s 64(3) read with s 68(1).

8.4 THE REGULATED AGREEMENT AND PRE-CONTRACT DISCLOSURE OF INFORMATION

Before a regulated agreement is made the debtor or hirer must be furnished with prescribed pre-contract disclosure of information. This is followed by the appropriate credit or hire agreement and (save in limited exceptions) together with a copy for the customer's retention. Depending upon whether the agreement is governed by the 1983 or the 2010 Agreements Regulations, the customer is then furnished with a copy of the executed agreement or relevant prescribed information following execution of the agreement.

8.4.1 Agreements governed by the Consumer Credit (Agreements) Regulations 2010, SI 2010/1014 ('Agreements Regulations 2010')

The Agreements Regulations 2010:[1]

'(1) apply in respect of a regulated consumer credit agreement, except as provided for in paragraphs (1A) to (5) below;

(1A) apply to an agreement to which section 58 of the Act applies where–

(a) before the creditor gives the debtor the unexecuted agreement for his signature the creditor gives the debtor a copy of the unexecuted agreement in compliance or purported compliance with regulations 3 and 7 of, and Schedules 1 and 2 to, these Regulations, and

(b) the copy of the unexecuted agreement contains a heading and notice as set out in regulation 4(a)(ii) and (b)(ii) respectively of the Consumer Credit (Cancellation Notices and Copies of Documents) Regulations 1983;

(2)　do not apply to an agreement mentioned in paragraph (3) unless pre-contract credit information has been disclosed in compliance (or in purported compliance) with the Information Regulations 2010.

(3)　The agreements referred to in paragraph (2) are–

(a) an agreement secured on land other than an agreement to which section 58 applies;

(b) an agreement under which the creditor provides the debtor with credit which exceeds £60,260 other than a residential renovation agreement;

(c) an agreement entered into by the debtor wholly or predominantly for the purposes of a business carried on, or intended to be carried on, by him.

(4)　Paragraph (2) and regulations 3 to 4 and 6 to 7 do not apply to an authorised non-business overdraft agreement or an authorised business overdraft agreement.

(5)　Regulation 5 [dealing with modifying agreements] does not apply to a regulated consumer credit agreement which is also a distance contract unless the agreement is entered into by the debtor wholly or predominantly for the purposes of a business carried on, or intended to be carried on, by him.

(6)　Article 60C(5) and (6) of the Financial Services and Markets Act 2000 (Regulated Activities) Order 2001 applies for the purposes of paragraphs (3)(c) and (5).'

Authorised non-business overdraft agreements and authorised business overdraft agreements are subject to separate regulation, namely regulation 8 of the Agreements Regulations 2010.

1　Agreements Regulations 2010, reg 2.

8.4.2　Pre-contract disclosure governed by the Agreements Regulations 2010

The Consumer Credit (Disclosure of Information) Regulations 2010[1] ('Disclosure Regulations 2010') prescribe the need for, and the form and content of, pre-contract credit information to be disclosed to the debtor, generally before a consumer credit agreement, within the scope of the regulations, is entered into. The information must be in writing. It appears that the form must follow the prescribed order and headings of the relevant schedule.

The regulations apply to agreements other than telephone contracts, non-telephone distance contracts, excluded pawn agreements and overdraft agreements.[2]

The information prescribed by reg 8 must be disclosed by means of the form contained in Schedule 1, namely 'Standard European Consumer Credit Information' (SECCI). If the information relates to an authorised non-business overdraft agreement, it must be disclosed in accordance with regs 10 and 11 and Sch 3, namely 'European Consumer Credit Information' (ECCI).

Truncated prescribed information may be furnished where the agreement is made by voice telephone communication and the debtor explicitly consents, or made at the debtor's request by non-telephone distance contract, and the pre-contract credit information prescribed by regulation 8 is supplied immediately after the agreement is made.

Regulation 6 of the regulations prescribes separate requirements for distance contracts for the purpose of a business (in circumstances where these regulations are brought into operation).

The Disclosure Regulations 2010 apply to all regulated consumer credit agreements, except to the following:[3]

(a) an agreement to which section 58 of the Act (opportunity for withdrawal from prospective land mortgage) applies;

(b) an authorised non-business overdraft agreement which is–

    (i) for credit which exceeds £60,260, or

    (ii) secured on land;

(c) except as stated in paragraph (cc) below, the regulations do not apply to an agreement–

    (i) under which the creditor provides the debtor with credit exceeding £60,260 unless it is a residential renovation agreement,

    (ii) secured on land,

    (iii) entered into by the debtor wholly or predominantly for the purposes of a business also carried on, or intended to be carried on, by him, or

    (iv) with limited exceptions, where the agreement was made before 1 February 2011;

(cc) the Regulations apply to an agreement mentioned in paragraph (c) (which is not also an agreement mentioned in paragraph (a) or (b)) where a creditor or, where applicable a credit intermediary, discloses or purports to disclose the pre-contract credit information in accordance with these Regulations rather than in accordance with the Consumer Credit (Disclosure of Information) Regulations 2004 or the Financial Services (Distance Marketing) Regulations 2004 (as the case may be).'

The Regulations also do not apply to an authorised business overdraft agreement (as opposed to an authorised non-business overdraft agreement), by virtue of s 55 (Disclosure of information) (under which these Regulations are made) as s 74(1B) omits the application of s 55 to such agreements.

1 SI 2010/1013.
2 Disclosure Regulations 2010, reg 3(1).
3 Ibid., reg 2.

8.4.3 Agreements governed by the Consumer Credit (Agreements) Regulations 1983, SI 1983/1553 ('Agreements Regulations 1983')

The Agreements Regulations 1983 apply:[1]

(a) to all regulated consumer hire agreements; and

(b)   to the following regulated consumer credit agreements:

    (i)   an agreement secured on land,

    (ii)   an agreement under which the creditor provides the debtor with credit exceeding £60,260 other than a residential renovation agreement, or

    (iii)   an agreement entered into by the debtor wholly or predominantly for the purposes of a business carried on, or intended to be carried on, by him.

except to the extent that the Consumer Credit (Agreements) Regulations 2010 apply to such agreements.

Article 60C(5) and (6) of the Financial Services and Markets Act 2000 (Regulated Activities) Order 2001 applies for the purposes of paragraph (b)(iii).

1   Agreements Regulations 1983, reg 8.

8.4.4   Pre-contract disclosure governed by the Agreements Regulations 1983

The Consumer Credit (Disclosure of Information) Regulations 2004[1] ('Disclosure Regulations 2004') apply to the following regulated agreements:[2]

(a)   consumer credit agreements secured on land except those to which section 58 of the Act (opportunity for withdrawal from prospective land mortgage) applies,

(b)   consumer hire agreements,

(c)   consumer credit agreements under which the creditor provides the debtor with credit which exceeds £60,260 other than residential renovation agreements,

(d)   consumer credit agreements entered into by the debtor wholly or predominantly for the purposes of a business carried on, or intended to be carried on, by him, and

(e)   small debtor-creditor-supplier agreements for restricted-use credit,

except to the extent the Consumer Credit (Disclosure of Information) Regulations 2010 apply to such agreements.

These Regulations do not apply to:

(a)   a distance contract;

(b)   an authorised non-business overdraft agreement;

(c)   an agreement which would be an authorised non-business overdraft agreement but for the fact that the credit is not repayable on demand or within three months.[3]

1   SI 2010/1481.
2   Disclosure Regulations 2004, reg 2.
3   See Consumer Credit (Amendment) Regulations 2010, SI 2010/1969, reg 24.

8.4.5 Summary of pre-contract information requirements

Before a regulated consumer credit agreement or a regulated consumer hire agreement is entered into by the customer he must be given pre-contract information. This obligation on the creditor or owner depends on the circumstances, as set out below.

(a) If the agreement is one to which s 58 of CCA 1974 applies (i.e. an agreement where the customer is given an opportunity to withdraw from a prospective land mortgage), the customer must be given an advance copy of the agreement and the information in (d) below, if applicable.[1]

(b) In all other cases the creditor or owner must give the customer pre-contract information as specified in, and in a document which accords with, the requirements of the relevant regulations referred to at **8.4.2** and **8.4.4** above, as appropriate. The information must be given in good time before the agreement is made, which although not further defined, it is submitted, means sufficient time to enable the debtor or hirer at least to read the information. This is also implied by sections 64(3) and 68(1) of the Consumer Rights Act 2015.

(c) In general terms (and each set of regulations has its own specific requirements) the information must be clear and easily legible. The document must be separate from any other information, including the document embodying the relevant agreement, on paper or in another durable medium and of a nature that enables the customer to remove it from the place where it is disclosed to him.

(d) If the agreement is a distance contract, the creditor or owner must also give the customer the pre-contract information specified by the Financial Services (Distance Marketing) Regulations 2004 in good time prior to the customer being bound by the contract.[2]

(e) The creditor or credit broker must also furnish the customer with so-called Adequate Explanations in accordance with CONC 4.2, as summarised at **8.5** below.

1 SI 1983/1557.
2 SI 1999/2083 reg 5(5), Sch 2, para 1(i) although this relates to non-core terms of the agreement.

8.5 PRE-CONTRACT DISCLOSURE AND ADEQUATE EXPLANATIONS (CONC 4.2)

(a) Maximise application (CONC 4.2.1R)

This section, unless otherwise stated in or in relation to a rule:

(1) applies to a firm with respect to consumer credit lending;

(2) applies to a firm with respect to credit broking where the firm has or takes on responsibility for providing the disclosures and explanations to customers required by this section;

(3)   does not apply to an agreement under which the lender provides the customer with credit which exceeds £60,260, unless the agreement is a residential renovation agreement;

(4)   does not apply to an agreement secured on land; and

(5)   does not apply to a borrower-lender agreement enabling the customer to overdraw on a current account other than such an agreement which would be an authorised non-business overdraft agreement, but for the fact that the credit is not repayable on demand or within three months.

(b)   CONC 4.2.2G

For the agreements referred to in CONC 4.2.1R (3), (4) and (5), a firm within CONC 4.2.1R (1) or CONC 4.2.1R (2) should consider whether it is necessary or appropriate to provide explanations of the matters in CONC 4.2.5R (2); in particular, a firm should consider highlighting the principal consequences to the customer including the consequences of missing payments or under-paying, including, where applicable, the risk of repossession of the customer's property.

(c)   CONC 4.2.3G

(1)   The disclosure regulations made under section 55 of the CCA which require information to be disclosed before a regulated credit agreement is made remain in force.

(2)   Failure to comply with the disclosure regulations has the effect that agreements are enforceable against a borrower or hirer (as defined in the CCA) only with an order of court and enforcement for that purpose includes a retaking of goods or land to which the agreement relates.

(3)   Other relevant disclosure requirements are found in CONC 2.7 (distance marketing) and CONC 2.8 (electronic commerce), the Financial Services (Distance Marketing) Regulations 2004 (SI 2004/2095), the Electronic Commerce (EC Directive) Regulations 2002 (SI 2002/2013) and the Consumer Protection from Unfair Trading Regulations 2008 (SI 2008/ 1277) and the Cancellation of Contracts made in the Consumer's home etc Regulations 2008 (SI 2008/1816).

(d)   CONC 4.2.4G

The pre-contractual information disclosed under the disclosure regulations and the pre-contractual explanations required under CONC 4.2.5R should take into account any preferences expressed, or information provided by, the customer where the firm would in principle agree to offer credit on such terms.

(e)   Pre-contractual adequate explanations (CONC 4.2.5R)

(1)   Before making a regulated credit agreement the firm must:

(a)   provide the customer with an adequate explanation of the matters referred to in (2) in order to place the customer in a position to assess whether the agreement is adapted to the customer's needs and financial situation;

(b) advise the customer:

(i) to consider the information which is required to be disclosed under section 55 of the CCA; and

(ii) where the information is disclosed in person, that the customer is able to take it away;

(c) provide the customer with an opportunity to ask questions about the agreement; and

(d) advise the customer how to ask the firm for further information and explanation.

(2) The matters referred to in (1)(a) are:

(a) the features of the agreement which may make the credit to be provided under the agreement unsuitable for particular types of use;

(b) how much the customer will have to pay periodically and, where the amount can be determined, in total under the agreement;

(c) the features of the agreement which may operate in a manner which would have a significant adverse effect on the customer in a way which the customer is unlikely to foresee;

(d) the principal consequences for the customer arising from a failure to make payments under the agreement at the times required by the agreement including, where applicable and depending upon the type and amount of credit and the circumstances of the customer:

(i) the total cost of the debt growing;

(ii) incurring any default charges or interest for late or missed payment or under-payment;

(iii) impaired credit rating and its effect on future access to or cost of credit;

(iv) legal proceedings, including reference to charging orders (or, in Scotland, inhibitions), and to the associated costs of such proceedings;

(v) repossession of the customer's home or other property; and

(vi) where an article is taken in pawn, that the article might be sold, if not redeemed; and

(e) the effect of the exercise of any right to withdraw from the agreement and how and when this right may be exercised.

(3) The adequate explanation and advice in (1) may be given orally or in writing, except where (4) applies.

(4)   Where the matters in (2)(a), (b) or (e) are given orally or to the customer in person, the explanation of the matters in (2)(c) and (d) and the advice required in (1)(b) must be given orally to the customer.

(5)   Paragraphs (1) to (4) do not apply to a lender if a credit broker has complied with those sub-paragraphs in respect of the agreement.

(6)   Where the regulated credit agreement is an agreement under which a person takes an article in pawn:

(a)   the requirement in (1)(a) only relates to the matters in (2)(d) and (e); and

(b)   the requirements in (1)(b) and (d) do not apply.

(7)   This rule does not apply to:

(a)   a non-commercial agreement;

(b)   a small borrower-lender-supplier agreement for restricted-use credit.

(8)   Where this rule applies to a borrower-lender agreement to finance the making of payments arising on or connected with the death of a person, the payments in question are set out in (9) …

(f)   CONC 4.2.6G

The explanation provided by a lender or a credit broker under CONC 4.2.5R should enable the customer to make a reasonable assessment as to whether the customer can afford the credit and to understand the key associated risks.

(g)   CONC 4.2.7R

In deciding on the level and extent of explanation required by CONC 4.2.5R, the lender or credit broker should consider (and each of them should ensure that anyone acting on its behalf should consider), to the extent appropriate to do so, factors including:

(1)   the type of credit being sought;

(2)   the amount and duration of credit to be provided;

(2A) the actual and potential costs of the credit;

(2B) the risk to the customer arising from the credit (the risk to the customer is likely to be greater the higher the total cost of the credit relative to the customer's financial situation);

(2C) the purpose of the credit, if the lender or (as the case may be) the credit broker knows what that purpose is;

(3)   to the extent it is evident and discernible, the customer's level of understanding of the agreement, and of the information and the explanation provided about the agreement; and

(4)   the channel or medium through which the credit transaction takes place.

(h) CONC 4.2.7AG

    (1) ... Where there is more than one customer acting together as 'joint borrowers', the lender or credit broker should consider whether it may be appropriate to give separate explanations to each customer and whether the explanation should be the same or different for each, rather than giving a single explanation to all of them jointly. (Where the borrower is a partnership or an unincorporated association, the members or partners may be treated as a single customer.) ...

(i) CONC 4.2.8R

Where the regulated credit agreement is high-cost short-term credit, the lender or a credit broker must explain under CONC 4.2.5R (1)(a) that entering into that agreement would be unsuitable to support sustained borrowing over long periods and would be expensive as a means of longer term borrowing. ...

(j) CONC 4.2.12R

The lender or the credit broker must enable a customer to request and obtain further information and explanation about a regulated credit agreement without incurring undue cost or delay.

(k) CONC 4.2.13R

Neither a lender nor a credit broker may require a customer to acknowledge that the information and explanations it has provided are adequate to satisfy the requirements of CONC 4.2.5R.

(l) CONC 4.2.14G

A lender or credit broker may require an acknowledgement that it has provided an explanation, and of receipt of any written information that forms a part of the explanation, but not an acknowledgement as to its adequacy. CONC 4.2.13R does not prevent the lender or credit broker asking if the customer has understood an explanation given.

(m) For adequate explanations in relation to particular regulated credit agreements, see CONC 4.2.15R.

(n) For guidance on adequate explanations where agreements are marketed by distance or electronic means, see CONC 4.2.17G.

(o) For credit agreements where there is a guarantor etc, see CONC 4.2.22R to 4.2.24G.

8.6 SIGNATURE AND COPIES OF THE AGREEMENT

8.6.1 Signing the agreement

A regulated agreement must be signed by both parties to the agreement and where two or more customers enter into the agreement, by each customer.[1] It may be signed by one person on behalf of a partnership or an unincorporated body of persons, as the debtor or hirer, under the agreement.[2] The agreement date must be inserted but the customer's signature need not be dated except in the case of a cancellable agreement.[3]

The provisions relating to the furnishing of copies of the agreement are complicated and are set out in detail below. The copy requirements apply in respect of each customer where more than one person enters into the agreement as the customer.[4]

1 CCA 1974, s 61(4) and the Consumer Credit (Agreements) Regulations 1983, reg 6(3)(a).
2 Consumer Credit (Agreements) Regulations 1983, reg 6(3)(a) and (c); Consumer Credit (Agreements) Regulations 2010, reg 4(3)(a) and (c).
3 CCA 1974, ss 63(5), (6) and 61A.
4 Ibid., s 185(1)(a).

8.6.2   Duty to supply a copy of the executed consumer credit agreement

Section 61A of CCA 1974 provides as follows:

'(1) Where a regulated consumer credit agreement, other than **an excluded agreement**, has been made, the creditor must give a copy of the executed agreement, and any other document referred to in it, to the debtor.

(2) Subsection (1) does not apply if–

(a) a copy of the unexecuted agreement (and of any other document referred to in it) has already been given to the debtor, and

(b) the unexecuted agreement is in identical terms to the executed agreement.

(3) In a case referred to in subsection (2), the creditor must inform the debtor in writing–

(a) that the agreement has been executed,

(b) that the executed agreement is in identical terms to the unexecuted agreement a copy of which has already been given to the debtor, and

(c) that the debtor has the right to receive a copy of the executed agreement if the debtor makes a request for it at any time before the end of the period referred to in section 66A(2).

(4) Where a request is made under subsection (3)(c) the creditor must give a copy of the executed agreement to the debtor without delay.

(5) If the requirements of this section are not observed, the agreement is not properly executed.

(6) For the purposes of this section, an agreement is **an excluded agreement** if it is–

(a) a cancellable agreement, or

(b) an agreement–

(i)   secured on land,

(ii) under which the creditor provides the debtor with credit which exceeds £60,260, or

(iii) entered into by the debtor wholly or predominantly for the purposes of a business carried on, or intended to be carried on, by him.

unless the creditor or a credit intermediary has complied with or purported to comply with regulation 3(2) of the Consumer Credit (Disclosure of Information) Regulations 2010.

(6A) An agreement is not an excluded agreement by virtue of subsection (6)(b) (ii) if it is a residential renovation agreement.'

8.6.3 Duty to supply a copy of the unexecuted consumer credit agreement where the agreement is an 'excluded agreement'

Section 62 of the Act provides as follows:

'(1) If in the case of a regulated agreement which is an excluded agreement the unexecuted agreement is presented personally to the debtor or hirer for his signature, but on the occasion when he signs it the document does not become an executed agreement, a copy of it, and of any other document referred to in it, must be there and then delivered to him.

(2) If the unexecuted agreement is sent to the debtor or hirer for his signature, a copy of it, and of any other document referred to in it, must be sent to him at the same time.

(3) A regulated agreement which is an excluded agreement is not properly executed if the requirements of this section are not observed.

(4) In this section, "excluded agreement" has the same meaning as in section 61A.'

8.6.4 Duty to supply a copy of an executed agreement in the case of an 'excluded agreement' or a regulated hire agreement

It appears from the wording of s 63 (as set out below), that this section applies both to an excluded agreement and a consumer hire agreement, although the opening words of the section only refer to an excluded agreement.

An excluded agreement is any of the following:[1]

(a) a cancellable agreement, or

(b) an agreement:

(i) secured on land,

(ii) under which the creditor provides the debtor with credit which exceeds £60,260, or

(iii) entered into by the debtor wholly or predominantly for the purposes of a business carried on, or intended to be carried on, by him, unless the creditor or a credit intermediary has complied with or purported to comply with reg 3(2) of the Consumer Credit (Disclosure of Information) Regulations 2010.

An agreement is not an excluded agreement by virtue of section 63(6)(b)(ii) if it is a residential renovation agreement.

Section 63 of the Act provides as follows:

'(1) If in the case of a regulated agreement which is an excluded agreement the unexecuted agreement is presented personally to the debtor or hirer for his signature, and on the occasion when he signs it the document becomes an executed agreement, a copy of the executed agreement, and of any other document referred to in it, must be there and then delivered to him.

(2) A copy of the executed agreement, and of any other document referred to in it, must be given to the debtor or hirer within the seven days following the making of the agreement unless–

(a) subsection (1) applies, or

(b) the unexecuted agreement was sent to the debtor or hirer for his signature and, on the occasion of his signing it, the document became an executed agreement.

(3) In the case of a cancellable agreement, a copy under subsection (2) must be sent by an appropriate method.

(4) In the case of a credit-token agreement, a copy under subsection (2) need not be given within the seven days following the making of the agreement if it is given before or at the time when the credit-token is given to the debtor.

(5) A regulated agreement which is an excluded agreement is not properly executed if the requirements of this section are not observed.

(6) In this section, "excluded agreement" has the same meaning as in section 61A.'

1 CCA 1974, s 63(6) read with s 61A(6) and (6A).

8.6.5 Meaning of expressions in the above regulations

(a) 'give' means 'deliver or send by an appropriate method';[1]

(b) an 'appropriate method'[2] means by post, or transmission in the form of an electronic communication if, in the latter case:

(i) the person to whom it is transmitted agrees that it may be delivered to him by being transmitted to a particular electronic address in a particular electronic form,

(ii) it is transmitted to that address in that form, and

(iii) the form in which the document is transmitted is such that any information in the document which is addressed to the person to whom the document is transmitted is capable of being stored for future reference for an appropriate period in a way which allows the information to be reproduced without change.

1 CCA 1974, s 189(1).
2 Ibid., s 189(1), read with s 176A(1).

8.6.6   Debtor's right of withdrawal

The debtor's right of withdrawal from a credit agreement, governed by the Agreements Regulations 2010, was introduced by the EU Directive. The withdrawal right is described in CCA 1974 as follows:[1]

'(1) The debtor under a regulated consumer credit agreement, **other than an excluded agreement,** may withdraw from the agreement, without giving any reason, in accordance with this section.

(2) To withdraw from an agreement under this section the debtor must give oral or written notice of the withdrawal to the creditor before the end of the period of 14 days beginning with the day after the relevant day.

(3) For the purposes of subsection (2) the relevant day is whichever is the latest of the following–

   (a) the day on which the agreement is made;

   (b) where the creditor is required to inform the debtor of the credit limit under the agreement, the day on which the creditor first does so;

   (c) in the case of an agreement to which section 61A (duty to supply copy of executed consumer credit agreement) applies, the day on which the debtor receives a copy of the agreement under that section or on which the debtor is informed as specified in subsection (3) of that section;

   (d) in the case of an agreement to which section 63 (duty to supply copy of executed agreement: excluded agreements) applies, the day on which the debtor receives a copy of the agreement under that section.

(4) Where oral notice under this section is given to the creditor it must be given in a manner specified in the agreement.

(5) Where written notice under this section is given by facsimile transmission or electronically–

   (a) it must be sent to the number or electronic address specified for the purpose in the agreement, and

   (b) where it is so sent, it is to be regarded as having been received by the creditor at the time it is sent (and section 176A does not apply).

(6) Where written notice under this section is given in any other form–

   (a) it must be sent by post to, or left at, the postal address specified for the purpose in the agreement, and

   (b) where it is sent by post to that address, it is to be regarded as having been received by the creditor at the time of posting (and section 176 does not apply).

(7) Subject as follows, where the debtor withdraws from a regulated consumer credit agreement under this section–

   (a) the agreement shall be treated as if it had never been entered into, and

   (b) where an ancillary service relating to the agreement is or is to be provided by the creditor, or by a third party on the basis of an agreement between the third party and the creditor, the ancillary service contract shall be treated as if it had never been entered into.

(8) In the case referred to in subsection (7)(b) the creditor must without delay notify any third party of the fact that the debtor has withdrawn from the agreement.

(9) Where the debtor withdraws from an agreement under this section–

   (a) the debtor must repay to the creditor any credit provided and the interest accrued on it (at the rate provided for under the agreement), but

   (b) the debtor is not liable to pay to the creditor any compensation, fees or charges except any non-returnable charges paid by the creditor to a public administrative body.

(10) An amount payable under subsection (9) must be paid without undue delay and no later than the end of the period of 30 days beginning with the day after the day on which the notice of withdrawal was given (and if not paid by the end of that period may be recovered by the creditor as a debt).

(11) Where a regulated consumer credit agreement is a conditional sale, hire-purchase or credit-sale agreement and–

   (a) the debtor withdraws from the agreement under this section after the credit has been provided, and

   (b) the sum payable under subsection (9)(a) is paid in full by the debtor,

   title to the goods purchased or supplied under the agreement is to pass to the debtor on the same terms as would have applied had the debtor not withdrawn from the agreement.

(12) In subsections (2), (4), (5), (6) and (9)(a) references to the creditor include a person specified by the creditor in the agreement.

(13) In subsection (7)(b) the reference to an ancillary service means a service that relates to the provision of credit under the agreement and includes in particular an insurance or payment protection policy.

(14) For the purposes of this section, an agreement is **an excluded agreement** if it is–

   (a) an agreement for credit exceeding £60,260, other than a residential renovation agreement,

   (b) an agreement secured on land,

   (c) a restricted-use credit agreement to finance the purchase of land, or

   (d) an agreement for a bridging loan in connection with the purchase of land.'

Significantly, a consumer credit agreement for business purposes for credit up to £25,000 is not an excluded agreement and is therefore subject to the debtor's right of withdrawal.

Where the debtor withdraws, he is obligated to repay the credit amount plus accrued interest to the creditor without undue delay and in any event within thirty days of the day after the notice of withdrawal was given. In the case of a conditional sale, hire-purchase or credit sale agreement, once such sum has been paid in full, title to the goods passes to the debtor on the same terms as would have applied had the debtor not withdrawn from the agreement. In the case of a credit sale agreement title passes to the debtor when the agreement is made and in the case of a conditional sale or hire-purchase agreement title only passes to the debtor upon full payment, including any option to purchase fee payable under a hire-purchase agreement. It follows that, pending full payment to the creditor, title to the goods in the case of a conditional sale or hire-purchase agreement continues to vest in the creditor who, if the debtor fails to make payment when due, can recover his goods and claim any diminution in their value.

1 CCA 1974, s 66A.

8.6.7 Cancellable agreements and the right of cancellation

A debtor or hirer may cancel a regulated agreement where the agreement is cancellable under s 67 and is not subject to the right of withdrawal under s 66A of CCA 1974.[1] In the case of a cancellable agreement, a notice in the prescribed form indicating the right of the debtor or hirer to cancel the agreement must be set out in every copy of the agreement.[2] Save where the agreement becomes an executed agreement upon the owner's or creditor's signature, a copy of the executed agreement, containing a notice of cancellation rights, must also be sent by an 'appropriate method' to the debtor or hirer within seven days following the making of the agreement.[3]

The second copy of a credit-token agreement may be sent by an 'appropriate method' to the debtor before the credit-token is given or sent together with the credit-token, even if this is after the foregoing seven-day period.[4] Save in the case of the first credit-token, on the issue of any subsequent credit-token the debtor must be given a copy of the executed agreement.[5] This will usually be set out in or with the card carrier.

The cancellation notice gives the debtor five days from the day after receipt of the copy agreement to notify the creditor or owner of his wish to cancel the same.[6] The convergence of the consumer credit regime and the distance marketing regime means that when the regulated agreement is a distance contract, the longer period for cancellation of the agreement specified by either regime, applies to the regulated agreement.

The Distance Marketing Regulations provide a cancellation period of 14 calendar days beginning with the day after the conclusion of the contract. In the case of a distance contract relating to life insurance, in place of the conclusion day there is substituted the day on which the consumer is informed that the distance contract has been concluded. In the case of an insurance contract or a personal pension, the cancellation period is 30 calendar days.[7]

There is no right of cancellation in relation to a consumer credit agreement secured by a land mortgage or a restricted-use credit agreement to finance the purchase of land or an existing building or a bridging loan in that connection.[8]

A distance contract is essentially a contract relating to financial services (services of a banking, credit, insurance, personal pension investment or payment nature) concluded between a supplier and a consumer without the simultaneous physical presence of the supplier and the consumer.[9] Financial services include most types of consumer hire agreements.

The relevant cancellation period must, in the case of all cancellable regulated agreements, be inserted in the statutory notice of cancellation rights.[10]

Exemptions from the need to supply notice of cancellation rights apply to certain mail order purchases.[11]

The cancellation of, or withdrawal from, a regulated agreement, will also effect the cancellation of, or withdrawal from, a linked transaction, unless the agreement provides otherwise[12] or the linked transaction is exempt from the consequences of cancellation.[13]

1　CCA 1974, s 67(2).
2　Ibid., s 64(1)(a).
3　Ibid., s 64(1)(b).
4　Ibid., s 63(4).
5　Ibid., s 85.
6　Ibid., s 68(1).
7　Financial Services (Distance Marketing) Regulations 2004, SI 2004/2095, reg 10.
8　Ibid., reg 11(1)(g).
9　Ibid., reg 2(1).
10　See the forms in Consumer Credit (Cancellation Notices and Copies of Documents) Regulations 1983, SI 1983/1557, Sch.
11　Consumer Credit (Notice of Cancellation Rights) (Exemptions) Regulations 1983, SI 1983/1558.
12　Consumer Credit (Linked Transactions) (Exemptions) Regulations 1983, SI 1983/1560.
13　See, in this connection, *Goshawk Dedicated (No 2) Ltd v Governor and Company of Bank of Scotland* [2005] GCCR 5431 and *Governor and Company of the Bank of Scotland v Euclidian (No 1) Ltd* [2007] All ER (D) 330.

8.6.8　Regulated agreements secured on land

Regulated agreements secured on land (subject to the qualifications stated in the paragraph below) follow a reverse sequence to that which applies to cancellable agreements. These transactions, under CCA 1974, s 58, are initiated by an advance copy of the agreement, setting out the customer's right of withdrawal from the proposed agreement.[1] This is followed, not less than seven days after the advance copy was given to the debtor or hirer, with the sending to the debtor by an 'appropriate method' of a copy of the signature copy of the agreement. The creditor or owner is not permitted to contact the customer during the period commencing with the giving of the advance copy and ending at the expiry of seven days after the day on which the unexecuted agreement is sent to the customer for his signature, or on its return by the customer after signature by him, whichever occurs first. This period is called the consideration period. This is intended to enable the customer to consider the merits and demerits of entering into the proposed agreement without being bothered by the creditor or owner, or any representative or professional appointee of the creditor or owner, such as a solicitor or surveyor. No communication may take place with the customer during the consideration period, whether in person, by telephone, letter or in any other way except in response to a specific request made by the customer after the beginning of the consideration period.[2] A failure to observe these requirements will render the resulting agreement improperly executed and unenforceable without an order of the court.[3]

These provisions do not apply to restricted-use credit agreements to finance the purchase of the mortgaged land or to an agreement for a bridging loan in connection with the purchase of mortgaged land or other land.[4] The exceptions are to facilitate the expeditious completion of such agreements.

It should be noted that the above applies to regulated agreements (subject to the exceptions noted) and does not apply to exempt agreements, as to which see **Chapter 6**.

1 CCA 1974, s 58.
2 Ibid., s 61(2) and (3).
3 Ibid., s 61 read with s 65.
4 Ibid., s 58(2).

8.7 STATUTORY INFORMATION REQUIRED BY THE REGULATIONS

8.7.1 Pre-contract information

Under the Disclosure Regulations 2004, the Pre-contract Information document practically duplicates the information required to be set out in the regulated agreement.

Under the Disclosure Regulations 2010 the information is that set out in Schedule 1 to the Regulations in respect of the SECCI and Schedule 3 in respect of the ECCI.

No additional information may be contained in the above documents.

8.7.2 The regulated agreement

CCA 1974 lays down essential requirements for a regulated agreement and requires regulations to be made to ensure that the debtor or hirer is made aware of:

(a) the rights and duties conferred or imposed on him by the agreement;

(b) the amount and rate of the total charge for credit (in the case of a consumer credit agreement);

(c) the protection and remedies available to him under the Act; and

(d) any other matters which, in the opinion of the Treasury [effectively the Financial Conduct Authority or FCA], it is desirable for [him] to know about in connection with the agreement.[1]

The Act states that regulations may in particular:

(a)   require specified information to be included in the prescribed manner in documents, and other specified material to be excluded;

(b)   contain requirements to ensure that specified information is clearly brought to the attention of the debtor or hirer, and that one part of a document is not given insufficient or excessive prominence compared with another.[2]

There is provision to apply to the Treasury if, in any particular case, it is impractical to comply with the Regulations.[3]

1   CCA 1974, s 60(1).
2   Ibid., s 60(2).
3   Ibid., s 60(3) to (5).

8.7.3   The regulated consumer credit agreement

8.7.3.1   The prescribed terms

As already noted at **8.3**, the prescribed terms no longer occupy the high ground which they did prior to 6 April 2007, when the absence of a prescribed term automatically rendered the agreement unenforceable. The prescribed terms, set out in Schedule 6 to the Consumer Credit (Agreements) Regulations 1983 and in regulation 4(1) of the Consumer Credit (Agreements) Regulations 2010 are no longer of more importance than the other elements of a regulated agreement, namely, that the document is in the prescribed form, conforms to regulations made under s 60(1), is signed in the prescribed manner by the debtor (or hirer) and by or on behalf of the creditor (or owner), embodies all the terms of the agreement other than implied terms and is, when presented or sent to the debtor (or hirer) for signature, in such a state that all its terms are readily legible.

The prescribed terms are the following: the amount of credit or, in the case of a running-account credit agreement, the credit limit or the manner in which it will be determined or a statement that there is no credit limit; the rate of interest; the repayments, which in the case of credit agreements under the Agreements Regulations 1983 are to be described by reference to a combination of any of the number, amount, frequency and timing of payments, dates of repayments, and the manner in which any of the foregoing may be determined and any power of the creditor to vary what is payable and, in the case of the Agreements Regulations 2010, are to be described by reference to the number (if applicable) and frequency of repayments to be made by the debtor.[1]

The case of *Dimond v Lovell*[2] affirmed the unenforceability of an agreement which did not contain all the prescribed terms; see also *Sutherland Professional Funding Ltd v Bakewells*.[3] These decisions were based on s 127(3), which has now been repealed, and offer no guidance on how the court might have construed the absence of a financial, as opposed to a prescribed, term. The same observation may be made in respect of *Watchtower Investments Ltd v Payne*,[4] *McGinn v Grangewood Securities Ltd*[5] and *London North Securities Ltd v Meadows*,[6] each of which dealt with the categorisation of, and differentiation between, credit and charges and whether the agreement in question contained the necessary prescribed terms. It is submitted that where, as now, a court is required to exercise its discretion under s 127(1), in circumstances such as those prevailing in the above cases, it will endeavour to uphold the agreement. Indeed, why otherwise should the legislature have found it fit to repeal s 127(3)?

1 Agreements Regulations 1983, SI 1983/1553, reg 6(1) and Sch 6; Agreements Regulations 2010, SI 2010/1014, reg 4.
2 [2001] GCCR 2751, [2002] 2 All ER 897, HL.
3 [2013] GCCR 11756, [2013] EWHC 2685 (QB).
4 [2001] GCCR 3055.
5 [2002] GCCR 4761.
6 [2005] GCCR 5381.

8.7.3.2 *Information prescribed by the Agreements Regulations 1983*

(1) A consumer credit agreement which is subject to the Agreements Regulations 1983 must contain the information set out in Schedule 1 to the Regulations, namely the following information and in the following order:[1]

    (a) the nature of the agreement, namely one of the statutory headings;

    (b) the parties to the agreement, namely the names and addresses of the parties;

    (c) specified financial and related particulars under the respective headings: 'Key Financial Information', 'Other Financial Information' and 'Key Information';

    (d) under the heading 'Key Information', the relevant statements of protection and remedies set out in Schedule 2 to the Regulations;

    (e) as prescribed by Schedules 2 and 5, the customer signature box and, where applicable, the separate box required where the agreement is one to which s 58(1) of CCA 1974 applies, or if the agreement is a cancellable agreement or is an agreement under which any person takes any article in pawn and under which the pawn-receipt is not separate from the document embodying the agreement, a separate box immediately above, below or adjacent to the signature box containing the appropriate statutory statement. It should be noted that where the agreement is a cancellable agreement, the notice of cancellation rights needs to be set out above the signature box by virtue of it being part of the 'Key Information' i.e. the 'Key Information' ends before the signature box;

    (f) as prescribed by Schedule 5, where the agreement embodies a debtor-creditor-supplier agreement which finances a premium under a contract of insurance under which a sum is payable in the event of the death of the debtor or the debtor suffering an accident, sickness or unemployment before the credit under the agreement becomes payable, or finances a premium under a contract of shortfall insurance or a contract of insurance relating to the guarantee of goods, the agreement must contain a statutory form of consent immediately below the customer signature box and which requires completion and signature by the customer.

The above financial information, statements of protection and remedies, signature and separate boxes, must be set out in the order prescribed by the regulations, shown together as a whole and not preceded by any information, apart from trade names, logos or the reference number of the agreement. The foregoing may not be interspersed with any other information or wording, apart from sub-totals of total amounts and cross-references to the terms of the agreement.

(2)   Aspects of the prescribed information

(a)   *Order of the information*: The general view, which was supported by the then Department for Business, Innovation and Skills (BIS, formerly BERR and DTI and now called the Department for Business, Energy and Industrial Strategy (BEIS))[2] is that, where the Regulations prescribe the ordering of particular information, the order is that which applies to the blocks of information i.e. 'Key Financial Information', 'Other Financial Information' and 'Key Information' rather than to the individual items of information within each block.

(b)   *Total charge for credit etc.*: Where the total charge for credit or rate of interest cannot be exactly ascertained, the creditor may insert information based on assumptions it may reasonably make in all the circumstances.[3] A statement of the assumptions should be included in the terms of the agreement and the terms on the face of the agreement should cross-refer to the assumptions.

In the case of a running-account credit agreement, the total charge for credit and APR must be calculated on the following assumptions:[4]

(i)   where there will be a credit limit but that limit is not known at the date of making the agreement, the credit amount is assumed to be £1,500 or where it will be less than £1,500, an amount equal to that limit;

(ii)   credit is provided for a year beginning with the relevant date (normally the date of the agreement);

(iii)   credit is provided in full on the relevant date;

(iv)   where the rate of interest will change at a time provided in the agreement within a period of three years beginning with the date of the making of the agreement, the rate should be taken to be the highest rate obtaining under the agreement in that period;

(v)   where the agreement provides credit to finance the purchase of goods, services, land or other things and also provides one or more of cash loans, credit to refinance existing indebtedness and credit for any other purpose, and the rates of interest and charges differ, the rate of interest and charges shall be those applying to the provision of credit for the purchase of goods etc.;

(vi)   the credit is assumed to be repaid in 12 equal instalments at monthly intervals, beginning one month after the relevant date.

The result of the above is that the credit agreement will show one APR even though it may also include provision for balance transfers and cash advances, each at different rates of interest and different charges.

(c) *Amount of repayments*: The amount of each repayment must be stated in the manner required by the Agreements Regulations. Paragraph 13 of Schedule 1 is more restrictive than para 5 of Schedule 6 in only permitting it to be stated in 'the manner in which the amount will be determined' if it cannot be stated in any of the alternative ways specified in para 13. Failure to comply will give rise to a court having to exercise its discretion in respect of the enforceability of the agreement under s 127(1).[5]

(d) *Allocation of payments*: Where different interest rates or different charges or both are at any time payable in respect of credit under the agreement pro- vided for different purposes or different parts of the agreement, the agree- ment must state the order or proportions in which any amount paid by the debtor, which is insufficient to discharge the total indebtedness, will be applied or appropriated towards the discharge of the sums due.[6] Examples are 'Any payments will be allocated first to pay off arrears, if any, then costs and charges accrued due, if any, and then to reduce the balance out- standing' or 'Payments are allocated first towards interest, second towards other charges and fees, next to balance transfers, followed by purchases, followed by cash advances'.

(e) *Charges*: The agreement must list any charges payable under the agreement upon failure by the debtor or a relative of his to do or refrain from doing anything which he is required to do or refrain from doing. It must also contain a statement indicating any term of the agreement which provides for charges not required to be shown as above or not included in the total charge for credit. This is understood to refer to a general charges provision rather than to a specific charge e.g. a clause requiring the debtor to pay all costs, charges and expenses relating to the enforcement of the credit agree- ment.[7] 'Charges' clearly does not mean the payment payable on termination of the agreement.

(f) *Cancellation rights*: In the case of a cancellable agreement, the agreement must set out the statutory form relating to the debtor's rights to cancel the agreement. Where the agreement is not a cancellable agreement, whether under CCA 1974, the Timeshare Act 1992 or the Financial Services (Distance Marketing) Regulations 2004, the agreement must contain a statement that the debtor has no right to cancel the agreement under those provisions.[8]

(g) *Amount payable on early settlement*: An agreement for fixed-sum credit for a term of more than one month must set out examples based on the amount of credit to be provided under the agreement, or the nominal amount of either £1,000 or £100, showing the amount that would be payable if the debtor exercises his right under s 94 of the Act to discharge his indebted- ness on the date when a quarter, half and three quarters of the term respec- tively has elapsed, or on the first repayment date after each of those dates. The amounts need to be described as only illustrative and as not taking account of any variation which might occur under the agreement.[9]

(h) *Statutory warnings:*[10] A notice alerting the debtor to the fact that missing payments could have severe consequences and make obtaining credit more difficult, must be inserted in the agreement.

A notice alerting the debtor to the fact that his home may be repossessed if he does not keep up repayments on a mortgage or other debt secured on it, must be inserted in an agreement which is secured on land.

1 SI 1983/1553, reg 2(4) read with Sch 1.
2 Guidance Notes, issued October 2004.
3 Agreement Regulations, SI 1983/1553, as amended, reg 2(2).
4 Ibid., Sch 7, para 1.
5 See *Hurstanger Ltd v Wilson* [2007] EWCA Civ 299, CA, which was decided before the repeal of s 127(3).
6 SI 1983/1553, Sch 1, para 14A.
7 Ibid., para 22.
8 Ibid., para 23.
9 Ibid., para 24.
10 Ibid., Sch 2, Forms 2 and 3.

8.7.3.3 Information prescribed by the Agreements Regulations 2010

A consumer credit agreement which is subject to the Agreements Regulations 2010 must contain the information set out in Schedule 1 to the Regulations.[1] The information is not subject to a prescribed order, nor to a restriction on interspersals.
The following should be noted:

(a) *Parties to the agreement*: This includes any credit intermediary, although clearly not 'a party' to the agreement.

(b) *Advance payment*: There is no specific requirement for a statement of any advance payment, although it is referred to in various items of information and should therefore be stated, where relevant.

(c) *Total charge for credit*: There is no requirement, although it is submitted that it is desirable, to include a separate item by way of a statement of the total charge for credit. Paragraph 12 refers to the total amount payable as including the total charge for credit and paras 18 and 19 refer to charges and interest respectively.

(d) *Goods or services*: The wording of paras 26 and 27 is restricted to goods or services and does not expressly include land etc (compare the SECCI and ECCI), raising the question whether the information is also required where the credit agreement finances the acquisition of land or a chose in action.

1 SI 2010/1014, reg 3(1).

8.7.4 The regulated consumer hire agreement

8.7.4.1 Prescribed terms

The (Consumer Credit) Agreements Regulations 1983 set out, in Schedule 6, the prescribed terms for a regulated hire agreement. These are surprisingly restricted in scope. They are limited to a statement of the term stating how the hirer is to discharge his obligations under the agreement to pay the hire payments. This may be expressed by reference to the combination of the number, amount, frequency and timing or dates of payments or the manner in which any of the foregoing may be determined and any power of the owner to vary what is payable.

8.7.4.2 Information to be contained in a regulated consumer hire agreement

A regulated consumer hire agreement must contain the information set out in Schedule 3 to the Consumer Credit (Agreements Regulations) 1983, namely the following information and in the following order:[1]

(a) the nature of the agreement, namely the statutory heading;

(b) parties to the agreement, namely the names and addresses of the parties;

(c) specified financial and related particulars under the respective headings 'Key Financial Information' and 'Key Information';

(d) under the heading 'Key Information', the relevant statements of protection and remedies set out in Sch 4 to the Regulations;

(e) the customer signature box and, where applicable, the separate box containing the appropriate statutory statement required where the agreement is one to which s 58(1) of the Act applies or is a cancellable agreement. Although the Regulations state that the separate box must be immediately above, below or adjacent to the signature box, where the hire agreement is a cancellable agreement it follows from the content of 'Key Information' that it must be set out above the customer signature box.

The financial information, statements of protection and remedies, signature and separate box, if any, must be set out in the order stated in the Agreements Regulations, shown together as a whole and not preceded by any information apart from trade names, logos or the reference number of the agreement. The foregoing may not be interspersed with any other information or wording, apart from sub-totals of total amounts and cross-references to the terms of the agreement.

1 SI 1983/1553, reg 3(4) read with Sch 3.

8.7.4.3 Aspects of the prescribed information

(a) Estimated information: Where any information relating to the hire payments or other payments (as specified in Schedule 3) cannot be exactly ascertained, estimated information based on such assumptions as the owner may reasonably make in all the circumstances of the case, and an indication of the assumptions made, may be included in the agreement.1 This would usually take the form of a cross-reference after the relevant information to the assumptions stated in the terms of the agreement.

(b) *Other payments*: One of the listed 'Other payments' is 'any payment payable on termination of the agreement (other than a payment on default to be shown under paragraph 10' of Schedule 3, namely the paragraph relating to the charges). It appears that this refers to the amount payable on termination of the agreement albeit that a similar provision does not exist in relation to credit agreements. In view of the uncertainty, it is advisable to include it by this description under 'Key Financial Information'.

(c) *Cancellation rights*: In contrast to the position in relation to cancellable credit agreements, the Agreements Regulations require the incorporation of a statement that the agreement is non-cancellable only where the agreement is not a cancellable agreement under CCA 1974 and not where it is not cancellable under the Financial Services (Distance Marketing) Regulations 2004.[2] The result is that the statement can be misleading and therefore should, it is submitted, be qualified where the latter regulations result in the agreement being a cancellable agreement.

(d) *Statutory warnings*: A notice alerting the hirer to the fact that missing payments could have severe consequences and may make obtaining credit more difficult, must be inserted in the agreement.

A notice alerting the hirer to the fact that his home may be repossessed if he does not keep up the payments on a hire agreement secured by a mortgage or other security on his home, must be inserted in an agreement which is secured on property.

It is unfortunate that there is inconsistency in the wording of these statutory notices as compared to those applying to a credit agreement.

1 SI 1983/1553, reg 3(2).
2 Ibid., Sch 3, para 11.

8.7.5   Modifying agreements

8.7.5.1   Prescribed terms

A modifying agreement revokes the earlier agreement and contains provisions reproducing the combined effect of the two agreements.[1] The prescribed terms of a modifying agreement are set out in the relevant regulations that apply to a credit agreement or a hire agreement, depending upon whether it is an agreement modifying a credit agreement or a hire agreement.

1 CCA 1974, s 82(2).

8.7.5.2   Information to be contained in an agreement modifying a credit agreement

A modifying agreement under the Agreements Regulations 1983 which modifies an earlier credit agreement must contain the information set out in Part I of Schedule 8 to those Regulations, namely the following information and in the following order:[1]

(a) the nature of the agreement, namely one of the statutory headings;

(b) the parties to the agreement, namely the names and addresses of the parties;

(c) specified financial and related particulars under the respective headings: 'Key Financial Information', 'Other Financial Information' and 'Key Information';

(d) under the heading 'Key Information', the relevant statements of protection and remedies set out in Schedule 2 to the Regulations;

(e) the customer signature box and, where applicable, the separate box referred to in regulation 2(7)(b).

There is provision for estimated information where certain information cannot be exactly ascertained.[2]

The financial information, statements of protection and remedies, signature and separate boxes, must be set out, in the order stated in the Agreements Regulations 1983, shown together as a whole and not preceded by any information, apart from trade names, logos or the reference number of the agreement. The foregoing may not be interspersed with any other information or wording, apart from sub-totals of total amounts and cross-references to the terms of the agreement.

A modifying agreement under the Agreements Regulations 2010 must contain the information referred to in regulation 5 of, and Schedule 1 to, the Regulations.

1 SI 1983/1553, reg 7(4).
2 Ibid., reg 7(3).

8.7.5.3 *Information to be contained in an agreement modifying a hire agreement*

An agreement modifying an earlier hire agreement must contain the information set out in Part II of Schedule 8 to the Agreements Regulations 1983, namely the following information and in the following order:[1]

(a) the nature of the agreement, namely the statutory heading;

(b) the parties to the agreement, namely the names and addresses of the parties;

(c) specified financial and related particulars under the respective headings: 'Key Financial Information' and 'Key Information';

(d) under the heading 'Key Information', the relevant statements of protection and remedies set out in Schedule 4 to the Regulations;

(e) the customer signature box and, where applicable, the separate box referred to in regulation 3(6).

There is provision for estimated information where certain information cannot be exactly ascertained.[2]

The financial information, statements of protection and remedies, signature and separate boxes, must be set out, in the order stated in the Agreements Regulations 1983, shown together as a whole and not preceded by any information, apart from trade names, logos or the reference number of the agreement. The foregoing may not be interspersed with any other information or wording, apart from sub-totals of total amounts and cross-references to the terms of the agreement.

1 SI 1983/1553, reg 7(4).
2 Ibid., reg 7(10).

8.7.6   Authorised overdraft agreement

The content of an authorised non-business overdraft agreement or an authorised business overdraft agreement is governed by regulation 8 of the Agreements Regulations 2010, although regard must also be had to the Agreements Regulations 1983.[1]

1   See further at **22.4** below.

8.8   CONTENTS OF THE AGREEMENT COPY

We have already discussed the requirement for the furnishing of copies of the agreement.[1] This paragraph deals with the contents of a copy of the agreement.

Every copy of an agreement must be a true copy of the original agreement.[2] Although the relevant regulation refers to a copy of an executed agreement, the principle applies equally to a copy of the unexecuted agreement i.e. the first copy or advance copy of the agreement, as the case may be. The copy agreements are governed by the Consumer Credit (Cancellation Notices and Copies of Documents) Regulations 1983 (the 'Copy Document Regulations').[3] The separate forms of notice of cancellation rights are set out in the Schedule to the Regulations.

Certain information may be omitted from a copy, notably any signature box.[4]

Where the agreement falls under s 58(1) of CCA 1974, the advance copy of the agreement must have a specified heading and contain a box indicating the right of the debtor or hirer to withdraw from the prospective agreement, in accordance with the statutory form. Where the agreement is a cancellable agreement, the agreement must include the debtor's or hirer's right to cancel, in statutory form.[5]

Where a notice indicating the right of the debtor or hirer to cancel does not appear prominently on the first page of the copy of the agreement, the copy of the agreement must show on its first page a box containing the statutory statement: 'This is a copy of your agreement for you to keep. It includes a notice about your cancellation rights which you should read'.[6] This requirement creates an anomaly, as the Agreements Regulations do not permit any information other than that which they prescribe, and this statement is not included or envisaged in the information, so that it constitutes a prohibited interspersal. However, it is submitted that the Copy Document Regulations supersede the Agreements Regulations in this respect, as otherwise this requirement would be incapable of fulfilment.

A regulated agreement must embody all the terms of the agreement, other than implied terms.[7] A document embodies a provision if the provision is set out either in the document itself or in another document referred to in it.[8]

The Copy Document Regulations set out general requirements as to the form and content of copy documents. In essence, every copy of an executed agreement, security instrument or other document referred to in CCA 1974, which is delivered or sent to a debtor, hirer or a surety, must be a true copy. This does not mean that it must be an identical or exact copy.[9] As stated by Waksman J in *Carey v HSBC Bank plc*, 'immaterial differences between the original and the copy which do not mislead the reader as to the contents can be ignored'.[10] Waksman J also held that the copy may take the form of a reconstituted version of the executed agreement which may be from sources other than the actual signed agreement,[11] and whether several pieces of paper constitute one document is a question of substance and not of form.[12]

The *Carey* case was cited, with approval, by the Court of Appeal in *Phoenix Recoveries (UK) Limited SARL v Kotecha*[13] stating that the obligation under s 78 requires delivery of a copy of the actual terms of the agreement (not necessarily an exact copy of the document itself) and that the copy supplied can be a reconstituted version made from sources other than the original signed document.

The Regulations dispense with the need to supply certain copies of documents, notably a document obtained by the debtor or hirer from a person other than the creditor or owner and supplied by the debtor or hirer to the creditor or owner or a document kept or to be kept by the debtor or hirer under the terms, or in consequence, of the agreement.[14]

Where more than one debtor or hirer enters into the agreement, the creditor or owner, as the case may be, must supply a copy of the agreement to each of them.[15]

1 At **8.6.2** to **8.6.4**.
2 SI 1983/1557, reg 3(1). See also **8.3**.
3 SI 1983/1557.
4 Ibid., reg 3(2)(b).
5 Ibid., reg 5.
6 Ibid., reg 5 and Sch, Part V.
7 CCA 1974, s 61(1)(b).
8 Ibid., s 189(4).
9 SI 1983/1557, reg 3(1).
10 [2009] GCCR 9951, [2009] EWHC 3417 (QB), at para 49.
11 Ibid., para 234.
12 Ibid., para 173.
13 [2011] GCCR 1101, [2011] EWCA Civ 105 at para 9.
14 SI 1983/1557, reg 11.
15 CCA 1974, s 185.

Chapter 9

Contract terms

9.1 OVERVIEW

Consumer credit agreements and consumer hire agreements are governed by an array of statutes, regulations, the FCA Handbook (notably CONC Sourcebook) and codes of practice. Indeed, the regulatory framework has become increasingly complex, intricate and all-embracing.

The following are the principal relevant statutory enactments:

- Consumer Credit Act 1974 ('CCA 1974'), as amended, notably by the Consumer Credit Act 2006 and the Consumer Credit (EU) Directive Regulations 2010 and the various regulations made under CCA 1974

- Financial Services and Markets Act 2000 ('FSMA')

- Consumer Rights Act 2015

- Financial Services (Distance Marketing) Regulations 2004

- Consumer Protection (Distance Selling) Regulations 2000

- Data Protection Act 1998

- Electronic Communications Act 2000

- Consumer Credit Act 1974 (Electronic Communications) Order 2004

- Supply of Goods and Services Act 1982

- Supply of Goods (Implied Terms) Act 1973

- Unfair Contract Terms Act 1977

- Financial Services and Markets Act 2000 (Regulated Activities) Order 2001

- Consumer Protection from Unfair Trading Regulations 2008

- Electronic Money Regulations 2011.

The following codes may also impact on the consumer agreement:

- The Lending Code

- The Codes of Practice of the Finance & Leasing Association

- The Code of Practice of the Consumer Credit Trade Association.

In general terms, the codes require the agreement terms to be clear and in plain intelligible language, that the agreement contains the information prescribed by the relevant Acts and regulations, and does not contain unfair contract terms.

The various controls which are listed above represent a far cry from the notion of freedom of contract and indeed epitomise the converse of the concept of 'caveat emptor', which has been buried in the distant past.

9.2   THE SHAPE OF A REGULATED AGREEMENT

Various provisions in the statutory enactments serve to give a regulated agreement a particular shape.

9.2.1   Consumer credit agreements and consumer hire agreements under the Consumer Credit (Agreements) Regulations 1983[1]

An agreement governed by these regulations[2] requires a prescribed heading and prescribed information relating to the financial and related particulars, which must be set out together and as a whole, without interspersals.

In general terms a regulated consumer credit agreement must set out, in the following sequence, 'Key Financial Information', 'Other Financial Information' and 'Key Information' followed by the customer's signature box, whilst a consumer hire agreement must set out, in the following order, 'Key Financial Information' and 'Key Information', followed by the customer's signature box. The content of each information section is prescribed. The agreement must contain statutory forms of statement of protection and remedies and in certain cases these must be set out adjacent to the financial and related particulars and in others, adjacent to the customer's signature box. Certain statutory forms or notices must be enclosed in a box.

Whilst there are no requirements governing the size of the lettering, the agreement must be easily legible and of a colour which is readily distinguishable from the background medium. Subject to limited exceptions, the lettering of the terms must be of equal prominence.[3] Prominence as such is not defined and is in some respects a subjective issue. Information regarding the customer's personal data, and how it may be used, should preferably be set out below, but near the customer's signature box, so that it can be shown that the customer consented to the same; alternatively, it may be set out in the agreement itself and the customer's attention drawn to it by a reference close to the signature box.

The reader is referred to the detailed discussion in Chapter 8.

1 Consumer Credit (Agreements) Regulations 1983, SI 1983/1553, as amended.
2 See **Chapter 2**.
3 See the above regulations.

9.2.2 Consumer credit agreements under the Consumer Credit (Agreements) Regulations 2010[1]

A credit agreement under these regulations is not subject to the same degree of formalistic regulation as a credit agreement under the 1983 Regulations. Apart from a statutory heading to the agreement, there are no prescribed headings to blocks of information, nor any prescribed form of signature. The agreement must, however, contain the prescribed information and the relevant statutory forms of statement of protection and remedies, set out in Schedules 2 and 3 to the Regulations.

The information in the agreement must be presented in a clear and concise manner, easily legible and of a colour which is readily distinguishable from the background medium.[2] In contrast with the 1983 regulations, there are no restrictions on interspersals.

The reader is referred to the detailed discussion in Chapter 8.

1 SI 2010/1014.
2 Ibid., reg 3.

9.3 CONTRACT TERMS

We review below some of the more common contract terms found in consumer agreements.

9.3.1 Time of performance

It is usual for an agreement to state that prompt payment is essential. The contract may also stipulate that prompt performance of other obligations is essential.

In general, in the absence of a contractual term that time is of the essence, or notice by one party to the other requiring performance within a reasonable time, prompt performance of a contractual obligation is not essential. Thus, although the party in breach may incur liability for damages or for interest on late payment, his late performance will not constitute a repudiatory breach of the agreement.[1]

We turn next to consumer contracts, namely a contract between a trader and a consumer, as defined in section 2 of the Consumer Rights Act 2015. The Act defines a consumer as an individual acting for purposes that are wholly or mainly outside that individual's trade, business, craft or profession.

In a sales contract, that is one under which a trader transfers or agrees to transfer ownership of goods to the consumer who pays or agrees to pay the price, in the absence of an agreed time or period, the contract is to be treated as including a term that the trader must deliver the goods without undue delay and in any event not more than 30 days after the day the contract was entered into.[2]

In a contract to supply a service, in the absence of an express term or information as to the time for the service to be performed or how the time is to be fixed, the contract is to be treated as including a term that the trader must perform the service within a reasonable time. What is a reasonable time is a question of fact.[3]

1 See *Chitty on Contracts* (32nd ed) vol. 1 at 21-011 ff.
2 Consumer Rights Act 2015, ss 5(1) and 28(3).
3 Ibid., s 52(2) and (3).

9.3.2 Contract terms imported by the Consumer Rights Act 2015

9.3.2.1 Contracts to supply goods

Chapter 2 of the Consumer Rights Act 2015 contains a list of statutory rights and duties under a goods contract, namely a contract for a trader to supply goods to a consumer, with a corresponding list of remedies if the statutory rights are not met.[1] The contract encompasses a sales contract (colloquially known as a contract of sale), a contract for the hire of goods, a hire-purchase agreement and a contract for the transfer of goods (which would include a contract of exchange).[2] The statutory rights are expressed not, as historically, by way of warranty, condition or implied terms but as terms which are included in the contract. The statutory wording expression is that the contract is to be treated as including the relevant term, so that the term is, in fact, an express term which is deemed to be incorporated in the contract.

The statutory rights and corresponding duties are expanded upon under the following heads:

- goods to be of satisfactory quality (s 9);

- goods to be fit for a particular purpose (s 10);

- goods to be as described (s 11);

- other pre-contract information included in the contract (s 12);

- goods to match a sample (s 13);

- goods to match a model seen or examined (s 14);

- installation as part of conformity of the goods with the contract (s 15);

- goods not conforming to the contract if the digital content does not conform (s 16);

- trader to have the right to supply the goods etc (s 17);

- no other requirement about quality or fitness to be treated as included unless expressly included in the contract (s 18);

- delivery of goods (s 28);

- the passing of risk (s 29).

The consumer's statutory remedies, if the statutory rights are not met, are set out in sections 19 to 27.

With limited exceptions in respect of s 17 under hire agreements, a trader's liability under sections 9 to 29 above cannot be excluded or restricted.[3]

Equivalent terms apply to digital content contracts[4] and to services contracts,[5] as discussed below.

1 Sections 3 and 9 to 24.
2 Section 3.
3 Section 31, and see s 32.
4 Sections 34 to 47.
5 Section 48 ff.

9.3.2.2 Other supply contracts

(A) CONTRACTS TO SUPPLY SERVICES

Chapter 4 of the Consumer Rights Act 2015 covers contracts for a trader to supply services to a consumer.

Services contracts include the following statutory rights and corresponding duties:[1]

- the service is to be performed with reasonable skill (s 49);

- information about the trader or service taken into account by the consumer is to be binding (s 50);

- in the absence of an expressly stated price, a reasonable price is to be paid for the service (s 51);

- in the absence of an expressed time for performance, the service is to be performed within a reasonable time (s 52);

- any enactment or rule of law imposing a stricter duty on the trader is unaffected (s 53).

The consumer's statutory remedies, if the statutory rights are not met, are as set out in sections 54 to 56.

With limited exceptions in respect of s 50, a trader's liability under the above sections cannot be excluded or restricted.[2]

'Services' would include the provision of a loan or the advance of credit.

(B) CONTRACTS TO SUPPLY DIGITAL CONTENT

Chapter 3 of the Consumer Rights Act 2015 covers contracts for a trader to supply digital content to a consumer.

Statutory rights and corresponding duties include the following:

- digital content to be of satisfactory quality (s 34);

- digital content to be fit for particular purpose (s 35);

- digital content to be as described (s 36);

- pre-contract information to be treated as included as a term of the contract (s 37);

- trader's right to supply content to the consumer (s 41).

Liability in respect of the above cannot be excluded or restricted.[3]

The consumer's statutory remedies, if the statutory rights are not met, are as set out in sections 42 to 46.

1 Sections 49 to 57.
2 Section 57.
3 Section 47.

9.3.2.3   Terms implied under other Acts

Various statutes import implied terms into contracts which fall outside the Consumer Rights Act 2015.[1] Thus, in the case of a contract of sale, the Sale of Goods Act 1979, ss 12, 13, 14 and 15 import various implied terms, previously called conditions, into the contract of sale. These relate to implied terms as to title, correspondence of the goods with their description, about the quality or fitness for any particular purpose of goods and that they are of satisfactory quality and, in a contract for sale by sample, that the bulk will correspond with the sample in quality and will be free from any defect which would not be apparent on reasonable examination of the sample. The above sections of the Sale of Goods Act 1979 contain express exclusions in respect of contracts which fall within the scope of the Consumer Rights Act 2015.

The Supply of Goods and Services Act 1982 introduces various implied terms into contracts which fall outside the scope of the Consumer Rights Act 2015, called 'relevant contract for the transfer of goods' relating to the transfer of property in goods, where ownership of goods will pass from the supplier to the customer, but which are not sale agreements. It also introduces implied terms into contracts for the hire of goods outside the scope of the 2015 Act, called 'relevant contract for the hire of goods' and into certain contracts for the supply of services outside the scope of the 2015 Act, called 'relevant contract for the supply of a service'.[2] The narrative below relates to contracts outside the scope of the Consumer Rights Act 2015.

The 1982 Act does not apply to a contract for the sale of goods (as to which see above), nor to a hire-purchase agreement (as to which see below). Implied terms about title on a transfer of property in goods are contained in s 2, implied terms as to the correspondence of the goods with their description in s 3, implied terms as to the goods' quality or fitness for any particular purpose in s 4, and, in the case of the transfer of goods by reference to a sample, the implied condition in s 5 that the bulk will correspond with a sample in quality, that the transferee will have a reasonable opportunity of comparing the bulk with the sample and that the goods will be free from any defect not apparent on a reasonable examination of the sample.

The Supply of Goods and Services Act 1982 also contains implied terms in relation to contracts of hire. Thus, in a contract for the hire of goods, there is an implied condition that the bailor (or owner) has a right to transfer possession of the goods by way of hire, that the bailee (or hirer) will enjoy quiet possession of the goods for the period of their hire (s 7), that where the bailor agrees to hire the goods by description, that the goods will correspond with their description (s 8), where the owner hires out the goods in the course of a business, that the goods supplied under the contract are of satisfactory quality (s 9), where the owner hires the goods by reference to a sample that the bulk will correspond with the sample in quality, that the hirer will have a reasonable opportunity of comparing the bulk with the sample and that the goods will be free from any defect which would not be apparent on a reasonable inspection of the sample (s 10).

Part 1A of the Supply of Goods and Services Act 1982 extends the application of the Act to the supply of goods with respect to Scotland.

As its title suggests, the Supply of Goods and Services Act 1982 also applies to the supply of services and it imports implied terms into such a contract. These are to the effect that there is an implied term that the supplier will carry out the service with reasonable care and skill (s 13), that the supplier will carry out the service within a reasonable time (s 14) and that the party contracting with the supplier will pay a reasonable charge (s 15).

Implied terms in relation to hire-purchase agreements outside the scope of the Consumer Rights Act 2015, called 'relevant hire-purchase agreement',[3] are contained in the Supply of Goods (Implied Terms) Act 1973. This sets out implied terms as to title (s 8), an implied term that the goods will correspond with their description (s 9), that where the creditor hires out goods under a hire-purchase agreement in the course of a business, the goods supplied under the agreement are of satisfactory quality (s 10) and an implied term that where goods under a hire-purchase agreement are hired by reference to a sample, that the bulk will correspond with the sample in quality, the person to whom the goods are hired will have a reasonable opportunity of comparing the bulk with the sample and that the goods will be free from any defect which would not be apparent on a reasonable examination of the sample (s 11).

Whereas originally the Sale of Goods Act 1979 and the Supply of Goods and Services Act 1982 imported what are now called 'terms' as 'conditions', it is now left to the courts to determine whether, in all the circumstances, the particular breach was a condition entitling the buyer to rescind a contract. Whether or not it is a condition is assisted by further provisions in each Act. Thus, the Sale of Goods Act states that, where in the case of contract of sale the buyer would have had the right to reject goods by reason of the breach on the part of the seller of terms implied by ss 13, 14 or 15, but the breach is so slight that it would be unreasonable for him to reject them, then if the buyer does not deal as consumer, the breach is not to be treated as a breach of condition but may be treated as a breach of warranty.[4] Similarly, in the Supply of Goods and Services Act, where in the case of a breach of contract for the transfer of goods, the transferee would have had the right to treat the contract as repudiated by reason of a breach on the part of the transferor of a term implied by s 3, 4 or 5(2)(a) or (c) but the breach is so slight that it would be unreasonable for him to do so, then if the transferee does not deal as consumer, the breach is not to be treated as a breach of condition but may be treated as a breach of warranty.[5] These sections apply unless a contrary intention appears in, or is to be implied from, the contract.

A term can also be implied into a contract via other routes, namely by custom or trade usage or terms implied by the courts. An example of the latter is the implied term that, where interest rates in an agreement are expressed to be variable, the rates would not be set dishonestly, for an improper purpose, capriciously or arbitrarily.[6] The reader is reminded that a regulated agreement is not required to set out implied terms even though they are contained in, and form part of, the agreement.[7]

Unless the particular implied terms cannot be excluded, by virtue of any of the provisions referred to below, implied terms can be overridden, superseded or indeed amplified by express terms set out in the agreement or varied by custom or trade usage.

1 (i) Unfair Contract Terms Act 1977, ss 6, 7(3A) and 20 and the provisions there referred to relating to contracts of sale and hire-purchase, namely the Sale of Goods Act 1979, ss 12, 13, 14 and 15 (re sale) and the Supply of Goods (Implied Terms) Act 1973, ss 8, 9, 10 and 11 (re hire-purchase); (ii) The Unfair Contract Terms Act 1977, ss 7 and 21 and the Supply of Goods and Services Act 1982, ss 2 and 7 (re contract for transfer of goods and contract for hire respectively).
2 Description inserted by Consumer Rights Act 2015, Sch 1, para 38.
3 Description inserted by Consumer Rights Act 2015, Sch 1, para 2.
4 Sale of Goods Act 1979, s 15A.
5 Supply of Goods and Services Act 1982, s 5A.
6 *Paragon Finance plc v Nash and Staunton* [2001] GCCR 3073D, [2002] 1 WLR 685, [2001] 2 All ER (Comm) 1025, CA.
7 CCA 1974, s 61(1)(b).

9.3.2.4   Other remedies for breach

Apart from the provisions of the Consumer Rights Act 2015, a breach of contract entitles the innocent party, whether creditor, owner or consumer, to institute an action for damages. The right to terminate the contract is dependent upon whether the defaulting party has repudiated the contract or otherwise committed a fundamental or repudiatory breach of the contract. To constitute a repudiatory breach, the default must be a breach of condition or go to the root of the contract. The agreement may provide that a particular breach is a fundamental breach which entitles the creditor or owner to terminate the agreement, or it may be so persistent a breach as to constitute a repudiatory breach.

It may be a question of degree whether or not the conduct of the debtor or hirer amounts to repudiation. Thus, non-payment of six months' instalments has been held to amount to a repudiation, whereas failure to make payment of two instalments was held not to amount to repudiation.[1] If time was expressed to be, or made, of the essence, or if an act or omission is expressed to amount to repudiation of the contract, the courts are likely to treat it as such.[2]

Where the debtor or hirer has neither repudiated the agreement nor committed a fundamental breach, but the creditor or owner terminates the agreement in the exercise of an express power to do so, the owner's damages are limited to loss suffered through any breaches up to the date of termination. Any greater compensatory measure would be void as a penalty.[3]

An agreement might provide for its automatic termination on the happening of certain events of default, such as the debtor's or the hirer's bankruptcy. Regulated credit or hire agreements cannot be terminated automatically, as they require the prior service of a default notice. The advantage of an automatic termination provision, where permitted, is that it serves to crystallise the creditor's claim on insolvency and can afford protection for the owner's goods that are the subject of a hire agreement, a conditional sale or a hire-purchase agreement.

Contract terms, including those specifying breaches and their consequences, are subject to the Unfair Contract Terms Act 1977, the unfair terms provisions of the Consumer Rights Act 2015, and the unfair relationships provisions of the Consumer Credit Act 1974, to which we turn next.

1 *Yeoman Credit Ltd v Waragowski* [1961] 3 All ER 145, CA; see further *Financings Ltd v Baldock* [1963] 2 QB 104; *Anglo-Auto Finance Co Ltd v James* [1963] 3 All ER 566, CA.
2 *Lombard North Central plc v Butterworth* [1987] 1 All ER 267, CA.
3 See *Chitty on Contracts: General Principles of Contract* (32nd edn, 2015) at para 26–200ff. esp. 26–141; *Financings Ltd v Baldock* [1963] 2 QB 104, CA; *Re Apex Supply Co* [1942] Ch 108.

9.3.3 Restrictions on exclusion clauses

9.3.3.1 Under the Consumer Rights Act 2015

A trader cannot contract out of his liability under the consumer's statutory rights listed at **9.3.2.1** above.[1]

That also means that a term of a contract to supply goods is not binding on the consumer to the extent that it would:

(a) exclude or restrict a right or remedy in respect of a liability under a provision so listed;

(b) make such a right or remedy or its enforcement subject to a restrictive or onerous condition;

(c) allow a trader to put a person at a disadvantage as a result of pursuing such a right or remedy, or

(d) exclude or restrict rules of evidence or procedure.[2]

As regards a contract of services, with limited exceptions in respect of s 50, a trader's liability with regard to the consumer's rights listed at **9.3.2.2** above cannot be excluded or restricted.[3]

That also means that a term of a contract to supply services is not binding on the consumer to the extent that it would:

(a) exclude or restrict a right or remedy in respect of a liability under a provision so listed;

(b) make such a right or remedy or its enforcement subject to a restrictive or onerous condition;

(c) allow a trader to put a person at a disadvantage as a result of pursuing such a right or remedy, or

(d) exclude or restrict rules of evidence or procedure.[4]

Liability in respect of the trader's statutory obligations in relation to a contract to supply digital data under the Consumer Rights Act 2015 cannot be excluded or restricted.[5]

1 Consumer Rights Act 2015, s 31(1).
2 Ibid., s 31(2).
3 Ibid., s 57(1) to (3).
4 Ibid., s 57(4).
5 Ibid., s 47.

9.3.3.2   The Unfair Contract Terms Act 1977

This Act generally does not apply to a term in a consumer contract or to a consumer notice, as such terms are defined in section 61 of the Consumer Rights Act 2015.

A person cannot, by reference to any contract term or to a notice given to persons generally or to particular persons, exclude or restrict his liability for death or personal injury resulting from negligence. In the case of other loss or damage, a person cannot so exclude or restrict his liability for negligence except in so far as the term or notice satisfies the requirement of reasonableness. Where a contract term or notice purports to exclude or restrict liability for negligence, a person's agreement to or awareness of it is not of itself to be taken as indicating his voluntary acceptance of any risk.[1]

The Unfair Contract Terms Act 1977 outlines the reasonableness test. The requirement is that the term must have been a fair and reasonable one, having regard to the circumstances which were, or ought reasonably to have been, known to or in contemplation of the parties when the contract was made.[2] In determining the reasonableness or otherwise of a term, regard must be had to the guidelines set out in Sch 2. In summary, they are the following:

(a)   the strength of the bargaining positions of the parties;

(b)   whether the customer received an inducement to agree to the term or had an opportunity of entering into a similar contract with other persons without having to accept a similar term;

(c)   whether the customer knew or ought reasonably to have known of the existence and extent of the term;

(d)   where the term excludes or restricts any relevant liability if some condition is not complied with, whether it was reasonable to expect that compliance with that condition would be practicable; and

(e)   whether the goods were manufactured, processed or adapted to the special order of the customer.

There are restrictions on the exclusion of a seller's implied undertakings as to title, as to conformity of goods with their description and their quality or fitness for a particular purpose, and on the corresponding rights and obligations in relation to hire purchase or the passing of possession or ownership of goods.[3]

In certain circumstances, exclusions have been upheld on the grounds that they were found to be fair and reasonable to incorporate in the contract.[4]

1 Section 2.
2 Section 11 read with Sch 2.
3 Sections 6, 7 and 13.
4 Unfair Contract Terms Act 1977, ss 2, 6 and 11 and Sch 2; *Photoprint v Forward Trust Group* (1993) 12 Tr LR 146.

9.3.3.3   Unfair contract terms

CONSUMER CONTRACTS

Part 2 of the Consumer Rights Act 2015 governs unfair terms in consumer contracts and unfair notices to consumers. An unfair term of a consumer contract and an unfair consumer notice are not binding on the consumer. A term is unfair if, contrary to the requirement of good faith, it causes a significant imbalance in the parties' rights and obligations under the contract to the detriment of the consumer. A notice is unfair if, contrary to the requirement of good faith, it causes a significant imbalance in the parties' rights and obligations to the detriment of the consumer. Part 1 of Schedule 2 to the Act contains an indicative and non-exhaustive list of terms of consumer contracts that may be regarded as unfair. Part 1 is subject to Part 2 of Schedule 2.[1]

As to the concept of good faith, see **9.3.3.4** below.

A term of a consumer contract may not be assessed for fairness under section 62 to the extent that it specifies the main subject matter of the contract or the assessment is of the appropriateness of the price payable under the contract by comparison with the goods, digital content or services supplied under it, provided the term is transparent and prominent. 'Transparent' means that it is expressed in plain and intelligible language and (if in writing) is legible. 'Prominent' means that it is brought to the consumer's attention in such a way that the average consumer would be aware of the term. 'Average consumer' means a consumer who is reasonably well-informed, observant and circumspect.[2]

A trader cannot exclude or restrict liability for death or personal injury resulting from negligence.[3]

Where a contract term is not binding, the contract continues, so far as practicable, to have effect in every other respect.[4]

The court must consider whether the term is fair even if none of the parties to the proceedings has raised the issue or indicated that it intends to raise it, provided that the court considers that it has sufficient legal and factual material before it to consider the fairness of the term.[5]

Separate controls on unfair business practices are imposed by CONC e.g. CONC 4.8R.

An instructive case on unfair contract terms under the earlier Unfair Terms in Consumer Contracts Regulations 1999 that preceded the Consumer Rights Act 2015, and which contained essentially similar provisions in this regard, and consideration too of the Consumer Protection from Unfair Trading Regulations 2008, is to be found in *Office of Fair Trading v Ashbourne Management Services Ltd*.[6]

NON-CONSUMER CONTRACTS

Unfair contract terms in non-consumer contracts are governed by the Unfair Contract Terms Act 1977, generally referred to as UCTA.

As between contracting parties, where one of them deals on the other's written standard terms of business, as against that party, the other cannot by reference to any contract term:

(a) when himself in breach of contract, exclude or restrict any liability of his in respect of the breach; or

(b) claim to be entitled:

    (i) to render a contractual performance substantially different from that which was reasonably expected of him, or

     (ii)   in respect of the whole or any part of his contractual obligation, to render no performance at all,

except in so far as the contract term satisfies the requirement of reasonableness.[7] The reader is also referred to **9.3.3.2** above.

1 Sections 61 to 63.
2 Section 64.
3 Section 65.
4 Section 67.
5 Section 71.
6 [2011] GCCR 11201, [2011] EWHC 1237 (Ch).
7 Section 3.

9.3.3.4 'Unfairness' and 'good faith'

The general rule in English contract law was succinctly stated in *Monde Petroleum SA v Westernzagros Ltd* as follows:

> 'There is no general doctrine of "good faith" in English contract law. A duty of good faith is implied by law as an incident of certain categories of contract (for example, contracts of employment and contracts between partners or others whose relationship is characterised as a fiduciary one). However, in all other categories of contract ... such a duty will only be implied where the contract would lack commercial or practical coherence without it and where all the other requirements for implication are met.'[1]

In the context of consumer contracts, the EU introduced the concept of good faith into such contracts in the UK, including consumer credit agreements and consumer hire agreements, via the Directives which gave rise to the Unfair Terms in Consumer Contracts Regulations 1994, the Unfair Terms in Consumer Contracts Regulations 1999 and the Consumer Rights Act 2015.

    In *Director General of Fair Trading v First National Bank plc*[2] the court dwelt at some length on the concepts of unfairness and good faith in the earlier Unfair Terms in Consumer Contracts Regulations 1994 Lord Bingham stated:[3]

> 'The requirement of good faith in this context is one of fair and open dealing. Openness requires that the terms should be expressed fully, clearly and legibly, containing no concealed pitfalls or traps. Appropriate prominence should be given to terms which might operate disadvantageously to the customer. Fair dealing requires that a supplier should not, whether deliberately or unconsciously, take advantage of the consumer's necessity, indigence, lack of experience, unfamiliarity with the subject matter of the contract, weak bargaining position or any other factor listed in or analogous to those listed in Schedule 2 of the regulations. Good faith in this context is not an artificial or technical concept; nor since Lord Mansfield was its champion, is it a concept wholly unfamiliar to British lawyers. It looks to good standards of commercial morality and practice.'

The Consumer Rights Act 2015 expressly employs the concept of good faith in Part 2 in relation to unfair terms. Thus, a contract term or notice is stated to be unfair if, contrary to the requirement of good faith, it causes a significant imbalance in the parties' rights and obligations to the detriment of the consumer.[4] It is submitted that good faith also comprises transparency, as prescribed by s 68 of the Act, avoiding the terms listed in Part 1 of Schedule 2 to the Act and not falling foul of the unfair relationships provisions of section 140A of CCA 1974.

The reader is also referred to *Office of Fair Trading v Abbey National plc*,[5] in relation to the then Unfair Contract Terms Regulations and bank charges.

1 [2016] EWHC 1472 (Comm) at para 249.
2 [2001] GCCR 3075, [2001] UKHL 52, [2002] 1 All ER 97, HL.
3 At para 17. See also the Opinion of Lord Steyn at para 36.
4 Section 62(4) and (6).
5 [2009] GCCR 9851, [2009] UKSC 6.

9.3.4.5   *Unfair relationships and contract terms*

The unfair relationships provisions of s 140A of the Act, discussed in **Chapter 24**, impact directly on consumer credit agreements. Section 140A(1)(a) provides that a court may make an order under s 140B in connection with a credit agreement if it determines that the relationship between the creditor and the debtor arising out of the agreement, or the agreement taken with any related agreement, is unfair to the debtor because, inter alia, any of the terms of the agreement or of any related agreement.

Whilst the unfair terms in consumer contracts under Part 2 of the Consumer Rights Act 2015 do not apply to terms to the extent that they specify the main subject matter of the contract or the assessment of the appropriateness of the price payable under it,[1] section 140A applies to all terms of the contract. Thus, unfairness and absence of good faith are criteria against which a credit agreement, whether or not a regulated agreement, might be tested under this provision.

1 Section 64.

9.4   DEFAULT

9.4.1   Default interest

Under a regulated consumer credit agreement, the creditor may not require the debtor to pay default interest, namely interest on sums which in breach of the agreement are unpaid by him, at a rate exceeding the interest rate applying to the agreement. Where the total charge for credit applying to the credit agreement does not include interest, the default interest rate may not exceed what would be the rate of the total charge if any items included by virtue of rules made by the FCA under article 60M of the RAO were disregarded.[1]

It follows that default interest cannot be charged in interest-free transactions. In variable rate transactions the maximum default interest rate will vary with the interest rate applying on the date of the default.

No restrictions apply to default interest in regulated hire agreements. Clearly such interest could not be circumscribed by reference to the total charge for credit (as this does not apply to hire agreements) although it might have been restricted by reference to bank base rate or some other objective rate.

Where the debtor is entitled to a rebate of charges on early settlement, any rebate to which the debtor is entitled is calculated as at the date of early payment.[2]

In the absence of a default interest clause, no interest would be chargeable on a judgment debt relating to a regulated agreement.[3]

The entitlement of a creditor to charge default interest at the contract rate after, as well as before, any judgment was the subject of a challenge by the Director General of Fair Trading under the Unfair Terms in Consumer Contracts Regulations 1994 in *Director General of Fair Trading v First National Bank plc*.[4] Lord Bingham in the House of Lords stated that it was trite law that, once judgment is obtained under the loan agreement for a principal sum and judgment is entered, the contract merges in the judgment and the principal becomes owing under the judgment. However, the parties to a contract may agree that a covenant to pay interest will not merge in any judgment and that contract interest will be charged on the principal sum even after judgment had been obtained. The court held that such a provision was not a core term as it did not define the main subject matter of the contract nor relate to the adequacy of price or remuneration.

1 CCA 1974, s 93; and see FCA Handbook CONC App 1.
2 *Forward Trust v Whymark* [1989] 3 All ER 915, CA.
3 County Courts (Interest on Judgment Debts) Order 1991, SI 1991/1184, art 2(3).
4 [2001] UKHL 52, [2001] GCCR 3075 at para 3.

9.4.2   Default charges

Standard default charges or a tariff of default charges is now commonplace in relation to financial products. They were the subject of the OFT's statement on 'Calculating fair default charges in credit card contracts'.[1] The OFT stated that in its view a fair default charge should:

(a)   be calculated on the basis of a reasonable pre-estimate of the net limited additional administrative costs which occur as a result of the specific breaches of contract and can be identified with reasonable precision;

(b)   reflect a fair attribution of those costs between defaulting consumers;

(c)   be based on a genuine estimate of the numbers of expected instances of default in the relevant period; and

(d)   treat costs other than those net limited additional administrative costs as a general overhead of the credit card business and disregard them for purposes of calculating a default fee.

The OFT effectively required credit card companies to limit their default charges to £12 per default, stating that, as a practical measure, to help encourage a swift change in market practice, it was setting a simple mandatory threshold for intervention by the OFT on default charges.[2]

In accordance with CONC, a firm must not impose charges on customers in default or arrears difficulties unless the charges are no higher than necessary to cover the reasonable costs of the firm.[3]

1 OFT 842, April 2006 at para 3.27. See also OFT Irresponsible Lending Guidance (ILG) and Debt
   Collection Guidance (DCG) referred to in CONC 7.15 and 3.7, 3.11 respectively.
2 At para 5.3.
3 CONC 7.7.5R.

9.5 VARIATION CLAUSES

9.5.1 General

A clause commonly found in financing agreements, whether of credit or hire, is the ability of the creditor or owner unilaterally to vary the charges or interest rates and in consequence, the regular payment amounts. Where s 82(1) of the CCA 1974 applies, notice of a variation must first be given to debtors and hirers. This section does not apply to the exceptions mentioned in s 82(1A) to (1E). The Agreements Regulations contain provision for the creditor in the case of consumer credit agreements and the owner in the case of consumer hire agreements, to vary the charges and rentals.

The Consumer Credit (Notice of Variation of Agreements) Regulations 1977[1] provide the manner in which notice of a variation of a regulated agreement must be given, namely the notice must set out the particulars of the variation and be served on the debtor or hirer in accordance with CCA 1974, s 176 (service of documents), before the variation takes effect. Prior to the Consumer Credit (Agreements) Regulations 2010,[2] which implemented the EU Directive, coming into force, not less than seven days' prior notice was required.[3]

An alternative procedure to the above is available in respect of the variation of the rate of interest under a regulated consumer credit agreement secured on land, where the amount of payment of interest charged under the agreement is calculated by reference to the daily outstanding balance. In that case the variation may be notified in a prescribed form by publication in at least three national daily newspapers.[4] Before implementation of the above statutory instrument, this procedure was available in respect of all regulated consumer credit agreements, whether or not secured.

Regard must be had to the Consumer Rights Act 2015, Sch 2, para 11, which posits, as a *prima facie* unfair term, one which has the object or effect of enabling the trader to alter the terms of the contract unilaterally without a valid reason which is specified in the contract.[5] This is qualified by a further paragraph to the effect that the foregoing provision does not include a term by which a supplier of financial services reserves the right to alter the rate of interest payable by or due to the consumer, or the amount of other charges for financial services without notice, where there is a valid reason, if the supplier is required to inform the consumer of the alteration at the earliest opportunity and the consumer is free to dissolve the contract immediately.[6] It also does not apply to a term under which a trader reserves the right to alter unilaterally the condition of a contract of indeterminate duration, if the trader is required to inform the consumer with reasonable notice and the consumer is free to dissolve the contract.[7]

In *Paragon Finance plc v Staunton and Nash*[8] the Court of Appeal stated that there was an implied term that a rate of interest described as being variable would not be set dishonestly, for an improper purpose, capriciously or arbitrarily.

The power to vary the rate of charge must be distinguished from provisions whereby consumers are locked into contract terms which may themselves constitute unfair contract terms. The Office of Fair Trading issued guidance on interest variation terms.[9] This set out, as examples of unfair interest variation terms, unrestricted interest variation terms in mortgage and savings products where consumers are locked in by a requirement to pay an early payment charge on a mortgage or suffer a loss of interest or a charge where consumers give insufficient notice of withdrawal of money from a savings account.

1 SI 1977/328, regs 2 and 3.
2 SI 2010/1014.
3 SI 1977/328, reg 48.
4 Ibid., reg 3.
5 Schedule 2, Part 1.
6 Ibid., para 22.
7 Ibid., para 23.
8 [2001] GCCR 3073D, [2001] EWCA Civ 1466, [2001] 2 All ER (Comm) 1025, CA.
9 Unfair Contract Terms Guidance: Interest Variation Terms (February 2000).

9.5.2   Restrictions on variations in the FCA Handbook

CONC specifically regulates the increase of interest rates, in the terms below. Under CONC 6.7.14R, where a firm has a right to increase the interest rate under a regulated credit agreement, the firm must not increase the interest rate unless there is a valid reason for doing so.

[**Note**: paragraph 6.20 of ILG]

Examples of valid reasons for increasing the rate of interest in CONC 6.7.14R include:

(1)   recovering the genuine increased costs of funding the provision of credit under the agreement; and

(2)   a change in the risk presented by the customer which justifies the change in the interest rate, which would not generally include missing a single repayment or failing to repay in full on one or two occasions.

[**Note**: paragraph 6.20 (box) of ILG]

Under CONC 6.7.16R, where a firm increases a rate of interest based on a change in the risk presented by the customer, the firm must:

(1)   notify the customer that the rate of interest has been increased based on a change in risk presented by the customer; and

(2)   if requested by the customer provide a suitable explanation which may be a generic explanation for such increases.

[**Note**: paragraph 6.20 (box) of ILG]

9.6 SET-OFF

The former common practice to exclude the customer's right of counterclaim and set-off in relation to payments due by the customer to the creditor or owner in regulated agreements is curtailed in relation to consumer contracts by the Consumer Rights Act 2015, and formerly by the Unfair Terms in Consumer Contracts Regulations 1999. A term is deemed to be unfair which has the object or effect of inappropriately excluding or limiting the legal rights of the consumer in relation to the trader or another party in the event of total or partial non-performance or inadequate performance by the trader of any of the contractual obligations, including the option of offsetting a debt owed to the trader against any claim which the consumer may have against the trader.[1] It is also an unfair term if a term has the object or effect of excluding or hindering the consumer's right to take legal action or exercise any other legal remedy, in particular by requiring the consumer to take disputes exclusively to arbitration not covered by legal provisions or by unduly restricting evidence available to the consumer or by imposing on the consumer a burden of proof which, according to the applicable law, should lie with another party to the contract.[2] A consumer contract may, however, legitimately provide for set-off by the creditor of any sum standing to the borrower's credit in a savings account with the creditor against any undisputed sum owing by the borrower to the creditor. In other words, offsetting is permissible to the extent that the customer is not in dispute with the other party to the contract.

1 Consumer Rights Act 2015, Sch 2, Part 1, para 2.
2 Ibid., para 20.

9.7 CONSOLIDATION

A provision, commonly known as a consolidation clause, entitles the creditor or owner under one agreement with his customer to terminate all other agreements with that customer in the event of his breach. It gives rise to practical problems in relation to regulated agreements. First, a consolidation clause which first appears in a later agreement cannot be imported as a term into an earlier agreement except by way of variation or modification of the earlier agreement. Secondly, in a regulated agreement a default notice is required before a party is entitled to exercise his rights arising from the default, so that a default notice would have to be served in respect of each agreement, so as to give a customer an opportunity to remedy the breach, before a consolidation clause could effectively be invoked. Thirdly, CONC contains provisions governing the appropriation of payments by the customer.[1] Finally, the right of consolidation is subject to the same objections as the right of set-off, as discussed at **9.6**, by virtue of the Consumer Rights Act 2015.

1 CONC 6.4.2R.

9.8 'ENTIRE AGREEMENT CLAUSE'

It used to be common practice for a consumer agreement to contain an 'entire agreement clause' to the effect that the agreement contained all the terms agreed between the parties relating to its subject matter. The inclusion of such a clause in consumer contracts was challenged by the Office of Fair Trading as constituting an unfair contract term, particularly as it limited the seller's or supplier's obligation to respect commitments undertaken by his agents.[1] The Office of Fair Trading was especially concerned with the attempted exclusion of representations which may have been made by the dealer or the dealer's representatives or agents prior to the conclusion of a contract.[2]

However, it is submitted that there is a justifiable ground for consumer credit agreements and consumer hire agreements to contain such a clause. Apart from putting the consumer on notice that it is the basis upon which the contract is entered into, it accords with the rationale of the Consumer Credit Act 1974 which stipulates that a regulated agreement is not properly executed unless the document embodies all the terms of the agreement, other than implied terms.[3] If the agreement had to be read with any additional written or oral terms or representations, it would, by definition, not have been properly executed. It is submitted that the correct approach is to assume that a regulated agreement does contain all its terms, that a clause in the agreement to that effect is not *prima facie* an unfair term but it would be advisable to draw the customer's attention to any such provision on the face of the agreement. If representations were made in connection with entry into the agreement, it would be more appropriate to challenge the agreement on the grounds that it does not contain all its terms.

1   OFT Unfair Contract Terms Guidance (2008) OFT 311, para 14.
2   Under the revoked Unfair Terms in Consumer Contracts Regulations 1999, Sch 2, para 1(n) and now contained in the Consumer Rights Act 2015, Sch 2, Part 1, para 17.
3   CCA 1974, s 61(1)(b).

9.9   ASSIGNABILITY[1]

Regulated agreements generally prohibit the customer assigning the agreement or assigning the customer's rights or duties under the agreement. On the other hand, the creditor or owner will usually assert his right to assign the benefit of the agreement and the right to transfer his obligations under the agreement. By concluding an agreement on these terms, the customer is deemed to have given his consent to the assignment.

The FCA Handbook at CONC 6.5.2R governs assignment in the following terms:

(1)   Where rights of a lender under a regulated credit agreement are assigned to a firm, that firm must arrange for notice of the assignment to be given to the customer:

(a)   as soon as reasonably possible; or

(b)   if, after the assignment, the arrangements for servicing the credit under the agreement do not change as far as the customer is concerned, on or before the first occasion they do.

[**Note**: this, and paragraph (2) below replicate repealed section 82A of CCA 1974]

(2)   Paragraph (1) does not apply to an agreement secured on land.

(3)   A firm may assign the rights of a lender under a regulated credit agreement to a third party only if:

(a)   the third party is a firm; or

(b)   where the third party does not require authorisation, the firm has an agreement with the third party which requires the third party to arrange for a notice of assignment in accordance with (1).

[**Note**: article 17 of the Consumer Credit Directive]

The right of assignment is subject to the provisions governing unfair contract terms in the Consumer Rights Act 2015. Under the 2015 Act, a term is regarded as unfair which has the object or effect of allowing the trader to transfer the trader's rights and obligations under the contract, where this may reduce the guarantees for the consumer, without the consumer's agreement.[2] In other words, without the customer's consent to a transfer or assignment, the customer's rights under the agreement must at least be assured. For example, if a clearing bank were to have the right to assign variable rate agreements to a sub-prime lender which might purport to exercise its right to vary the interest rate unfairly, the customer would be unduly prejudiced. For this reason, the right of assignment or transfer needs to be qualified, possibly by a direct reference to the wording of the paragraph, e.g. provided that the assignment does not reduce the guarantees for the consumer, without the latter's agreement. In passing, it might also be noted that the relevant paragraph makes reference to the right of the trader to transfer not only his rights, but also his obligations, under the contract.

1   See **7.7**.
2   CRA 2015, Sch 2, Pt 1, para 19.

Chapter 10

Duties of creditor or owner and rights of debtor or hirer, prior to and during the lifetime of a regulated agreement

This chapter outlines the duties of a creditor and, in some but not all respects, of an owner before entering into a regulated agreement and the rights of a debtor or hirer, including to documents and information, prior to and in the course of the agreement. **Chapter 11**, by contrast, addresses the obligations of a creditor or owner to keep the customer informed of the state of his agreement by the issue of notices and statements of account.

This chapter does not address information prescribed by CCA 1974, s 55 and regulations made under that section which, if not complied with, render the agreement enforceable against the debtor or hirer on an order of the court only. The regulations, discussed in **Chapter 8**, are:

- the Consumer Credit (Disclosure of Information) Regulations 2004;[1] and

- the Consumer Credit (Disclosure of Information) Regulations 2010.[2]

1 SI 2004/1481.
2 SI 2010/1013.

10.1 PRE-CONTRACT INFORMATION UNDER THE FCA CONSUMER CREDIT SOURCEBOOK (CONC)

10.1.1 Quotations

CCA 1974 originally envisaged extensive use being made of quotations, with their contents prescribed by regulations. The regulations have been repealed and, whilst the issue of quotations remains voluntary and continues to be relatively rare, except in the case of mortgages, their content is prescribed by CONC.

A 'quotation' is defined as any document by which a person gives a customer information about the terms on which the person or a lender or owner is prepared to do business, but does not include:

(a)   a communication which is also a financial promotion;

(b)   any document given to a customer under section 58 of CCA 1974 (opportunity for withdrawal from prospective land mortgage);

(c)   any document sent to a customer for signature which embodies the terms or such of them as it is intended to reduce to writing of a credit agreement or a consumer hire agreement; or

(d)   any copy of an unexecuted agreement delivered or sent to a customer under section 62 of CCA 1974 (duty to supply copy of unexecuted agreement).[1]

As with quotations issued under the earlier regulations in respect of credit agreements secured by mortgage on a customer's home,[2] CONC 4.1.3R and 4.1.4R specify warning statements that must appear in such quotations.

1 CONC 4.1.5R.
2 SI 1999/2725.

10.1.2   Pre-contract disclosure and adequate explanations

CONC 4.2 requires a creditor and, where applicable, a credit broker to furnish the customer with pre-contract disclosure and adequate explanations. The latter originated in the now repealed CCA 1974, s 55A.[1] In general, this obligation:

(1)   applies to a firm with respect to consumer credit lending;

(2)   applies to a firm with respect to credit broking where the firm has or takes on responsibility for providing the disclosures and explanations to customers;

(3)   does not apply to an agreement under which the lender provides the customer with credit which exceeds £60,260, unless the agreement is a residential renovation agreement;

(4)   does not apply to an agreement secured on land; and

(5)   does not apply to a borrower-lender agreement enabling the customer to overdraw on a current account other than such an agreement which would be an authorised non-business overdraft agreement, but for the fact that the credit is not repayable on demand or within three months.[2]

The adequate explanation must include:

(a)   the features of the agreement which may make the credit to be provided under the agreement unsuitable for particular types of use;

(b)   how much the customer will have to pay periodically and, where the amount can be determined, in total under the agreement;

(c)   the features of the agreement which may operate in a manner which would have a significant adverse effect on the customer in a way which the customer is unlikely to foresee;

(d)   the principal consequences for the customer arising from a failure to make payments under the agreement at the times required by the agreement including, where applicable and depending upon the type and amount of credit and the circumstances of the customer:

(i)   the total cost of the debt growing;

(ii) incurring any default charges or interest for late or missed payment or under-payment;

(iii) impaired credit rating and its effect on future access to or cost of credit;

(iv) legal proceedings, including reference to charging orders (or, in Scotland, inhibitions), and to the associated costs of such proceedings;

(v)   repossession of the customer's home or other property; and

(vi) where an article is taken in pawn, that the article might be sold, if not redeemed; and

(e)   the effect of the exercise of any right to withdraw from the agreement and how and when this right may be exercised.[3]

The adequate explanation and advice may be given orally or in writing, except where certain specified explanation and advice has been given orally, when it must likewise be given orally to the customer.[4]

Additional specified information must be provided in relation to credit token agreements, credit card cheques, home credit loan agreements, high-cost short-term credit agreements, bills of sale loan agreements, hire purchase and conditional sale agreements, credit consolidating agreements and credit agreements requiring to be secured by a guarantor.[5]

Separate additional requirements apply to P2P agreements,[6] credit brokers[7] and with regard to specified matters, such as continuous payment authorities (CPA).[8]

1   Inserted in CCA 1974 by SI 2010/1010, following implementation of the Consumer Credit Directive 2008/48/EC art 8.
2   CONC 4.2.1R.
3   CONC 4.2.5R.
4   CONC 4.2.5(4).
5   CONC 4.2.15R and 4.2.22R.
6   CONC 4.3R.
7   CONC 4.4R.
8   CONC 4.5R to 4.7R.

10.2   CREDITWORTHINESS ASSESSMENT

The relevant provisions in CONC 5.2 are a successor to the now repealed CCA 1974, s 55B and were introduced following implementation of the Consumer Credit Directive 2008/48/EC. Before making a regulated credit agreement, a firm must undertake an assessment of the creditworthiness of the customer.[1] The extent and scope of the assessment should be proportionate, including to factors listed in CONC 5.2.3G. Creditworthiness extends to affordability and sustainability, including if the customer experiences financial difficulties or significant adverse consequences.[2] This is setting a high expectation on the assessor and one which cannot be met with any great certainty, especially in relation to a customer in need of credit as opposed to one who seeks credit to enhance his financial position. Special provisions apply to P2P agreements.[3]

A creditor's obligation to assess a debtor's creditworthiness also applies during the course of the agreement. Thus, CONC 6.2 requires a lender to undertake such an assessment before significantly increasing either the amount of credit to be provided under a regulated credit agreement or the credit limit under a regulated running-account credit agreement. The rule also sets out the considerations which are to be taken into account.

1   CONC 5.2.1R.
2   CONC 5.3.1G.
3   CONC 5.5.

10.3   OTHER RELEVANT DISCLOSURE REQUIREMENTS

Other relevant disclosure requirements are set out in:

- CONC 2.7 relating to distance marketing;

- CONC 2.8 on electronic commerce;

- Financial Services (Distance Marketing) Regulations 2004;

- Electronic Commerce (EC Directive) Regulations 2002; and

- Consumer Protection from Unfair Trading Regulations 2008.

10.4   ENTITLEMENT TO COPIES OF THE AGREEMENT AND TO DOCUMENTS

The Consumer Credit Directive 2008/48/EC and the regulations made pursuant to it[1] created a bifurcation of the rights of a debtor under a regulated consumer credit agreement, namely rights under a credit agreement within the scope of the Directive and rights under a credit agreement outside its scope. Hire agreements are not governed, and therefore not affected, by the Directive.

A debtor under a regulated consumer credit agreement within the scope of the Directive is entitled to receive a copy of the prospective agreement before the agreement is made, unless the creditor is unwilling to proceed with the agreement.[2] The debtor is also entitled to receive a copy of the executed agreement and any other document referred to in it, unless a copy of the unexecuted agreement has already been given to him, is in identical terms to the executed agreement and the creditor informs the debtor accordingly in the terms prescribed by s 61A(3).[3] The debtor may still request a copy of the executed agreement before expiry of the withdrawal period.

A debtor under a regulated consumer credit agreement outside the scope of the Directive or a hirer under a regulated hire agreement, is entitled to receive at least one copy of the agreement. In the ordinary case, where the debtor or hirer signs first and the creditor or owner signs second, two copies of the agreement must be supplied to the customer. One copy, of the unexecuted agreement, must be supplied with the original agreement which the customer is to sign and a second copy, of the executed agreement, signed by both parties, must be given to the debtor or hirer within seven days following the making of the agreement.[4] A debtor and hirer are also entitled to receive a copy of the executed credit agreement on request.[5]

'Give', in respect of a document whether within or outside the scope of the Directive, means deliver or send by an appropriate method. 'Appropriate method' means post or transmission in the form of an electronic communication in accordance with s 176A(1).[6]

As a general rule the copy agreement must also be accompanied by a copy of any document referred to in the agreement.[7] There are exceptions to this rule and the following need not be supplied: a document obtained by the customer from a third party and supplied to the creditor or owner (e.g. an insurance policy); a copy of a mail order catalogue where the agreement complies with the description specified in the Schedule to the Consumer Credit (Notice of Cancellation Rights) (Exemption) Regulations 1983; a document, not being a security, which relates to title to property or to the rights or duties of the debtor or hirer in respect of such property (e.g. a title deed or a lease); a document to be kept by the customer under the terms of, or in consequence of, the agreement (e.g. premium receipts, life policy, vehicle registration documents). The latter could not be used as a device to overcome a statutory requirement, e.g. a subsequent fresh regulated agreement which refers to the earlier agreement, requires the earlier agreement to be copied, notwithstanding a term in the earlier agreement to the effect that the customer must retain it. Other copies of documents that need not be supplied are the following:

(a) a copy of an entry in a register contained by or on behalf of a government department or other body charged with a public administrative or statutory function and open to public inspection (e.g. birth, marriage and death certificates, charge certificates and an extract from the Land Register);

(b) an enactment (subject to a limited exception); a document, other than an enactment, published by or on behalf of a government department or other body charged with a public administrative or statutory function; in the case of a modifying agreement, a document embodying the terms of the earlier agreement (subject to various exceptions);

(c) in the case of an unexecuted agreement, where the agreement is to be or is secured on land, any document referred to in the agreement where the debtor or hirer has earlier been supplied with a copy of that document in an identical form by virtue of any requirement of the CCA 1974. This dispensation only applies where the document was supplied pursuant to a requirement of the CCA 1974 and therefore excludes a situation, for example, where the document was supplied under an earlier agreement. Thus, where an advance copy of an agreement secured on land is supplied with a mortgage, a mortgage deed in an identical form need not be copied again with the signature copy of the agreement. However, if the customer enters into a subsequent loan agreement secured by the original all-monies mortgage, the mortgage deed must again be copied with the second loan agreement.[8]

Where the creditor or owner signs first and the debtor or hirer signs second, so that an executed agreement comes into being upon the customer's signature, there is an obligation to supply only one copy of the agreement, namely a copy of the executed agreement and not also a copy of the unexecuted agreement. Professor Goode extends this to the situation where both parties sign on the same occasion, notwithstanding that the customer signs first and the creditor or owner signs second, giving a wider interpretation to the words 'on the *occasion* of his [the customer] signing it [the document] became an executed agreement'.[9] Where a second copy of an agreement is not required then, in the case of a cancellable agreement, the creditor or owner must send a separate notice of cancellation rights to the customer within seven days of the making of the agreement.[10] The notice must be sent either by post or by transmission in the form of an electronic communication in accordance with s 176A(1).[11]

In the case of an agreement outside the scope of the Directive, a copy of the unexecuted agreement is not required to be given where the agreement is neither presented personally nor sent to the customer for signature. An example of such a case is where the customer takes a leaflet form containing a regulated agreement, usually a credit-token agreement, from a leaflet dispenser in a store, colloquially known as a 'take-one'.[12] (This exception does not apply to credit agreements for credit not exceeding £60,260, i.e. credit agreements within the scope of the Directive.)

In the case of a credit-token agreement, the second copy may be sent by post or by electronic communication even after the seven-day period has expired if it is sent together with the credit-token.[13] The notice of cancellation rights may likewise be sent by post or electronic communication before or with the credit-token.[14]

1 See **Chapter 2**.
2 CCA 1974, s 55C.
3 Ibid., s 61A(1), (2) and (3).
4 Ibid., s 62.
5 Ibid., ss 77, 78 and 79.
6 Ibid., s 64(1) read with s 189(1).
7 Ibid., s 62.
8 Consumer Credit (Cancellation Notices and Copies of Documents) Regulations 1983, SI 1983/1557, reg 11.
9 CCA 1974, s 63(2)(b) and *Goode: Consumer Credit Law and Practice*, para IC [30.62].
10 Ibid., s 64(1).
11 Ibid., s 64(1) read with s 189(1).
12 Ibid., s 63(1) and (2).
13 Ibid., s 63(4).
14 Ibid., s 64(2).

10.5 RIGHT OF WITHDRAWAL FROM A CONSUMER CREDIT AGREEMENT

The debtor's right to withdraw from a consumer credit agreement applies to a credit agreement within the scope of the Directive or, exceptionally, to a consumer credit agreement for business purposes for credit up to £25,000.

The right of withdrawal is embodied in CCA 1974, s 66A, as follows:

'(1) The debtor under a regulated consumer credit agreement, other than an excluded agreement, may withdraw from the agreement, without giving any reason, in accordance with this section.

(2) To withdraw from an agreement under this section the debtor must give oral or written notice of the withdrawal to the creditor before the end of the period of 14 days beginning with the day after the relevant day.

(3) For the purposes of subsection (2) the relevant day is whichever is the latest of the following–

(a) the day on which the agreement is made;

(b) where the creditor is required to inform the debtor of the credit limit under the agreement, the day on which the creditor first does so;

(c) in the case of an agreement to which section 61A (duty to supply copy of executed consumer credit agreement) applies, the day on which the debtor receives a copy of the agreement under that section or on which the debtor is informed as specified in subsection (3) of that section;

(d) in the case of an agreement to which section 63 (duty to supply copy of executed agreement: excluded agreements) applies, the day on which the debtor receives a copy of the agreement under that section.

(4) Where oral notice under this section is given to the creditor it must be given in a manner specified in the agreement.

(5) Where written notice under this section is given by facsimile transmission or electronically–

(a) it must be sent to the number or electronic address specified for the purpose in the agreement, and

(b) where it is so sent, it is to be regarded as having been received by the creditor at the time it is sent (and section 176A [relating to electronic transmission of documents] does not apply).

(6) Where written notice under this section is given in any other form–

(a) it must be sent by post to, or left at, the postal address specified for the purpose in the agreement, and

(b) where it is sent by post to that address, it is to be regarded as having been received by the creditor at the time of posting (and section 176 [relating to service of documents] does not apply).

(7) Subject as follows, where the debtor withdraws from a regulated consumer credit agreement under this section–

(a) the agreement shall be treated as if it had never been entered into, and

(b) where an ancillary service relating to the agreement is or is to be provided by the creditor, or by a third party on the basis of an agreement between the third party and the creditor, the ancillary service contract shall be treated as if it had never been entered into.

(8) In the case referred to in subsection (7)(b) the creditor must without delay notify any third party of the fact that the debtor has withdrawn from the agreement.

(9) Where the debtor withdraws from an agreement under this section–

    (a) the debtor must repay to the creditor any credit provided and the interest accrued on it (at the rate provided for under the agreement), but

    (b) the debtor is not liable to pay to the creditor any compensation, fees or charges except any non-returnable charges paid by the creditor to a public administrative body.

(10) An amount payable under subsection (9) must be paid without undue delay and no later than the end of the period of 30 days beginning with the day after the day on which the notice of withdrawal was given (and if not paid by the end of that period may be recovered by the creditor as a debt).

(11) Where a regulated consumer credit agreement is a conditional sale, hire-purchase or credit-sale agreement and–

    (a) the debtor withdraws from the agreement under this section after the credit has been provided, and

    (b) the sum payable under subsection (9)(a) is paid in full by the debtor,

title to the goods purchased or supplied under the agreement is to pass to the debtor on the same terms as would have applied had the debtor not withdrawn from the agreement.

(12) In subsections (2), (4), (5), (6) and (9)(a) references to the creditor include a person specified by the creditor in the agreement.

(13) In subsection (7)(b) the reference to an ancillary service means a service that relates to the provision of credit under the agreement and includes in particular an insurance or payment protection policy.

(14) For the purposes of this section, an agreement is an excluded agreement if it is–

    (a) an agreement for credit exceeding £60,260,

    (b) an agreement secured on land,

    (c) a restricted-use credit agreement to finance the purchase of land, or

    (d) an agreement for a bridging loan in connection with the purchase of land.'

It will be observed from subsections (9)(a) and (11) above that withdrawal from a hire-purchase or conditional sale agreement results in the debtor being obligated to pay the full credit price plus any accrued interest, whereupon title to the goods will pass to him. This contrasts with cancellation of such an agreement outside the scope of the Directive where cancellation of such agreement cancels the underlying transaction; the debtor is under a duty to return the goods to the creditor, thereby effectively ending his liability under the agreement.[1]

CCA 1974, ss 176 (Service of documents) and 176A (Electronic transmission of documents) are overridden by subsections (6)(b) and(5)(b) above, respectively.

1 CCA 1974, s 72.

10.6   RIGHT TO CANCEL A REGULATED AGREEMENT

A cancellable agreement, as described at **4.5**, must include a notice of the customer's cancellation rights in the original agreement and in each copy of the agreement. Where a second copy of the agreement is not required, a separate notice of cancellation rights must still be provided.[1] In each case, the second copy of the agreement or the notice must be sent to the customer by post or by electronic transmission (i.e. by email).[2] The latter applies if:

(a)   the person to whom it is transmitted agrees that it may be delivered to him by being transmitted to a particular electronic address in an electronic form;

(b)   it is transmitted to that address in that form, and the form in which the document is transmitted is such that any information in the document is capable of being stored for future reference for an appropriate period in a way which allows the information to be reproduced without charge.[3]

If the customer wishes to cancel the agreement he may do so by completing and forwarding the statutory cancellation form within the so-called 'cooling-off' period ending five days after receipt of the second copy of the agreement or of the notice, as appropriate.[4] A notice in any other form indicating the customer's intention to cancel the agreement will also operate as a cancellation notice.

A notice of cancellation sent by post is deemed to be served at the time of posting and if sent by email at the time of transmission and otherwise on the working day immediately following the day of transmission.[5]

Cancellation will have the effect of cancelling the agreement and any linked transaction and of withdrawing any offer by the customer to enter into a linked transaction.[6] Effectively the transaction is undone, *void ab initio*, and each party must reimburse the other for any sums paid under or in contemplation of the transaction and return any goods given in part-exchange or make a payment in lieu of the same.[7]

If, under the cancelled agreement, the customer is in possession of any goods, he has a lien on those goods until any payment due to him by the trader has been made.

In the case of a debtor-creditor-supplier agreement for restricted-use credit which is used to finance the doing of work or the supply of goods to meet an emergency or for the supply of goods which, before the cancellation became effective, had become incorporated or affixed to any land or things not comprised in the agreement, the customer is liable for payment of only the cash price of the goods. So, for example, where a trader installs kitchen equipment with the customer's consent (provided the equipment constitutes goods within the meaning of the Sale of Goods Act 1979, s 61(1)), the customer will only be liable for payment of the cash price and not for any credit charge, if he cancels the agreement within the prescribed time. It is therefore prudent for traders to wait for the cancellation or cooling-off period to expire before supplying goods or services under a cancellable agreement.[8]

The cancellation period is extended where the agreement is a distance contract under the Financial Services (Distance Marketing) Regulations 2004.[9] The cancellation period is 14 calendar days beginning with the day after the distance contract is concluded.[10] A contract is concluded when the offeror is made aware of the offeree's acceptance. In the case of a distance contract relating to life insurance or a personal pension, the cancellation period is 30 calendar days in place of 14 calendar days.[11]

Withdrawal rights analogous to those under CCA 1974 are to be found in the Timeshare, Holiday Products, Resale and Exchange Regulations 2010.[12] Cancellation rights similar to those in CCA 1974 are contained in the Cancellation of Contracts made in a Consumer's Home or Place of Work etc Regulations 2008,[13] which regulations do not apply to cancellable agreements under CCA 1974.

1 CCA 1974, s 64.
2 Ibid., ss 63(3), 64(1)(b), 189(1) and 176A(1).
3 Ibid., s 176A(1).
4 Ibid., s 68.
5 Ibid., s 69(7)(b).
6 Subject to the Consumer Credit (Linked Transactions) (Exemptions) Regulations 1983, SI 1983/1560. See also *Goshawk Dedicated (No 2) Ltd v Governor and Company of Bank of Scotland* [2005] EWHC 2906 (Ch), [2005] GCCR 5431; *Governor and Company of the Bank of Scotland v Euclidian (No 1) Ltd* [2007] EWHC 1732 (Comm), [2007] GCCR 6051.
7 CCA 1974, s 69(1) and (4); *Colesworthy v Collman Services* [1993] CCLR 4.
8 Ibid., s 69(2).
9 SI 2004/2095.
10 Ibid., reg 10(1) and (2).
11 Ibid., reg 10(5).
12 SI 2010/2960.
13 SI 2008/1816.

10.7   RIGHT OF WITHDRAWAL UNDER S 58

The withdrawal rights under CCA 1974, s 58 are cancellation rights in reverse, namely a customer's right to withdraw from an agreement before entering into it. They are provided in respect of agreements secured on land. The customer is given a so-called 'consideration period' in which to decide whether or not he wishes to proceed with the agreement. The consideration period begins with the furnishing of the advance copy of the agreement and ends at the expiry of seven days after the day on which the unexecuted agreement is sent to him for signature, or on its return by the customer after signature by him, if earlier.[1]

The withdrawal rights do not apply to a restricted-use credit agreement to finance the purchase of the mortgaged land or to an agreement for a bridging loan in connection with the purchase of the mortgaged land or other land.[2]

1 CCA 1974, s 61(2) and (3).
2 Ibid., s 58(2).

10.8 ENTITLEMENT TO INFORMATION

The debtor, hirer and surety are each entitled, on written request and payment of a nominal fee, to copies of the executed agreement and of any document referred to in the agreement and to a signed statement by the creditor setting out prescribed financial information regarding the state of the account under the agreement. The obligations of the creditor or owner are:[1]

- s 77(1): duty to give information to debtor under fixed-sum credit agreement;

- s 78(1): duty to give information to debtor under running-account credit agreement;

- s 79(1): duty to give information to hirer under consumer hire agreement;

- s 103(1): duty to give debtor or hirer a termination statement or serve a counter-notice;

- s 107(1): duty to give information to surety under fixed-sum credit agreement;

- s 108(1): duty to give information to surety under running-account credit agreement;

- s 109(1): duty to give information to surety under consumer hire agreement; and

- s 110(1): duty to give debtor or hirer a copy of any security instrument executed in relation to agreement after making of agreement.

The creditor or owner must comply with any request for information under the above within the prescribed period of 12 working days. If a creditor or owner defaults, he is not entitled to enforce the agreement whilst the default continues.[2]

In the leading case of *Carey v HSBC Bank plc*,[3] HHJ Waksman QC held that the supply of a reconstituted version of the executed agreement, which may be created from sources other than the signed agreement, is sufficient to satisfy the duty to provide a copy of the agreement under s 78. The copy must contain the name and address of the debtor as at the time of the agreement, but may be taken from any source the creditor has. If the agreement has been varied, the creditor must provide a copy of the original and of the varied terms. The court also held that the prescribed terms of the agreement may be contained in a separate piece of paper referred to in the agreement and supplied together with the agreement at the point of signature. Whether several pieces of paper constitute one document is a question of substance and not of form. A breach of s 78 does not itself give rise to an unfair relationship under s 140A. A court has jurisdiction to make a declaration that there has been a breach of s 78.

Subject to the court's power to grant relief under CCA 1974, s 172, a statement by a creditor or owner of information to a debtor or hirer under s 77(1), 78(1) or 79(1), of a figure for early settlement under s 97(1) or of information to sureties under s 107(1), 108(1) or 109(1), is binding on the creditor or owner.

Further obligations upon a creditor are discussed in the next chapter. They include the obligation to provide annual statements under fixed-sum credit agreements[4] and a statement of account on request.[5] A creditor under a running-account credit agreement must also provide the debtor with a statement of account on a request in writing.[6] Failure to provide the debtor with an annual statement under s 77A is met with serious consequences for the creditor, referred to in **Chapter 11**. Breach of the duty imposed by s 77B is actionable as a breach of statutory duty.

In general, a debtor under a variable rate credit agreement must be notified in writing of the variation of the rate of interest and payments, before the variation can take effect.[7]

There are exceptions to the above general rules, set out in the relevant sections referred to above.

1 See also CONC 13 for guidance on the duty to give information under ss 77, 78 and 79.
2 See the sections cited and the Consumer Credit (Prescribed Periods for Giving Information) Regulations 1983, SI 1983/1569. See also CONC 13.1.6G.
3 [2009] GCCR 9951, [2009] EWHC 3417 (QB). See also CONC 13.1.4G.
4 CCA 1974, s 77A.
5 Ibid., s 77B.
6 Ibid., s 78.
7 Ibid., s 78A.

10.9   EARLY PAYMENT BY THE DEBTOR

A debtor under a regulated consumer credit agreement is entitled to discharge his indebtedness under the agreement in whole or, except where the agreement is secured on land, in part, at any time.[1] The debtor must give the creditor notice of his intention which, unless the agreement is secured on land or is notice to discharge part of his indebtedness, need not be in writing. The notice to discharge his whole indebtedness may also incorporate other information, such as the exercise of an option to purchase goods under a hire-purchase agreement or deal with any other matter arising on, or in relation to termination of the agreement e.g. cancellation of an insurance policy.[2]

Where the debtor gives notice to repay part of the outstanding balance, the repayment must be made within 28 days from the day after that on which the creditor receives the notice or on or before any later date specified in the notice.[3]

On the debtor's request, the creditor must furnish a settlement statement within seven working days of the request, setting out the prescribed information. In relation to an agreement secured on land, the request must be in writing.[4]

To counter-balance the effect of the rebate which the creditor is obliged to give the debtor, and particularly to compensate the creditor for initial setting-up costs, the creditor is entitled notionally to postpone the settlement date for purposes of the rebate calculation to the date of expiration of a period of 28 days after the day on which the creditor received a request for a statement from the debtor, unless a later date is requested by the debtor.[5] A request need not be in writing unless the agreement is secured on land. The settlement date may be further postponed for purposes of calculating the rebate.[6]

A debtor or hirer ('the customer') may serve on the creditor or owner ('the trader') a termination notice, stating that the customer has discharged his indebtedness to the trader and that the agreement has ended, and requiring the trader to provide, within the prescribed period of 12 working days, a notice confirming that those statements are correct or a counter-notice setting out the particulars in request of which the termination notice is alleged to be wrong.[7] The counter-notice is binding on the trader, even if erroneous, unless a court is prepared to grant relief.[8]

1 See CCA 1974, s 94(1) and (3).
2 Ibid., s 94(2).
3 Ibid., s 94(4)(c).
4 Ibid., s 97 read with the Consumer Credit (Settlement Information) Regulations 1983, SI 1983/1564.
5 SI 1983/1564, reg 3.
6 See **10.10.2** below.
7 CCA 1974, s 103 read with SI 1983/1569.
8 Ibid., s 172(2); see *Lombard North Central plc v Stobart* [1990] CCLR 53, CA, The Times, 2 March 1990.

10.10 REBATE ON EARLY SETTLEMENT

10.10.1 Entitlement to a rebate

Upon early repayment, in whole or in part, of a debtor's indebtedness under a regulated consumer credit agreement, the debtor has a statutory entitlement to a rebate of charges attributable to the repaid credit amount in the period after the early settlement date, calculated in accordance with the Consumer Credit (Early Settlement) Regulations 2004.[1] Early settlement takes place where:

(a) the indebtedness of the debtor is discharged or becomes payable before the time fixed by the agreement:

  (i) under s 94(1) of the Act;

  (ii) on refinancing;

  (iii) on breach of the agreement; or

  (iv) for any other reason;

(b) the indebtedness of the debtor is discharged in part under section 94(3) of the Act, or

(c) any sum becomes payable by the debtor before the time fixed by the agreement.[2]

A debtor who voluntarily pays early, must give notice of his intention to do so, but no period is prescribed for the notice and the notice may accompany the payment.[3] The notice may embody the exercise by the debtor of an option to purchase goods under the agreement and deal with any other matter arising on, or in relation to, termination of the agreement.[4]

There is no entitlement to a rebate when the debtor terminates a hire-purchase agreement or conditional sale agreement under s 99 of CCA 1974 as, in that case, the debtor's liability is limited by s 100 of the Act.[5]

The creditor will usually be entitled to compensation for early discharge by the debtor of all or part of his indebtedness. The compensation is an amount equal to the cost incurred by the creditor if the amount of early payment exceeds £8,000 or the total of early payments in any 12-month period exceeds £8,000.[6] The amount claimed by the creditor must be fair, objectively justified and not exceed a specified ceiling.[7]

1 SI 2004/1483.
2 Ibid., reg 2(1A).
3 CCA 1974, s 94 and Consumer Credit (Early Settlement) Regulations 2004, SI 2004/1483.
4 Ibid., s 94(2).
5 SI 2004/1483, reg 2(3).
6 CCA 1974, s 95A.
7 Ibid., s 95A(3)(c).

10.10.2   Calculation of the rebate

The rebate is calculated on the charges element only, and not the credit amount, and specifically on the charges which would have arisen after the settlement date under the agreement but for early payment.

For the purposes of calculating the rebate, the settlement date is calculated in accordance with regulation 5 of the Consumer Credit (Early Settlement) Regulations and may be deferred by one month, or 30 days, where the credit is repayable over a period of more than one year after the agreement date.[1]

The rebate is calculated in accordance with the formula set out in regulation 4, and 4A where the indebtedness is discharged in part, of the Consumer Credit (Early Settlement) Regulations.[2] The statutory rebate is the minimum rebate the creditor is required to grant the debtor, the creditor being free to offer the debtor a greater rebate.

In *Forward Trust v Whymark*[3] the court held that a creditor was entitled to claim the unrebated payment due by the debtor, as the debtor's entitlement to a rebate arises only upon actual discharge of the indebtedness and not when the demand for payment is made.

1 Consumer Credit (Early Settlement) Regulations 2004, SI 2004/1483, reg 6.
2 Ibid., reg 4.
3 [1989] 3 All ER 915, CA.

10.10.3   Exclusions from the rebate calculation

Certain items may be excluded from the rebate calculation. They include so much of taxes, duties, fees etc.as is attributable to the period before the settlement date, sums paid under linked transactions before the settlement date and sums payable under linked transactions for insurance contracts, for guarantees of goods or for the operation of current or deposit accounts and so much of any fee or commission payable under a credit brokerage contract as is attributable to the period before the settlement date.[1]

1 Consumer Credit (Early Settlement) Regulations 2004, SI 2001/1483, reg 3(2).

10.10.4 Settlement statement

A debtor is entitled to a settlement statement on request, to be provided within seven working days of his request, setting out, inter alia, details of the agreement, parties to the agreement, the amount of payment required to be made before taking into account any rebate, any compensatory amount claimed by the creditor, the amount of any rebate on early settlement or a statement that the debtor is not entitled to a rebate, the rebated settlement amount and the compensatory amount, the settlement date and the statement explaining how the rebate has been calculated.[1]

Where a debtor makes payment of part of his indebtedness, he may request the creditor to provide him with a statement within seven working days, containing specified particulars.[2]

1 CCA 1974, s 97 and the Consumer Credit (Settlement Information) Regulations 1983, SI 1983/1564, reg 2 and Schedule. See also *Home Insulation v Wadsley* [1988] CCLR 25.
2 CCA 1974, s 97A.

10.10.5 Hire agreements

Although, as already noted, in certain instances a hirer may terminate a hire agreement once it has run for 18 months, there is otherwise no statutory entitlement to early termination or to a rebate on the termination sum payable in the event of early settlement of a hire agreement. However, at common law and under the rules of equity, there are limitations upon the sum recoverable by the owner on early settlement. Thus, whilst it is open to the parties to stipulate in the contract a sum to be paid as liquidated damages in the event of a breach, the sum so fixed as at the date of the contract must be a reasonable pre-estimate of the loss or damages likely to result from the breach. The sum may not constitute a penalty, such as a sum which is intended to deter the hirer from terminating the agreement or to give the owner an additional windfall in the event of breach.[1]

1 See, for example, *Bridge v Campbell Discount Co Ltd* [1962] 1 All ER 385; *Volkswagen Financial Services (UK) Ltd v Ramage* [2007] GCCR 6181.

10.11 PROTECTED GOODS

Once a debtor under a regulated hire-purchase or a regulated conditional sale agreement has paid the creditor one-third or more of the total cost of the goods and ownership of the goods remains in the creditor, the creditor may only recover possession of the goods from the debtor with an order of the court.[1] The goods falling within this section are referred to as 'protected goods'. Where the agreement also provides for an amount to be paid in respect of the installation of goods, reference to one-third of the total price is construed as a reference to the aggregate of the installation charge plus one-third of the remainder of the total price of the goods.[2]

There is an important provision to the effect that once goods have become protected goods and are comprised, whether alone or with other goods, in a later agreement or a modifying agreement, they remain protected goods and also 'infect' the remaining goods under the new or modifying agreement so that all the goods become protected goods.[3] This is important in relation to add-on agreements.

'Payment' includes tender,[4] and includes payment pursuant to a judgment. However, both payment and tender mean payment and tender of the full amount which is due, so that if the debtor merely offers to pay sufficient to make up one-third of the total purchase price of the goods at a time when a greater amount is owing, e.g. a larger instalment or the full outstanding balance, the creditor is entitled to reject such payment or tender, with the result that the goods do not become protected goods and can be recovered without an order of the court. A tender of money is ineffective unless the money is actually produced.[5]

If the creditor or owner breaches the foregoing provisions by recovering protected goods without obtaining a court order, the regulated agreement, if not previously terminated, terminates automatically and the debtor is released from all liability under the agreement and is entitled to recover from the creditor all sums paid under the agreement.[6] Sums payable under the agreement include sums paid by way of deposit or part-exchange allowance.[7]

It has been suggested that goods are not protected goods, even though one-third or more of the total price may have been paid, unless the debtor is in breach of the agreement.[8] This cannot be the case as it would be absurd to suggest that a debtor who had paid more than one-third and was not in breach is in a worse position than a debtor who had defaulted under his agreement. The reference in CCA 1974, s 90 to the debtor being in breach is simply a statement of the circumstances in which a creditor would normally be impelled to recover possession of his goods as, in the absence of default by the debtor, the creditor would have no reason to do so.

In appropriate circumstances a court may grant equitable relief against forfeiture of the goods upon a customer's breach of an agreement when the sum forfeited was out of all proportion to the damage suffered and when it would be unconscionable for the creditor or owner to retain the money. In exercising its discretion a court will take into account the following factors:

(a)   whether or not the debtor or hirer is in default under the agreement;

(b)   whether significant prejudice would be caused to the creditor or owner by the grant of the relief; and

(c)   whether the refusal of relief would give the creditor or owner a substantial windfall profit or cause the debtor or hirer a disproportionate loss.[9]

---

1   CCA 1974, s 90(1).
2   Ibid., s 90(2).
3   Ibid., s 90(3) and (4).
4   Ibid., s 189(1).
5   See Treitel, *The Law of Contract* (12th edn), at 17-003 and *Dixon v Clarke* (1848) 5 CB 365; *Read's Trustee in Bankruptcy v Smith* [1951] Ch 439, [1951] 1 All ER 406.
6   CCA 1974, s 91.
7   *Branwhite v Worcester Works Finance Ltd* [1969] 1 AC 552, [1999] GCCR 397, HL.
8   *Chitty on Contracts* (32nd edn, Sweet & Maxwell, 2015) vol 2 at 39–362.
9   Ibid., 39–343 and see *Barton, Thompson & Co Ltd v Stapling Machines Co* [1966] 2 All ER 222 and *Transag Haulage Ltd v Leyland DAF Finance plc and Lease Plan UK Ltd* [1999] GCCR 1819; *Goode: Consumer Credit Law and Practice* at [47.222].

10.12   DEBTOR'S RIGHT TO APPROPRIATE PAYMENTS

At common law a debtor or hirer who has several agreements with a creditor or owner may appropriate payments made by him in such order and manner as he deems fit. If, however, the debtor makes no such appropriation, the creditor may do so.[1]

Originally, the CCA 1974 preserved this right and also provided that, if the debtor or hirer did not appropriate his payments to different agreements, the payments had to be appropriated towards satisfaction of the sums due under the various agreements in the proportions which those sums bore to one another.[2] Those sections of CCA 1974 have been repealed and replaced, to the same effect, by CONC 6.4.2R, as follows:

(1)   Where a firm is entitled to payments from the same customer in respect of two or more regulated agreements, the firm must allow the customer, on making any payment in respect of those agreements which is not sufficient to discharge the total amount then due under all the agreements, to appropriate the sum paid by him:

   (a)   in or towards the satisfaction of the sum due under any one of the agreements; or

   (b)   in or towards the satisfaction of the sums due under any two or more of the agreements in such proportions as the customer thinks fit.

(2)   If the customer fails to make any such appropriation where one or more of the agreements is:

   (a)   a hire-purchase agreement or conditional sale agreement; or

   (b)   a consumer hire agreement; or

   (c)   an agreement in relation to which any security is provided;

   the firm must appropriate the payment towards satisfaction of the sums due under the agreements in the proportions which those sums bear to one another.

1   *Chitty on Contracts* (32nd edn) vol 1 at 21-061.
2   CCA 1974, s 81(1) and (2).

10.13   TIME ORDERS

A debtor or hirer is given various opportunities to apply to a court for a time order. A time order may provide for payment by the debtor, hirer or any surety of any sum owed under a regulated agreement or a security, by such instalments and at such times as the court considers reasonable, having regard to the means of the debtor, hirer or surety. It may also provide for remedy by the debtor or hirer of any breach of a regulated agreement (other than for non-payment) within such period as the court may specify.[1]

A time order may be applied for, either in response to an application or action by a creditor or owner for an enforcement order or an order to recover possession of goods or land, or at the instance of the debtor or hirer, including after his receipt of a notice of sums in arrears or default sums.[2] In the latter case, the debtor or hirer may make an application only after giving notice to the creditor or owner under s 129A(2) and a period of at least 14 days has elapsed after the day on which he gave notice.[3]

1 CCA 1974, s 129(2).
2 CCA 1974, s 129(1).
3 CCA 1974, s 129A.

10.14 PROHIBITION ON CONTRACTING OUT

In the context of a customer's rights, a term is void if it is inconsistent with a provision for the protection of the debtor or hirer, his relative or any surety. This will also apply to a waiver by a debtor or hirer of any protection afforded to him by the regulatory regime.[1]

In *Wood v Capital Bridging Finance Ltd*[2] the credit agreement wrongly incorporated a declaration for the borrower's business purposes which, had it been correctly incorporated, would have exempted the agreement from regulation under the provisions of CCA 1974. It was alleged that the defendant was estopped by her declaration from denying that the agreement was unregulated. The Court of Appeal held, per Lord Justice Briggs, that contractual estoppel cannot prevail against the clear prohibition of contracting out of CCA 1974 in s 173(1).

Where a provision specifies the duty or liability of the debtor or hirer, or his relative or surety, in certain circumstances, a term is inconsistent with s 173(1) if it purports to impose an additional duty or liability on him in those circumstances.[3]

1 CCA 1974, s 173(1).
2 [2015] EWCA Civ 451, [2015] GCCR 13013.
3 CCA 1974, s 173(2).

Chapter 11

Post-contract information

11.1 BACKGROUND

Whilst CCA 1974 originally made provision for the furnishing of statements in relation to running-account credit agreements, government was of the view that there was a lack of ongoing information provided to debtors under consumer credit agreements. As the perspective was from the angle of the escalation of debt, it is perhaps not surprising that more emphasis was placed upon the need for information for debtors rather than for hirers under regulated hire agreements, albeit that the problem applied equally to hirers. To quote from the White Paper:[1]

> 'A contributory fact identified in relation to the escalation of debt, has been the lack of ongoing information that many borrowers receive concerning their credit agreement. This is a particular concern to consumers who fall into arrears, as they are often unaware of the consequences of charges on their account, default costs for missed payments, compound interest on the amount owed or underpayment on the accumulation of their debt. At present, although the CCA contains some duties on the lender to provide information, these are generally only triggered by a request from the consumer. There is no obligation on the lender to provide regular statements or, crucially, to inform consumers when payments have been missed.'

In consequence, the Consumer Credit Act 2006 ('CCA 2006') introduced various new post-contract information requirements, as follows:

(a) annual statements to be provided in relation to fixed-sum credit agreements, but not in respect of hire agreements;

(b) additional provisions to be contained in statements relating to running-account credit agreements;

(c) notice of sums in arrears under fixed-sum credit agreements and hire agreements;

(d) notice of default sums;

(e) notice of interest payable on judgment debts; and

(f) information sheets on arrears and defaults, prepared by the Office of Fair Trading, to accompany notices of arrears and notices of default respectively.

---

1 White Paper: Fair, Clear and Competitive: The Consumer Credit Market in the 21st Century (Cm 6040 December 2003).

11.2   ANNUAL STATEMENTS OF ACCOUNT UNDER FIXED-SUM CREDIT AGREEMENTS

This requirement was introduced by s 6 of CCA 2006 (s 77A of CCA 1974). A creditor under a regulated agreement for fixed-sum credit must furnish the debtor with an annual statement of account, the first relating to the period of one year beginning with the day on which the agreement is made or the first day on which there is a movement in the account, and thereafter at intervals of not more than one year. Each statement must be given before the end of 30 days, beginning with the day after the end of the period to which the statement relates.

A creditor who fails to comply with this obligation is not entitled to enforce the agreement during the period of non-compliance, and the debtor has no liability to pay any sum of interest or any default sum during the period of non-compliance.[1]

As 'give' is defined in the Act to mean 'deliver or send by an appropriate method'[2] ('appropriate method' means post or transmission in the form of an electronic communication)[3] it is only necessary for the statement to be posted, and not received, by the relevant date.

The prescribed content of the statement is set out in Parts 1 and 2 of Sch 1 to the Consumer Credit (Information Requirements and Duration of Licences and Charges) Regulations 2007[4] and includes the period to which the statement relates, details of the creditor, information specific to the agreement and specified statutory forms of wording under the following headings:

(a)   'Settling your credit agreement early'

(b)   'Dispute resolution'

(c)   'Paying less than the agreed sum'

and where the statement relates to a hire-purchase or conditional sale agreement, a statutory form of wording under the heading 'Termination: Your rights'.[5]

Where the fixed-sum credit agreement relates to a home credit loan agreement, it must include certain additional information and a statutory statement.[6]

The duty to provide annual statements applies equally to agreements entered into before the relevant regulations came into force, i.e. before 1 October 2008, and in that the case the first statement must be provided within one year beginning with that date. Provision is made for certain information to be omitted from the statement relating to agreements entered into before such date.[7]

Statements must be in plain, intelligible language[8] and certain specified forms of wording are required to appear together as a whole and not interspersed with any other information or wording.[9] The wording must be easily legible and of a colour which is readily distinguishable from the background medium upon which it is displayed.[10] There are prescribed rules regarding prominence of the information and wording.[11]

A non-compliant statement does not constitute a statement under s 77A, with the result that the creditor is deemed not to have provided the debtor with a statement at all.[12] Non-compliance with the statement requirements means that the debtor is entitled to recover payments made during the period of non-compliance.[13]

1 CCA 1974, s 77A.
2 Ibid., s 189(1).
3 Ibid., s 189(1) read with s 176(1).
4 SI 2007/1167, as amended by SI 2008/1751.
5 Ibid., Part 3.
6 Ibid., reg 12.
7 Ibid., regs 46 to 50 and CCA 2006, Sch 3, para 2.
8 Ibid., reg 36.
9 Ibid., reg 37.
10 Ibid., reg 39.
11 Ibid., reg 40.
12 *JP Morgan Chase Bank, National Association v Northern Rock (Asset Management) plc* [2014] EWHC 291 (Ch), [2014] GCCR 12000.
13 *NRAM Plc v McAdam and another* [2014] EWHC 4174 (Comm), [2014] GCCR 12103; and on appeal at [2015] EWCA Civ 751, [2015] GCCR 13187.

11.3 STATEMENTS OF ACCOUNT UNDER RUNNING-ACCOUNT CREDIT AGREEMENTS

From the very outset, CCA 1974 obligated creditors under running-account credit agreements to furnish regular statements of account.[1] The contents of statements under running-account credit agreements is prescribed by the Consumer Credit (Running-Account Credit Information) Regulations 1983 and the Schedule to those regulations.[2] These requirements have been supplemented by those under the Consumer Credit (Information Requirements and Duration of Licences and Charges) Regulations 2007.[3]

The statement of account must also contain the prescribed form of wording relating to the order or proportions in which any amount paid by the debtor which is insufficient to discharge the total debt then due, will be applied by the creditor towards the discharge of the sums due in respect of amounts of credit provided for different purposes or different parts of the agreement. This corresponds to a similar requirement in the Agreements Regulations.

There is additional statutory wording which must be included in statements under running-account credit agreements as prescribed by the above regulations.[4] Depending upon the circumstances, the specified statutory forms of wording relate to the following:[5]

(a) 'Minimum payments'

(b) 'You have failed to make a minimum payment'

(c) 'Dispute resolution'.

Statutory periods are laid down for the sending of statements of account. Where the statement includes a demand for payment, the statement must be sent within one month from the end of the period to which the statement relates. Where the statement does not include a demand for payment and there is a nil balance throughout the period to which the statement relates or at the end of the period to which the statement relates, a 12-monthly statement must be sent. Where it does not include a demand for payment and there is a debit or credit balance on the account at the end of the period, the statement must be sent within six months of the end of the period to which the statement relates.[6]

The rules regarding the form and formalities set out above apply equally to statements under running-account credit agreements.

The failure by a creditor to provide statements may be taken into account by the FCA in exercising its functions under CCA 1974.[7] However, there is no equivalent to the sanction on creditors which fail to provide annual statements under fixed-sum credit agreements.

Although periodic statements are not binding on the creditor,[8] estoppel may apply.[9]

1 CCA 1974, s 78(4).
2 Consumer Credit (Running-Account Credit Information) Regulations 1983, SI 1983/1570, reg 2.
3 SI 2007/1167, regs 13 to 18 read with Sch 2.
4 Ibid., regs 13 to 18.
5 Ibid., Sch 2.
6 Consumer Credit (Running-Account Credit Information) Regulations 1983, SI 1983/1570, reg 3.
7 CCA 1974, s 170(2).
8 Ibid., ss 170 and 172.
9 See *United Overseas Bank v Jiwani* [1977] 1 All ER 733.

11.4   NOTICE OF SUMS IN ARREARS

A notice of sums in arrears is an innovation introduced by CCA 2006.[1] It applies to fixed-sum credit agreements, running-account credit agreements and hire agreements. Fixed-sum credit agreements include hire-purchase agreements and conditional sale agreements.

Under fixed-sum credit agreements or hire agreements the creditor or owner respectively must, within 14 days when two contractual payments are in arrears, and thereafter at six monthly intervals whilst the account is in arrears, send the debtor or hirer respectively a notice of arrears. Where the payment is due at weekly or shorter intervals, the trigger is four rather than two contractual payments in arrears. The obligation to issue the arrears notice only applies if the shortfall is no less than the sum of the last two payments which the debtor or hirer is required to have made. The obligation ceases once the debtor or hirer is no longer in arrears or a judgment is given in relation to the agreement requiring a payment to be made by the debtor or hirer.[2]

In the case of running-account credit agreements, the creditor is obliged to issue an arrears notice within 14 days when two contractual payments have been missed and the last two payments have not been made. The obligation continues even after the grant of a judgment, whilst there is still a sum to be paid under the judgment.

If the creditor or owner fails to issue an arrears notice when required, he is not entitled to enforce the agreement during the period of non-compliance and the debtor or hirer does not incur any liability to pay any sum of interest or default sum during the period of non-compliance.[3]

As regards agreements entered into before the statutory requirement for notices of arrears, the start date for determining any arrears is the coming into force of CCA 2006, s 9. In other words the relevant arrears are those arising after 1 October 2008, the relevant date for the commencement of CCA 2006, s 9.[4]

The content of the notice of sums in arrears is prescribed by the Consumer Credit (Information Requirements and Duration of Licences and Charges) Regulations 2007.[5] The notice must contain the information set out in the Regulations, which includes the following:

(a) a form of wording to the effect that the notice is given in compliance with the 1974 Act because the debtor or hirer is behind with his payments under the agreement;

(b) a form of wording encouraging the debtor or hirer to discuss the state of his account with the creditor or owner;

(c) the information specified in the relevant Regulations read with Sch 3;

(d) in the case of an arrears notice under a fixed-sum credit agreement or hire agreement, the amount of the shortfall under the agreement which gave rise to the duty to give the notice. This information appears to apply only to the first arrears notice. On receipt of a request for further information about the shortfall, the creditor or owner must give the debtor or hirer in relation to each of the sums comprising the shortfall, notice of the amount of the sums, the date on which they became due and the amounts paid by the debtor or hirer;[6]

(e) in arrears notices under fixed-sum credit and hire agreements, other than the first arrears notice, additional prescribed information must be set out.[7]

Only minor non-compliance with the requirements of the Act's information requirements would save an arrears notice.[8]

The information to be included in notice of sums in arrears under running-account credit agreements is set out in the relevant Regulations.[9] The notice of arrears relating to a running-account credit agreement, but inexplicably not that relating to a fixed-sum credit agreement or a hire agreement, may be incorporated in a statement or other notice which the creditor gives the debtor in relation to the agreement by virtue of any other provision of CCA 1974.[10] In such a case the notice need not contain so much of the information as is required to be included in the other notice or under CCA 1974 under which the notice is given.[11]

Arrears notices must be accompanied by the current information sheet on arrears prepared by the Financial Conduct Authority[12] and must include a statutory notice drawing the customer's attention to its inclusion.[13]

As regards agreements entered into before the relevant sections come into force, the obligation to give the first notice does not arise under a fixed-sum credit agreement or hire agreement until at least two payments have fallen due after the section has come into force and the arrears are at least in the sum of the last two (or four, as the case may be) payments that the debtor or hirer has been required to make.[14]

In the case of running-account credit agreements, the obligation in relation to pre-existing agreements does not arise until at least two payments have fallen due after the section has come into force and the last two payments have not been made.[15]

The FCA Handbook, Consumer Credit sourcebook (CONC) at CONC 7 generally covers, amongst other matters, arrears policies and procedures, the treatment of customers in default or arrears, and the obligation to provide debtors and hirers with information on the amount of any arrears and the balance owing.

Special provisions apply to notices of sums in arrears under P2P agreements. They are set out at CONC 7.17 for fixed-sum credit and at CONC 7.18 for running-account credit.

1 Sections 9 to 12, inserting ss 86B, 86C and 86D of CCA 1974 with effect from 1 October 2008, by virtue of SI 2007/1167.
2 CCA 1974, s 86B(4).
3 Ibid., s 86D.
4 CCA 2006, Sch 3, paras 6(2) and 7(2).
5 Consumer Credit (Information Requirements and Duration of Licences and Charges) Regulations 2007, SI 2007/1167, regs 19 to 24 read with Sch 3.
6 CCA 1974, s 86B(2)(a) read with reg 19(2)(a) and Sch 3, Part 2 of the above Regulations.
7 Ibid., s 86B(2)(b) read with reg 19(3) and Sch 3, Part 3 of the above Regulations.
8 Consumer Credit (Information Requirements and Duration of Licences and Charges) Regulations 2007, SI 2007/1167, reg 41; see *JP Morgan Chase Bank, National Association v Northern Rock (Asset Management) plc* [2014] EWHC 291(Ch), [2014] GCCR 12000 at paras [41] to [44].
9 Regulation 24 read with Sch 3 of the above Regulations.
10 CCA 1974, s 86C(4).
11 Regulation 25 of the above Regulations.
12 CCA 1974, ss 86B(6) and 86C(3); regs 19(1)(e) and 24(1)(e) and Sch 3, Part 5 of the above Regulations.
13 Regulations 19(1)(e) and 24(1)(e) and Sch 3, Part 5 of the above Regulations.
14 CCA 2006, Sch 3, para 6(1) and (2).
15 Ibid., Sch 3, para 7.

11.5   DEFAULT NOTICES

Service of a default notice on the debtor or hirer is necessary before the creditor or owner may, by a reason of breach by the debtor or hirer of a regulated agreement, terminate the agreement, demand earlier payment of any sum, recover possession of any goods or land or treat any right conferred on the debtor or hirer by the agreement as terminated, restricted or deferred, or enforce any security.[1]

This does not prevent a creditor from treating the debtor's right to draw upon any credit as restricted or deferred and taking such steps as may be necessary to make the restriction or deferment effective.[2]

The default notice must be in paper form and comply with the relevant regulations.[3] The notice must specify the nature of the alleged breach, if the breach is capable of remedy, what action is required to remedy it and the date before which that action is to be taken; if the breach is not capable of remedy, the sum, if any, required to be paid as compensation for the breach and the date before which it is to be paid.[4] A date specified for the date of remedy must be not less than 14 days after the date of service of the default notice.[5]

The default notice might also set out what action the creditor or owner will take if the debtor or hirer respectively fails to remedy the breach within the prescribed period within the prescribed time.[6]

The form and contents of a default notice are set out in the Consumer Credit (Enforcement, Default and Termination Notices) Regulations 1983, as amended.[7] These Regulations were materially amended by the Consumer Credit (Information Requirements and Duration of Licences and Charges) Regulations 2007.[8] Notably, the latter prescribe a statutory notice of the customer's right under a hire-purchase or conditional sale agreement to end the agreement at any time before the final payment falls due and a warning that this right may be lost if the customer does not act before the date shown. They also require a statement in statutory form where the creditor or owner is entitled to charge post-judgment interest in connection with a judgment sum. The default notice must be accompanied by the current Financial Conduct Authority information sheet on default and must include a statutory notice drawing the customer's attention to its inclusion.[9]

The 1983 Regulations and the 2007 Regulations require the lettering in default notices to be easily legible, of a colour which is readily distinguishable from the background medium and prescribe the prominence of wording in the notice.

The treatment of customers in default or arrears is dealt with in CONC 7.3, with an emphasis on dealing with customers fairly, showing forbearance and due consideration, not taking disproportionate action, and exercising restraint in enforcing a debt or repossessing a customer's house. Likewise, CONC 7.7 imposes restraints on the application of interest and charges, requiring firms to consider their obligations under Principle 6 of the Principles for Businesses in the FCA Handbook (PRIN) to pay due regard to the interests of customers and to treat them fairly.[10]

1 CCA 1974, s 87(1).
2 Ibid., s 87(2).
3 Consumer Credit (Enforcement, Default and Termination Notices) Regulations 1983, SI 1983/1561, and see the Schedules to the Regulations. 'Paper form' is prescribed by reg 2(4A).
4 CCA 1974, s 88(1).
5 Ibid., s 88(2).
6 Ibid., s 85(5).
7 SI 1983/1561.
8 CCA 1974, s 88(4A) and the Consumer Credit (Information Requirements and Duration of Licences and Charges) Regulations 2007, SI 2007/1167.
9 CCA 1974, s 88(4A) and SI 2007/1167, reg 33(3)(c).
10 CONC 7.7.1G.

11.6 NOTICE OF DEFAULT SUMS

CCA 2006 introduced the new concept of a notice of default sums. A default sum is a sum (other than a sum of interest) which is payable by a debtor or hirer under a regulated agreement in connection with a breach of the agreement by him, but does not include a sum which, as a consequence of the breach of an agreement, is payable earlier than it would otherwise have been.[1] In short, it is a fee or charge, such as an administration charge, payable in respect of the customer's default under the agreement.

The creditor or owner must give the customer notice of the default sum within 35 days of the default sum becoming payable.[2] The content of the notice is set out in the Consumer Credit (Information Requirements and Duration of Licences and Charges) Regulations 2007.[3] Significantly, interest on default sums may only be charged at a simple rate even if, as is usually the case, interest on the principal debt is calculated at a compound rate of interest.[4] There is no liability to pay interest on the default sum in respect of the period of 29 days following the day on which the debtor or hirer is given notice of the default sum.[5]

The restriction of interest to simple interest also applies to agreements entered into before the section came into force, but only as regards default sums payable after the commencement of CCA 2006, s 13, namely 1 October 2008.[6]

The notice of default sum may be incorporated in a statement or other notice which the creditor or owner gives the debtor or hirer in relation to the agreement by virtue of another provision of CCA 1974.[7] In such a case there is no need to duplicate the information which is required to be included in the other notice by virtue of a provision of CCA 1974.[8]

If the creditor or owner fails to give the notice, he is not entitled to enforce the agreement until the notice of default sum has been given.[9]

Notice of default sums under P2P agreements is specifically addressed in CONC 7.19.

The Office of Fair Trading, while it was in control of consumer credit, adopted a strident approach to default charges, initially with its statement on 'Calculating fair default charges in credit card contracts' in April 2006.[10] The OFT considered default charge provisions to be open to challenge on grounds of unfairness if they had the object of raising more in revenue than was reasonably expected to be necessary to recover certain limited administrative costs incurred by the credit card issuer. It maintained that credit card default fees had been set at a significantly higher level than was fair for the purposes of the then Unfair Terms in Consumer Contracts Regulations 1999. In the view of the OFT, a default charge should:

(a)   be calculated on the basis of a reasonable pre-estimate of the net limited additional administrative costs which occur as a result of the specific breaches of contract and can be identified with a reasonable precision;

(b)   reflect a fair attribution of those costs between defaulting consumers;

(c)   be based on a genuine estimate of the total number of expected instances of default in the relevant period; and

(d)   treat costs other than those net of limited administrative additional costs as a general overhead of the credit card business and disregard them for purposes of calculating a default fee.[11]

To help encourage a swift change in market practice, the OFT set a simple monetary threshold for intervention by the OFT on default charges, at £12, which has remained in force ever since it was introduced. The OFT considered that the basic principles enunciated by it in its statement applied also to other analogous default charges in consumer contracts, for example agreements for bank overdrafts, mortgages and store card agreements. The FCA has unsurprisingly adopted the OFT's position by prescribing that a firm must not impose charges on customers in default or arrears unless the charges are no higher than necessary to cover the reasonable costs of the firm.[12]

The OFT's decision created a sea-change in the treatment of default charges on the part of creditors, from card issuers in relation to credit card agreements to banks in respect of charges for overdraft facilities and a backlash on the part of credit institutions in their approach to levying charges for services which were previously free or at a low rate of charge, e.g. charges for balance transfers, annual fees for credit cards and the like.

1 CCA 1974, s 187A.
2 SI 2007/1167, reg 28.
3 Ibid., regs 29 to 32.
4 CCA 1974, ss 86F(2) and 86E(4).
5 CCA 2006, Sch 3, para 9(1) and (2).
6 CCA 1974, s 86E(4).
7 Ibid., s 86E(3).
8 SI 2007/1167, reg 32.
9 CCA 1974, s 86E(5).
10 OFT 842.
11 Ibid., para 3.27.
12 CONC 7.7.5.

11.7 NOTICE OF INTEREST ON JUDGMENT DEBTS

CCA 2006 introduced a new requirement that creditors and owners must give notice to judgment debtors of interest payable on the judgment amount, following the grant of judgment, before becoming entitled to the same. Interest may be interest at the contract rate or at the judgment rate. The notice must be given after the obtaining of judgment and subsequently at intervals of not more than six months. No liability to pay post-judgment interest accrues before the day on which the first required notice is given or subsequently in respect of the period in which any required notice has not been given.[1]

The notice may be incorporated in a statement or other notice which the creditor or owner gives to the debtor or hirer in relation to the agreement by virtue of any other provision of the Act.[2]

The requirement to give notice does not apply in relation to post-judgment interest which is required to be paid by virtue of s 74 of the County Courts Act 1984, s 4 of the Administration of Justice (Scotland) Act 1972 or Art. 127 of the Judgments Enforcement (Northern Ireland) Order 1981.[3]

The content of notices of intention to recover post-judgment interest is set out in the Consumer Credit (Information Requirements and Duration of Licences and Charges) Regulations 2007.[4]

1 CCA 1974, s 130A(1) to (3).
2 Ibid., s 130A(5).
3 Ibid., s 130A(7).
4 SI 2007/1167, reg 34 read with Sch 5.

11.8 INFORMATION SHEETS FOR ARREARS AND DEFAULT NOTICES

Information sheets, as prescribed by the FCA and in the form in force from time to time, must accompany arrears notices and default notices. Specific information sheets are prescribed for high-cost short-term loans and for high-cost short-term loans for issue by peer-to-peer lenders (P2P).

11.9 PROVISIONS APPLICABLE TO VARIOUS NOTICES

11.9.1 'Agreement to aggregate'

This is a new concept, introduced by the Consumer Credit (Information Requirements and Duration of Licences and Charges) Regulations 2007.[1] An 'agreement to aggregate' is defined as an agreement, whether arising by conduct or otherwise, made between the creditor and the debtor:

(a) concerning two or more agreements for fixed-sum credit between the creditor and the debtor where at least one such agreement is a regulated credit agreement; and

(b) which permits or requires the debtor to aggregate all individual payments under the agreements mentioned in paragraph (a) above and pay them at the same time.

It will be noted that the concept does not apply to agreements for running-account credit, nor to hire agreements. Various concessions are made in respect of agreements to aggregate, including in relation to the content of statements[2] and notices of sums in arrears.[3]

1 SI 2007/1167, reg 2.
2 Ibid., regs 7 to 9.
3 Ibid., regs 19(2)(d) to 23.

11.9.2 Formalities

Many rules as to formalities are common to notices and statements. Enforcement, default and termination notices must be in paper form[1] but all other notices and statements may be sent by an 'appropriate method', meaning by post (and hence in a paper form) or by electronic communication, where the recipient agrees to the latter.[2] Notices must set out the prescribed information together as a whole, not interspersed with any other information or wording. They must be easily legible and of a colour which is readily distinguishable from the background medium. Information and wording must be equally prominent except for certain specified wording which may be more prominent than other wording.[3]

1 SI 2007/1167, reg 39 and the Consumer Credit (Enforcement, Default and Termination Notices) Regulations 1983, SI 1983/1561, reg 2(4A).
2 CCA 1974, ss 189(1) and 176A.
3 SI 2007/1167, regs 36 to 40.

11.9.3 Charges for notices etc

No charge may be levied for statements or notices.[1] This prohibition does not extend to default notices. A charge imposed on customers in default or in arears difficulties may not exceed what is necessary to cover the reasonable costs of the firm.[2]

1 CCA 1974, s 77A(3) re statements under fixed-sum credit agreements (there is no equivalent provision for statements under running-account credit agreements); ss 86B(7) and 86C(5) re notice of sums in arrears; s 86E(6) re notice of default sums; and s 130A(4) re notice of judgment interest.
2 CONC 7.7.5R.

11.9.4 Errors and omissions

Where a notice or statement contains an error or omission which does not affect the substance of the information or forms of wording which it is required to contain, it does not on that ground alone constitute a breach of the relevant regulations.[1] A breach which affects the substance would have the effect of that notice or statement being considered not to have been given. The court in *JP Morgan Chase Bank, National Association v Northern Rock (Asset Management) plc* held that, unless the error or omission is minor, there is a breach of the regulations, specifically regulation 41.[2] It is submitted that there is a middle ground between an error or omission which does not affect the substance of the information or forms of wording which the notice or statement is required to contain (which, alone, does not constitute a breach of the regulations), on the one hand, and an error or omission which is minor, on the other hand, which the court did not address.

In contrast, s 172 of CCA 1974 deems certain statements, however defective, to be binding on the creditor or owner, namely statements given in response to a debtor, hirer or surety exercising his entitlement under the Act to request information in relation to the state of his agreement. Whilst s 172(2) states that the notice is binding on the trader, s 172(3) provides that, where the statement or notice is shown to be incorrect, the court may direct such relief, if any, to be given to the creditor or owner as appears to it to be just.[3]

1 Consumer Credit (Information Requirements and Duration of Licences and Charges) Regulations 2007, SI 2007/1167, reg 41.
2 [2014] EWHC 291 (Ch), [2014] GCCR 12000 at paras [41] to [44].
3 But estoppel may apply: *United Overseas Bank v Jiwani* [1977] 1 All ER 733.

11.9.5 Joint debtors or hirers

Where a regulated agreement has two or more debtors or hirers, not being a partnership or unincorporated body of persons, anything required by CCA 1974 to be done to or in relation to the debtor or hirer must be done in relation to each of them.[1] Likewise anything done by one of them shall be deemed to have been done by or on behalf of all of them.

1 CCA 1974, s 185(1).

11.9.6 Dispensing notice

Where an agreement is entered into by two or more debtors, any (but not all) of the debtors may sign a dispensing notice, dispensing with the creditor's need to send a statement to him under s 77A or 78(4). The dispensing notice ceases to be operational if it is revoked or any of the debtors dies.[1] A dispensing notice which is operative in relation to an agreement, is also operative in relation to any modifying agreement.[2]

1 CCA 1974, s 185(2), 2(A) and (2C).
2 Ibid., s 185(2D).

11.10 PROVISIONS APPLICABLE TO SPECIFIC AGREEMENT TYPES

11.10.1 Store card agreements

Specific provision relating to store cards was introduced as a result of the Store Cards Market Investigation conducted by the Competition Commission following a referral to it by the Office of Fair Trading under the Enterprise Act 2002 in March 2004.

Store card statements must contain certain prescribed information.[1] In summary form, the information is: the current APR on purchases; an estimate of the amount of interest payable for the next month if the customer only makes the minimum payment; the minimum payment warning; the amount of each insurance charge accompanied by a description of the charge on the basis of its calculation; a list of any charges payable in the event of late payment or default; an explanation and the basis of the calculation of the interest amount; the relevant annual rates of interest; the payment options including payment by direct debit; how any insurance cover relating to the store card account can be reviewed.

Where the APR is 25% or more the store card provider must also prominently display an APR warning on the face of each monthly statement.

1 Store Cards Market Investigation Order, 27 July 2006, Sch 2.

11.10.2 Home credit loan agreements

Specific requirements apply to information relating to home credit loan agreements. This was introduced by the Consumer Credit (Information Requirements and Duration of Licences and Charges) Regulations 2007[1] as a result of recommendations made by the Competition Commission following its enquiry into the Home Credit Market pursuant to a referral to it by the Office of Fair Trading under the Enterprise Act 2002, in December 2004.

A home credit loan agreement is a debtor-creditor agreement which satisfies either or both of the following conditions:

(a)   the agreement provides that all or most of the sums payable by the debtor are to be collected by or on behalf of the creditor at the debtor's home or the home of a natural person who makes payments to the creditor on the debtor's behalf or, to be so collected if the debtor so wishes;

(b)   at the time the agreement is entered into, the debtor could reasonably expect, from representations made by or on behalf of the creditor at or before that time, that all or most of the sums payable will be collected as set out above, or so collected if the debtor so wished.[2]

A statement under s 77A relating to a home credit agreement must contain the additional information prescribed by reg 12 of the above regulations.

In addition to the above, the Competition Commission's Home Credit Market Investigation Order 2007 (as varied by the Home Credit Market Investigation Order 2007 Variation Order 2011)[3] imposed a duty on a creditor under a home credit loan agreement, within 7 days after receiving a request to that effect, to give the debtor a statement complying with the Order. The Order contains provisions requiring early settlement rebates to be calculated on the assumption that early settlement will take place not later than 13 days, rather than 28 days, under an ordinary credit agreement. A creditor is required to supply product information to a debtor on request and positive, delinquent and default data at least monthly to credit reference agencies on all accounts it has entered into.

The provisions applying to home credit accounts are attributable to the desire to open up the market to greater competition. The message is intended to be relayed both to consumers and to other suppliers. Indeed, the Order requires lenders to publish information on the price of loans on a website, making it easier for customers in particular to shop around and compare offers.

1 SI 2007/1167.
2 Ibid., reg 2; and see FCA Handbook, Glossary.
3 Home Credit Market Investigation Order 2007, dated 13 September 2007 (as varied by the Home Credit Market Investigation Order 2007 Variation Order 2011, dated 24 February 2011). The 2007 Order is still referred to in the above reg 12(3) although much of the Order, as varied, has been superseded by FSMA and the FCA Handbook. See the trenchant criticism in *Goode: Consumer Credit Law and Practice* at 34.110 onwards.

11.10.3 General observation

Notwithstanding the imposition of further requirements on store card and home credit providers, their markets have remained relatively intact, although customers are being urged by the FCA to consider utilising a cheaper form of credit facility.

11.11 POST-CONTRACTUAL BUSINESS PRACTICES

CONC 6.7 sets out rules and guidance that apply to post-contractual business practices. A firm must monitor a customer's repayment record and take appropriate action here there are signs of actual or possible repayment difficulties. The action should generally include notifying customers of the risk of escalating debt, additional interest or charges, potential financial difficulties and providing details of not-for-profit debt advice bodies.[1]

1 CONC 6.7.2R and 6.7.3G.

Chapter 12

Linked transactions

12.1 MEANING OF A 'LINKED TRANSACTION'

Inevitably it was necessary for CCA 1974 to provide for transactions which are related, or ancillary, to the principal credit or hire agreement. The need for this is especially present where the principal agreement is a cancellable agreement and where it is in fact cancelled. The question then arises as to the impact that it has on the related transaction.

A linked transaction is defined as a transaction entered into by the debtor or hirer, or his relative, with another person, in relation to an actual or prospective regulated agreement ('the principal agreement') of which it does not form part, if it falls within one or other of the following alternative heads. First, if the transaction is entered into in compliance with a term of the principal agreement. Second, if the principal agreement is a debtor-creditor-supplier agreement and the transaction is financed, or to be financed, by the principal agreement. Third, if the transaction was suggested to the debtor or hirer or his relative by one of a specified number of persons (essentially the creditor or owner) and the debtor or hirer enters into the agreement for one of a specified range of purposes. The purposes are inducing the creditor or owner to enter into the principal agreement, any other purpose related to the principal agreement or where the principal agreement is a restricted-use credit agreement, a purpose related to a transaction financed, or to be financed, by the principal agreement.[1]

A notable exception from linked transactions is any agreement for the provision of security but it appears that s 113(8) of the CCA 1974 brings security for linked transactions back into the 'linked transaction syndrome'.[2] However, RAO art 60E(8)(b) provides otherwise.

The principal agreement is the regulated credit or hire agreement. In practice a linked transaction might take the form of one or other of a life assurance contract, an insurance contract, a contract relating to the guarantee or warranty of goods, a maintenance and service agreement or a contract for the purchase of goods or the supply of services ancillary to the principal contract such as supplemental health insurance, a regular savings plan, an agreement for a current account and the like.

1 CCA 1974, s 19(1) and (2).
2 Ibid., s 19(1). See also ss 105 to 124 and especially s 113(8).

12.2   DUPLICATION OF TREATMENT OF A 'LINKED TRANSACTION'

The Financial Services and Markets Act 2000 (Regulated Activities) Order 2001 ('RAO'),[1] with minor differences, replicates the provisions of CCA 1974 and the Exemptions Regulations referred to at **12.4** below, in RAO art 60E(8) to (10). The FCA's references to linked transactions are to provisions in the RAO. Like so many other examples of duplication in the FCA regime of provisions in the CCA regime (i.e. CCA 1974 and regulations under that Act), the grounds for such duplication seem inexplicable.

1   SI 2001/544.

12.3   LEGAL ASPECTS OF A LINKED TRANSACTION

A linked transaction entered into before the making of the principal agreement has no effect until such time as that agreement is made.[1] Thus, although on the face of it the agreement constituting the linked transaction might appear to be valid and binding, it is in fact inchoate and in suspense until the main agreement to which it relates is made. It follows that the linked transaction is unenforceable by either party until such time. When the principal agreement comes into force, it will also trigger the coming into force of the linked transaction and, apparently, may not do so with retrospective effect to the date when the linked transaction was entered into.

It would appear to follow, *a fortiori* from the foregoing, that the withdrawal of a party from a prospective regulated agreement will also constitute a withdrawal from any linked transaction. Although this would appear to be an obvious inference, it is expressly provided for.[2] Notice of withdrawal may be oral or in writing.

In the case of a cancellable agreement, notice by the debtor or hirer of cancellation of the agreement will also serve as cancellation of any linked transaction.[3] The result is that the hirer or debtor is entitled retrospectively to the extinction of his liability and to repayment of all sums paid. However, in certain circumstances the debtor will remain liable for payment of the cash price. This will be so where the agreement is a debtor-creditor-supplier agreement for restricted-use credit financing the doing of work or supply of goods to meet an emergency or the supply of goods which, before service of the notice of cancellation, had by the act of the debtor or his relative, become incorporated in any land or thing not comprised in the agreement or any linked transaction. In those circumstances any cancellation by the debtor will cancel any agreement or linked transaction in so far as it relates to credit or the payment of any charge for credit, leaving the debtor liable for payment of the cash price of the goods or services.

The effect of the debtor's exercise of the right to cancel the credit agreement is that the agreement and any linked transaction, including the contract of supply, are treated as though they had never been entered into and any money paid by the debtor under or in contemplation of the agreement or the linked transaction is recoverable by him and he is released from all liability for future payments. Except in the situation mentioned, the supplier under a linked transaction would not be entitled to the return of his goods as there is no common law restitutionary principle to fall back on.[4]

In other circumstances where the debtor or hirer cancels the credit agreement, hire agreement or linked transaction after he has obtained possession of the goods, he is required to return the goods and in the meanwhile to take reasonable care of them.[5]

Where a debtor discharges his liability under a regulated consumer credit agreement, he and his relative will at the same time be discharged from any liability which has not yet accrued due under a linked transaction.[6] This flows from the fact that a linked transaction rides on the back of the principal agreement.

Any charges payable under a linked transaction which is entered into in compliance with a term of the principal agreement (but not charges under other linked transactions), are included in the total charge for credit under the principal agreement.[7]

The 'linked agreement' provisions of CCA 1974 can have absurd results. Fortunately these were avoided in the case of *Citibank International plc v Schleider*,[8] which is nevertheless illustrative of the potential absurdities arising from the sections of the Act. In that case it was argued that a relatively minor agreement, a regulated interest credit agreement, had been improperly executed, with the result that the main mortgage transaction, which was a linked transaction in relation to it, was unenforceable, the main mortgage being ancillary to the regulated agreement which CCA 1974 deems to be the principal agreement. The court rejected the argument on the grounds that the credit agreement was not a restricted-use credit agreement and therefore not a debtor-creditor-supplier agreement within s 12, with the result that the main mortgage loan was not a linked transaction within s 19(1)(b).

1 CCA 1974, s 19(3).
2 Ibid., s 57(1).
3 Ibid., s 69.
4 Ibid., s 69(2).
5 Ibid., s 72.
6 Ibid., s 96.
7 See CONC App 1.1.5R and the definition of 'transaction', which includes any transaction which is a linked transaction, as defined in RAO art 60E.
8 [2001] GCCR 2281.

12.4   EXEMPT LINKED TRANSACTIONS

The following linked transactions are excluded from most of the above provisions applying to linked transactions (but not from inclusion in the total charge for credit):

(a)   contracts of insurance;

(b)   other contracts in so far as they contain a guarantee of goods;

(c)   transactions comprising or effected under:

(i) any agreement for the operation of any account (including any savings account) for the deposit of money; or

(ii) any agreement for the operation of a current account.[1]

As noted above, a contract of insurance is excluded from the meaning of 'linked transactions' for certain purposes, but these purposes do not include the calculation of the total charge for credit. Indeed, a premium under a contract of insurance payable under the transaction (which includes a linked transaction under CCA 1974, s 19(1)(a)) is now expressly included in the total charge for credit where the making or maintenance of the contract of insurance is required by the creditor as a condition of the making of the agreement and for the sole purpose of ensuring complete or partial repayment of the credit and of the charges included in the total charge for credit in the event of the debtor's death, invalidity, illness or unemployment.

Specified linked transactions are excluded from:

(a) the operation of s 19(3) of the Act, which provides that a linked transaction entered into before the making of the regulated consumer credit agreement or regulated hire agreement to which it relates has no effect until such time, if any, as that agreement is made;

(b) s 69(1)(ii) which provides that a notice of cancellation served by the debtor or hirer under a cancellable agreement shall operate to cancel any linked transaction and to withdraw any offer by the debtor or hirer or his relative, to enter into a linked transaction; and

(c) the operation of s 96(1) which provides that where the indebtedness of the debtor under a regulated consumer credit agreement is discharged before the time fixed by the agreement, he and any relative of his, shall be discharged from any liability under a linked transaction other than a debt which has already become payable.

In *Goshawk Dedicated (No 2) Ltd v Governor and Company of Bank of Scotland*[2] it was held that cancellation of the credit agreement did not result in cancellation of the insurance policy, by virtue of the Consumer Credit (Linked Transactions) (Exemptions) Regulations 1983, which had the effect of excluding the policy from constituting a linked transaction. The relevant 'Note' to the cancellation notice in the regulated credit agreement was therefore applicable and the bank was correct in appending it to the notice of the customer's cancellation rights. This case was followed in *Governor and Company of the Bank of Scotland v Euclidian (No 1) Ltd*.[3] However, with respect, it is not clear that the cases were correctly decided, not least because the parties to a regulated consumer credit or regulated consumer hire agreement are at liberty to contract otherwise, namely to agree that cancellation of the credit or hire agreement will affect the linked transaction, so that the 'Note' would make no sense if it indicated the contrary.[4]

1 Consumer Credit (Linked Transactions) (Exemptions) Regulations 1983, SI 1983/1560.
2 [2005] GCCR 5431.
3 [2007] GCCR 6051.
4 See the writer's comments on the case at note 3 above.

12.5   UNFAIR RELATIONSHIPS AND LINKED TRANSACTIONS

The unfair relationships provisions are extensive and discussed in detail in **Chapter 24**. For present purposes it should be pointed out that linked transactions are subject to the provisions of sections 140A and 140B of CCA 1974, which set out the meaning and consequences of unfair relationships arising between creditors and debtors. References in those sections to an agreement related to a credit agreement, and which are likewise subject to those provisions, are deemed to refer also to a linked transaction in relation to the credit agreement or a linked transaction in relation to a credit agreement consolidated by a subsequent credit agreement.[1]

The unfair relationships provisions apply to a credit agreement of any amount and to both regulated credit agreements and exempt agreements.[2] There is a corresponding provision relating to linked transactions, so that a transaction is a linked transaction even if the credit agreement to which it relates is not a regulated consumer credit agreement.[3]

1   CCA 1974, s 140C(4)(b).
2   Ibid., s 140C(1).
3   Ibid., s 140C(5).

12.6   DISTINGUISHING 'LINKED TRANSACTIONS' FROM OTHER CONNECTED AGREEMENTS

A linked transaction is to be distinguished from a 'linked credit agreement' and from an 'ancillary service', both of the latter being concepts introduced upon the implementation of the Consumer Credit Directive.[1]

A 'linked credit agreement' is a regulated consumer credit agreement which serves exclusively to finance an agreement for the supply of specific goods or the provision of a specific service and where the creditor uses the services of the supplier in connection with the preparation or making of the agreement, or where the specific goods or provision of a specific service are explicitly specified in the agreement.[2] The significance of this is set out in s 75A and **Chapter 15**.

An 'ancillary service' is a service that relates to the provision of credit under a regulated consumer credit agreement and includes, in particular, an insurance or payment protection policy.[3] Its relevance is to be found in s 66A and **30.2** below.

1   As inserted by SI 2010/1010.
2   CCA 1974, s 75A(5).
3   Ibid., s 66A(13).

Chapter 13

Credit brokers

13.1 MEANING OF 'CREDIT BROKING'

13.1.1 Activities involving credit broking

Provisions relating to credit broking were originally contained in Part X of CCA 1974, s 145(2) and were extended under the Financial Services and Markets Act 2000 (Regulated Activities) Order 2001 ('RAO'), with effect from 1 April 2014,[1] also to include the category of credit intermediary, originally provided for under the repealed CCA 1974, s 160A. As a result, RAO article 36A(1) defines credit broking by reference to each of the following:[2]

(a) effecting an introduction of an individual or relevant recipient of credit who wishes to enter into a credit agreement to a person ('P') with a view to P entering into by way of business as lender a regulated credit agreement (or an agreement which would be a regulated credit agreement but for any of the relevant provisions referred to below);

(b) effecting an introduction of an individual or relevant recipient of credit who wishes to enter into a consumer hire agreement to a person ('P') with a view to P entering into by way of business as owner a regulated consumer hire agreement or an agreement which would be a regulated consumer hire agreement but for RAO article 60O (exempt agreements: exemptions relating to the nature of the agreement) or 60Q (exempt agreements: exemptions relating to the nature of the hirer);

(c) effecting an introduction of an individual or relevant recipient of credit who wishes to enter into a credit agreement or consumer hire agreement (as the case may be) to a person who carries on an activity of the kind specified in sub-paragraph (a) or (b) by way of business;

(d) presenting or offering an agreement which would (if entered into) be a regulated credit agreement (or an agreement which would be a regulated credit agreement but for any of the relevant provisions referred to below);

(e) assisting an individual or relevant recipient of credit by undertaking preparatory work with a view to that person entering into a regulated credit agreement (or an agreement which would be a regulated credit agreement but for any of the relevant provisions referred to below);

(f)   entering into a regulated credit agreement (or an agreement which would be a regulated credit agreement but for any of the relevant provisions referred to below) on behalf of a lender.[3]

'Relevant recipient of credit' means (a) a partnership consisting of two or three persons not all of whom are bodies corporate, or (b) an unincorporated body of persons which does not consist entirely of bodies corporate and is not a partnership.[4] It is to be noted that 'relevant recipient of credit' may also include a recipient of hire facilities, reference to 'credit' in this term being misleading.

References to 'the relevant provisions' referred to in paragraphs (d) to (f) above are to exempt agreements which fall under the following heads in RAO:[5]

(a)   exemptions relating to the nature of the agreement (article 60C);

(b)   exemptions relating to the purchase of land for non-residential purposes (article 60D);

(c)   exemptions relating to the nature of the lender (article 60E), except for paragraph (5) of that article;

(d)   exemptions relating to the total charge for credit (article 60G);

(e)   exemptions relating to the nature of the borrower (article 60H).

The exclusions that apply to exempt agreements are limited to the activities mentioned in paragraphs (d) to (f) above; credit broking covers effecting an introduction to an exempt credit agreement, an exempt consumer hire agreement or to a person carrying on such a business, as described in paragraphs (a) to (c) above.

1 Financial Services and Markets Act 2000 (Regulated Activities) Order 2001, SI 2001/544 ('RAO'), inserted by the Financial Services and Markets Act 2000 (Regulated Activities) (Amendment) (No 2) Order 2013, SI 2013/1881.
2 Carrying on any such activity by way of business requires authorisation and the necessary permission by the FCA; see **13.7** below.
3 Essentially, paras (a) to (c) constituted credit brokerage, under CCA 1974, s 145(2); and paras (d) to (f) constituted acting as credit intermediaries, under CCA 1974, s 160A.
4 RAO art 60L.
5 Ibid., art 36A(4). See also FCA Handbook, PERG 2.7.7F G.

13.1.2   Operating an electronic system in relation to lending

Credit broking does not apply in relation to operating an electronic system in relation to lending.[1] However, authorisation of an electronic money institution, being a payment service provider, is required by the Payment Services Regulations 2017.[2] The Regulations implement Directive (EU) 2015/2366 of the European Parliament and of the Council on payment services in the internal market. Note that the provisions of reg 76, which govern a payment service provider's liability for unauthorised payment transactions, do not apply to specified transactions covered by a credit line provided under a consumer credit agreement.[3]

It is immaterial whether the credit agreement or consumer hire agreement is subject to the law of a country outside the UK.[4]

1 RAO art 36A(2). See also FCA Handbook, PERG 2.7.7G G.
2 SI 2017/752; see the relevant definitions in reg 2, and see Sch 1.
3 Ibid., reg 64.
4 RAO art 36A(3).

13.1.3 Activities in relation to certain agreements relating to land

RAO article 36E excludes from article 36A above:[1]

(a) activities carried on with a view to an individual or a relevant recipient of credit entering into an investment property loan, as defined in RAO article 61A(6) (mortgage contracts which are not regulated mortgage contracts);

(b) activities of a kind specified by article 25A (arranging regulated mortgage contracts) or 25C (arranging regulated home purchase plans);

(c) other activities not excluded by paragraph (a) or (b) above which consist of effecting an introduction with a view to an individual or relevant recipient of credit entering into a relevant agreement (namely, a regulated mortgage contract or a home purchase plan), if the person to whom the introduction is made is an authorised person who has permission to:

   (i) enter into such an agreement as lender or home purchase provider (as the case may be), or

   (ii) make an introduction to an authorised person who has permission to enter into such an agreement as lender or home purchase provider (as the case may be).

(4) In paragraph (3) 'relevant agreement' means a regulated mortgage contract or a regulated home purchase plan.

1 RAO art 36E.

13.2 MEANING OF 'EFFECTING AN INTRODUCTION'

Credit brokerage under CCA 1974 was defined by reference to the effecting of introductions of individuals whereas, under RAO article 36A, credit broking is defined, in terms of the singular number, as effecting an introduction of an individual. In practice, little will to turn on the distinction as the regulated activity is the business of credit broking, which is unlikely to involve the introduction of only an individual.

To effect introductions of prospective debtors to prospective creditors or owners is to bring them into contact with each other, whether personally, by correspondence, by telephone, via the internet or in any other manner. Although the relevant provision only refers in terms to one-way introductions, namely introductions of individuals desiring to obtain credit to those in business to provide it,[1] it appears that credit broking includes introductions moving the other way, namely introductions of prospective creditors or owners to prospective debtors or hirers respectively.[2]

An intermediary does not act as a credit broker merely by advertising credit facilities as a result of which an individual makes contact with the provider of credit or hire. Nor does an intermediary effect an introduction to a credit grantor by making the latter's application forms available in display boxes, but presenting or offering a regulated agreement or assisting a customer to enter into a regulated agreement would now constitute credit broking.[3] In the case of an estate agent it has been held that merely sending particulars of a property to a potential purchaser does not amount to introducing the purchaser to the vendor.[4] However, on the credit scene, sending details of a loan offer in the name of the lender to a potential borrower would, it is submitted, amount to an introduction to the lender. Whether a particular action amounts to the effecting of an introduction is largely a question of fact to be determined on the merits of each case. If the criteria were to be too widely cast, then every bank, hotel or restaurant in the country advertising the services of a credit card issuer and providing leaflets relating to the services it offers would need to be authorised. This could not be what the law intended.[5]

A person is engaged in credit broking not only when he directly effects an introduction but also when the introduction is effected by his agent.[6] It is therefore not possible to bypass a refusal of authorisation by appointing an agent to act as credit broker on behalf of oneself.

No credit broking business is involved in a trader simply accepting payment by credit card or trading check. However, if a retailer conducts his own in-house credit card scheme in conjunction with a third party as the credit provider, the retailer will be carrying on a credit broking business. If a trader actively recruits customers to a credit card scheme he will also need to be authorised as a credit broker.

It is not credit broking business to recommend a source of credit where no commission or other arrangement exists between the party recommending the source of credit and the credit provider. The same applies to consumer hire. The activity of introducing only corporate customers to a source of credit or hire is also not credit broking.

The role of the credit broker may be pivotal to the categorisation of the credit agreement. Thus, if the credit broker is the supplier under the credit agreement and the creditor has entered into, or proposes entering into, arrangements or an agreement with the supplier, the credit agreement entered into between the creditor and the debtor will be a debtor-creditor-supplier/borrower-lender-supplier agreement, with all the consequences that flow from that categorisation.[7]

A credit broker's introduction may take the form of an automatic referral by the credit broker of all enquirers for credit to a credit provider, without any active intervention on the part of the credit broker. Indeed, the introduction may be effected by an automated system.

---

1   See **13.1** above.
2   Compare *Goode: Consumer Credit Law and Practice* (LexisNexis Butterworths), para IC [48.25]; Bennion, *Consumer Credit Act Manual* (3rd edn, Sweet & Maxwell), p 153; and Guest, *Encyclopaedia of Consumer Credit Law* (Sweet & Maxwell), 2–146.
3   *Brookes v Retail Credit Cards Ltd* (1985) 150 JP 131, [1986] CCLR 5, but see the expanded meaning of credit broking at **13.1** above.
4   *Christie Owen & Davis plc v King* 1998 SCLR 786.
5   See note 1 above.

6 *Hicks v Walker* (1984) 148 JP 636, [1999] GCCR 721.
7 CCA 1974, s 12(b) and (c).

13.3 CREDIT BROKING BUSINESS

13.3.1 The business of credit broking

'Business' has been described in general terms as including every trade, occupation or profession and so as to apply to single transactions as well as long-term ventures.[1]

Although the Act defines 'business' as including a profession or trade, it also provides that a person is not to be treated as carrying on a particular type of business merely because occasionally he enters into transactions belonging to a business of that type. In addition, no credit broking is involved where the individual is introduced to the provider of non-commercial agreements as, by definition, the provider is not engaged in a consumer credit business, a business involving exempt agreements, a consumer hire business or a business involving exempt hire agreements.[2]

Particular circumstances may support the notion of a business, whether of credit broking or otherwise, even in the case of just one introduction or transaction.

In *R v Marshall*[3] the court had to consider whether a double-glazing salesman, who offered financial arrangements to customers in the form of credit facilities, at a time when he was unlicensed, was carrying on an unlicensed credit brokerage business in breach of CCA 1974, ss 39(1) and 145. The Court of Appeal quashed the conviction of the court of first instance. The trial court had been too restrictive in its direction to the jury when it stated that, if all that the defendant did was occasionally make introductions, not as part of his way of selling his goods or services, but only because he was assisting customers who wanted that help, he did not break the law. The court cited with approval a passage in *Consumer Credit Legislation* (now *Consumer Credit Law and Practice*) that 'regularity of activity is necessary before that activity can be regarded as a business activity so as to attract the licensing provisions. Thus, a person making occasional bridging loans for his clients or customers would not, on that account alone, be carrying on a consumer credit business'.[4]

It is submitted that the test as to whether a person is carrying on a business is more sophisticated than a question of regularity of activity. For example, a person may set up in business with the declared intention of conducting a certain type of business, although he merely enters into one transaction of that type, after which, say, the business folds. Thus the declared purpose of a business, including where a person advertises or announces himself as carrying on a business, is relevant to the determination of whether that person is in fact carrying on such business. This was also the view of the Court of Appeal in *Conroy v Kenny*.[5]

1 *Cornelius v Phillips* [1918] AC 199.
2 See CCA 1974, ss 189(1) and 145(1), (2) and (3).
3 [1999] GCCR 1345, CA.
4 *Goode: Consumer Credit Law and Practice*, para 1C [48.12]; see now IC [27.15].
5 [1999] 1 WLR 1340, [1999] All ER (D) 146, CA.

13.3.2   The conduct of credit broking business

A firm, duly authorised by the FCA with permission to carry on the activity of a credit broking business, must:[1]

(1) where it has responsibility for doing so, explain the key features of a regulated credit agreement to enable the customer to make an informed choice as required by CONC 4.2.5R [Note: paras 4.27 to 4.30 of CBG[2] and 2.2 of ILG];[3]

(2) take reasonable steps to satisfy itself that a product it wishes to recommend to a customer is not unsuitable for the customer's needs and circumstances [Note: para 4.22 of CBG];

(3) advise a customer to read, and allow the customer sufficient opportunity to consider, the terms and conditions of a credit agreement or consumer hire agreement before entering into it [Note: para 3.9l of CBG];

(4) before referring the customer to a third party which carries on regulated activities or to a claims management service (within the meaning of section 4 of the Compensation Act 2006) or other services, obtain the customer's consent, after having explained why the customer's details are to be disclosed to that third party [Note: para 3.9r of CBG];

(5) before effecting an introduction of a customer to a lender or owner in relation to a credit agreement or consumer hire agreement, or before entering into such an agreement on behalf of the lender or owner, disclose (where applicable) the fact that the lender or owner is linked to the firm by being a member of the same group as the firm [Note: para 3.9y of CBG];

(6) bring to the attention of a customer how the firm uses the customer's personal data it collects, in a manner appropriate to the means of communication used [Note: para 3.9q of CBG];

A firm may comply with (6) above by presenting to the customer a privacy notice. The Information Commissioner's Office has prepared the Privacy Notices Code of Practice.

(7) provide customers with a clear and simple method to cancel their consent for the processing of their personal data [Note: para 3.9u of CBG];

(8) at the request of a customer, disclose from where the customer's personal data was obtained [Note: para 3.9w of CBG];

(9) take reasonable steps not to pass a customer's personal data to a business which carries on a credit-related regulated activity for which the business has no permission [Note: para 3.9x of CBG];

(10) in giving explanations or advice, or in making recommendations, pay due regard to the customer's needs and circumstances. In complying with the foregoing a firm must pay due regard to whether the credit product is affordable and whether there are any factors that the firm knows, or reasonably ought to know, that may make the product unsuitable for that customer (CONC 5.4.2R) [Note: paras 4.32 to 4.36 of CBG];

(11) before undertaking to search the product market or a part of it before effecting an introduction, search the product market to the extent stated to the customer (CONC 5.4.3R).

Rules relating to quotations are set out in CONC 4.1.4R and relating to pre-contract disclosure and adequate explanations in CONC 4.2.

1 CONC 2.5.3R.
2 CBG means the Office of Fair Trading's Credit Brokers and Intermediaries Guidance, OFT 1388, dated November 2011
3 ILG means the Office of Fair Trading's Irresponsible Lending Guidance, OFT 1107, dated March 2010, and updated February 2011.

13.3.3 Credit broking and unfair business practices

The general position is that credit brokers must comply with the principles in the FCA Handbook at PRIN 2.1.

The FCA Handbook, CONC, lists some 22 rules relating to unfair business practices at 2.5.8R, together with Guidance at 2.5.9G. Significantly they are couched as rules, in contrast with guidance standards, on which they are based, as originally set out in the Office of Fair Trading's Credit Brokers and Intermediaries Guidance, OFT 1388, dated November 2011 (identified as CBG in CONC).

A credit broker must also comply with rules relating to disclosure of fees and commission contained in CONC 4.4 and 4.5.

13.4 FINANCIAL PROMOTIONS AND COMMUNICATIONS

CONC 3.7 contains obligations relating to credit brokers' financial promotions and communications, as briefly outlined below.

A firm must, in a financial promotion or a document which is intended for individuals which relates to its credit broking, indicate the extent of its powers and, in particular, whether it works exclusively with one or more lenders or works independently (CONC 3.7.3R). By way of guidance, a firm should, in a financial promotion or in a communication with a customer:

(a) make clear, to the extent an average customer of the firm would understand, the nature of the service that the firm provides;

(b) indicate to the customer in a prominent way the existence of any financial arrangements with a lender that might impact upon the firm's impartiality in promoting a credit product to a customer;

(c) only describe itself as independent if it is able to provide access to a representative range of credit products from the relevant product market on competitive terms and is not constrained in providing such access, for example, because of one or more agreements with lenders; and

(d) ensure that any disclosure about the extent of its independence is prominent and, in accordance with the clear, fair not misleading rule in CONC 3.3.1R, clear and easily comprehensible (CONC 3.7.4G).

A firm must ensure that a financial promotion or a communication with a customer specifies the legal name of the firm as it appears in the Financial Services Register and not merely a trading name (CONC 3.7.5R). This requires that all financial promotions and communications with customers specify the legal name of the firm. The rule does not prohibit the use of trading names, but requires the legal name to be given in addition to any trading name used. If the firm is a company registered under the Companies Act 2006, the firm's legal name will be the name under which it is registered (CONC 3.7.6G).

As regards disclosure of acting as a credit broker, CONC 3.7.7R provides that:

(a) a firm which is a credit broker and not a lender must ensure that any financial promotion states prominently that the firm is a credit broker and that it is not a lender;

(b) a firm which is both a credit broker and a lender must ensure that any financial promotion that solely promotes its services as a credit broker states prominently that the financial promotion is promoting the firm's services as a credit broker and not its services as a lender.

A statement will not be treated as prominent unless it is presented, in relation to other content of the financial promotion, in such a way that it is likely that the attention of the average person to whom the financial promotion is directed would be drawn to it (CONC 3.7.8G).

The above are separate and distinct from general requirements relating to promotions and communications. These include obligations in respect of promotions that are not in writing. CONC 3.10.2R provides that a firm must not communicate a solicited or unsolicited financial promotion, that is not in writing, to a customer outside the firm's premises, unless the person communicating it only does so at an appropriate time of the day, identifies that person and the firm represented at the outset and makes clear the purpose of the communication. Separate requirements for promotions about credit agreements not secured on land are contained in CONC 3.5 and about credit agreements secured on land in CONC 3.6.

13.5   CREDIT BROKING AND UNFAIR RELATIONSHIPS BETWEEN CREDITOR AND DEBTOR

The conduct of credit brokers is relevant in determining whether the relationship between the creditor and debtor is unfair because of anything done, or not done, by the credit broker acting on behalf of the creditor, either before or after the making of the agreement or any related agreement.[1]

In deciding whether to make a determination, the court must have regard to all matters it thinks relevant. A creditor transacting on an ongoing basis with a specific credit broker should therefore procure undertakings from the credit broker to conduct himself lawfully, fairly, and in accordance with the rules in the FCA Handbook. Moreover, as any claim would lie against the creditor, without an automatic right of recourse against the credit broker, the creditor should obtain an appropriate indemnity from the credit broker, including in respect of any acts, omissions and representations by the credit broker on the creditor's behalf.

Turning to the case law, the Supreme Court in *Plevin v Paragon Personal Finance Ltd*[2] considered, amongst other matters, the meaning of CCA 1974, s 140A(1)(c). This section permits the court to take into account, in determining the existence or otherwise of unfair relationships between creditor and debtor, 'any other thing done (or not done) by, or on behalf of, the creditor (either before or after the making of the agreement or any related agreement).' The court held that 'by, or on behalf of the creditor' is to be construed so as to limit the relationship in question to that of agency or deemed agency. A credit broker *per se* and without more is not to be considered as acting on behalf of the creditor. On the other hand, in respect of antecedent negotiations conducted by a credit broker, s 56(1)(c) read with s 56(2) of CCA 1974 deems them to be conducted by the credit broker negotiator in the capacity of agent of the creditor as well as in his actual capacity. As a result, s 56 triggers the application of s 140A(1)(c), as indeed was held to be the case in *Scotland v British Credit Trust Ltd*.[3]

1 CCA 1974, s 140A.
2 [2014] UKSC 61, [2014] GCCR 12085.
3 [2014] EWCA Civ 790, [2014] GCCR 12141 especially at para [74]; see also the Comment on the report in GCCR.

13.6 CREDIT BROKER AS AGENT

13.6.1 The position at common law

At common law, in the absence of an agreement establishing the credit broker as agent of the finance company, the credit broker acting in his capacity as the dealer or supplier of the goods or equipment is not the agent of the finance company. This was the decision in the leading case of *Branwhite v Worcester Works Finance*.[1]

The House of Lords approved the following statement of Pearson LJ in *Mercantile Credit Co Ltd v Hamblin*:[2]

> 'There is no rule of law that in a hire-purchase transaction the dealer never is, or always is, acting as agent for the finance company or as agent for the customer. In a typical hire-purchase transaction the dealer is a party in his own right, selling his car to the finance company, and he is acting primarily on his own behalf and not as a general agent for either of the other two parties. There is no need to attribute to him an agency in order to account for his participation in the transaction. Nevertheless the dealer is to some extent an intermediary between the customer and the finance company, and he may well have in a particular case some ad hoc agencies to do particular things on behalf of one or the other or it may be both of those two parties. For instance, if the car is delivered by the dealer to the customer after the hire-purchase agreement has been concluded, the dealer must be making delivery as agent of the finance company.'

The Court in *Branwhite* held that the mere possession by the dealer of the finance company's forms was not enough to constitute an agency and that neither filling in the forms on behalf of the intending purchaser, nor receiving a deposit from him, amounted to acting as agent for the finance company. It is also clear from the cases that the dealer's mere receipt of commission from the finance company does not make him an agent of the finance company.

It follows that the finance company is also not fixed with any knowledge that the dealer (which is not its agent) may have of defective title in the goods.[3]

The principle in *Branwhite's* case was applied to a leasing agreement in *Woodchester Equipment (Leasing) Ltd v British Association of Canned and Preserved Foods Importers and Distributors Ltd*[4] where Millett LJ stated:

> 'There is no rule of law that in a hire-purchase transaction that the supplier is the agent of the finance company for the purpose of procuring the customer to offer to acquire goods on hire-purchase. There is equally no rule of law that the supplier is not the agent of the finance company for that purpose. The question is a question of fact in every case. This was settled by the decision of the House of Lords in *Branwhite v Worcester Works Finance Ltd* ([1969] 1 AC 552).
>
> That case also decided that the facts that the finance company has provided the supplier with a stock of its forms to enable him to provide one to a prospective customer, and that it has also provided the supplier with the information necessary to enable him to calculate and inform the customer of the amounts of the initial payment and subsequent periodic payments which the finance company will require, neither constitute the supplier [and] the agent of the finance company as a matter of law, nor amount to evidence that he is such an agent in fact. These facts are entirely consistent with all parties acting as principals in their own interests.
>
> In my judgment the same applies to a leasing agreement; see the decision of this court in *J D Williams & Co v McCauley* ([1994] CCLR 78). In such a case, the supplier wishes to sell goods and the customer wishes to hire them. These conflicting objectives can both be accommodated only by the interposition of a third party, such as a finance company, which buys the goods from a supplier and in turn lets them on hire to the customer. Such a transaction involves three parties and two contracts, one of sale and the other of hire. These contracts are capable of being concluded by the parties without the interposition of any agency, so that a finding of agency requires, in my judgment, to be supported by clear evidence.'

1 *Branwhite v Worcester Works Finance Ltd* [1969] 1 AC 552, [1999] GCCR 397, HL; see also *Mynshul Asset Finance v Clarke (t/a Peacock Hotel)* referred to in [1992] CLY 487; *Moorgate Mercantile Leasing v Isobel Gell and Ugolini Dispensers (UK) Ltd* [1988] CCLR 1. Compare *Woodchester Leasing Equipment Ltd v R M Clayton and D M Clayton (t/a Sudbury Sports)*, decision of the Sudbury County Court (October 1993) where the court found the suppliers to be the agent of the plaintiff leasing company, resulting in a cancellable lease under CCA 1974, s 67. It drew the rather forced inference from the fact that the agreement was highly advantageous to the supplier and the leasing company. See also Chapter 14 on 'Agency'.
2 [1965] 2 QB 242, CA at 269.
3 *Car and Universal Finance Co Ltd v Caldwell* [1964] 1 All ER 290, CA.
4 [1999] GCCR 1923, CA at 1932.

13.6.2   Agency under CCA 1974

In the common 'three-party' hire-purchase or instalment sale agreement the dealer is a credit broker who sells the goods which are the subject of the proposed credit agreement to the creditor. The creditor then delivers those goods on credit terms to the debtor. That agreement, being a hire-purchase or instalment sale agreement, is a debtor-creditor-supplier/borrower-lender-supplier agreement and any negotiations conducted by the dealer in relation to those goods or to the transaction financed or to be financed by the credit agreement are deemed to be conducted by the dealer in his capacity as agent of the creditor as well as in his actual capacity.[1] This means that the creditor is bound by any statements or representations made by the dealer in relation to the goods or the transaction. This might include an associated or linked agreement.[2]

Included in such negotiations, known as 'antecedent negotiations', are statements made when the credit broker first enters into communications with the debtor or hirer, namely advertisements, discussions and correspondence.[3] 'Antecedent negotiations' are any negotiations with a debtor conducted by a credit broker in relation to goods sold or proposed to be sold by the credit broker to the creditor before forming the subject matter of a debtor-creditor-supplier agreement under s 12(a) of CCA 1974.[4] As stated in CCA 1974, s 56:

'(1) In this Act "antecedent negotiations" means any negotiations with the debtor or hirer–

(a) conducted by the creditor or owner in relation to the making of any regulated agreement, or

(b) conducted by a credit-broker in relation to goods sold or proposed to be sold by the credit-broker to the creditor before forming the subject-matter of a debtor-creditor-supplier agreement within section 12(a), or

(c) conducted by the supplier in relation to a transaction financed or proposed to be financed by a debtor-creditor-supplier agreement within section 12(b) or (c),

and "negotiator" means the person by whom negotiations are so conducted with the debtor or hirer.

(2) Negotiations with the debtor in a case falling within subsection (1)(b) or (c) shall be deemed to be conducted by the negotiator in the capacity of agent of the creditor as well as in his actual capacity.'

In *Forthright Finance Ltd v Ingate*,[5] Mrs Ingate, the debtor, had agreed to buy a motor car under a three-party conditional sale agreement with the third party, Carlyle Finance. The car dealer, who set up the agreement, also agreed to take the debtor's existing car, which was the subject of a conditional sale agreement with Forthright Finance under which a sum of money was still owed, by way of part exchange. The car dealer also undertook to pay the balance owing under that agreement but before doing so, went into liquidation.

The Court of Appeal found, on the facts, that there were not two independent transactions, one relating to the discharge of the sum owing in respect of the part exchanged vehicle and the other relating to the financing of the new vehicle, but that the two transactions were linked aspects of one transaction. In the court's judgment, s 56(1)(b) meant that there must be goods sold or proposed to be sold by the credit broker to the creditor which will form the subject matter of a debtor-creditor-supplier/borrower-lender-supplier agreement. If that condition is fulfilled, one next enquires whether there were negotiations in relation to those goods. If there were, then all that was said by the credit broker in those negotiations is deemed to have been said on behalf of the creditor. On the other hand, what is said in any other negotiations which do not relate to those goods, is not deemed to have been said on behalf of the creditor.

The court held that the negotiations, including those in respect of the part exchange, related to the goods to be sold because they were all part of one transaction. In the circumstances, the finance company of the second vehicle, Carlyle Finance Ltd, was vicariously liable for representations by the dealer as a negotiator within s 56. As stated by Henry J:

> 'Using the old familiar language of "hirer, dealer and finance company" the clear statutory effect of s 56 of the Consumer Credit Act of 1974 is to make the dealer, in addition to his liability in his "actual capacity", the finance company's agent in situations where he would not be at common law because he would not have had the authority express or implied so to act. The machinery for doing this is to be found in s 56(2) of the Act, making him the finance company's agent in negotiations with [the hirer] ....'

In contrast to *Forthright Finance Ltd v Ingate* is the case of *Black Horse Ltd v Langford*[6] where the court held that the phrase 'sold or proposed to be sold' in CCA 1974, s 56(1)(b) only applies to the credit broker which actually sold or proposed to sell the goods to the creditor and not to any intermediate credit broker. In this case the credit broker which made the representations, Castleford Trade Car Centre, introduced the transaction to another credit broker, North Riding Finance, which in turn introduced the defendant, Langford, to the finance company, Black Horse, the supplier on hire-purchase of the motor vehicle to Langford. It was held that the original credit broker's promise to discharge the outstanding balance under an existing hire-purchase agreement of Langford, was not deemed to have been made by him as agent of the claimant, Black Horse, under s 56 as that credit broker did not sell the vehicle to Black Horse. The decision appears to be correct but will be of little comfort to any person relying on the original dealer's representation as binding the ultimate creditor or supplier.

An error in the drafting of s 56 has given rise to the anomalous position that it does not extend to negotiators of hire agreements, so that s 56 does not bind the owner under a hire agreement to antecedent negotiations entered into by the negotiator, unless the negotiator was in fact the owner's agent.[7] This result is dramatically different from that in relation to a negotiator in respect of a credit agreement where the creditor is bound by the antecedent negotiations of the negotiator.

Section 56 does not exclude situations where, as a matter of fact, one party negotiated as agent of another, including a dealer as agent of the hiring company. Thus, in *Woodchester Leasing Equipment Ltd v Clayton*[8] the court was satisfied that the defendant had been induced to enter into the leasing agreement by the representations made to him by the supplier and concluded that in all the circumstances of the case it defied belief that the plaintiff leasing company did not know of the kind of inducements which the supplier would hold out, approve of their use and encourage the supplier to make them. Accordingly, it found that the supplier was acting as agent for the leasing company.

A credit broker is deemed to be the agent of the creditor or hiring company for various other purposes, such as receiving various notices, including a notice of withdrawal from a prospective agreement, a notice of cancellation in respect of a cancellable agreement and a notice rescinding the agreement. These deemed agency provisions may not be excluded by agreement as they are intended for the protection of the debtor or hirer.[9]

An intention made known to a credit broker by a consumer may be imputed to the creditor or leasing company. For example, if a customer makes known to a credit broker the purpose for which he proposes purchasing goods or hiring goods under a hire-purchase agreement, there is an implied condition that the goods supplied under the agreement are reasonably fit for that purpose. The credit broker's knowledge is imputed to the creditor. The presumption can be dislodged if it can be shown that the hirer or buyer has not relied upon, and that it would be unreasonable for him to rely upon, the skill or judgement of the creditor or credit broker.[10]

It is submitted that, outside the provisions of CCA 1974 set out above and in the absence of an express or implied agency agreement, the limited agency of the credit broker under CCA 1974 will not result in the creditor incurring liability for the credit broker's wrongful or tortious acts or omissions, including any under the Consumer Protection from Unfair Trading Regulations 2008 or the Consumer Protection Act 1987.

1 CCA 1974, s 56(2).
2 *UDT v Whitfield* [1987] CCLR 60. Cf *Northgran Finance Ltd v Ashley* [1963] 1 QB 476.
3 CCA 1974, s 56(4).
4 Ibid., s 56(1)(b).
5 [1999] GCCR 2213, at 2220, CA. Compare this decision to *Powell v Lloyds Bowmaker Ltd* [1999] GCCR 3523 (Sheriff's Court).
6 [2007] EWHC 907 (QB), [2007] All ER (D) 214, [2007] GCCR 6001.
7 *Moorgate Mercantile Leasing v Isobell Gell and Ugolini Dispensers (UK) Ltd* [1988] CCLR 1; *Lloyds Bowmaker Leasing Ltd v John R MacDonald* [1999] GCCR 3443 (Sheriff's Court).
8 Reported in Consumer Credit Trade Association Journal, January 1994, vol 48 no 5, p 2; for *UDT v Whitfield* see note 2 above.
9 CCA 1974, s 173.
10 Sale of Goods Act 1979, s 14(3); Supply of Goods (Implied Terms) Act 1973, s 10(3); and see *R&B Customs Brokers Co Ltd v United Dominions Trust Ltd* [1999] GCCR 1195, CA.

13.7 CONSEQUENCES OF CARRYING ON UNAUTHORISED CREDIT BROKING BUSINESS

Section 19 of the Financial Services and Markets Act 2000 ('FSMA') provides that no person may carry on a regulated activity in the United Kingdom or purport to do so, unless he is an authorised person, or an exempt person. This prohibition is referred to as the general prohibition. Breach of the general prohibition is an offence (FSMA, s 23(1)).

FSMA, s 22 provides that an activity is a regulated activity for purposes of FSMA if it is an activity of a specified kind which is carried on by way of business and relates, among other things, to an investment (i.e. any asset, right or interest) specified in an order made by the Treasury (for practical purposes, the RAO). Credit broking is a specified kind of activity, being specified in RAO article 36A.[1]

An agreement made by a person in the course of carrying on a regulated activity in contravention of the general prohibition is unenforceable against the other party. The other party is entitled to recover any money or property paid or transferred by him and to compensation for any loss (FSMA, s 26). In addition, breach of a rule made by the FCA is actionable at the suit of a private person who suffers loss as a result of the breach (FSMA, s 138D(2)).

Whilst a creditor or owner is only concerned to ensure that his immediate introducer is authorised, each credit broker in a chain of credit brokers must be authorised. Thus, it does not avail a person whose application for authorisation has been declined to avoid such refusal by introducing applicants for credit through an ultimately authorised credit broker. Indeed, he and all those involved in any such scheme are liable for breach of FSMA and the RAO.[2]

1 See RAO art 36A(1)(c) and **13.1** above.
2 Compare *Hicks v Walker* [1984] Crim LR 495, [1999] GCCR 721 relating to licensing offences under CCA 1974.

13.8   CREDIT BROKERS' CHARGES

Credit brokers are entitled to levy charges, fees or commission on their customers or the creditor or owner to whom they introduce the customer. The latter will be the case where the credit is interest-free as then, by definition, no charge is levied on the customer.

Where a credit broker levies a charge on the customer for his services, the credit brokerage fee forms part of the total charge for credit and the annual percentage rate of charge ('APR'), and must be shown in the credit agreement. An anomaly is that credit brokerage fees charged in respect of hire agreements are reflected in neither the hire charge nor the hire agreement.

If a customer does not enter into a relevant agreement within six months of the introduction, the credit broker must reimburse the customer with the amount of any credit brokerage fee in excess of £5, a fee which has even defied inflation, since being set in 1998! This also applies to cancelled regulated agreements.[1]

A customer's right to a reimbursement of charges applies to an individual who sought an introduction for a purpose which would have been fulfilled by his entry into:

(a)   a regulated agreement, or

(b)   in the case of an individual desiring to obtain credit to finance the acquisition or provision of a dwelling occupied or to be occupied by that individual or a relative of that individual, an agreement for credit secured on land,

(c)   a credit agreement which is an exempt agreement for the purposes of Chapter 14A of Part 2 of the Regulated Activities Order, or

(d)   an agreement which is not a regulated credit agreement or a regulated consumer hire agreement but which would be such an agreement if the law applicable to the agreement were the law of a part of the United Kingdom;

but does not apply where:

(i)   the fee or commission relates to the effecting of an introduction of a kind mentioned in article 36E of the Regulated Activities Order (activities in relation to certain agreements relating to land); and

(ii)   the person charging that fee or commission is an authorised person or an appointed representative, within the meaning of the Financial Services and Markets Act 2000.[2]

The provisions relating to the right to recover credit brokerage fees also apply to any other fee or commission for the services charged by a credit broker. In the case of an individual desiring to obtain credit under a consumer credit agreement, any sum payable or paid by him to a credit broker, otherwise than as a fee or commission for the credit broker's services, is treated as such a fee or commission for the purposes of the right to recover brokerage fees, if it enters into, or would enter into, the total charge for credit.[3]

Whilst there is no stipulated upper limit on the amount which a credit broker can charge a customer, credit brokerage charges and commission are restricted by virtue of their impact on the APR, by the need to apply fair business practices, the potential fiduciary duty of a credit broker owed to its customer, and the unfair relationships provisions of CCA 1974 sections 140A to 140C. The duty to disclose the existence and rate of a credit broker's charges and commission has been the subject of various recent cases, and the reader is referred to **13.9** below and to *Plevin v Paragon Personal Finance Ltd*[4] and *McWilliam v Norton Finance (UK) Ltd*.[5]

The above is mainly relevant to consumer credit agreements, rather than to consumer hire agreements.

1 CCA 1974, s 155. The sum is variable by Order.
2 Ibid., s 155(2) and (2A).
3 Ibid., s 155(4).
4 [2014] UKSC 61, [2014] GCCR 12085.
5 [2015] EWCA Civ 186, [2015] GCCR 13027, CA.

13.9   CREDIT BROKER AND FIDUCIARY RELATIONSHIP

Where a credit broker receives payment of a fee from his customer, whether a debtor or hirer, it places the credit broker in a fiduciary relationship with his customer. As a fiduciary he is required to act loyally for the customer, in the customer's best interest, and not to put himself in a position where he has a conflict of interest with his customer. If he also receives commission or a fee from the lender, he can only discharge his fiduciary duty to his customer by obtaining his customer's informed consent with the full knowledge of all the material circumstances and of the nature and the extent of his interest, including disclosure of the fact that he is to receive a commission from the lender and the amount of the commission. The consent should be accompanied by a warning to the effect that payment of the commission to the broker might mean that he is not in a position to give unbiased advice. This was the principle of the decision in *Hurstanger Ltd v Wilson*.[1] A fiduciary relationship might also arise in circumstances where the customer relies upon the broker to advise him. Merely recommending a particular finance company is not, it is submitted, tantamount to advice and does not create a fiduciary relationship between the finance company and the customer.

The remedy for breach of the fiduciary duty lies in equity. The court has a discretion as to whether or not to grant rescission of the contract resulting from the credit broker's introduction or to grant compensation to the customer for the broker's breach of fiduciary duty. In the circumstances of *Hurstanger* the court considered that the defendants were adequately compensated by awarding them the sum of £240, equal to the commission which the credit broker received from the lender, plus interest. It held that to rescind the transaction altogether would be unfair and disproportionate.

The principle in *Hurstanger* has been accepted and followed by the courts, as in *McWilliam v Norton Finance (UK) Ltd (t/a Norton Finance) (in liquidation)*, where Tomlinson LJ stated:[2]

> 'More generally, as it seems to me, the circumstance that the Claimants were not looking to Norton for any advice or recommendation other than that to which I have referred is not relevant to the question whether a fiduciary duty was assumed. As pointed out in *Jackson and Powell on Professional Liability* (7th edn, 2011) para 2–141, the reliance upon which the trust and confidence which gives rise to fiduciary obligations is based is not the same sort of reliance as gives rise to a tortious duty of care:

> Rather, it is the fact that the principal so relies on the fiduciary as to leave the principal vulnerable to any disloyalty by the fiduciary and so reliant on his good faith.

> Nor do I regard it as conclusive of the question whether a fiduciary duty was owed that the Insurance Conduct of Business Rules in force at the time did not require disclosure by an insurance intermediary to a borrower of the amount of commission. In *Hurstanger* the relevant OFT regulatory materials encouraged, but did not require, disclosure of the amount or percentage figure of commission.

> In my judgment the judge was bound by *Hurstanger* to find that the relationship between Norton and the Claimants was a fiduciary one, and so are we.'

> In the recent case of *Commercial First Business Ltd v Pickup & Vernon*[3] the High Court (Chancery Division), after reviewing the authorities, distinguished *Hurstanger* and found, on the facts, that the customer could not reasonably have expected the broker's undivided loyalty, with the result that no fiduciary or agency relationship arose between the broker and the customer.

The provisions of the FCA Handbook, CONC sourcebook, stipulate that a credit broker must disclose to a customer, in good time before a credit agreement or a consumer hire agreement is entered into, the existence of any commission or fee or other remuneration payable to the credit broker by the lender or owner or a third party in relation to a credit agreement or a consumer hire agreement, where knowledge of the existence or amount of the commission could actually or potentially:

(1) affect the impartiality of the credit broker in recommending a particular product; or

(2) have a material impact on the customer's transactional decision.[4]

In contrast with the rule highlighted in the next paragraph, the above rule is not dependent upon the customer's prior request. At the request of the customer, a credit broker must disclose to the customer, in good time before a regulated credit agreement or a regulated consumer hire agreement is entered into, the amount (or, if the precise amount is not known, the likely amount) of any commission or fee or other remuneration payable to the credit broker by the lender or owner or a third party.[5]

1 [2007] All ER (D) 66, [2007] GCCR 5951, CA.
2 [2015] EWCA Civ 186, [2015] GCCR 13027, CA, paras [46] to [48]. See also *Nelmes v NRAM Plc* [2016] EWCA Civ 491, [2016] GCCR 14081, CA, at [34].
3 [2016] GCCR 14171.
4 CONC 4.5.3R.
5 CONC 4.5.4R.

13.10 OTHER REGULATED ACTIVITIES OF CREDIT BROKERS

Credit brokers often act as independent financial advisers or intermediaries in relation to activities regulated under the Financial Services and Markets Act 2000 (Regulated Activities) Order 2001.[1] These activities include accepting deposits, issuing electronic money, effecting and carrying out contracts of insurance, dealing in investments as principal, dealing in investments as agent, arranging deals in investments, managing investments, assisting in the administration and performance of a contract of insurance, safeguarding and administering investments and advising on investments. Investments include deposits, electronic money, contracts of insurance, regulated mortgage contracts, regulated home reversion plans, regulated home purchase plans and regulated sale and rent back agreements.

A person conducting any of the above activities by way of business must be authorised by the Financial Conduct Authority under the Financial Services and Markets Act 2000 ('FSMA') or, for more limited purposes, be an appointed representative or agent of an authorised person.[2] The appointed representative or agent must have a contract with an authorised person permitting him to carry on business of a prescribed description. The principal must accept responsibility in writing for the activities of the appointed representative and the principal is responsible, to the same extent as if it had expressly permitted it, for anything done or omitted by the appointed representative or agent in carrying on the business for which it has accepted responsibility.

If the contract does not prohibit the representative from acting for persons other than his principal, it must contain provision allowing the principal to prohibit him from doing so, or to restrict the extent to which he can do so.[3]

An introducer appointed representative is an appointed representative appointed by a firm whose scope of appointment is limited to effecting introductions and distributing non real-time financial promotions. An introducer appointed representative must enter into an agreement with his principal, similar to an appointed representative, and broadly similar rules apply to him. However, whilst an appointed representative must register as an approved person with the Financial Conduct Authority, an introducer appointed representative is not required to do so.

1 SI 2001/544, as amended.
2 FSMA, ss 39 and 59.
3 Financial Services and Markets Act 2000 (Appointed Representative) Regulations 2001, SI 2001/1217, as amended.

13.11   DISCLOSURE OF DETAILS OF A CREDIT INTERMEDIARY

The Consumer Credit (Disclosure of Information) Regulations 2010[1] and the Consumer Credit (Agreements) Regulations 2010[2] require the pre-contract information documents and the credit agreement respectively to state the identity and geographical address of the credit intermediary, which would include a credit broker, where the agreement involves a credit intermediary.

1 SI 2010/1013, Schs 1 and 3.
2 SI 1010/1014, Sch 1.

Chapter 14

Agency

14.1 AGENCY AT COMMON LAW

The relationship of principal and agent may be constituted (a) by the conferring of authority by the principal on the agent, which may be express or implied from the conduct or situation of the parties; or (b) retrospectively, by subsequent ratification by the principal of acts done on his behalf. A person may also be estopped from denying that another person acted as his agent. Finally, a person may be liable under the doctrine of apparent authority in respect of another who is not his agent at all.[1]

An agent who undertakes to act for another, in circumstances giving rise to a relationship of trust and confidence, owes fiduciary duties to prefer his principal's interests to his own.[2] As stated by Millett LJ in *Bristol & West Building Society v Mothew*:[3]

> 'A fiduciary is someone who has undertaken to act for or on behalf of another in a particular matter in circumstances which give rise to a relationship of trust and confidence. The distinguishing obligation of a fiduciary is the obligation of loyalty. The principal is entitled to the single-minded loyalty of his fiduciary. This core liability has several facets. A fiduciary must act in good faith; he must not make a profit out of his trust; he must not place himself in a position where his duty and his interest may conflict; he may not act for his own benefit or the benefit of a third person without the informed consent of his principal. This is not intended to be an exhaustive list, but it is sufficient to indicate the nature of fiduciary obligations. They are the defining characteristics of the fiduciary. As Dr Finn pointed out in his classic work *Fiduciary Obligations* (1977) p 2, he is not subject to fiduciary obligations because he is a fiduciary; it is because he is subject to them that he is a fiduciary.'

The fiduciary relationship between a principal and an agent was the subject of *Hurstanger Ltd v Wilson*[4] where the court held that a credit broker who receives a payment from the debtor for acting as his agent and also has an arrangement with the creditor to receive commission (whether or not he in fact receives such commission) is under a fiduciary duty to make full disclosure to the debtor and to obtain his informed consent to receiving such payment from the creditor. In the absence of such disclosure and consent, the agent will have received a secret commission in breach of his fiduciary duty.[5] As the fact, but not the amount, of commission was disclosed, the customer was awarded equitable relief for the amount of the commission, rather than rescission of the agreement.

In *McWilliam v Norton*[6] the Court of Appeal considered the issue of a credit broker's fiduciary duty to its customers in circumstances in which the broker was paid commission by the lender in addition to receiving an agreed broker fee from the customers. The court followed *Hurstanger* and held that the broker should not have placed itself in a position where its duty and its interest might conflict, nor profit out of the trust reposed in it to get the best possible deal, nor act for its own benefit without the Claimants' informed consent. The claimant customers were not told how much commission would be paid and hence did not give their informed consent. The court awarded the customers the commissions received, together with interest.

1   *Bowstead & Reynolds on Agency* (Sweet & Maxwell, 20th edn, 2014), para 2-001.
2   *Chitty on Contracts*, vol 2, 32nd edn, para 31-118.
3   [1996] 4 All ER 698 at 712, cited by *Chitty* at para 31-120.
4   [2007] All ER (D) 66, CA.
5   See also the discussion at **13.9**.
6   [2015] EWCA Civ 186, [2015] GCCR 13027 at [43]; see also *obiter* in *Nelmes v NRAM Plc* [2016] EWCA Civ 491, [2016] GCCR 14081.

14.2   CONTRACTS (RIGHTS OF THIRD PARTIES) ACT 1999

Before turning to the statutory provisions creating an agency relationship under the CCA 1974, it should be mentioned that a contract might, directly or indirectly, confer upon a person who is not a party to the contract, namely a third party, the right to enforce a term of the contract. It will do so if the contract expressly provides such right or if the term purports to confer a benefit on a third party unless, in the latter case, it appears on a proper construction of the contract, that the parties to the contract did not intend the term to be enforceable by the third party. The third party must be expressly identified in the contract by name, as a member of a class or as answering a particular description or the agreement must purport to confer a benefit on him. The third party need not be in existence when the contract is made.

In a leasing or hire-purchase contract, if rights are conferred upon identifiable third parties in the event of a breach of the contract, for example upon the provider of maintenance of a motor vehicle, they would be enforceable by that provider.

14.3   RELATIONSHIP BETWEEN THE DEALER OR RETAILER AND THE FINANCE COMPANY

In the leading case of *Branwhite v Worcester Works Finance Ltd*,[1] the House of Lords stated that a dealer may, in some circumstances, be held out by a finance company as its agent. However, the court approved the following statement in *Mercantile Credit Co Ltd v Hamblin*:[2]

> 'There is no rule of law that in a hire-purchase transaction the dealer never is, or always is, acting as agent for the finance company or as agent for the customer. In a typical hire-purchase transaction the dealer is a party in his own right, selling his car to the finance company, and he is acting primarily on his own behalf

and not as general agent for either of the other two parties. There is no need to attribute to him an agency in order to account for his participation in the transaction. Nevertheless, the dealer is to some extent an intermediary between the customer and the finance company, and he may well have in a particular case some ad hoc agencies to do particular things on behalf of one or the other or it may be both of those two parties. For instance, if the car is delivered by the dealer to the customer after the hire-purchase agreement has been concluded, the dealer must be making delivery as agent of the finance company.'

The case was cited with approval in *Hudson v Shogun*[3] and also applied to leasing agreements in *JD Williams & Co v McCauley*[4] and *Woodchester Equipment (Leasing) Ltd v British Association of Canned and Preserved Foods Importers and Distributors Ltd*.[5] In the latter the court stated that the authority of *Branwhite* establishes beyond peradventure that unless some very exceptional factual material is present, a relationship of principal and agent does not arise between a finance company entering into a hire-purchase agreement and the dealer or retailer. This principle, the court held in *Woodchester*, applied equally to leasing agreements. It is irrelevant that a finance company supplied the dealer with a stock of its forms for use by the dealer's prospective customer and that it has supplied the dealer with information enabling him to calculate the financial details; these do not constitute the supplier as the agent of the finance company in law, nor amount to evidence that he is such an agent in fact. The court held that these facts are entirely consistent with all parties acting as principal in their own interest. The interposition of the supplier or dealer between the finance company and the customer is necessitated simply by the fact that the finance company sells the goods to the supplier, who in turn lets them on hire or hire-purchase to the customer. Such a transaction necessarily involves three parties and two contracts, one of sale and the other of lease or hire-purchase. These contracts are capable of being concluded by the parties without the interposition of any agency. A finding of agency requires to be supported by clear factual evidence and is not to be assumed merely from the relationship between the parties.[6] A dealer may, for some *ad hoc* or specific purpose, or at some particular moment in time, be the agent of the finance company.[7] If, on the other hand, the finance company in fact appoints the supplier or dealer as its agent, an agency relationship will exist by virtue of the express contractual term.

1 [1968] 3 All ER 104, [1999] GCCR 397, HL.
2 [1964] 3 All ER 592, at 600.
3 [2001] GCCR 3035, CA, at [16]; [2003] UKHL 62.
4 [1999] GCCR 1375, CA.
5 [1999] GCCR 1923, at 1926 and 1932, CA.
6 The reader is also referred to *Goode on Commercial Law* (5th edn, 2016) at paras 27.23 to 27.26.
7 *Black Horse Ltd v Langford* [2007] EWHC 907 (QB), [2007] GCCR 6001 at [37].

14.4 AGENCY UNDER THE CONSUMER CREDIT ACT 1974

14.4.1 Antecedent negotiations

CCA 1974, s 56 importantly provides that certain negotiations by a credit broker or by the supplier are deemed to be conducted by such person in the capacity of agent of the creditor as well as in his actual capacity. The negotiations are so-called antecedent negotiations, namely negotiations with a debtor or hirer conducted by a credit broker in relation to goods sold or proposed to be sold by the credit broker to the credit or, before forming the subject matter of a debtor-creditor-supplier agreement in the form of a restricted-use agreement to finance a transaction between the debtor and the creditor. Likewise, negotiations are deemed to be conducted by the supplier as agent for the creditor where the negotiations relate to a transaction financed or to be financed by a debtor-creditor-supplier agreement to finance a transaction between the debtor and a supplier, other than the creditor.[1] An agreement is void if, and to the extent that, it purports to provide that a person acting as, or on behalf of a negotiator, is to be treated as the agent of the debtor or hirer or to relieve a person from liability for acts or omissions of any person acting as, or on behalf of, a negotiator.[2]

The limitation of the scope of the s 56 agency provision is evidenced by *Black Horse Ltd v Langford*.[3] The court held that the phrase 'goods sold or proposed to be sold', in s 56(1)(b) applies only to the credit broker who actually sells or proposes to sell the goods to the creditor and not to any other credit broker in the chain of credit brokers leading to the conclusion of the transaction. Ironically, it highlights the advantage to finance companies of dealing with intermediary credit brokers, rather than directly with the supplier credit broker.

The provisions of s 56, though not for any logical reason, do not apply the relationship of agency to a dealer involved in antecedent negotiations in relation to the making of a regulated hire agreement (as opposed to a regulated credit agreement).

The agency relationship, where it exists, extends to the entire spectrum of negotiations which precede entering into the agreement, including negotiations by the dealer relating to the part-exchange of a vehicle prior to the creditor entering into a conditional sale agreement.[4]

Antecedent negotiations commence when the negotiator and the debtor or hirer first enter into communication, including communication by advertisement and, although the CCA 1974 describes them as 'antecedent negotiations' they may even include negotiations following the making of the agreement.[5]

1 CCA 1974, s 56(1)(b), (c) and (2).
2 Ibid., s 56(3).
3 [2007] All ER (D) 214.
4 *Forthright Finance Ltd v Ingate (Carlyle Finance Ltd, third party)* [1999] GCCR 2213, CA.
5 CCA 1974, s 56(4).

14.4.2 Agent relating to disclosure of borrower's/hirer's business purposes

An agreement is an exempt agreement under the Financial Services and Markets Act 2000 (Regulated Activities) Order 2001, SI 2001/544 ('RAO'), article 60C, and therefore not a regulated credit agreement, if the creditor/lender provides the debtor/borrower with credit exceeding £25,000, or a consumer hire agreement that requires the hirer to make payments exceeding £25,000 if, in each case, the agreement is entered into by the debtor/borrower or hirer, wholly or predominantly for the purposes of a business carried on, or intended to be carried on, by him.

This presumption does not apply if, when the agreement is entered into, the creditor/lender or owner, or any person acting on his behalf in connection with the entering into of the agreement, knows or has reasonable cause to suspect that the agreement is not entered into wholly or predominantly for the purposes of a business carried on, or intended to be carried on, by the debtor/borrower or hirer.[1] Such knowledge or suspicion may be held by a credit broker or intermediary who enters into regulated credit agreements with individuals on behalf of creditors.

It follows that, where a person acts as an agent for the creditor/lender or the owner and is informed by the debtor/borrower or hirer that he is entering into the agreement wholly or predominantly for the purpose of his business, the agreement will be an unregulated agreement. There is no need to prove that the information was actually passed to the creditor/lender or owner.

The words 'acted on his behalf in connection with the entering into the agreement' are not entirely clear but it would be safe to assume that the restricted interpretation applied to such phrase by the Supreme Court in *Plevin*, discussed below, in relation to CCA 1974, s 140A would be applied here too, complemented by reference to the decision in *Branwhite v Worcester Works Finance Ltd* that ordinarily a dealer is not to be construed as the agent of the creditor/lender or owner.

1   RAO art 60C(3), (5) and (6) relating to credit agreements, and art 60O relating to consumer hire agreements.

14.4.3   Relevance to unfair relationships between creditor and debtor

The relevance of any act or omission by an agent of the creditor to the issue of unfair relationships between creditor and debtor appears from the provisions governing the same. Thus, in considering whether the relationship between the creditor and the debtor arising out of the agreement is unfair to the debtor under CCA 1974, s 140A, one of the grounds to be taken into account is anything done, or not done, on behalf of the creditor either before or after the making of the agreement or any related agreement. The court is bound to take into account all matters it thinks relevant. Accordingly, the conduct of any person acting as agent of the creditor, whether as a credit broker, credit intermediary (entering into the consumer credit agreement on behalf of the creditor) or as a contractual agent, would be a relevant consideration.

After considerable debate regarding the meaning of the phrase 'by, or on behalf of, the creditor' in s 140A(c) and whether it should include anything done for the benefit of the creditor, the Supreme Court, in the unanimous judgment delivered by Sumption LJ in *Plevin v Paragon Personal Finance Ltd*,[1] rejected such suggestion, stating:

> 'The only limitation on the extreme breadth of sub-paragraph (c) is that the action or inaction in question must be "by or on behalf of the creditor". Putting the matter at its very lowest, those words envisage a relationship between the creditor and the person whose acts or omissions have made the relationship unfair. If it had been intended to extend the sub-paragraph to any conduct beneficial to the creditor or contributing to bringing about the transaction, irrespective of that

person's relationship with the creditor, it would have been easy enough to say so, and very strange to use the language which the legislator actually employed.

In their ordinary and natural meaning the words "on behalf of" import agency, which is how the courts have ordinarily construed them: see *Gaspet Ltd v Elliss (Inspector of Taxes)* [1985] STC 572, [1985] 1 WLR 1214, 1220, 60 TC 91 (Peter Gibson J); *Clixby v Pountney (Inspector of Taxes)* [1968] Ch 719, at paras 728–729, [1968] 1 All ER 802, [1968] 2 WLR 865 (Cross J). I would accept that a special statutory or contractual context may require the phrase "on behalf of" to be read more widely as meaning "in the place of", or "for the benefit of" or "in the interests of": see *R (Cherwell District Council) v First Secretary of State* [2005] 1 WLR 1128 (Chadwick LJ); *R(S) v Social Security Commissioner* [2009] EWHC 2221 (Admin), [2010] PTSR 1785, at paras 27–28; *Rochdale Metropolitan Borough Council v Dixon* [2011] EWCA Civ 1173, [2012] LGR 251, [2012] PTSR 1336, at paras 49–50 (Rix J). But there is nothing in the present statutory context to suggest any of these wider meanings, and much that is inconsistent with them.'

1 [2014] UKSC 61, [2014] GCCR 12085, especially at [29], [30] ff.

14.4.4 Agent for receiving notices etc

The Act deems certain persons to be the agent of the creditor or owner for specified purposes. Each of the following is deemed to be the agent of the creditor or owner for the purpose of receiving a notice of withdrawal from a prospective regulated agreement, a cancellation notice in respect of a cancellable agreement or a notice rescinding the agreement:

(a) a credit broker or supplier who is the negotiator in antecedent negotiations; and

(b) any person who, in the course of a business carried on by him, acts on behalf of the debtor or hirer in any negotiations for the agreement.[1]

The hirer under a regulated consumer hire agreement is entitled to terminate the agreement by giving notice to any person entitled or authorised to receive the rental payments.[2] Likewise, a debtor under a hire-purchase or conditional sale agreement may terminate the agreement by giving notice to any person entitled or authorised to receive the sums payable under the agreement.[3]

A credit broker or supplier who is the negotiator in antecedent negotiations is also deemed to be the agent of the creditor in respect of any repayments of credit or of interest and for the re-delivery of any goods under a cancelled agreement.[4]

Where a person is deemed to receive a notice or payment as agent of the creditor or owner under a regulated agreement, he is deemed to be under a contractual duty to the creditor or owner to transmit the notice or remit the payment to him forthwith.[5]

1 CCA 1974, ss 57(3), 67, 69(6), 73 and 102(1).
2 Ibid., s 101(1).
3 Ibid., s 99(1).
4 Ibid., ss 71(4) and 72(6).
5 Ibid., s 175.

14.4.5 Debtor's agent

The debtor under a regulated consumer credit agreement is not liable to the creditor for any loss arising from any use made of the credit facility by another person not acting, or to be treated as acting, as the debtor's agent.[1] However, the debtor under a credit-token agreement can be made liable for £50 of the creditor's loss.[2]

1 CCA 1974, s 83.
2 Ibid., s 84.

14.4.6 Contracting out

Finally, it should be mentioned that the various deemed agency provisions cannot be excluded or negated by contract, as this would offend CCA 1974, s 173. Subject to limited exceptions, this section provides that a term in a regulated agreement or linked transaction or in any other agreement relating to an actual or prospective regulated agreement or linked transaction is void if and to the extent that it is inconsistent with a provision for the protection of the debtor or hirer, his relative or any surety.

14.5 AGENCY UNDER THE FINANCIAL SERVICES AND MARKETS ACT 2000 ('FSMA')

The most relevant aspect of FSMA in the context of our analysis is the potential impact of rules made by the Financial Conduct Authority ('FCA') on the fiduciary duty of an agent. Thus, Part 9A contains rule-making powers requiring firms to disclose to their customers details of charges, remuneration and commission. Section 137P provides for the withholding of information which one party would otherwise be required to disclose to another. However, where there is a direct conflict between rules of law and FCA Rules, the former are likely to prevail. To quote *Bowstead & Reynolds on Agency*: 'It seems very doubtful, however, whether the power to alter basic protective rules of law could be conferred on a rule-making body in this way and by such general wording. Compliance with such standards might, however ... be evidence of statutory reasonableness; or be a guide to the extent of the fiduciary obligation; to trade usage; or more simply as to the understanding of the parties to a contract'.[1]

1 Loc. cit., para 6-060.

Chapter 15

The supplier and related supplies

15.1 THE SUPPLIER UNDER THE CONSUMER CREDIT ACT 1974

In relation to the supply of goods or services on credit, as we have already noted,[1] there are two types of debtor-creditor-supplier (d-c-s) agreements, also known as borrower-lender-supplier agreements, namely two-party and three-party d-c-s agreements. In a two-party d-c-s agreement the supplier is also the provider of the credit. This is the case in credit sale, conditional sale and hire-purchase agreements.

In a three-party d-c-s agreement the credit facility and the title to the goods pass from different sources. Thus, where a retailer supplies goods which are financed by a separate finance company, the retailer passes the title and the finance company provides the credit.

The CCA 1974 identifies the supplier obliquely, by reference to the third person to a credit transaction, namely as the party to the transaction with the debtor, other than the creditor, in the case of a three-party d-c-s agreement and as the creditor himself in the case of a two-party d-c-s agreement.

A useful distinction between the two kinds of supplier is provided by the Consumer Protection Act 1987. This refers to the supplier in a two-party d-c-s agreement as the ostensible supplier and the supplier in a three-party d-c-s agreement as the effective supplier. Section 46(2) of the Consumer Protection Act 1987 provides that in the case of a hire-purchase agreement, conditional sale agreement or credit sale agreement or an agreement for the hiring of goods, the effective supplier and not the ostensible supplier will be treated as supplying goods to the customer for the purposes of that Act.

The identity of the legal supplier is not always immediately apparent. In *Sutherland Professional Funding Ltd v Bakewells*[2] the court had to determine whether the service provider in respect of disbursements, or the solicitors firm Bakewells, were the supplier under the funding agreement with the client. As the contract between Bakewells and their client required the client to make good the disbursements to, and paid by, the firm, Bakewells, which had the primary responsibility for meeting disbursements, it was held to be the supplier.

CCA 1974, s 75 renders the creditor liable for any misrepresentation or breach of contract by the supplier. The creditor is entitled to a statutory indemnity by the supplier for any loss suffered by the creditor in satisfying such liability, including costs reasonably incurred by him in defending proceedings instituted by the debtor.[3] It is submitted that a creditor facing potential claims under CCA 1974, s 75 might apply to the court under the Contracts (Rights of Third Parties) Act 1999 or the Third Parties (Rights against Insurers) Act 1930, as appropriate, for the purpose of establishing rights transferred to, or vested in, the creditor.[4]

Section 75A(1) provides that a debtor who has a claim against the supplier for breach of contract under a linked credit agreement (as defined in sub-section (5)) may pursue that claim against the creditor if the conditions of sub-section (2) are met.

The expressions 'dealer' and 'supplier' are used as terms of art in one context and interchangeably in another. The Glossary in the FCA Handbook defines 'dealer' as, in relation to a hire-purchase agreement, credit-sale agreement or conditional sale agreement under which this person is not the lender, a person who sells or proposes to sell goods, land or other things to the lender before they form the subject matter of any such agreements; and, in relation to any other agreements, it means a supplier or the supplier's agent.

The Glossary defines 'supplier' as:

(a)   the person referred to as the supplier in the definitions of borrower-lender agreement, borrower-lender-supplier agreement and restricted-use credit agreement; and

(b)   in relation to a credit agreement falling within (2)(a) of the definition of restricted-use credit agreement [i.e. a credit agreement to finance a transaction between the borrower and the lender, whether forming part of that agreement or not], the lender; and

(c)   including a person to whom the rights and duties of a person falling within (a) or (b) above have passed by assignment or operation of law.

In commercial parlance, 'dealer' is used in preference to 'supplier'.

1   See **4.4**.
2   [2013] EWHC 2685 (QB); [2013] GCCR 11756.
3   CCA 1974, s 75. See further **17.4.4**.
4   See *Re OT Computers* [2004] 1 All ER (Comm) 320, [2003] GCCR 4951.

15.2   DEALER AGREEMENTS

Creditors and providers of leasing facilities often enter into agreements with dealers to govern their relationship, including the terms of supply, commission arrangements, credit criteria, compliance with laws and regulations, recourse and buy-back arrangements and, in the case of leasing agreements, for the sale of equipment as the lessor's agent on expiry of the agreement.

It is common practice to require the dealer to give warranties and indemnities, either in a master agreement or in respect of each credit or lease agreement entered into in respect of goods or equipment supplied by the dealer. Thus, the dealer might be required to warrant that any initial payment or deposit had been received by him, that the agreement was correctly completed before it was signed by the customer, the requisite statutory copies were supplied to the customer, the goods or equipment were the dealer's unencumbered property and that, upon acceptance of the supply by the dealer, their ownership will pass to the creditor or the lessor, as the case may be.

Dealer agreements may contain restrictive covenants seeking to prevent the dealer from transacting with other finance companies during the term of the dealer's agreement with the finance company.

In view of the value attached to customer lists, dealer agreements might contain provisions seeking to protect the confidentiality of, and rights of ownership to, customer names and addresses.

A typical dealer agreement would contain terms governing the substantive relationship between the parties including provisions relating to:

(i)   submission of agreements;

(ii)   credit referencing, credit criteria and credit assessment;

(iii)   controls on the dealer as a credit intermediary;

(iv)   controls and procedure on pre-contractual explanations and making of agreements;

(v)   reimbursement by the finance company of the cash price of goods or equipment and payment of commission to the dealer;

(vi)   marketing and advertising;

(vii)   operation of a negative stop list especially in the case of credit card transactions;

(viii) debt collection procedures where the dealer is involved in the same;

(ix)   restrictions on the use of customer information;

(x)   confidentiality provisions;

(xi)   compliance with the law, the FCA regime and relevant codes of practice;

(xii)   customer complaints procedure;

(xiii) dispute resolution procedure;

(xiv)   rights of assignment;

(xv)   provisions applying on termination;

(xvi)   governing law and jurisdiction.

15.3 EXTENDED WARRANTIES

In addition to statutory warranties and guarantees, which may not be excluded or restricted in the case of consumer agreements, suppliers might offer customers additional protection by way of extended warranties to cover their supplies. Typically this cover extends the warranty or guarantee applying to the goods for a period after the manufacturer's guarantee has expired.

Following a reference by the Office of Fair Trading in July 2002 under the Fair Trading Act 1973, the Competition Commission investigated the market for extended warranties on electrical goods. In consequence of the Competition Commission's Report, an Order was made in January 2005, which came into force on 6 April 2005,[1] and essentially relates to a product designed to be connected to an electricity supply or powered by batteries for domestic purposes. The Order requires a person who offers to supply a consumer with an extended warranty, either directly or on behalf of a third party, to display the price of the extended warranty, provide specified information and produce a written quotation in store, in newspaper advertisements and other media, catalogues and websites. Written quotations must be available for acceptance for 30 days. The consumer has 45 days to cancel the extended warranty if it is to apply for more than one year.

Arranging, advising on and selling extended warranties is a regulated activity and requires the principal which offers the same to be authorised under the Financial Services and Markets Act 2000. However, an agent offering this will usually be exempt from the requirement to be authorised as an agent, as the sale by an agent of a 'connected insurance product' is not a regulated activity.[2] The exemption only applies to the sale of a contract of insurance which is complementary to non-motor goods.

Other insurance which 'piggy backs' on credit or hire agreements is mechanical breakdown insurance which might be sold 'as an optional extra' in respect of agreements involving motor vehicles and fraud protection cover which might be offered free of charge as an incentive to applicants for credit cards. The provider of such insurances, and the intermediary, will generally need to be authorised under the Financial Services and Markets Act 2000.

1   The Supply of Extended Warranties on Domestic Electrical Goods Order 2005, SI 2005/37. Note that the cancellation and termination rights under art 8 do not apply to a distance contract.
2   Financial Services and Markets Act 2000 (Regulated Activities) Order 2001, SI 2001/544, as amended, art 72B(2).

15.4   INSURANCE AND THE REGULATED AGREEMENT

Insurance companies offer insurance in connection with credit or hire transactions in respect of associated insurable risks. These include third party motor vehicle insurance, comprehensive insurance cover and Guaranteed Asset Protection (GAP) insurance in the case of motor vehicles, insurance of goods, usually in the form of comprehensive insurance cover and property insurance in respect of mortgaged land. In addition, life assurance may be taken up on the life of the borrower in the context of an endowment mortgage or as collateral security for a loan. Arranging, advising on and selling insurance products is a regulated activity under the Financial Services and Markets Act 2000 and requires authorisation by the FCA.

Contracts of insurance are excluded from the normal rule that linked transactions entered into before the regulated agreement have no effect until that agreement is made. It follows that cancellation of a regulated agreement will not (at least, in the writer's view, in the absence of a contractual term to the contrary), terminate a contract of insurance.[1]

Included in the total charge for credit, and consequently in the APR of the credit agreement, is a premium under a contract of insurance, payable under the transaction by the borrower or a relative of his, where the making or maintenance of the contract of insurance is required by the lender (i) as a condition of making the credit agreement, and (ii) for the sole purpose of ensuring complete or partial repayment of the credit or of payment to the lender of such of the charges included in the total charge for credit as are payable to him under the transaction, in the event of the death, invalidity, illness or unemployment of the borrower.[2]

1 CCA 1974, s 19 and Consumer Credit (Linked Transactions) (Exemptions) Regulations 1983, SI 1983/1560, reg 2(1) and (2)(a).
2 FCA Handbook, CONC App 1.1.5R.

15.5 PAYMENT PROTECTION INSURANCE ('PPI')

Payment protection insurance encompasses various categories of cover intended to protect the customer against liability to make repayments under credit or hire agreements when unable to do so. It may include insuring the customer against his inability to pay if he is made redundant, suffers an accident, falls ill, ceases to be employed or dies.

PPI has undergone radical reform in the way in which it is permitted to be sold to consumers. Originally it was commonly sold to borrowers and hirers by way of a negative option, whereby the customer was asked to make an election only if he did not wish to take out such insurance, as opposed to positively electing for PPI. This incurred the wrath of the consumer lobby, which persuaded the then Director General of Fair Trading to declare that he would regard the continuing sale of payment protection insurance by negative option as calling into doubt the licensee's licence under CCA 1974.[1]

Life assurance and general insurance were transferred from the authority of the then Department of Trade and Industry to the Treasury in December 2001 and January 2005 respectively, when they came under the regulatory powers of the Financial Services Authority, now the Financial Conduct Authority (FCA). Accordingly, arranging, advising on and selling insurance products, such as PPI, are regulated activities and require authorisation by the FCA. Regulation of PPI falls under the Insurance: Conduct of business sourcebook (ICOBS) of the FCA Handbook generally. The Rules govern all aspects of the insurance, including identifying client needs, advising, product information, customer's rights of cancellation, claims handling and complaints.

Payment protection insurance may be dealt with in various different ways. First, it may be financed and constitute the main or only subject matter of the agreement. In this case it invariably needs to be documented as a regulated debt-orcreditorsupplier agreement. Second, it may be ancillary to the main subject matter of a regulated agreement. Finally, payment protection insurance may be paid for by regular, usually monthly, cash premiums, in which event it is not financed. It will then take the form of a regular periodical policy, in respect of which failure to pay the premium will result in the policy lapsing.

In February 2004 the OFT made a reference to the Competition Commission under the Enterprise Act 2002 for an investigation into the supply of PPI. This ultimately led to a prohibition on the sale of PPI from the time of an application for credit until the seventh day following the day when the credit sale ends.[2]

In August 2010 the then FSA issued a Policy Statement 10/12 after it and the Financial Ombudsman Service (FOS) had agreed to notify each other of complaint issues where there may be a need to consider regulatory action to ensure that consumers who had suffered widespread detriment did not lose out. FOS had drawn attention to issues arising from past payment protection sales and evidence of widespread and regular failure on the part of many firms to comply with FSA's rules and insurance law. The FSA Policy Statement included amendments to the Handbook introduced by the Dispute Resolution: Complaints (Payment Protection Insurance) Instrument 2010, now in Appendix 3 to DISP.

The watershed decision, by way of judicial review, that entrenched the basis of claims totalling billions of pounds for the mis-selling of PPI, is *R (on the application of the British Bankers Association) v Financial Services Authority and another*.[3] The claimant challenged the lawfulness of the Policy Statement as it treated FSA Principles in the Handbook as giving rise to obligations owed by firms to customers, leading to compensation being payable for their breach when, it was argued, Principles are not actionable in law. The court held, however, that the Principles are the substrata to which the specific rules are added and might augment specific rules. The Principles always have to be complied with. The rules are specific applications of the Principles to the particular requirements they cover. The Principles are not ousted by the provisions of s 404 of FSMA.

1 Press Release of 28 October 1992.
2 Payment Protection Insurance Market Investigation Order 2011, made by the Competition Commission, which came into effect on 6 April 2011.
3 [2011] EWHC 999 (Admin), [2011] GCCR 11251.

15.6   CARD PROTECTION COVER

The credit industry has spawned a secondary industry which is involved in all aspects of the protection of credit cards. In return for a premium or membership fee card protection companies or card notification organisations will provide a range of services such as the confidential registration of all the member's cards; an emergency helpline to notify card issuers of the loss or theft of cards to stop their further use; payment of a sum, by way of protection against fraudulent use of cards; an emergency cash loan; arrangements for the replacement of cards; lost key registration; valuable property and document protection; lost luggage recovery etc.

Taking advantage of opportunities created by cards being lost or stolen, these agencies also offer to replace lost keys, pay hotel bills, replace airline tickets and provide emergency car hire.

In *Card Protection Plan Ltd v Commissioners of Customs and Excise*[1] the House of Lords held that arrangements of this kind constitute insurance business, as the dominant purpose is one of insurance. Accordingly, the transaction is to be regarded for VAT purposes as comprising a principal exempt insurance supply, with the other supplies in the transaction being ancillary, so that they are to be treated as exempt for VAT purposes.[2]

1 [2001] 2 All ER 143, HL.
2 Value Added Tax Act 1983, ss 2(1) and (2), 17(1), Sch 6, Group 2 – Insurance.

15.7 PROVIDERS OF MAINTENANCE SERVICES

Debtors and hirers are ordinarily required to maintain goods in proper working condition, fair wear and tear excepted and, in the case of the hire of motor vehicles, to have them serviced regularly.

Where, under the agreement, the owner makes arrangements for the maintenance of the vehicles, routine servicing costs will often be included in the rentals. Where they are not, the owner will collect the maintenance payments by way of monthly cash sums, other than financed monthly payments, to avoid problems in relation to the categorisation of the agreement as a credit agreement.

A separate maintenance contract in conjunction with the hire or credit agreement will usually be a linked transaction with the result that cancellation of the regulated agreement will also result in cancellation of the maintenance contract.

15.8 DISTANCE CONTRACTS AND OFF-PREMISES CONTRACTS

15.8.1 Distance contracts for goods or services

Distance contracts are governed by the Consumer Contracts (Information, Cancellation and Additional Charges) Regulations 2013.[1] A 'distance contract' is a contract concluded between a trader and a consumer under an organised distance sales or service-provision scheme without the simultaneous physical presence of the trader and the consumer, with the exclusive use of one or more means of distance communication up to and including the time at which the contract is concluded.[2] 'Consumer' is defined as an individual acting for purposes which are wholly or mainly outside that individual's trade, business, craft or profession, and 'trader' means a person acting for purposes relating to that person's trade, business, craft or profession, whether acting personally or through another person acting in the trader's name or on the trader's behalf.[3]

An 'off-premises contract' is a contract between a trader and a consumer which is any of the following:

(a) a contract concluded in the simultaneous physical presence of the trader and the consumer, in a place which is not the business premises of the trader;

(b) a contract for which an offer was made by the consumer in the simultaneous physical presence of the trader and the consumer, in a place which is not the business premises of the trader;

(c) a contract concluded on the business premises of the trader or through any means of distance communication immediately after the consumer was personally and individually addressed in a place which is not the business premises of the trader in the simultaneous physical presence of the trader and the consumer;

(d)   a contract concluded during an excursion organised by the trader with the aim or effect of promoting and selling goods or services to the consumer.[4]

The Regulations do not apply to various excluded contracts, notably contracts for services of a banking, credit, insurance, personal pension, investment or payment nature and contracts, in general terms, relating to immovable property.[5]

The Regulations set out, amongst other matters, information to be provided in connection with a distance contract, an on-premises contract and an off-premises contract and on the right to cancel a distance contract or an off-premises contract.

1   SI 2013/3134.
2   Ibid., reg 5.
3   Ibid., reg 4.
4   Ibid., reg 5.
5   Ibid., reg 6(1).

15.8.2   Distance contracts for financial services

The Financial Services (Distance Marketing) Regulations 2004[1] apply to distance contracts for financial services, i.e. any service of a banking , credit, insurance, personal pension, investment or payment nature.[2] There is a statutory obligation to provide prescribed information prior to the conclusion of the contract, other than in relation to a consumer credit agreement, or an authorised non-business overdraft agreement where there has been compliance with the Consumer Credit (Disclosure of Information) Regulations 2010.[3] The regulations provide a cancellation period of 14 calendar days, beginning with the day after the conclusion of the contract. There are various exceptions to the right to cancel, including a contract under which the supplier provides credit to a consumer under an agreement secured by a legal mortgage on land and a restricted-use credit agreement to finance the purchase of land or an existing building or an agreement for a bridging loan in connection with the same.[4] In general, cancellation of a distance contract for the provision of a financial service to a consumer also has the effect of cancelling any secondary or attached distance contract for the provision of a further financial service.[5]

1   SI 2004/2095.
2   Ibid., reg 3(2) read with reg 2(1).
3   Ibid., reg 7.
4   Ibid., reg 11(1)(d).
5   Ibid., reg 12.

15.9   TIMESHARE AGREEMENTS

Timeshare agreements are governed by the Timeshare, Holiday Products, Resale and Exchange Contracts Regulations 2010,[1] which came into force on 23 February 2011 and implement the EU Directive on the subject.[2] The regulations revoked, *inter alia*, the Timeshare Act 1992 and the Timeshare Regulations 1997. Amongst other matters, the regulations prescribe key information which must be given to a consumer in writing before entering into a contract, require the agreement to be in writing and confer on a consumer the right to withdraw from the contract within a 14-day period, which also has the effect of withdrawal from an ancillary contract and any related credit agreement. Breach of certain of the regulations constitutes an offence under the regulations and may also constitute an offence under the Consumer Protection from Unfair Trading Regulations 2008.

Where a timeshare agreement is financed by a regulated debtor-creditor-supplier agreement, the creditor under the agreement assumes obligations pursuant to CCA 1974, ss 56 and 75, notwithstanding that the property which is the subject of the timeshare agreement is situated outside the jurisdiction of the United Kingdom. So it was held in *Jarrett v Barclays Bank plc; Jones v First National Bank plc; Peacock v First National Bank plc*.[3] Morritt LJ stated that the claims against the defendants, as lenders, on grounds of misrepresentation and breach of contract, did not have as their object the tenancies of immovable property (i.e. the timeshare accommodation). Rather, the foundation of the claims under CCA 1974, ss 56 and 75 was the debtor-creditor-supplier agreement, to which the personal statutory rights conferred on the debtor by CCA 1974 were attached. It followed that the debtors under the various credit agreements were able to institute proceedings against their respective creditors for misrepresentation or breach of contract by the sellers of the timeshares.

It is submitted that a regulated agreement may not import the law of the jurisdiction where the timeshare properties are situated if the effect would be to exclude rights conferred on the debtor by CCA 1974. This would conflict with the anti-avoidance provisions of CCA 1974, s 173 and constitute an unfair term under s 62, read with paragraph 2 of Schedule 2 to the Consumer Rights Act 2015.

1 SI 2010/2960.
2 Directive 2008/122/EC of the European Parliament and of the Council on the protection of consumers in respect of certain aspects of timeshare, long-term holiday product, resale and exchange contracts.
3 [1999] QB 1, [1999] GCCR 2151, CA.

Chapter 16

Ancillary credit businesses

16.1 MEANING OF 'ANCILLARY CREDIT BUSINESS'

The CCA 1974 defines an ancillary credit business as any business insofar as it comprises or relates to credit broking, debt adjusting, debt counselling, debt collecting, debt administration, the provision of credit information services, or the operation of a credit reference agency.[1]

'Business' includes a profession or trade, but a person is not to be treated as carrying on a particular type of business merely because occasionally he enters into transactions belonging to a business of that type.[2]

The FCA regime, which now informs the above definitions, reshaped the regulatory landscape by separating out credit broking under its own heading in chapter 6A of the Financial Services and Markets Act 2000 (Regulated Activities) Order 2001, SI 2001/544 ('RAO'), activities in relation to debt in RAO chapter 7B and specified activities in relation to information in Part 3A of RAO. Thus, debt adjusting, debt counselling, debt collecting and debt administration are now grouped together under the heading 'activities in relation to debt' in RAO chapter 7B, whilst the provision of credit information services and providing credit references fall under the heading of 'specified activities in relation to information' in Part 3A of RAO.

The activities of debt counselling and debt adjusting apply to credit agreements and consumer hire agreements, whether they are regulated or not.

The business of credit broking was discussed in **Chapter 13** and we shall now consider each of the other ancillary credit businesses in turn.

1 CCA 1974, s 145(1).
2 Ibid., s 189(1) and (2).

16.2 DEBT ADJUSTING, DEBT COUNSELLING, DEBT COLLECTING AND DEBT ADMINISTRATION

These specified kinds of activity (within the meaning of FSMA, s 22) bear the somewhat convoluted meanings below, subject to the exceptions and exclusions that follow.

Principles for Businesses (PRIN) of the FCA's Handbook apply as a whole to firms with respect to debt counselling, debt adjusting and providing credit information services.

16.2.1   Debt adjusting (RAO art 39D and CCA 1974, s 145(5))

(1)   When carried on in relation to debts due under a credit agreement:

    (a)   negotiating with the lender, on behalf of the borrower, terms for the discharge of a debt,

    (b)   taking over, in return for payments by the borrower, that person's obligation to discharge a debt, or

    (c)   any similar activity concerned with the liquidation of a debt.

(2)   When carried on in relation to debts due under a consumer hire agreement:

    (a)   negotiating with the owner, on behalf of the hirer, terms for the discharge of a debt,

    (b)   taking over, in return for payments by the hirer, that person's obligation to discharge a debt, or

    (c)   any similar activity concerned with the liquidation of a debt.

The FCA's Handbook Consumer Credit Sourcebook (CONC) at CONC 2.6 stipulates rules governing the conduct of business in relation to debt counselling, debt adjusting and providing credit information services.

A firm must provide a customer with a written contract setting out its terms and conditions for the provision of its debt solution services (CONC 8.4). Charging for debt counselling, debt advice and related services are covered in CONC 8.7 and debt management plans in CONC 8.8.

16.2.2   Debt counselling (RAO art 39E and CCA 1974, s 145(6))

(1)   Giving advice to a borrower about the liquidation of a debt due under a credit agreement.

(2)   Giving advice to a hirer about the liquidation of a debt due under a consumer hire agreement.

CONC 2.6 stipulates rules governing the conduct of business in relation to debt counselling, debt adjusting and providing credit information services. A firm must provide a customer with a written contract setting out its terms and conditions for the provision of its debt solution services (CONC 8.4). Charging for debt counselling, debt advice and related services is covered in CONC 8.7 and debt management plans in CONC 8.8.

The scope of debt counselling (or consumer credit debt counselling, as it is also called) is amplified in PERG 17 of the FCA Handbook and summarised below.

(a) Meaning of 'liquidation of a debt' (PERG 17.3)

This has a wide meaning and would cover any of the following: paying off the debt in full and in time; agreeing a rescheduling or a temporary halt to paying off the debt; the debtor being released from the debt; agreeing a reduced repayment amount (including the creditor agreeing to accept token repayments); a third party taking over the debtor's obligation to discharge the debt; and discharging the debt or making it irrecoverable through personal insolvency procedures such as bankruptcy, a voluntary arrangement or a debt relief order.

(b) Meaning of 'debt due'

This should be interpreted fairly broadly and should not be limited to debts that are immediately payable (for example, where the debtor is in default). Therefore, for instance, it would cover present obligations to make payments in the future.

(c) Advice given to the public in general rather than to a particular debtor (PERG 17.4)

The advice must relate to the debts of a particular debtor or debtors. So, for example, it would not generally cover advice in a newspaper, periodical publication, journal, magazine, publication or a radio or television broadcast. General advice open to everyone on a website is unlikely to be debt counselling for the same reason.

(d) Meaning of 'advice' (PERG 17.5)

Advice means giving an opinion as a guide to action to be taken, in this case the liquidation of debts. It either explicitly or implicitly steers the customer to a particular course of action.

The concept of advice is broad enough to include any communication with the debtor which, in the particular context in which it is given, goes beyond the mere provision of information and is objectively likely to influence the debtor's decision whether or not to undertake the course of action in question. In general terms, simply giving balanced and neutral information, without making any comment or value judgement on its relevance to decisions which a debtor may make, is not advice. The provision of purely factual information does not become regulated advice merely because it feeds into the debtor's own decision-making process and is taken into account by him. Therefore, a neutral and balanced explanation of the implications of entering into different debt solutions need not, itself, involve debt counselling. However, information is likely to constitute advice if the circumstances in which it is provided give it, expressly or by implication, the force of a recommendation. For example, the adviser may provide information on a selected, rather than balanced and neutral, basis that would tend to influence the decision of the debtor.

Undertaking the process of scripted questioning gives rise to particular issues concerning debt counselling. If the process involves identifying one or more particular courses of action then, to avoid debt counselling, the critical factor is likely to be whether the process is limited to, and likely to be perceived by the debtor as, assisting the debtor to make his own choice of how to liquidate his debts. The questioner will need to avoid making any judgement on the suitability of one or more courses of action for the debtor.

The medium used to give advice is immaterial as to whether or not the advice is debt counselling.

16.2.3 Debt collecting (RAO art 39F and CCA 1974, s 145(7))

(1) Taking steps to procure the payment of a debt due under a credit agreement or a relevant article 36H agreement.

(2) Taking steps to procure the payment of a debt due under a consumer hire agreement.

(3) Paragraph (1) does not apply insofar as the activity is an activity of the kind specified by article 36H (operating an electronic system in relation to lending).

(4) In this article, 'relevant article 36H agreement' means an article 36H agreement (within the meaning of article 36H) which has been entered into with the facilitation of an authorised person with permission to carry on a regulated activity of the kind specified by that article.

The collection and administration of debts is governed by CONC 7.3.

16.2.4 Debt administration (RAO art 39G and CCA 1974, s 145(7A))

(1) Subject to paragraph (3), taking steps:

(a) to perform duties under a credit agreement or relevant article 36H agreement on behalf of the lender, or

(b) to exercise or enforce rights under such an agreement on behalf of the lender.

(2) Subject to paragraph (3), taking steps:

(a) to perform duties under a consumer hire agreement on behalf of the owner, or

(b) to exercise or enforce rights under such an agreement on behalf of the owner.

(3) Paragraphs (1) and (2) do not apply insofar as the activity is an activity of the kind specified by article 36H (operating an electronic system in relation to lending) or article 39F (debt collecting).

A 'relevant article 36H agreement' means an article 36H agreement [relating to operating an electronic system in relation to lending] which has been entered into with the facilitation of an authorised person with permission to carry on a regulated activity of the kind specified by that article.

The collection and administration of debts is governed by CONC 7.3.

16.2.5   Exclusions (RAO art 39H)

(1)   There are excluded from RAO articles 39D(1), 39E(1) and 39F(1) activities carried on by a person who is:

(a)   the lender under the agreement,

(b)   the supplier in relation to that agreement,

(c)   a person carrying on an activity of the kind specified by article 36A [credit broking] by way of business and who has acquired the business of the person who was the supplier in relation to the agreement, or

(d)   a person who would be carrying on an activity of the kind specified by article 36A by way of business but for the exclusion in article 36B where the agreement was made in consequence of an introduction (by that person or another person) to which article 36B applies.

(2)   There are excluded from articles 39D(2), 39E(2) and 39F(2) activities carried on by a person who is:

(a)   the owner under the consumer hire agreement, or

(b)   a person who would be carrying on an activity of the kind specified by article 36A by way of business but for the exclusion in article 36B where the agreement was made in consequence of an introduction (by that person or another person) to which article 36B applies.

(3)   There is excluded from article 39G(1) steps taken under or in relation to an agreement by a person who is, in relation to that agreement, a person falling within paragraph (a) to (d) in the first paragraph above.

(4)   There is excluded from article 39G(2) steps taken under or in relation to a consumer hire agreement by a person who is, in relation to that agreement, a person falling within paragraph (2)(a) or (b) above.

(5)   In the first paragraph above, 'supplier', in relation to an agreement, means:

(a)   a person, other than the lender, whose transaction with the borrower is, or is to be, financed by the agreement, or

(b)   a person to whom the rights and duties of a person falling within subparagraph (a) have been passed by assignment or operation of law.

16.2.6   Further exclusions

There are further specific exclusions under the following heads:

(1)   Activities carried on by certain energy suppliers (RAO art 39I).

(2)   Activities carried on in relation to a relevant agreement in relation to land ((RAO art 39J).

(3)   Activities carried on by members of the legal profession (RAO art 39K).

(4)   Activities carried on by pensions guidance providers (RAO art 39KA).

(5)   Exclusions in:

    (a)   art 72A relating to information society services,

    (b)   art 72G relating to local authorities, and

    (c)   art 72H relating to insolvency practitioners (RAO art 39L).

16.3   PROVISION OF CREDIT INFORMATION SERVICES (RAO PART 3A, ART 89A(1) AND (2) AND CCA 1974, S 145(7B))

The types of specified activity comprised under this head in RAO art 89A are:

(1)   Taking any of the steps in paragraph (3) on behalf of an individual or relevant recipient of credit.

(2)   Giving advice to an individual or relevant recipient of credit in relation to the taking of any of the steps specified in paragraph (3).

(3)   Subject to paragraph (4), the steps specified in this paragraph are steps taken with a view to:

    (a)   ascertaining whether a credit information agency holds information relevant to the financial standing of an individual or relevant recipient of credit;

    (b)   ascertaining the contents of such information;

    (c)   securing the correction of, the omission of anything from, or the making of any other kind of modification of, such information;

    (d)   securing that a credit information agency which holds such information:

        (i)   stops holding the information, or

        (ii)   does not provide it to any other person.

(4)   Steps taken by a credit information agency in relation to information held by that agency are not steps specified in paragraph (3).

(5)   Paragraphs (1) and (2) do not apply to an activity of the kind specified by article 36H (operating an electronic system in relation to lending).

(6)   'Credit information agency' means a person who carries on by way of business an activity of the kind specified by any of the following:

    (a)   article 36A (credit broking);

    (b)   article 39D (debt adjusting);

    (c)   article 39E (debt counselling);

    (d)   article 39F (debt collecting);

    (e)   article 39G (debt administration);

(f) article 60B (regulated credit agreements) disregarding the effect of article 60F;

(g) article 60N (regulated consumer hire agreements) disregarding the effect of article 60P;

(h) article 89B (providing credit references).

CONC 2.6 contains rules governing the conduct of business in relation to debt counselling, debt adjusting and providing credit information services.

CONC 8 covers all firms with respect to debt counselling, debt adjusting and providing credit information services, which includes profit-seeking as well as not-for-profit bodies which hold such permissions and, in that case, include those bodies with permission by virtue of RAO article 62 (arranging administration by an authorised person).

CONC 8.1 applies, unless otherwise stated in or in relation to a rule, to every firm with respect to:

(1) debt counselling;

(2) debt adjusting; and

(3) to the extent of giving the advice referred to in RAO article 89A(2), providing credit information services.

CONC 8.10 (Conduct of business: providing credit information services) applies to every firm with respect to providing credit information services and with respect to operating an electronic system in relation to lending in relation to activities specified in RAO article 36H(3)(e) to (h) which are similar to providing credit information services.

16.4 PROVIDING CREDIT REFERENCES (RAO PART 3A, ART 89B(1) TO (3))

This head comprises furnishing persons with information relevant to the financial standing of individuals or relevant recipients of credit, and is a specified kind of activity if the person has collected the information for that purpose (RAO art 89B). Activities carried on in the course of a business which does not primarily consist of activities of the kind described also do not constitute the specified kind of activity.

It is not a specified kind of activity if the activity is of the kind specified by article 36H (relating to operating an electronic system in relation to lending).

16.5 CREDIT REFERENCE AGENCY (CCA 1974, S 145(8) AND RAO ART 89B)

A credit reference agency is a person providing credit references.[1] Thus, that definition does not envisage the necessity, in all circumstances, of a credit reference agency having to be authorised, as a firm, by the FCA. On the other hand, CCA 1974 states that a person ('P') operates a credit reference agency if P carries on, by way of business, an activity of the kind specified by article 89B of RAO.[2]

There are three limbs to the activity of credit referencing: collecting information, furnishing information to others, and that the information must relate to the financial standing of individuals, i.e. their creditworthiness.

It follows from article 89B that, if information is only gathered for the collector's own use, e.g. a bank or leasing company, the activity does not constitute the operation of a credit reference agency business. However, if a company in a group of companies furnishes its associate companies with information regarding the credit status of individuals, it will be conducting a credit reference agency business. If an organisation only serves the purpose of controlling personal data, e.g. by setting up and operating a data system, without both collecting information on the financial standing of others and imparting that information to other persons, it is not conducting the business of a credit reference agency.

Whilst there are numerous operations which conduct ancillary credit businesses and a vast number which carry on credit broking businesses, there are three main credit reference agencies in the United Kingdom: Experian Ltd, Equifax plc and Callcredit Information Group Ltd.

The landscape for obtaining information from credit reference agencies remains shambolic. Some rights under CCA 1974 only apply to debtors and not hirers, some only apply to a consumer other than a natural person, some rights specifically apply to business consumers but not to a sole trader, and some rights only arise under the Data Protection Act 1998. Thus, CCA 1974, s 157 below applies to debtors, excluding debtors under credit agreements secured by land mortgage:

'157   Duty to disclose name etc of agency

(A1) Where a creditor under a prospective regulated agreement, other than an excluded agreement, decides not to proceed with it on the basis of information obtained by the creditor from a credit reference agency, the creditor must, when informing the debtor of the decision—

(a) inform the debtor that this decision has been reached on the basis of information from a credit reference agency, and

(b) provide the debtor with the particulars of the agency including its name, address and telephone number.

(1) In any other case, a creditor, owner or negotiator, within the prescribed period after receiving a request in writing to that effect from the debtor or hirer, shall give him notice of the name and address of any credit reference agency from which the creditor, owner or negotiator has, during the antecedent negotiations, applied for information about his financial standing.

(2) Subsection (1) does not apply to a request received more than 28 days after the termination of the antecedent negotiations, whether on the making of the regulated agreement or otherwise.

(2A) A creditor is not required to disclose information under this section if such disclosure–

(a) contravenes the Data Protection Act 1998,

(b) is prohibited by any EU obligation,

(c) would create or be likely to create a serious risk that any person would be subject to violence or intimidation, or

(d) would, or would be likely to, prejudice–

    (i) the prevention or detection of crime,

    (ii) the apprehension or prosecution of offenders, or

    (iii) the administration of justice.

(3) If the creditor, owner or negotiator fails to comply with subsection [(A1) or] (1) he commits an offence.

(4) For the purposes of subsection (A1) an agreement is an excluded agreement if it is–

(a) a consumer hire agreement, or

(b) an agreement secured on land.'

The statutory duty embodied in s 157 above has been incorporated in Schedules 1 and 3 to the Consumer Credit (Disclosure of Information) Regulations 2010 and, by a recent amendment, in reg 3(1A) of the Consumer Credit (Disclosure of Information) Regulations 2004.

The obligation to disclose names and addresses of credit reference agencies consulted in relation to consumer credit lending and consumer hiring is underscored and extended in CONC 2.4R, as follows:

(1)   Not later than the lender ('L') informs a credit broker that L is not willing to make a regulated credit agreement, L must, unless L informs the customer directly that L is not willing to make the agreement, inform the credit broker of the name and address (including an appropriate e-mail address) of any credit reference agency from which L has, during the negotiations relating to the proposed agreement, applied for information about the financial standing of the customer.

(2)   Not later than the owner ('O') informs a credit broker that O is not willing to make a regulated consumer hire agreement, O must, unless O informs the customer directly that O is not willing to make the agreement, inform the credit broker of the name and address (including an appropriate e-mail address) of any credit reference agency from which O has, during the negotiations relating to the proposed agreement, applied for information about the financial standing of the customer.

Section 158 of CCA 1974 only applies to a consumer other than a natural person or sole trader, as evidenced by the section below:

'158 Duty of agency to disclose filed information

(1) A credit reference agency, within the prescribed period after receiving–

(a) a request in writing to that effect from a consumer,

(b)   such particulars as the agency may reasonably require to enable them to identify the file, and

(c)   a fee of [£2],

shall give the consumer a copy of the file relating to it kept by the agency.

(2) When giving a copy of the file under subsection (1), the agency shall also give the consumer a statement in the prescribed form of the consumer's rights under section 159.

(3) If the agency does not keep a file relating to the consumer it shall give [the consumer] notice of that fact, but need not return any money paid.

(4) If the agency contravenes any provision of this section it commits an offence.

(4A) In this section "consumer" means–

(a)   a partnership consisting of two or three persons not all of whom are bodies corporate; or

(b)   an unincorporated body of persons which does not consist entirely of bodies corporate and is not a partnership.

(5) In this Act "file", in relation to an individual, means all the information about him kept by a credit reference agency, regardless of how the information is stored and "copy of the file", as respects information not in plain English, means a transcript reduced into plain English.'

Section 160 of CCA 1974 governs the furnishing of a request for information from a business consumer other than a sole trader.

Finally, an individual consumer or trader may access the personal data held on him by a credit reference agency pursuant to sections 7 and 9 of the Data Protection Act 1998.

An individual who has been given information by a credit reference agency under the Data Protection Act 1998, s 7 or CCA 1974, s 158 which he considers to be incorrect, and if not corrected likely to prejudice him, may give notice to the agency requiring it either to remove the entry from the file or to amend it. The credit reference agency is required to act on that instruction within 28 days. If a dispute cannot be satisfactorily resolved, the consumer can invoke the assistance of the FCA or the Information Commissioner, as appropriate.[3] The Consumer Credit (Credit Reference Agency) Regulations 2000[4] provide statutory notices that must accompany an agency's disclosure of information.

Credit reference agencies may, with the approval of the Financial Conduct Authority, refuse to disclose information to consumers who carry on a business where disclosure would adversely affect the service provided by them to customers.[5]

Information held by credit reference agencies in relation to an individual includes information about the individual on the electoral roll (in order to check the address), and judgments supplied by Registry Trust Ltd, an independent organisation established by the Lord Chancellor's Department for keeping the Register of County Court Judgments (CCJs) entered for sums of money in the county courts in England and Wales. The agency also holds records of Scottish judgments, called decrees. These records are usually kept on file for six years.

Credit reference agencies might supply a payment profile service, providing details of the financial commitments and payment performance of an individual, which is a valuable aid to underwriting. They will supply a copy of the mortgage possession register, confirming details of properties which have been surrendered to, or repossessed by, mortgage lenders, and hold records on non-registered businesses, such as sole traders and partnerships. They might also offer underwriting services and credit account services, such as the production of statements for customers, and control and audit reports for credit companies.

In 1992 the then Data Protection Registrar (now the Information Commissioner) instituted proceedings against the main credit reference agencies with a view to preventing them from furnishing information about persons living at the same address as the data subject about whom a credit reference was sought, on the grounds that such information was irrelevant. As a result of those hearings before the Data Protection Tribunal, an Enforcement Notice was issued under the terms of which lenders are restricted to searching credit reference agencies for information only about an applicant for credit and other people with the same surname, or with a different name if it is reasonable to believe that such person is the data subject or has been living as a member of the same family as the data subject in a single household.[6]

Needless to say, credit reference agencies must comply with the Data Protection Principles set out in Schedule 1 to the Data Protection Act 1998. These principles include the requirements that personal data: should be processed fairly and lawfully; shall be obtained only for one or more specified and lawful purposes; must be adequate, relevant and not excessive in relation to the purposes for which they are processed; need to be accurate and kept up to date; may not be kept for longer than is necessary; and must be processed in accordance with the rights of data subjects. Appropriate technical and organisational measures must be taken against unauthorised or unlawful processing of personal data and against accidental loss or destruction of, or damage to, personal data. Personal data may not be transferred to a country outside the European Economic Area unless that country ensures an adequate level of protection of the rights and freedoms of the subjects in relation to the processing of personal data.

In general, credit reference agencies retain records for six years. Records of bankruptcies are held for six years after the date of bankruptcy, County Court Judgments are held for six years after the date of the judgment, and account records are held for six years from the date of the last entry on that account.

Data controllers must ensure that the necessary security measures are in place to safeguard personal data. If a controller uses the services of a data processor, the security arrangements must be recorded in a written agreement between the parties.[7]

1 FCA Handbook, Glossary.
2 CCA 1974, s 145(8).
3 Ibid., ss 158 and 159 and the Consumer Credit (Credit Reference Agency) Regulations 2000, SI 2000/290.
4 SI 2000/290.
5 CCA 1974, s 160(1).
6 See *Goode: Consumer Credit Law and Practice* (LexisNexis Butterworths), at para VIII, D [23.1].
7 Data Protection Act 1998, Sch 1, Pt 1, reg 7; Pt II, para 12(a).

16.6 EXCLUSIONS

There are excluded from articles 89A and 89B (see **16.3** and **16.4** above) members of the legal profession, as described in article 89C. Articles 89A and 89B above are also subject to the exclusion in article 72A (information society services), and article 89A is subject to the further exclusions in articles 72G (local authorities) and 72H (insolvency practitioners) (RAO art 89D).

16.7 DEBT MANAGEMENT

The FCA Handbook, Glossary, defines 'debt management activity' as the activities of debt counselling or debt adjusting, alone or together, carried on with a view to an individual entering into a particular debt solution or in relation to any such debt solution, and activities connected with those activities. A 'debt management firm' is defined as:

(a) a firm which carries on the activities of debt counselling or debt adjusting, alone or together, with a view to an individual entering into a particular debt solution; or

(b) a firm which carries on the activity of debt counselling where an associate carries on debt adjusting with the aim in (a) in view; or

(c) a firm which carries on the activity of debt adjusting where an associate carries on debt counselling with the aim in (a) in view; and

in each case, other than a not-for-profit debt advice body.

A typical debt management plan is a voluntary arrangement where a client enters into an agreement with a debt management firm which will administer the client's debts on the client's behalf, normally by collecting monthly payments from the client and passing them to the client's creditors.

CONC 8.3.2R lays down that a firm must ensure that:

(1) all advice given and action taken by the firm or its agent or its appointed representative:

   (a) has regard to the best interests of the customer;

   (b) is appropriate to the individual circumstances of the customer; and

   (c) is based on a sufficiently full assessment of the financial circumstances of the customer;

(2) customers receive sufficient information about the available options identified as suitable for the customers' needs; and

(3) it explains the reasons why the firm considers the available options suitable and other options unsuitable.

CONC 8.8 sets out prescriptive rules that apply to debt management plans.

CASS 11 of the FCA Handbook, which is the chapter that deals with the debt management of client money, applies to debt management firms that receive or hold client money.

The FCA carried out a thematic review of the quality of debt management advice on which it reported in June 2015.[1] It has ordered firms to grant redress to customers who had overpaid for their services and has instituted criminal proceedings where client monies were misappropriated.

1 TR 15/8.

16.8 ANCILLARY CREDIT BUSINESS AND UNFAIR RELATIONSHIPS

The manner in which ancillary credit business, of whatever kind, is carried on, may have an impact upon a credit agreement by virtue of the unfair relationships provisions of CCA 1974.[1] Section 140A expressly states that the relationship between the creditor and the debtor arising out of the agreement may be unfair to the debtor because of the way in which the creditor has exercised or enforced any of his rights under the agreement or any related agreement or because of any other thing done, or not done, by or on behalf of the creditor, either before or after making the agreement or any related agreement. Thus, in addition to the FCA's powers in relation to authorising firms, the courts may, in the event of misconduct on behalf of a provider of ancillary credit business services, make an order in any of the terms set out in s 140B. It therefore behoves a creditor to ensure that it, and any party carrying on ancillary credit business on its behalf, does so in a lawful and unimpeachable manner.

1 CCA 1974, s 140A ff.

16.9 CLAIMS MANAGEMENT COMPANIES

Claims management companies are not part of 'ancillary credit business' but merit mention in the context of consumer credit business generally.

Claims management companies act on claims by debtors against creditors. They are licensed by the Ministry of Justice under Part 2 of the Compensation Act 2006 in respect of regulated claims management activities and are subject to the Compensation (Claims Management Services) Regulations 2006, as amended.[1] They are regulated by the Claims Management Regulator, a unit of the Ministry of Justice. The Ministry of Justice has laid down rules for the operation of this business, principally the Conduct of Authorised Persons Rules 2007 and the Complaints Handling Rules 2006.

1 SI 2006/3322, as amended by SI 2008/1441, SI 2014/3239 and SI 2015/42.

Chapter 17

Credit cards and other payment cards

17.1   STRUCTURE OF CREDIT CARD TRANSACTIONS

Credit card transactions fall into one of two structures. The first is a three-party structure which involves (i) an agreement between the card issuer and the cardholder to extend credit by paying for goods or services purchased by the cardholder from suppliers or merchants who have agreed to honour the card and, where applicable, advancing cash and/or agreeing to discharge the amount owing under other cards of the cardholder by way of balance transfers; (ii) an agreement between the card issuer and the supplier under which the supplier or merchant agrees to accept the card in payment and the card issuer agrees to pay the supplier or merchant; (iii) an agreement between the cardholder and the supplier or merchant for the purchase of goods or services and any other benefits (such as cash advances and balance transfers).

A three-party scheme is described in *Asda Stores Limited and Others v MasterCard Incorporated and Others*[1] in the following terms:

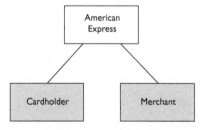

'The operator of a three-party scheme deals directly with cardholders and merchants. It issues the cards to cardholders, who pay it a fee. It also charges the merchant a fee. Payments are cleared through the operator: the cardholder uses his card to buy goods or services from the merchant; the merchant is paid by the operator the price less the merchant fee; the operator recovers the full price of the goods or services from the cardholder, typically having provided credit. As the diagram suggests, the leading example of a three-party scheme in the UK is American Express ("Amex"). Another smaller three-party scheme is operated by Diners Club.'

The second type of structure is a so-called four-party structure which has developed out of the use made by card issuers of merchant acquirers to recruit new suppliers willing to accept the issuer's card. In this situation, there is interposed between the card issuer and the supplier the merchant acquirer acting as an independent party. The merchant acquirer and supplier enter into an agreement under which the supplier undertakes to honour the card and the merchant acquirer undertakes to pay the supplier. The merchant acquirer and the card issuer enter into an agreement under which the merchant acquirer agrees to pay the supplier and the card issuer undertakes to reimburse the merchant acquirer. There is no direct contractual link between the card issuer and the supplier.

A further development of the four-party structure is the interposition of large international credit card operating networks, such as VISA and MasterCard, which involves the addition of a clearing house system. Under the rules of the VISA and MasterCard networks, the card issuer enters into an agreement with its customer to extend credit in connection with the purchase of goods or services (and/or the advance of cash and provision of balance transfers) from any supplier who has agreed to honour the network card. The merchant acquirers recruit suppliers to the network, rather than to an individual card issuer, and the supplier undertakes to honour the network card regardless of the identity of the issuer. The card issuer undertakes to reimburse the merchant acquirer even though unaware of his identity or existence.[2]

The four-party structure is described diagrammatically and graphically in *Asda Stores Limited and Others v MasterCard Incorporated and Others*[3] as follows:

> 'The MasterCard payment card scheme, like that of Visa, is often described as a "four-party" scheme, although it involves five parties. It is to be distinguished from "three-party" schemes which involve three parties.

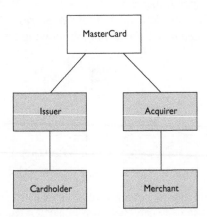

> The four parties in grey in the diagram are each necessarily involved in the flow of payments arising from a transaction: the issuer issues the payment card to the cardholder; the cardholder "pays" for the goods or services provided by the merchant by card; the acquirer provides the "acquiring" service to the merchant which allows it to receive card payments, and pays the merchant for the goods and services, less a discount. The acquirer obtains payment from the issuer, who charges the cardholder for the transaction. MasterCard charges a fee to both issuers and acquirers for their ability to participate in the scheme.
>
> The financial dynamics for those participating in the scheme are as follows:

(1) When the cardholder purchases goods or services from the merchant, he does not immediately make any payment. In the case of a credit card he does not have to pay the issuer until the end of the period of credit agreed with the issuer. Typically in the UK he will receive free credit until the end of the month. In the case of a debit card, the debit from his account is swift but not instantaneous because it is made by the issuer in response to clearing via the acquirer.

(2) Following a sale, the merchant recovers the price from the acquirer, who services the payment. The acquirer charges a merchant service charge ("MSC") for the service which is deducted from the price paid to the merchant.

(3) The acquirer recovers his outlay, plus a profit, from the issuer; the issuer does not pay the acquirer the full price of the goods or services, but deducts an amount by way of interchange fee.

(4) The issuer charges the full value of the transaction to its cardholder customer. In theory therefore the issuer recovers in full from the customer and earns potentially profit making revenue in the form of (a) any fees charged to the cardholder for the issue or use of the card (b) the interchange fee and (c) any profit on the interest rate charged to the customer for credit. In practice there falls to be set against such potential profit (a) the costs of issuing cards and processing recovery from the customer (b) the cost of benefits or rewards offered to cardholders which attach to the use of particular cards in particular ways (c) the cost of free credit for the interest free period and (d) losses due to cardholder default or fraud, which under the terms of the scheme fall on the issuers rather than the merchants or acquirers.

(5) MasterCard has a contractual relationship with both the issuers and acquirers, who are licenced to participate in the scheme and undertake to abide by a single set of scheme rules set by MasterCard. These are detailed and prescriptive, and updated from time to time ... MasterCard's income is derived from the fees it charges to issuers and acquirers in return for licencing their use of the cards.

Interchange fees can in theory be agreed bilaterally between issuers and acquirers. In practice this is not how the interchange fee is determined. Under the Scheme Rules (Rule 8.3), MasterCard sets the interchange fees which are to apply compulsorily in default of bilateral agreements. These are the multilateral interchange fees or "MIFs". In practice there are no material bilateral agreements, and so the MIF always applies. This is not surprising: in a putative bilateral negotiation between an issuer and an acquirer the issuer has no incentive to accept less than the default MIF and the acquirer no incentive to offer more.'

As a matter of practice, VISA and MasterCard will not permit card issuers to join their operating networks unless they are authorised by the Financial Conduct Authority under the Financial Services and Markets Act 2000 with authority to collect deposits (i.e. banks) or the card issuer is ultimately owned by such an institution or a similar authorised financial institution abroad.

---

1 *Asda Stores Limited and Others v MasterCard Incorporated and Others* [2017] EWHC 93 (Comm) para 5.

2 See *Office of Fair Trading v Lloyds TSB Bank plc* [2006] GCCR 5701, CA, at 5704-5; *Re Charge Card Services Ltd* [1983] 3 All ER 289, at 301, [2000] GCCR 1231; *Customs and Excise Commissioners v Diners Club Ltd* [1999] GCCR 1213, CA.
3 *Asda Stores Limited and Others v MasterCard Incorporated and Others* [2017] EWHC 93 (Comm) paras 6 to 9.

17.2   LEGAL CHARACTERISATION OF PAYMENT BY CREDIT CARD

In contrast to payment by cheque, which operates as a conditional payment, payment by credit card is an absolute, unconditional payment of the relevant amount on the date the payment is effected.[1] It is unaffected by any subsequent failure of the card issuer or merchant acquirer to effect payment to the supplier. If the supplier fails to recover payment from the card issuer or merchant acquirer, he has no right of recovery against the cardholder.

There is no possibility of making a post-dated payment by credit card, as there is in the case of payment by cheque. From the point of view of the supplier this underlines the need to check, prior to accepting payment by credit card, that the cardholder's account does in fact have the necessary funds in place to enable the credit card payment to be effected. If the cardholder exceeds his credit limit and the card issuer subsequently refuses to meet the liability, the supplier will have accepted the risk of loss of recovery of payment. From the point of view of the cardholder who wishes to order goods on day one but to postpone payment until receipt of delivery of the goods, he is unable to achieve this where payment is made by credit card but he is protected against any breach of contract, including non-receipt of the goods or misrepresentation by the supplier, by virtue of the card issuer's (creditor's) joint and several liability with the supplier under sections 75 and 75A of CCA 1974. Section 75 protection, and presumably by analogy protection under s 75A, also extends to the use made of a credit card abroad.[2]

1 *Re Charge Card Services Ltd* [1999] GCCR 95, [2000] GCCR 1231, CA.
2 *Office of Fair Trading v Lloyds TSB Bank plc* [2006] GCCR 5701, CA, at 5738-9.

17.3   LIABILITY FOR THEFT, LOSS OR MISUSE OF A CREDIT CARD

The debtor under a regulated consumer agreement is not liable to the creditor for loss arising from use of the credit facility by another person not acting, or to be treated as acting, as the debtor's agent.[1] However, the debtor under a credit-token agreement is liable to the creditor for loss to the extent of £50 (or the credit limit if lower) arising from use of the credit-token by other persons prior to the creditor being given notice that the credit-token has been lost or stolen or is for any other reason liable to misuse. On the other hand, where the credit-token is acquired by another person with the debtor's consent, the debtor's liability for loss to the creditor, arising out of use made of the credit-token, is unlimited.[2]

If the debtor alleges that any use made of the credit-token has not been authorised by him, the onus of proof falls on the creditor to prove either that the use was so authorised or that the use occurred before the creditor had been given notice of the loss, theft or misuse.[3]

The Lending Code, for banks, building societies and credit card providers which subscribe to it, spells out the respective liabilities of creditor and debtor for unauthorised credit card transactions as follows:[4]

'Unless the subscriber can show that the customer acted fraudulently, their liability for their credit card being misused will be limited as follows:

- If someone else uses the card, before the customer informs the subscriber that it has been lost or stolen or that someone else knows the PIN, the most the customer will have to pay is £50.

- If someone else uses the card details without the customer's permission, and the card has not been lost or stolen, the customer will not have to pay anything; this would include where a customer's card has been cloned.

If the card is used before the customer has received it, the customer will not have to pay anything, unless the subscriber can show that the customer acted fraudulently.

In the event that the card details are used by someone else, without the customer's permission, for a transaction where the cardholder does not need to be present, the customer will not have to pay anything.

Unless the subscriber can show that the customer acted fraudulently, where a credit card transaction has not been authorised by the customer then any interest or other changes that may have been applied as a result of the transaction will be refunded.

In relation to unauthorised transactions, the burden of proof lies with the subscriber and not with the customer, so the subscriber will have to provide proof if necessary.'

The Code contains numerous other provisions governing credit cards. They include controls over pre-sale information, point of contact information, issuance and protection of Chip and PIN, communication of interest rates, setting credit limits, credit card statements (including by reference to the UK Cards Association Best Practice Guidelines for the Cardholder Statement Summary Box), credit card repayments and credit card cheques.[5]

Liability of the debtor for misuse of credit-tokens, as described in the first paragraph above, shall not apply if the credit agreement does not contain particulars of the name, address and telephone number of the person to whom theft, loss or misuse of a credit-token is to be notified, set out prominently and so as to be easily legible.[6] Notice takes effect when received, but where the agreement requires confirmation of loss in writing, oral notice shall not be treated as taking effect if not confirmed in writing within seven days.[7]

1 Consumer Credit Act 1974, s 83.
2 Ibid., s 84(2).
3 Ibid., s 171(4).
4 March 2011 (revised September 2015), section 6, paras 138 to 142.
5 Ibid., section 6.
6 Consumer Credit Act 1974, s 84(4) and Consumer Credit (Credit-Token Agreements) Regulations 1983, SI 1983/1555.
7 Ibid., s 84(5).

17.4   ASPECTS OF THE REGULATORY REGIME

17.4.1   Unsolicited credit-tokens

A firm must not give a person a credit-token if he has not asked for it. A request must be in a document signed by the person making the request, unless the credit-token agreement is a small borrower-lender-supplier agreement. This does not apply to the giving of a credit-token to a person for use under a credit-token agreement already made, or in renewal or replacement of a credit-token previously accepted by that person under a credit-token agreement which continues in force, whether or not varied.[1]

The prohibition was previously contained in section 51 of CCA 1974 but was repealed by article 20(15) of the Financial Services and Markets Act 2000 (Regulated Activities) (Amendment) (No 2) Order 2013,[2] save for the purposes of regulation 52 of the Payment Services Regulations 2009[3] (the effect being that section 51 continues to apply in relation to a regulated credit agreement in place of regulation 58(1)(b) of the Payment Services Regulations).

In *Elliott v Director General of Fair Trading*,[4] which turned on the meaning of section 51 of CCA 1974, the court held that a document may constitute a credit-token even though the creditor's undertaking to supply cash, goods or services has no contractual force. It would also be a credit-token notwithstanding that the customer's entitlement to credit is still subject to credit vetting and approval. Furthermore, it would be a credit-token even if the undertaking to grant credit is in fact false. If, on the other hand, without prior solicitation, the customer is furnished with a document to assist in identifying him to a credit grantor as a privileged customer or as a customer entitled to be granted credit, for example by reference to an account number or other means of identification, the provision or furnishing of such information, as it is not a document or other tangible item, would not constitute an unsolicited credit-token.

As unsolicited credit-tokens now fall under the FCA regime and are governed by FCA rules, notably CONC 2.9, their issue is no longer a criminal offence but could give rise to FCA financial penalties.

1 CONC 2.9.2R.
2 SI 2013/1881.
3 SI 2009/2009.
4 [1980] 1 WLR 977.

17.4.2   Credit card cheques

Draconian restrictions on the issue of credit card cheques, aimed at eliminating the rampant issue of cheques that incurred the higher charges of a credit card account as against a bank account, were originally contained in section 51A of CCA 1974. This section was repealed on 1 April 2014 with the transfer of the consumer credit regime from the OFT to the FCA. It was replaced by CONC 2.3.5R, which provides as follows:

(a)   a firm may provide credit card cheques only to a customer who has asked for them;

(b) a firm may provide credit card cheques only on a single occasion in respect of each request that is made;

(c) the number of credit card cheques provided in respect of a request must not exceed three (or, if less, the number requested);

(d) where a single request is made for the provision of credit card cheques in connection with more than one credit-token agreement, (b) and (c) apply as if a separate request had been made for each agreement;

(e) where more than one request for the provision of credit card cheques is made in the same document or at the same time:

(i) they may be provided in respect of only one of the requests, but

(ii) if the requests relate to more than one credit-token agreement, in relation to each agreement they may be provided only in respect of one of the requests made in relation to that agreement.

CONC 2.3.5R does not apply to credit card cheques provided in connection with a credit-token agreement entered into by the customer wholly or predominantly for the purposes of a business carried on, or intended to be carried on, by the customer. If a credit-token agreement includes a declaration made by the customer to the effect that the agreement is entered into for the business purposes mentioned, the agreement is treated as having been so entered into, unless the lender, or any person who has acted on behalf of the lender in connection with the entering into of the agreement knows, or has reasonable cause to suspect, that the agreement is not entered into for such purposes. The declaration must be in the relevant form and content set out in CONC App 1.

17.4.3 The total charge for credit and APR

Running-account credit agreements within the scope of the Consumer Credit Directive are governed by the Consumer Credit (Agreements) Regulations 2010.[1] Schedule 4 contains provisions relating to the calculation and disclosure of the total charge for credit and APR, and refers to the relevant rules in CONC. The Schedule states, among other matters, that where credit is to be provided subject to a maximum credit limit of less than £1,200, the credit limit shall be assumed to be an amount equal to that maximum limit. CONC App 1.1.12R states that where the amount of the credit to be provided under the credit agreement cannot be ascertained at the date of the making of the credit agreement, in the case of a credit agreement for running-account credit under which there is a credit limit, that amount shall be taken to be such credit limit; and in any other case, that amount shall be taken to be £100. It is not clear how these two propositions can be reconciled.

The Schedule also provides for permissible tolerances in the disclosure of the APR, about which CONC App 1 is strangely silent.

The Consumer Credit (Agreements) Regulations 1983[2] apply to consumer credit agreements outside the scope of the Directive and contain different and more extensive assumptions about running-account credit, as follows:

(i)   in any case where there will be a credit limit, but that limit is not known at the date of the making of the agreement, the amount of the credit to be provided shall be taken to be £1,500 or, in a case where the credit limit will be less than £1,500, an amount equal to that limit;

(ii)   the credit is provided for a period of one year beginning with the relevant date;

(iii) the credit is provided in full on the relevant date;

(iv)   where the rate of interest will change at a time provided in the agreement, within a period of three years beginning with the date of the making of the agreement, the rate shall be taken to be the highest rate at any time obtaining under the agreement in that period;

(v)   where the agreement provides credit to finance the purchase of goods, services, land or other things and also provides one or more of cash loans, credit to refinance existing indebtedness of the debtor's, whether to the creditor or another person and credit for any other purpose, and either or both different rates of interest and different charges are payable in relation to the credit for all or some of those purposes, the rate of interest and charges payable in relation to the whole of the credit are those applicable to the provision of credit for the purchase of goods, services, land or other things; and

(vi)   the credit is repaid in 12 equal instalments and at monthly intervals beginning one month after the relevant date.

The APR is the mathematical representation of the total charge for credit and is calculated in accordance with CONC App 1. Once again, CONC App 1 does not provide for any permitted tolerance in the statement of the APR, in contrast with the Agreements Regulations, which set out permitted tolerances in the disclosure of the APR in various stated circumstances. There is also a general permissible tolerance insofar as the APR may be shown at a rate which exceeds the APR by not more than one, or a rate which falls short of the APR by not more than 0.1.

1   SI 2010/1014, Sch 4.
2   SI 1983/1553, Sch 7.

17.4.4   Debtor's rights, and creditor's liability, under sections 75 and 75A

Section 75 of CCA 1974 provides that if the debtor under a debtor-creditor-supplier agreement falling within s 12(b) or (c) has, in relation to a transaction financed by the agreement, any claim against the supplier in respect of a misrepresentation or breach of contract, he has a like claim against the creditor who, with the supplier, is accordingly jointly and severally liable to the debtor. The section does not apply to a claim under a non-commercial agreement or so far as the claim relates to any single item to which the supplier has attached a cash price not exceeding £100 or more than £30,000.[1] The creditor is entitled to a statutory indemnity by the supplier for loss suffered by the creditor in satisfying any such claim, including costs incurred by him in defending proceedings instituted by the debtor.[2]

It will be noted that s 75 liability attaches to a debtor-creditor-supplier agreement falling within s 12(b) or (c) of the Act. It therefore does not apply to a cash withdrawal or to goods or services paid by cash withdrawn by means of a credit card, which is an unrestricted-use debtor-creditor agreement under s 13(c). Section 75 also does not apply to a balance transfer or to an agreement to refinance any existing indebtedness of the debtor, which is a restricted-use debtor-creditor agreement under s 13(b). A balance transfer does not extinguish the s 75 liability of the original creditor under a debtor-creditor-supplier agreement preceding the balance transfer, albeit that the original indebtedness is refinanced.

CCA 1974, s 75A(1), which was introduced pursuant to Consumer Credit Directive 2008/48/EC, confers on a debtor under a linked credit agreement, a claim against the creditor, where the debtor has a claim for breach of contract against the supplier. The agreement in question may, but need not, be a debtor-creditor-supplier agreement. A s 75A claim is subject to fulfilment of one or more of the following conditions: that the supplier cannot be traced; that the debtor has contacted the supplier but the supplier has not responded; that the supplier is insolvent; or that the debtor has taken reasonable steps, which need not include litigation, to pursue his claim against the supplier but has not obtained satisfaction for his claim.[3]

The new concept of 'linked agreement' introduced by s 75A, means a regulated consumer credit agreement (other than an agreement excluded by s 75A(6) or (8)), which serves exclusively to finance an agreement for the supply of specific goods or the provision of a specific service and where the creditor uses the services of the supplier in connection with the preparation or making of the agreement (i.e. the supplier is also a credit broker or credit intermediary) or the specific goods or services are explicitly specified in the agreement.[4]

Section 75(A)(1) does not apply, and hence no claim lies against the creditor, in relation to a breach of contract by the supplier, where:

(a)   the cash value of the goods or service is £30,000 or less (this is the corollary to s 75(3)(b) above and avoids a duplication of remedies);

(b)   the linked credit agreement is for credit which exceeds £60,260 and is not a residential renovation agreement;

(c)   the linked credit agreement is entered into by the debtor wholly or predominantly for the purposes of a business carried on, or intended to be carried on, by him; or

(d)   the credit agreement is secured on land.

Exclusions (b), (c) and (d) are due to the fact that the s 75A remedy is confined to credit agreements within the scope of the Directive.

In relation to credit card transactions, the long-standing issue as to whether a creditor is liable under s 75 for purchases made by a borrower under a credit card transaction entered into outside the United Kingdom, was resolved by the House of Lords in *Office of Fair Trading v Lloyds TSB Bank plc.*[5] Lord Hoffmann stated that there was nothing in the language of s 75(1) to exclude foreign transactions. In so far as it was alleged that the section had the effect of legislating extra-territorially, he stated that extra-territorial effect means seeking to regulate the conduct or affect the liabilities of people over whom the United Kingdom has no jurisdiction. In this case the Office of Fair Trading accepted that s 75(1) applied only to agreements with a creditor carrying on business in the United Kingdom. The effect of the section was equivalent to the statutory implication of a term in the contract between a United Kingdom creditor and the debtor by which the former accepts joint and several liability with the supplier. If the supplier is foreign, the Act does not purport to regulate his conduct or impose liabilities upon him. It is only the United Kingdom creditor who is affected. As regards the argument that s 75(1) was dependent upon the enforceability of the statutory indemnity of the creditor by the supplier under s 75(2), Lord Hoffmann stated that if this was Parliament's intention, it would have said so and that it was not obvious why there should be such a link.

In his Opinion, Lord Mance emphasised the need for consumer protection, which was the fundamental purpose of the Consumer Credit Act 1974. He referred to the Crowther Committee Report, which led to the enactment of the Act, and its observation that the law's task was to maintain a fair balance between the creditor and the debtor and that in considering which of two innocent parties should bear the greater loss, it was much easier for the business creditor to do so than the individual debtor. In distinguishing between so-called 'connected' and 'unconnected' loans, the Committee had felt that the connected lender should incur a primary liability for supplier's misrepresentation or breach along the lines reflected in s 75(1). Commenting on the expression 'arrangements' in the definition of a debtor-creditor-supplier agreement, Lord Mance stated that the language of 'arrangements' used in the Act is well capable of embracing the modern relationships between card issuers and suppliers under networks like VISA and MasterCard. Finally, the statutory indemnity in s 75(2) did no more than reflect a well-recognised restitutionary right at English common law.

There is no reason why the extra-territorial jurisdiction over creditors situated in the UK should not also apply to claims against suppliers under s 75A.

The obvious problem of a creditor (and corresponding benefit to a debtor) with s 75 is that it imposes virtual unlimited liability on a creditor for use made by the debtor of the credit card, whether in the United Kingdom or abroad. Liability arises even if only the deposit, or part of the purchase price in a transaction, is paid for by means of the credit card.

Charge card transactions and debit card transactions, including electronic transfers of funds at point of sale, and cash withdrawals, do not attract the provisions or protection of s 75 or s 75A as they are not debtor-creditor-supplier agreements. For the avoidance of doubt the Act expressly excludes arrangements for the electronic transfer of funds from a current account at a bank, from the scope of arrangements between a creditor and a supplier.[6] A second or additional cardholder who is authorised by the debtor to make purchases (by means of a separate card) under a debtor-creditor-supplier agreement cannot invoke the provisions of s 75 or s 75A as such a person is not the 'debtor' under the agreement.[7]

1 CCA 1974, s 75(3)(b).
2 Ibid., s 75(1), (2) and (3).
3 Ibid., s 75A(2) and (3).
4 Ibid., s 75A(5).
5 [2007] All ER (D) 466, [2007] GCCR 6101, HL.
6 CCA 1974, s 187(3A).
7 See further **17.4.5** below.

17.4.5   Additional cardholders

The terms of a credit-token agreement commonly permit cards to be used by authorised users or additional cardholders. However, an additional cardholder is not a debtor under a credit agreement. It follows that in a contract of supply entered into by an authorised user or additional cardholder, they would not enjoy the protection afforded by s 75 or s 75A, as these sections only extend to a transaction financed by a debtor-creditor-supplier agreement where the debtor, and not any other person, has a claim against the supplier. In any event, 'debtor' in s 189(1) is the individual receiving credit under a consumer credit agreement or the person to whom his rights and duties under the agreement have passed by assignment or operation of law.

In February 2001 the OFT issued a note on s 75 under the heading 'Transactions by Authorised Second Users'[1] and refers to its views in an earlier report on Connected Lender Liability (March 1994), stating:

> 'Most card-issuers allow a second card to be issued on a single account, usually to the spouse of the account holder. The holder of the second card thus becomes an authorised user of the account. The Office's view in such cases is that the second card-user is acting as the agent of the principal cardholder and that any claims under s 75 in relation to purchases made by the second user should be made by the principal cardholder. It is a well-established principle of agency law that a person who is entitled to pledge the credit of another, acts as that other's agent.
>
> Card-issuers are evidently keen, for commercial reasons, to promote the use of second cards. Moreover, they can recover from the principal cardholder any debts arising from transactions entered into by an authorised second card-user. In these circumstances card-issuers cannot reasonably argue that they should have no s 75 liability in respect of authorised users. The evidence available to the Office suggests that, in practice, card-issuers may offer to settle some s 75 claims on an *ex gratia* basis. In contested cases, however, it appears that card-issuers have sometimes relied upon the second user not being the debtor, as defined in the Act, and sought to ignore the agency connection between him and the principal cardholder. Some county court judges, moreover, appear to have accepted this. It is the Office's view that card-issuers should act on the basis of the agency connection that undoubtedly exists, and meet claims arising from transactions of authorised second users.'

It is submitted that the OFT's reasoning is flawed. The entitlement of an additional cardholder or authorised person to utilise the principal cardholder's credit under the account is the extension of a facility and not the creation of an agency relationship. The additional cardholder is neither the debtor under the transaction nor the beneficiary of any rights in respect of misrepresentation or breach of contract, whether as 'debtor' or agent of the debtor.

The corollary of the foregoing is that the debtor's claim under s 75 only lies against the creditor under the debtor-creditor-supplier agreement and not the creditor's agent, as was confirmed by the Supreme Court in *Plevin v Paragon Personal Finance Ltd*:[2] 'Section 75 does not provide for a deemed agency, but it imposes liability under a debtor-creditor-supplier agreement for the misrepresentations and breaches of contract of the supplier'.

'Creditor' is defined in s 189 as including the person to whom the creditor's right and duties under the agreement have passed by assignment or operation of law so that, it is submitted, the debtor would have an equal claim against the creditor's assignee. Furthermore, the creditor may not avoid liability by assignment, as this would amount to an unfair contract term.[3]

1 Consumer Credit Act 1974: Section 75 – Transactions by Authorised Second Users (February 2001).
2 [2014] UKSC 61, [2014] GCCR 12085 at para 31.
3 Consumer Rights Act 2015, Sch 2, Pt 1, para 19.

17.5   TYPES OF CREDIT CARD AND CREDIT CARD USER

Credit cards are distinguished either by their purpose or by the method by which the outstanding balance is to be discharged.

17.5.1   Types of credit card user

The card industry distinguishes between two types of credit card user: 'revolvers' and 'transactors'. Transactors pay off their bill in full at the end of every month, and so do not make use of a credit facility above and beyond the interest-free period. Revolvers, on the other hand, roll over some or all of their debt at the end of the month, and thus pay interest. Premium cards and reward cards are generally aimed at transactors, who by definition have no real need of extended credit: the rewards are an incentive for them to use credit cards despite that fact.[1]

1 *Asda Stores Limited and Others v MasterCard Incorporated and Others* [2017] EWHC 93 (Comm) para 22.

17.5.2   Store card

A store card is a payment card, usually in the form of a credit card, issued for use in one retailer or more retailers or group of retail outlets which are part of a single group of interconnected corporate bodies or belong to a store card network which trades under a common name or operates in the same shopping centre. The card will usually carry associated benefits, such as special discounts, card-holder offers and retail promotions. Store cards take the form of either an Option Account card or, less frequently, a Budget Account.

Following the Store Cards Market Investigation by the Competition Commission, the latter made an Order entitled the 'Store Cards Market Investigation Order', which came into force on 1 May 2007.[1]

The Order imposes the following obligations on issuers of store cards:

(a)   Information on statements must include:

(i)   a statement of the current APR applicable to purchases;

(ii)   an estimate of interest payable in the following month if the card-holder only makes a minimum payment;

(iii) a warning outlining the consequences of only making minimum payments;

(iv) the basis of insurance charges;

(v) late payment or default of charges;

(vi) the basic assumptions used in calculating the estimate of interest payable in the following month;

(vii) contact details for amending or cancelling insurance sold with the store card and a brief summary of insurance cover.

(b) The APR warning, to the effect that the rate of interest on the account may be higher than on other sources of credit and that it may be costly to leave balances owing on the account after the interest-free period.

(c) Provision and display of the facility to pay outstanding balances by direct debit.

(d) The requirement that insurances which are generally offered in conjunction with credit cards, such as payment protection insurance, price protection and purchase protection, be sold as separate insurances.

1 Store Cards Market Investigation Order – Date of Report – 7 March 2006. Date of Order – 27 July 2006. Note that the Order applies to all store cards, whether in the form of payment or credit cards.

17.5.3 Option account card

An option account card is sometimes mistakenly called a charge card. It is a credit card issued in respect of a running-account or revolving credit agreement under which the borrower selects the credit limit which is to apply to his account. The borrower must then make a monthly payment in a minimum sum, usually 5% of the outstanding balance from time to time. He may also at any time pay more than this amount or discharge the outstanding balance in full.

17.5.4 Budget account card

Budget accounts have largely been overtaken by option accounts. A budget account card is a credit card issued in connection with an account under which the borrower agrees to pay a fixed monthly amount, selected by him, and the credit limit is set as a multiple of that fixed monthly payment. The credit limit is usually 24 times the monthly payment, based on the deceptive assumption that the fully utilised credit limit would be discharged within two years.

17.5.5 Affinity card

This is a card where the issuer undertakes to pay a specified percentage of the transaction costs to a charity, either of the customer's or the creditor's choice.

17.5.6   Charge card

A charge card is descriptive of two quite distinct types of credit card. In the strict sense it is the description of a card that requires the customer under the terms of his account to settle the outstanding balance in full by one payment within a prescribed period not exceeding three months following the date of his monthly statement, resulting in a limited period of interest-free credit. The agreement for such an account is an exempt agreement, which is not regulated by the RAO.1

A charge card is also the description applied to a 't and e' (travel and entertainment) card. Typical examples are American Express and Diners Club Cards.

1 RAO art 60F(3).

17.5.7   Co-branded or loyalty card

This is a card, usually a credit card, whose utilisation earns the cardholder points which can then be exchanged for discounts, purchases or services, either from the card issuer or from a related or sponsoring supplier. It is in fact no more than a marketing device to win or preserve market share or customer loyalty.

17.6   OTHER PAYMENT CARDS

17.6.1   Cash card/prepaid card

Issuers of cash cards or prepaid cards are registered and supervised by the Financial Conduct Authority under the Financial Services and Markets Act 2000, the Financial Services and Markets Act 2000 (Regulated Activities) Order 2001 ('RAO'),[1] the Payment Services Regulations 2017[2] and the Electronic Money Regulations 2011 ('2011 Order').[3]

Prepaid cards constitute 'electronic money'. Electronic money is a specified investment under RAO art 74A, and the issuing of electronic money is a regulated activity under RAO. 'Electronic money' is defined in reg 2(1) of the 2011 Order as:

> 'electronically (including magnetically) stored monetary value as represented by a claim on the electronic money issuer which—
>
> (a) is issued on receipt of funds for the purpose of making payment transactions;
>
> (b) is accepted by a person other than the electronic money issuer; and
>
> (c) is not excluded by regulation 3.'

Regulation 3 of the 2011 Order provides as follows:

> **'3 Electronic money: exclusions**
>
> For the purposes of these Regulations electronic money does not include–
>
> (a) monetary value stored on instruments that can be used to acquire goods or services only–

    (i)   in or on the electronic money issuer's premises; or

    (ii) under a commercial agreement with the electronic money issuer, either within a limited network of service providers or for a limited range of goods or services;

(b) monetary value that is used to make payment transactions executed by means of any telecommunication, digital or IT device, where the goods or services purchased are delivered to and are to be used through a telecommunication, digital or IT device, provided that the telecommunication, digital or IT operator does not act only as an intermediary between the payment service user and the supplier of the goods and services.'

The 2011 Order sets out the regime requirements for registration by the FCA of an authorised electronic money issuer or a small electronic money institution and the permitted activities and obligations of the issuer or institution.

The prepaid card, known colloquially as an electronic purse, has become increasingly popular. It includes cards such as the Oyster card, prepaid telephone cards, travel cards, travel money and foreign currency cards, which may also be part of the MasterCard or VISA network, and prepaid gift or book token cards issued by retailers.

It is submitted that prepaid cards are not credit-tokens within the meaning of s 14 of CCA 1974 as no credit is involved and the card issuer does not undertake payment to a third party in return for payment by the cardholder.[4] On the contrary, the third party undertakes to pay no more than what the cardholder has already paid into the card.

1 SI 2001/544, as amended.
2 SI 2017/752.
3 SI 2011/99 which implements Directive 2009/110/EC of the European Council and of the European Parliament of 16 September 2009.
4 Consumer Credit Act 1974, s 14(1). See also *Goode: Consumer Credit Law and Practice* (LexisNexis Butterworths), paras 1C [25.69] to [25.80].

17.6.2   Debit card

The trend in relation to card usage is markedly in favour of debit cards over credit cards. This evolution could not have taken place but for the increasing number of consumers who hold current accounts, the consequence of a development from weekly to monthly wage payments. The lower cost of an overdraft on a current account than a credit card account is also a reason for the increasing popularity of non-credit cards.

A debit card is used in conjunction with a current account to obtain cash at an automated teller machine ('ATM'), or to effect payment and obtain cash by electronic funds transfer at point of sale ('EFTPOS'). It dispenses with the need for cheques. The account holder's bank account is debited and funds transferred in about the time that it takes to clear a cheque, approximately three working days. The card has no pre-set transaction limit. The only limit is the amount available to the customer under his current account. A major advantage to the supplier is the speed with which he receives payment, albeit in return for a commission payable by him, usually at a lower rate than under a credit card transaction.

There is controversy as to whether or not a debit card is a credit-token for the purposes of CCA 1974. According to Professor Guest such a card is a credit-token under CCA 1974, s 14(1)(b), as a deemed provision of credit will arise under s 14(3). The regulated agreement for the provision of such credit will be a debtor-creditor-supplier agreement. On the other hand, Professor Goode maintains that an agreement for the issue of a debit card is not a credit agreement but merely an agreement providing for a convenient payment mechanism and that in all probability a debit card is not a credit-token.[1] These arguments also extend to cash cards.[2] Whatever the position may be, banks have endeavoured to structure their debit card agreements as exempt agreements under RAO.

The most common debit card schemes in place in the United Kingdom are those operated by Switch Card Services, backed by various banks and building societies, the Connect Scheme operated by the VISA network and the Delta debit card.

1 Guest, *Consumer Credit Law* (Sweet & Maxwell), 2–015; *Goode: Consumer Credit Law and Practice* (LexisNexis Butterworths), para 1C [24.84].
2 Guest, *Consumer Credit Law* (Sweet & Maxwell), 2–015; *Goode: Consumer Credit Law and Practice* (LexisNexis Butterworths), paras 1C [25.69] to [25.80].

Chapter 18

Security (including mortgages)

18.1 TYPES OF 'SECURITY'

The CCA 1974 envisages a range of security in relation to an actual or prospective consumer credit agreement, consumer hire agreement or any linked transaction. 'Security' means a mortgage, charge, pledge, bond, debenture, indemnity, guarantee, bill, note or other right provided by the debtor or hirer, or at his request, express or implied, to secure the carrying out of the obligations of the debtor or hirer under the agreement.[1] Whilst the Act limits the meaning of 'security' to any of the above provided by, or at the request of, the debtor or hirer, the meaning of 'security' has become obscured in relation to consumer credit agreements under the Consumer Credit (Agreements) Regulations 2010 as a result of the requirement to state any security or guarantee to be provided by the debtor or on his behalf (that is, whether or not requested by the debtor).[2]

Article 60L of the Financial Services and Markets Act 2000 (Regulated Activities) Order 2001 ('RAO') reinforces the original definition in CCA 1974 by defining 'security' in relation to a credit agreement as a mortgage, charge, pledge, bond, debenture, indemnity, guarantee, bill, note or other right provided by the borrower or at the implied or express request of the borrower to secure the carrying out of the obligations of the borrower under the agreement.

A regulated agreement must embody any security provided in relation to it by the debtor or hirer.[3]

1 CCA 1974, s 189(1).
2 SI 2010/1014, Sch 1, para 23. See also the confused insertion in the Consumer Credit (Disclosure of Information) Regulations 2010, SI 2010/1013, Sch 1, para 2.
3 This is the effect of s 105(9). See also the definition of 'embody' in s 189(4).

18.2 FORM AND CONTENT OF SECURITY DOCUMENTS

Any security provided in relation to a regulated agreement by the debtor, hirer or a third party must be in writing. Whilst guarantees and indemnities are further regulated,[1] there are no specific regulations covering other forms of security, except for the European Standardised Information Sheet (ESIS) which relates to regulated mortgage contracts.[2] A regulated agreement must embody any security provided in relation to the agreement by the debtor or hirer.[3] This means that the agreement must set out all the provisions of the security or expressly refer to the security document.[4] As mentioned above, in relation to a regulated agreement under the 1983 Regulations this requirement only applies to security provided by, or at the request of, the debtor or hirer.

Where the agreement is secured on land, the words 'secured on' followed by the address of the land must appear at the end of the statutory heading to the regulated agreement.[5] The agreement must also contain the statutory form of statement: 'YOUR HOME MAY BE REPOSSESSED etc.'.[6]

The CCA 1974's provisions relating to the form of security document are additional to those provided for elsewhere.

1 CCA 1974, s 105 and Consumer Credit (Guarantees and Indemnities) Regulations 1983, SI 1983/1556.
2 See **18.2.3.3** below.
3 CCA 1974, s 105(9); Consumer Credit (Agreements Regulations) 1983, SI 1983/1553, as amended, Sch 1, para 20 and Sch 3, para 9, and see footnote 2 at **18.1** above.
4 CCA 1974, s 189(4).
5 SI 1983/1553, Sch 1, para 1; Sch 3, para 1; SI 2010/1014, Sch 1, para 1(5).
6 SI 1983/1553, Sch 2, para 3; Sch 4, para 3; SI 2010/1553, Sch 2, para 2.

18.2.1   Guarantee and indemnity[1]

Section 4 of the Statute of Frauds (1677) requires a guarantee to be in writing and signed by the party to be charged or by some other person lawfully authorised by him. The section only applies to guarantees and not to indemnities, which constitute primary obligations. However, in the case of guarantees or indemnities securing obligations under regulated or linked transactions, the Consumer Credit (Guarantees and Indemnities) Regulations require any security to be in writing and prescribe the form and formalities that apply to them. They include the following:

(i)   a prescribed heading;

(ii)   prescribed terms and certain minimum information;

(iii) a statement of the surety's rights in statutory form;

(iv) a statutory form of signature box.

As with regulated agreements, there are requirements relating to the prominence of certain lettering and the legibility of the document.

A guarantee or indemnity must be signed by or on behalf of the surety. The document must embody all the terms of the security other than implied terms, and when presented to the surety for his signature must be accompanied by a copy of the document, together with a copy of any other document referred to in it (e.g. the agreement secured by it). Where the security is provided before the regulated agreement is made, a copy of the subsequently executed agreement, together with a copy of any other document referred to in it, must be given to the surety within seven days of the regulated agreement being made. Otherwise a copy of the executed agreement and of any document referred to in it must be given to the surety when the security is provided. Failure to comply with these requirements will ordinarily result in the security being unenforceable against the surety save on an order of the court.[2]

Save for certain exceptions relating to registered charges, in respect of ineffective securities:

(a) the security, so far as it is so provided, shall be treated as never having effect;

(b) any property lodged with the creditor or owner solely for the purposes of the security as so provided shall be returned by him forthwith;

(c) the creditor or owner shall take any necessary action to remove or cancel an entry in any register, so far as the entry relates to the security as so provided; and

(d) any amount received by the creditor or owner on realisation of the security shall, so far as it is referable to the agreement, be repaid to the surety.[3]

A weakness of the regulations is that they do not make specific provision for continuing guarantees.

The foregoing requirements are in addition to the common law requirement that a guarantee or indemnity must either be given for consideration or executed as a deed, in accordance with the Law of Property (Miscellaneous Provisions) Act 1989.

The FCA Handbook, CONC sourcebook, chapter 7, dealing with arrears, default and recovery, including repossessions, also applies to guarantors and indemnifiers.

1 CCA 1974, s 105 and Consumer Credit (Guarantees and Indemnities) Regulations 1983, SI 1983/1556.
2 Ibid., s 105(5) and (7).
3 Ibid., ss 106 and 177.

18.2.2 Mortgage and land mortgage

A mortgage, in the case of goods, is a transfer of ownership to the creditor by way of security, upon the express or implied condition that the asset will be reconveyed to the debtor when the sum secured has been paid. Where the debtor wishes to remain in possession of the mortgaged goods or chattels, he must register a bill of sale under the Bills of Sale Acts 1878 to 1891.

Mortgages or charges of property, whether of goods or land, by a company are registrable under the Companies Act 2006, ss 860, 861, 870 and 874.

The more usual type of mortgage used to secure a regulated agreement is a land mortgage. There are two types of land mortgages, a mortgage by demise for a term of years absolute (i.e. a lease) or the more usual form of charge by way of legal mortgage.

The mortgage deed might itself provide for the method of payment or, alternatively, the credit agreement secured by it will provide for the method of payment. The two main methods are the 'repayment mortgage' and the 'endowment', or so-called 'interest only' mortgage. The former requires repayment of the loan during the term by regular, usually monthly, payments of capital and interest. The latter provides for the payment of the loan by regular, usually monthly, instalments of interest only and repayment of the capital sum of the loan by one lump sum at the end of the term. In the case of an endowment mortgage the capital sum is repaid out of the proceeds of a life assurance policy on the life of the mortgagor or a third party which is assigned to the mortgagee at the time of the execution of the mortgage. Within this broad framework, there are various variations of the theme, either in relation to the mode of payment or the form of security.

There are many payment methods which are offered as distinct mortgage products. These include a fixed-rate mortgage (interest charged at a fixed rate in the early years), a low start or discounted mortgage, a tracker mortgage (a variable-rate mortgage with payments linked to the Bank of England Base Rate), a capped mortgage, a collateral or offset mortgage (which is linked to a savings account and only charges interest on the net balance between the two accounts) and a cash-back mortgage. Often, these descriptions simply refer to the beneficial mortgage terms which apply in the early years of the mortgage, usually the first two to five years. The objective is to assist the mortgagor financially at a time when ordinarily his earnings would be low. The beneficial terms are, however, invariably linked to some 'lock-in' provision requiring the mortgagor to compensate the mortgagee for its support by payment of a redemption charge if the mortgagor redeems the security during the beneficial period. The particular term and payment amount may be open to challenge as an unfair contract term under Part 2 of, and Schedule 2 to, the Consumer Rights Act 2015.

A flexible mortgage is one which, during the mortgage term, entitles the mortgagor to make payments, as and when he pleases, in excess of the instalment payment, to take payment holidays (without the non-payment of the monthly instalment constituting a breach of the mortgage), to obtain a re-advance of repaid principal and so on. An offset mortgage is a mortgage which entitles the mortgagor to set off interest accrued on his savings account against the accrued interest charged on his mortgage, thereby saving the income tax which would otherwise be payable on the interest earned on the savings account.

Mortgages can be combined with repayment vehicles such as a unit trust, ISA (Individual Savings Account) and a pension policy. Each of these involves payment by the mortgagor into an additional investment or pension scheme, the ultimate proceeds of which are utilised towards discharge of the loan secured on the mortgaged property.

The Mortgage Credit Directive Order 2015[1] sets out a framework for regulating buy-to-let mortgage lending to consumers. It makes provision for a register of firms involved in such lending, prescribes requirements for such firms, and assigns to the FCA the role to monitor and enforce such requirements.

A mortgage or charge of land or an interest in land, including an equitable charge, is subject to the Law of Property (Miscellaneous Provisions) Act 1989, which requires the document to be by way of deed and executed as a deed in accordance with its provisions.

1 SI 2015/910.

18.2.3   Regulated mortgage contracts and unregulated mortgage contracts

18.2.3.1   Regulated mortgage contract, home reversion plan, home purchase plan, and regulated sale and rent back agreement

The Financial Services and Markets Act 2000 ('FSMA'), the Financial Services and Markets Act 2000 (Regulated Activities) Order 2001 ('RAO')[1], the Mortgage Credit Directive Order 2015[2] and the Mortgage Conduct of Business Sourcebook ('MCOB') together create a complex web of regulation under the supervision and control of the Financial Conduct Authority ('FCA').

A regulated mortgage contract[3] is a contract which, at the time it is entered into, meets the following conditions:

(a)   the lender provides credit to an individual or to trustees ('the borrower');

(b)   the contract provides for the obligation of the borrower to repay to be secured by a mortgage on land in the EEA; and

(c)   at least 40% of the land is used, or is intended to be used:

   (i)   in the case of credit provided to an individual, as or in connection with a dwelling; or

   (ii)   in the case of credit provided to a trustee which is not an individual, as or in connection with a dwelling by an individual who is a beneficiary of the trust, or by a related person;

but such a contract is not a regulated mortgage contract if it falls within RAO article 61A(1) or (2) below.

A regulated mortgage contract includes a first, second or later mortgage contract and also an equitable mortgage contract.

It is noteworthy that, in contrast with the definition of an 'individual' in CCA 1974, an 'individual' (borrower) under RAO article 61(3) does not appear to include a partnership of two or three persons or other unincorporated body of persons not consisting entirely of bodies corporate.

'Related person' is defined in RAO article 61(4)(c) with respect to the borrower or the beneficiary of the trust, but surprisingly RAO article 61(3)(a) makes no mention of a related person in relation to credit to an individual.

A regulated home reversion plan[4] is an arrangement under which the plan provider (the investor) buys all or part of a qualifying interest in land (other than timeshare accommodation) in the United Kingdom from the reversion seller. The reversion seller (if he is an individual) or an individual who is a beneficiary of the trust (if the reversion seller is a trustee), or a related person, is entitled under the arrangement to occupy at least 40% of the land as or in connection with a dwelling and intends to do so. The arrangement ends on the happening of a specified qualifying termination event.

A regulated home purchase plan[5] is an arrangement under which: a person (the home purchase provider) buys a qualifying interest or an undivided share of a qualifying interest (held on trust for the home purchase provider and the individual or trustees constituting the home purchaser) in land (other than timeshare occupation) in the United Kingdom; the home purchaser is obliged to purchase the interest bought by the home purchase provider during or at the end of a specified period; and the home purchaser or a beneficiary of the trust or a related person is entitled under the arrangement to occupy at least 40% of the land as or in connection with a dwelling and intends to do so.

A regulated sale and rent back agreement[6] is an arrangement under which a person (the agreement provider) buys all or part of the qualifying interest in land (other than timeshare accommodation) in the United Kingdom from an individual or trustees (the agreement seller) and the latter, if an individual, or an individual who is a beneficiary of the trust or a related person is entitled under the arrangement to occupy at least 40% of the land as or in connection with a dwelling and intends to do so.

1 SI 2001/544.
2 SI 2015/910.
3 RAO art 61(3). See further **18.2.3.2** below.
4 Ibid., art 63B(3).
5 Ibid., art 63F(3).
6 Ibid., art 63J(3).

18.2.3.2   *Mortgage contracts which are not regulated mortgage contracts*

As set out in RAO, a mortgage contract is not a regulated mortgage contract if it is one of the following:[1]

(a)   a regulated home purchase plan;

(b)   a limited payment second charge bridging loan;

(c)   a second charge business loan;

(d)   an investment property loan; ...

(e)   an exempt consumer buy-to-let mortgage contract; ...

(f)   an exempt equitable mortgage bridging loan; or

(g)   an exempt housing authority loan.

Furthermore, a mortgage contract is not a regulated mortgage contract if:[2]

(a)   it is a limited interest second charge credit union loan;

(b)   the borrower receives timely information on the main features, risks and costs of the contract at the pre-contractual stage; and

(c)   any advertising of the contract is fair, clear and not misleading.

If an agreement includes a declaration which:[3]

(a)   is made by the borrower, and

(b)   includes:

   (i)   a statement that the agreement is entered into by the borrower wholly or predominantly for the purposes of a business carried on, or intended to be carried on, by the borrower,

(ii) a statement that the borrower understands that the borrower will not have the benefit of the protection and remedies that would be available to the borrower under the Act if the agreement were a regulated mortgage contract under the Act, and

(iii) a statement that the borrower is aware that if the borrower is in any doubt as to the consequences of the agreement not being regulated by the Act, then the borrower should seek independent legal advice,

the agreement is to be presumed to have been entered into by the borrower wholly or predominantly for the purposes specified in sub-paragraph (b)(i) unless, when the agreement is entered into:[4]

(a) the lender (or, if there is more than one lender, any of the lenders), or

(b) any person who has acted on behalf of the lender (or, if there is more than one lender, any of the lenders) in connection with the entering into of the agreement,

knows or has reasonable cause to suspect that the agreement is not entered into by the borrower wholly or predominantly for the purposes of a business carried on, or intended to be carried on, by the borrower.

A borrower is to be regarded as entering into an agreement for the purposes of a business carried on, or intended to be carried on, by the borrower if the agreement is a buy-to-let mortgage contract and:[5]

(a)

(i) the borrower previously purchased, or is entering into the contract in order to finance the purchase by the borrower of, the land subject to the mortgage;

(ii) at the time of the purchase the borrower intended that the land would be occupied as a dwelling on the basis of a rental agreement and would not at any time be occupied as a dwelling by the borrower or by a related person, or where the borrower has not yet purchased the land the borrower has such an intention at the time of entering into the contract; and

(iii) where the borrower has purchased the land, since the time of the purchase the land has not at any time been occupied as a dwelling by the borrower or by a related person; or

(b) the borrower is the owner of land, other than the land subject to the mortgage, which is:

(i) occupied as a dwelling on the basis of a rental agreement and is not occupied as a dwelling by the borrower or by a related person; or

(ii) secured by a mortgage under a buy-to-let mortgage contract.

The reader's attention is also drawn to **Chapter 6**, especially at **6.3**.

1 RAO art 61A(1) to (5).
2 Ibid., art 61(2).
3 Ibid., art 61(3).
4 Ibid., art 61(4).
5 Ibid., art 61(5).

18.2.3.3 Application of the Mortgages and Home Finance Conduct of Business Sourcebook (MCOB)

The MCOB sourcebook of the FCA's Handbook applies to:

(a) every firm that carries on a home finance providing activity,[1] which comprises any of the following:

- entering into a regulated mortgage contract;

- entering into a regulated sale and rent back agreement;

- entering into a home purchase plan;

- entering into a home reversion plan; or

- agreeing to carry on a regulated activity in any of the first three categories above,

subject to the business loan and loans to high net worth mortgage customers application provisions; and

(b) every firm that communicates or approves a financial promotion of qualifying credit, of a home purchase plan, of a home reversion plan or of a regulated sale and rent back agreement.

The core MCOB provisions are contained in:

- MCOB 3A – Financial promotions and communications with customers

- MCOB 3B – MCD general information

- MCOB 4 – Advising and selling standards

- MCOB 4A – Additional MCD advising and selling standards

- MCOB 5 – Pre-application disclosure

- MCOB 5A – MCD Pre-application disclosure

- MCOB 6 – Disclosure at the offer stage

- MCOB 6A – MCD disclosure at the offer stage

- MCOB 7 – Disclosure at start of contract and after sale.

MCOB 5A Annex 1 sets out the European Standardised Information Sheet (ESIS), and Annex 2 sets out the Instructions to complete the ESIS. Both forms have their origin in Directive 2014/17/EU.

The FCA also regulates promotional literature and advertising for 'qualifying credit' as defined in paragraph 10 of Schedule 1 to the Financial Services and Markets Act 2000 (Financial Promotion) Order 2005,[2] namely credit, including a cash loan and any other form of financial accommodation, provided in accordance with an agreement under which (a) the lender is a person who enters into or administers regulated mortgage contracts; and (b) the obligation of the borrower to repay is secured, in whole or in part, on land. Advertising and promotions are subject to controls under MCOB.

Enforcement of a regulated mortgage continues to be subject to the need for a court order under the enforcement of the land mortgages provision of CCA 1974, s 126.

The reader is also referred to **Chapter 4**, especially at **4.8.1** and **4.8.2**.

1 MCOB 1.2.
2 SI 2005/1529.

18.2.4   The charge

A charge does not depend on delivery of possession or transfer of ownership of the property charged, but comprises an agreement between the creditor and the debtor by which a particular asset is appropriated to the satisfaction of the debt, so that the creditor is entitled to look to the asset and its proceeds to discharge the indebtedness in priority to the claims of unsecured creditors.

In the case of a receivable, a charge will take the form either of an assignment of rights or a negotiation, namely delivery, for example of a bill of exchange, negotiable certificate of deposit or other instrument, together with an endorsement. In order to vest a receivable in the assignee at law and to enable the assignee to sue solely in his own name, the assignment must be in writing, under the hand of the assignor, absolute and not by way of charge, relate to the whole of the debt and be notified to the debtor in writing.[1]

1 Law of Property Act 1925, s 136.

18.2.5   Mortgage on goods

18.2.5.1   The current law: bills of sale

Bills of sale are governed by the Bills of Sale Act 1878 and Bills of Sales Act (1878) Amendment Act 1882 (together called the Bills of Sale Acts 1878 and 1882). The former defines a bill of sale in lengthy terms but it is essentially a form of security over a personal chattel, whereby the owner and possessor of the chattel retains possession of the chattel but assigns to the holder of the bill of sale the property he has in the same.[1] This rather dated legislation is still utilised by creditor grantors, especially by way of logbook loans in the motor finance industry, largely in order to avoid the consequences of the one-third ('protected goods') and one-half ('total liability on termination') rules which apply to hire-purchase and conditional sale agreements under CCA 1974, ss 90 and 100 respectively. In contrast with the position under a regulated hire-purchase or conditional sale agreement, if a personal loan agreement is secured by a bill of sale the borrower is not entitled to terminate the agreement and pay only one half of the total sum payable under the agreement.

Bills of sale must take the form set out in the Bills of Sale Acts 1878 and 1882 and follow the form of attestation, affidavit and mode and place of registration specified. Registration serves as notice to the world of the chattel mortgage, which is essential in view of the fact that the mortgagor remains in possession of the mortgaged chattel.

A bill of sale creates practical difficulties where it secures a regulated agreement for the reason that the statutory form of the bill of sale only allows for repayment of the principal sum, together with interest and no other charges, by equal payments. Failure to comply with the requisite form renders the bill of sale void.

The execution of the bill of sale by the grantor must be attested by 'one or more credible witness or witnesses, not being a party or parties thereto'.[2] It has been held that a bill of sale is rendered void in circumstances where its execution by the grantor (the customer) is attested by the employee of the grantee of the bill (the creditor) who negotiates, agrees and signs on behalf of the grantee, the credit agreement between the customer and the grantee.[3] The bill of sale, together with an affidavit of due execution made by the attesting witness or anyone having knowledge of the facts deposed to, must be filed at the Central Office of the High Court of Justice.

In December 2009 the government published a consultation on its proposal to prohibit bills of sale for consumer lending. In response, the credit industry proposed a voluntary code of practice, which the government then approved, together with the introduction of a consumer information sheet on how bills of sale work.

Apart from meeting legislative requirements, with effect from 1 February 2011 lenders utilising bills of sale are required to comply with obligations in the code of practice applying to bills of sale, such as that of the Consumer Credit Trade Association, and which includes an obligation to provide customers with an industry standard 'Bill of Sale Borrower Information Sheet'.

The use of bills of sale has grown from 3,000 in 2001 to over 37,000 in 2015, largely by way of so-called 'logbook loans' in the form of security for motor vehicle finance.[4]

1 See also *Johnson v Diprose* [1893] 1 QB 512, CA; and generally on Bills of Sale, see *Halsbury's Laws of England* (5th edn), Vol. 50, para 1620ff.
2 Bills of Sale Act (1878) Amendment Act 1882, s 10.
3 *Log Book Loans Ltd v The Office of Fair Trading; Nine Regions Ltd (trading as Log Book Loans) v The Office of Fair Trading* [2010] UKFTT 643 (GRC).
4 The Law Commission, Responses to Consultation Paper No 225, February 2016.

18.2.5.2   Goods Mortgages Bill

A welcome proposal for change, which has reached the advanced stage of a draft Goods Mortgages Bill, is the result of the Law Commission's proposals for the repeal and replacement of the Bills of Sale Acts 1878 and 1882 (Consultation Paper No 225 of September 2015). The proposed changes relate to mortgages of tangible moveable property (subject to limited exclusions) and include the simplification of the goods mortgage documentation, the application of the one-third rule that currently applies to hire-purchase and conditional sale agreements, the mortgagor's right to terminate the goods mortgage and deliver the goods to the mortgagee, the mortgagee's right to take possession of, and sell, the mortgaged goods if certain conditions are met, and a duty on the mortgagor of the goods to disclose to a purchaser of the goods the existence of the goods mortgage.

The proposed 'Goods Mortgages Act' would apply to transactions where individuals, including unincorporated businesses, mortgage goods including vehicles in which they hold title, as security for loans or other non-monetary obligations, while retaining possession of them. It is proposed that registration would not be mandatory but that failure to register a goods mortgage would, in general, result in the purported mortgage being void. It is also proposed that innocent private purchasers in good faith and without notice of a registered charge will be protected in the same way as is currently the case with a private purchaser of a motor vehicle in good faith and without notice of a hire-purchase agreement or conditional sale agreement, under Part III of the Hire Purchase Act 1964. Registration alone would not serve as constructive notice of registration of a vehicle mortgage or mortgage of goods.

A register of goods mortgages is to be kept by the Secretary of State in accordance with regulations to be made under the proposed Act. The regulations may, but need not, provide for the register to be kept in the High Court.

A proposal for a simpler form of registration of a general assignment of book debts, in order to address, and prevent, avoidance of book debts under s 344 of the Insolvency Act 1986 for failure to register under the Bills of Sale Act 1878, appears to have been dropped.

The Law Commission's proposals constitute a significant advance towards achieving a more secure, transparent and efficient registration system for chattel mortgages.

18.2.6 Contractual set-off

Contractual set-off is not a true security interest, although it fulfils a security function. It gives no right over the creditor's asset (i.e. the debt), but merely an entitlement to set off one personal obligation against another and is therefore not registrable as a security interest.[1]

Contractual set-off is wider than equitable set-off. Contractual set-off is an arrangement for the mutual setting-off of personal obligations between parties. However, in the case of the debtor's insolvency, the Insolvency Act 1986 does not permit the creditor to obtain for himself a better position by virtue of the set-off arrangements than those to which he is entitled under the Insolvency Act.[2]

1 Goode, *Commercial Law* (5th edn, LexisNexis Butterworths, 2016), para 22.39, referring to *Re Charge Card Services Ltd (No 2)* [1987] Ch 150.
2 Goode, *Commercial Law* (5th edn, LexisNexis Butterworths, 2016); Insolvency Rules 1986, SI 1986/1925, r 4.90. See also *British Eagle International Airlines Ltd v Compagnie Nationale Air France* [1975] 2 All ER 390, [1975] 1 WLR 758, HL.

18.2.7 Charge over a credit balance

In *Re Charge Card Services Ltd (No 2)*,[1] Millett J (as he then was) held that it was conceptually impossible for a debtor (e.g. a bank with whom monies are deposited by its customer) to become its own creditor. It follows that a depositor of monies in a savings account cannot effectively charge such monies, or the credit balance, in favour of the bank. Legal opinion remained divided on the issue.[2] However, in *Re Bank of Credit and Commerce International SA (No 8)*,[3] Lord Hoffmann, delivering the decision of the House of Lords, held that a bank could take a charge over its customer's deposit. To quote Goode:[4] 'It is therefore likely that in future cases courts will uphold the charge-back as an effective security, and presumably the same is true of pledge-backs – for example, the pledge of a negotiable instrument or a negotiable security back to the issuer'.

1 [1987] Ch 150.
2 See Goode, *Commercial Law* (loc. cit.), para 22.42.
3 [1998] AC 214 (see the criticism of this case in Goode, 'Commercial Law in the Next Millennium', *The Hamlyn Lectures* (49th Series, Sweet & Maxwell)).
4 Loc. cit., para 22.42.

18.2.8   'Flawed asset' and negative pledge clauses

A 'flawed asset' is the description given to an agreement between a depositor of monies and the depositee by which the depositor agrees not to withdraw the monies on deposit except on fulfilment of certain conditions. This does not amount to a security interest but merely qualifies the bank's repayment obligation.[1]

In a negative pledge, the obligor undertakes in favour of the obligee not to grant any other security over the asset without the obligee's consent. A mortgagor's undertaking not to enter into any other mortgage without the first mortgagee's consent is an example of a negative pledge. Breach of such negative pledge gives rise to a personal liability and is therefore not a security interest.[2]

1 See Goode, *Commercial Law* (loc. cit.), para 22.43.
2 Ibid., para 22.46.

18.2.9   Pledge

A pledge is the actual or constructive delivery of possession of an asset to the creditor by way of security. Ownership remains with the pledgor but the pledgee enjoys a limited legal interest in the asset which includes the right to use the asset at his own risk so long as this will not impair the asset, to sell his interest as pledgee or assign it by way of gift, to deliver the asset to another for safekeeping, to sub-pledge the asset on the same conditions as he holds it and to sell the asset in the event of default in payment by the pledgor.

As equity considers as done that which ought to be done, an agreement for the pledge of specified property together with the passing of consideration, will result in the creation of a security interest.

18.2.10   Assignment

Security may be created by assignment. Thus, a life policy or other insurance policy may be assigned by way of security. This is done in one of two ways. First, it may be effected by written assignment together with notice of assignment to the insurer.[1] Alternatively, it may be effected by endorsement of the policy under the Policies of Assurance Act 1867 or by assignment in the form prescribed in the Schedule to that Act.

1 Law of Property Act 1925, s 136.

18.2.11 Contractual lien

A possessory lien may be created at common law or by contract. The essential distinction between a contractual lien and a pledge is that in a pledge possession is given for the purpose of security, whereas in the case of a lien, possession is given for some independent purpose, usually to secure payment or performance of some obligation, such as a repairer's lien to secure payment for his services. A lien entitles its holder to withhold possession of the asset as security for payment or performance and, in the absence of a term to the contrary, does not confer upon its holder the right of sale.

18.2.12 Pawn

A pawn is any article subject to a pledge.[1] The earlier Pawnbrokers Acts 1872–1960 were repealed by CCA 1974, with sections 114 to 122 dealing with pledges and pawns.

When a person takes an article by way of pawn under a regulated agreement, he must give a pawn-receipt in the form prescribed by the Consumer Credit (Pawn-Receipts) Regulations 1983 and, where the pawn-receipt forms part of a document embodying a regulated consumer credit agreement or modifying agreement, in accordance with the Consumer Credit (Agreements) Regulations 2010.[2]

A pawn is redeemable within a period of not less than six months from the time it is taken and until the expiry of such longer period as the parties may stipulate or the expiry of the agreement secured by the pledge if earlier. Even then, it remains redeemable until it is realised by the pawnee. Special provision is made for a statutory declaration or, in certain circumstances, a written statement to replace a pawn-receipt, where the latter has been lost or stolen.

In *Wilson v Robertsons (London) Ltd*,[3] Wilson appealed against a decision of the county court and claimed that the credit agreements were invalid owing to the inclusion of the document fee in the amount of credit and further, as some of the agreements had been backdated, that this resulted in a failure to provide the statutory redeemable period of six months. The appeal succeeded on both grounds. The court referred to s 116 of CCA 1974 which provides for a minimum redemption period of six months and to s 173 of the Act which stipulates that it is not possible to contract out of the statutory protections accorded by the Act. Reliance was placed on the House of Lords decision in *Wilson v Secretary of State for Trade and Industry/First County Trust Ltd (No 2)*,[4] where the House of Lords opined that CCA 1974 was, like the Moneylenders Act 1927 before it, designed to tackle a significant social problem. The activities of some money lenders had given the money lending business a bad reputation. Something had to be done to protect the borrower, who frequently, indeed normally, would be in a weak bargaining position. Protection of borrowers was the social policy behind the legislation. Part of that policy was to be achieved by setting stringent rules which had to be complied with by the lender if his money lending agreement was to be enforceable.

When a pawn has become realisable by the pawnee, the latter may sell it after giving the pawnor not less than 14 working days' notice of his intention. Within 20 working days after the sale takes place, the pawnee must give the pawnor the prescribed information in writing as to the sale, its proceeds and expenses.[5]

1   CCA 1974, s 189(1).
2   SI 1983/1566 and SI 2010/1014 respectively.
3   [2005] GCCR 5301, esp at 5305.
4   [2003] GCCR 4931, [2003] 4 All ER 97, HL.
5   CCA 1974, s 121(1) and (2).

18.2.13   Negotiable instruments

In order to prevent the circumvention of the CCA 1974's provisions, a creditor may not take a negotiable instrument other than a bank note or cheque, in discharge of any sum payable under a regulated agreement or by any surety in relation to the agreement.[1] Likewise, a creditor or owner may not take a negotiable instrument as security for the discharge of any such sum payable to him.[2] A contravention of these provisions will result in the agreement or security being enforceable only on an order of the court.[3]

1   CCA 1974, s 123(1).
2   Ibid., s 123(3).
3   Ibid., s 124(1) and (2).

18.2.14   Rights of surety during lifetime of security

A surety is entitled to require the creditor or owner to furnish him, within 12 working days, with a copy of the executed agreement, or any document referred to in it, a copy of the security instrument and a statement signed by, or on behalf of, the creditor or owner showing, inter alia, the amount outstanding to him under the secured agreement.[1]

Where a creditor or owner defaults with any of these obligations, the security is unenforceable whilst the default continues.[2]

A creditor or owner is also obliged to furnish the surety with a copy of any default notice, enforcement notice or notice of termination in non-default cases served on the debtor or hirer. If he fails to do so, the security is enforceable against the surety only on an order of the court.[3]

1   CCA 1974, ss 107 to 111 and Consumer Credit (Cancellation Notices and Copies of Documents)
    Regulations 1983, SI 1983/1557, as amended, reg 10.
2   Ibid., s 107(4).
3   Ibid., s 111.

18.3 PRECAUTIONS WHEN TAKING SECURITY

The long line of cases since *Barclays Bank plc v O'Brien*[1] highlights the precautions to be taken by a creditor or owner when put on enquiry as to the circumstances in which a person agrees to stand surety, especially where there is an emotional relationship or a relationship of trust between the surety and the debtor. The court stated that a creditor was put on enquiry when a wife offered to stand surety for her husband's debts by the combination of two factors. These are the fact that the transaction is, on its face, not to the financial advantage of the wife and, secondly, that there is a substantial risk that in such a transaction the husband had committed a legal or equitable wrong that entitles the wife to set aside the transaction. In other words, the dual risk of undue influence and misrepresentation. In the court's opinion, for a creditor to avoid being fixed with constructive notice, it should take steps to draw the wife's attention to the risks she was running by standing surety and advise her to take independent advice. A creditor would satisfy those requirements if it insisted that the wife attend a private meeting, in the absence of her husband, with a representative of the creditor at which she was told of the extent of her liability as surety, warned of the risks she was running and urged to take independent legal advice.

The above situation, involving persons having a special relationship and one standing as surety for the other, giving rise to constructive notice on the part of the bank lender, contrasts with the situation where the wife enters into a joint borrowing with her husband. If a wife is induced by the undue influence of her husband to charge the matrimonial home as security for a loan made to her husband and herself jointly, the lender would not be affected by the undue influence if the husband was not the lender's agent, the lender had no actual knowledge of any undue influence and there was no indication that the transaction was anything other than a normal loan to a husband and wife for their joint benefit.[2]

The leading decision on a creditor's duty in relation to a proposed charge by a wife of her interest in favour of the bank as security for the indebtedness of her husband or his business, is *Royal Bank of Scotland plc v Etridge (No 2)*.[3] This case involved consolidated appeals in eight cases, each arising out of a transaction in which a wife charged the interest in her home in favour of a bank, one of which was the Royal Bank of Scotland, under the undue influence of her husband. The House of Lords ruled that where it was proposed that a wife should charge her interest in her home in favour of a bank as security for the indebtedness of her husband or his business, specific clear and simple procedures should be followed, as minimum requirements, to protect the wife and reduce to an acceptable level the risk that she had been misled or coerced by her husband, so that the lender might make the advance in reasonable confidence that, if necessary, the security would be enforceable.

The decision is the climax to the long line of decisions commencing with *Barclays Bank plc v O'Brien* in 1993 and held, in summary:

(a) The bank is put on inquiry whenever a wife offers to stand surety for her husband's debts and vice versa and likewise in the case of unmarried couples where the bank is aware of the relationship. On the other hand, where the money is advanced to the parties jointly, the bank is not put on inquiry unless it is aware that the loan is not being made for joint purposes.

However, cases where the wife stands surety for the debts of a company, even when she is a shareholder in the company, are not to be equated with joint loans. The bank is put on inquiry in such cases even when the wife is a director or company secretary.

(b)   In *O'Brien* it was stated that a bank could reasonably be expected to take steps to bring home to the wife the risks she was running and to advise her to take independent advice. The House of Lords held that this was applicable to past transactions. For the future a bank was to insist that the wife attend a private meeting with its representative at which she would be told of the extent of her liability and of the risk she was running and she would be urged to take independent advice. Exceptionally, to be safe, the bank had to insist on the wife being separately advised.

(c)   As regards the content of the legal advice, it was not for a solicitor to veto the transaction by declining to confirm to the bank that he had explained the documents and the attendant risks to the wife. If he considered the transaction not in her best interests, he should give her reasoned advice to that effect. However, if it was clear that the wife was being grievously wronged, the solicitor should decline to act further. At the very least, the solicitor should:

(i)   explain the nature of the documents and the practical consequences they would have for her if she signed them;

(ii)   point out the seriousness of the risks involved. He should discuss the wife's financial means and her understanding of the value of the property concerned and whether she or her husband had assets from which repayment could be made if the business failed;

(iii)   make it clear that the wife has a choice and that the decision is hers alone;

(iv)   check whether the wife wishes to proceed and whether she is content for him to write to the bank confirming the various matters or whether, for instance, she would prefer him to negotiate on the terms with the bank.

(d)   The solicitor might also act for the husband or the bank provided that he was satisfied that it was in the wife's best interest and that it would not give rise to any conflict of duty or interest.

(e)   If the solicitor failed to act properly, the wife had a remedy in damages for negligence against him. The mere fact that the bank asked the solicitor, for its own purposes, to advise the wife did not make him the bank's agent in giving that advice. In the ordinary case deficient advice was a matter between the wife and the solicitor.

The bank was entitled to proceed on the assumption that the solicitor had done his job by advising the wife properly.

(f)   As regards obtaining the solicitor's confirmation:

(i)   the bank should check directly with her the name of the solicitors who wished to act for her and communicate directly with her for that purpose;

(ii)   as the bank was likely to have a better picture of the husband's financial affairs, it should provide the solicitor with the financial information he needs for that purpose. The bank would first need to obtain the consent of its customer to the disclosure of that confidential information and if it is not forthcoming, the transaction would not be able to proceed;

(iii)   if the bank believed that the wife had been misled, it must notify the wife's solicitors of the facts giving rise to the belief or suspicion; and

(iv)   the bank should in every case obtain from the wife's solicitor written confirmation to the effect that he had fully explained to her the nature of the documents and the practical implications they would have for her. She should be told that the purpose of the requirement was to prevent her being able to dispute that she was legally bound by the documents once she had signed them.

An illustrative case, where the court found that a wife had not been properly advised by an independent solicitor of the risks involved in giving up her house and investments to assist her husband, is *Padden v Bevan Ashford Solicitors*.[4]

1   [1994] 1 AC 180, [1999] GCCR 1693, HL.
2   *CIBC Mortgages plc v Pitt* [1994] 1 AC 200, [1999] GCCR 1711, HL.
3   [2001] UKHL 44, [2001] 4 All ER 449, [2001] GCCR 3105, HL.
4   [2011] EWCA Civ 1616, CA.

18.4   UNFAIR RELATIONSHIPS AND SECURITY

The provisions of sections 140A to 140C of CCA 1974, relating to unfair relationships between creditors and debtors, which are discussed in detail in **Chapter 24**, also apply to security taken for a credit agreement or for a credit agreement consolidated by the main credit agreement or for a linked transaction.[1] Thus, reference in those sections to an agreement related to a credit agreement includes a security provided in relation to a credit agreement or to security taken for an agreement which is subsequently consolidated by a further credit agreement or to a linked transaction in relation to either such agreement. As the provisions relating to unfair relationships apply to a credit agreement in any amount, and whether or not an exempt agreement, the unfair relationships provisions likewise apply to security taken for any such agreement.[2]

It would appear to be trite law that the relevant provisions are restricted to a credit agreement as defined in s 140C(1), namely between an individual, as the debtor, and any other person, as the creditor. 'Individual' excludes a registered company, as was confirmed in *Bank of Ireland (UK) plc v Dermot McLaughlin*.[3]

1   CCA 1974, s 140C(4)(c).
2   Ibid., s 140C(6).
3   [2014] GCCR 12167.

18.5   GENERAL OBSERVATIONS

The regulatory regime applying to security is somewhat ambivalent. So far as documentation is concerned, it veers from being highly regulated in the case of guarantees and pawns, to being restricted to prescribed pre-contract information in relation to mortgages, and no requirements in respect of assignments.

A surety is inextricably involved from the outset in the making of the agreement and in any subsequent proceedings which may be brought for its enforcement. In the case of an agreement secured on land, where the debtor is not the mortgagor, the surety as third party mortgagor will be furnished with advance copies of the credit agreement and the mortgage. Similarly, where a guarantee is provided in advance of a regulated agreement being entered into, the guarantor is involved with the transaction before it is made. In other situations, the surety only becomes involved at the time when the agreement is entered into by the debtor or hirer.

Care needs to be taken in relation to an all-monies mortgage or charge or a continuing guarantee to ensure that it does not unwittingly catch within its grasp agreements between creditor and debtor, or between owner and hirer, which were not intended to be secured by it.

Where security is provided by a third party and it is a condition of the making of the agreement, the provision of the security is not a term of the agreement and does not require to be embodied in the regulated agreement.

The provisions of CCA 1974 may not be evaded by the use of any security.[1]

1   CCA 1974, s 113.

Chapter 19

The total charge for credit and APR

19.1 RELEVANCE OF THE TOTAL CHARGE FOR CREDIT

The Crowther Committee considered that it was of primary importance for borrowers to be able to compare different costs of credit so as to be able to make an informed choice. The result was a set of regulations governing the constituents of charges and formulae for the calculation of the total charge for credit (TCC). With effect from April 2000 the various formulae for calculation of the TCC were replaced by a single equation.[1]

The TCC is expressed by reference to an annual percentage rate of charge (APR). This must be stated in credit agreements, in the pre-contract credit information documents (note that this is required in the SECCI, although not in the ECCI) and in promotions. The relevant Agreements Regulations provide permissible tolerances in the disclosure of the APR. Thus, the APR may be stated at a rate which exceeds the APR by not more than one, or falls short of the APR by not more than 0.1.[2]

The amount of credit and the total charge for credit are mutually exclusive, so that an item entering into the total charge for credit may not be treated as credit even though time is allowed for its payment.[3] This was also the core of the decision in *Wilson v First County Trust Ltd (No 1)*[4] where the court held that the inclusion of a document fee as part of the loan amount had the effect that the credit amount was misstated. The imposition of interest on an amount of charge does not convert the charge into an amount of credit, as was conceded by the Supreme Court in *Southern Pacific Securities v Walker.*[5]

Charges which by law are required to be excluded from the total charge for credit might properly be included in the amount of credit if they are financed.

Traditionally, with the exception of running-account credit agreements, the APR has become recognised as an objective yardstick of the cost of credit. Indeed, provided that the APR is applied in a uniform manner there is no need for the public to be aware of how it is composed. In Consultation Paper CP 98 issued by the FSA in June 2001 on the subject of future control of residential mortgages, it stated that the APR is a long-established tool for enabling consumer comparison of the total costs of alternative forms of credit and that, in response to an earlier consultation paper, most respondents supported the use of the APR and continuity of the approach in the consumer credit regime. The reasons given included the view that the APR is the best measure available, that it enjoys some consumer recognition, and that it allows comparison between secured and unsecured credit although it worked best as a comparator between like products.

1 Consumer Credit (Total Charge for Credit Regulations) 1980, SI 1980/51, reg 7 as amended by the Consumer Credit (Total Charge for Credit, Agreements and Advertisements) (Amendment) Order 1999, SI 1999/3177.
2 Consumer Credit (Agreements) Regulations 1983, SI 1983/1553, as amended, Sch 7, para 1A; Consumer Credit (Agreements) Regulations 2010, SI 2010/1014, reg 1(2), Sch 4, para 2.
3 CCA 1974, s 9(4).
4 [2001] QB 407, [2001] GCCR 2901, CA and see [2003] GCCR 4931, HL.
5 [2010] GCCR 10151, [2010] UKSC 32.

19.2   EVOLUTION OF THE TCC REGULATIONS

The Consumer Credit Directive 2008/48/EC[1] introduced a revised basis for calculating the total charge for credit and APR in respect of consumer credit agreements governed by it. This basis was extended by the UK government to apply to all consumer credit agreements except for those secured on land, unless the Consumer Credit (Disclosure of Information) Regulations 2010 applied to such agreements.[2] As a result, two different sets of TCC regulations, the original Consumer Credit (Total Charge for Credit) Regulations 1980 ('1980 TCC Regulations') and the new Consumer Credit (Total Charge for Credit) Regulations 2010 ('2010 TCC Regulations') applied to their respective agreements.

The 1980 TCC Regulations and the 2010 TCC Regulations were revoked by the Financial Services and Markets Act 2000 (Regulated Activities) (Amendment) (No 2) Order 2013[3] and replaced by Rules in CONC Appendix 1.1 (Total charge for credit rules for certain agreements secured on land) and Appendix 1.2 (Total charge for credit rules for other agreements).

1 Directive 2008/48/EC, Art 19 and Annex 1, as amended by Commission Directive 2011/90/EU.
2 Consumer Credit (Total Charge for Credit) Regulations 1980, SI 1980/51, reg 1A and Consumer Credit (Total Charge for Credit) Regulations 2010, SI 2010/1011, reg 3, as amended by the Consumer Credit (Total Charge for Credit) (Amendment) Regulations 2012, SI 2012/1745, in force from 1 January 2013.
3 SI 2013/1881, Pt 6.

19.3   THE APR

19.3.1   Calculation of the total charge for credit ('TCC') and the annual percentage rate of charge ('APR')

There are two sets of TCC rules: CONC App 1.1 applies to agreements secured on land (except to the extent that the Consumer Credit (Disclosure of Information) Regulations 2010 apply to such agreements); and CONC App1.2 applies to other agreements. The APR for agreements secured on land is calculated in accordance with an equation which takes account of the factors mentioned in CONC App 1.1.8R to CONC App 1.1.10R.[1] The APR for other agreements is calculated in accordance with the equation in CONC App 1.2.6R, described as equating, on an annual basis, the total present value of drawdowns with the total present value of repayments and payments of charges. Although not defined as such, a drawdown means a drawdown of the amount of credit. The equation has its origin in Council Directive 2008/48/EC.

CONC App 1.1 provides for rounding to one decimal place. Where the figure at the second place is greater than or equal to 5, the figure at the first decimal place must be increased by one and the decimal places following the first decimal place are to be disregarded. Where the figure at the second decimal place is less than 5, that decimal place and any following it, is to be disregarded.[2] CONC App1.2 admits of more than one decimal place (i.e. described as 'expressed with an accuracy of at least one decimal place') except where the figure in the second decimal place is greater than or equal to 5, when the figure at the first decimal place is to be increased by one.[3]

Both CONC App 1.1 and CONC App 1.2 contain assumptions for the purposes of the calculations.

1 CONC App 1.1.7R.
2 CONC App 1.1.8R.
3 CONC App 1.2.6R (3)(f).

19.3.2 Statement of the APR

The Agreements Regulations permit limited deviations from the APR. They contain provisions relating to permissible tolerances in the disclosure of the APR, deeming there to be compliance with the requirements to show the APR if the APR is stated at a rate which exceeds the APR by not more than one, or a rate which falls short of the APR by not more than 0.1, or a rate determined as set out in the next paragraph.[1]

Where all repayments but one are equal and that one repayment does not differ from the others by more whole pence than there are repayments of credit, the APR may be calculated as if that one repayment were equal to the other repayments. Where three or more repayments are to be made at equal intervals and the interval between the relevant date (i.e. the date of the agreement) and the first repayment is greater than that between the repayments, the APR may be calculated as if the interval between the relevant date and the first repayment were shortened so as to be equal to the intervals between the repayments.[2]

Schedule 7 to the Agreements Regulations 1983[3] and Schedule 4 to the Agreements Regulations 2010[4] contain assumptions to be applied in the calculation and disclosure of the total charge for credit and APR in running-account credit agreements. The former includes a credit limit of not less than £1,500 and the latter a minimum credit limit of £1,200. The former will now rarely apply as most running-account credit agreements are not secured on land.

Where the stated interest rate did not produce the stated APR, it was held in *Sternlight v Barclays Bank plc*[5] that the determining factor as to whether the interest rate was properly stated for the purposes of the prescribed terms in Sch 6 to the Consumer Credit (Agreements) Regulations 1983 is the interest rate and not the APR. In other words, provided the interest rate is correctly stated, misstatement of the APR does not render the agreement defective by not containing the prescribed term of the rate of interest.

CONC and MCOB provide for a statement of the 'representative APR' and the 'APRC' respectively. It is confusing and unhelpful for there to be two apparently disparate yardsticks and acronyms.

The 'representative APR' is the APR at or below which the firm communicating or approving the financial promotion reasonably expects, at the date on which the promotion is communicated or approved, that credit would be provided under at least 51% of the credit agreements which will be entered into as a result of the promotion.[6]

The 'APRC' is defined in the Glossary to the FCA Handbook as the total cost of the credit to the consumer, expressed as an annual percentage of the total amount of credit, where applicable, including the costs referred to in MCOB 10A.1.2R, and equates, on an annual basis, to the present value of all future or existing commitments (drawdowns, repayments and charges) agreed, or which would be agreed, if the MCD[7] credit agreement is entered into, by the MCD creditor and the consumer.[8] There is no equivalent provision to the 51% above that relates to credit agreements not secured on land.

1 Schedule 1, para 2 and Sch 7, para 1, respectively.
2 SI 1983/1553, Sch 7.
3 SI 1983/1553, but see the assumption about the amount of credit at **19.3.5** below.
4 SI 2010/1014, but see the assumption about the amount of credit at **19.3.5** below.
5 [2010] GCCR 10201, [2010] EWHC 1865 (QB).
6 FCA Handbook, Glossary.
7 Mortgage Credit Directive, Directive 2014/17/EU on credit agreements for consumers relating to residential immovable property.
8 Ibid., based on Arts 4(15) and 17(2) of the Mortgage Credit Directive 2014/17/EU.

19.3.3 Charges included in the total charge for credit

It should be mentioned at the outset that **19.3.3** to **19.3.5** are based on CONC App 1.1 which is entitled 'Total charge for credit rules for certain agreements secured on land'. However, it appears that CONC App 1.1.5R and 1.1.6R are equally applicable to credit agreements which are not secured on land and the text proceeds on this assumption.

The total charge for credit comprises three elements of charge.[1] They are first, the total of the interest on the credit which may be provided under the agreement; second, other charges at any time payable under the transaction by or on behalf of a debtor or relative of his whether to the creditor or any other person(e.g. legal fees, documentation charge, credit brokerage charges); and third, any premium under a contract of insurance, payable under the transaction by the debtor or a relative of his, where the making or maintenance of the contract of insurance is required by the creditor:

(a)   as a condition of making the agreement; and

(b)   for the sole purpose of ensuring complete or partial repayment of the credit, and complete or partial payment to the creditor of those charges included in the total charge for credit as are payable under the transaction in the event of the death, invalidity, illness or unemployment of the debtor. The various charges are included notwithstanding that the whole or part of the charge may be repayable at any time or that the consideration may include matters not within the transaction or subsisting at a time not within the duration of the agreement.

'Transaction', in respect of which charges are included, is widely defined as a credit agreement, any transaction which is a linked transaction, any contract for the provision of security relating to the credit agreement, any credit broking contract relating to the credit agreement, and any other contract to which the borrower or his relative is a party and which the lender requires to be made or maintained as a condition of the making of the credit agreement.[2]

There is some confusion in CCA 1974 as to whether an option to purchase fee in a hire-purchase agreement is part of the total charge for credit. Notwithstanding the wording of s 9(3), read with the definition of 'total price' in s 189(1), it is submitted that it is part of the total charge for credit and not part of the credit amount.[3]

1 CONC App 1.1.5R.
2 FCA Handbook, Glossary.
3 *Goode: Consumer Credit Law and Practice* (LexisNexis Butterworths), IC [29.149] and *Humberclyde Finance Ltd v Thompson* [1999] ECCR 2141, CA.

19.3.4 Charges not included in the total charge for credit

Certain charges are excluded from the total charge for credit with the result that, even though they are payable under the agreement, they are not included in the total charge for credit in relation to a credit agreement.[1] They are the following:

'(a) any charge payable under the transaction to the lender upon failure by the borrower or a relative of his to do or to refrain from doing anything which he is required to do or to refrain from doing, as the case may be;

(b) any charge:

(i) which is payable by the lender to any person upon failure by the borrower or a relative of his to do or to refrain from doing anything which he is required under the transaction to do or to refrain from doing, as the case may be, and

(ii) which the lender may under the transaction require the borrower or a relative of his to pay to him or to another person on his behalf;

(c) any charge relating to a credit agreement which is a credit agreement to finance a transaction of a description referred to in (2)(a) or (b) of the definition of restricted-use credit agreement, being a charge which would be payable if the transaction were for cash;

(d) any charge (other than a fee or commission charged by a credit broker) not within (c) above:

(i) of a description which relates to services or benefits incidental to the credit agreement and also to other services or benefits which may be supplied to the borrower, and

(ii) which is payable pursuant to an obligation incurred by the borrower under arrangements effected before he applies to enter into the credit agreement, not being arrangements under which the borrower is bound to enter into any credit agreement;

(e) subject to (2) below, any charge under arrangements for the care, maintenance or protection of any land or goods;

(f) charges for money transmission services relating to an arrangement for a current account, being charges which vary with the use made by the borrower of the arrangement;

(g) any charge for a guarantee other than a guarantee:

(i) which is required by the lender as a condition of making the credit agreement, and

(ii) the purpose of which is to ensure complete or partial repayment of the credit, and complete or partial payment to the lender of such of those charges included in the total charge for credit as are payable to him under the transaction, in the event of the death, invalidity, illness or unemployment of the borrower;

(h) charges for the transfer of funds (other than charges within (f) above) and charges for keeping an account intended to receive payments towards the repayment of the credit and the payment of interest and other charges, except where the borrower does not have reasonable freedom of choice in the matter and where such charges are abnormally high; but this sub-paragraph does not exclude from the total charge for credit charges for collection of the payments to which it refers, whether such payments are made in cash or otherwise;

(i) a premium under a contract of insurance other than a contract of insurance referred to in CONC App 1.1.5R (c).'

1 CONC App 1.1.6R.

19.3.5 Assumptions for calculation of the total charge for credit for agreements secured on land[1]

The following assumptions apply to the calculation of the total charge for credit:[2]

(a) Where one or more other provisions of CONC App 1.1.11R to CONC App 1.1.18R would fall to be applied, CONC App 1.1.12R shall be applied first.

(b) Where the amount of the credit to be provided under the credit agreement cannot be ascertained at the date of the making of the credit agreement,

(i) in the case of a credit agreement for running-account credit under which there is a credit limit, that amount shall be taken to be such credit limit; and

(ii) in any other case, that amount shall be taken to be £100. (CONC App 1.1.12R)

It is to be noted that this assumption conflicts with that referred to at **19.3.2** above.

(c)   Where the period for which credit is to be provided is not ascertainable at the date of the making of the credit agreement, it shall be assumed that credit is provided for one year beginning with the relevant date. (CONC App 1.1.13R)

(d)   Subject to CONC App 1.1.15R referred to below, where the rate or amount of any item included in the total charge for credit or the amount of any repayment of credit under a transaction falls to be ascertained thereunder by reference to the level of any index or other factor in accordance with any formula specified therein, the rate or amount, as the case may be, shall be taken to be the rate or amount so ascertained, the formula being applied as if the level of such index or other factor subsisting at the date of the making of the credit agreement were that subsisting at the date by reference to which the formula is to be applied. (CONC App 1.1.14R)

CONC App 1.1.15R applies to variable rates of interest, as follows:

(1)   This rule applies to any land-related agreement which provides for the possibility of any variation of the rate of interest if it is to be assumed, by virtue of CONC App 1.1.3R (1)(e), that the variation will take place but the amount of the variation cannot be ascertained at the date of the making of the credit agreement.

(2)   'Initial standard variable rate' means:

(a)   the standard variable rate of interest which would be applied by the lender to the credit agreement on the date of the making of the credit agreement if the credit agreement provided for interest to be paid at the lender's standard variable rate with effect from that date, or

(b)   if there is no such rate, the standard variable rate of interest applied by the lender on the date of the making of the credit agreement in question to other land-related agreements or, where there is more than one such rate, the highest such rate,

taking no account (for the avoidance of doubt) of any discount or other reduction to which the borrower would or might be entitled; and

'varied rate' means any rate of interest charged when a variation of the rate of interest is to be assumed to take place by virtue of CONC App 1.1.3R (1)(e).

(3)   Where a land-related agreement provides a formula for calculating a varied rate by reference to a standard variable rate of interest applied by the lender, or any other fluctuating rate of interest, but does not enable the varied rate to be ascertained at the date of the making of the credit agreement, because it is not known on that date what the standard variable rate will be or (as the case may be) at what level the fluctuating rate will be fixed when the varied rate falls to be calculated, it shall be assumed that that rate or level will be the same as the initial standard variable rate.

(4)   Where a land-related agreement provides for the possibility of any variation in the rate of interest (other than a variation referred to in (3) above) which it is to be assumed, by virtue of CONC App 1.1.3R (1)(e) will take place but does not enable the amount of that variation to be ascertained at the date of the making of the credit agreement, it shall be assumed that the varied rate will be the same as the initial standard variable rate.

(e)   Where:

(i)   the period for which the credit or any part thereof is to be or may be provided cannot be ascertained at the date of the making of the credit agreement; and

(ii)   the rate or amount of any item included in the total charge for credit will change at a time provided in the transaction within one year beginning with the relevant date,

the rate or amount shall be taken to be the highest rate or amount at any time obtaining under the transaction in that year. (CONC App 1.1.16R)

(f)   Where the earliest date on which credit is to be provided cannot be ascertained at the date of the making of the credit agreement, it shall be assumed that credit is provided on that date. (CONC App 1.1.17R)

(g)   In the case of any transaction it shall be assumed:

(i)   that a charge payable at a time which cannot be ascertained at the date of the making of the credit agreement shall be payable on the relevant date or, where it may reasonably be expected that a borrower will not make payment on that date, on the earliest date at which it may reasonably be expected that he will make payment; or

(ii)   where more than one payment of a charge of the same description falls to be made at times which cannot be ascertained at the date of the making of the credit agreement, that the first such payment will be payable on the relevant date (or, where it may reasonably be expected that a borrower will not make payment on that date, at the earliest date on which it may reasonably be expected that he will make payment), that the last such payment will be payable at the end of the period for which credit is provided and that all other such payments (if any) will be payable at equal intervals between such times,

as the case may require. (CONC App 1.1.18R)

1   FCA Handbook: CONC App 1.1.2, except to the extent that the Consumer Credit (Disclosure of Information) Regulations 2010 apply to such agreements. This appears to refer specifically to the assumptions in Schedule 2 to the Regulations.
2   CONC App 1.1.11R to App 1.1.18R.

19.3.6   Assumptions for calculation of the total charge for credit for agreements not secured on land[1]

For the purposes of calculating the total charge for credit and the annual percentage rate of charge in these agreements:

(a)   it shall be assumed that the regulated credit agreement is to remain valid for the period agreed and that the lender and the borrower will fulfil their obligations under the terms and by the dates specified in that agreement;

(b)   in the case of a regulated credit agreement allowing variations in:

   (i)   the rate of interest, or

   (ii)   where applicable, charges contained in the annual percentage rate of charge,

   where these cannot be quantified at the time of calculation, it shall be assumed that they will remain at the initial level and will be applicable for the duration of the agreement;

(c)   where not all rates of interest are determined in the regulated credit agreement, a rate of interest shall, where necessary, be assumed to be fixed only for the partial periods for which the rate of interest is determined exclusively by a fixed specific percentage agreed when the agreement is made;

(d)   where different rates of interest and charges are to be offered for limited periods or amounts during the regulated credit agreement, the rate of interest and the charge shall, where necessary, be assumed to be at the highest level for the duration of the agreement;

(e)   where there is a fixed rate of interest agreed in relation to an initial period under a regulated credit agreement, at the end of which a new rate of interest is determined and subsequently periodically adjusted according to an agreed indicator, it shall, where necessary, be assumed that, at the end of the period of the fixed rate of interest, the rate of interest is the same as at the time of making the calculation, based on the value of the agreed indicator at that time;

(f)   where the regulated credit agreement gives the borrower freedom of drawdown, the total amount of credit shall, where necessary, be assumed to be drawn down immediately and in full;

(fa) where the regulated credit agreement imposes, amongst the different ways of drawdown, a limitation with regard to the amount of credit and period of time, the amount of credit shall, where necessary, be assumed to be the maximum amount provided for in the agreement and to be drawn down on the earliest date provided for in the agreement;

(g)   where the regulated credit agreement provides different ways of drawdown with different charges or rates of interest, the total amount of credit shall, where necessary, be assumed to be drawn down at the highest charge and rate of interest applied to the most common drawdown mechanism for the credit product to which the agreement relates;

(h)   for the purposes of (g), the most common drawdown mechanism for a particular credit product shall be assessed on the basis of the volume of transactions for that product in the preceding 12 months, or expected volumes in the case of a new credit product;

(i)   in the case of an overdraft facility, the total amount of credit shall, where necessary, be assumed to be drawn down in full and for the entire duration of the regulated credit agreement;

(j)   for the purposes of (i), if the duration of the overdraft facility is not known, it shall, where necessary, be assumed that the duration of the facility is three months;

(k)   in the case of an open-end regulated credit agreement, other than an overdraft facility, it shall, where necessary, be assumed that the credit is provided for a period of one year starting from the date of the initial drawdown, and that the final payment made by the borrower clears the balance of capital, interest and other charges, if any;

(l)   for the purposes of (k):

    (i)   the capital is repaid by the borrower in equal monthly payments, commencing one month after the date of initial drawdown;

    (ii)   in cases where the capital must be repaid in full, in a single payment, within or after each payment period, successive drawdowns and repayments of the entire capital by the borrower shall, where necessary, be assumed to occur over the period of one year;

    (iii)   interest and other charges shall be applied in accordance with those drawdowns and repayments of capital and as provided for in the regulated credit agreement;

(m)   in the case of a regulated credit agreement, other than an overdraft facility, or an open-end regulated credit agreement:

    (i)   where the date or amount of a repayment of capital to be made by the borrower cannot be ascertained, it shall, where necessary, be assumed that the repayment is made at the earliest date provided for under the regulated credit agreement and is for the lowest amount for which the regulated credit agreement provides;

    (ii)   where it is not known on which date the regulated credit agreement is made, the date of the initial drawdown shall, where necessary, be assumed to be the date which results in the shortest interval between that date and the date of the first payment to be made by the borrower;

(n)   where the date or amount of a payment to be made by the borrower cannot be ascertained on the basis of the regulated credit agreement or the assumptions set out in (i) to (m), it shall, where necessary, be assumed that the payment is made in accordance with the dates and conditions required by the lender and, when these are unknown:

    (i)   interest charges are paid together with repayments of capital;

    (ii)   a non-interest charge expressed as a single sum is paid on the date of the making of the regulated credit agreement;

(iii) non-interest charges expressed as several payments are paid at regular intervals, commencing with the date of the first repayment of capital, and if the amount of such payments is not known they shall, where necessary, be assumed to be equal amounts;

(iv) the final payment clears the balance of capital, interest and other charges, if any;

(o) in the case of an agreement for running-account credit, where the credit limit applicable to the credit is not yet known, that credit limit shall, where necessary, be assumed to be £1,200.

1 CONC App 1.2.5R.

19.4   MCOB: TCC, APR AND APRC

To add further to the confusion, MCOB 10 has its own rules for calculating the total charge for credit and APR, and MCOB 10A has its own rules for calculating the APRC. (These are not set out in this text.)

MCOB applies to every firm that:

(a) carries on a home finance activity (subject to the business loan and loans to high net worth mortgage customers application provisions); or

(b) communicates or approves a financial promotion of qualifying credit, of a home purchase plan, of a home reversion plan or of a regulated sale and rent back agreement.

19.5   REFLECTIONS ON THE TCC AND THE APR

It will be apparent from various recent Directives on the subject of the total charge for credit and APR, namely Directive 87/102/EEC, Directive 2008/48/EC and Directive 2011/90/EU, that the composition of the APR is not a mathematical or universal certainty, but subject to change as envisaged and imposed by the EU legislator and by the FCA to the extent that it enjoys freedom in this regard. However, as a result of the composition of the APR being compulsory and uniform across the EU Member States, some degree of uniformity and comparability is achieved.

It is noteworthy that the Directives, like UK legislation that preceded them, do not regulate the method used for calculating interest charges. Thus, even within the UK, different creditors remain free to calculate the interest charge, which of course is a constituent of the APR, in their own way. This has always been, and will doubtless remain, an issue of contention with the consumer lobby.

Ultimately the law, and now the relevant FCA Rules, must be judged by their simplicity and workability. In this regard they leave much to be desired, as is evident from the observations made in the text above.

Chapter 20

Advertising and promoting credit and hire facilities and ancillary credit business

20.1 BACKGROUND

Advertising is the showcase or introduction to a credit or hire agreement. Originally, the Consumer Credit Act 1974 ('CCA 1974'), together with the Advertisements Regulations under that Act, controlled the advertising of consumer credit and consumer hire, but the pendulum has now swung to rules made by the Financial Conduct Authority in the FCA Handbook. The transformation has been from complex and prescriptive advertisements regulations to broader purposive rules relating to promotions. Notwithstanding the repeal of sections 43 to 47 of CCA 1974 dealing with advertising, the definition of 'advertisement' in section 189(1) has been retained but is not reflected in corresponding relevant legislation.

CCA 1974 defines an 'advertisement' as including every form of advertising, whether in a publication, by television or radio, by display of notices, signs, labels, showcards or goods, by distribution of samples, circulars, catalogues, price lists or other material, by exhibition of pictures, models or films or in any other way, and references to the publishing of advertisements shall be construed accordingly.[1]

As will be observed, an advertisement is defined by reference to form rather than substance. It does mean that any form of representation is capable of being construed as an advertisement.

Whilst 'advertise' is not defined in the Act, it clearly refers to making something known to the public or drawing something to the attention of members of the public. The Concise Oxford Dictionary defines 'advertise' as 'make (thing) generally or publicly known'.

The question arises as to what is meant by 'the public'. In *R v Delmayne*[2] the Court of Appeal held that a circular sent to a members of a mutual benefit society on his joining the society, inviting him to deposit money with the society, and which was printed as a circular inviting any person to whom it was addressed, was issued to the public for the purpose of s 2(1) of the Protection of Depositors Act 1963. The court could not accept that once Mr Lake (the recipient of the circular) joined the society he ceased to be a member of the public, nor that when he received this document he received it purely in his capacity as a member of the society and not as a member of the public; he obviously received it as a member of the public. Thus, a section of the public, namely members of a mutual benefit society, was construed as constituting 'the public'.

The question whether existing customers can be categorised as members of the public as, for example, where they receive a circular or messages *en masse,* was considered by the First-tier Tribunal in *Log Book Loans Ltd v The Office of Fair Trading* and *Nine Regions Ltd (t/a Log Book Loans) v The Office of Fair Trading.*[3] The Tribunal held that the sending of text messages to selected existing customers whose payment history indicated that they might qualify for a top-up loan, constituted the publication of a credit advertisement. It opined that there was nothing in the legislation (relating to publishing an advertisement) which justified a line being drawn between new and existing customers or between those with no track record and those with a previous track record.

As will be seen below, control and regulation are extended to financial promotions and to communications, which are much wider concepts than advertisements.

1   CCA 1974, s 189(1).
2   [1969] 2 All ER 980.
3   [2010] GCCR 10501; CCA/2009/0010 & CCA/2009/0011.

20.2   THE REGULATORY LANDSCAPE

Regulation of the advertising and promotion of consumer credit, consumer hire and ancillary credit businesses is governed by a combination of the following:

(1)   Consumer Credit Act 1974;

(2)   Financial Services and Markets Act 2000;

(3)   Financial Services and Markets Act 2000 (Financial Promotion) Order 2005;[1] and

(4)   FCA Handbook, especially CONC and MCOB.

Regulation of advertisements and promotions of regulated mortgage contracts, regulated home reversion plans, regulated home purchase plans and regulated sale and rent back agreements falls under (2) to (4) above.

The Consumer Protection from Unfair Trading Regulations 2008[2] may also be of relevance.

1   SI 2005/1529.
2   SI 2008/1277.

20.3   CONSUMER CREDIT ACT 1974

Originally, Part IV of CCA 1974, sections 43 to 54 (relating to advertising credit and hire facilities) and sections 151 to 156 (relating to advertising ancillary credit business), together with the Advertisements Regulations made under the Act, controlled all such advertising. Only vestiges of the Act remain, in the form of sections 48 and 49 (prohibition of canvassing debtor-creditor agreements off trade premises), section 50 (prohibition of circulars to minors), sections 153 and 154 (prohibition of canvassing off trade premises agreements for ancillary credit business) and section 155 (enabling recovery of credit brokerage fees). All Advertisements Regulations have been repealed.

20.4   FINANCIAL SERVICES AND MARKETS ACT 2000

Section 21 of FSMA is the principal provision that governs financial promotion. 'Financial promotion' is described in the Glossary of the FCA Handbook as:

(1)   an invitation or inducement to engage in investment activity that is communicated in the course of business;

(2)   in addition to (1) above (in relation to COBS 3.2.1R (3), COBS 4.3.1R, COBS 4.5.8R and COBS 4.7.1), a marketing communication within the meaning of MiFID made by a firm in connection with its MiFID or equivalent third country business;

(3)   in addition to (1) (in MCOB 3A), any advertising or marketing communications within the meaning of Article 10 or 11 of the MCD made by an MCD firm in relation to an MCD credit agreement.

An 'invitation or inducement to engage in investment activity' has its origin in section 21(1) of FSMA. Section 21(1) precludes anyone, in the course of business, from communicating an invitation or inducement to engage in investment activity unless that person is an authorised person or the content of the communication is approved by an authorised person. Contravention of this prohibition is a criminal offence.[1]

In the case of a communication originating outside the United Kingdom, the prohibition applies only if the communication is capable of having an effect in the United Kingdom.

The Treasury may by Order specify circumstances in which a person is to be regarded as acting in the course of business or not acting in the course of business. The Treasury may by order specify circumstances (which may include compliance with financial promotion rules) in which the above does not apply.

'Engaging in investment activity' means:

(a)   entering or offering to enter into an agreement the making or performance of which by either party constitutes a controlled activity; or

(b)   exercising any rights conferred by a controlled investment to acquire, dispose of, underwrite or convert a controlled investment.[2]

An activity is a controlled activity if:

(a)   it is an activity of a specified kind or one which falls within a specified class of activity; and

(b)   it relates to an investment of a specified kind, or to one which falls within a specified class of investment.[3]

1   FSMA, ss 19 and 23.
2   Ibid., s 21(8).
3   Ibid., s 21(9).

20.5   FINANCIAL SERVICES AND MARKETS ACT 2000 (FINANCIAL PROMOTION) ORDER 2005[1] ('FINANCIAL PROMOTION ORDER')

This Order specifies the kinds of activities and investments which are controlled activities and investments for the purposes of s 21 of FSMA.

'Controlled activities'

A controlled activity is an activity which falls within any of paragraphs 1 to 11, Part 1, of Schedule 1 to the Financial Services and Markets Act 2000 (Financial Promotion) Order 2005.[2] It includes: debt adjusting; debt counselling; providing, arranging, advising on qualifying credit; providing, advising on relevant consumer credit; providing consumer hire; providing, arranging, advising on a regulated home reversion plan; providing, advising on a regulated home purchase plan; providing, arranging, advising on a regulated sale and rent back agreement; and agreeing to carry on specified kinds of activity.

'Controlled investments'

An investment is a controlled investment if it is an investment of a specified kind or one which falls within a specified class of investment. It is an investment which falls within any of paragraphs 12 to 27, Part 2, of Schedule 1 to the above Order.[3]

There are various exemptions, including promotions of credit for business purposes,[4] promotions to certified high net worth individuals,[5] promotions to self-certified sophisticated investors,[6] and credit agreements offered to employees by employers.[7]

1   SI 2005/1529.
2   Schedule 1, Pt 1.
3   See also FSMA, s 21(10).
4   SI 2005/1529, art 46A.
5   Ibid., art 48 and Sch 5.
6   Ibid., art 50A and Sch 5.
7   Ibid., art 72F.

20.6   THE FCA HANDBOOK

20.6.1   The primary sources

The primary sources, for present purposes, are PERG, CONC and MCOB.

PERG 8 contains advice as to whether communications are subject to, or comply with, FSMA and whether financial promotions are regulated activities.

It is largely an overview of the Financial Promotion Order. PERG 8.17A sets out guidance about financial promotions relating to consumer credit (other than a regulated mortgage contract or a regulated home purchase plan) and consumer hire.

CONC 3 is dedicated to financial promotions and communications of consumer credit with customers. CONC 3.1 deals with communications with customers, CONC 3.2 with financial promotions, CONC 3.3 addresses the requirement that a communication or a financial promotion must be clear, fair and not misleading, CONC 3.5 covers financial promotions about credit agreements not secured on land, and CONC 3.6 deals with those secured on land. Financial promotions and communications regarding credit brokers are covered by CONC 3.7, those regarding P2P agreements by CONC 3.7A, those concerning lenders by CONC 3.8, and debt counsellors and debt adjusters by CONC 3.9. PERG 8.17AG has guidance about financial promotions concerning relevant consumer credit.

MCOB 3A applies to: financial promotions and communications with customers in relation to a home finance transaction; or communicating, or approving, a financial promotion of qualifying credit, a home reversion plan, a home purchase plan or a regulated sale and rent back agreement. A financial promotion relates to qualifying credit if it communicates information to a customer in relation to a home finance transaction or communicates or approves a financial promotion of qualifying credit, a home reversion plan, a home purchase plan or a regulated sale and rent back agreement. PERG 8.17.1G to PERG 8.17.16G contains guidance about financial promotion of agreements for qualifying credit.

In passing, the description of qualifying credit in MCOB and PERG appears to be much wider and more embracing that its definition in the Financial Promotion Order, Schedule 1, Part 1, paragraph 10(2), which refers to article 61 of the Regulated Activities Order.

A financial promotion is not subject to CONC 3 to the extent that it relates to qualifying credit.

Where a firm makes a communication which consists of a financial promotion of qualifying credit and also a financial promotion of a different form of lending that is not qualifying credit (for example, an unsecured personal loan), the content of the latter will need to comply with CONC 3.

PERG 8.17.21G contains the following table, which must be read together with PERG 8.17.20:

	Subject of promotion	MCOB 3A may apply	CONC 3 may apply
(1)	regulated mortgage contracts	Yes	No
(2)	credit agreements secured on land where the lender also enters into regulated mortgage contracts as lender	Yes	No
(3)	credit agreements not secured on land, whether or not the lender also enters into regulated mortgage contracts as lender	No	Yes
(4)	credit agreements secured on land where the lender does not enter into regulated mortgage contracts as lender	No	Yes

	Subject of promotion	MCOB 3A may apply	CONC 3 may apply
(5)	credit agreements partly secured on land that include some unsecured credit and where the lender enters into regulated mortgage contracts as lender	Yes	No
(6)	credit agreements with features as in (1), (2) or (5) promoted in combination with other unsecured credit agreements	Yes	Yes

20.6.2 Meanings of expressions

(a) The Glossary defines 'financial promotion' as:

(1) an invitation or inducement to engage in investment activity that is communicated in the course of business; [Note: section 21 of FSMA (Restrictions on financial promotion)]

(2) (in relation to COBS 3.2.1R (3), COBS 4.3.1R, COBS 4.5.8R and COBS 4.7.1R) (in addition to (1)) a marketing communication within the meaning of MiFID made by a firm in connection with its MiFID or equivalent third country business;

(3) (in MCOB 3A), in addition to (1), any advertising or marketing communications within the meaning of article 10 or 11 of the MCD made by an MCD firm in relation to an MCD credit agreement. [Note: articles 10 and 11 of the MCD]

(b) 'Communicate' is defined in the Glossary as (in relation to a financial promotion) to communicate in any way, including causing a communication to be made or directed.

[Note: section 21(13) of FSMA (Restrictions on financial promotion) and article 6(d) of the Financial Promotion Order (Interpretation: communications)]

FCA Guidance in PERG expands on the meaning of 'communicate', as follows:[1]

The expression 'communicate' is extended under section 21(13) of the Act [FSMA] and includes causing a communication to be made. This means that a person who causes the communication of a financial promotion by another person is also subject to the restriction in section 21. Article 6(d) of the Financial Promotion Order also states that the word 'communicate' has the same meaning when used in exemptions in the Order. Article 6(a) also states that the word 'communication' has the same meaning as 'financial promotion'. It appears to the FCA that a person is communicating where he gives material to the recipient or where, in certain circumstances (see PERG 8.6.5G), he is responsible for transmitting the material on behalf of another person. As both causers and communicators communicate under section 21 the distinction between them is not usually of great significance.

What is important is whether a person who is not himself communicating is or is not causing a communication to be made by another. In the FCA's view, primary responsibility for a communication to which section 21 applies and which is capable of being read will rest with its originator. This is the person responsible for its overall contents.

(c) An 'invitation' is described in PERG² as something which directly invites a person to take a step which will result in his engaging in investment activity. It follows that the invitation must cause the engaging in investment activity. Examples of an invitation include a direct offer of a financial promotion and internet promotions by brokers where the response by the recipient will initiate the activity (such as 'register with us now and begin dealing online').

A communication may contain a statement that it is not an invitation. Such statements may be regarded as evidence that the communication is not an invitation unless its contents indicate otherwise.

(d) An 'inducement' is described in PERG³ as a link in a chain where the chain is intended to lead ultimately to an agreement to engage in investment activity. But this does not mean that all the links in the chain will be an inducement or that every inducement will be one to engage in investment activity. Only those that are a significant step in persuading or inciting or seeking to persuade or incite a recipient to engage in investment activity will be inducements under section 21. The FCA takes the view that the mere fact that a communication may be made at a preliminary stage does not, itself, prevent that communication from being a significant step. However, in many cases a preliminary communication may simply be an inducement to contact the communicator to find out what he has to offer. For example, an advertisement which merely holds out a person as having expertise in or providing services about investment management or venture capital will not be an inducement to engage in investment activity. It will merely be an inducement to make contact for further material and will not be a significant step in the chain. However, that further material may well be a significant step and an invitation or inducement to engage in investment activity. In contrast, an advertisement which claims that what the recipient should do in order to make his fortune is to invest in securities and that the communicator can provide him with the services to achieve that aim will be a significant step and an inducement to engage in investment activity.

In the writer's view, a distinction must be made between a product description and a product promotion. If a description is an inherent characteristic of the credit facility advertised, it is not an incentive. Examples of the former are a credit agreement with an initial interest-free or payment-free period, a loan with a specified payment holiday and a payday loan available within 24 hours of application. Advertising any of such credit products is no more than advertising a quality or characteristic of the credit agreement and no more of an incentive than a statement of the customer's option to purchase under a hire-purchase agreement. This was also the conclusion of the First-tier Tribunal, at **20.1** above, in holding that advertisements which extolled the speed with which loans can be obtained did not in the context constitute an incentive requiring a statement of the typical APR and merely constituted a description of the product.

(e)   Inducements and links on a website[4] may take different forms. Some of these will be inducements under section 21 and others not. Links which are activated merely by clicking on a name or logo will not be inducements. The links may be accompanied by or included within a narrative or, otherwise, referred to elsewhere on the site. Whether or not such narratives or references are inducements will depend upon the extent to which they may seek to persuade or incite persons to use the links. Simple statements such as 'these are links to stockbrokers' or 'click here to find out about stockmarkets – we provide links to all the big exchanges' will either not amount to inducements or be inducements to access another site to get information. If they are inducements, they will be inducements to engage in investment activity only if they specifically seek to persuade or incite persons to use the link for that purpose. Where this is the case, but the inducement does not identify any particular person as a provider of a controlled investment or as someone who carries on a controlled activity, the exemption in article 17 of the Financial Promotion Order (Generic promotions) may be relevant (see PERG 8.12.14G).

1   PERG 8.6.1G.
2   PERG 8.4.5G.
3   PERG 8.4.7G.
4   PERG 8.4.11G.

20.6.3   General requirements

A firm must ensure that a communication or a financial promotion is clear, fair, and not misleading. CONC stipulates various sets of requirements, which are set out below. In the first instance:

(1A) A firm must ensure that each communication and each financial promotion:

(a)   is clearly identifiable as such;

(b)   is accurate;

(c)   is balanced and, in particular, does not emphasise any potential benefits of a product or service without also giving a fair and prominent indication of any relevant risks;

(d)   is sufficient for, and presented in a way that is likely to be understood by, the average member of the group to which it is directed, or by which it is likely to be received; and

(e)   does not disguise, omit, diminish or obscure important information, statements or warnings.

(1B) A firm must ensure that, where a communication or financial promotion contains a comparison or contrast, the comparison or contrast is presented in a fair and balanced way and is meaningful.

(2) If, for a particular communication or financial promotion, a firm takes reasonable steps to ensure it complies with (1), (1A) and (1B), a contravention does not give rise to a right of action under section 138D of the Act.[1]

Secondly, a firm must ensure that a communication or a financial promotion:

(1) uses plain and intelligible language;

(2) is easily legible (or, in the case of any information given orally, clearly audible);

(3) specifies the name of the person making the communication or communicating the financial promotion or the person on whose behalf the financial promotion is made; and

(4) in the case of a communication or financial promotion in relation to credit broking, specifies the name of the lender (where it is known).[2]

Finally:

(1) A firm must not, in a financial promotion or a communication to a customer, state or imply that credit is available regardless of the customer's financial circumstances or status.

(2) This rule does not apply to a financial promotion or communication relating to a credit agreement under which a person takes an article in pawn and the customer's total financial liability (including capital, interest and all other charges) is limited under the agreement to the proceeds of sale which would represent the true market value (within the meaning of section 121 of the CCA) of the article or articles pawned by the customer.[3]

1 CONC 3.3.1R.
2 CONC 3.3.2R.
3 CONC 3.3.3R.

20.6.4 Requirements as to form and expression

Every communication or financial promotion must be clear, fair and not misleading.[1] This includes accuracy, a balanced presentation, sufficient clarity to enable it to be understood by the average member of the group to which it is addressed and disclosure of important information, statements or warnings. Where a communication or financial promotion contains a comparison or contrast, it must be presented in a fair, balanced and meaningful way.[2] Where applicable, the financial promotion must make it clear that the credit is secured on the customer's home and make clear important items, statements or warnings.[3]

Every communication or financial promotion must use plain and intelligible language, be easily legible or audible, as the case may be, specify the name of the person making the communication or financial promotion and the lender, where made by a credit broker on a lender's behalf.[4]

Guidance on 'clear, fair and not misleading' is set out in CONC 3.3.6G to 3.3.10G.

Specific requirements relating to risk warnings for high-cost, short-term credit are contained in CONC 3.4. Specific requirements for financial promotions and communications by credit brokers are set out in CONC 3.7, for P2P agreements in CONC 3.7A, for lenders in CONC 3.8, and for debt counsellors and debt adjusters in CONC 3.9.

1　CONC 3.3; MCOB 3A.2 and 3A.2.5R.
2　CONC 3.3.1R; MCOB 3A.2.4R and 3A.3.
3　MCOB 3A.2.4R and 3A.3.
4　CONC 3.3.2R.

20.6.5　Prescribed content of financial promotions

The required content of financial promotions about credit agreements not secured on land is set out in CONC 3.5, and that relating to credit agreements secured on land in CONC 3.6.

The required content of financial promotions relating to an MCD regulated mortgage contract that indicate an interest rate or any figure relating to the cost of credit is set out in MCOB 3A.5.

MCOB 9.4 regulates the content of an equity release illustration.

20.6.6　Restricted expressions

Use of the following expressions in financial promotions is restricted:[1]

(a)　the word 'overdraft' or any similar expression describing any agreement for running-account credit except an agreement enabling the customer to overdraw on a current account;

(b)　the expression 'interest free' or any similar expression indicating that a customer is liable to pay no greater amount in respect of a transaction financed by credit than he would be liable to pay as a cash purchaser for the like transaction, except where the total amount payable does not exceed the cash price;

　　　The statement of the exception here appears superfluous.

(c)　the expression 'no deposit' or any similar expression, except where no advance payments are to be made;

(d)　the expression 'gift', 'present' or any similar expression, except where there are no conditions which would require the customer to repay the credit or return the item that is the subject of the claim;

(e)　the expression 'weekly equivalent' or any expression to the like effect or any other periodical equivalent, unless weekly payments or other periodical payments are provided for under the agreement.

MCOB sets out restrictions on the use of terms, essentially restricting the user to descriptions of credit products used in the legislation and the FCA Handbook.[2]

A firm must not, in a financial promotion or a communication, state or imply that credit is available regardless of the customer's financial circumstances or status, or that credit is guaranteed or pre-approved or not subject to any credit checks or other assessment of creditworthiness.[3]

1 CONC 3.5.12R and 3.6.8R.
2 MCOB 3A.2.6R.
3 CONC 3.3.3R and 3.3.4R.

20.7   BREACH OF FINANCIAL PROMOTION PROVISIONS

CCA 1974, s 46, which originally made it an offence to publish false or misleading advertisements, was repealed and effectively replaced by the Consumer Protection from Unfair Trading Regulations 2008.[1] The Financial Conduct Authority might intervene under its enforcement powers where it considers the advertiser to be in breach of FSMA, regulations under FSMA or FCA Rules.[2]

FSMA, s 19(1) prohibits a person carrying on a regulated activity in the United Kingdom, or purporting to do so, unless he is an authorised person or an exempt person. FSMA, s 21(1), read with s 21(2), provides that a person must not, in the course of business, communicate an invitation or inducement to engage in investment activity unless he is an authorised person, or the content of the communication is approved (for the purposes of this section) by an authorised person. The restrictions must be read with the Financial Services and Markets Act 2000 (Financial Promotion) Order 2005.[3]

A consumer might pursue an action for damages under FSMA, s 138D for breach of an FCA Rule or under the Misrepresentation Act 1967 for false or misleading financial promotions.

The Advertising Standards Authority ('ASA') will often uphold objections to advertisements on the grounds that they are misleading, in circumstances where the courts or regulatory authorities might be reluctant to intervene. However, the ASA's role is quite different from that of the courts or regulatory authorities, as it acts as an arbiter of what is legal, decent, honest and truthful, rather than as a judge of the advertiser's intent.

The following are examples of cases relating to breaches of the original advertising provisions in CCA 1974 and the Advertising Regulations under that Act. As these provisions have now been repealed, the cases merely serve a comparative purpose.

In *Jenkins v Lombard North Central plc*[4] it was successfully argued on the finance company's behalf that an advertisement stating the cash price of a vehicle in a sticker attached to the vehicle was not a credit advertisement at all as it did not indicate the advertiser's willingness to provide credit. The court referred to *Maurice Binks (Turf Accountants) Ltd v Huss*[5] where it was stated that a suggestion derived from the knowledge of the advertiser's business which was obtained not from the advertisement itself did not amount to an indication. As the House of Lords refused leave to appeal, it can be assumed that it concurred in the view that surrounding circumstances should not be taken into account in determining the construction of the expression 'indicating a willingness to provide credit'.

Contrasting circumstances are to be found in *R v Kettering Magistrates' Court, ex p MRB Insurance Brokers Ltd*.[6] This case turned on whether a wrongly stated

APR in a regulated agreement constituted a misleading indication as to price, in contravention of s 20 of the Consumer Protection Act 1987. The court found that the statement of an APR as 28.3% when in fact it was an APR of approximately 64% was a misleading price indication.

In *Metsoja v H Norman Pitt & Co Ltd*[7] it was held that an advertisement for 0% APR where the purchaser was in fact given a less favourable part-exchange allowance than was available to a cash purchaser, constituted a misleading advertisement. The court also found that the advertisement contravened reg 7(c) of the then Consumer Credit (Advertisements) Regulations 1989. This regulation prohibited the use of the expression 'interest free' (or any expression to the like effect) indicating that a customer is liable to pay no greater amount in respect of a transaction financed by credit than he would be liable to pay as a cash purchaser, except where the total amount payable does not exceed the cash price.

Where 'interest free' credit is advertised but a purchaser for cash, unlike a credit purchaser, may, with the aid of a dividend card, receive back cash in due course, the court in *Holman v Co-operative Wholesale Society Ltd*[8] held that this contravened reg 7(c) above.

In *Roller Group Ltd and Roller Finance Ltd v Sumner*[9] an advertisement was found to be misleading where the price quoted for a new car was stated exclusive of the cost of delivery, road fund tax and number plates. A contravention of CCA 1974, s 46 did not require the false or misleading information to relate to the terms of credit.

In *Currys Ltd v Jessop*[10] an advertisement containing the phrase 'nothing to pay for three months' was held to be misleading in circumstances where payments only commenced after three months but interest in fact began to accrue immediately from the date of purchase. In contrast, in *Dudley Metropolitan Borough v Colorvision plc*[11] the court found that the expression 'Your purchase absolutely free. If we cannot meet our competitors' price ask for details' would be interpreted by the average citizen as not meaning that he could expect a free item but rather a price reduction if a rival offered better terms.

1 SI 2008/1277; see **21.12** below.
2 See **Chapter 25** on enforcement and dispute resolution.
3 SI 2005/1529.
4 [1999] GCCR 623.
5 [1971] 1 All ER 104.
6 [2000] GCCR 2701.
7 [1999] GCCR 1339.
8 [2001] GCCR 2777.
9 [1995] CCLR 1.
10 [1999] GCCR 3407.
11 [1999] GCCR 2135.

20.8 CONSUMER PROTECTION FROM UNFAIR TRADING REGULATIONS 2008 ('CPRS')[1]

These regulations implemented Directive 2005/29/EC on unfair business-to-consumer commercial practices. They repealed *inter alia* CCA 1974, s 46 (false or misleading advertisements) and removed hire advertisements from CCA 1974. Advertisements for hire are now governed by these regulations.

1 SI 2008/1277.

20.8.1 Concepts embodied in the Regulations

The Regulations apply to commercial practices, namely any act, omission, course of conduct, representation or commercial communication, including advertising and marketing, by a trader, directly connected with the promotion, sale or supply of a product to or from consumers. 'Product' means any goods or services and includes immovable property, rights and obligations. 'Consumer' means any individual who in relation to a commercial practice is acting for purposes which are outside his business. 'Commercial practice' is any act, omission, course of conduct, representation or commercial communication (including advertising and marketing) by a trader, which is directly connected with the promotion, sale or supply of a product to or from consumers, whether occurring before, during or after a commercial transaction (if any) in relation to a product.[1]

The standard of conduct required is one which evidences professional diligence, meaning the standard of special skill and care which a trader may reasonably be expected to exercise towards consumers, which is commensurate with honest market practice or the general principle of good faith, in each case in the trader's field of activity.[2]

Reference in the Regulations to the concept of 'materially distorting the economic behaviour' means, in relation to an average consumer, appreciably to impair the average consumer's ability to make an informed decision, causing him to take a transactional decision he would not have taken otherwise.[3]

'Average consumer' is defined by reference to the material characteristics of such an average consumer, including his being reasonably well informed, reasonably observant and circumspect. Due regard must be had to the members of a vulnerable group of consumers.[4]

1 SI 2008/1277, reg 2(1).
2 Ibid., reg 2(1).
3 Ibid., reg 2(1).
4 Ibid., reg 2(2) to (6).

20.8.2 Meaning of unfair commercial practice

A commercial practice is unfair in relation to goods (including immovable property) or services if:

(a) it contravenes the requirements of professional diligence; and

(b) materially distorts or is likely to materially distort the economic balance of the average consumer with regard to the goods or services.[1]

1 SI 2008/1277, reg 3(2).

20.8.3 Specific unfair commercial practices

(1)   Misleading action

A commercial practice is unfair if:

(a)   it is a misleading action.[1] This includes:

    (i)   if it contains false information in relation to matters listed in reg 5(4) or in any way deceives or is likely to deceive the average consumer in relation to the matters listed; and

    (ii)   causes or is likely to cause the average consumer to take a transactional decision he would not have taken otherwise;[2]

(b)   it concerns any marketing of goods or services, including comparative marketing, which creates confusion with any goods, services, trade marks, trade names etc. of a competitor; or

(c)   it concerns any failure by a trader to comply with a commitment in a code of conduct if the trader indicates that he is bound by that code and it causes or is likely to cause the average consumer to take a transactional decision he would not have taken otherwise.[3]

1   SI 2008/1277, reg 3(4)(a).
2   Ibid., reg 5(2).
3   Ibid., reg 5(3).

(2)   Misleading omission

A commercial practice is unfair if it is a misleading omission.[1] It is a misleading omission if, in its factual context, taking into account the matters specified in reg 6(2), the commercial practice:

(i)   omits material information;

(ii)   hides material information;

(iii)   provides material information in a manner which is unclear, unintelligible, ambiguous or untimely; or

(iv)   fails to identify its commercial intent, unless this is apparent from the context.[2]

1   SI 2008/1277, reg 3(4)(b).
2   Ibid., reg 6(1).

(3)   Aggressive commercial practices

A commercial practice is unfair if it is an aggressive commercial practice,[1] that is, in its factual context, taking into account all of its features and circumstances:

(a)   it significantly impairs or is likely significantly to impair the average consumer's freedom of choice or conduct in relation to the goods or services through the use of harassment, coercion or undue influence; and

(b) it thereby causes or is likely to cause him to take a transactional decision he would not have taken otherwise.[2]

Factors to be taken into account are listed in reg 7(2).

1 SI 2008/1277, reg 3(4)(c).
2 Ibid., reg 7(1).

(4) Specific unfair commercial practices

Schedule 1 to the Regulations lists 31 practices which in all circumstances are considered unfair.

(5) Offences and defences

The Regulations contain a prohibition on unfair commercial practices – that is, commercial practices which include advertising and marketing that contravene the requirements of professional diligence, misleading actions, misleading omissions, aggressive commercial practices and unfair commercial practices (reg 3). A trader is guilty of an offence if:

(a) he knowingly contravenes, or recklessly engages in, a commercial practice which contravenes the requirements of professional diligence and the practice materially distorts or is likely to distort the economic behaviour of the average consumer; or

(b) he engages in a commercial practice which is a misleading action or omission (including a commercial communication containing false information), or in an aggressive commercial practice or in any of the 28 (out of the 31) commercial practices listed in Sch 1 to the Regulations which in all circumstances is considered unfair (reg 8).

Regulation 18 contains an 'innocent publication of advertisement defence'.

The prohibitions are enforceable through the enforcement of Community Infringements under Part 8 of the Enterprise Act 2002.

20.9 OTHER STATUTORY CONTROLS

Various statutory controls apply to advertising and promotions, whether or not relating to credit, regulated or unregulated.

Relevant legislation includes the Misrepresentation Act 1967, the Unfair Contract Terms Act 1977, the Property Misdescriptions Act 1991, the Property Misdescriptions (Specified Matters) Order 1992, the Consumer Protection Act 1987 and the Electronic Commerce (EC Directive) Regulations 2002.[1]

The Business Protection from Misleading Marketing Regulations 2008[2] provide that a trader is guilty of an offence if he engages in advertising which is misleading with respect to other traders.

1 See further **23.2**.
2 SI 2008/1276, reg 6.

20.10   NON-STATUTORY CONTROLS

The Advertising Standards Authority ('ASA') is the independent body set up by the advertising industry to monitor the rules laid down in the advertising codes. It has the support of the advertising industry and operates through the Committee of Advertising Practice ('CAP'). The ASA is the general regulator of the content of advertisements, sales promotions and direct marketing in the UK. The UK Code of Non-broadcast Advertising, Sales Promotion and Direct Marketing ('CAP Code') is the rule book for non-broadcast marketing communications which are not regulated by the FCA or Trading Standards.

The UK Code of Broadcast Advertising ('BCAP Code') applies to broadcast advertising. It originally came into force on 1 September 2010 and replaced the four previous separate BCAP Codes for broadcast advertising. The Code applies to all broadcast advertisements, including teleshopping, content on self-promotional television channels, television text and interactive television advertisements as well as to programme sponsorship credits on radio and television services licensed by Ofcom. The main principles of the advertising codes are that advertisements should not mislead, cause harm or offend. All marketing communications should be legal, decent, honest and truthful and should be prepared with a sense of responsibility to consumers and to society. The ASA has responsibility regarding non-technical elements of communications, such as statements which might cause serious or widespread offence and in respect of social responsibility and the truthfulness of claims that do not relate to specific characteristics of financial products; although, with regard to the latter, the ASA has widened its jurisdiction in conjunction with reference to the FCA and its governance of financial promotion.

The ASA, CAP and BCAP do not adopt a legalistic approach towards sanctions but endeavour to ensure that non-compliant marketing communications are amended, withdrawn or stopped as early as possible. The ASA publishes rulings, which itself might adversely affect an advertiser. It also maintains a rapport with the FCA and other bodies with responsibility for administering laws relating to advertising and, if necessary, those bodies might be urged to take further action.

The Lending Code 2011, adopted by the British Bankers' Association, the Building Societies Association and the UK Cards Association, requires its subscribers, namely banks, building societies and card issuers, to ensure that all communications to customers are clear, fair and not misleading. The Code contains a section on Communications and Financial Promotions, including marketing and advertising, and requires customers' consent to be given for certain purposes and the opportunity for customers to opt out of receiving marketing information.

Chapter 21

Credit marketing and responsible lending

21.1 ENTITLEMENT TO CREDIT

Some of the greatest dilemmas faced by the socio-economic foundations of society are to be found in the credit arena, namely how to match the expectations of individuals' entitlement to credit on the one hand with the willingness of credit grantors to advance credit at affordable rates on the other hand; to meet the expectations of individuals in a consumer society given to spending without resulting in over-indebtedness and holding creditors accountable for the same. These contradictions mirror those on the international plane where we have in the past witnessed sovereign states borrow beyond their means only subsequently to appeal for their indebtedness to be written off.

The problems are exacerbated by the fact that credit has become an essential constituent of everyday life. Most individuals have a need to borrow at one time or another, whether in order to pursue their studies, a business or profession, to purchase a dwelling, motor vehicle, assist with expenses associated with a holiday, wedding and general living expenses. Indeed, credit supplies the means to enable individuals to achieve their multifarious goals. Given that the grant of credit is generally not an act of charity but a function of business, it needs to be profitable. Consumer credit law is concerned with the governance of the wants and desires of the parties at opposite ends of the spectrum.

The situation is well described in the following extract from the Quinquennial Review of the Insolvency Service 2000:[1]

> 'Credit is an essential element of everyday life. Business involves taking risks and all who invest recognise that businesses may fail for a variety of reasons, from bad luck to incompetence and fraud. Over the last century the level of personal indebtedness has been rising; and more people have entered business on their own account or using a limited company. Most people are in debt one way or another whether by having a mortgage, paying for essential services in arrears, using credit cards or taking out specific loans; and most businesses are funded at least in part by bank overdrafts and loans, hire, hire purchase and supplier credit.'

This theme, but with the ultimate consequence of over-indebtedness, was the subject of the Over-indebtedness Summit Conference held in London in October 2000 when the Minister for Consumer Affairs stated:[2]

> 'The availability of credit is a key, possibly essential, requirement for consumers in today's society. For most it brings a means of easier access to services and goods, and provides consumers with greater flexibility in making best use of their income. I do not want to clamp down on the innovation which has enabled many consumers safely to realise their dreams. But for some consumers it can, often through a change of circumstance but also on occasions through over-commitment, result in over-indebtedness ... The average debt for a consumer with repayment problems has increased by a quarter since 1997, and now stands at £21,000. The overall level of unsecured debt has risen 70% in just five years ... I want us to gain a greater understanding of the causes and effects of over-indebtedness and by means of a constructive dialogue, look at how we can encourage, through practical solutions, more responsible lending and borrowing.'

These sentiments were also echoed by the Council of the European Union which, on 26 November 2001, passed a resolution on consumer credit and indebtedness. The resolution notes that over-indebtedness affects a significant and growing number of consumers in all the Member States. It advocates that consideration be given at Community level to implementing measures to develop cross-border credit with measures to prevent over-indebtedness throughout the credit cycle. It further recommends the harmonisation of preventive measures, cooperation on the study and prevention of over-indebtedness and finding ways of monitoring over-indebtedness within the internal market.[3] The opportunity for cross-border credit has since been enhanced by Directive 2008/48/EC, implemented in the UK with effect from 1 February 2011, and by Directive 2014/17/EU, implemented in the UK with effect from 21 March 2016. It appears doubtful whether these Directives will have any impact in reducing over-indebtedness.

In the UK, it was noted in the White Paper on Consumer Credit Market in the 21st Century, that while the majority of consumers do not experience any difficulties with borrowing, 20% of households who have credit, experience difficulties, while 7% have levels of credit use associated with over-indebtedness.[4] The longer-term trend would appear to suggest that debt is becoming a problem for an increasing number of households with the debt to disposable income ratio across the household sector continuing to rise, driven by the growth in secured lending. On the other hand, the household debt to total assets ratio, which includes both financial and housing wealth in total assets, has remained little changed since 2002 and the data for 2006 shows that the ratio is just under 17%. Household wealth, including both housing and financial assets, was £7.5 trillion in 2006, with household secured and unsecured debt equal to approximately 17% of this figure.[5]

A report produced for the Department for Business, Innovation and Skills ('BIS') in October 2010[6] concluded that, with the caveat that the analysis was based on households already in debt as opposed to those about to fall into over-indebtedness, there was a fall in the prevalence of over-indebtedness among those in the most over-indebted households between 2006–2008 and a year later, but an increase in the depth of over-indebtedness. Whilst there is no generally accepted definition of over-indebtedness, it has been defined in terms of a household having 25% of its annual income spent on repaying consumer debt or 50%

on repaying consumer credit agreements and mortgages, or having at least four credit commitments.[7]

At the end of 2015, UK households owed £1.27 trillion in mortgages and £179 billion in consumer credit; average household debt to income was 142% and predicted to rise to 149% by 2021.[8]

The Bank of England's Financial Policy Committee reported in 2017 that domestic credit had grown broadly in line with nominal GDP over the past two years, and the share of households with mortgage debt-servicing costs exceeding 40% of their income (the percentage likely to give rise to repayment difficulties) was just 1%.[9]

1 Published by the Department of Trade and Industry.
2 Speech of Dr Kim Howells given on 30 October 2000.
3 Official Journal of the European Communities (2001/C 364/01).
4 CM 6040 December 2003, p 5.
5 Household Debt Monitoring Paper HI 2007: BERR Consumer and Competition Policy Directorate (December 2007 URN 07/401A), pp 5 and 17.
6 Mark Bryan, Mark Taylor and Michail Veliziotis, *Over-indebtedness in Great Britain: An analysis using the wealth and assets survey and household annual debtors survey* (Institute for Social and Economic Research, University of Essex, October 2010).
7 White Paper on The Consumer Credit Market in the 21st Century (CM 6040, December 2003, para 5.5).
8 FCA's Sector Views 2017.
9 Statement from its meeting on 20 September 2017.

21.2 CREDIT GRANTORS

21.2.1 Lending institutions

The common institutions that grant loans to individuals are banks, building societies and finance companies. The latter include specialist dedicated finance companies as well as the credit arms of insurance companies and other institutions which finance their respective products and services, such as insurance company subsidiaries that finance insurance premiums.

Most mainstream lenders belong to one or other association, such as the British Bankers Association, the Building Societies Association, the Finance & Leasing Association and the Consumer Credit Trade Association.

21.2.2 Credit unions

The availability of credit to those less able to afford it is being facilitated by the expansion of credit unions. A credit union is a financial cooperative owned and controlled by its individual members. It is a body corporate registered under the Industrial and Provident Societies Act 1965 as a credit union in accordance with the Credit Unions Act 1979, which is an authorised person.[1] Credit union members are encouraged to save their money by purchasing shares in the credit union out of which funds loans are made to members. Credit unions are a worldwide phenomenon found in approximately 100 countries, comprising some 46,000 credit unions serving over 170 million members.

As at April 2017 there were 462 authorised credit unions in the United Kingdom, with a combined adult membership exceeding 1.6 million individuals.[2] Although the number of credit unions decreased from 557 in September 2006, total membership has increased from about half a million individual members at that time.[3]

Credit unions operate under the provisions of the Credit Unions Act 1979, as amended by the Financial Services and Markets Act 2000, and are regulated and supervised by the Financial Conduct Authority. Under the rules of a particular society which operates as a credit union, admission to membership must be restricted to persons who fall within one or more common bonds appropriate to a credit union (whether or not any other qualifications for admission to membership are required under the rules). The common bonds appropriate to a credit union are:

(a)   following a particular occupation;

(b)   being employed by a particular employer;

(c)   residing or being employed in a particular locality;

(d)   being a member of a bona fide organisation or being otherwise associated with other members of the society for a purpose other than that of forming a society to be registered as a credit union;

(e)   any other common bond for the time being approved by the Financial Conduct Authority.[4]

Lending by credit unions is governed by the FCA Handbook. Lending powers are determined by whether the credit union is a so-called Version 1 credit union or a Version 2 credit union. A credit union must not lend more than £15,000 or such lesser amount as may be specified, in excess of a member's shareholding, the credit limit depending upon whether the credit union is a Version 1 or Version 2 credit union.[5] Member's shareholding means any shares held by a member in the credit union. Notwithstanding the above, a Version 1 credit union may not lend more than £7,500 in excess of the borrowing member's shareholding unless it has a capital to total assets ratio of at least 5%. A Version 1 credit union must not lend for a period of more than five years unsecured and ten years secured. A Version 2 credit union must not lend for a period of more than ten years unsecured and 25 years secured. A credit union with permission to enter into a regulated mortgage contract must not enter into such a contract for a term of more than 25 years.[6]

1   See Glossary definition in the FCA Handbook.
2   See Bank of England Report on credit unions, dated 28 April 2017.
3   See FCA Financial Returns Data on Credit Unions.
4   Credit Unions Act 1979, s 1A.
5   FCA Handbook CREDS 7.3 Lending Limits.
6   Ibid.

21.2.3   Peer-to-peer lending platforms

In a peer-to-peer lending platform, a person ('A') will be operating an electronic system in relation to lending which enables him to facilitate persons ('B' and

'C') becoming the lender and borrower under an article 36H agreement.[1] *Inter alia* the agreement must be for credit not exceeding £25,000 or for an agreement not entered into by the borrower wholly or predominantly for the purposes of a business carried on or intended to be carried on by him.[2]

1 FCA Handbook PERG 2.7.7H G and Financial Services and Markets Act 2000 (Regulated Activities) Order 2001, SI 2001/544 ('RAO') art 36H.
2 RAO art 36H(4) to (6).

21.2.4 Loan-based crowdfunding

Crowdfunding involves a firm (a) that is subject to the client money rules in CASS 7, and (b) whose designated investment business includes operating an electronic system in relation to lending.[1]

1 FCA Handbook CASS 7, especially 7.10.7A ff.

21.2.5 Student loans

Special arrangements for providing financial support to students are contained in the Teaching and Higher Education Act 1998.[1] The scheme operates on the borderline between public and private law and student loans are statutory rather than contractual in character. The loans are made by the Student Loans Company acting as agent of the Secretary of State and, being statutory rather than contractual, CCA 1974 does not apply to them. Loans are subject to the Education (Student Loans) (Repayment) Regulations 2009.[2]

1 As amended, notably by the Higher Education and Research Act 2017.
2 SI 2009/470. See also Further Education Loans Regulations 2012, SI 2012/1818.

21.2.6 Miscellaneous

Certain housing associations, in partnership with banks or building societies, provide low cost credit to tenants. There are also schemes to provide loans to those who cannot obtain loans elsewhere. Short term payday lenders are subject to additional restrictive rules set out in the FCA Handbook, discussed in the next chapter.

21.3 RESPONSIBLE LENDING

21.3.1 Pre-contractual requirements

Responsible lending is a concomitant of assessing creditworthiness, a far from easy task as it involves assessing the customer's present and future ability to pay and to meet the customer's commitments in a sustainable manner. As laid down by the FCA:[1]

(1) Before making a regulated credit agreement the firm must undertake an assessment of the creditworthiness of the customer.

(2) A firm carrying out the assessment required in (1) must consider:

    (a) the potential for the commitments under the regulated credit agreement to adversely impact the customer's financial situation, taking into account the information of which the firm is aware at the time the regulated credit agreement is to be made; and

    (b) the ability of the customer to make repayments as they fall due over the life of the regulated credit agreement, or for such an agreement which is an open-end agreement, to make repayments within a reasonable period.

(3) A creditworthiness assessment must be based on sufficient information obtained from:

    (a) the customer, where appropriate; and

    (b) a credit reference agency, where necessary.

(4) This rule does not apply to:

    (a) an agreement secured on land; or

    (b) an agreement under which a person takes an article in pawn.

By way of FCA Guidance, rather than a Rule, the credit assessment may include:[2]

(1) the type of credit;

(2) the amount of the credit;

(3) the cost of the credit;

(4) the financial position of the customer at the time of seeking the credit;

(5) the customer's credit history, including any indications that the customer is experiencing or has experienced financial difficulties;

(6) the customer's existing financial commitments including any repayments due in respect of other credit agreements, consumer hire agreements, regulated mortgage contracts, payments for rent, council tax, electricity, gas, telecommunications, water and other major outgoings known to the firm;

(7) any future financial commitments of the customer;

(8) any future changes in circumstances which could be reasonably expected to have a significant financial adverse impact on the customer;

(9) the vulnerability of the customer, in particular where the firm understands the customer has some form of mental capacity limitation or reasonably suspects this to be so because the customer displays indications of some form of mental capacity limitation.

Where the loan agreement is to be guaranteed by a guarantor, an assessment must also be made of the guarantor's creditwothiness.[3]

A creditworthiness assessment must also be made in relation to a P2P agreement, although this is provided for separately.[4]

1 CONC 5.2.1R.
2 CONC 5.2.3G.
3 CONC 5.2.5R.
4 CONC 5.5.

21.3.2 Assessment of creditworthiness during the agreement

A corresponding, though less onerous, regime to that described above applies before the credit amount or credit limit is raised during the lifetime of the agreement.[1]

1 CONC 6.2.

21.3.3 Responsible lending and MCOB

MCOB 11.6 sets out the requirements regarding responsible lending and financing in relation to regulated mortgage contracts and home purchase plans.

Apart from interest-only mortgages, business purpose mortgages and loans for high net worth mortgage customers (for which there are special provisions), before entering into, or agreeing to vary, a regulated mortgage contract or home purchase plan, a firm must assess whether the customer, and any guarantor of the customer's obligations, will be able to pay the sums due. A firm must not enter into the transaction unless it can demonstrate that the new or varied regulated mortgage contract or home purchase plan is affordable by the customer and any guarantor.[1]

When assessing affordability, a firm must not base its assessment on the equity in the property used as security or take account of an expected increase in property prices. A firm must take full account of the customer's income, expenditure and household expenses.[2] It must also take into account likely future interest rate increases over a minimum period of five years, unless the regulated mortgage contract is for a shorter period.[3]

A firm must put in place, and operate, a policy approved by its governing body, setting out the factors it will take into account in assessing a customer's ability to pay. The factors are prescribed in a Rule so that, unlike in CONC, they are not discretionary.[4]

A firm must have systems and controls (including management information and key performance indicators) in place to monitor the effectiveness of its affordability assessments.[5]

There are specific provisions for mortgages for business purposes, high net worth mortgage customers, interest-only mortgages, bridging loans and interest roll-up mortgages.

1 MCOB 11.6.2R.
2 MCOB 11.6.5R.
3 MCOB 11.6.18R.
4 MCOB 11.6.20R.
5 MCOB 11.6.22R.

21.4   CREDIT SCORING

One of the yardsticks used by lenders to determine a borrower's capacity to borrow is credit scoring. This evaluates information provided by the borrower and other information obtained by the creditor and allocates points for each item of relevant information. Creditors operate different types of credit scoring systems, very often of their own creation, and dependent upon the experience they have gained in their sector of business over a period of time.

The Guide to Credit Scoring Practice (2000)[1] agreed between different organisations, lays down principles applying to the design, implementation and operation of scorecards as they relate to decisions following a request for a credit facility or amendment to an existing facility. The Guide describes 'scoring' as a process used by credit grantors to evaluate risk, which embraces the principles of credit, behavioural and collection scoring.

If an application for credit is declined on the basis of credit scoring, the Guide requires the proposed creditor to notify the applicant of such fact, together with an indication of the type of information that was included in the scorecard and to give the applicant an opportunity to request a reconsideration of the decision.

Credit grantors may not discriminate on the grounds of sex, race, religion, disability or colour. Creditors must have regard to all relevant legislation including the following: CCA 1974, the Sex Discrimination Act 1975, the Race Relations Act 1976, the Fair Trading Act 1973, the Employment Protection Act 1975, the Employment Protection Consolidation Act 1978, the Data Protection Act 1998 and the Equality Act 2010, each as amended and the regulations made under the various Acts.

There are other types of credit scoring techniques such as artificial intelligence or behavioural scoring. These are statistically derived assessments of the future credit risk of an existing customer based on the characteristics relating to his conduct of an existing account. Another technique takes the form of computer programs which incorporate a body of useful human knowledge in such a way that they can provide support in decision making.

Credit grantors will usually procure credit references from one of the principal credit reference agencies operating in the United Kingdom. The most important types of information held by such credit reference agencies are electoral roll information, public information about past debts and account information. The Data Protection Act 1998 lays down controls on automated credit processing. It confers the right on an individual at any time, by notice in writing to a data controller, to require the data controller to ensure that no decision taken by or on the data controller's behalf, which significantly affects the individual, is based solely on the processing by automatic means of personal data in respect of the individual's creditworthiness. Moreover, even where no such notice has been served, but the credit decision has been made on that basis, the data controller must, as soon as reasonably practicable, notify the individual that the decision was taken on that basis. The individual is then entitled, within 21 days of receiving such notice, to require the data controller to reconsider that decision or to take a new decision on a different basis, and if the data controller fails to take such action, the individual is entitled to compensation for damage or distress suffered as a result.[2]

21.5   CUSTOMER'S ENTITLEMENT TO PRE-CONTRACT INFORMATION

21.5.1   Credit reference agency information

CCA 1974 requires a creditor under a prospective regulated credit agreement, but not an owner under a prospective hire agreement, where the prospective creditor has decided not to proceed with the agreement on the basis of information obtained from a credit reference agency, to inform the debtor of such fact when it notifies him of its decision, together with the particulars of the agency, including its name, address and telephone number.[1] In addition, unless the creditor or owner informs the applicant borrower or hirer directly that he is not willing to enter into a regulated agreement, he must inform the credit broker of such fact and of any agency from whom, during the negotiations relating to the proposed agreement, he applied for information about the financial standing of the applicant.

Not later than when the lender or owner informs a credit broker that the lender/owner is not willing to make a regulated credit agreement or regulated consumer hire agreement, the lender/owner must, unless it informs the customer directly that it is not willing to make the agreement, inform the credit broker of the name and address (including an appropriate e-mail address) of any credit reference agency from which it has, during the negotiations relating to the proposed agreement, applied for information about the financial standing of the customer.[2]

Where a credit broker ('B') is a negotiator (within the meaning of section 56(1) of CCA 1974), B must, at the same time as B gives notice to a customer, under section 157(1) of CCA 1974 (which relates to the duty to disclose on request the name and address of any credit reference agency consulted by B) also give the customer notice of the name and address of any credit reference agency of which B has been informed under CONC 2.4.2R.[3]

Where a credit broker ('B') is not a negotiator (within the meaning of section 56(1) of CCA 1974), B must, within seven working days after receiving a request in writing for any such information, which is made by a customer within 28 days after the termination of any negotiations relating to a regulated credit agreement or a regulated consumer hire agreement, whether on the making of the agreement or otherwise, give to the customer notice of: the name and address of any credit reference agency from which B has during those negotiations applied for information about the financial standing of the customer; and the name and address of any credit reference agency of which B has been informed under CONC 2.4.2R.[4]

The credit broker must, on request, furnish a debtor or hirer with the details of any credit reference agency consulted by him.[5] Debtors and hirers are entitled to

require their creditors and owners respectively to notify them of any credit reference agency to which the creditor, owner or negotiator during antecedent negotiations, applied for information about their financial standing.[6] A credit reference
agency must, within seven working days, respond to the consumer's request by
giving the consumer a copy of the file relating to the consumer together with a
statement in the prescribed form of the consumer's rights to require any incorrect
information to be corrected.[7]

Reference to 'consumer' in this context is to a partnership of two or three persons not all of whom are bodies corporate or an unincorporated body of persons
not consisting entirely of bodies corporate.[8] But this is too limited a description and clearly also includes an individual or natural person, as is evident from
s 159(1). 'File', in relation to an individual, means all the information kept about
him by the credit reference agency, regardless of how the information is stored;
and 'copy of the file', in respect of information not in plain English (for example,
in computer language), means a transcript reduced into plain English.[9] Similar
rights to those under CCA 1974 are conferred on a consumer who is a natural person in respect of information held by a data controller, under the Data
Protection Act 1998.[10]

A consumer given information under either the Data Protection Act or
CCA 1974 who considers that an entry in his file is incorrect, and that if not corrected it is likely to cause him prejudice, may give notice to the credit reference
agency requiring it either to remove the entry from the file or to amend it. Within
28 days after receiving such notice, the credit reference agency must by notice
inform the objector that it has removed the entry from the file, amended it or
taken no action. The objector is given further rights dependent upon what action
the agency takes.[11] The credit reference agency must also, within ten days after
giving notice of having removed or corrected a file, notify the relevant particulars to every person to whom it has, in the six months preceding the individual's
request, furnished information relevant to the financial status of the individual
concerned.[12]

1 CCA 1974, s 157(A1).
2 CONC 2.4.2R.
3 CONC 2.5.5R.
4 CONC 2.5.6R.
5 CONC 2.5.5R and 2.5.6R.
6 CCA 1974, s 157(1).
7 Ibid., ss 158 and 159.
8 Ibid., s 158(4A).
9 Ibid., s 158(5).
10 Data Protection Act 1998, s 7.
11 CCA 1974, s 159.
12 Consumer Credit (Conduct of Business) (Credit References) Regulations 1977, SI 1977/330,
    as amended by the Consumer Credit (Conduct of Business) (Credit References) (Amendment)
    Regulations 2000, SI 2000/291.

21.5.2   Quotations, illustrations and disclosure

The CCA 1974 envisaged that credit grantors and providers of hire facilities
might provide customers with written quotations on request before entering into

agreements. The Act originally made provision for regulations governing the form and content of any document by which a person, who carries on a consumer credit business or consumer hire business, or a business in the course of which he provides credit to individuals secured on land, gives prospective customers information about the terms on which he is prepared to do business.[1]

The original regulations were the Consumer Credit (Quotations) Regulations 1989. Although businesses expended considerable sums in ensuring that they were in a position to provide quotations, potential borrowers and hirers rarely requested quotations with the result that this entire section of the Act effectively became a dead letter. The regulations were repealed with effect from March 1997.[2]

The Quotations Regulations were resurrected a year later, but solely in respect of land mortgages, only to be subsequently revoked.

Providing quotations remains voluntary but, where provided, they and their content, or at least minimum content, are prescribed by CONC 4.1. The content of quotations by lenders and owners is governed by CONC 4.1.3R, and by credit brokers by CONC 4.1.4R.

Illustrations, in the form of a Key Facts Illustration Document, preceding mortgages are mandatory and their content, order and format are prescribed by MCOB 5 (Pre-application disclosure) and, in particular, by MCOB 5.6.2R read with MCOB 5 Annex 1R. There is also a requirement for disclosure by way of illustration at the offer stage (MCOB 6) and for disclosure at the start of the contract (MCOB 7.4).

1 CCA 1974, s 52.
2 Consumer Credit (Quotations) (Revocation) Regulations 1997, SI 1997/211.

21.5.3 Pre-contract disclosure of contractual information

The innovation of a Pre-Contract Information document largely displaced quotations, which were rarely requested by consumers. The requirement for Pre-Contract Information was introduced, in relation to all regulated consumer credit agreements and consumer hire agreements not secured on land, by the Consumer Credit (Disclosure of Information) Regulations 2004[1] and, in relation to distance contracts, by the Financial Services (Distance Marketing) Regulations 2004.[2]

Following the implementation of the Consumer Credit Directive, the Consumer Credit (Disclosure of Information) Regulations 2010[3] replaced the Consumer Credit (Disclosure of Information) Regulations 2004 in respect only of regulated consumer credit agreements within the scope of the Directive. The prescribed information, ordinarily to be disclosed to debtors in good time before the agreement is made, is set out in regulations 8(1) and Schedule 1 (Standard European Consumer Credit Information or 'SECCI') and regulation 11(1) and Schedule 3 (European Consumer Credit Information or 'ECCI').

The above is in addition to any quotations, illustrations and disclosure of information referred to at **21.5.2** above.

1 SI 2004/1481.
2 SI 2004/2095.
3 SI 2010/1013.

21.5.4   Copy of draft consumer credit agreement

Before a regulated consumer credit, but not a consumer hire agreement, is made the debtor is entitled to a copy of the draft agreement which must be given to him without delay. There are exceptions to this obligation, including in respect of an agreement secured on land. Breach of this obligation is actionable as a breach of statutory duty.[1]

1 CCA 1974, s 55C.

21.6   CONDUCTING BUSINES OFF TRADE PREMISES

It is an offence to canvass debtor-creditor agreements (as opposed to debtor-creditor-supplier agreements) off trade premises. Canvassing involves soliciting the entry by the customer into a regulated agreement by making oral representations during a visit by the canvasser carried out for the purpose of making such representations.[1]

A person does not engage in canvassing if the visit takes place in response to a written signed request made by or on behalf of the person making it and the request was made on a previous occasion. There is also no canvassing if the place at which the oral representations are made are the premises where business is carried on by the creditor or owner, the supplier, the canvasser or the person whose employee or agent the canvasser is, or the consumer. The inclusion of the consumer's premises is significant as it is excluded from business premises for determining whether an agreement is cancellable.

Two interesting practical problems arise. First, it is necessary to establish whether the visit was in fact carried out for the purpose of making such oral representations or for some other purpose in the course of which the opportunity arose to canvass a debtor-creditor agreement. Second, what is meant by a 'previous occasion', in relation to the request for the visit? It is submitted that sufficient time and purpose must distinguish the two visits and that ideally, though not necessarily, the visits should be made on separate days.

Unlawful canvassing or soliciting does not affect the validity or enforceability of the agreement.[2]

1 CCA 1974, ss 48 and 49.
2 Ibid., s 170(1).

21.7   CIRCULARS TO MINORS

Persons under 18 years of age do not have contractual capacity.[1] The capacity of a person to enter into a consumer hire or consumer credit agreement is governed by the ordinary rules of contract. A minor may enter into such an agreement but it will be unenforceable against him unless it relates to necessaries and the contract is beneficial to the minor. However, if the contract is ratified by the minor on attaining majority, it becomes an enforceable contract. Prior to that time the court has the power to order restitution by the minor of property acquired by him under the contract.

It is an offence, for financial gain, to send to a minor any document inviting him to borrow money, to obtain goods on credit or hire, to obtain services on credit or to apply for information or advice on borrowing money or otherwise obtaining credit or hiring goods.[2] Rather strangely, it is not an offence to invite a minor orally to apply for credit.

Codes of practice generally advocate that special care is taken in relation to applications for credit from young people (those aged between 18 and 21).

In practice, finance companies publish the fact that credit or hire facilities are not available to persons under 18 years of age. This alone would not suffice if traders in fact solicit business from minors or do not take sufficient care to avoid doing so. Credit advertisements and insertions in such magazines or periodicals which are predominantly read by minors would create a presumption that they were addressed to minors. Where a document is received by a minor at a school or educational establishment for minors, there is an assumption that it was sent to the minor.

By way of defence, a person charged may prove that he did not know or had no reasonable cause to suspect that the recipient was a minor. Thus, in the case of *Alliance and Leicester Building Society v Babbs*[3] the Society sent circulars for loans to 750,000 account holders without seeking to distinguish between recipients above and below the age of 18. The circular did, however, state that loans were not available to applicants under the age of 18 years of age and the Society's computer program was also written so as to prevent loans being granted to persons under age. The court acquitted the Society on the grounds that the document, read as a whole, was not an invitation to persons under 18 years and that it was not the Society's intention to obtain financial gain from minors. The only logical inference to be drawn from the evidence was that when the brochures were sent out, indiscriminately though that may have been, it was not the Society's intention to obtain financial gain from any person who at the time of receipt of such brochure was a minor.

1 Family Law Reform Act 1969, s 1.
2 CCA 1974, s 50.
3 [1999] GCCR 1657.

21.8 UNSOLICITED CREDIT-TOKENS

CONC 2.9.2R provides as follows:

'(1) A firm must not give a person a credit token if he has not asked for it.

(2) A request in (1) must be in a document signed by the person making the request, unless the credit-token agreement is a small borrower-lender-supplier agreement.

(3) Paragraph (1) does not apply to the giving of a credit token to a person–

(a) for use under a credit-token agreement already made; or

(b) in renewal or replacement of a credit token previously accepted by that person under a credit-token agreement which continues in force, whether or not varied.'

The above Rule reiterates original s 51 of CCA 1974. Section 51 was repealed by article 20(15) of the Financial Services and Markets Act 2000 (Regulated Activities) (Amendment) (No 2) Order 2013 (SI 2013/1881). However, section 51 was saved for the purposes of regulation 52 of the Payment Services Regulations 2009,[1] the effect being that the section continued to apply in relation to a regulated credit agreement in place of regulation 58(1)(b) of the Payment Services Regulations 2009. However, as the 2009 Regulations have since been revoked and replaced by the Payment Services Regulations 2017,[2] without a saving of CCA 1974, s 51, the current position is that the above Rule in CONC alone prevails.

A 'credit token' is as a card, cheque, voucher, coupon, stamp, form, booklet or other document or thing given to an individual by a person carrying on a consumer credit business who undertakes:

(a)   that on the production of it (whether or not some other action is also required) he will supply cash, goods and services (or any of them) on credit; or

(b)   that where, on the production of it to a third party (whether or not any other action is also required), the third party supplies cash, goods and services (or any of them) he will pay the third party for them (whether or not deducting any discount or commission), in return for payment to him by the individual.[3]

Thus, in *Elliott v Director General of Fair Trading*[4] the trader was convicted notwithstanding that the card was merely designed to entice customers to enter the shop and customers still had to meet various criteria before they became entitled to credit. The card was a credit-token even though it was not capable of contractually binding its issuer.

1   SI 2009/209.
2   SI 2017/752.
3   CCA 1974, s 14(1). See an equivalent definition in the FCA Handbook, Glossary.
4   [1980] 1 WLR 977, [1999] GCCR 537.

21.9   CODES OF PRACTICE

Codes of Practice, whilst still in place and relevant, have lost much of their preeminence as a result of more extensive consumer protective legislation and the FCA regime, principally in the form of the FCA Handbook. With the advent of more innovative codes, the emphasis has shifted from rules to outcomes. Thus, The Standards of Lending Practice of UK Finance states that it represents a move away from its predecessor, which was focused more on compliance with provisions than customer outcomes.

Codes of practice of various trade associations lay down principles and guidelines for the marketing of, and entry into, credit and hire agreements and debt collection. They include the Lending Code (for lending to micro-enterprises), The Standards of Lending Practice[1] of UK Finance, relating to personal customers, and codes of the Finance & Leasing Association, the Consumer Credit Trade Association and the Consumer Credit Association of the United Kingdom.

In general, all codes advocate the use of plain English in communications with customers and the disclosure of relevant information to customers, with due notice being given to customers of any variations to contract terms. Members of the relevant associations are urged to act responsibly and prudently in marketing, both in relation to advertising and the granting of facilities. Members are urged to satisfy themselves as to the customers' ability to repay and to encourage customers in financial difficulties to inform them of their difficulties at the earliest opportunity. Various codes lay down minimum standards for credit brokers and for monitoring their business practices, provisions for the protection of confidential customer information, procedures for dealing with customer complaints and arbitration and standards for debt collection procedures.

The Lending Code[2] is a self-regulatory code that sets minimum standards of good practice for banks, building societies and credit card providers when lending to micro-enterprises (a business that employs fewer than 10 persons and has a turnover or balance sheet not exceeding 2 million euros) and charities with an annual income of less than £1 million. The Code covers good practice in relation to loans, credit cards, charge cards and current account overdrafts.

1 Effective from 1 October 2016.
2 Dated March 2011 (Revised 1 May 2012).

21.10 DISTANCE SELLING AND DISTANCE MARKETING

21.10.1 Distance selling of goods or services

The Consumer Contracts (Information, Cancellation and Additional Charges) Regulations 2013[1] apply to contracts entered into on or after 13 June 2014. The Regulations do not, however, apply to a contract for services of a banking, credit, insurance, personal pension, investment or payment nature.

A 'distance contract' means a contract concluded between a trader and a consumer under an organised distance sales or service-provision scheme without the simultaneous physical presence of the trader and the consumer, with the exclusive use of one or more means of distance communication up to and including the time at which the contract is concluded.[2]

1 SI 2013/3134.
2 Ibid., reg 5.

21.10.2 Distance marketing of financial services

The Financial Services (Distance Marketing) Regulations 2004[1] apply to distance contracts in respect of financial services. 'Financial services' means any service of a banking, credit, insurance, personal pension, investment or payment nature.

A distance contract is a contract concerning one or more financial services concluded between a supplier and a consumer under an organised distance sales or service-provision scheme run by the supplier or by an intermediary who, for the purposes of that contract, makes exclusive use of one or more means of distance communication up to and including the time at which the contract is concluded. 'Distance communication' is any means which, without the simultaneous physical presence of the supplier and the consumer, may be used for the marketing of the service between those parties.

The Regulations prescribe, inter alia, pre-contract information which must be provided by the supplier to the consumer in good time prior to the latter being bound by the contract. They also prescribe a cancellation period of 14 calendar days, beginning with the day after the day on which the consumer receives the contract. In the case of life assurance or a personal pension, the cancellation period is 30 calendar days.

1   SI 2004/2095.

21.11   PLAIN ENGLISH

The Plain English Campaign was founded in 1979 as a non-profit making and independent institution for the promotion of documents in plain English. Documents achieving such standards are awarded the so-called Crystal Mark. To date it has been awarded for documents produced, inter alia, by finance and leasing organisations, banks, building societies and insurance companies.

The campaign for plain intelligible language received indirect statutory recognition by the Unfair Terms in Consumer Contracts Regulations 1994, subsequently replaced by the Unfair Terms in Consumer Contracts Regulations 1999.[1] The latter was, in turn, repealed by the Consumer Rights Act 2015. This emphasises the need for transparency in agreement terms. A term is transparent if it is expressed in plain and intelligible language and, in the case of a written term, is legible.[2] In 2000, HM Treasury set so-called 'CAT Standards' for mortgages and credit card agreements. 'CAT' is an acronym for fair Charges, easy Access and decent Terms, but the essential features of such compliant products are much more detailed. They are voluntary standards which constitute a benchmark against which standard terms of mortgages and credit card products can be measured and are intended as a form of reassurance to customers. CAT standards do not convey a government assurance in respect of the terms to which they apply.

1   SI 1994/3159; SI 1999/2083.
2   Consumer Rights Act 2015, ss 64 and 68.

21.12   OTHER STATUTORY CONTROLS

Various other statutes govern the marketing of credit and hire facilities, directly or indirectly, notably the Consumer Protection from Unfair Trading Regulations 2008, the Prices Acts 1974 and 1975 and the Consumer Protection Act 1987. They are wide-ranging enactments and include controls on unfair commercial practices and aggressive commercial practices.[1]

1   See further **Chapter 20**.

21.13 THE COMMON LAW

From time to time the courts impose breaks on 'the unruly marketing horse'. Where a finance company had 'personalised' its standard agreement forms by utilising a trading style similar to that of a well-known equipment supplier and, with its consent, created the impression that the customer was dealing with the supplier and not the finance company, it was held that the finance company had adopted a deliberately misleading trading practice, without intending to defraud the customer, and the court granted the customer relief on the basis of estoppel.[1]

1 *Lease Management Services v Purnell Secretarial Services (Canon (South West)) Ltd* [1994] CCLR 127.

Chapter 22

Discrete consumer credit agreements

This chapter describes unique aspects of some specific consumer credit agreements. Matters common to regulated consumer credit agreements generally are covered by the text as a whole.

22.1 HIGH-COST SHORT-TERM CREDIT AGREEMENT

22.1.1 FCA duty-bound

The FCA is obliged to make rules in relation to one or more specified descriptions of regulated credit agreement appearing to the FCA to involve the provision of high-cost short-term credit, with a view to securing an appropriate degree of protection for borrowers against excessive charges.[1] The Rules appear in the CONC sourcebook of the FCA Handbook.

High-cost short-term credit is defined in the Glossary of the FCA Handbook as a regulated credit agreement:

(a) which is a borrower-lender agreement or a P2P agreement;

(b) in relation to which the APR is equal to or exceeds 100%;

(c) either:

    (i) in relation to which a financial promotion indicates (by express words or otherwise) that the credit is to be provided for any period up to a maximum of 12 months or otherwise indicates (by express words or otherwise) that the credit is to be provided for a short term; or

    (ii) under which the credit is due to be repaid or substantially repaid within a maximum of 12 months of the date on which the credit is advanced;

(d) which is not secured by a mortgage, charge or pledge; and

(e) which is not:

    (i) a credit agreement in relation to which the lender is a community finance organisation; or

(ii) a home credit loan agreement, a bill of sale loan agreement or a borrower-lender agreement enabling a borrower to overdraw on a current account or arising where the holder of a current account overdraws on the account without a pre-arranged overdraft or exceeds a pre-arranged overdraft limit.

1 FSMA, s 137C(1)(a)(ii) and (b).

22.1.2   Cost caps

A firm must not enter into an agreement for high-cost short-term credit that provides for the payment by the borrower of one or more charges that, alone or in combination with any other charge under the agreement or a connected agreement, exceed or are capable of exceeding the amount of credit provided under the agreement.[1]

A firm must not enter into an agreement for high-cost short-term credit that provides for the payment by the borrower of one or more charges that, alone or in combination with any other charge under the agreement or a connected agreement, exceed or are capable of exceeding 0.8% of the amount of credit provided under the agreement calculated per day from the date on which the borrower draws down the credit until the date on which repayment of the credit is due under the agreement, but if the date of repayment is postponed by an indulgence or waiver, the date to which it is postponed.[2]

In the event of a contravention of the above cost caps:

(a)   the agreement is unenforceable against the borrower; and

(b)   the borrower may choose not to perform the agreement and if that is the case:

(i)   at the written or oral request of the borrower, the lender must, as soon as reasonably practicable following the request and in any case within 7 days of the request, repay to the borrower any charges paid by the borrower under the agreement or confirm by notice in writing to the borrower that there are no charges to pay;

(ii)   where the lender complies with (i), the borrower must repay any credit received by the borrower under the agreement to the lender within a reasonable period from the day on which the charges in (i) are received by the borrower or the day on which the notice of confirmation in (i) is received; and

(iii)   in any case, the lender must not demand payment of the sum in (ii) in less than 30 days from the day in (ii).[3]

1 CONC 5A.2.2R.
2 CONC 5A.2.3R.
3 CONC 5A.5.2.

22.2 P2P AGREEMENT

22.2.1 Definition

A P2P agreement is:

(a) (in relation to a borrower) in accordance with article 36H of the Regulated Activities Order [see below], an agreement by which one person provides another person with credit (within the meaning of article 60L of the Regulated Activities Order) and in relation to which:

 (i) the operator of the electronic system in relation to lending which facilitates the agreement does not provide credit (within that meaning), assume the rights (by assignment or operation of law) of a person who provided credit, or receive credit under the agreement;

 (ii) the borrower is an individual; and

 (iii) either condition (A) or (B) is satisfied:

 (A) the lender provides credit (within that meaning) of less than or equal to £25,000; or

 (B) the agreement is not entered into by the borrower wholly or predominantly for the purposes of a business carried on, or intended to be carried on, by the borrower;

(b) (in relation to a lender) in accordance with article 36H of the Regulated Activities Order, an agreement by which one person provides another person with credit (within the meaning of article 60L of the Regulated Activities Order) and in relation to which either:

 (i) the lender is an individual or was an individual at the time the agreement was entered into; or

 (ii) if the lender is not an individual or was not an individual at the time the agreement was entered into, either condition (A) or (B) is satisfied, or was satisfied at the time the agreement was entered into:

 (A) the lender provides credit (within that meaning) of less than or equal to £25,000; or

 (B) the agreement is not entered into by the borrower wholly or predominantly for the purposes of a business carried on, or intended to be carried on, by the borrower;

provided, in either case, that the operator of the electronic system in relation to lending which facilitates the agreement does not provide credit (within that meaning), assume the rights (by assignment or operation of law) of a person who provided credit, or receive credit under the agreement.[1]

1 FCA Handbook, Glossary.

22.2.2   Operating an electronic system in relation to lending (RAO art 36H)[1]

RAO article 36H, in truncated form, provides as follows:

(1)   Where the conditions in paragraphs (2), (2A) and (2C) are satisfied, operating an electronic system which enables the operator ('A') to facilitate persons ('B' and 'C') becoming the lender and borrower under an article 36H agreement is a specified kind of activity.

(2)   The condition in this paragraph is that the system operated by A is capable of determining which agreements should be made available to each of B and C (whether in accordance with general instructions provided to A by B or C or otherwise).

(2A) The condition in this paragraph is that A, or another person ('X') acting under an arrangement with A or at A's direction, undertakes to:

(a)   receive payments in respect of either interest or capital or both due under the article 36H agreement from C, and

(b)   make payments in respect of either interest or capital or both due under the article 36H agreement to B.

(2B) For the purposes of paragraph (2A):

(a)   an agreement by A to appoint X to perform the activities in that paragraph is to be treated as an undertaking by A within the meaning of that paragraph;

(b)   it is immaterial that:

(i)   payments may be subject to conditions;

(ii)   A, or X, may be entitled to retain a portion or the entirety of any payment received from C.

(2C) The condition in this paragraph is that A, or another person ('X') acting under an arrangement with A or at A's direction, undertakes to perform, or A undertakes to appoint or direct another person to perform, either or both of the following activities:

(a)   taking steps to procure the payment of a debt under the article 36H agreement;

(b)   exercising or enforcing rights under the article 36H agreement on behalf of B.

(2D) Where A carries on an activity of the kind specified in paragraph (1), it is a specified kind of activity for A to operate an electronic system where:

(a)   that system enables A to facilitate a person ('B') assuming the rights of the lender under an article 36H agreement by assignment or operation of law, and

(b) the conditions in paragraphs (2), (2A) and (2C) are satisfied where C is the borrower under the agreement in sub-paragraph (a).

1 SI 2001/544.

22.2.3 FCA Handbook provisions

Among the specific provisions in CONC governing P2P agreements are: CONC 3.7A (promotions); CONC 4.3 (pre-contractual requirements and adequate explanations); CONC 5.5 (creditworthiness assessments); and CONC 6.7 (post-contract business practices).

22.3 AGREEMENT SECURED BY BILL OF SALE OR 'GOODS MORTGAGE'

The existing regime characterised by a charge, by way of security, on goods, is identified as a bill of sale.

A bill of sale loan, commonly known as a logbook loan where the loan agreement is secured on a motor vehicle, is a personal loan secured by a bill of sale on goods which remain in the possession of the debtor, who transfers ownership of the goods, by way of security, to the creditor together, in the case of a vehicle, with the logbook/V5C registration certificate. Requirements for bills of sale are discussed at **18.2.5.1** above. Whilst they may be used for personal chattels and goods generally, in the context of consumer credit, bills of sale are essentially used as security for high-value assets such as motor vehicles, yachts and works of art.

The loans are subject to the voluntary code relating to loans secured on bills of sale and to the requirement that the creditor issues to the customer a 'Bill of Sale Information Sheet' in the form prescribed by BIS, at the time the Pre-contractual Information or Standard European Consumer Credit Information ('SECCI') relating to the credit agreement is provided to the customer. Where the bill of sale involves a motor vehicle, the creditor must register his interest in the vehicle, within 24 hours of the making of the agreement, with a recognised asset finance register, such as HPI Limited.

It is anticipated that the Goods Mortgages Bill, when enacted, will simplify documentation and the procedure for registration, at least in relation to motor vehicles, impose restrictions on mortgagees taking possession of goods, and afford protection to innocent third party purchasers.[1]

1 See **18.2.5.2**.

22.4 STUDENT LOANS

Student loans for higher and further education are governed by Part II (primarily s 22) of the Teaching and Higher Education Act 1998, as amended by ss 43 and 50 of the Higher Education Act 2004 and s 76 of the Education Act 2011, the

Higher Education and Research Act 2017 and various regulations which include the Education (Student Loans) (Repayment) Regulations 2009,[1] the Education (Student Loans) (Repayment) (Amendment) Regulations 2013,[2] and the Further Education Loans Regulations 2012.[3]

The above statutes require the interest rates prescribed by the regulations to be lower than those prevailing on the market or no higher than those prevailing on the market where the other terms on which such loans are provided are more favourable to borrowers than those prevailing on the market.

The Student Loans Company is a UK public sector organisation that provides loans, grants, allowances and bursaries to over one million Further Education and Higher Education students annually. The scheme operates on the borderline between public and private law and student loans are statutory rather than contractual in character. The loans are made by the Student Loans Company acting as agent of the Secretary of State and, being statutory rather than contractual, CCA 1974 does not apply to them.

A borrower may repay the student loan at any time. He is not required to repay any part of the student loan before the start of the following tax year commencing on 6 April after he ceases to be eligible for financial support pursuant to regulations made under s 22 of the Teaching and Higher Education Act 1998, whether by reason of having completed that course or otherwise. Repayments may be made directly or by deduction by the employer under the PAYE system.

1 SI 2009/470.
2 SI 2013/607.
3 SI 2012/1818.

22.5 OVERDRAFTS ON CURRENT ACCOUNT

22.5.1 How overdrafts came to be regulated

Before 1 February 2011 an overdraft on a current account, whilst subject to CCA as a debtor-creditor agreement, was only regulated lightly. It was exempt from Part V of the Act, which governs entry into credit or hire agreements (save for s 56 relating to antecedent negotiations). A creditor was only required to inform the OFT in writing of its general intention to enter into agreements of this type and to furnish the debtor with the limited information set out in the Determination made by the OFT under s 74(3), at the time or before the agreement was concluded or where the debtor overdrew with the creditor's tacit consent, within seven days of the agreement remaining overdrawn for three months.

As the Consumer Credit Directive[1] also governs overdraft agreements that fall within its scope,[2] Parliament was compelled to alter the regulatory regime which applied to an agreement for an overdraft on a current account. At the same time it extended the regulation so as to apply also to overdraft agreements outside the scope of the Directive, including business overdraft agreements.

CCA 1974 defines authorised 'non-business' and 'business' overdraft agreements in the following terms:[3]

"'authorised non-business overdraft agreement" means a debtor-creditor agreement which provides authorisation in advance for the debtor to overdraw on a current account where–

(a) the credit must be repaid on demand or within three months, and

(b) the agreement is not entered into by the debtor wholly or predominantly for the purposes of the debtor's business (see subsection (2A));

"authorised business overdraft agreement" means a debtor-creditor agreement which provides authorisation in advance for the debtor to overdraw on a current account, where the agreement is entered into by the debtor wholly or predominantly for the purposes of the debtor's business (see subsection (2A)).'

1 Directive 2008/48/EC of the European Parliament and of the Council of 23 April 2008.
2 The Directive distinguishes between, and regulates, an 'overdraft facility' ,which is defined as an explicit credit agreement whereby a creditor makes available to a consumer funds which exceed the current balance in the consumer's current account , and an 'overrunning' which is defined as a tacitly accepted overdraft whereby a creditor makes available to a consumer funds which exceed the current balance in the consumer's current account or the agreed overdraft facility (Article 3(c) and (d)).
3 CCA 1974, s 189(1).

22.5.2 The applicable statutory provisions

Following the implementation of the Directive, from 1 February 2011 onwards Part V of CCA 1974 in general does not apply to a debtor-creditor agreement enabling the debtor to overdraw on a current account, except for the following sections of Part V:[1]

(1) Where such an agreement is an authorised business overdraft agreement the following provisions apply:

(a) section 55B (assessment of creditworthiness);

(b) section 56 (antecedent negotiations);

(c) section 60 (regulations on form and content of agreements);

(d) section 61B (duty to supply copy of overdraft agreement).

(2) Where such an agreement is an authorised non-business overdraft agreement the following provisions apply:

(a) section 55 (regulations on disclosure of information);

(b) section 55B (assessment of creditworthiness);

(c) section 55C (copy of draft consumer credit agreement);

(d) section 56 (antecedent negotiations);

(e) section 60 (regulations on form and content of agreements);

(f) section 61B (duty to supply copy of overdraft agreement).

(3) Where such an agreement would be an authorised non-business overdraft agreement but for the fact that the credit is not repayable on demand or within three months the following provisions apply:

(a)   section 55 (regulations on disclosure of information);

(b)   section 55A (adequate explanations);

(c)   section 55B (credit assessment);

(d)   section 55C (copy of draft consumer credit agreement);

(e)   section 56 (antecedent negotiations);

(f)   section 60 (regulations on form and content of agreements);

(g)   section 61 (signing of agreement);

(h)   section 61A (duty to supply copy of executed agreement);

(i)   section 66A (withdrawal from consumer credit agreement).

1 CCA 1974, s 74(1B), (1C), (1D).

22.5.3   FCA Handbook, CONC Sourcebook

The statutory controls of CCA 1974 in sections 74A and 74B were repealed, transferred from the OFT to the FCA and replicated in the FCA Handbook, CONC Sourcebook,[1] as set out below.

1 SI 2013/1881.

22.5.3.1   *Information on entering into a current account*[1]

(1)   When a firm enters into a current account agreement where:

(a)   there is a possibility that the account-holder may be allowed to over-draw on the current account without a pre-arranged overdraft or exceed a pre-arranged overdraft limit; and

(b)   if the account-holder did so, this would be a regulated credit agreement;

the current account agreement must contain the information in (2) and (3).

(2)   The information required by (1) is:

(a)   the rate of interest charged on the amount by which the account-holder overdraws on the current account or exceeds the pre-arranged over-draft limit;

(b)   any conditions applicable to that rate;

(c)   any reference rate on which that rate is based;

(d)   information on any changes to that rate of interest (including the peri-ods that the rate applies to and any conditions or procedure applicable to changing that rate); and

(e)   any other charges payable by the account holder under the agreement (and the conditions under which those charges may be varied). [Note: section 74A(2) of CCA]

(3) Where different rates of interest are charged in different circumstances, the firm must provide the information in (2)(a) to (d) in respect of each rate.

1 CONC 4.7.2R.

22.5.3.2 *Information to be provided on significant overdrawing without prior arrangement*[1]

(1) A firm must inform the account-holder in writing of the matters in (2) without delay where:

    (a) the account-holder overdraws on the current account without a pre-arranged overdraft, or exceeds a pre-arranged overdraft limit, for a period exceeding one month;

    (b) the amount of that overdraft or excess is significant throughout that period;

    (c) the overdraft or excess is a regulated credit agreement; and

    (d) the account-holder has not been informed in writing of the matters in (2) within that period.

(2) The matters in (1) are:

    (a) the fact that the account is overdrawn or the overdraft limit has been exceeded;

    (b) the amount of that overdraft or excess;

    (c) the rate of interest charged on it; and

    (d) any other charges payable by the customer in relation to it (including any penalties and any interest on those charges).

(3) For the purposes of (1)(b) the amount of the overdraft or excess is significant if:

    (a) the account-holder is liable to pay a charge for which he would not otherwise be liable; or

    (b) the overdraft or excess is likely to have an adverse effect on the customer's ability to receive further credit (including any effect on the information about the customer held by a credit reference agency); or

    (c) it otherwise appears significant, having regard to all the circumstances.

(4) Where the overdraft or excess is secured on land, (1)(a) is to be read as if the reference to one month were a reference to three months.

1 CONC 6.3.4R.

22.5.4 The regulatory provisions

The Consumer Credit (Disclosure of Information) Regulations 2010[1] and the Consumer Credit (Agreements) Regulations 2010 contain specific provisions governing overdraft agreements. The former set out the information required to be disclosed in good time before an authorised non-business overdraft agreement is entered into.[2] They provide that information requirements may be met by disclosing the information by means of the form set out in Schedule 3 (namely, 'European Consumer Credit Information' or 'ECCI') in accordance with the regulation.[3] The Regulations make separate provision for such agreements entered into by means of distance communication and for the disclosure of information where a current account is held by two or more debtors jointly.

As to the Consumer Credit (Agreements) Regulations 2010,[4] the specific provisions are contained in regulation 8.

1   SI 2010/1013.
2   Regulation 10.
3   Regulation 11.
4   SI 2010/1014.

22.6   RESIDENTIAL RENOVATION AGREEMENT

A residential renovation agreement is a consumer credit agreement entered into on or after 21 March 2016 which is unsecured and the purpose of which is the renovation of residential property, as described in Article 2(2a) of Directive 2008/48/EC on credit agreements for consumers.[1] The date of 21 March 2016 is when the Mortgage Credit Directive 2014/17/EU was implemented.

The reference to Article 2(2a) is perplexing as it does not at all describe 'residential property' but refers to 'credit agreements which are secured either by a mortgage or by another comparable security commonly used in a Member State on immovable property or secured by a right related to immovable property'.

The definition is further confused in the Glossary of the FCA Handbook, which defines a residential renovation agreement as a credit agreement entered into on or after 21 March 2016 the purpose of which is the renovation of residential property, as described in paragraph 2a of article 2 of the Consumer Credit Directive, and which is not secured on land. Thus, whilst CCA 1974 describes the agreement as 'unsecured', the FCA Handbook describes it as 'not secured on land'. It follows that an agreement whose purpose is the renovation of residential property and which is secured other than on land is not a residential renovation agreement under CCA 1974 but is a residential renovation agreement for the purposes of the FCA Handbook.

The main purpose of the introduction of the concept of a residential renovation agreement is to bring it within the parameters of a regulated credit agreement, when otherwise it would have been exempt from the particular provisions. Examples are:

- CONC 4.2 and 4.3 (Pre-contract disclosure and adequate explanations);
- CCA 1974, s 55C(4) (Copy of draft consumer credit agreement);
- CCA 1974, s 60(5) (Form and content of agreements);
- CCA 1974, s 61A (Duty to supply copy of executed agreement);

- CCA 1974, s 66A(14) and CONC 11.1.3 (Right of withdrawal);

- CCA 1974, s 75A (Further liability of creditor for breaches); and

- CCA 1974, s 77B(9) (Statement of account on request).

The reader is also referred to PERG 2.7 and 2.9.

1 CCA 1974, s 189(1).

22.7 BUY-TO-LET FINANCE

22.7.1 Buy-to-let credit agreement

A buy-to-let credit agreement is a contract that:[1]

(a) at the time it is entered into:

    (i) is one under which a lender provides credit to an individual or to trustees (the 'borrower');

    (ii) provides for the obligation of the borrower to repay to be secured by a mortgage on land in the EEA;

    (iii) at least 40% of the land is used, or is intended to be used:

        (A) (in the case of credit provided to an individual) as or in connection with a dwelling; or

        (B) (in the case of credit provided to a trustee which is not an individual) as or in connection with a dwelling by an individual who is a beneficiary of the trust or a related person; and

    (iv) provides that the land secured by the mortgage cannot at any time be occupied as a dwelling by the borrower or a related person;

    and is to be occupied as a dwelling on the basis of a rental agreement; or

(b) is a regulated credit agreement which is an article 3(1)(b) credit agreement and provides that the land, or existing or projected building, to which it relates;

    (i) cannot at any time be occupied as a dwelling by the borrower or a related person; and

    (ii) is to be occupied as a dwelling on the basis of a rental agreement.

Article 72I of the Financial Services and Markets Act 2000 (Regulated Activities) Order 2001 ('RAO')[2] excludes from certain provisions of the Order consumer buy-to-let mortgage business entered into after 21 March 2016 carried on by a registered consumer buy-to-let mortgage firm, as defined in article 4 of the Mortgage Credit Directive Order 2015.[3]

1 FCA Handbook, Glossary.
2 SI 2001/544.
3 SI 2015/910.

22.7.2   Buy-to-let mortgage contract

A buy-to- let mortgage contract is a contract that:[1]

(a)   at the time it is entered into:

    (i)   meets the conditions in paragraphs (i) to (iii) of article 61(3)(a) of the Regulated Activities Order (regulated mortgage contracts); and

    (ii)   provides that the land subject to the mortgage cannot at any time be occupied as a dwelling by the borrower or by a related person, and is to be occupied as a dwelling on the basis of a rental agreement; or

(b)   is a regulated credit agreement within the meaning of article 60B of the Regulated Activities Order which:

    (i)   falls within Article 3(1)(b) of the mortgages directive; and

    (ii)   provides that the land, or existing or projected building, to which it relates cannot at any time be occupied as a dwelling by the borrower or by a related person, and is to be occupied as a dwelling on the basis of a rental agreement.

1   SI 2015/910, art 4(1).

22.7.3   Consumer buy-to-let mortgage contract

A consumer buy-to-let mortgage contract is a buy-to-let mortgage contract which is not entered into by the borrower wholly or predominantly for the purposes of a business carried on, or intended to be carried on, by the borrower.[1]

Part 3 of the Mortgage Credit Directive Order 2015[2] governs the regime applying to consumer buy-to-let mortgages and makes provision for registration of firms involved in such lending and for their regulation by the FCA.[3]

1   SI 2015/910, art 4(1).
2   SI 2015/910.
3   See FCA Handbook, especially PERG 4.10B.

Chapter 23

Electronic communications

23.1 ENTERING INTO THE REGULATED AGREEMENT ONLINE

Whilst the Consumer Credit Act 1974, in its original form, preceded the advent of common electronic communications, amendments to the Act and the Regulations under the Act have brought it up to date with the electronic age. Thus, a regulated agreement might be in electronic form and signed by an electronic signature.

Section 61(1)(c) of CCA 1974 requires the terms of the agreement to be readily legible. The Consumer Credit (Agreements) Regulations 1983 and the Consumer Credit (Agreements) Regulations 2010 refer to the agreement being easily legible and of a colour which is readily distinguishable from the background medium upon which the information is displayed.[1] A similar requirement applies to the copy of the agreement.[2]

The agreement copies, whether of the unsecured agreement, or the agreement secured on land, must be sent by an appropriate method.[3] The expression 'appropriate method' means post or transmission in the form of an electronic communication if:[4]

(a) the person to whom it is transmitted agrees that it may be delivered to him by being transmitted to a particular electronic address in a particular electronic form,

(b) it is transmitted to that address in that form, and

(c) the form in which the document is transmitted is such that any information in the document which is addressed to the person to whom the document is transmitted is capable of being stored for future reference for an appropriate period in a way which allows the information to be reproduced without change.

Where a document is transmitted electronically, as above, unless the contrary is proved, it is treated (save in respect of notice of withdrawal or notice of cancellation, as to which see below) as having been delivered on the working day immediately following the day on which it is transmitted.[5]

Where notice of withdrawal from a regulated consumer credit agreement under the Agreements Regulations 2010 is given electronically, it is regarded as having been received by the creditor at the time it is sent (and s 176A does not apply).[6] The disapplication of s 176A also means that paragraph (c) above does not apply.

Where an agreement is cancellable, a notice in the prescribed form indicating the right of the debtor or hirer to cancel the agreement and how and when that right is exercisable, must be included in every copy of the agreement and sent by an appropriate method, as described above, to the debtor within seven days following the making of an agreement.[7] Whether or not the notice of a cancellation is actually received by the creditor or owner, it is deemed to have been served on the creditor or owner in the case of a notice transmitted by electronic communication, at the time of the transmission. This equates to the time when a notice of cancellation sent by post is deemed to have been served, namely at the time of the posting.[8]

Signature of a regulated agreement may be effected by electronic signature. This is impliedly recognised by reg 6(5) of the Agreements Regulations 1983 which provides that, where an agreement is intended to be concluded by the use of an electronic communication, there might be included in the signature box information about the process or means of providing, communicating or verifying the signature to be made by the debtor or hirer.[9] It is likewise implicit in the Agreements Regulations 2010 which provide that, where an agreement is intended to be concluded by the use of electronic communication, nothing in the regulation dealing with signing of the agreement shall prohibit the inclusion in the document of information about the process or means of providing, communicating or verifying the signature to be made by the debtor.[10]

1 SI 1983/1553, reg 6(2)(a); SI 2010/1014, reg 3(3).
2 SI 1983/1557, reg 2(1).
3 CCA 1974, s 63(2) and (3); s 61(2(b).
4 Ibid., s 189(1) and s 176A(1).
5 Ibid., s 176A(2) and s 189(1).
6 Ibid., s 66A(5).
7 Ibid., s 64(1)(b) and see also s 64(2).
8 Ibid., s 69(7).
9 SI 1983/1553, reg 6(5).
10 SI 2010/1014, reg 4(5).

23.2 ELECTRONIC (EC DIRECTIVE) REGULATIONS 2002[1]

These overarching regulations apply, in general terms, to all online commercial communications designed to promote, directly or indirectly, the goods or services or image of any person.[2] They prescribe the information which a service provider must supply to the consumer with the commercial communication.[3] They also prescribe the information that a service provider must provide to the consumer where contracts are concluded by electronic means, including terms and conditions in a way that allows the recipient to store and reproduce them.[4]

1 SI 2002/2013.
2 Ibid., reg 2(1).
3 Ibid., reg 6.
4 Ibid., reg 9.

23.3 DISTANCE CONTRACT

It follows from the above that one would expect the various sets of regulations to specifically accommodate distance contracts. Whilst there is no mention of distance contracts in the Consumer Credit (Agreements) Regulations 1983, the term is defined in the Consumer Credit (Disclosure of Information) Regulations 2004,[1] but only for the purposes of disapplying the regulations to distance contracts.[2] In contrast, the Consumer Credit (Agreements) Regulations 2010 and the Consumer Credit (Disclosure of Information) Regulations 2010 both accommodate distance contracts, defined as follows:[3]

> '"distance contract" means any regulated agreement made under an organised distance sales or service-provision scheme run by or on behalf of the creditor who, in any such case, for the purpose of that agreement makes exclusive use of one or more means of distance communication up to and including the time at which the agreement is made. For this purpose, "means of distance communication" means any means which, without the simultaneous physical presence of the creditor or a person acting on behalf of the creditor and of the debtor, may be used for the making of a regulated agreement between the parties to that agreement.'

The Consumer Credit (Disclosure of Information) Regulations 2010 specifically address requirements for pre-contract disclosure in the case of distance contracts. However, it is not clear whether they permit the Disclosure of Information document in the form of the 'SECCI' to be in electronic form, as the pre-contract credit information form must be in writing and of a nature that enables the debtor to remove it from the place where it is disclosed to him.[4]

As already mentioned, the Agreements Regulations envisage the possibility of agreements entered into by way of distance contracts but do not specifically regulate them any differently to non-distance contracts, save in respect of signature by the debtor in the case of electronic communication.

It is useful to refer to the Financial Services (Distance Marketing) Regulations 2004[5] for the source of the various concepts and definitions relating to distance contracts in the consumer credit area.

1 SI 2004/1481, reg 1(2).
2 Ibid., reg 2(3).
3 SI 2010/1014, reg 1(3) and SI 2010/1013, reg 1(2) respectively.
4 SI 2010/1013, reg 8(2).
5 SI 2004/2095.

23.4 POST-CONTRACT INFORMATION

Statements, notice of sums in arrears, notice of default sums, notice of interest payable on judgment debts and notice of termination may all be given electronically if:

(a) the person to whom it is transmitted agrees that it may be delivered to him by being transmitted to a particular electronic address in a particular electronic form;

(b)   it is transmitted to that address in that form; and

(c)   the form in which the document is transmitted is such that any information in the document which is addressed to the person to whom the document is transmitted is capable of being stored for future reference for an appropriate period in a way which allows the information to be reproduced without change.[1]

By way of exception to the general position that a document may be sent in electronic form, an enforcement, default or termination notice must be given to the debtor or hirer in paper form.[2]

1   CCA 1974, s 189(1): definitions of 'give', 'serve', 'appropriate method'; and s 176A.
2   SI 1983/1561, reg 2(4A).

23.5   ELECTRONIC SIGNATURE

An electronic signature is associated with an electronic document. It is used to give the recipient of the document confirmation that the communication comes from the person who it purports to come from. It is also essential to ensure that the electronic signature has not been tampered with.

The procedure known as encryption is used to create a digital signature by the holder of a private key issued specifically for the individual. Encryption is a way of encoding information and turning (or locking) normal readable text into something which is unreadable (a coded series of numbers and/or letters) which can be unlocked by the holder of the relevant key (decoding device) which will then transfer it back into normal readable form.[1]

Electronic signatures give rise to various problems, not least the difficulty in proving that the individual named as the borrower or hirer has actually signed the agreement. The Electronic Communications Act 2000 describes how an electronic signature may be admitted in evidence and taken as a valid means of establishing the authenticity of documents. Section 7 provides that in any legal proceedings an electronic signature incorporated into, or logically associated with, a particular electronic communication or particular electronic data and the certification by any person of such signature, is admissible in evidence in relation to any question as to the authenticity of the communication or data or as to the integrity of the communication or data. The section sets out the meaning of an electronic signature and how the signature is to be certified. Section 7 provides for the admissibility in any legal proceedings of an electronic document as evidence in relation to any question as to the authenticity of an electronic transaction.

The Act also contains provision for a register of approved providers of cryptography support services.

The Electronic Identification and Trust Services for Electronic Transactions Regulations 2016[2] implement Regulation (EU) No 910/2014 of the European Parliament and of the Council of 23 July 2014 on electronic identification and trust services for electronic transactions in the internal market ('the eIDAS Regulation').

1   See generally Amanda C. Brook and Rafi Azim-Khan, *E-Business: The practical guide to the laws* (2nd edn, Spiramus Press, 2008).
2   SI 2016/696.

23.6   ONLINE SERVICES

Various websites provide online services, including credit broking and comparative sites of charges and features of credit products. These sites are subject to the usual legislative and contract law provisions, including in relation to data protection and privacy policy, advertising and marketing, offer and acceptance, distance contracts, rights of cancellation, payment by card, protection against fraudulent use of a payment card and electronic communications.

23.7   'DURABLE MEDIUM'

Given that various documents relating to consumer credit and hire agreements may take the form of distance contracts and be produced in electronic form it is surprising and ironic that only the Consumer Credit (Disclosure of Information) Regulations 2004 expressly refer to disclosure being contained in a document which is 'on paper or on another durable medium which is available and accessible to the debtor or hirer'.[1]

Based upon the definition in the Financial Services(Distance Marketing) Regulations 2004, 'durable medium' is defined as 'any instrument which enables a consumer to store information addressed personally to him in a way accessible for future reference for a period of time adequate for the purposes of the information and which allows the unchanged reproduction of the information stored'.[2] Its inclusion is ironic as the above Disclosure of Information Regulations do not apply to distance contracts, which are the subject of the above Distance Marketing Regulations.[3]

Whilst it appears that pre-contract disclosure and the regulated credit agreement under the 2010 Consumer Credit Regulations can also be effected electronically in the case of a distance contract, the requirement for such contract to be in a durable medium, where not on paper, is derived from the above Distance Marketing Regulations.[4]

The meaning of 'durable medium' was considered by the European Court of Justice which opined that 'Where a medium allows the consumer to store the information which has been addressed to him personally, ensures that its content is not altered and that the information is accessible for an adequate period, and gives consumers the possibility to reproduce it unchanged, that medium must be regarded as "durable" within the meaning of that provision' (i.e. Directive 97/7/EC on the protection of consumers in respect of distance contracts).[5]

1   SI 2004/1481, reg 4(d)(iv).
2   Ibid., reg 1(2) and SI 2004/2095, reg 2(1).
3   SI 2004/1481, reg 2(3).

4 SI 2004/2095, reg 8(1).
5 Judgment of the Court (Third Chamber) of 5 July 2012 in *Content Services Ltd v Bundesarbeitskammer* ECJC-05.07.2012 C-49/11.

23.8   FCA HANDBOOK

The FCA Handbook contains rules and guidance on e-commerce and electronic communications, notably in CONC 2.8 and MCOB 2.7 and 2.7A.

Chapter 24

Unfair relationships

24.1 THE STATUTORY PROVISIONS

Sections 19 to 22 of the Consumer Credit Act 2006 introduced the concept of unfair relationships between creditors and debtors, originally in the form of ss 140A to 140D of the Consumer Credit Act 1974. Section 140D was repealed with the abolition of the Office of Fair Trading. The provisions mark a radical departure from the provisions on extortionate credit bargains which they replaced and which were generally considered to be ineffective, principally because of the heavy burden of proof placed on the debtor. In order to establish that an agreement constituted an extortionate credit bargain the debtor had to prove that the transaction required him to make payments which were grossly exorbitant or that the transaction otherwise grossly contravened ordinary principles of fair dealing.

Section 140A(1) empowers the court to make an order in connection with a credit agreement if it determines that the relationship between the creditor and the debtor arising out of the agreement (or the agreement taken with any related agreement) is unfair to the debtor because of one or more of the following:

(a)   any of the terms of the agreement or of any related agreement;

(b)   the way in which the creditor has exercised or enforced any of his rights under the agreement or any related agreement;

(c)   any other thing done (or not done) by, or on behalf of, the creditor either before or after the making of the agreement or any related agreement.[1]

In deciding whether to make a determination a court must have regard to all matters it thinks relevant (including matters relating to the creditor and matters relating to the debtor. Except to the extent that it is not appropriate to do so, a court must treat anything done (or not done) by, or on behalf of, or in relation to, an associate or a former associate of the creditor as if done (or not done) by, or on behalf of, or in relation to, the creditor. A court may make a determination in relation to a relationship notwithstanding that it may have ended.[2]

Where a court finds that a credit agreement gives rise to unfair relationships, it is given extensive powers. They include requiring the creditor, or any associate or former associate of the creditor, to repay in whole or in part any sum paid by the debtor or by a surety under or in relation to the agreement, or to do or to refrain from doing anything in connection with the agreement or any related agreement. A court may reduce or discharge any sum payable by the debtor or a surety in respect of the agreement or any related agreement, set aside any duty imposed on the debtor or a surety and alter the terms of the agreement or any related agreement. It may order the return to the surety of any property provided by him by way of security.[3]

As section 140A(1) applies to a 'credit agreement' between a creditor and a debtor, it is not restricted to regulated credit agreements under CCA 1974. For the purposes of these provisions, 'creditor' and 'debtor' include persons to whom their respective rights and duties under the agreement have passed by assignment or operation of law.[4] In fact this provision is superfluous as it is provided for in the definitions of 'creditor' and 'debtor' in s 189(1).

Where two or more persons are the creditor or the debtor, the provisions apply to any one or more of such persons.[5]

A 'related agreement' is a credit agreement which is consolidated by a subsequent credit agreement, or a linked transaction in relation to the credit agreement or a security provided in relation to either such agreement.[6]

The unfair relationships provisions came into force on 6 April 2007.[7] The provisions are retrospective to an agreement whenever made, except for an agreement completed before 6 April 2007,[8] that is one under which no sum is payable or will still become payable.[9]

The provisions reflect a swing of the pendulum in favour of the debtor to the detriment of the creditor. As will have been noted, 'unfair relationships' is very widely defined, the courts are given extensive powers in relation to agreements which are found to contravene the sections and a debtor or surety need merely allege that the relationship between the creditor and the debtor arising out of the agreement is unfair to the debtor, in order for the onus of proof to pass to the creditor to prove the contrary.[10]

1 CCA 1974, s 140A(1).
2 Ibid., s 140A(2), (3) and (4).
3 Ibid., s 140B.
4 Ibid., s 140C(2)(a).
5 Ibid., s 140C(2)(b).
6 Ibid., s 140C(4).
7 SI 2007/123, art 3(2) read with Sch 2.
8 CCA 2006, s 69 read with Sch 3, para 14(2).
9 Ibid., s 69 read with Sch 3, para 1.
10 CCA 1974, s 140B(9).

24.2 INTERPRETATION AND APPLICATION OF THE PROVISIONS

24.2.1 Plevin v Paragon Personal Finance Ltd

The starting point in a consideration of the meaning of the unfair relationship provisions is the seminal Supreme Court decision of *Plevin v Paragon Personal Finance Ltd*.[1] Whilst the decision is authority both on the meaning of unfair relationships and of the expression 'by, or on behalf of, the creditor', it is essentially concerned with omissions, in the form of undisclosed commission, rather than with an act or commission.

Outlining the basis of s 140A, Lord Sumption, who delivered the judgment of the court, stated:[2]

'Section 140A is deliberately framed in wide terms with very little in the way of guidance about the criteria for its application, such as is to be found in other provisions of the Act conferring discretionary powers on the courts. It is not possible to state a precise or universal test for its application, which must depend on the court's judgment of all the relevant facts. Some general points may, however, be made. First, what must be unfair is the relationship between the debtor and the creditor. In a case like the present one, where the terms themselves are not intrinsically unfair, this will often be because the relationship is so one-sided as substantially to limit the debtor's ability to choose. Secondly, although the court is concerned with hardship to the debtor, subsection 140A(2) envisages that matters relating to the creditor or the debtor may also be relevant. There may be features of the transaction which operate harshly against the debtor but it does not necessarily follow that the relationship is unfair. These features may be required in order to protect what the court regards as a legitimate interest of the creditor. Thirdly, the alleged unfairness must arise from one of the three categories of cause listed at sub-paragraphs (a) to (c). Fourthly, the great majority of relationships between commercial lenders and private borrowers are probably characterised by large differences of financial knowledge and expertise. It is an inherently unequal relationship. But it cannot have been Parliament's intention that the generality of such relationships should be liable to be reopened for that reason alone.'

The court opined that the fairness or unfairness of a debtor-creditor relationship may legitimately be influenced by the standard of commercial conduct reasonably to be expected of the creditor. It held that the non-disclosure of commission payable out of Mrs Plevin's PPI premium made her relationship with Paragon unfair. A sufficiently extreme inequality of knowledge and understanding was a classic source of unfairness in any relationship between a creditor and a non-commercial debtor. It was a question of degree and necessary to determine at which point the non-disclosure of information exceeded the tipping point. Thus:

'Mrs Plevin must be taken to have known that some commission would be payable to intermediaries out of the premium before it reached the insurer. The fact was stated in the FISA borrowers' guide and, given that she was not paying LLP for their services, there was no other way that they could have been remunerated. But at some point commissions may become so large that the relationship cannot be regarded as fair if the customer is kept in ignorance. At what point is difficult to say, but wherever the tipping point may lie the commissions paid in this case are a long way beyond it. Mrs Plevin's evidence, as recorded by the recorder, was that if she had known that 71·8% of the premium would be paid out in commissions, she would have "certainly questioned this". I do not find that evidence surprising. The information was of critical relevance. Of course, had she shopped around, she would not necessarily have got better terms. As the Competition Commission's report suggests, this was not a competitive market. But Mrs Plevin did not have to take PPI at all. Any reasonable person in her position who was told that more than two thirds of the premium was going to intermediaries, would be bound to question whether the insurance represented value for money, and whether it was a sensible transaction to enter into. The fact that she was left in ignorance in my opinion made the relationship unfair.'[3]

The fact that the information omitted went beyond the so-called tipping point made the relationship unfair. It is therefore the tipping point that must be established on the facts in any case that relates to omitted information.

The court next considered whether the state of affairs arising from omitted information was 'something done or not done by or on behalf of Paragon' and opined:

> 'Bearing in mind the breadth of s 140A and the incidence of the burden of proof according to s 140B(9), the creditor must normally be regarded as responsible for an omission making his relationship with the debtor unfair if he fails to take such steps as (i) it would be reasonable to expect the creditor or someone acting on his behalf to take in the interests of fairness, and (ii) would have removed the source of that unfairness or mitigated its consequences so that the relationship as a whole can no longer be regarded as unfair.'[4]

> 'On that footing, I think it is clear that the unfairness which arose from the non-disclosure of the amount of the commissions was the responsibility of Paragon. Paragon was the only party who must necessarily have known the size of both commissions. It could have disclosed them to Mrs Plevin. Given its significance for her decision, I consider that in the interests of fairness it would have been reasonable to expect it to do so. Had it done so this particular source of unfairness would have been removed because Mrs Plevin would then have been able to make a properly informed judgment about the value of the PPI policy.'[5]

The court analysed the expression 'by, or on behalf of' in the following terms:[6]

(a) in their ordinary and natural meaning, the words import agency and there is nothing in the present statutory context to suggest a wider meaning;

(b) when the Consumer Credit Act imputes responsibility to the creditor for the acts or omissions of others who are not necessarily the creditor's agents, it does so in express and clear terms, with the notable exception of s 140A itself; and

(c) if the expression was meant to extend beyond simple agency and deemed agency, there are no coherent criteria by which to determine what, if any, connection is required between the creditor and acts or omissions causing the unfairness.

Some of the writer's post *Plevin* observations:

(a) The deemed agency provisions of CCA 1974, s 56(1)(b) and (c) would, in the circumstances described in those sections, visit any omission or commission of the credit broker or supplier in antecedent negotiations on the creditor. Indeed, so it was held in *Scotland v British Credit Trust Ltd*[7] and *Townson v FCE Bank plc (t/a Ford Credit)*.[8] *Scotland* also considered the question of a related agreement under s 140C(4) in relation to a PPI policy, sold with a loan agreement in the course of antecedent negotiations.

(b) Section 140A enables the court to take into account relevant misrepresentations attributable to the creditor, even if some of them occurred more than 12 years before the date of the claim, this being the limitation period for an action on a specialty.[9]

(c) *Axton v GE Money Mortgages Ltd*[10] is an example of a case where the facts were distinguishable from those in *Plevin*, whilst *Brookman v Welcome Financial Services Ltd*[11] is an illustration of a case involving similar facts to those in *Plevin.*

(d) Sections 140A to 140C (initially also s 140D) were introduced into CCA 1974 in 2006, following extensive Parliamentary debate which intentionally left the scope of s 140A wide open for determination and application by the courts. Ironically, *Plevin* has set parameters which narrow the scope of the expression 'by, or on behalf of' in s 140A.

1 [2014] GCCR 12085, [2014] UKSC 61.
2 At para [10].
3 At para [18].
4 At para [19].
5 At para [20].
6 At paras [30] to [32].
7 [2014] GCCR 12141, [2014] EWCA Civ 790, CA, especially at para 65.
8 [2016] GCCR 14155, County Court, Birmingham
9 [2014] GCCR 12141, [2014] EWCA Civ 790, CA, especially at para 82.
10 [2015] GCCR 13105, [2015] EWHC 1343 (QB).
11 [2015] GCCR 13267, County Court, Cardiff (Mercantile List).

24.2.2 Further illustrative cases

We turn to briefly consider some illustrative cases relating to the issue of unfair relationships in the context of consumer and commercial credit agreements.

In *Paragon Mortgages Ltd v McEwan-Peters*[1] the court held that there is no unfairness within the meaning of s 140A where demand for repayment of a mortgage debt is made in circumstances where this is commonplace in the industry, is not based on an arbitrary decision and is not prompted by an improper motive.

In the commercial context, the cases of *Mohamad Khodari v Fahad Al Tamimi*[2] and *Shafik Rahman v HSBC Bank*[3] indicate that the courts will give primary credence to commercial considerations and prevailing industry practice in ruling on an allegation of unfair relationships. In the former, Blair J stated:[4]

> 'The Defendant's case is that a claim to a 10% return on lending which might be outstanding only for a matter of days in circumstances where he was led to believe that half of that return would be used to meet the Claimant's own borrowing costs is manifestly unfair: see ss 140A(1)(a) and (c). If the court agrees, then it has power to "reduce or discharge" the profit element claimed.
>
> I do not accept this submission. I have already held that the Defendant was not led to believe that 5% was attributable to the Claimants' own borrowing costs when dealing with the misrepresentation allegation. The size of the charge is plainly very large compared to the short period of the loan, but this has to be seen in the light of the credit risk assumed in making the loan, as this litigation shows very clearly. The Defendant wanted these loans, and could well afford to repay them. There was nothing unfair to him in the relationship between the parties which would justify invoking s 140A.'

In *Shafik Rahman v HSBC Bank*, HHJ Behrens, sitting as a judge of the High Court, opined:[5]

'The terms of the Agreements

This was commercial lending involving very substantial sums of money. There is no suggestion that Mr Rahman had the weaker bargaining position. He was quite willing to take his business elsewhere and threatened to do so on a number of occasions. Indeed much of his case was predicated on the submission that he was in a strong bargaining position.

At no stage did he complain about the terms that are now suggested to be unfair whereas he did complain about a number of other terms. As Mr Wilson pointed out he plainly read the terms and conditions with some care.

In the light of my findings none of the terms were inconsistent with what was discussed at the meeting of 28 June 2006. I agree with David Steel J that the repayment of overdraft facilities on demand cannot remotely be considered to be unfair. It is commonplace in the industry and in the nature of an overdraft. The five year facility was not repayable on demand. It was repayable after five years. There is nothing unfair about that. A term entitling a mortgagee to appoint an LPA receiver on breach is also standard in the industry and cannot in my view be regarded as unfair.

Equally I do not regard the cross default clause as being unfair. It is not clear whether such a clause is standard but at least one of the other banks offering terms to Mr Rahman would have included such a clause. It has to be remembered that there were multiple facilities offered to various costs centres all of which were supported by multiple securities. In such a case there are sound commercial reasons for the cross default clause.

The Manner of Enforcement

I have set out the history of enforcement in some detail so as to demonstrate that this is not a case where HSBC have arbitrarily decided to serve a demand for immediate repayment and then appointed Receivers. On the contrary through Mr Barreau HSBC have since February 2011 adopted a patient attitude and have tried to find a solution to the dispute …

In my view HSBC's decision to enforce its securities at the end of August cannot remotely be described as unfair. It is true that Mr Rahman always paid the interest due under the facility letters. However I agree with Mr Wilson that this does not assist him. The obligation on the Trustees, and Mr and Mrs Rahman was to repay the capital after five years. If they could avoid enforcement by simply paying the interest after this time they would be able to convert a five year term to a term of indefinite length.

I also agree with Mr Wilson that when the whole of the correspondence is looked at it was not unfair of HSBC to refuse to accede to the requests in Mrs Rahman's letter of 19 August 2011 and the solicitors' letter of 30 August 2011. In my view Mr Rahman had been given more than sufficient time to make proposals since May 2011 and had declined to do so.

In all the circumstances I reject the application for an order under s140A of the Act.'

It was held in *Barnes v Black Horse Limited*[6] that s 140A permits the court to take into account related agreements which are no longer in operation, in determining whether unfair relationships have arisen in respect of an agreement which is still in force.

The Court of Appeal held, in *Graves v Capital Homes Ltd,*[7] that it would have to be an exceptional case for a court to find that a mortgagee, whose power of sale had become exercisable, had acted unfairly in realising its security.

In *McMullon v Secure The Bridge Ltd*[8] the Court of Appeal rejected the appeal from the County Court which had found that the facts did not support the conclusion that the relationship between lender and borrower breached the unfair relationships test. Although parts of the agreement were inappropriate, the appellant borrower had not been misled or influenced by the respondent claimant. On the facts, as found by Hildyard J in the County Court, the appellant was fully aware of the interest of her coach and trainer in the claimant company, he had not abused his position or given any wrong or misleading advice and, insofar as the appellant entered into a high-risk transaction, she did so with her eyes open and was willing to take a risk.

Nelmes v NRAM Plc[9] involved a credit broker who acted for the borrower but, unbeknown to the borrower, was paid commission by the creditor. Finding that this gave rise to unfair relationships, Lord Justice Christopher Clarke, delivering the judgment of the Court of Appeal, stated:[10]

'The claim against NR [NRAM Plc] in the present action is not a claim that it should account for the commission or for rescission of the credit agreement, but that relief should be given because of the unfair nature of the relationship. That claim raises different, and broader, considerations. I am, however, quite satisfied that in this respect the relationship between NR, the creditor, and Mr Nelmes, the debtor, arising out of the loan agreements was unfair on account of the combination of the following: (i) the term of the credit agreement that Mr Nelmes should pay NR an arrangement fee; (ii) the related agreement that NR should pay commission of half that amount to Mr Nelmes' broker; (iii) the payment of that commission; and (iv) the failure of NR to tell Nelmes about the payment. A relationship between lender and borrower which involves such a payment deprives the borrower of the disinterested advice of his broker and is, for that reason, unfair.'

A useful precis of criteria which determine whether subject matter gives rise to unfairness and unfair relationships is to be found in *Deutsche Bank (Suisse) SA v Khan*,[11] as follows:

'In considering the test of unfairness guidance is provided by the following authorities in particular: *Maple Leaf Macro Volatility Master Fund and another v Rouvroy and others* [2009] EWHC 257 (Comm), [2009] 2 All ER (Comm) 287, [2009] 1 Lloyd's Rep 475 ("*Maple Leaf*"); *Paragon Mortgages Ltd v McEwan-Peters* [2011] EWHC 2491 (Comm) ("*Paragon Mortgages*"); and *Rahman and others v HSBC Bank plc and others* [2012] EWHC 11 (Ch) ("*Rahman*").

These authorities suggest that the matters likely to be of relevance include the following:

(1) In relation to the fairness of the terms themselves:

    a.   whether the term is commonplace and/or in the nature of the product in question (*Rahman* [277]);

b.   whether there are sound commercial reasons for the term (*Rahman* [278]);

c.   whether it represents a legitimate and proportionate attempt by the creditor to protect its position (*Maple Leaf* [288]);

d.   to the extent that a term is solely for the benefit of the lender, whether it exists to protect him from a risk which the debtor does not face (*Maple Leaf* [289]);

e.   the scale of the lending and whether it was commercial or quasi-commercial in nature (*Rahman* [275]) (a court is likely to be slower to find unfairness in high value lending arrangements between commercial parties than in credit agreements affecting consumers); and

f.   the strength (or otherwise) of the debtors bargaining position (*Rahman* [275]);

g.   whether the terms have been individually negotiated or are pro forma terms and, if so, whether they have been presented on a "take it or leave it" basis (*Rahman* [275]);

(2)   In relation to the creditor's conduct before and at the time of formation:

a.   whether the creditor applied any pressure on the borrowers to execute the agreement (if an agreement has been entered into with a sense of urgency it will be relevant to consider to what extent responsibility for this lay with the debtor, as distinct from the creditor) (*Maple Leaf* [274]);

b.   whether the creditor understood and had reasonable grounds to believe that the borrower had experience of the relevant arrangements and had available to him the advice of solicitors (*Maple Leaf* [274]);

c.   whether the creditor had any reason to think that the debtor had not read or understood the terms (*Maple Leaf* [274]); and

d.   whether the debtor demurred at the time of formation over the terms he now suggests are unfair (this point has particular force if he did complain over other terms) (*Maple Leaf* [274]; *Rahman* [276]).

(3)   In relation to the creditor's conduct following formation and leading up to enforcement:

a.   whether any demand was prompted by an "improper motive" or was the consequence of an "arbitrary decision" (*Paragon Mortgages* [54(b)]);

b.   whether the creditor has shown patience and, before leaping to enforcement, has taken steps in the hope of reaching some form of accommodation (for example by attending meetings, engaging in correspondence and/or inviting proposals) (*Rahman* [280]–[281]); and

c.   whether the debtor has resisted attempts at accommodation by raising unfounded claims against the creditor (*Rahman* [280]–[281]).'

1 [2011] GCCR 11367, [2011] EWHC 2491 (Comm).
2 [2008] GCCR 8561, [2008] EWHC 3065 (QB).
3 [2012] EWHC 11 (Ch).
4 At paras 45–46.
5 At paras 275–285.
6 [2011] GCCR 11301.
7 [2014] GCCR 12047, [2014] EWCA Civ 1297.
8 [2015] GCCR 13159, [2015] EWCA Civ 884.
9 [2016] GCCR 14081, [2016] EWCA Civ 491.
10 At para 35.
11 [2013] EWHC 482 (Comm) at paras 345 and 346.

24.3   THE BURDEN OF PROOF

Where the debtor or a surety alleges that the relationship between the creditor and the debtor is unfair to the debtor, it is for the creditor to prove the contrary.[1] The question arises as to what is meant by 'alleges'; does the debtor or surety have to provide more information in support of his allegation or will a bare allegation suffice?

In *Bevin v Datum Finance Limited*[2] the court held that it is not incumbent on the debtor to show a *prima facie* case as to unfairness. All he has to do is to make an allegation of unfairness.

It is respectfully submitted that a claim of unfair relationships must at the very least be amplified by a statement of allegedly relevant facts. It is difficult to see how a bare allegation of unfair relationships can require the creditor to answer the same, as he might justifiably ask what it is that he is required to answer.

1 CCA 1974, s 140B(9).
2 [2011] EWHC 3542 (Ch).

24.4   REFLECTIONS ON THE UNFAIR RELATIONSHIPS PROVISIONS

The provisions relate to the relationship between the creditor and the debtor, something more enduring and permanent than the underlying cause of unfairness or imbalance in the rights and obligations arising under the contract, to the detriment of the consumer.[1] The status of unfair relationships is a deduction a court is required to consider on the basis of the existence of one or more of the factors set out in s 140A(1). Unfair relationships arise as a result of one or more of the underlying causes or factors in s 140A(1)(a), (b) and (c) but are not to be equated with those factors, as otherwise the statutory provisions would have omitted all mention of unfair relationships and merely referred to unfairness as between the creditor and the debtor by reason of one or more of those factors. As was stated in *Harrison v Black Horse Ltd*,[2] 'it is the relationship between the parties which must be determined to be unfair, not their agreement, although it is envisaged that the terms of the agreement may themselves give rise to an unfair relationship'.

In passing, the expression 'related agreement' is not defined, although 'an agreement related to a credit agreement' is described in s 140C(4); definitions of 'associate' and 'linked transaction' are to be found in s 189(1).

Some lawyers maintain that the unfair relationships provisions are so vaguely drafted that they are unlikely to comply with Article 1, Protocol 1, of the European Convention on Human Rights, which was incorporated into UK law by the Human Rights Act 1998 and that they violate the constitutional principle of legal certainty. An Opinion to this effect[3] was considered by the Joint Committee on Human Rights of the UK Parliament. It concluded that EU case law expressly acknowledges that some laws are required by their subject matter to be flexible, that there is suitable guidance available as to the meaning of 'unfair' in the case law and that, while citizens must be able to foresee the consequences of their conduct, if needs be with appropriate advice, creditors can and should be able to obtain sufficient advice about the meaning of 'unfairness' by seeking the meaning of that term in other closely analogous contexts. Whilst specific guidance as to the meaning of 'unfair' in relation to the 'unfair relationships' provisions might be desirable, the Committee considered that the absence of such guidance in the Act did not render the unfair relationship provisions incompatible with Article 1, Protocol 1, of the European Convention on Human Rights.[4]

We next turn to briefly consider the three separate limbs of s 140A(1).

The first test or limb of unfair relationships is whether the relationship arising out of the agreement is unfair to the debtor because of any of the terms of the agreement or of any related agreement. As the relationship is linked to the terms of the agreement, the courts are required to determine the fairness of the contractual relationship between creditor and debtor by reference to the agreement or any regulated agreement. This can be done by referring to other relevant legislation, such as the Unfair Contract Terms Act 1977, Part 2 of the Consumer Rights Act 2015, the common law and relevant case law. Courts might also resort to the law of equity in the context of mortgages (admittedly a creature of equity). Equity will give relief if the contractual terms are unfair, oppressive or unconscionable. For example, in *Multiservice Bookbinding Ltd v Marden*,[5] the court stated that the classic example of an unconscionable bargain is where advantage is taken of a young, inexperienced or ignorant person to introduce a term which no sensible, well advised person would have accepted.

In *Director General of Fair Trading v First National Bank plc*[6] the House of Lords had to consider the provision in the then Unfair Terms in Consumer Contracts Regulations 1994 that a contractual term which has not been individually negotiated is unfair if, contrary to the requirement of good faith, it causes a significant imbalance in the parties' rights and obligations to the detriment of the consumer. It opined that good faith in this context was not an artificial or technical concept, nor a concept unfamiliar to British lawyers. The law looked to good standards of commercial morality and practice.

The government's eleventh hour amendment to the Bill, by way of the introduction of s 25(2B) of CCA 1974, now prescribed by the FCA in CONC 5, requiring creditors to lend responsibly, will provide further support for this limb.

The unfair relationships provisions also apply to the terms of any related agreement.[7] A credit agreement may therefore give rise to unfair relationships because of any of the terms of the underlying agreement financed by the credit agreement. The connection between a supply agreement and a financing agreement is well recognised in hire-purchase, conditional sale, credit sale and connected loan or debtor-creditor-supplier agreements. Whilst the new provision marks a considerable shift in emphasis, as it encompasses all personal loan agreements, and of necessity puts financiers on their guard in relation to the terms of supply agreements financed by them, it is already in the reasonable expectation of creditors that their potential liability extends to the terms of transactions financed by their credit agreements. However, it should be noted in this regard that the unfair relationships provisions effectively impose on creditors liability equivalent to that under s 75 of CCA 1974 in circumstances where the statutory indemnity under that section may not be available to them.

The second test or limb of 'unfair relationships' is whether the relationship is unfair to the debtor because of the way in which the creditor has exercised or enforced any of his rights under the agreement or any related agreement. This means that the fairness of an agreement can be tested not merely by what is stated in the agreement on the date it is entered into, but also on how the agreement is operated and enforced in practice. This would include any variation of the agreement, its terms and debt collection procedures. For example, where an interest rate under a credit agreement starts at a fair and competitive rate but is varied frequently and to rates unconnected to generally prevailing interest rates, the agreement will be open to challenge under this section.

The House of Lords in *Wilson v First County Trust Ltd*[8] stated that inherent in Article 1 of the First Protocol of the European Convention on Human rights is the need to hold a fair balance between the public interest and the protection of the fundamental rights of creditors. The fairness of a system of law governing the contractual or proprietary rights of private persons is a matter of public concern and Parliament is charged with the primary responsibility for deciding whether the means chosen to deal with a social problem are both necessary and appropriate. The court added that the more severe the sanction, the more important it is that the law should be unambiguous.

Given that s 140B of CCA 1974 confers on the court a wide range of remedies, it appears likely that this limb will be considered to be not unduly wide or uncertain in its ambit, as the court will order a remedy which fits the particular circumstances. Moreover the section is restricted to the manner in which the creditor, and not any person under the related agreement, has exercised or enforced his rights.

The third test or limb of 'unfair relationships' is whether the relationship arising out of the agreement is unfair to the debtor because of any other thing done or not done by or on behalf of the creditor (or by any associate or former associate of the creditor) either before or after the making of the agreement or any related agreement. The act or omission in question need not be limited, or necessarily linked, to the credit agreement. Indeed, the inference must be that this test or limb extends to circumstances beyond the first two limbs.

It is submitted that this limb is so widely couched as to impose obligations upon creditors which are incapable of certainty or circumscription. Indeed, that is the very object of the provision. In the words of Lord Sainsbury in Grand Committee considering the Bill:[9]

'I believe it would assist noble Lords if I briefly explain the Government's position in relation to the test and the need to define unfair relationships.

The new test is general so that it can catch all unfair relationships. It does not exist in a vacuum – Parliament and Ministers have already specified in other legislation those terms and practices that are unfair when considered alone. The new test is broader and is directed at looking at the substance of the relationship between the debtor and the creditor. This consideration will depend on the circumstances of the particular case. The court can consider anything that is relevant in deciding that there is an unfair relationship. Therefore, we do not want to give undue emphasis to some things by spelling them out, as this could mean that in practice the range of issues that the court considers is limited. It is not possible to define an unfair relationship as being certain things, or combinations of specific types of conduct, without limiting it in some way. That would serve to reduce the effectiveness of the test and the ability of the court to tackle unfair relationships – whatever form they take.'

In the writer's view the breadth and vagueness of this provision and the fact that it gives no indication of the type of conduct which is relevant (even though s 140A(2) obliges the court only to have regard to matters it thinks relevant), or the time preceding or following the contract within which the act or omission must have occurred, results in imposing obligations on creditors which are uncertain and unquantifiable. Arguably, the third limb creates a fiduciary relationship between creditor and debtor, something which is beyond the scope of a credit agreement. It is submitted that the third limb produces an unfair balance between the public interest and the protection of the fundamental rights of creditors, and conflicts with the provisions of Article 1, Protocol 1, of the European Convention on Human Rights. It appears to fail the tests in *Wilson v First County Trust Ltd*.[10]

One might usefully contrast the third limb with the more specific test in the Consumer Protection from Unfair Trading Regulations 2008. Under these regulations a commercial practice is unfair if it contravenes the requirements of professional diligence and it materially distorts or is likely to materially distort the economic behaviour of the average consumer with regard to the product.[11]

There are exceptional factors which ought to influence a court in adopting a restrictive approach to the interpretation of s 140A(1). The first is the fact that the provisions apply retrospectively to a credit agreement whenever made (CCA 2006, Sch 3, para 14)) as well as to an agreement or relationship which has ended (s 140A(4) of CCA 1974). The second is the fact that the 'unfair relationships' provisions can be invoked merely on application or assertion of the same by the debtor or surety. Thirdly, Parliament had the opportunity to set parameters to the law in the interest of fairness and certainty for both debtor and creditor when it is a principle of legal policy that law should be certain and predictable.[12]

1 Compare the requirement for contract terms to be unfair in the Consumer Rights Act 2015, s 62.
2 [2011] GCCR 11327, [2011] EWCA Civ 1128 at para 37.
3 By Michael Beloff QC and Andrew Hunter in their Opinion. See *Hansard*, vol 674, No 47, p 1040.
4 Joint Committee on Human Rights First Report dated 24 October 2005.
5 [1978] 2 All ER 489.
6 [2001] GCCR 3075.
7 CCA 1974, s 140A(1).

8 [2003] GCCR 4931.
9 *Hansard*, vol 675, No 56, GC 159.
10 See note 8 above.
11 SI 2008/1277, reg 3(3) based on Directive 2005/29/EC of 11 May 2005 concerning unfair busi-ness-to-consumer commercial practices, Art 5, para 2(b).
12 Bennion, *Statutory Interpretation* (4th edn, LexisNexis Butterworths), s 266 and *Halsbury's Laws of England* (LexisNexis Butterworths), vol 44(1) para 1434.

Chapter 25

Enforcement, dispute resolution and damages claims

25.1 MEANING OF 'ENFORCEMENT'

'Enforcement' is used in at least three senses in CCA 1974. Thus:

(a) Section 65 provides that an improperly executed agreement is enforceable against the debtor or hirer only on an order of the court.[1] A retaking of goods or land to which the agreement relates is an enforcement of the agreement.[2]

(b) Section 76 regulates the creditor's or owner's entitlement to enforce a term of a regulated agreement.[3]

(c) Although not expressly referring to enforcement, s 87, which prescribes the need for a statutory default notice before a creditor or owner can act upon the debtor's or hirer's default, is clearly addressing the enforcement of the underlying agreement.[4]

The meaning of 'enforcement' in CCA 1974 was considered in some detail by Flaux J in *McGuffick v Royal Bank of Scotland plc*,[5] where he opined:[6]

> 'The Consumer Credit Act does not define what constitutes "enforcement" and therefore does not define what actions a creditor may not undertake during a period when the agreement is unenforceable. Both sections 76 (dealing with provisions in agreements which entitle a creditor to take certain steps when an event, such as bankruptcy, occurs, but there is no breach of contract by the debtor) and 87 (dealing with the entitlement of the creditor to take such steps where there has been a breach) contemplate that those steps will amount to enforcement. Those steps include matters which might be said to be obviously enforcement such as (under section 87), enforcing security or (under both sections) recovering possession of goods or land.
>
> Both sections also include two steps which might be said less obviously to amount to enforcement: (i) demanding earlier repayment of any sum and (ii) treating any right conferred on the debtor by the agreement as terminated, restricted or deferred. The former of these is referring to a provision in the agreement which provides that on the occurrence of the triggering event (in a non-breach case within section 76) or of default amounting to breach under section 87, the creditor is entitled to demand immediate repayment of the total amount outstanding under the

agreement. It was no doubt because the agreement in the present case contained such a provision that the bank served the default notice as it did on 16 May 2007.

However, nothing in either sections 76 or 87 can be said to give one any real clue as to the parameters of the concept of enforcement, for the purposes of determining what, if any, action by the creditor is permissible during the period when the agreement is unenforceable by virtue of section 77(1), let alone whether, as the claimant contends, reporting to the CRAs [credit reference agencies] amounts to enforcement and so is not permitted during that period.'

Flaux J, as he then was, considered whether the specific actions in the case amounted to enforcement and stated:[7]

'In contrast, the bank invited the court (as set out in the list of issues) to conclude not only that reporting to the CRAs did not amount to enforcement, but that a number of other activities did not constitute enforcement: (i) reporting to CRAs without also telling them that the agreement is currently unenforceable; (ii) disseminating or threatening to disseminate the claimant's personal data in respect of the agreement to any third party; (iii) demanding payment from the claimant; (iv) issuing a default notice to the claimant; (v) threatening legal action and (vi) instructing a third party to demand payment or otherwise to seek to procure payment.

So far as activities (iii) to (vi) are concerned, it was accepted on behalf of the claimant that these did not amount to enforcement or actions to enforce the agreement. That concession seems to me to be correct: at most these activities are steps preparatory to subsequent enforcement. Furthermore, in a recent decision, *Rankine v American Express Services Europe Ltd* [2009] CCLR 3, HHJ Simon Brown QC (sitting as a Deputy High Court Judge) concluded that the bringing of proceedings is only a step taken with a view to enforcement and not actually enforcement. It seems to me that that conclusion must be correct. Were it otherwise, as Mr Handyside pointed out, one would be left with the conundrum that the creditor could not apply to the court for an enforcement order under section 127(1), because to do so would amount to enforcement, not permitted by section 65(1).

Once it is recognised that the bringing of proceedings is not enforcement, it necessarily follows that activities (iii) to (vi) do not constitute enforcement, since they are all steps taken prior to the commencement of proceedings and therefore by definition, at most, steps taken with a view to enforcement.

I do not consider that either reporting to the CRAs or the related activities referred to in (i) and (ii) come anywhere near amounting to enforcement if activities (iii) to (vi) are not enforcement. These activities are concerned with reporting to CRAs or other third parties and are not even steps taken prior to enforcement such as threatening proceedings would be. Even if one accepted (which for reasons given earlier in this judgment I do not) the claimant's somewhat pejorative categorisation of reporting to CRAs as being motivated by the desire to pressurise the claimant into paying the outstanding balance, at its highest that is an attempt by indirect means to persuade the claimant to pay. If demanding payment directly or through a third party does not amount to enforcement, it is difficult to see how such indirect means could do so, even if the claimant were right as to the relevant motive of the bank.

It follows that, in my judgment the reporting to CRAs and related activities do not constitute enforcement for the purposes of the Consumer Credit Act.'

1   CCA 1974, s 65(1).
2   Ibid., s 65(2).
3   See further **25.2** below.
4   Ibid., s 87(1).
5   [2009] GCCR 9551, [2009] EWHC 2386 (Comm).
6   Ibid., at paras 74 to 76.
7   Ibid., at paras 79 to 82 and 85.

25.2   ENFORCING A TERM OF THE AGREEMENT

As a general rule, by virtue of s 76, a creditor or owner is not entitled to enforce a term of a regulated agreement without giving the debtor or hirer the prescribed notice, namely not less than seven days' written[1] notice in paper form.[2] The notice must be in the prescribed form.[3]

Enforcement of a term of a regulated agreement means demanding earlier payment of any sum, or recovering possession of any goods or land, or treating any right conferred on the debtor or hirer by the agreement as terminated, restricted or deferred, in each case not by reason of the debtor's or hirer's breach of the regulated agreement.[4]

By way of exception, there is no need to give such prior written notice of enforcement where the agreement is not for a specified duration, as in the case of a running-account credit agreement, and the period has not ended when the creditor or owner does an act as described in the preceding paragraph.[5]

A creditor may treat a debtor's right to draw on any credit as restricted or deferred and take steps to enforce such restriction or deferment without giving the debtor prior notice of any kind.[6] Thus, in a running-account credit card agreement the creditor is entitled to put a stop on the further use of the account or the further use of a credit-token without prior notice to the debtor.

Having regard to the creditor's general obligation to treat customers fairly, it is always advisable to give the debtor a reasonable period of notice, which may be a longer period than that prescribed by the legislation.

Consumer credit claims generally are subject to CPR 7.9, as supplemented by paragraph 7 of CPR PD 7B.

1   CCA 1974, s 76(1) and Consumer Credit (Enforcement, Default and Termination Notices) Regulations 1983, SI 1983/1561 (as amended).
2   Ibid., reg 2(4A).
3   CCA 1974, s 76(3) and the above Regulations, reg 2(1), Sch 1.
4   Ibid., s 76(1) and (6).
5   Ibid., s 76(2).
6   Ibid., s 87(2).

25.3   ENFORCEMENT FOLLOWING DEFAULT

25.3.1   CCA 1974 and statutory controls

A creditor or owner may not proceed against a debtor or hirer, where the debtor or hirer is in default under the agreement, without first serving a notice of default in the prescribed form.[1] The notice must be in paper form, give the debtor or hirer at least 14 days to remedy any breach capable of remedy and be accompanied by the current OFT default information sheet.[2] *Brandon v American Express Services Europe Limited*[3] reversed the decision of the County Court to the effect that, where a default notice did not provide the requisite 14 days' notice, the defect could be remedied by the creditor giving the debtor appropriate time before instituting enforcement action. That decision would have rendered nugatory any requirement to give the debtor the prescribed period of notice. The Appeal Court held that the 14 day notice was mandatory and that any shorter period of notice could not be condoned as *de minimis.*

A default notice is required before the creditor or owner is entitled, by reason of any breach by the debtor or hirer of a regulated agreement, to terminate the agreement, to demand earlier payment of any sum, to recover possession of any goods or land, to treat any right conferred on the debtor or hirer by the agreement as terminated, restricted or deferred, or to enforce any security.[4] Where a creditor or owner seeks to recover goods under a regulated hire-purchase, conditional sale or hire agreement, he must prove that the hirer's or buyer's possession would be adverse to his rights. This necessitates that the creditor or owner makes a demand for delivery of the goods in the default notice under s 88(5) or makes a request in writing for the surrender of the goods.[5]

As in the case of enforcement proceedings, a notice is not required for the creditor to treat a debtor's right to draw upon any credit as restricted or deferred and to take such steps as may be necessary to make the restriction or deferment effective.[6]

When a default notice overstated the amount due it has been held to be ineffective.[7]

In the case of a material or repudiatory breach (or a breach which is of the essence) of a regulated agreement which entitles the creditor to terminate the agreement, the creditor can recover, as damages (and the agreement will usually so stipulate), the unpaid balance of the total price, less the value of any repossessed goods and a discount in respect of the creditor's receipt of accelerated payment.[8] Any agreement may, by its terms, provide that a particular breach is of the essence.[9]

A creditor or owner may not harass his debtor or hirer or send letters which cause the debtor or hirer anxiety or stress.[10]

Consumer credit claims generally, are subject to CPR 7.9 as supplemented by CPR PD 7B.

1 CCA 1974, s 87; and see the regulations referred to at **25.2** above.
2 Ibid., s 88(2), (4A); and reg 2(4A). See also **Chapter 11**.
3 [2011] GCCR 11353, [2011] EWCA Civ 1187.
4 CCA 1974, s 87(1).
5 Ibid., s 134(1).
6 Ibid., s 87(2).
7 *Woodchester Lease Management Services Ltd v Swain & Co* [1998] All ER (D) 339, [1999] ECCR 2255, CA.
8 *Yeoman Credit Ltd v Waragowski* [1961] 3 All ER 145; see further *Financings Ltd v Baldock* [1963] 1 All ER 443.
9 *Lombard North Central plc v Butterworth* [1987] 1 All ER 267, CA.
10 Administration of Justice Act 1970, s 40 and Malicious Communications Act 1988.

25.3.2   FCA Handbook, CONC

CONC 7.3 regulates the treatment of customers in default or arrears, including repossessions. The rules and guidance apply to lenders, owners and debt collectors. The provisions cover:

(a)   dealing fairly with customers in arrears or default;

(b)   forbearance and due consideration;

(c)   proportionality; and

(d)   enforcement of debts.

25.4   TERMINATION OF AGREEMENT IN NON-DEFAULT CASES

A creditor or owner who wishes to terminate a regulated agreement which contains a contractual right of termination where the customer is not in default, must give the debtor or hirer not less than seven days' written notice of termination in the prescribed form.[1] This applies when the agreement is for a specified period and that period has not ended when the notice is given.[2]

The above requirements do not prevent the creditor from treating the debtor's right to draw on any credit as restricted or deferred and taking steps to enforce the same.[3]

1   CCA 1974, s 98(1); and see the regulations referred to at **25.2** above.
2   Ibid., s 98(2)(a) and (b).
3   Ibid., s 98(4).

25.5   NOTICE ON SURETY

Where a default notice or termination notice is served on a debtor or hirer, a copy of the notice, in paper form, must also be served by the creditor or owner on any surety.[1] Failure to serve such notice will result in the security being enforceable against the surety on an order of the court only.

1   CCA 1974, s 111.

25.6   RECOVERY OF POSSESSION OF GOODS OR LAND

A creditor or owner is not entitled to enter into any premises to take possession of goods which are the subject of a regulated hire-purchase agreement, a regulated conditional sale agreement or a regulated consumer hire agreement except on an order of the court.[1]

A creditor is not entitled to recover possession of land from a debtor under a regulated conditional sale agreement relating to land except on an order of the court.[2]

An entry in contravention of the foregoing is actionable as a breach of statutory duty giving rise to a claim in damages.[3] However, by virtue of s 173(3), an order of the court is not required in respect of any of the above actions if it is done at any time with the consent of the relevant person (debtor, hirer or owner/lessee or occupier of premises, as the case may be) given at that time, but the refusal of consent does not give rise to any liability.[4] Where goods have been lawfully repossessed following the termination of an agreement and the hirer or debtor pays the arrears the court may, as a matter of equity, grant relief.[5]

Where the hirer has abandoned the goods, the owner is entitled to retake possession of them without a court order as in that event he does not recover the goods 'from the hirer'.[6]

The reader is also referred to **25.3.2** above.

1 CCA 1974, s 92(1).
2 Ibid., s 126.
3 Ibid., s 92(2).
4 Ibid., s 173(3).
5 *Goker v NWS Bank plc* [1990] CCLR 34; see also **25.7** below.
6 *Bentinck Ltd v Cromwell Engineering Co* [1971] 1 QB 324.

25.7   RETAKING 'PROTECTED GOODS'

Where the debtor is in breach of a regulated hire-purchase or a regulated conditional sale agreement relating to goods and has paid to the creditor one-third or more of the total price of the goods, and the property in the goods remains in the creditor, the creditor is not entitled to recover possession of the goods, so called 'protected goods', from the debtor except on an order of the court.[1] If the creditor does recover the goods without a court order, the regulated agreement is deemed to be terminated and the debtor released from all liability under the agreement. In addition the debtor is entitled to recover from the creditor all sums paid by him under the agreement.[2] If, however, the hirer consents to recovery at the time when repossession is sought, the creditor may take the goods without an order of the court.[3] It will be necessary for the creditor to show that the hirer's consent was informed and voluntary.[4]

Proceedings for the recovery of protected goods must comply with the Consumer Credit Act Procedure set out in Practice Direction 7B at CPR PD 7B, as applied in *Hunter v Lex Vehicle Finance Ltd*.[5]

Where the hirer of protected goods has in fact and in law abandoned all his rights to possession of the goods, it was held that the recovery by the owner of possession of the goods otherwise than by action was not illegal or in breach of the equivalent provisions under the Hire Purchase Act 1965.[6] Lord Denning stated that the retaking in such case does not amount to recovering possession from the hirer, but the abandonment must be abandonment of all rights in the car so as to evince quite clearly that the hirer no longer has an interest in it.

The reader is also referred to **25.3.2** above.

1 CCA 1974, s 90(1).
2 Ibid., s 91.
3 Ibid., s 173(3) and see *Chartered Trust plc v Pitcher* [1988] RTR 72, [1987] LS Gaz 1147.

4 See above.

5 [2005] EWHC 223 (Ch).

6 *Bentinck Ltd v Cromwell Engineering Co* [1971] All ER 33, CA. Compare *Kassam v Chartered Trust plc* [1999] GCCR 2245, CA.

25.8   EQUITABLE RELIEF

In *Transag Haulage Ltd v Leyland DAF Finance plc and Lease Plan UK Ltd,*[1] the facts were that the owner terminated the agreements, as it was entitled to do, upon the appointment of an administrative receiver to the hirer under hire-purchase agreements; the administrative receiver wished to carry on the business as a going concern and sought relief in order to retain the fleet of 12 vehicles under the hire-purchase agreements to enable it to fulfil contracts for the transportation of goods. The court (in the Chancery Division) held that although it had no jurisdiction to grant relief from forfeiture of merely contractual rights, it had equitable jurisdiction to grant relief from forfeiture of proprietary rights, namely the hirer's contingent right to purchase the vehicles under the hire-purchase agreements and would grant such relief where the hirer had been guilty of no default in payment, no financial loss would be caused to the creditor and to refuse relief would result in a substantial windfall profit for the creditor and a disproportionate loss for the hirer. There appears to be no reason why such equitable relief should not be similarly available in the case of regulated agreements.

Relief from forfeiture was extended by the House of Lords to apply also to monies held in an escrow account, pending resolution of claims to it, in *On Demand Information plc (in administrative receivership) v Michael Gerson (Finance Credit) plc.*[2] A court had previously acceded to an application for an interim order for the sale of the equipment pursuant to RSC Order 29, r 4. In reversing the decision of the Court of Appeal and allowing the appeal, Millet LJ stated that, given the purpose of the rule, it was clear that the conversion of the property into money effected by the sale of the equipment was not intended to prejudice the parties' rights. The whole purpose of the sale was to preserve the value of their rights and particularly the rights of the ultimate successful party.

If a claimant believes it is entitled to relief from forfeiture, it should act expeditiously and where necessary, as in the above case, obtain an order of the court for the sale of the goods and payment of the proceeds into an escrow account pending resolution of the conflicting claims to the monies.

1 [1999] GCCR 1819, [1994] 2 BCLC 88 and see *BICC plc v Burndy Corpn* [1985] Ch 232, [1985] 1 All ER 417.

2 [2002] All ER (D) 116 (April), [2003] GCCR 4651, HL.

25.9   CONSEQUENCE OF FAILURE TO COMPLY WITH THE STATUTORY NOTICE REQUIREMENTS

The 14 day period for remedy of a breach in a default notice, as prescribed by s 88(2) of CCA 1974, is mandatory and a shorter period cannot be condoned as *de minimis* (or negligible).[1]

Where a creditor or owner takes action without complying with the requisite notice provisions, including failure to give the debtor or hirer the prescribed period of notice for remedying any remediable breach, the debtor or hirer may be entitled to one or more of the following: to recover damages; to recover possession of goods or land removed from him; to a prohibitory injunction to restrain the creditor or owner from taking action or a mandatory injunction to restore the position to what it was before the creditor or owner took action.

It is usually open to a creditor or owner to remedy any failure to serve a compliant enforcement or default notice by subsequently serving a fresh correct notice. The creditor or owner may, however, be estopped from proceeding in this way and where this is not the case, the fresh notice may impact on the amount of the claim and require fresh proceedings to be instituted.

1 *Brandon v American Express Services Ltd* [2011] GCCR 1153, [2011] EWCA Civ 1187.

25.10 WHERE FORMAL NOTICE IS NOT REQUIRED

Where the creditor or owner is entitled to rescind the agreement on grounds, for example, of the debtor's or hirer's misrepresentation (whether fraudulent, negligent or innocent) he is not obliged to serve a default notice before rescinding the agreement. A default notice is also not required where the creditor or owner wishes to sue for accrued arrears (although an arrears notice will be required) or for damages, unless he also proceeds against the surety.

Creditors and owners, or agents on their behalf, will operate debt collection procedures. Letters issued prior to formal default or enforcement notices which are not, and do not purport to be, a notice of arrears, a notice of default sums, a default notice or an enforcement notice, are permissible and do not need to comply with any formalities.

25.11 LAND MORTGAGES

Subject to the exception of the consent of the debtor or hirer under s 173(3), a land mortgage securing a regulated agreement is enforceable on an order of the court only.[1]

Possession claims relating to mortgaged residential property are subject to CPR 55.

The reader is also referred to **25.3.2** above.

1 See **25.6** above and CCA 1974, s 126.

25.12 JUDICIAL CONTROL

Court proceedings to enforce regulated agreements, or linked transactions, must be brought in the County Court. Any action instituted in a High Court will be transferred to the County Court.[1]

1 CCA 1974, s 141; *Sovereign Leasing plc v Ali; Sovereign Leasing plc v Martindale* [1992] CCLR 1.

25.13   ENFORCEMENT ORDERS IN CASE OF INFRINGEMENT

The court's discretion in cases of infringement of the CCA 1974's provisions is governed by s 127. This provides that in the case of an application for an enforcement order relating to improperly executed agreements, improperly executed security instruments, failure to serve a copy of a notice on a surety or the taking of negotiable instruments in contravention of s 122 (which prohibits a creditor or owner taking a negotiable instrument, other than a bank note or cheque in discharge of any sum payable under a regulated agreement) the court must dismiss the application if it considers it just to do so. In deciding whether it is just to do so the court must have regard, inter alia, to the prejudice caused to any person by the contravention in question and the degree of culpability for it.[1]

In making an enforcement order the court may reduce or discharge any sum payable by the debtor or hirer or any surety, to compensate him for any prejudice suffered.[2] Thus, in *National Guardian Mortgage Corporation v Wilkes*[3] where the creditor failed to serve an advance copy of the secured loan agreement, the court held that as the borrower might have borrowed at a lower rate were she to have had the benefit of the consideration period, the borrower should be awarded credit equivalent to 40% of the interest claimed.

Where an enforcement order has been refused, the debtor or hirer can apply for a declaratory order that the creditor or owner is not entitled to do such thing and subsequently no application for an enforcement order in respect of the same shall be entertained.[4] Although such an order appears superfluous, it may serve the purpose of stopping a harassing creditor or owner.

The court's power to make a declaration only exists where the court could grant an enforcement order.[5]

Paragraph 7 of CPR PD 7B prescribes the content of an application for an enforcement order.

1   CCA 1974, s 127(1).
2   Ibid., s 127(2).
3   [1993] CCLR 1.
4   CCA 1974, s 142.
5   See *Rankine v American Express Services Europe Ltd* [2008] GCCR 7701.

25.14   TIME ORDERS

A debtor or hirer may apply for a time order after he has received a notice of sums in arrears.[1] Application for a time order may only be made if he has given notice of his intention to apply for a time order to the creditor or owner and a period of at least 14 days has elapsed after the day on which such notice was given.[2] The notice must set out details of the proposal by the debtor or hirer.[3]

Where a creditor or owner applies to the court for an enforcement order or an order to enforce any security or to recover possession of any goods or land to which a regulated agreement relates or on an application by a debtor or hirer following service of a default, enforcement or termination notice, the court may, in its discretion, make a time order.

A time order relates either to payments or to the remedying of a breach. A time order relating to payments may be made by the court, in its discretion, under which the debtor, hirer or surety is ordered to make payment of the sum owed under a regulated agreement or a security, by such instalments and at such times, as the court deems reasonable. A time order in relation to the remedying of a breach is an order on the debtor or hirer to remedy a breach, other than non-payment of money, within such period as the court may specify.

In making time orders courts might reduce both the rate of interest and the amount of monthly instalments. A court is unlikely to make a time order where there has been a history of default, where the instalments which the debtor can afford will not meet the accruing interest and where there is no realistic prospect of the debtor's financial position improving. In considering making a time order the court must have regard to both the creditor's and the debtor's position.[4]

A concomitant of the court's power to make time orders is the court's power to vary agreements and securities under CCA 1974, s 136. This enables a court, in an order made by it, to include such provision as it considers just for amending any agreement or security in consequence of a term of the order. The issue of time orders and the court's power to vary under s 136, was considered in the context of default interest at the contract interest rate (rather than the judgment rate) in the case of *Director General of Fair Trading v First National Bank plc*.[5]

In *Southern and District Finance plc v Barnes; J & J Securities v Ewart and Equity Home Loans Ltd v Lewis*[6] the Court of Appeal laid down three principles relating to time orders. First, a time order relates to a sum owed under a regulated agreement or a security and means any sum which the lender is entitled to recover by action, in other words, a sum which is due and payable. If the full loan has not been called in, the only sum owed is the outstanding arrears. Second, the power to vary agreements in s 136 can only be exercised in consequence of the term of a time order and where the making of the variation is just. Third, where application is made for a time order or a possession order of property mortgaged as security for a regulated agreement, the court must first consider whether it is just to make a time order by taking into account all the circumstances and the position of the creditor as well as the debtor. The Court of Appeal upheld the judgment of the court of first instance which had rescheduled the instalments due under the agreement over a fresh period of 15 years and reduced the rate of interest to nil. In so doing, the court exercised its power under s 136 to amend the agreement in consequence of a term of a time order under s129.

A time order may provide for the rescheduling of future instalments which have not yet fallen due, grant time for the payment of arrears or vary the rate of interest.[7]

Paragraph 7 of CPR PD 7B prescribes the content of an application for a time order.

1 CCA 1974, s 129(1)(ba).
2 Ibid., s 129A(1).
3 Ibid., s 129A(2).
4 *First National Bank plc v Syed* [1991] 2 All ER 250, [1999] GCCR 1533, CA.
5 [2000] GCCR 2601, CA.
6 [1999] GCCR 1935, CA.
7 *Cedar Holdings Ltd v Thompson* [1993] CCLR 7. See the contrary decision in *Ashbroom Facilities v Bodley* [1992] CCLR 31 which was not followed.

25.15 FINANCIAL RELIEF FOR HIRER

Where the owner under a regulated consumer hire agreement recovers possession of goods, the subject of the agreement, otherwise than by action, the hirer
may apply to the court for relief. Relief includes the repayment of the whole or
part of any sum paid by the hirer to the owner in respect of the goods and termination of the obligation to continue to make rental payments.[1] If, however, the
hirer consents to recovery at the time when repossession is sought, the owner
may take the goods without an order of the court. It will be necessary for the
creditor to show that the hirer's consent was informed and voluntary.[2]

1 CCA 1974, s 132.
2 Ibid., s 173(3) and see *Chartered Trust plc v Pitcher* [1988] RTR 72, [1987] LS Gaz 1147.

25.16 CLAIMS FOR DELIVERY OF GOODS UNDER A HIRE-PURCHASE AGREEMENT/CONDITIONAL SALE AGREEMENT

Where a claimant claims the delivery of goods let under a hire-purchase agreement or sold under a conditional sale agreement, the claimant must set out specified particulars in a prescribed order, including whether notice under s 76(1) or
s 98(1) of CCA 1974 has been served and the date that it was served.[1]

Where, in relation to a regulated hire-purchase or conditional sale agreement,
it appears to the court just to do so, the court may make a 'return order', namely
an order for return to the creditor of goods to which the agreement relates, or a
'transfer order' for the transfer to the debtor of the creditor's title to the goods.[2]

None of the foregoing provisions derogates from the provisions of the Torts
(Interference with Goods) Act 1977 and indeed s 3(8) of that Act specifically
states that it is without prejudice to the remedies afforded by CCA 1974, s 133.

Paragraph 7 of CPR PD 7B prescribes the content of a claim for the delivery
of goods to enforce a hire-purchase agreement or conditional sale agreement.

1 CPR 16 and CPR PD 7B.
2 CCA 1974, s 133.

25.17 DISTRESS FOR RENT BY LANDLORD OF DEBTOR OR HIRER

At common law the landlord is entitled to distrain on any goods on the leased
premises, whether or not they are owned by the tenant. This right also applies
to goods under a hire-purchase or conditional sale agreement unless it has been
terminated or is a regulated agreement in respect of which a default or termination notice is in force. The owner of goods comprised in any such agreement,
whether within or outside the CCA 1974, should therefore serve a declaration on
the landlord of the premises notifying the landlord that the tenant has no right of
property or beneficial interest in the goods.

The Tribunals, Courts and Enforcement Act 2007 gives enforcement agents
powers to take control of, and sell, goods. Schedule 12, para 60 of the Act gives

rights to a third party claiming goods, to apply to the court to safeguard his interest in them. After receiving notice of the application the enforcement agent may not sell the goods unless directed by the court.

25.18   ADDITIONAL POWERS OF THE COURT

(a)   On an application of the creditor or owner under a regulated agreement the court may make a protection order, namely an order protecting the property of the creditor or owner, or property subject to any security, pending the determination of any proceedings.[1]

(b)   The CCA 1974 empowers a court to impose conditions in any order or to suspend the operation of any term of the order, if it considers it just to do so. The court may also include such provision as it considers just for amending any agreement or security in consequence of a term of the order.[2]

(c)   The court may only make a declaration where a thing can be done by a creditor or owner on an enforcement order and not, for instance, where a defective default notice had been served.[3]

(d)   Under the Torts (Interference with Goods) Act 1977, in addition to remedies available to a creditor or owner under CCA 1974, an action will also lie against a bailee in conversion for any loss or destruction of goods which he has allowed whilst the goods were in his care.

(e)   The remedies and measures discussed in this chapter are in addition to those available to the parties at common law for breach of contract or misrepresentation, whether fraudulent, negligent or innocent.

(f)   The court may order the set-off of the claimant's money judgment against the award of costs, whether by applying the test of equitable set-off, or set-off by judgment or as a matter of discretion under s 51 of the Senior Courts Act 1981.[4]

(g)   An order of the court in relation to a regulated agreement may not include interest on the judgment debt. However, there is no bar to a creditor or owner suing for both the principal amount and any default interest due under the regulated agreement[5] provided that this would not amount to seeking to enforce an unfair contract term.[6] In addition, the creditor or owner must have served the statutory notices prescribed by CCA 1974, s 130A.

1   CCA 1974, s 131.
2   Ibid., ss 135 and 136 and see *Cedar Holdings Ltd v Jenkins* [1988] CCLR 34.
3   Ibid., s 142(1) and see *Rankine v American Express Services Europe Ltd* [2008] GCCR 7701; *Carey v HSBC Bank Plc* [2009] GCCR 9951, [2009] EWHC 3417 (QB) at para 156.
4   *Black Horse Ltd v Dickinson*, Luton County Court, 16 December 2011, Case No. OLS 04381.
5   County Court (Interest on Judgment Debts) Order 1991, SI 1991/1184 and see *Forward Trust Ltd v Whymark* [1990] 2 QB 670, [1999] GCCR 1363, CA.
6   See *Director General of Fair Trading v First National Bank plc* [2000] GCCR 2601, CA.

25.19 A NOTE ON PROCEDURE

CPR Practice Direction 7B supplements CPR rule 7.9 and sets out the claims under the provisions of CCA 1974, including unfair relationships, to which it applies.

In an application for disclosure under CPR 31.16, the applicant must show that he has a *prima facie* case which is more than speculative.[1] The exercise of the court's discretion under this rule involves taking account of the issues, the nature of the documents sought to be disclosed, the provisions of any relevant protocol and the applicant's prospects of bringing the proceedings without the disclosure being sought.[2]

The Defence Form raises the question as to whether, in the case of a regulated agreement, the defendant wants the court to consider whether the terms of the original agreement are fair. The borrower is also reminded of the right to apply for a time order in the form: 'Do you intend to apply to the court for an order changing the terms of your loan agreement?'.

Notwithstanding the fact that the burden of proof in a claim based on unfair relationships under s 140A of CCA 1974 rests on the creditor, it is open to the creditor to discharge the same in summary judgment proceedings under CPR 24.2, as was the case in *Axton v GE Money Mortgages Ltd*.[3]

1 *Kneale v Barclays Bank plc (t/a Barclaycard)* [2010] GCCR 10401, [2010] EWHC 1900 (Comm).
2 *Black v Sumitomo Corp* [2001] EWCA Civ 1819.
3 [2015] GCCR 13105, [2015] EWHC 1343 (QB).

25.20 CONSEQUENCES OF DEATH OF THE DEBTOR OR HIRER

If the regulated agreement is fully secured, the creditor or owner under a regulated agreement is not entitled, by reason of the death of the debtor or hirer, to terminate the agreement, demand earlier payment of any sum, recover possession of any goods or land, treat any right conferred on the debtor or hirer as terminated, restricted or deferred or enforce any security.[1] If the agreement was only partly secured or unsecured, the creditor or owner may do any of the foregoing on an order of the court only.[2]

1 CCA 1974, s 86. Note that this section employs the expressions 'fully secured', 'partly secured' or 'unsecured'. It is submitted that 'fully secured' means security to the full value of the outstanding indebtedness under the agreement.
2 Ibid., s 86.

25.21 SURETIES

Where an agreement has been secured by a surety, whether a guarantor or indemnifier, a copy of any enforcement notice under s 76(1), termination notice under s 98(1) or default notice under s 87(1) must also be served in paper form on the surety, containing the prescribed heading, stating that it is the surety's copy of such notice. Failure to comply will result in the security being enforceable against the surety on an order of the court only.[1]

There is no obligation to serve a on the surety a copy of a notice of sums in arrears or a copy of a notice of default sums.

1 CCA 1974, s 111 and Consumer Credit (Cancellation Notices and Copies of Documents) Regulations 1983, SI 1983/1557, reg 10.

25.22   FINANCIAL OMBUDSMAN SERVICE

25.22.1   Background

The complaint handling jurisdiction of the Financial Ombudsman Service (FOS) was extended with effect from 6 April 2007 to cover consumer credit complaints and now forms part of its compulsory jurisdiction under Part 16 of, and Schedule 17 to, FSMA, as follows:

'**226 Compulsory jurisdiction**

(1) A complaint which relates to an act or omission of a person ("the respondent") in carrying on an activity to which compulsory jurisdiction rules apply is to be dealt with under the ombudsman scheme if the conditions mentioned in subsection (2) are satisfied.

(2) The conditions are that–

(a)   the complainant is eligible and wishes to have the complaint dealt with under the scheme;

(b)   the respondent was an authorised person, or an electronic money issuer within the meaning of the Electronic Money Regulations 2011 or a payment service provider within the meaning of the Payment Services Regulations 2009, at the time of the act or omission to which the complaint relates; and

(c)   the act or omission to which the complaint relates occurred at a time when compulsory jurisdiction rules were in force in relation to the activity in question.

(3) "Compulsory jurisdiction rules" means rules–

(a)   made by the FCA for the purposes of this section; and

(b)   specifying the activities to which they apply.

(4) Only activities which are regulated activities, or which could be made regulated activities by an order under section 22, may be specified.

(5) Activities may be specified by reference to specified categories (however described).

(6) A complainant is eligible, in relation to the compulsory jurisdiction of the ombudsman scheme, if he falls within a class of person specified in the rules as eligible.'

25.22.2 FCA Handbook: Compulsory jurisdiction of FOS[1]

The compulsory jurisdiction covers the following activities by a firm (as 'firm' is defined in the FCA Handbook, Glossary):

(1) regulated activities;

(2) consumer buy-to-let (CBTL) business;

(3) lending money secured by a charge on land;

(4) lending money (excluding restricted credit where that is not a credit-regulated activity);

(5) paying money by a plastic card (excluding a store card where that is not a credit-regulated activity); and

(6) providing ancillary banking services;

or any ancillary activities, including advice, carried on by the firm in connection with them.

The compulsory jurisdiction of FOS also applies to:

(a) activities by payment service providers;

(b) activities by electronic money issuers;

(c) activities by CBTL firms;

(d) consumer redress schemes;

(e) activities by designated credit reference agencies; and

(f) activities by designated finance platforms.

1 FCA Handbook, DISP 2.3.

25.22.3 The Alternative Dispute Resolution for Consumer Disputes (Competent Authorities and Information) Regulations 2015[1]

These Regulations implemented most of the provisions of EU Directive 2013/11/EU,[2] which require all traders selling to consumers to provide access to a certified provider of ADR services in their sector, thereby obviating the need for court proceedings. FOS was already established as an ADR provider in the financial services sector. In addition to the requirements which already applied, with effect from 9 July 2015 the FOS website address must be displayed:

(a) on the firm's website and in the firm's terms and conditions for services with its customers;

(b) in a firm's final written response to a customer complaint informing the complainant, in accordance with wording in the FCA Handbook, whether it consents to FOS considering a complaint that is referred outside of the specified time limits.

The reader is referred to the DISP section of the Handbook for more detailed requirements.

1 SI 2015/542.
2 As amended by SI 2015/1392 and SI 2015/1972.

25.22.4 FCA Handbook: Dispute Resolution: Complaints (DISP)

The FCA Rules are set out in the FCA Handbook, Redress: Dispute Resolution: Complaints (DISP).

DISP 3, and in particular 3.5, sets out the procedure and approach of FOS. Before the ombudsman can consider a complaint, he must be satisfied that the firm was given the requisite eight weeks to consider the complaint. Where a firm fails to send a final response to the complainant by the end of eight weeks or fails to resolve the complaint, the ombudsman will consider the complaint. The ombudsman will attempt to resolve the complaint at the earliest possible stage and by whatever means appears appropriate.

25.23 ENFORCEMENT BY THE FINANCIAL CONDUCT AUTHORITY

The FCA Handbook, Enforcement Guide (EG) sets out the FCA's enforcement powers, which are summarised as follows:[1]

> 'This guide describes the FCA's approach to exercising the main enforcement powers given to it by the Financial Services and Markets Act 2000 (the Act) and by other legislation. It is broken down into two parts. The first part provides an overview of enforcement policy and process, with chapters about the FCA's approach to enforcement (chapter 2), the use of its main information gathering and investigation powers under the Act and the CRA [Consumer Rights Act 2015] (chapter 3), the conduct of investigations (chapter 4), settlement (chapter 5) and publicity (chapter 6). The second part contains an explanation of the FCA's policy concerning specific enforcement powers such as its powers to: vary a firm's Part 4A permission and impose requirements on its own initiative (chapter 8); make prohibition orders (chapter 9); prosecute criminal offences (chapter 12); and powers which the FCA has been given under legislation other than the Act (chapter 19)'.

Examples of cases involving the FCA's powers in relation to Part 4A permissions are *PDHL Ltd v Financial Conduct Authority*[2] and *Koksal t/a Arcis Management Consultancy v Financial Conduct Authority*.[3]

The FCA's policy with respect to the prosecution of criminal offences is set out in EG 12 and applies to the prosecution of CCA 1974 offences under section 401 of FSMA. The FCA will not prosecute a person for an offence under CCA 1974 in respect of an act or omission where it has already disciplined the person under section 66, 205, 206 or 206A of FSMA in respect of that act or omission.[4]

1 EG 1.1.1.
2 [2016] GCCR 14001, 14013 and 14045.
3 [2016] GCCR 14059 and 14117.
4 EG 20.5.101.

25.24 ACTION FOR DAMAGES

FSMA provides a remedy for breach by an authorised person of a rule made by the Financial Conduct Authority or the Prudential Regulation Authority. Thus, s 138D(2) to (4) of FSMA provides that, unless otherwise specified, a contravention by an authorised person of a rule made by the FCA is actionable at the suit of a private person who suffers loss as a result of the contravention, subject to the defences and other incidents applying to actions for breach of statutory duty. In prescribed cases, a contravention would also be actionable at the suit of a person who is not a private person. (Similar consequences flow from a breach of s 56(6) or s 59(1) and (2) of FSMA.)

Section 138D(1) of FSMA contains a similar provision in relation to contravention of a rule made by the PRA.

'Private person' is defined in article 3 of the Financial Services and Markets Act 2000 (Rights of Action) Regulations 2001.[1]

An action for breach of statutory duty is analogous to an action in tort. It remains an open question as to who bears the onus of proof in an action under s 138D.[2]

1 SI 2001/2256.
2 See *Goode: Consumer Credit Law and Practice* at [47.242]ff.

Chapter 26

Fraud, money laundering, criminal offences and civil penalties

26.1 FRAUD: THE EXTENT OF THE PROBLEM

It is trite to state that fraud is a cancerous virus which pervades all sectors of the credit industry: payment and credit cards, retail credit, mortgage finance, motor and asset finance and the banking sector generally. The fraudster might operate alone or as a member of an organised group, nationally or internationally.[1]

The annual cost of fraud across all sectors in the UK is estimated to be as high as £193 billion, which includes mortgage losses of more than £1 billion. Fraud perpetrated against individuals is estimated at £9.7 billion, of which identity fraud accounts for about £5.4 billion.[2]

1 For a survey and analysis of part of the problem, see 'The Prevention of Cheque and Credit Card Fraud' by Michael Levi, Paul Bissell and Tony Richardson, Paper No 26 issued by the Home Office Crime Prevention Unit (June 1991).
2 University of Portsmouth: Annual Fraud Indicator 2016.

26.2 FRAUD: THE LAW

26.2.1 Criminal offences

The legislation governing fraud was dramatically simplified by the Fraud Act 2006 which received Royal Assent on 8 November 2006 and came fully into force on 15 January 2007. It changed the face of anti-fraud legislation in the United Kingdom, largely by simplifying the definition of fraud and closing loopholes which existed previously.

The Fraud Act 2006 sets out various fraud offences, as follows:

(a) Fraud by false representation. In essence this involves dishonestly making a false representation and intending, by making the representation, to make a gain for oneself or to cause a loss to another. The representation may be express or implied and made in any form to any system or device designed to receive, convey or respond to communications.[1]

(b)   Fraud by failing to disclose information. This essentially takes place where a person dishonestly fails to disclose to another, information which he is under a legal duty to disclose and intends, by so doing, to make a gain for himself or to cause loss to another.[2]

(c)   Fraud by abuse of position. This is essentially caused where a person who occupies a position in which he is expected to safeguard, or not to act against, the financial interests of another person, dishonestly abuses that position and intends, by so doing, to make a gain for himself or to cause loss to another.[3]

(d)   Participating in a fraudulent business carried on by a sole trader etc. A person commits this offence if he is knowingly a party to the carrying on of a business which is outside the reach of section 993 of the Companies Act 2006 (offence of fraudulent trading) and with the intent to defraud creditors of any person or for any other fraudulent purpose.[4]

(e)   Obtaining services dishonestly. Essentially this offence is committed if a person obtains services for himself or another by a dishonest act in that he has no intention of making payment for them in full or at all.[5]

Some offences appertaining to fraud remain governed by legislation which preceded the Fraud Act 2006 and has not been repealed. The offences include:

(a)   dishonestly retaining a wrongful credit;[6]

(b)   unauthorised access to computer material with intent to commit or facilitate the commission of offences;[7]

(c)   conspiracy to defraud or conspiracy to commit an offence;[8]

(d)   false accounting;[9]

(e)   forgery.[10]

Mention might also be made of the Bribery Act 2010 which, inter alia, sets out two cases involving the offence of bribing another person (s 1), four cases relating to the offence of being bribed (s 2) and the offence of failure by a commercial organisation to prevent bribery (s 7).

1 Fraud Act 2006, s 2.
2 Ibid., s 3.
3 Ibid., s 4.
4 Ibid., s 9.
5 Ibid., s 11.
6 Theft Act 1968, s 24A.
7 Computer Misuse Act 1990, ss 1 to 3A as amended by the Police and Justice Act 2006.
8 Criminal Justice Act 1987, s 12; Criminal Law Act 1977, s 1.
9 Theft Act 1968, s 17.
10 Forgery and Counterfeiting Act 1981.

26.2.2   Proceeds of crime

The Proceeds of Crime Act 2002 ('POCA') established the Assets Recovery Agency and makes provision for confiscation or civil recovery orders in relation to persons who benefit from criminal conduct and for restraint orders to prohibit dealing with property, to allow the recovery of property which is or represents property obtained through unlawful conduct or which is intended to be used in unlawful conduct, including by money laundering. The Act was amended by the Criminal Finances Act 2017 to cover terrorist property and to create corporate offences where a person associated with a body corporate or partnership facilitates the commission by another person of a tax evasion offence.

26.3 FRAUD PREVENTION

Various organisations, systems and procedures have been established and techniques introduced in order to prevent, or at least limit, fraud.

In order to combat fraud it is essential to nip it in the bud by early detection. This is especially so where the fraudulent activity is being undertaken by conspirators, whether local, national or international. Combating fraud effectively presupposes the following:

(a) the sharing and exchange of information;

(b) rapid reaction and response;

(c) co-operation and action on the part of the police and the enforcement authorities;

(d) an effective and up to date civil and criminal law; and

(e) the fraudsters being brought to justice.

The law on fraud must be clear, firm, uncompromising and effective, and perceived as such, so that fraud prevention and control is not viewed by the criminal fraternity as the achilles heel of the criminal system.

26.3.1 Organisations established to combat fraud

Financial Fraud Action UK co-ordinates efforts to prevent and detect fraud. Its membership includes the major banks, credit, debit and charge card issuers and card payment acquirers (with whom it works in partnership with their association, the UK Cards Association). It is now integrated into UK Finance which represents the banking and finance industry in the UK.

Financial fraud losses across payment cards, remote banking and cheques totalled £768.8 million in 2016, and prevented fraud totalled £1.38 billion. The fraud losses included £618 million on UK issued cards and £62.8 million on retailer face-to-face purchases in the UK. The latter was, however, significantly lower than the peak of £218.8 million in 2004, prior to the introduction of CHIP and PIN in the UK. The fraud losses also included an estimated £308.8 million of e-commerce fraud on cards (accounting for 50% of all card fraud and 71% of total remote purchase fraud).[1]

CIFAS is a system for preventing fraud. Established in 1991, it facilitates the exchange of information by its members, particularly by sharing data on allegedly fraudulent applications for credit and other services. Members can also exchange information about accounts suspected of being used fraudulently and insurance claims suspected of being made fraudulently. When a CIFAS member identifies a fraud, a warning is placed against the address linked to the applicant or account, thereby alerting other CIFAS members when they check against that address. In 2016, CIFAS members prevented £1.03 billion in fraud losses.[2] The principal credit reference agencies provide software packages which enable their subscribers to identify suspected fraud.

HPI Limited and Car Data Check are registering and information service businesses which enable creditors with security interests in vehicles, arising under hire-purchase, conditional sale or loan agreements, to register their interests on a register. Potential purchasers of vehicles can check whether the vehicles they propose purchasing have security interests registered against them. HPI Limited also holds a so-called 'condition alert register' relating to vehicles which have been the subject of a major damage insurance claim and where the insurer has declined to have the vehicle repaired as the vehicle has been written off. It serves as an alert to potential purchasers in relation to the condition of the vehicle. Other registers held relate to stolen vehicles, vehicles that are at risk from fraud or theft, vehicles which have undergone registration plate changes since April 1990 and a register recording dates of first registration.

The Finance & Leasing Association (FLA) and the Driver and Vehicle Licensing Agency (DVLA) jointly launched a vehicle recovery scheme, in September 2012, for financed cars which have been impounded by the DVLA because of the driver's default .The scheme mirrors a similar scheme operated between the FLA and the majority of police forces in the UK which facilitates the recovery of financed vehicles impounded by the police.

The Joint Fraud Taskforce was established by the government in 2016 to use the collective powers and resources of government, law enforcement and industry to combat financial fraud.

1 Financial Fraud Action UK: Fraud The Facts 2017.
2 CIFAS Annual Report 2017.

26.3.2   Procedures to combat fraud

Procedures for combating fraud are limitless. They cover, amongst other precautions, applying prudent checks on, and identifying customers, ensuring that goods proposed to be leased exist and are not already the subject of an existing lease agreement, implementing floor limits in stores to ensure that credit approvals are required for purchases above a pre-set limit, personal delivery of credit cards to customers at their bank branches and safeguards in relation to PINs.

26.3.3   Fraud prevention techniques

At the basic level, the most effective measure to prevent credit fraud is for credit grantors to share information on persons who have made fraudulent applications for credit or have otherwise evidenced fraudulent misuse of credit. Such information is clearly enhanced by the comprehensiveness and exhaustiveness of the data base.

CHIP and PIN technology is at the forefront of the fight against plastic card fraud. As early as January 2007 the UK banks and card companies had issued 138 million CHIP and PIN cards, representing 97% of the UK's 142 million payment cards.[1]

A CHIP card is a plastic card containing a microchip which has highly secure memory and processing capabilities. Chip cards are also known as integrated circuit cards ('ICCs') or smart cards and are designed to international specifications set by the international card schemes. Europay, MasterCard and Visa have established EMV, a standard for the inter-operation of chip-embedded cards with Point of Sale (POS) terminals and ATMs used to authenticate transactions. As of early 2011, 1.2 billion EMV cards were in issue in the world.[2]

A PIN is a personal identification number ('PIN') which enables customers to withdraw cash and use other services at a cash machine or at the point of sale.

Another method of tackling fraud is by way of knowledge-based systems, namely checking for unusual purchasing patterns in order to detect the fraudulent use of cards.

Personal identification methods such as iris scanning and fingerprint recognition have been promoted from time to time but it appears that such technology is not sufficiently reliable or cost effective to meet the current requirements of the UK card industry.

Most internet fraud involves using card details which have been obtained fraudulently in order to make card-not-present transactions. Various methods and devices exist to prevent or detect fraud, notably the automated address and card security code checking system which allows merchants to verify the billing address of card holders and to cross-check coded digits on cards. In order to protect data against being intercepted by hackers, certified organisations encrypt data.[3]

1 *Fraud: The Facts 2007*, published by APACS.
2 See the excellent article on CHIP and PIN: Douglas King, 'Success and Challenges in Reducing Fraud' (Retail Payments Risk Forum, Federal Reserve Bank of Atlanta, January 2012).
3 See further **Chapter 23**.

26.4 MONEY LAUNDERING

The prevention and detection of money laundering and terrorist financing in the financial system is now governed by the Money Laundering, Terrorist Financing and Transfer of Funds (Information on the Payer) Regulations 2017.[1] They implement the Fourth Money Laundering Directive 2015/849/EU and the Funds Transfer Regulation (EU) 2015/847. The Regulations came into force on 26 June 2017 and replace the Money Laundering Regulations 2007 (SI 2007/2157) and the Transfer of Funds (Information on the Payer) Regulations 2007 (SI 2007/3298).

The Regulations apply to 'persons' acting in the course of business carried on by them. The 'persons' are:

(a)   credit institutions;

(b)   financial institutions;

(c)   auditors, insolvency practitioners, external accountants and tax advisers;

(d)   independent legal practitioners;

(e)   trust or company service providers;

(f)   estate agents;

(g)   high value dealers; and

(h)   casinos.

The Regulations set out separate requirements, related to the degree of risk of money laundering and terrorist financing, for general customer due diligence, enhanced due diligence and simplified due diligence. Customer due diligence and transaction records and information must be kept for a minimum period of five years following completion of the transaction.[2] The Regulations also contain specific data protection measures.[3]

Among the Regulations' extensive provisions, the FCA and the Commissioners for HMRC are empowered to impose civil penalties by way of fines, suspension and removal of authorisation and prohibitions on management. In addition, a person who contravenes a relevant requirement imposed on that person commits an offence.

The FCA's powers for monitoring and enforcing compliance with the Regulations is set out in the FCA Handbook, Enforcement Guide at EG 19.14, and its procedures in conducting investigations at EG 19.15 and 19.18.

1   SI 2017/692.
2   Ibid., reg 40.
3   Ibid., reg 41.

26.5   CCA 1974 AND FCA: OFFENCES AND CIVIL PENALTIES AND DATA SUBJECT'S RIGHTS

26.5.1   Overview

The criminal law is the remedy of last resort in relation to the enforcement of consumer credit law, so that the sparsity of prosecutions under CCA 1974 should not be viewed as evidence of the ineffectiveness of criminal sanctions. The enforcement powers of the Financial Conduct Authority have significantly reduced the criminal law to a subsidiary position in relation to the enforcement of consumer credit law.

26.5.2   Offences

There are now only 11 offences (as compared to the original 35 offences) under CCA 1974. Together with their mode of prosecution and the sentences they carry, the offences are summarised in Schedule 1 to the Act. It is submitted that there is a basic flaw in consumer credit law, insofar as certain fundamental breaches of CCA 1974 and the regulations give rise simultaneously to both criminal and civil sanctions, the civil sanctions sometimes resulting in the unenforceability of the agreement. As a higher degree of proof is required in criminal cases, it may result in an acquittal in circumstances where a civil court, deciding the same issue, might find that there had been a breach of the relevant regulations. The decision of the court in *National Westminster Bank v Devon County Council and Devon County Council v Abbey National plc*,[1] which was a successful appeal from a criminal conviction, is an illustration. This case had far-reaching consequences, not least of which was the amendment of the Consumer Credit (Total Charge for Credit) Regulations 1980.

The existence of criminal offences for infringements of CCA 1974 has from time to time aroused views of disbelief on the part of the judiciary that reputable institutions, which acted in good faith, find themselves prosecuted for breaches of abstruse and difficult regulations.[2] The reputation of an institution is not, however, a relevant factor, and reference to it distorts the issue in question.

1 [1999] GCCR 1685.
2 See the above decision, at p 1692.

26.5.3 Civil penalties

Civil penalties and enforcement by the Financial Conduct Authority have largely overtaken the criminal law. They are essentially set out in the Financial Services Act 2012 (Consumer Credit) Order 2013,[1] which extends provisions of FSMA and powers of the FCA to requirements under CCA 1974, and in the FCA Handbook at EG, sections 7 to 12 and section 20.

1 SI 2013/1882.

26.5.4 Defences and the approach of the courts

It is not intended to deal with defences generally but to highlight a specific defence under CCA 1974 and to outline the approach of the courts.

It is a defence for a person charged with an offence under CCA 1974 to prove both:

(a) that the act or omission was due to a mistake or to reliance on information supplied, or to an act or omission by another person, or to an accident or some other cause beyond the person's control; and

(b) that the person took all reasonable precautions and exercised all due diligence to avoid such an act or omission by the person or any other person under his control.[1]

The defence was pleaded in the case of *Coventry City Council v Lazarus*.[2] The respondents traded in partnership as a garage and advertised credit for used motor vehicles without complying with the Consumer Credit (Advertisements) Regulations 1989. Failure to comply was not in issue, but the respondents argued that they had relied upon advice given by the Retail Motor Industry's Federation and had received a visit from the Area Manager who had offered advice concerning the advertisements. According to the evidence, the respondents relied on the information but the court found that they had not exercised all due diligence to avoid the publication of the offending advertisements.

An interesting analogous case is *Tesco Supermarkets Ltd v Nattrass*.[3] This involved a prosecution under the Trade Descriptions Act 1968 which provides a defence for the person charged to prove that the commission of the offence was due to a mistake or to reliance on information supplied to the person or to the act or default of another person and that the accused took all reasonable precautions and exercised all due diligence to avoid the commission of the offence. The court stated that the defence was plainly intended to make a just and reasonable distinction between an employer who is wholly blameless and ought to be acquitted and an employer who was in some way at fault. Although on the facts, a chain of command was set up through regional and district supervisors, the acts and omissions of shop managers was found not to constitute those of the company itself which was therefore acquitted.

Where a person deliberately flouts the law, the courts will usually impose a custodial sentence. In *R v Curr*[4] an unlicensed trader advanced moneys to customers by way of loan and acted in deliberate defiance of the law. In addition to imposing a fine, the court considered a sentence of imprisonment justified because of the appellant's attitude to the law. Similarly, in *R v Priestly*[5] which involved offences under the Trade Descriptions Act 1968 and unlicensed trading under CCA 1974, where the trader had engaged in activities in a manner which, with his experience, he knew was contrary to the law and did so quite brazenly, the court considered it appropriate to impose a prison sentence.

A misstated APR in a credit agreement was held to be a misleading indication as to price in breach of the Consumer Protection Act 1987, s 21 in the case of *R v Kettering Magistrates' Court, ex p MRB Insurance Brokers Ltd*.[6] The court stated that CCA 1974, s 170(1), which provides that a breach of any requirement under the Act will incur no civil or criminal sanction except to the extent expressly provided by or under the Act, is merely intended to clarify (by disapplying) the common law rules relating to breaches of an Act of Parliament. It does not prevent a person being charged under legislation other than the Act itself and did not preclude a prosecution under the Consumer Protection Act 1987. The rationale for the decision was approved by the Court of Appeal in *R v Chapman*,[7] where Cranston J stated:

> 'The *Kettering Magistrates' Court* case established that section 170 has a very narrow ambit. The court in that case endorsed the views of the two leading experts on the Consumer Credit Act, Mr Francis Bennion, who drafted it, and Professor Sir Roy Goode QC, who sat on the Crowther Committee which devised it, and whose *Encyclopaedia of Consumer Credit Law* is the pre-eminent work on the subject. They both took the view, and this was endorsed by the court, that section 170 was limited in scope, designed specifically to preclude common law actions on the back of a breach of the Act, essentially actions for breach of statutory duty.'

1 CCA 1974, s 168(1).
2 [1999] GCCR 1909.
3 [1971] 1 QB 133.
4 [1999] GCCR 533, CA.
5 [1999] GCCR 641, CA.
6 [2001] GCCR 2701.
7 [2015] EWCA Crim 694, [2015] GCCR 13181 at para 17.

26.5.5　Data subject's rights

The following is a key to Articles in the GDPR on the data subject's rights in relation to the processing of personal data:

- 4:　Definitions of 'controller' and 'processor';

- 5:　Principles;

- 6:　Grounds for processing personal data;

- 13: Information to be provided where personal data collected from data subject;

- 15: Right of access;

- 16: Right to rectification;

- 17: Right to erasure (right to be forgotten);

- 18: Right to restriction of privacy;

- 20: Right to data portability, especially Article 20(1)(a); and

- 21: Right to object, especially Article 21(2) to (4).

Chapter 27

Data protection

27.1 BACKGROUND

Directive 95/46/EC of the European Parliament and of the Council sought to harmonise the protection of fundamental rights and freedoms of natural persons in respect of the processing of personal data and to ensure the free flow of personal data between Member States. It gave rise to the Data Protection Act 1998 ('DPA 1998') which is relevant to the consumer credit regime in two respects: it imposes obligations on credit grantors and providers of hire facilities; and it confers rights on consumers. Its application is confined to personal data, being data which relate to a living individual and who can be identified from those data or from those data and other information which is in the possession, or likely to come into the possession, of the data controller.

DPA 1998 will be superseded by a new Data Protection Act which is expected to incorporate the General Data Protection Regulation, Regulation (EU) 2016/679 of the European Parliament and of the Council of 27 April 2016 on the protection of natural persons with regard to the processing of personal data and on the free movement of such data ('GDPR'). The GDPR repeals Directive 95/46/EC and is especially geared to addressing concerns in the new digital economy. It is directly applicable to the UK from 25 May 2018. The government has confirmed that the UK's decision to leave the EU will not affect the commencement of the GDPR.[1]

1 Overview of GDPR published online by the Information Commissioner's Office.

27.2 EU DATA PROTECTION REGULATION

EU data protection regulation comprises the following three limbs:

(1) the General Data Protection Regulation ('GDPR');[1]

(2) the Data Protection Law Enforcement Directive;[2] and

(3) the Council of Europe Convention for the Protection of Individuals with regard to Automatic Processing of Personal Data.[3]

The GDPR applies to 'controllers' and 'processors'. An outline of its principal subject matter, by way of a precis of the recitals to the GDPR, is set out below.

(a) Right to the protection of personal data.

(b) Protection of natural persons with regard to the processing of personal data.

(c) The need for a strong and more coherent data protection framework backed by strong enforcement.

(d) The need for high level protection of natural persons and the removal of obstacles to the flow of personal data within the EU.

(e) Principles of data protection should apply to natural persons identifiable from personal data which have undergone pseudonymisation (anonymisation).

(f) Exceptions applying to personal data disclosed to public authorities.

(g) Consent to processing of personal data to be by way of a clear affirmative act, freely given, specific, informed and unambiguous. Special protective provisions apply to consent given on behalf of children.

(h) Consent should not provide a valid legal ground for processing where there is a clear imbalance between the data subject and the controller.

(i) Processing of personal data should be lawful and fair and to the extent necessary and proportionate for the purpose of ensuring network and information security.

(j) Sensitive personal data (i.e. sensitive in relation to fundamental rights and freedoms) should not be processed except as permitted by the Regulation.

(k) Principles of fair and transparent processing require that the data subject is informed of the existence and purpose of the processing operation.

(l) The data subject should have the right to access personal data collected about him or her and to have it rectified if necessary and a right for it to be forgotten.

(m) The data subject should have the right to object to certain processing, e.g. direct marketing or decisions based on profiling.

(n) Processing should only be by persons providing sufficient guarantees to implement measures which meet the requirements of the Regulation.

(o) Controllers of personal data must communicate to a data subject a personal data breach without delay.

(p) The EU Commission may decide whether a third country offers an adequate level of data protection.

(q) Supervisory authorities must be established in Member States.

(r) A European Data Protection Supervisor must be established.

(s) Data subjects should be entitled to compensation for infringements. There should also be penalties or fines for infringements, and Member States should have the right to lay down criminal penalties.

The following are of some of the principal Articles in GDPR:

(a) Article 5: Principles relating to processing of personal data.

(b) Article 6: Lawfulness of processing.

(c) Article 7: Conditions for consent.

(d) Article 16: Right to rectification.

(e) Article 17: Right to erasure ('right to be forgotten').

1 Regulation (EU) 2016/679.
2 Directive 2016/680/EU.
3 ETS no 108.

27.3   GDPR: PRINCIPAL DEFINITIONS

The following are some of the more important definitions in the General Data Protection Regulation:[1]

"personal data" means any information relating to an identified or identifiable natural person ("data subject"); an identifiable natural person is one who can be identified directly or indirectly, in particular by reference to an identifier sych as a name, an identification number, location data, an online identifier or to one or more factors specific to the physical, physiological, genetic, mental, economic, cultural or social identity of that natural person;

"processing" means any operation or set of operations which is performed on personal data or sets of personal data, whether or not by automated means such as collection, recoding, organisation, structuring, storage, adaptation or alteration, retrieval, consultation, use, disclosure by transmission, dissemination or otherwise making available , alignment or combination, restriction, erasure or destruction;

"controller" means the natural or legal person, public authority, agency or other body which, alone or jointly with others, determines the purposes and means of the processing of personal data; where the purposes and means of such processing are determined by Union or Member State law, the controller or the specific criteria for its nomination may be provided for by Union or Member State law;

"processor" means a natural or legal person, public authority, agency or other body which processes personal data on behalf of the controller;

"consent" of the data subject means any freely given, specific, informed and unambiguous indication of the data subject's wishes by which he or she, by a statement or by a clear affirmative action, signifies agreement to the processing of personal data relating to him or her;

"personal data breach" means a breach of security leading to the accidental or unlawful destruction, loss, alteration, unauthorised disclosure of, or access to, personal data transmitted, stored or otherwise processed.'

1 Article 4.

27.4   GDPR: PROCESSING PERSONAL DATA

The following is a precis of the data protection principles.

Personal data shall be:[1]

(a)   processed lawfully, fairly and in a transparent manner in relation to the data subject;

(b)   collected for specified, explicit and legitimate purposes and not further processed in a manner that is incompatible with those purposes;

(c)   adequate, relevant and limited to what is necessary in relation to the purposes for which they are processed;

(d)   accurate and, where necessary, kept up to date; every reasonable step must be taken to ensure that personal data that are inaccurate, having regard to the purposes for which they are processed, are erased or rectified without delay;

(e)   kept in a form which permits identification of data subjects for no longer than is necessary for the purposes for which the personal data are processed; and

(f)   processed in a manner that ensures appropriate security of the personal data, including protection against unauthorised or unlawful processing and against accidental loss, destruction or damage, using appropriate technical or organisational measures.

The controller is responsible for, and must be able to demonstrate compliance with, the above principles.[2]

The GDPR sets out the conditions precedent for lawful processing which, in brief, are that:[3]

(a)   the data subject has given consent to the processing of his or her personal data for one or more specific purposes;

(b)   processing is necessary for the performance of a contract to which the data subject is party or to take steps at the request of the data subject prior to entering into a contract;

(c)   processing is necessary for compliance with a legal obligation binding the controller;

(d)   processing is necessary in order to protect the vital interests of the data subject or another natural person;

(e)   processing is necessary for performance of a task carried out in the public interest or the exercise of official authority vested in the controller;

(f)   processing is necessary for purposes of the legitimate interests pursued by the controller or by a third party.

Processing certain special categories of personal data (previously described as 'sensitive personal data') is prohibited unless there is compliance with specific requirements, including that the data subject gives his or her explicit consent.[4]

There are controls on processors.[5]
Specific obligations pertain to the security of personal data.[6]

1 GDPR, Article 5(1).
2 Ibid., Article 5(2).
3 Ibid., Article 6.
4 Ibid., Article 9.
5 Ibid., Article 28.
6 Ibid., Article 32.

27.5   GDPR: SOME INNOVATIVE PROVISIONS

Among the data subject's innovative rights are:

(a) the right to rectification of inaccurate personal data concerning him or her;[1]

(b) the right to erasure of specified personal data concerning him or her;[2] and

(c) the right to restrict the processing of personal data in specified circumstances.[3]

Processors of personal data must maintain records of personal data and processing activities and are responsible for a breach.[4]

1 GDPR, Article 16.
2 Ibid., Article 17.
3 Ibid., Articles 18 to 22.
4 Ibid., Article 6.

27.6   GDPR: TRANSFER OF PERSONAL DATA

Chapter V of GDPR governs the transferability of personal data to third countries or international organisations.

27.7   CONSENT CLAUSES

Before personal data relating to an individual is accessed, whether at the application or agreement stage, the person obtaining that information, usually the creditor
or lessor, must provide the following information to the proposed customer: the
identity of the data controller and if he has a nominated representative the identity
of that representative; the purposes for which the data are intended to be processed;
and any further information which is necessary, having regard to the specific circumstances in which the data are to be processed, to enable the data processing to
be fair. This includes information as to the source of any personal data.

A typical notification clause in an agreement might read as follows:

'Data Protection: Use of Your Information

In considering whether to enter into this agreement we will search your record
at credit reference agencies. They will add to their record about you details of
our search and your application and this will be seen by other organisations

that make searches. We will also add to your record with the credit reference agencies details of your agreement with us and your payment record under this agreement. These records will be shared with other organisations and may be used by them to consider your further applications for credit and credit related services and to trace debtors, recover debts and for fraud prevention. We may also check your details with fraud prevention agencies and if you provide us with false information or we suspect fraud, this may be recorded. Fraud prevention agencies will also share their records with other organisations to help make decisions. We may also use information about you for marketing our other products to you. If you do not wish to receive such information, you should write to us at any time.

Please telephone us on freephone .... if you want to have details of the credit reference and fraud prevention agencies from whom we obtain and to whom we pass information about you. You have a legal right to these details. You also have a right to receive a copy of the information we hold about you if you apply to us in writing. A fee will be payable.'

27.8   ASSOCIATED RECORDS

For some time the Information Commissioner's Office expressed concern at the credit industry's use of so-called 'third party data', the assumption of a financial connection on the basis of shared surname and current or previous address.

The credit industry duly recognised the need for change, reinforced by the DPA 1998, and the Human Rights Act 1998. A working party was set up in 1999 comprising representatives of various trade associations resulting in agreement on an additional data protection notice to be included in the general data protection notice. It reads as follows:

'Use of Associated Records

Before entering into any agreement with you we may search records at credit reference agencies which may be linked to records relating to your spouse/ partner or other persons with whom you are linked financially and other members of your household. For the purposes of this application you may be treated as financially linked and you will be assessed with reference to "associated records".

Where any search or application is completed involving joint parties, you both consent to our recording details at credit reference agencies. As a result, an "association" will be created which will link your financial records and your associate's information may be taken into account when future searches are made by us or another lender unless you file a "disassociation" at the credit reference agencies.'

This practice will need to be reconsidered in the light of the GDPR.

Consent clauses in applications and agreement forms have become almost as lengthy as the forms themselves and will often necessitate an extra page being appended to the form. Where applications are entered into over the internet, the data protection notice must be included on the relevant page of the trader's website and there must be evidence that the customer read and consented to that notice, especially where explicit consent is required to sensitive personal data. Applications over the telephone must likewise be preceded by the consent notice being read to the customer. In these cases the notice can be replicated in the agreement form itself so as to make the customer's consent abundantly clear.

Doubtless the GDPR will give rise to new forms of consent clause having the approval of the Information Commissioner's Office.

27.9   NOTIFICATION/REGISTRATION

The current system of notification under the DPA 1998 replaced the registration scheme under the Data Protection Act 1984 and produced a register of data controllers. No personal data may be processed unless an entry in respect of the data controller is included in the register maintained by the Information Commissioner. When a notification is made by a data controller, in addition to the registrable particulars, the general description of the security measures taken to protect the personal data must be notified.

Apart from general information relating to the data controller, the notification form requires the data controller to include the purposes for which personal data are being or are to be processed, a description of the data subjects about whom data are to be held, a description of the data classes, a list of the recipients of the data, and information as to where the data are to be transferred outside the European Economic Area.

The GDPR requires each Member State to provide one or more independent public authorities to be responsible for monitoring the application of the Regulation.[1] This will doubtless be the Information Commissioner's Office in the UK. A likely change following the Regulation is that more emphasis will be placed on self-regulation, including the abolition of the current form of notification to the Information Commissioner, mentioned above.

1   GDPR Chapter VI.

27.10   FREEDOM OF INFORMATION ACT 2000

This Act provides individuals with access to information held by public authorities, as defined in Schedule 1 to the Act. They include government departments, the House of Commons, the House of Lords, local government bodies, bodies falling under the National Health Service, maintained schools and other educational institutions, police forces and specified Advisory Committees, Boards, Councils and Agencies. Various items of information are exempt from the duty to provide information, either absolutely exempt or conditionally exempt.[1]

1   See s 2 and Part 11; see s 2(3) for absolute exemptions.

27.11   OTHER RIGHTS OF INDIVIDUALS

The DPA 1998 and CCA 1974 permit individuals to find out what information is held about them on computer and certain paper records. This is known as the right of subject access. The provisions of DPA 1998 will be replaced by GDPR Chapter III, entitled 'Rights of the Data Subject', which includes right of access by the data subject to personal data.

An individual or partnership is entitled to receive information held by credit reference agencies. This entitlement and its source are somewhat muddled, as will be seen below.

Under CCA 1974 a creditor under a prospective regulated credit agreement (but not an owner or lessor under a hire agreement) who decides not to proceed with the agreement on the basis of information obtained from a credit reference agency must, when informing the prospective debtor of the decision, inform him that it was reached on the basis of such information and provide him with the particulars of the agency.[1] A creditor, owner or negotiator must, within seven working days after receiving a written request, furnish a debtor or hirer with the name and address of any credit reference agency to which it applied for information about the applicant's financial standing.[2]

The duty of the credit reference agency to supply information is set out in CCA 1974 in relation to requests received from partnerships or any other unincorporated body of persons and in the DPA 1998 in respect of requests received from a living individual. Why this unnecessary bifurcation was resorted to is unclear.

Under CCA 1974 a credit reference agency must, within the period of seven working days after receiving a written request and the prescribed fee, furnish the consumer with a copy of the file relating to it kept by the agency, failure to do so constituting an offence.[3] Under the DPA 1998 the individual is entitled to be given a description of the personal data held, the purposes for which they are held, the recipients to whom they are to be disclosed, and the source of those data. Further, where processing by automatic means of personal data is undertaken, e.g. credit scoring, the data subject is entitled to be informed of the logic involved in taking that decision. The information must be requested in writing and the prescribed fee paid.[4]

An individual who considers an entry in his file to be incorrect, and if not corrected that he is likely to suffer prejudice, may give notice to the agency requiring it to be removed.[5]

Where there is information on the individual's file about people in his family with whom he has no financial connection, he can write to the agency to disassociate himself from them.

1 CCA 1974, s 157(A1).
2 Ibid., s 157(1).
3 Ibid., s 158(1), read with the Consumer Credit (Credit Reference Agency) Regulations 1977, SI 1977/329.
4 Data Protection Act 1998, s 7(1) and (2) read with the Data Protection (Subject Access) (Fees and Miscellaneous Provisions) Regulations 2000, SI 2000/191.
5 CCA 1974, s 159 and the procedure set out there.

27.12   CODES OF PRACTICE

Codes of practice of various trade associations contain provisions relating to data protection. The codes will usually have received the approval of the Information Commissioner.

New codes are to be produced by the Information Commissioner under the proposed Data Protection Act (clauses 119 and 120 of the Data Protection Bill).

27.13 OTHER CONFIDENTIALITY SAFEGUARDS

27.13.1 The Tournier principle and exceptions

In the leading case of *Tournier v National Provincial and Union Bank of England*[1] the court held that there is a contractual duty of secrecy implied in the relationship of banker and customer. It enunciated four exceptions, namely:

(a) where disclosure is under compulsion by law;

(b) where there is a duty to the public to disclose;

(c) where the interests of the bank require disclosure; and

(d) where the disclosure is made by the express or implied consent of the customer.

1 [1924] 1 KB 461, CA. See also *Christofi v Barclays Bank plc* [1999] 4 All ER 437, *Robertson v Canadian Imperial Bank of Commerce* [1995] 1 All ER 824, *Barclays Bank plc v Taylor* [1989] 3 All ER 563.

27.13.2 Use of the electoral register

The refusal by an electoral registration officer to allow an elector to have his name removed from an electoral register before it was sold to a commercial concern for marketing purposes was held to constitute both a breach of his right to respect for his private and family life under Art 8 of the European Convention on Human Rights and an invalid interference with his right to vote.[1] The issues raised by the *Robertson Case* were resolved by the Representation of the People (England and Wales) (Amendment) Regulations 2002.[2] These regulations provide for the creation of two versions of the register – a full version and an edited version. The full version is supplied to a limited number of organisations, principally government departments and credit reference agencies. The edited version is available for sale to anyone, although individuals may object to their details being included in the edited version.[3]

1 *R (on the application of Robertson) v City of Wakefield Metropolitan Council* [2001] All ER (D) 243.
2 SI 2002/1871.
3 See *Encyclopedia of Data Protection & Privacy* (Sweet & Maxwell), at 1–165.

27.14 THE NEW DATA PROTECTION ACT

The proposed UK reforms, in the form of a new Data Protection Act, will replace DPA 1998 and complement GDPR. In outline, it is intended to cover the following:[1]

(a)   *Protecting individuals*

Individuals will be given more control over their digital footprint, their personal data, how it is used and passed on by companies. Specifically, parents or guardians will be required to give consent to information services where a child is under 13 years of age.

There will be improved data access. New rules will make it easier for customers to move data between service providers.

There will be a right to be forgotten.

Individuals will have a greater say regarding their profiling, decision making about them based on automated processing.

(b)   *Protecting organisations*

There will be greater accountability with less bureaucracy. Businesses will need to notify the Information Commissioner's Office (ICO) within 72 hours of a data breach taking place if the breach risks the rights and freedoms of an individual.

(c)   *Stronger enforcement*

The ICO will be empowered to request information from data controllers and carry out investigations and impose civil sanctions by way of fines up to £17m or 4% of global turnover. The ICO or the Crown Prosecution Service and equivalent services in Scotland and Northern Ireland will continue to prosecute offenders.

Journalists and whistleblowers will be protected.

(d)   *A bespoke regime for law enforcement purposes*

There will be a requirement for a mandatory Data Protection Officer (DPO), for controls on charges for, and refusals of, data protection requests, and the need for a full audit trail of specific operations of automated processing systems.

It would not be surprising if the GDPR or the new Data Protection Act will have the effect of overturning the decision of the Court of Appeal in *Durant v Financial Services Authority*[2] on the restrictive meaning of disclosable 'personal data'.

1 'A New Data Protection Bill: Our Planned Reforms: Statement of Intent', published by the Department for Digital, Culture Media & Sport, 7 August 2017.
2 [2003] EWCA Civ 1746.

Chapter 28

Funding and outsourcing

28.1 INTRODUCTION

It is not possible to do justice to this vast subject which falls more properly within the scope of corporate finance. Nevertheless, it is appropriate to include brief mention of the methods whereby credit and hire facilities are financed and a note on the outsourcing of services.

Credit grantors and providers of hire facilities do not enjoy a free hand in raising funds. Increased regulatory and compliance requirements on banks, building societies and other lending institutions, especially in recent years following the international banking crisis, have resulted in a slow-down of lending both to business and the consumer.

Companies are restricted by virtue of the provisions of their constitution, memoranda and articles of association (although greatly reduced by the virtual extinction of the *ultra vires* doctrine) and associations and institutions by their rules and constitutions. Leasing companies which are banks fall under the supervision of the FCA and leasing transactions are ordinarily treated as loans for the purposes of calculating the institution's risk/asset ratio.

28.2 METHODS OF FINANCING

The primary criteria which apply to the selection of sources of funding are their availability, cost, efficiency (including accounting treatment) and tax effectiveness. These, in their various orders of priority, will ultimately dictate the method of funding adopted.

28.2.1 Equity

Equity or share capital is the risk-bearing capital of a company and can take the form of various classes of shares such as ordinary, preference or deferred shares, each with their separate rights. Every company, unless it is a company limited by guarantee (and which is usually utilised for non-profit making associations or charities) is required to have a share capital.

28.2.2   Deposits

Banks, building societies and other authorised institutions will utilise the monies received by way of deposit from customers and their members for lending on to borrowers. The importance of this source of funding was highlighted by the funding crisis involving Northern Rock plc which relied almost exclusively on the availability of wholesale funding. When banks ceased to lend to each other Northern Rock's funding resource dried up.

28.2.3   Borrowing

There are, in theory, many types and sources of loans ranging from simple bank loan facilities, such as sterling dealing lines, to Eurocurrency floating rate loans. The appropriate type of loan facility will be determined by the factors already mentioned, the amount to be raised and the ease with which this can be achieved. In practice, opportunities for fund-raising have been severely curtailed by increased regulation and unfavourable economic conditions. This has, in turn, created opportunities for investment funds and the so-called shadow banking sector.

A new type of lending that currently operates outside the circle of constraints applying to banks but is subject to authorisation and regulation by the FCA is so-called peer-to-peer, or P2P, lending. A type of P2P lending, by way of fund-raising for the purpose of lending, is so-called crowdfunding such as that facilitated by Zopa Ltd and the Funding Circle Ltd. In essence, loans are made to borrowers by groups of individual lenders who choose to lend to borrowers of a pre-selected status, at interest rates set by the lenders and for a pre-determined purpose, namely for the borrowers' business or non-business purposes. A loan-based crowdfunding firm is a firm authorised by the FCA that is subject to the client money rules in CASS 7 and whose designated investment business includes operating an electronic system in relation to lending.[1]

P2P lending has grown rapidly in the UK. In 2015, it accounted for 13% of the supply of new loans to small enterprises (those with turnover of £1 million or less). It still accounts for only a small share of the market for unsecured consumer loans.[2] A loan may be a fixed sum loan or an overdraft or other revolving credit facility and may be raised from one or several lenders, in the form of a syndicated loan. In the case of more mature and larger companies, borrowings may be effected by the issue of debenture loan stock, secured on the assets of the borrowing company. Eurobonds, debt securities denominated in a foreign currency, might also be used to raise funds abroad.

The capacity of a company to raise funds is dependent upon its ability to provide security, its gearing ratio (the relationship between its indebtedness and its equity capital) and its ability to meet its repayment obligations. Together these will affect the borrower's credit rating which will, in turn, have a direct bearing on the cost of loan finance; in simple terms, the higher the credit rating of the borrower, the cheaper will be its cost of funding.

The Bank of England itself sought to facilitate lending, notably by its Funding for Lending scheme which was launched in August 2012 and which, by early December 2012, accounted for £4.4 billion of cheaper funding to the banks.

1 FCA Handbook, CASS 7.
2 See the detailed and thoroughly researched paper 'The Business Models and Economics of Peer-to-Peer Lending' by Alistair Milne and Paul Parboteeah, School of Business, Loughborough University, UK, 5 April 2016. The paper also contains a valuable comparison of the situation in the UK with that in the USA.

28.2.4   Funding of leasing companies

Whilst many of the methods of funding described above apply equally to leasing companies, they also enjoy certain unique methods of raising finance.

Head-lease finance involves interposing the leasing company between a superior lessor and the ultimate lessee. The head-lease takes the form of a master lease corresponding to a wholesale funding line of credit, and sharing all the characteristics of a lease. The leasing company can be certain of the availability of leasing finance provided that the lease agreement entered into by the leasing company with its lessee mirrors the provisions of the head lease agreement and that the tax and capital allowance provisions of the lease agreement match the corresponding provisions of the head lease. The ultimate sub-lessee may or may not be aware or made aware of the existence of the head lease agreement at the outset or at all.

At the other end of the spectrum, leasing finance may be raised after leases have already been concluded with the lessees. This would normally involve an assignment by the lessor, either by way of security or outright assignment, of the underlying lease receivables on their own or together with the transfer of the leased equipment. Depending upon the commercial considerations, a lessor might enter into a total refinancing package substituting the financier as the lessor in new leasing agreements with the lessee, by way of a novation of the original leases.

Accounting for leases and hire-purchase contracts, including sale and lease-back transactions, is subject to section 20 of FRS 102 and IAS 17.

28.2.5   Stock-in-trade finance

The expression 'stock-in-trade finance' is a generic description of on-going funding arrangements available to a dealer who provides his own finance. Examples are unit-stocking finance and block discounting or periodical assignments of agreements.

Unit-stocking finance is the arrangement whereby vehicles are supplied on consignment to dealers with the consignor invariably retaining title to the vehicles. The consignment may take the form of conditional sale under which the dealer only incurs liability for the purchase price of a vehicle when the dealer effects a sale of the vehicle to a customer. Unit-stocking finance is in fact a method of subsidised extended credit.

Block discounting is a form of receivables financing. It takes place after the dealer has entered into the relevant finance or lease agreements. Under a block discounting agreement the dealer might sell the receivables under the agreements (alone or together with title to the underlying goods) to a financier. The dealer may then continue to collect the receivables as disclosed or undisclosed agent for the financier. Commercial considerations will often dictate that no notice of the assignment is given to the customers so that the arrangement constitutes merely an equitable assignment. Where notice of the assignment is given to customers (e.g. where the purchaser of the receivables collects payments directly from customers), the arrangement constitutes a legal assignment. Block discounting might also take the form of a loan by a financier secured by a charge on the finance and leasing agreements.

The Business Contract Terms (Assignment of Receivables) Regulations 2017[1] will assist this process, insofar as they provide that a term in a contract has no effect to the extent that it prohibits the assignment of a receivable under that contract or any other contract. Certain contracts, including a contract for prescribed financial services, are excluded from the Regulations.

1 Draft SI.

28.2.6   Refinancing techniques

28.2.6.1   Securitisation

Securitisation is a financing technique whereby the originator of a pool of assets (such as residential or commercial mortgages, credit card or other receivables, personal loans or leases) sells or transfers such assets to a special-purpose vehicle ('SPV') which funds the purchase by issuing debt securities (typically medium-term notes or commercial paper) into the capital markets. The debt securities are typically divided into several different layers or 'tranches' with the junior tranche absorbing any losses first and attracting the highest rate of return as compensation. The transaction is structured so that the income produced by the purchased assets is sufficient for the issuing vehicle to fund the payment obligations arising under the debt securities and to redeem them at maturity.

There are many reasons why an originator might choose securitisation over other financing techniques, including the opportunity to remove assets from its balance sheet for regulatory (in the case of a bank originator) and/or accounting purposes (in some cases without the need for an actual sale of the assets) thereby freeing up capital for further investment, the opportunity to access diverse funding sources and the opportunity to access the cheaper funding often offered by the capital markets. The rules governing structures for originators which are UK banks are set out in the FSA Handbook. Originators in the UK looking to remove assets from their balance sheet for accounting purposes using securitisation will have to do so in accordance with either IFRS or UK GAAP.

Securitisation is usually associated with refinancing of assets which have already been originated, but this is not necessarily the case. A variation of the theme is the creation, in advance of the credit or leasing agreements coming into existence, of a SPV which acts as a borrowing company, whose sole activity is to purchase and fund selected credit and leasing receivables. It is possible to structure the transaction so that the SPV would be off balance sheet to all parties to the transaction.

28.2.6.2 Swaps

The swap market assists traders to solve financial problems arising out of variations in interest rates and currency exchange rates, different taxation regimes, rates of inflation and degrees of creditworthiness.

In its simplest form a swapped contract is an agreement between two parties by which one agrees to pay the other on a specified date amounts calculated by reference to the interest which would have accrued over a given period on the same notional principal sum, assuming different rates of interest to be payable.[1]

1 *Hazell v Hammersmith and Fulham London Borough Council* [1991] 2 WLR 372, at 378–9, HL.

28.2.6.3 Cash settlement systems

Grantors of credit facilities which operate internationally, such as credit card companies, might enter into a multilateral netting agreement in order to avoid duplicated foreign exchange deals and so as to avoid additional fund transfer costs. Each party to the agreement settles its position by a transfer in the local currency to a local netting centre and all local netting centres settle their positions vis-à-vis the international netting centre. In this way the number and amount of cross-border remittances and the volume of foreign exchange transactions required to effect the settlement of outstanding liability is reduced.

28.2.6.4 Government funding: Student Loans Company

In the financial year 2015–16, the number of borrowers stood at 5 million and the amount lent was £11.8 billion, an increase of 11% on 2014–15.

28.3 OUTSOURCING

A common practice is the outsourcing by consumer lending firms of IT and telecommunications, business process or facilities management services.

Outsourcing is defined as:[1]

> 'an arrangement of any form between a firm and a service provider by which that service provider performs a process, a service or an activity which would otherwise be taken by the firm itself.'[2]

The FCA has always expressed concern that outsourcing creates operational risk. The central theme to the FCA's approach is set out in SYSC 3.2. In simple terms a firm cannot contract out of its regulatory obligations. Outsourcing should not be considered a method for reducing a firm's regulatory obligations and a firm should take reasonable care to supervise the discharge of outsourced functions by its contractor.

The implementation of the Markets in Financial Instruments Directive[3] ('MiFID') and the Capital Requirements Directive[4] ('CRD') has not altered the FCA's general approach but has introduced additional regulatory provisions derived directly from the EU legislation, with which firms must comply. These additional regulatory provisions cover issues such as the following:

- obligation to avoid undue additional operational risk;

- obligation to have adequate policies and procedures;

- notification to the FCA;

- due diligence;

- service management;

- disclosure, audit and maintenance of records;

- confidential information;

- business continuity and termination; and

- written agreement.

The FCA Handbook, in SYSC 13.9, sets out a firm's obligations in respect of outsourcing. Included in these obligations, a firm:

(a) should take particular care to manage material outsourcing arrangements and, as SUP 15.3.8G (1)(e) explains, a firm should notify the FCA when it intends to enter into a material outsourcing arrangement;

(b) should not assume that, because a service provider is either a regulated firm or an intra-group entity, an outsourcing arrangement with that provider will, in itself, necessarily imply a reduction in operational risk;

(c) before entering into, or significantly changing, an outsourcing arrangement, should:

   (1) analyse how the arrangement will fit with its organisation and reporting structure, business strategy, overall risk profile, and ability to meet its regulatory obligations;

   (2) consider whether the agreements establishing the arrangement will allow it to monitor and control its operational risk exposure relating to the outsourcing;

   (3) conduct appropriate due diligence of the service provider's financial stability and expertise;

   (4) consider how it will ensure a smooth transition of its operations from its current arrangements to a new or changed outsourcing arrangement (including what will happen on the termination of the contract); and

   (5) consider any concentration risk implications, such as the business continuity implications that may arise if a single service provider is used by several firms.

A more detailed consideration of this topic is outside the scope of this book.[5]

1 Commission Directive 2006/73/EC implementing Directive 2004/39/EC of the European Parliament and of the Council as regards organisational requirements and operating conditions for investment firms and defined terms for the purposes of that Directive ('MiFID Implementing Directive').
2 Article 2(6) of the MiFID Implementing Directive.
3 Directive 2004/39/EC of the European Parliament and of the Council on the markets in financial instruments amending Council Directives 85/611/EC and 93/6/EEC and Directive 2000/12/EC of the European Parliament and of the Council and repealing Council Directive 93/22/EEC ('MiFID'); repealed by MiFID II, Directive 2014/65/EU.
4 Capital Requirements Directive.
5 See Amanda Lewis, *Outsourcing Contracts – a Practical Guide* (City & Financial Publishing), which provides a comprehensive description of the business and legal issues relating to outsourcing, and includes a chapter on all FCA guidance relevant to outsourcing.

Chapter 29

Miscellaneous accounting and tax aspects

29.1 ACCOUNTING FOR LEASES

The subject is currently governed by section 20 'Leases' of FRS 102[1] and IAS 17. A new leasing standard, IFRS 16, will be effective from 1 January 2019. This will fundamentally change the accounting for leases, preventing off balance sheet finance from taking place. Section 20 of FRS 102 codifies accepted practice for some aspects of lease accounting and requires assets held under finance leases and the related leasing obligations to be capitalised on a company's balance sheet. Capitalisation of assets held under finance leases results in the company's assets and obligations being readily apparent. Hire-purchase contracts which are of a financing nature are to be accounted for on a similar basis to finance leases.

A lease is a finance lease if it transfers substantially all the risks and rewards incidental to ownership. A lease is classified as an operating lease if it does not.[2]

Whether a lease is classified as one or the other depends on the substance of the transaction rather than the form of the contract. A lease would normally be classified as a finance lease if the lease term is for the major part of the economic life of the asset or if the lease transfers ownership of the asset to the lessee by the end of the lease term. Alternatively, if, at the inception of the lease, the present value of the minimum lease payments, including any initial payment, amounts to substantially all of the fair value of the leased asset, it would be classified as a finance lease.[3] Since a lessor and lessee are obliged to apply the test independently, each may treat the asset differently in their accounts.

1 September 2015.
2 FRS 102 para 20.4.
3 FRS 102 para 20.5.

29.1.1 Accounting by lessee

At commencement of the lease term, a finance lease should be recorded in the balance sheet of the lessee as an asset and a liability at the lower of the fair value of the asset and the present value of the minimum lease payments (discounted at the interest rate implicit in the lease, if practicable, or else at the entity's incremental borrowing rate).[1] In practice the fair value of the asset will often be a sufficiently close approximation to the present value of the minimum lease payments and may then be substituted for it.

The total finance charge under a finance lease should be allocated to accounting periods during the lease term so as to produce a constant periodic rate of charge on the remaining balance of the liability.[2] The depreciation policy for financed assets should be consistent with that for owned assets. The asset should be depreciated over the shorter of the lease term and the asset's useful life. A lessee must also assess at each reporting date whether an asset leased under a finance lease is impaired.[3]

The rentals under an operating lease should be recognised as an expense in the income statement over the lease term on a straight-line basis, unless another systematic basis is more representative of the time pattern of the user's benefit.[4]

1 FRS 102 paras 20.9, 20.10.
2 FRS 102 para 20.11.
3 FRS 102 para 20.12, section 27.
4 FRS 102 para 20.15.

29.1.2   Accounting by lessor

A lessor must recognise assets held under a finance lease in its statement of financial position and present them as a receivable at an amount equal to the net investment in the lease. The net investment in a lease is the lessor's gross investment in the lease discounted at the interest rate implicit in the lease. The gross investment in the lease is the aggregate of:

(a)   the minimum lease payments receivable by the lessor under a finance lease; and

(b)   any unguaranteed residual value accruing to the lessor.

The payments should be allocated to accounting periods so as to give a constant periodic rate of return on the lessor's net cash investment and release in each period.

Tax-free grants which are available to the lessor against the purchase price of assets for leasing should be spread over the period of the lease.[1]

In the case of operating leases, the asset should be recorded as a fixed asset and depreciated over its useful life. Rental income should be recognised on a straight-line basis over the period of the lease unless another systematic basis is more representative of the hire pattern.[2]

1 FRS 102 para 20.17.
2 FRS 102 paras 20.24–20.26.

29.1.3   Accounting by manufacturer or dealer lessor

A manufacturer or dealer lessor must recognise sales revenue at the commencement of the lease as the fair value of the asset or, if lower, the present value of minimum lease payments accruing to the lessor, computed at a market rate of interest. The cost of sale recognised at the commencement of the lease term is the cost, or carrying amount if different, of the leased asset less the present value of the unguaranteed residual value. The difference between the sales revenue and the cost of sale is the selling profit, which is recognised in accordance with the entity's policy for outright sales.[1]

1 FRS 102 para 20.21.

29.2   SALE AND LEASEBACK TRANSACTIONS

29.2.1   Accounting by the seller/lessee

FRS 102 provides that, in a sale and leaseback transaction which results in a finance lease, any apparent profit or loss should be deferred and amortised in the financial statements of the seller/lessee over the lease term.[1]

In the case of an operating lease, if the transaction is established at fair value, any profit or loss should be recognised immediately. Separate rules apply where the sale price is below or above fair value.[2]

Finance Act 2004 introduced anti-avoidance legislation to prevent double tax benefits arising in the leaseback of plant or machinery by retention of capital allowances at the same time as obtaining a deduction for the leaseback rentals.[3]

1 FRS 102 para 20.33.
2 FRS 102 para 20.34.
3 Capital Allowances Act 2001, ss 228A to 228M.

29.2.2   Accounting by the buyer/lessor

A buyer/lessor should account for a sale and leaseback in the same way as he accounts for other leases.

29.3   LEASING AND TAXATION

Costs incurred in leasing or hiring an asset to be used in a trade will be allowable for tax purposes. However, no capital allowances can be claimed by the lessee, as the lessor is the legal owner.

Whether the lease is an operating lease or a finance lease, the amount charged to the P&L account is an allowable expense for tax purposes. There is a difference between an operating lease and a finance lease in respect of what will be charged to the P&L account. Under an operating lease, the lease rentals are charged to the P&L account; while, under a finance lease, the lease interest and lease depreciation will both be charged to the P&L account and will be allowable for tax purposes.

29.4　CAPITAL ALLOWANCES

Capital allowances are the amount of depreciation allowed by HMRC to be offset against taxable profits and are governed by the Capital Allowances Act 2001. Allowances can be claimed on the cost of plant or machinery (qualifying expenditure) purchased for use in a qualifying activity (e.g. a trade).[1] Qualifying expenditure in respect of each item is allocated to a pool on which the owner claims the allowances.

Special provisions apply to cars. If a car's CO_2 emissions exceed 130g/km, it must be allocated to the special rate pool and it attracts annual writing down allowances of 8%. Cars with CO_2 emissions of between 76g/km and 130g/km are allocated to the taxpayer's main pool, for capital allowances purposes, and attract an annual writing down allowance of 18%. New and unused cars with CO_2 emissions of no more than 75g/km are eligible for a 100% first year allowance.

The special rate pool is also used to capture total expenditure relating to integral features,[2] long-life assets and thermal insulation expenditure. Long-life assets[3] are plant or machinery with a useful economic life of at least 25 years. The special rate pool only attracts annual writing down allowances of 8%. All other assets are allocated to the main pool which attracts writing down allowances of 18%. The annual writing down allowance on short-life assets is 18%.[4]

An annual investment allowance currently provides for a 100% allowance on the first £200,000 of expenditure on plant and machinery. This excludes expenditure incurred on cars. A 100% first year allowance is available for expenditure on energy-saving plant and machinery.

As regards hire-purchase agreements, the plant or machinery is treated as owned by the person who hires and shall or may become the owner of the asset at any time when he is entitled to the benefit of the contract, so far as it relates to the plant and machinery. At the time that the plant and machinery is brought into use by the hirer for the purposes of a qualifying activity, he is treated as having incurred all capital expenditure in respect of the same.[5] However, this does not apply to expenditure incurred on plant or machinery which is a fixture.[6]

The lessor, as owner of equipment under the lease, is generally entitled to all allowances in relation to the assets. An exception is made where the plant or machinery is provided by the lessee, the lessee incurs capital expenditure for the purposes of a qualifying activity, and the lessee does not own the plant or machinery.[7]

Allowances under the Capital Allowances Act 2001 are only available if the person carries on a qualifying activity, notably a trade, profession or vocation or the special leasing of plant or machinery.[8]

1　'Qualifying activity' is defined in Chapter 2 of Part 2 of the Act.
2　Capital Allowances Act 2001, s 33A.
3　Ibid., s 91 for meaning of 'long-life asset' and s 102.
4　Ibid., s 83 for meaning of 'short-life asset' and s 56.
5　Ibid., s 67.
6　Ibid., ss 69 and 173.
7　Ibid., s 70.
8　Ibid., ss 11 and 15.

29.5 'FUNDING LEASE' AND 'LONG FUNDING LEASE'

Finance Act 2006 introduced the new concepts of a 'funding lease' and a 'long funding lease' into the Capital Allowances Act 2001.[1] The intention of the regime is to treat lease finance and loan finance in the same way and the regime is therefore restricted to leases which are essentially financing transactions.

A 'funding lease' is a lease of plant or machinery which, at its inception, meets one or more of the following tests: a finance lease test, a lease payments test or the useful economic life test, subject to specified exceptions.[2]

A 'long funding lease' is a funding lease which meets the following conditions: it is not a short lease, it is not an excluded lease of so-called background plant or machinery for a building and it is not excluded by the *de minimis* provision for plant or machinery leased with land.[3]

Under the new regime, capital allowances in respect of long funding leases are given to the lessee rather than to the lessor. The lessee may qualify for first year allowances in respect of expenditure on the provision of the leased plant or machinery. Only those sums which, in accordance with generally accepted accounting practice would be treated as finance charges, can be deducted from the lessee's taxable profits. The lessor is disabled from claiming allowances which he would otherwise have been entitled to in respect of the leased plant or machinery and the rental earnings for the relevant period is the amount which, in accordance with generally accepted accounting practice, would be treated as the gross return on the investment.

1 Capital Allowances Act 2001, ss 70A to 70YJ.
2 Ibid., s 70J.
3 Ibid., s 70G.

29.6 VALUE ADDED TAX[1]

29.6.1 Loans

The making of loans and the granting of credit are exempt from VAT. This includes credit granted in connection with the supply of goods or services, provided that a separate charge is made for the credit and disclosed to the customer.[2]

1 Value Added Tax Act 1994, s 31 and Sch 9, Part II, Group 5; Value Added Tax Regulations 1995, SI 1995/2518; HMRC Notice 701/49 VAT: Finance (30 January 2013, updated 7 June 2017).
2 See HMRC Notice 701/49 para 4.2 and also *Customs & Excise Comrs v Diners Club Ltd* [1989] 2 All ER 385, CA.

29.6.2 Supplies by credit, debit and charge card companies

Charges made by credit or charge card companies to retailers who accept the cards in payment for goods or services they have provided are exempt. This includes interchange fees and charges in the form of a discount on the amount reimbursed to the retailer or other outlet. Charges made by a debit card issuer to the retailer or outlet which accepts the cards are also exempt.

Charges payable by cardholders such as interest, annual membership and the like, are exempt.[1]

The following charges by ATM providers are also exempt supplies: charges for the facility to obtain money, the provision of money, transaction processing or the operation of accounts.[2]

1 HMRC Notice 701/49 para 4.8.
2 Ibid., para 2.9.

29.6.3   Instalment credit finance

The charges for credit supplied under a hire-purchase, conditional sale or credit sale agreement, without involving a finance company, are exempt from VAT if the amount of such charges is separately disclosed to the customer.[1]

If the transaction is financed by a finance company which becomes the owner of the goods, the retailer's supply of goods to the finance company is taxable. The finance company's supply of the goods to the customer is taxable but the separate supply of credit is exempt if the credit charge is disclosed separately to the customer.

Option fees in a hire-purchase agreement, documentation fees, arrangement fees and similar additional fees in conditional sale and credit sale agreements are exempt from VAT provided that the fees are specified in the agreement and do not exceed a total of £10 and the agreement includes an exempt supply of instalment credit finance.[2]

In *Primback Ltd v Comrs of Customs & Excise*[3] the Court of Appeal held that retailers who sold furniture on interest free credit to customers with the finance company buying the furniture at a lower price than that paid by customers, were not obliged to pay VAT on the full retail price but only on the sums received from the finance company. It was the court's view that to require retailers to pay VAT on the full price paid by the customers rather than on the sum the retailers actually received from the finance company was to require payment of VAT on an exempt supply, in conflict with art 27 of the Sixth Directive of 17 May 1977 on the Harmonisation of Turnover Taxes (77/388/EEC). The House of Lords referred the matter to the European Court for a preliminary ruling. The European Court overruled the Court of Appeal finding that, since an agreement between the claimant retailer and the customer in each case was that the customer would pay the full advertised price, which was known in advance and invoiced as such and did not vary according to the method of payment, that price was the consideration for the goods and the taxable amount.[4]

In a recent judgment of the European Court of Justice, following a request for a preliminary ruling by the Court of Appeal (England and Wales) (Civil Division), the Court (First Chamber) held as follows in relation to the imposition of VAT in a hire-purchase agreement:[5]

> 'The words "contract for hire which provides that in the normal course of events ownership is to pass at the latest upon payment of the final instalment", used in Article 14(2)(b) of Council Directive 2006/112/EC of 28 November 2006 [the VAT Directive] on the common system of value added tax, must be interpreted

as applying to a leasing contract with an option to purchase if it can be inferred from the financial terms of the contract that exercising the option appears to be the only economically rational choice that the lessee will be able to make at the appropriate time if the contract is performed for its full term, which it is for the national court to ascertain.'

1 Value Added Tax Act 1994, Sch 9, Group 5, Item 3.
2 Ibid., Sch 9, Group 5, Item 4.
3 [1996] CCLR 81, CA.
4 [2001] 1 WLR 1693.
5 *Commissioners for Her Majesty's Revenue & Customs v Mercedes-Benz Financial Services UK Ltd* (4 October 2017).

29.6.4   Credit brokerage and intermediary services[1]

A supplier of an exempt intermediary service is a person who:

- brings together a person seeking a financial service with a person who provides a financial service;

- stands between the parties to a contract and acts in an intermediary capacity; and

- undertakes work preparatory to the completion of a contract for the provision of financial services, whether or not it is completed.

A 'financial service' for the purposes of the intermediaries' exemption is a service listed in the VAT Act, Schedule 9, Group 5, items 1 to 4 and 6.

Work preparatory to the completion of a contract refers to work done of a specialised nature. This could include helping to set the terms of the contract or making representations on behalf of a client, but would not include work done of a general nature, such as administrative or clerical formalities.

Special provisions apply to persons in different capacities, including Independent Financial Advisors (IFAs).

1 HMRC Guidance on VAT and Finance (HMRC 701/49 para 9).

29.6.5   Equipment leasing

Rentals under leasing or hire agreements are subject to VAT, whether the agreement is a finance lease or an operating lease. VAT must be charged on each rental due under the lease agreement. The tax point, namely the date which determines when the tax must be paid by the finance company, is usually the earlier of the issue of a VAT invoice or receipt of the rental payment.

Where the lease or hire agreement contains an option to purchase clause, i.e. where it is a hire-purchase or lease purchase agreement, no VAT is payable in respect of the finance charges, provided that such charges are disclosed to the recipient of the goods.[1]

1 Value Added Tax Act 1994, Sch 9, Part II, Group 5, item 3.

29.6.6   Taxable services

The supply of credit management services, when the supplier does not grant the credit, is taxable.[1] The supply of debt collection services is taxable.[2]

1 Value Added Tax Act 1994, Sch 9, Group 5, Item 5; HMRC Notice 701/49 para 4.10.
2 HMRC Notice 701/49 para 5.10.

29.6.7   Bad debt relief

Bad debt relief can be claimed on supplies of goods made by way of hire-purchase or conditional sale where the customer has defaulted. Supplies have two components: a supply of goods; and a supply of associated finance. Suppliers are permitted to allocate each payment received from defaulting customers to goods and to finance in the same ratio as the total costs of goods and the total cost of finance to the customer.[1] In the case of repossessed goods, where the disposal of the repossessed goods are subject to VAT, a supplier need not deduct the proceeds of the disposal from the outstanding debt of the customer when claiming bad debt relief.[2] No debt relief is allowable in respect of an agreed reduction in the price.

1 Customs and Excise Business Brief 19/2001 issued 7 December 2001.
2 Regulation 170A of the Value Added Tax Regulations 1995 (SI 1995/2518) and see Revenue & Customs Brief 14/07 issued 13 February 2007.

Chapter 30

FCA authorisation and permission

30.1 INTRODUCTION

The original aim of the Financial Conduct Authority (FCA), when it was established, was to create a more robust regulatory regime that protects consumers while encouraging innovative businesses that meet its regulatory standards.

The FCA statutory objectives are the foundation for the FCA approach to regulating firms and, in its engagement with those firms, the FCA seeks to ensure that the fair treatment of consumers is at the heart of the business and that the activities of the business do not adversely affect market integrity and competition.

In order to achieve its original aim, and to meet its objectives, the FCA continually engages with firms, which takes place through four main activities:

- creating rules that firms must follow (through FCA Policy work);

- considering whether firms should be authorised by the FCA under Part 4A with specific permissions for particular activities (led by the FCA Authorisations Division);

- ongoing supervision of regulated firms' activities (led by the FCA Supervision Division); and

- the use of enforcement powers in instances where egregious misconduct has been identified (led by the FCA Enforcement Division).

This chapter deals with the FCA activity, led by its Authorisations Division, of considering whether consumer credit firms should be authorised by the FCA for particular activities.

'Authorisation' is defined in the Glossary to the FCA Handbook thus: 'authorisation as an authorised person for the purposes of FSMA'.

An 'authorised person', as defined in the Glossary, means, in accordance with section 31 of FSMA (Authorised persons), one of the following:

(a) a person who has a Part 4A permission to carry on one or more regulated activities;

(b) an incoming EEA firm;

(c) an incoming Treaty firm;

(d)   a UCITS qualifier;

(e)   an investment company with variable capital (ICVC);

(f)   the Society of Lloyd's.

Part 4A permission in (a) means, as defined in section 55A of FSMA (Application for permission), a permission (permission to carry on regulated activities) given by the FCA or PRA under Part 4A of FSMA (permission to carry on regulated activities), or having effect as if so given.

Part 4A of FSMA provides for regulation by both regulators, namely the FCA and the PRA. PRA regulation is not particularly relevant to this text and therefore consideration will be given to FCA regulation and, in this chapter, to persons who are seeking Part 4A permission from the FCA, to carry on one or more regulated activities.

In simple terms, authorisation means: if the FCA approves an application from a person for Part 4A permission, that person (the applicant firm or individual) will be regarded as 'authorised'.

Authorisation is regarded as the FCA's equivalent of the now repealed consumer credit licensing regime (previously controlled by the OFT under Part III of CCA 1974), but operates somewhat differently.

First, the consumer credit licensing regime, under the provisions of CCA 1974, began on the principle that a licence was required, by any trader, to carry on a consumer credit business, a consumer hire business or an ancillary credit business, and then went on to provide for sanctions (including offences under Part III of CCA 1974) for traders who carried on those specified businesses without a licence.

Authorisation under FSMA, however, commences under section 19 with a 'general prohibition' on *all* regulated activities, but then provides for authorisations and exemptions, both of which operate by converting an otherwise unlawful activity into an activity permitted by the FCA. Section 19 effectively prohibits the carrying on of any regulated activities by unauthorised persons, establishing criminal offences on the way, which means that firms that wish to carry on regulated consumer credit-related activities must apply to the FCA for authorisation to do so (unless an exemption exists).

Secondly, CCA 1974 was only concerned with licensing the business, namely the legal entity that carried on the business such as a body corporate, an incorporated body of persons, a partnership or an individual in the case of a sole trader. In deciding whether to issue a licence to the business, the OFT had the power to consider the fitness and propriety of those who managed the business, but it was the legal entity that carried on the business that became the licensee.

The FCA, however, under s 59 of FSMA, is not only concerned with authorising the business itself as a legal entity but is also concerned in giving 'approval', which in a sense is personal authorisation, to senior persons of the business to carry out certain management functions for the business. A person in respect of whom approval is given is known as an 'approved person', and the decision of who that person should be is determined not by choice but by that person's role in the business.

For consumer credit firms this means that, under s 59 of FSMA, the FCA must approve at least one individual in all consumer credit firms, except for most not-for-profit debt advice bodies and some sole traders, when a firm applies to be authorised. (See **Chapter 31** on the current FCA 'approved person' regime and on the high-level review of the new Senior Managers and Certification (SM&CR) regime.)

30.2   THE 'GENERAL PROHIBITION'

Section 19 of Part II of FSMA sets out what is referred to as 'the general prohibition' and provides that no person may carry on a regulated activity in the United Kingdom unless that person is authorised or exempt. For an activity to be a regulated activity under FSMA, it must be 'carried on by way of business', as stated in section 22(1).

In essence, as with all other financial services firms, the general prohibition makes it unlawful for any consumer credit firm or individual to carry on, or purport to carry on, a regulated activity in the United Kingdom unless it is authorised by the FCA to carry on one or more regulated activities or is an exempt person.

Firms, including individuals, who carry on an unauthorised business do so in breach of section 19, are guilty of an offence under section 23(1) of FSMA, and are liable:

(a)   on summary conviction, to imprisonment for a term not exceeding six months or a fine not exceeding the statutory maximum, or both; and

(b)   on conviction on indictment, to imprisonment for a term not exceeding two years or a fine, or both.

It is noteworthy that an authorised person is also guilty of an offence under section 23(1A) of FSMA if that person carries on a credit-related regulated activity in the UK or purports to do so, otherwise than in accordance with permission given to that person under Part 4A.

Furthermore, agreements made by unauthorised lenders or made as a result of introductions by unauthorised credit brokers may be unenforceable against the borrower under sections 26, 26A and 27 of FSMA.

Section 19 applies fully to firms or individuals that wish to offer consumer credit, or have interim permission to do so, and need to apply for authorisation. The section reads:

'(1) No person may carry on a regulated activity in the United Kingdom, or purport to do so, unless he is–

(a)   an authorised person; or

(b)   an exempt person.

(2) The prohibition is referred to in this Act as the general prohibition.'

For the purposes of this chapter, and as defined in the Glossary to the FCA Handbook:

'Person' means (in accordance with the Interpretation Act 1978) any person, including a body of persons corporate or unincorporate (that is, a natural person, a legal person and, for example, a partnership).

'Regulated activity' means (in accordance with section 22 of FSMA (Regulated activities)), the activities specified in Part II of the Financial Services and Markets Act 2000 (Regulated Activities) Order 2001.[1]

(A full description of each regulated activity relating to consumer credit can be found in the FCA Handbook at PERG 2.7.)

'Authorised person' means (in accordance with section 31 of FSMA (Authorised persons)) a person who has a Part 4A permission to carry on one or more regulated activities.

'Exempt person' means:

(1)   (as defined in section 417(1) of FSMA (Definitions)) (in relation to a regulated activity) a person who is exempt from the general prohibition in respect of that activity as a result of:

   (a)   the Exemption Order (The Financial Services and Markets Act 2000 (Exemption) Order 2001);[2] or

   (b)   being an appointed representative; or

   (c)   section 285(2) or (3) of FSMA (Exemption for recognised investment exchanges and clearing houses); and

(2)   a person who is exempt from the general prohibition as a result of section 312A(2) of FSMA (Exercise of passport rights by EEA market operator).

1 SI 2001/544 (Specified Activities).
2 SI 2001/1201.

30.3   PRINCIPALS AND APPOINTED REPRESENTATIVES: AN ALTERNATIVE TO AUTHORISATION

The most common way a business can qualify for an exemption and become an exempt person is to become what is referred to in FSMA as an Appointed Representative (AR) of an authorised person.

A person, which includes a firm or individual, wishing to carry on certain regulated activities in the UK without authorisation, may, under section 39 of FSMA, qualify as an exempt person for the purposes of section 19(1)(b) of FSMA by becoming an AR; that is, acting as an agent for an authorised person (the principal) where the principal agrees to take full responsibility, under a written contract, for the regulated activities carried on by the AR, including responsibility for any acts or omissions of the AR.

In broad terms an AR is a firm that carries on certain regulated activities under the supervision of another firm that is authorised by the FCA: the AR has no direct relationship with the FCA on an ongoing basis. (See the Glossary to the FCA Handbook for the full definition of an AR.)

A person will only qualify for exemption as an AR if that person satisfies the conditions specified in section 39(1) of FSMA, as follows:

'39 Exemption of appointed representatives

(1) If a person (other than an authorised person)–

(a) is a party to a contract with an authorised person ('his principal') which–

    (i) permits or requires him to carry on business of a prescribed description, and

    (ii) complies with such requirements as may be prescribed, and

(b) is someone for whose activities in carrying on the whole or part of that business his principal has accepted responsibility in writing,

he is exempt from the general prohibition in relation to any regulated activity comprised in the carrying on of that business for which his principal has accepted responsibility.'

The expressions 'prescribed description' and 'prescribed requirements' above are substantiated by the Financial Services and Markets Act 2000 (Appointed Representatives) Regulations 2001.[1]

The supervision manual (SUP 12 (Appointed Representatives)), under the title 'Regulatory Processes' in the FCA Handbook, sets out the FCA's rules and guidance that apply to a firm in relation to ARs. SUP 12 specifically provides guidance on how the provisions of section 39 of FSMA operate, by providing guidance on the conditions that must be satisfied in order for a person to be appointed an AR. It also provides guidance on the implications, for an authorised firm, of appointing an AR, including the formal requirement of completing a form (see SUP 12.7).

The main purpose of the FCA rules and associated guidance in SUP 12 is to place responsibility on an authorised firm to ensure that:

(1) its ARs are fit and proper persons to deal with clients in its name; and

(2) clients dealing with its ARs are afforded the same level of protection as if they had dealt with the authorised firm itself.

In conclusion, the AR regime creates statutory and regulatory responsibilities on both the principal and the AR, which can be summarised as follows.

1 SI 2001/1217.

30.3.1 Responsibilities of a principal

- The principal is fully responsible for ensuring that ARs comply fully with FCA rules and requirements.

- A written contract must exist between the principal and the AR that documents the arrangements between them.

- Before entering into an agreement with an AR, the principal is required to carry out sufficient checks to ensure that the AR is financially stable and that the AR has achieved, and is maintaining, a satisfactory level of competence.

- The principal must notify the FCA of any firm that is appointed as an AR and, where applicable, must approve individuals who carry out a controlling function within the AR firm, before they in fact carry out regulated activities.

Once an authorised person agrees to be a principal, it is fully accountable for the range of activities the AR carries out, including:

- the products the AR sells and brokers;

- any advice the AR gives to customers; and

- ensuring that the AR delivers the six 'treating customers fairly' outcomes in the same way as a directly authorised firm would. (See **Chapter 32** on the current 'Treating Customers Fairly' (TCF) regime.)

30.3.2   Responsibilities of an AR

ARs are required by the FCA to understand and comply with the regulatory requirements for the business that they conduct and must allow the principal access to its staff, premises and records so that the principal can carry out the necessary oversight and monitoring of the business.

A business cannot be an AR for a regulated activity if:

- it does not have a contract with a principal firm covering its regulated business;

- its principal firm has not accepted responsibility in writing for the regulated activity the business undertakes;

- the firm that the business wants to act as its principal holds only an interim permission for the relevant credit activity;

- it operates a credit reference agency;

- it provides credit (unless the credit is free of interest and any other charges); and

- it is authorised for another activity.

The exception to this is that a firm with limited permission for certain credit activities will be able to be an AR for other regulated activities. For example, a motor dealer with limited permission to carry on credit broking can also be an AR insurance intermediary (section 39(1D) of FSMA).

30.4   APPLYING FOR PERMISSION

Broadly, the aim of the FCA is to ensure that firms wanting to offer consumer credit products and services are well run by fit and proper persons and have appropriate business models. As such, those firms are required to undergo the same process in obtaining authorisation as all other financial services firms, albeit in a more proportionate manner.

1 April 2014, being the date the FCA took on regulatory responsibility for consumer credit, heralded the commencement of the FCA accepting applications for Part 4A permission (authorisation) from consumer credit firms.

30.4.1   Interim permission: the transition from licence to authorisation

Firms that were previously licensed under CCA 1974 and regulated by the OFT were given the opportunity, within a strict timeframe, to register with the FCA and obtain what is referred to as 'interim permission' (IP).

The FCA introduced the IP registration procedure, in accordance with articles 56 to 59 of the Financial Services and Markets Act 2000 (Regulated Activities) (Amendment) (No 2) Order 2013[1] ('RAO 2013'), specifically for existing CCA 1974 licence holders to enable them to continue carrying on credit-related regulated activities for which they were licensed, after 1 April 2014. Any person not holding a CCA licence preserved by the IP regime was required to seek authorisation directly from the FCA.

The registration procedure was deliberately designed to allow for a smooth transition to the new consumer credit regime, as it was not feasible for the FCA to process applications for authorisation from the large number of CCA licence holders before the FCA assumed responsibility for consumer credit.

Affected firms were required to register for IP with the FCA by 31 March 2014 and, once registered, which was confirmed by the issue of an IP number (formerly the CCA licence number), IP remained valid until a firm's application for authorisation under FSMA had been submitted and approved or declined by the FCA, or until a firm cancelled its permission. Any firm that failed to register with the FCA before 31 March 2014 could not legally continue carrying out credit-related regulated activities and was required to cease doing so until an application was made to the FCA to become directly authorised and that application had been granted.

Staged 'application periods' were set and allocated to firms by the FCA, running from 1 October 2014, with the final one ending on 31 March 2016. Allocation of application periods took place by way of an FCA direction made under article 58 of RAO 2013. The allocation procedure enabled the FCA to manage and control the large number of applications during those staged application periods.

If firms did not submit their application for authorisation within their allocated application period, their IP lapsed at the end of that period and, as a consequence, they were not able to carry on credit-related regulated activities previously covered by their IP. Any affected firms could still submit an application for direct authorisation but were not able to carry on credit-related regulated activities until the FCA granted the application. At the time of writing it is known that a number of consumer credit firms remain on IP.

1   SI 2013/1881.

30.4.2   Applying for permission: the starting point

Applications for permission (authorisation) under Part 4A of FSMA commence under s 55A, which provides that an application for permission to carry on one or more regulated activities may be made to the appropriate regulator (for current purposes, the FCA) by an individual, a body corporate, a partnership or an unincorporated association. Subsection (3) prevents an authorised person who already has permission under Part 4A from making a further application. However, once permission has been granted, it can be varied by way of an application for a 'variation of permission' to include further (or exclude certain) regulated activities (section 55H of FSMA).

30.5   THRESHOLD CONDITIONS

The regulatory framework within which the FCA works is set by FSMA. Part of that regulatory framework consists of high-level standards that apply to all firms, including what are referred to in FSMA as 'threshold conditions'.

A threshold condition is defined in the Glossary to the FCA Handbook as '(in relation to a regulated activity) any of the conditions set out in or under Schedule 6 to the Act (FSMA) (Threshold conditions), including the additional conditions in the Financial Services and Markets Act 2000 (Variation of Threshold Conditions) Order 2001 (SI 2001/2507)'.

The threshold conditions in Schedule 6 to FSMA represent the minimum conditions for which the FCA is responsible, which a firm is required to satisfy and to continue to satisfy, in relation to all of the regulated activities for which it has or will have Part 4A permission (authorisation).

Section 55B of Part 4A of FSMA requires the FCA to ensure that the applicant for permission satisfies and will continue to satisfy the relevant 'threshold conditions'.

Section 137O of FSMA gives the FCA the power to create a 'threshold condition code'.

The FCA provides such a code in the form of guidance on its application of the threshold conditions in the module entitled 'COND Threshold Conditions' of the FCA Handbook. Thus, when applying the threshold conditions, the FCA applies both statutory requirements and its own 'code' (COND), by way of minimum standards that the FCA expects from regulated firms.

The majority of the guidance in COND is intended to assist all firms to understand how the FCA will approach its assessment of the applicable FCA threshold conditions, and the guidance in COND 2 explains, in some detail, each FCA threshold condition in Schedule 6 to FSMA and how the FCA will interpret it in practice.

Section 55C of Part 4A of FSMA empowers HM Treasury, for certain purposes, to amend Schedule 6 to FSMA. HM Treasury exercised this power by making the Financial Services and Markets Act 2000 (Threshold Conditions) Order 2013 (SI 2013/555), which came into force on 1 April 2013 (the 'TC Order'). The TC Order created separate sets of threshold conditions for each regulator (the PRA and the FCA).

For present purposes, this chapter deals solely with the separate threshold conditions that are relevant to the discharge by the FCA of its functions in relation to firms authorised and regulated by it. The relevant FCA threshold conditions are set out in paragraphs 2B to 2F of Schedule 6 to FSMA, together with the corresponding COND cross-references, as follows:

- 2B – Location of offices (COND 2.2)

- 2C – Effective supervision (COND 2.3)

- 2D – Appropriate resources (COND 2.4)

- 2E – Suitability (COND 2.5)

- 2F – Business model (COND 2.7).

In relation to the specific threshold conditions in paragraphs 2D to 2F above, the FCA will consider whether a firm is ready, willing and organised to comply, on a continuing basis, with the requirements and standards which apply, or will apply, to the firm if it is granted Part 4A permission, or a variation of its permission.

The FCA will consider the individual circumstances of each firm on a case-by-case basis and assess whether a firm satisfies, and will continue to satisfy, the threshold conditions in the context of the size, nature, scale and complexity of the business which the firm carries on or will carry on if the relevant application is granted. The risks of the firm's business model to consumers will also be considered.

In summary, the FCA will only authorise a firm if satisfied that it meets and will continue to meet the threshold conditions. The FCA will consider the specific information which firms are required to provide in the 'Application for Consumer Credit Full/Limited Permissions Authorisation'.

Once a firm is granted Part 4A permission, the threshold conditions remain and will continue to be applied as a key FCA supervisory tool, providing the basis for triggering certain powers of intervention in relation to the firm (including the power to vary or cancel permission under s 55J of FSMA).

30.6   FCA APPROACH TO AUTHORISATION

The FCA approach to authorisation of consumer credit firms is based on whether the firm requires 'full permission' or can benefit from what is known as 'limited permission'.

The Government was committed to designing a tailored and proportionate consumer credit regime, and this commitment was reflected in the October 2013 FCA Consultation paper CP13/10, 'Detailed proposals for the FCA regime for consumer credit'. In CP13/10 the FCA stated that the two main objectives of the FCA regime are to protect consumers and to deliver a proportionate risk-based approach to the supervision of firms, and that it would focus its resources on dealing with the risks it regards as having the potential to cause the most harm to consumers. This proportionate approach is said to help the FCA focus more intense scrutiny on higher-risk firms and problems that have a greater impact on consumers, while ensuring consumers have access to the products and services they need.

A result of the two objectives in CP13/10 was the creation of a two-tiered regulatory approach that enables the FCA to identify which firms are carrying out activities that pose a higher risk to consumers and which are carrying out lower-risk activities. Once identified, the FCA approach to regulation and supervision differs depending on which category a firm falls into. This difference in the levels of risk resulted in authorisation of regulated activities being split into two categories, known as 'full permission' and 'limited permission'. Full permission firms (carrying on higher-risk activities) attract a higher degree of regulation by the FCA and, as a consequence, are subject to more scrutiny and have more conditions to meet for authorisation and subsequently. On the other hand, firms carrying on only lower-risk activities are able to apply for limited permission, instead of full permission, and benefit from a lesser degree of regulation both at the time of authorisation and when carrying out consumer credit-related activities.

In the Glossary to the FCA Handbook, the definition of 'limited permission' is a Part 4A permission for a relevant credit activity as defined in paragraph 2G of Schedule 6 to FSMA (guidance on which is given in COND 1.1A.5A G).

30.6.1   Limited permission credit firms

Applying for limited permission involves a shorter application process and lower application fee, and the threshold conditions for limited permission credit firms are modified. In addition, a business plan may not be required by the FCA with the application for limited permission.

Pursuant to article 10(19) of the Financial Services and Markets Act 2000 (Regulated Activities) (Amendment) (No 2) Order 2013,[1] certain threshold conditions, set out in Schedule 6 to FSMA, are modified for a firm that carries on, or is seeking to carry on, only relevant credit activities within paragraph 2G of Schedule 6 to FSMA and therefore has, or is applying for, limited permission (see COND 1.1A.5A G).

The modifications are:

1. In relation to paragraph 2C of Schedule 6 to FSMA (Effective supervision), paragraphs (a), (b) and (e) of sub-paragraph (1) do not apply (see COND 2.3).

2. In relation to paragraph 2D of Schedule 6 to FSMA (Appropriate resources), the person has adequate financial resources if it is capable of meeting its debts as they fall due (see COND 2.4).

3. Paragraph 2F of Schedule 6 to FSMA (Business model) does not apply (see COND 2.7).

1. SI 2013/1881 ('RAO 2013').

30.6.2   Regulated activities that only need limited permission (limited permission activities)

The broad categories of limited permission activities are:

- Consumer hire.

- Credit broking (other than by a domestic premises supplier) where the sale of goods or non-financial services is the main business, and broking is a secondary activity to help finance the purchase of those goods or services (such as certain motor dealerships and high-street retailers that introduce customers to a finance provider).

- Credit broking in relation to consumer hire and hire purchase agreements.

- Consumer credit lending where the sale of goods or non-financial services is the main business, and there is no interest or charges, excluding hire purchase or conditional sale agreements (such as certain golf clubs or gyms allowing deferred payment for membership).

- Consumer credit lending by local authorities (where lending is within the scope of the Consumer Credit Directive).

- Not-for-profit bodies providing debt counselling and/or debt adjusting, including those that also provide credit information services.

30.6.3 Full permission regulated activities

The broad categories of full permission activities are:

- Credit broking where introducing customers to lenders is a main business activity.

- Credit broking where the sale of goods or services takes place in the customer's home (such a supplier is known as a 'domestic premises supplier').

- Consumer credit lending which is not limited permission (such as personal loans, credit cards, overdrafts, pawnbroking, hire-purchase or conditional sale agreements).

- Debt counselling and debt adjusting on a commercial basis.

- Debt collection and debt administration.

- Providing credit information services.

- Providing credit reference agency services.

- Operating an electronic system (peer-to-peer lending).

30.7 THE APPLICATION PROCEDURE

The general procedure in relation to applications for Part 4A permission (authorisation), and the process that the FCA must follow in its decision-making, are governed and set out in a series of sections of FSMA, commencing at section 55U.

Sections 55U to 55W relate to the making, form and content of applications and the timescale for the FCA to determine such applications, which is six months from the date of receipt of the application where the application is complete, and within 12 months of receiving an incomplete application (or six months from when an incomplete application becomes completed).

The application process, governed by s 55U, simply sets out the framework and lays down the basic requirements. The FCA is provided with a statutory power under that section to determine the detailed requirements for all applications.

In practice, the FCA provides a set of online application forms and accompanying guidance notes for applicants, relevant to the nature of the business to be authorised. The applicant is expected to source the relevant application form from the FCA website, together with all the information required to enable it to prepare and submit an application. Completion of the online application form is carried out using the FCA online portal known as 'Connect'.

For assistance to applicants, the FCA has produced and provided 11 step-by-step informative and instructional video guides which explain how a consumer credit firm should complete and submit an application, including how to register and log in to 'Connect'.

When an application for authorisation is made, the applicant is required to provide complete and detailed information about the business, including its structure, its key individuals and its financial resources. The FCA states that it offers five commitments in return, namely the FCA will:

1. Advise the applicant as soon as the application has been assigned to a case officer, who will be the single point of contact for the applicant from then on.

2. Acknowledge any communication from the applicant within two working days.

3. Provide a substantive response (or an indication of when this can be expected) to any communication from the applicant within ten working days.

4. Provide clear deadlines if it requests any additional information.

5. Provide an update on the progress of the application at least once a month.

30.7.1 Regulatory business plan (RBP)

A fundamental component of the 'application for authorisation' which an applicant is required to prepare and provide (where necessary) is a 'Regulatory Business Plan' (RBP), providing specific detailed information about the applicant's business. The FCA, in its published 'CREDIT READY Jargon Buster', defines an RBP as a document that:

> '…will set out your business aims and objectives and detail how you will organise your resources to achieve them. The level of detail that your plan goes into should be proportionate to the complexity and scale of your business. Your business plan will help us assess the adequacy of your resources and the suitability of your business model. If you apply for full permission you must attach this to the online application form. If you apply for limited permission you will not need to include it with your application but you should be able to provide it later if we request it.'

The FCA states that the RBP should include detailed information about the applicant's business in relation to specific matters such as business strategy, governance (including the experience of the senior management and their responsibilities), culture and the firm's proposals in relation to the customer journey, risk assessment and internal control, all of which are conveniently arranged under the following headings:

- General information;

- Information on customers; and

- Information on products and procedures.

The preparation and submission of an RBP is regarded by the FCA as an important component of the overall application and is integral to its decision-making process. Moreover, the FCA regards the RBP as an important regulatory tool, not just for the regulator but also for the applicant firm itself, in measuring the firm's business risk and control over any regulatory concerns.

Risks of regulatory concerns are those risks that may pose any threat to the FCA's operational objectives, namely: the protection of consumers (including the fair treatment of the firm's customers), effective competition and the integrity of the UK financial system, which include risks that relate to the firm's soundness, stability, resilience and system in connection with financial crime.

The FCA provides guidance in relation to the control of risks of regulatory concern in that part of the FCA Handbook in High Level Standards, bearing the title: 'SYSC Senior Management Arrangements, Systems and Controls' and, more specifically, in SYSC 3.2. In that guidance, regulatory expectations in relation to the control of risks of regulatory concern are made clear. Thus, a firm should plan its business appropriately so that it and its governing body are able to identify, measure, manage and control those risks by having appropriate management information (MI) that is relevant, reliable and timely and, subject to the nature, scale and complexity of their business, to have business strategy plans documented and updated on a regular basis to take account of changes in the business environment.

The FCA does not provide applicants with RBP templates for the reason that the content must be specific to the firm to which it relates. However, the FCA does provide, in its sample application form, a guide to the expected content, comprising common information requirements for all applicant firms, common information requirements for all lenders, and additional specific information requirements for applicant firms who wish to operate in specified sectors.

The detailed information required to be provided by firms is accessible in the section headed 'Regulatory business plan' in the FCA's published 'Jargon Buster' and on that part of the FCA website which deals with consumer credit authorisation and, more specifically, in section 7 of the Full Permission Application Sample Form. A separate sample form is available at the same location for Limited Permission applications.

30.7.2 In summary

The aim of the FCA when assessing an application for authorisation is to ensure that firms wanting to offer consumer credit products and services are well organised, run by fit and proper persons, have appropriate business models and have the interests of customers and market integrity at the heart of how the applicant's business is run.

Being mindful of the threshold conditions, the FCA needs to be satisfied that the applicant can:

- identify all the regulated activities and any unregulated activities it intends to carry on;

- identify all the likely business and regulatory risk factors, including the adequacy of its resources and their suitability;

- explain how it will monitor and control those business and regulatory risks; and

- take into account any intended future developments.

Further guidance on the subject of authorisation can be found in the Perimeter Guidance Manual (PERG) of the FCA Handbook. PERG 1.1.2 G states: 'The purpose of PERG is for the FCA to give guidance about the circumstances in which authorisation is required, or exempt person status is available, including guidance on the activities which are regulated under the Act and the exclusions which are available'.

Chapter 31

FCA 'Authorised Persons' regime

31.1   INTRODUCTION

The Financial Services and Markets Act 2000 ('FSMA'), when enacted, provided the framework within which a single regulator for the financial services industry, the Financial Services Authority ('FSA'), would operate. It equipped the FSA with a full range of statutory powers and introduced, among other things, a statutory regime for the approval and regulation of named key individuals who perform certain key activities for authorised firms. The arrangements under which those individuals were approved were referred to as the 'Approved Persons Regime'.

The current regulatory regime, operated by the Financial Conduct Authority ('FCA') under FSMA, includes Part 4A permission (authorisation) and, in ensuring that certain standards for authorisation are met, the FCA has adopted and applied the 'Approved Persons Regime' to all regulated firms. This includes consumer credit firms but applied in a modified and proportionate way. As part of the authorisation process, firms are required to identify the individuals who will be performing key activities within the business and so must seek regulatory approval from the FCA before taking up their positions. The decision of who that individual should be is determined not by choice but by that person's role in the business. Non-approval prior to taking up the role may lead to FCA enforcement action against the firm and/or the individual.

In broad terms an 'approved person' is an individual approved by the FCA to perform one or more key activities on behalf of an authorised firm. The FCA refers to these activities as 'controlled functions'. A controlled function is a function, role or position within a regulated business that has particular regulatory significance in that it requires a high degree of skill and experience and specific regulatory oversight. Twelve controlled functions potentially apply to a consumer credit firm, depending on the nature of the business and its legal status.

Controlled functions need to be carried out by approved persons who are closely involved in running the firm and who possess the appropriate skills, capabilities and behaviours. The FCA therefore expects firms, at the time candidates are nominated, to be able to demonstrate that they have a robust recruitment process in place and procedures to carry out the appropriate level of due diligence on all of their candidates. The FCA approves an individual only if it is satisfied that the individual is a fit and proper person to perform the controlled function(s) applied for.

31.2   THE STATUTORY FRAMEWORK FOR APPROVAL

The statutory basis for the current regime is found in Part V of FSMA (Performance of Regulated Activities), commencing at section 56. For present purposes the most relevant sections can be summarised as follows:

Section 59 (Approval for particular arrangements) requires firms (authorised persons) to take reasonable care not to allow persons to perform controlled functions without the approval of the FCA. Subsection (2) similarly requires firms to take reasonable steps to ensure that any contractor (typically an appointed representative) does not allow a person to perform such controlled functions without the approval of the FCA. The FCA is also provided under this section with a statutory power to determine and specify in its rules the nature and description of the controlled functions requiring approval (see **31.3** below).

Section 60 (Applications for approval) requires an application for approval to be submitted by the authorised person concerned or, in the case of new firms awaiting authorisation, a prospective authorised person. Subsection (2) gives the FCA the powers to specify the information it will require to support applications and the manner in which those applications are made. Subsection (3) enables the FCA to request any additional information it needs to assess the suitability of each candidate in order to determine the application. Applications for approval of an individual are made electronically through 'Connect', and the FCA provides a useful summary of forms, and their use for applications, in Annex 2 to SUP 10A of the Supervision Manual in the FCA Handbook.

Section 61 (Determination of applications) sets out the basis on which the FCA is to assess the suitability of a candidate for approval. Subsection (1) requires the FCA to be satisfied that a candidate is fit and proper to perform the function(s) to which the application relates before it is able to give its approval. Section 61 does not prescribe the matters that the FCA should take into account when determining fitness and propriety. However, subsection (2) states that the FCA may have regard (among other things) to whether the candidate or approved person:

(a)   has obtained a qualification;

(b)   has undergone, or is undergoing, training;

(c)   possesses a level of competence; or

(d)   has the personal characteristics,

required by general rules made by the FCA.

The FCA is thus provided with a statutory power under this section to determine and specify in its rules its criteria for assessing the suitability of a candidate for approval (see **31.4** below).

Section 63 (Withdrawal of approval) gives the FCA power to withdraw the approval granted for the purposes of section 59 where it no longer considers that the person is a fit and proper person to carry out the functions for which the person had been approved (for example, because the FCA had obtained new information which cast doubt on its initial assessment).

Section 64A (Rules of conduct) gives the FCA the power, as part of its wider rule-making functions, to issue 'statements of principle', setting out in general terms the kinds of behaviour which it requires from approved persons in respect of any particular type of function. Statements of principle issued under this section have been elaborated upon by a non-exhaustive 'code of practice', which illustrates the circumstances in which the FCA would regard a principle as having been complied with or not complied with, as the case may be (see **31.5** below).

Section 66 (Disciplinary powers) gives the FCA power to take disciplinary action against an approved person when the two conditions set out in subsection (1) have been met:

(a)   it appears to the FCA that he is guilty of misconduct; and

(b)   the FCA is satisfied that it is appropriate in all the circumstances to take action against him.

The FCA may take disciplinary action against an approved person where the individual acts in a manner inconsistent with FCA regulatory requirements, in particular if the individual has failed to comply with a 'statement of principle' (as evidenced by a breach of the code of practice) issued by the FCA under section 64A of FSMA. Such disciplinary action may include an appropriate fine, suspension or restriction, or the publication of a statement relating to the misconduct; and, in circumstances where the FCA has concluded that an approved person is no longer fit and proper to perform the individual's role, it may withdraw approval and prohibit the individual from holding a controlled function in the future.

31.3   CONTROLLED FUNCTIONS

Controlled functions are those roles within an FCA regulated business that have a particular regulatory significance and are required to be carried out by approved persons who are closely involved in the running of the firm. Approved persons that perform controlled functions for authorised consumer credit firms are usually those that can exert significant influence over the firm's conduct – for example, those performing the controlled functions that include being a director of a regulated firm, overseeing the firm's systems and controls, and being responsible for compliance with statutory requirements and FCA rules.

It is permissible for an individual to hold more than one controlled function, but the authorised firm must be able to evidence in its application that the individual has the ability to manage multiple roles. Similarly, it is permissible for an individual to be an approved person performing controlled functions for more than one authorised firm, provided that each firm takes appropriate responsibility for ensuring that the individual manages the risks involved and the firm can demonstrate this in its application. The FCA will consider the application against how the individual plans to undertake this, including how the risks associated with being an approved person for more than one firm will be managed (for example, the availability of time). This is the responsibility of each respective firm.

It is unlikely that authorised firms can outsource these roles and still meet the standards that the FCA expects, although it will assess this on a case-by-case basis. However, outsourcing of resources for guidance and support for approved persons performing controlled functions is permissible.

Different controlled functions exist, relevant to different businesses. Twelve controlled functions potentially apply to a consumer credit firm, depending on the nature of the business and its legal status. No firm will need to perform all the functions.

The primary source of rules and guidance relating to FCA controlled functions can be found in Chapter 10 of the Supervision Manual (SUP) of the FCA Handbook. SUP 10A.3 to SUP 10A.11 specify, under section 59 of FSMA, descriptions of the FCA controlled functions which are listed in the 'Table of controlled functions in SUP 10A.4.4 R' (www.handbook.fca.org.uk/handbook/glossary/G1659.html – see below). The descriptions are further elaborated by a detailed explanation of each one commencing from SUP 10A.6.

FCA Table of controlled functions (SUP 10A.4.4 R)

(amended to show only the 12 controlled functions for consumer credit)

Part 1 (FCA controlled functions for FCA authorised persons and appointed representatives)		
Type	**Controlled Function**	**Description of FCA controlled function**
FCA governing functions	1	Director function
	2	Non-executive director function
	3	Chief executive function
	4	Partner function
	5	Director of unincorporated association function
	6	Small friendly society function
FCA required functions	8	Apportionment and oversight function
	10	Compliance oversight function
	10A	CASS operational oversight function
	11	Money laundering reporting function
Systems and controls function	28	Systems and controls function
Significant management function	29	Significant management function

The functions listed above in the table of controlled functions for consumer credit are FCA 'significant-influence functions'. A significant-influence function, in relation to the carrying on of a regulated activity by a firm, means a function that is likely to enable the person responsible for its performance to exercise a significant influence on the conduct of the firm's affairs, so far as relating to the activity (SUP 10A.5.3).

Whether an FCA controlled function is likely to result in the person responsible for its performance exercising significant influence on the conduct of the firm's affairs is a question of fact in each case. The FCA has identified the FCA significant-influence functions listed above as satisfying this condition (SUP 10A.5.5).

31.4 FITNESS AND PROPRIETY OF APPROVED PERSONS (FIT)

Under section 61(1) of FSMA (Determination of applications), the FCA may grant an application for approval of approved person status made under section 60 (Applications for approval) only if it is satisfied that the nominated candidate is fit and proper to perform the controlled function(s) to which the application relates; and, in any re-assessment of existing approved persons, the same standards also apply. The FCA achieves the expected standards by applying a 'Fit and Proper Test' which approved persons must meet and comply with on an ongoing basis. The fit and proper test is not an examination that is to be passed but is a benchmark the FCA uses to assess whether individuals are suitable to perform a controlled function.

In addition, the FCA expects individuals nominated for approved person status to have a full understanding of the importance of establishing an honest and open relationship with the FCA at the start of the application process and in any future interactions with the FCA.

The application form (currently 'Form A', sourced from the FCA Handbook Reference: SUP 10A Annex 4D) incorporates a 'fitness and propriety' section asking questions of fact requiring 'yes' or 'no' answers. (Various questions include the word 'ever', meaning that the answers that are required to be given are not restricted to any specified period.) Firms are precluded from making an assessment on whether to disclose a matter and are therefore required to disclose all information in the supplementary information section of the application. Where it is the opinion of the firm that a particular disclosure may not affect the individual's fitness and propriety, it should make this clear by providing additional information explaining why.

FSMA does not prescribe the matters which the FCA should take into account when determining fitness and propriety. However, section 61(2) states that the FCA may have regard (among other things) to whether the candidate: has obtained a qualification; or has undergone, or is undergoing, training; or possesses a level of competence; or has the personal characteristics, required by general rules made by the FCA (FIT 1.2.4).

The primary source of information and guidance relating to the main assessment criteria for the 'Fit and Proper Test for Approved Persons' can be found in Chapter 2 of FIT in the FCA Handbook. The purpose of FIT generally is to set out and describe the criteria that the FCA will consider when assessing the fitness and propriety of a candidate for a controlled function and may consider when assessing the continuing fitness and propriety of approved persons (FIT 1.1.2).

The FCA will have regard to a number of factors when assessing the fitness and propriety of a person to perform a particular controlled function, as more particularly described in FIT 2 (Main assessment criteria) (FIT 1.3.1).

In the FCA's view, the most important considerations will be the person's:

(1) honesty, integrity and reputation (including openness regarding any self-disclosure) (FIT 2.1);

(2) competence and capability (FIT 2.2); and

(3) financial soundness (FIT 2.3).

31.5   STATEMENTS OF PRINCIPLE AND CODE OF PRACTICE FOR APPROVED PERSONS (APER)

Section 64A (Rules of conduct) of FSMA gives the FCA the power, as part of its wider rule-making functions, to issue 'statements of principle', setting out in general terms the kinds of behaviour which it requires from approved persons in respect of any particular type of function. Once approved, therefore, approved persons must perform the controlled function(s) they have been approved to perform in compliance with the standards set out in FCA high-level conduct rules, namely the 'Statements of Principle', and the accompanying 'Code of Practice for Approved Persons', both under 'APER' in the FCA Handbook.

The Statements of Principles align somewhat with the eleven 'Principles for Businesses' (the 'general statements of the fundamental obligations of firms under the regulatory system') which apply to the regulated firm under PRIN in the FCA Handbook, and cover not dissimilar matters, such as acting with integrity and due skill, care and diligence, and dealing with regulators in an open and cooperative way.

The Statements of Principle, contained in chapter 2 of APER, are the rules (Rules of Conduct) made under section 64A(1)(a) of FSMA. These rules are accompanied by the 'Code of Practice for Approved Persons' which sets out descriptions of conduct which, in the opinion of the FCA, do or do not comply with a Statement of Principle. The Code of Practice for Approved Persons also sets out, in certain cases, factors which, in the opinion of the FCA, are to be taken into account in determining whether or not an approved person's conduct complies with a Statement of Principle.

APER 2.1A.3R sets out the Statements of Principle issued by the FCA and to which the provisions of the Code of Practice for Approved Persons in APER 3 (Code of Practice for Approved Persons: general) and APER 4 (Code of Practice for Approved Persons: specific) apply.

31.5.1   Statements of Principle issued under section 64A(1)(a) of the Act (APER 2.1A.3R)

Statement of Principle 1
An approved person must act with integrity in carrying out his accountable functions.

Statement of Principle 2
An approved person must act with due skill, care and diligence in carrying out his accountable functions.

Statement of Principle 3
An approved person must observe proper standards of market conduct in carrying out his accountable functions.

Statement of Principle 4
An approved person must deal with the FCA, the PRA and other regulators in an open and cooperative way and must disclose appropriately any information of which the FCA or the PRA would reasonably expect notice.

Statement of Principle 5

An approved person performing an accountable higher management function must take reasonable steps to ensure that the business of the firm for which they are responsible in their accountable function is organised so that it can be controlled effectively.

Statement of Principle 6

An approved person performing an accountable higher management function must exercise due skill, care and diligence in managing the business of the firm for which they are responsible in their accountable function.

Statement of Principle 7

An approved person performing an accountable higher management function must take reasonable steps to ensure that the business of the firm for which they are responsible in their accountable function complies with the relevant requirements and standards of the regulatory system.

Of the seven Statements of Principle, Statements of Principle 1 to 4 apply to all Approved Persons, and Statements of Principle 5 to 7 apply only to those performing significant-influence functions. All of the functions listed in the table of controlled functions (SUP 10A.4.4R) for consumer credit are FCA 'significant-influence functions'; therefore, all seven Statements of Principle apply to approved persons performing controlled functions for consumer credit firms.

31.5.2 Code of Practice for Approved Persons

The purpose of the Code of Practice for Approved Persons is to help an approved person to determine whether or not that person's conduct complies with a Statement of Principle. The code sets out descriptions of conduct which, in the FCA's opinion, do or do not comply with the relevant Statements of Principle. The code also sets out certain factors which, in the opinion of the FCA, are to be taken into account in determining whether an approved person's conduct complies with a particular Statement of Principle (APER 3.1.1A).

An approved person will only be in breach of a Statement of Principle where he is personally culpable. Personal culpability arises where an approved person's conduct was deliberate or where the approved person's standard of conduct was below that which would be reasonable in all the circumstances (see DEPP 6.2.4G (Action against approved persons under section 66 of the FSMA)).

In summary, being an approved person brings with it a number of important and critical responsibilities, including a duty to be aware of and comply with FCA regulatory requirements and expectations and understand how they apply to the carrying out of each controlled function. More specifically, approved persons must:

- comply with, and continue to comply with, the FCA 'Fit and Proper test' for Approved Persons (FIT);

- comply with the 'Statements of Principle', which describe the conduct that the FCA requires and expects of individuals that it approves, and the 'Code of Practice for Approved Persons' (APER); and

- report to the authorised firm and to the FCA any matter that may affect their ongoing fitness and propriety (using 'Form D' sourced from the FCA Handbook Reference: SUP 10A Annex 7R).

Importantly, the FCA has the ability, through the Approved Persons Regime, to hold senior management of regulated firms accountable for their conduct and competence.

31.6   THE SENIOR MANAGERS AND CERTIFICATION REGIME (SM&CR)

The banking crisis of 2008 and conduct failings, such as the manipulation of the London Interbank Offered Rate (LIBOR), prompted government to set up the Parliamentary Commission for Banking Standards (PCBS) to consider and report on professional standards and culture of the UK banking sector, lessons to be learned about corporate governance, transparency and conflicts of interest and their implications for regulation and for Government policy, and to make recommendations for legislative and other action.

PCBS, in its report, was very critical of the Approved Persons Regime and recommended a new accountability framework focused on senior management. It also recommended that firms should take more responsibility for employees being fit and proper, and that there should be better standards of conduct at all levels in banking firms. In response to the recommendations of PCBS, Government brought forward legislative reforms to the way individuals who work in banking are regulated through a series of amendments to FSMA which were included in the Financial Services (Banking Reform) Act 2013. These reforms led to the PRA and the FCA applying what is now known as the 'Senior Managers and Certification Regime' ('SM&CR') to the banking sector, of which the main rules came into effect on 7 March 2016.

In October 2015, HM Treasury announced, in its paper entitled 'Senior Managers and Certification Regime: extension to all FSMA authorised persons', its intention to extend SM&CR to all FSMA-authorised firms and, as a result, the Bank of England and Financial Services Act 2016 was passed and included provisions extending SM&CR to all FSMA authorised firms including consumer credit firms regulated by the FCA. SM&CR will replace the Approved Persons Regime.

The aim of SM&CR is to reduce harm to consumers and strengthen market integrity by making individuals more accountable for their conduct and competence, thus introducing a new regulatory framework for individual accountability to replace the Approved Persons Regime. At the time of writing, the extension of SM&CR to firms which offer financial services and are authorised by the FCA under FSMA is under consultation by the FCA by a published consultation paper (CP17/26), which sets out how the FCA proposes to implement the new regime. The FCA proposes that the new SM&CR framework will have essentially three components:

(1) The 'Senior Managers Regime', in which the responsibilities of Senior Managers will be clearly set out and, should something in their area of

responsibility go wrong, they could be personally held to account. The Senior Managers will be approved by the FCA and appear on the FCA Register.

(2)   The 'Certification Regime' under which firms will certify individuals for their fitness, skill and propriety at least once a year, if they are not covered by the Senior Managers Regime but their jobs significantly impact customers, firms or markets.

(3)   'Conduct Rules' that will apply to all financial services staff at FCA authorised firms. This simple set of rules means that individuals must act with integrity, with due care, skill and diligence, be open and cooperative with regulators, pay due regard to customer interests and treat them fairly, and observe proper standards of market conduct. There will be further conduct rules for Senior Managers.

In CP17/26, the FCA stressed that it does not think it is appropriate to take exactly the same approach with consumer credit firms as it did with the banks, and went on to state that, while it wants to have consistent principles applied across financial services, it also wants the new regime to be proportionate and flexible enough to accommodate the different business models and governance structures of firms.

The government intends that implementation of the newly extended regime should come into operation during 2018. This is to allow the regulators to engage effectively with all affected stakeholders and to consider in detail important issues such as proportionality and the lessons learned through the implementation of the SM&CR for banking sector firms.

Chapter 32

FCA 'Treating Customers Fairly' regime

32.1 INTRODUCTION AND HISTORY

The concept of 'Treating Customers Fairly' ('TCF') is not new. It is steeped in, but not confined to, history and can be traced as far back as the office of the Director General of Fair Trading established by the Fair Trading Act 1973. The general concept of 'fairness' is apparent in various pieces of legislation, most notably in the Consumer Credit Act 1974 in relation to the 'Unfair Relationships' provisions in section 140A, the Unfair Contract Terms Act 1977, the consumer contract terms which may be regarded as unfair in the Consumer Rights Act 2015, and the Consumer Protection from Unfair Trading Regulations 2008.

More recently, in a document entitled 'Journey to The FCA' published by the Financial Services Authority ('FSA') in October 2012, John Griffith-Jones, the then FCA Chairman-Designate, stated in his foreword, 'This document sets out how we [the FCA] will approach our regulatory objectives; how we intend to ensure firms put consumers at the heart of their business'. In relation to 'Ensuring firms continue to meet our standards', he stated:

> 'The new approach [by the FCA] will be underpinned by judgement-based supervision. This means that we will be making supervisory judgements about a firm's business model and forward looking strategy, and will intervene if we see unacceptable risks to the fair treatment of customers. Essentially, we will be looking for firms to base their business model, their culture, and how they run the business, on a foundation of fair treatment of customers as set out in the "Treating Customers Fairly (TCF) initiative". While we recognise that firms need to be sustainable, we will not let a firm compromise fair treatment of customers to achieve financial success.'

It is significant to note at this point that the 'TCF initiative' was not an invention of the current regulator, the FCA, but was the 'brainchild' of the previous financial services regulator, the FSA. It followed completion of a study project as part of the 'New Regulator for the New Millennium' programme and was initiated by the publication of a 'Discussion Paper' in June 2001 entitled 'Treating retail customers fairly after the point of sale'. The TCF initiative ran for no less than eight years, resulting in the FSA setting a deadline by which firms, by the end of

December 2008, were expected to be able to demonstrate to themselves and the FSA that they were consistently treating their customers fairly.

In June 2008, in its TCF progress update, the FSA stipulated that firms should:

- be able to demonstrate that senior management had instilled a culture whereby they understand what the fair treatment of customers means; where they expect their staff to achieve this at all times; and where (a relatively small number of) errors are promptly found, that they be put right and learnt from;

- be appropriately and accurately measuring performance against all customer fairness issues materially relevant to their business, and be acting on the results;

- be demonstrating through those measures that they are delivering fair outcomes; and

- have no serious failings, whether seen through management information (MI) or known to the FSA directly, including in areas of regulatory interest previously publicised by the FSA.

In November 2008 the FSA published a further update, reaffirming that TCF was a hugely important part of its retail agenda for consumer protection and was to remain central to the overall FSA retail strategy, and adding that it had gained enormous buy-in from firms and their senior management. The update informed firms that the FSA had made the decision to realise the benefits of the TCF initiative more quickly than it first envisaged by moving TCF assessment of firms into its core supervisory work from January 2009, rather than September 2009 as originally intended. TCF was therefore embedded within the FSA's core supervisory work. Firms' delivery of the TCF outcomes (and consequently their compliance with the December deadline) would be formally assessed by the FSA using its risk-responsive operating framework (ARROW); and, where failings were identified, the FSA would use and continue to use its full range of regulatory powers to take tough action.

32.2   THE FCA'S APPROACH

In today's consumer credit market the FCA operates the (TCF regime almost entirely consistently with the standards and requirements set in the TCF initiative by the FSA. Martin Wheatley, the then FCA Chief Executive-Designate, stated in his introduction to the publication 'Journey to The FCA' (FSA October 2012):

> 'Through our new style of supervision we will increase our focus on the conduct at the very top of firms. Firms' senior management teams set the culture of their organisations so we must ensure that the targets and aspirations set at the top turn into good outcomes for consumers. The six retail consumer outcomes that were set out in the Treating Customers Fairly (TCF) initiative remain core to how we expect firms to treat their customers. These outcomes will be part of the normal focus of the FCA, part of our approach and our language. We will continue to use them as an important factor in guiding our regulatory decisions and actions.'

During the period of the TCF initiative, the FSA published a plethora of TCF documents, including progress reports and updates in relation to specific matters such as customer outcomes, culture in firms and management information (MI), all of which are relevant in today's consumer credit market. The FCA expects regulated firms to refer to those publications in their pursuit of complying with their regulatory responsibility for making sure their customers are treated fairly.

The entire FSA TCF library is still relevant and available and is accessible at www.fsa.gov.uk/doing/regulated/tcf.

32.3 TREATING CUSTOMERS FAIRLY AND TODAY'S CONSUMER CREDIT MARKET

Section 1L of Chapter 1, Part 1A of FSMA places an obligation on the FCA to 'maintain arrangements for supervising authorised persons'. These arrangements, whose design is shaped by the statutory objectives given to the FCA by Parliament, are the foundation for its approach to regulating firms. In its relationship with firms the FCA wants to ensure that firms do not adversely affect market integrity and competition and, particularly relevant to this chapter, that fair treatment of consumers is at the heart of a firm's business.

The FCA's statutory objectives are set out in section 1B of Chapter 1, Part 1A of FSMA. The FCA has one strategic objective of ensuring that the relevant markets function well and, in discharging its general functions, the FCA must, so far as is reasonably possible, act in a way which is compatible with its strategic objective and which advances one or more of its three operational objectives of:

(1) securing an appropriate degree of protection for consumers (the 'consumer protection' objective, as defined in section 1C of Chapter 1 aforesaid);

(2) protecting and enhancing the integrity of the UK financial system (the 'integrity' objective, as defined in section 1D of Chapter 1 aforesaid); and

(3) promoting effective competition in the interests of consumers (the 'competition' objective, as defined in section 1E of Chapter 1 aforesaid).

TCF, with its focus on consumer outcomes, is central to the work of the FCA in ensuring a fair deal for consumers. It underpins the delivery of its statutory consumer protection objective, and firms must not divert attention away from a focus on risks to the fair treatment of customers.

On its website, under the heading 'Tasks for regulated firms', the FCA has published only minimal information on the subject of TCF under the headings 'Fair treatment of customers', 'Culture' and 'Management information'. We consider each of these heads in turn.

32.4 FAIR TREATMENT OF CUSTOMERS

Under the heading 'Fair treatment of customers', the FCA states that regulated firms have a regulatory responsibility for making sure their customers are treated fairly and that the FCA's 'Principles for Businesses' (PRIN) includes explicit and implicit guidance on the fair treatment of customers. PRIN are high-level principles that reflect the statutory objectives of the FCA and are a general statement of the fundamental obligations of firms under the regulatory system. Principle 6 (the 'treating customers fairly' principle) states: 'A firm must pay due regard to the interests of its customers and treat them fairly', but other principles also apply to this area of business behaviour. The further principles most relevant to TCF are:

- Principle 1 – A firm must conduct its business with integrity.

- Principle 2 – A firm must conduct its business with due skill, care and diligence.

- Principle 3 – A firm must take reasonable care to organise and control its affairs responsibly and effectively, with adequate risk management systems.

- Principle 7 – A firm must pay due regard to the information needs of its clients, and communicate information to them in a way which is clear, fair and not misleading.

- Principle 8 – A firm must manage conflicts of interest fairly, both between itself and its customers and between a customer and another client.

- Principle 9 – A firm must take reasonable care to ensure the suitability of its advice and discretionary decisions for any customer who is entitled to rely upon its judgment.

The former Office of Fair Trading (OFT) recognised and referred to the relevant principles in Annex E of its guidance entitled 'Unfair relationships – Enforcement action under Part 8 of the Enterprise Act 2002' (OFT854Rev – May 2008 (updated August 2011)). The OFT stated that such principles might also be relevant to an assessment of unfairness in an individual case under section 140A of CCA 1974.

Breaching a principle renders a firm liable to disciplinary sanctions by the FCA. The reader is referred to the FCA Handbook in the Decision Procedure and Penalties Manual (DEPP) and the FCA's Enforcement Guide (EG) on how the FCA operates in relation to regulatory breaches and its approach to decision making and the use of its regulatory, civil and criminal powers.

The FCA requires firms to be able to demonstrate that fair treatment of customers is consistently at the heart of their business model. The FCA expects firms to strive to achieve the six TCF outcomes (as defined by the FSA under its TCF initiative) to ensure fair treatment of customers. The outcomes are:

- **Outcome 1:** Consumers can be confident they are dealing with firms where the fair treatment of customers is central to the corporate culture.

- **Outcome 2:** Products and services marketed and sold in the retail market are designed to meet the needs of identified consumer groups and are targeted accordingly.

- **Outcome 3:** Consumers are provided with clear information and are kept appropriately informed before, during and after the point of sale.

- **Outcome 4:** Where consumers receive advice, the advice is suitable and takes account of their circumstances.

- **Outcome 5:** Consumers are provided with products that perform as firms have led them to expect, and the associated service is of an acceptable standard and as they have been led to expect.

- **Outcome 6:** Consumers do not face unreasonable post-sale barriers imposed by firms to change product, switch provider, submit a claim or make a complaint.

The FCA does not elaborate any further on the topic of 'Fair treatment of customers' except to say that, 'Above all, customers expect financial services and products that meet their needs from firms they trust'. Further information on the 'Principles for Businesses' is available in the FCA Handbook under the chapter entitled 'PRIN', and further information on the topic of 'consumer outcomes' is available from the FSA TCF library at www.fsa.gov.uk/doing/regulated/tcf.

32.5 'CULTURE'

Under the heading 'Culture', the FCA states that senior management must establish the right culture to convert good intentions into fair outcomes for consumers. The FCA considers that there are six critical areas of management behaviour that can influence a firm's culture of customer treatment:

- **Leadership:** all managers should make clear in their practices and communication that the fair treatment of customers is fundamental to the firm's operation. Controls and monitoring should be applied to other staff.

- **Strategy:** the firm can articulate a clear vision featuring fair treatment of customers. Strategic decisions, such as change management and outsourcing, reflect the centrality of customers to the firm's future. Risk levels should reflect customer concerns and feedback.

- **Decision-making:** at all levels, decisions should reflect on the fair treatment of customers. Feedback from staff, customers and other external sources should be used, where appropriate. This management information should feed into properly balancing customers' interests against shareholders.

- **Recruitment, training and competence:** Staff selection should reflect the importance of customer treatment to the firm. Management should then train and maintain staff knowledge, behaviour and values to accord with fair customer treatment. Managers should also reward good staff performance in this regard and act on poor performance.

- **Reward:** The firm's reward framework (such as incentives and bonuses) should be transparent, recognise good quality and support the fair treatment of customers. In other words, firms should not concentrate on sales, volumes and profit without considering quality and controls to mitigate this risky framework.

- **Controls:** The firm should have controls that reflect the fair treatment of customers. These should be integral to the firm's risk framework.

The FCA does not elaborate any further on the topic of 'Culture', except to say: 'We do not consider it reasonable for firms to compromise on fair treatment of customers in the name of financial success'. However, still relevant today is the concept of firms addressing the fair treatment of customers through their product life-cycle, as outlined in an FSA document entitled 'Treating customers fairly – towards fair outcomes for consumers (published July 2006). In that document, the FSA reaffirmed to firms that their product life-cycle offers a practical framework for considering TCF. Relying on its general regulatory approach of the responsibility of senior management, the FSA looked to senior management to embed the principle of TCF in their corporate strategy (as does the FCA today) and to build it into their firms' culture and day-to-day operations.

Addressing the fair treatment of customers through the product life-cycle includes:

- product design and governance;

- identifying target markets;

- marketing and promoting the product;

- sales and advice processes;

- after-sales information and services; and

- complaint handling.

Further information on the topic of 'Culture' is available in an FSA document entitled 'Treating customers fairly – culture', accessed from the FSA TCF library at www.fsa.gov.uk/doing/regulated/tcf.

32.6   MANAGEMENT INFORMATION

Under the heading 'Management information', the FCA states that it regards MI as a very important resource in analysing trends, helping firms to forecast the future and solving any identified problems.

As part of the TCF initiative, the FSA expected firms to demonstrate that:

(1) they had the appropriate MI or measures in place to test whether they were treating their customers fairly, including by delivering the six TCF consumer outcomes;

(2) the MI evidenced that they were consistently treating customers fairly and delivering the consumer outcomes; and

(3) processes were in place that monitored the MI to enable the right people to take action.

It appears that the FCA has adopted the same expectations of firms in relation to the use of MI. The FCA expects firms to have appropriate MI or other measures in place, proportionate to the size and complexity of their business, to test whether they are delivering the six TCF outcomes. However, how firms use and collect MI is the responsibility of the firm and not the regulator, although it should be used to monitor customer treatment, expectations and outcomes. MI can come in many different forms such as: new business register, business persistency, training and competence records, file reviews, customer feedback, and compliance reports; and, whether MI is anecdotal or quantified, it should be proactive rather than merely reactive. It should address future risks rather than dealing with only known problems and should be acted on when necessary.

The FCA's MI expectations directly reflect the position under the FCA rules that firms need to have information to enable them to comply with their regulatory obligations. Guidance is set out in the Senior Management Arrangements, Systems and Controls Manual (SYSC) in the FCA Handbook under 'Management information' (SYSC 3.2.11A and SYSC 3.2.12).

The FCA does not elaborate any further on the topic of MI but refers to a historical document published by the FSA entitled 'Treating Customers Fairly – guide to Management Information'. This document was produced by the FSA in 2007 under its 'TCF initiative' but, as quoted by the FCA, remains relevant. The document can be accessed from the FSA TCF library at www.fsa.gov.uk/doing/regulated/tcf.

32.7 CONCLUSION

To conclude, it is evident that both regulators, the former FSA and the FCA, have resisted making prescriptive rules relating to TCF or providing firms with a definition of 'fairness'. No definition of either 'Treating Customers Fairly' or 'fairness' exists in the Glossary to the FCA Handbook. The only defining reference to TCF is in the FCA Jargon Buster which states:

> '"Treating Customers Fairly": This is one of our most fundamental principles for businesses, which are the principles that all FCA-regulated firms must comply with at all times. Principle six says "A firm must pay due regard to the interest of its customers and treat them fairly"'.

Principle 6, therefore, is the primary regulatory requirement for FCA-regulated firms to treat their customers fairly. The subjective nature of Principle 6 can create difficulty for firms, as it places the onus on firms to determine what is 'fair' in each particular set of circumstances. What is clear is that the ultimate decision on whether a firm's application of Principle 6 evidences fairness is that of the regulator, the FCA; and, if the FCA makes a supervisory judgement to the effect that a firm has not treated its customers fairly, it can take regulatory action against that firm.

Chapter 33

FCA supervision and regulatory reporting

33.1 INTRODUCTION

In the exercise of its functions under FSMA, the FCA takes a proactive approach to monitoring markets and engaging with the firms it regulates. The regulatory process by which this is carried out is referred to as 'supervision'. Although intrinsically linked, supervision is not the same as regulation; regulation relates to the FCA's legal framework, rules and regulatory standards that govern the way in which regulated firms operate, whereas supervision is effectively the proactive pursuit of the FCA's statutory objectives, through oversight of the conduct by firms of regulated activities.

As already identified in previous chapters, the statutory objectives bestowed upon the FCA by Parliament are the foundation of the FCA's approach to regulating firms. In its relationship with firms the FCA seeks to ensure that the fair treatment of consumers is at the heart of the firm's business and that the firm's conduct and activities do not adversely affect market integrity and competition. Ultimately, however, it remains the responsibility of the firm and its senior managers to identify and mitigate the risk of not complying with the rules, detail and spirit of FCA regulation.

Consistent with its aim to deliver a sustainable supervision programme, the FCA operates a proportionate, judgement-based, forward-looking supervisory approach that is market-based rather than firm-specific, concentrating its resources on the greatest potential risks to its statutory objectives. It aims to ensure that consumers are at the centre of a firm's business and that firms take appropriate action in relation to any identified key risks before they cause harm. This approach is achieved by:

(1) ongoing proactive supervision of regulated firms through the FCA's supervision division, driven by a supervisory focus and by applying risk-based judgements on: how firms are run, including how they make their money; business models; financial health; and how their strategy and culture uphold market integrity and support fairness for consumers; and

(2) the use of FCA enforcement powers, through the FCA's enforcement division, in instances where it identifies egregious misconduct.

33.2   THE STATUTORY FRAMEWORK

Section 1L ('Supervision, monitoring and enforcement') of Chapter 1, Part 1A of FSMA places an obligation on the FCA to 'maintain arrangements for supervising authorised persons [i.e. firms]'. The design of these arrangements is shaped by the FCA's statutory objectives[1] in relation to the conduct supervision of financial services firms as well as the prudential supervision of firms not supervised by the PRA. Conduct supervision includes the FCA ensuring that firms comply with relevant statutory and regulatory requirements.

Section 1K ('Guidance about objectives') of Chapter 1, Part 1A of FSMA requires the FCA to include, in its general guidance (under section 139A of FSMA), guidance on how it intends to advance its operational objectives in discharging its general functions in relation to different categories of authorised person or regulated activity.

The 'arrangements' for supervising firms, including firms' reporting obligations, are set out in rules and guidance in the 'Supervision Manual' ('SUP') of the FCA Handbook. SUP is the primary source of information and regulatory guidance for regulated firms, including consumer credit firms, in relation to FCA supervision and describes both the operation of the FCA's supervisory function and the requirements on firms relating to that supervisory function. One purpose of the guidance in SUP is to discharge the duties of the FCA set out in sections 1L and 1K of FSMA. The FCA's approach to supervision is also designed to enable it to meet its supervisory obligations in accordance with EU legislation, where applicable, including in relation to requirements arising otherwise than under FSMA – as, for example, under directly applicable EU regulations.[2]

In its approach to supervision, the FCA refers to the application of its 'regulatory principles' set out in section 3B of FSMA – in particular, to focus and reinforce the responsibility of the senior management of each firm (section 3B(1)(d) of FSMA) so as to ensure that 'it takes reasonable care to organise and control the affairs of the firm responsibly and effectively, and develops and maintains adequate risk management systems'. It is the responsibility of management to ensure that the firm acts in compliance with its regulatory requirements.[3]

1 Section 1B of Chapter 1 Part 1A of FSMA.
2 SUP 1A.1.2.
3 SUP 1A.1.4.

33.3   THE SUPERVISION MANUAL (SUP)

SUP, together with the 'Decision Procedure and Penalties Manual' ('DEPP'), form the 'Regulatory Processes' part of the FCA Handbook. SUP sets out the relationship between the FCA and authorised persons (referred to in the Handbook as 'firms') and, as a general rule, contains material that is of continuing relevance after a firm has been authorised.

SUP is an extensive work that runs, at the time of writing, to no less than 1,230 pages comprising: 25 chapters (SUP); two specialist 'application' chapters (SUP App); six chapters relating to specific transitional provisions (SUP TP); and four Schedules (SUP Sch).

Not all of the SUP module will apply to all firms. A firm should refer to the 'Application and purpose' sections at the start of each SUP chapter in the FCA Handbook in order to determine if a particular chapter or section applies to it, taking in account matters such as the nature of the firm's business, its regulated activities, and its permissions under Part 4A of FSMA ('Permission to carry on regulated activities').

DEPP sets out the FCA's decision-making procedures that involve, among other things, the giving of statutory notices and the FCA's policy in respect to the imposition and amount of penalties.

33.4   THE FCA'S APPROACH TO SUPERVISION (SUP IA.3.2)

The overall approach to supervision is based on ten principles, which form the basis of the FCA's interaction with firms:

(1)   forward-looking and interventionist;

(2)   focused on judgment, not process;

(3)   consumer-centric;

(4)   focused on the big issues and causes of problems;

(5)   interface with executive management/boards;

(6)   robust when things go wrong;

(7)   focused on business models and culture as well as product supervision;

(8)   viewing poor behaviour in all markets through the lens of the impact on consumers;

(9)   oriented towards firms doing the right thing; and

(10) externally focused, engaged and listening to all sources of information.

In its application of the ten principles, the FCA adopts a proportionate pre-emptive approach, concentrating its resources on the greatest potential risks to its statutory objectives, based on making forward-looking judgments about firms' business models, product strategy and how they run their business. This enables the FCA to identify and intervene earlier to prevent problems crystallising. In addition, where serious consumer detriment has been identified, the FCA will robustly seek redress for consumers.

33.5   CONDUCT CLASSIFICATION: 'FIXED PORTFOLIO' AND 'FLEXIBLE PORTFOLIO' FIRMS

In its assessment of a firm's application for authorisation, the FCA assigns firms an indicative prudential classification (P1, P2, P3 and P4), and an indicative conduct classification as either 'fixed portfolio' or 'flexible portfolio'. The prudential categories reflect the impact that the disorderly failure of a firm could have on markets and consumers. According to the FCA, the vast majority of firms, including consumer credit firms, fall into the P3 category. Immediately following authorisation, the FCA informs firms of their indicative 'conduct classification', which determines the nature and intensity of the FCA's ongoing conduct supervisory approach and the extent of a firm's engagement with the FCA's supervision division.

Firms in the 'fixed portfolio' category are a small number of firms (out of the total number regulated by the FCA) that, based on factors such as size, market presence and customer footprint, require the highest level of supervisory attention. These firms are proactively supervised using a firm-specific continuous assessment approach and are allocated a named individual supervisor.

Firms in the 'flexible portfolio' category account for the vast majority of credit firms (out of the total number regulated by the FCA) and are supervised through a combination of market-based thematic work and programmes of communication, engagement and education activity aligned with the key risks identified for the sector in which the firms operate. These firms are not allocated a named individual supervisor, and their first point of contact with the FCA is the Customer Contact Centre. For further details, the reader is referred to www.fca.org.uk/publication/corporate/supervision-guide-flexible.pdf.

33.6   THE FCA'S THREE-PILLAR SUPERVISION MODEL

The FCA supervision model risk assessment process[1] applies to all firms, irrespective of the assigned conduct classification, and is based on three pillars of activity, namely:

(1)   **The firm systematic framework (proactive supervision)**

Pillar 1 involves the FCA carrying out proactive preventative work through structured conduct assessment of individual fixed portfolio firms, addressing potential risks on a firm-by-firm basis. The FCA does not carry out work under Pillar 1 to assess flexible portfolio firms individually, but takes a market-based approach to assess the sector as a whole (see Pillar 3).

(2)   **Event-driven work (reactive supervision)**

Pillar 2 involves the FCA dealing with problems that are emerging or have already crystallised, and securing customer redress or other remedial work (e.g. to secure the integrity of the market) where necessary. When the FCA becomes aware of significant risks to consumers or markets, or when damage has already been done, the FCA responds swiftly and robustly to ensure the offending firm mitigates risks, prevents further damage and addresses the root causes of problems. If necessary, the FCA will use its formal powers to hold the firm and individuals to account and gain redress for those consumers who have been treated unfairly. The FCA can discover risks or problems through a number of sources, including information from the firm (particularly under principle 11 of the FCA's Principles for Businesses (PRIN)), data analysis, whistleblowers, consumer complaints, and 'baseline monitoring' of the regulatory data that firms are required to submit to the FCA under SUP 16.

(3) **Issues and products supervision**

Pillar 3 relates to FCA 'thematic work' on sectors of the market or products within a sector that are putting or may put consumers at risk of harm. Thematic work is regarded by the FCA as fundamental to its forward-looking and pre-emptive market-based approach in identifying and mitigating risks across multiple firms or whole sectors. In this work, the FCA views each sector as a whole to analyse current events and investigate potential drivers of poor outcomes for consumers and markets. Thematic work is carried out on an ongoing basis in order to address risks common to more than one firm or sector before they can cause widespread damage.

The FCA three-pillar supervision model is described in more detail in its supervisory approach document for flexible portfolio firms, accessible at www.fca.org.uk/publication/corporate/supervision-guide-flexible.pdf.

1 SUP 1A.3.4.

33.7 TOOLS OF SUPERVISION

In order to meet its statutory objectives and address any identified risks to those objectives, the FCA has, at its disposal, a range of supervisory tools[1] that can be conveniently grouped under the following four headings:

(1) diagnostic: designed to identify, assess and measure risks;

(2) monitoring: to track the development of identified risks, wherever these arise;

(3) preventative: to limit or reduce identified risks and so prevent them crystallising or increasing; and

(4) remedial: to respond to risks when they have crystallised, including the power to impose financial penalties.

The FCA tools of supervision are designed to serve more than one purpose: in the first instance, remedial; and, in the second, preventative. The FCA also makes use of a variety of tools to monitor whether a firm, once authorised, remains compliant with regulatory requirements and to address particular risks identified in firms. The specific tools are presented in separate lists in SUP 1A.4.5 and SUP 1A.4.6 of the FCA Handbook, and they include the use of so-called 'skilled persons' where, following an event or development relating to a firm or as part of a risk mitigation programme, the FCA is concerned that a firm is not meeting its regulatory obligations.

1 SUP 1A.4.

33.8 REPORTS BY 'SKILLED PERSONS'

In the exercise of its supervisory function, the FCA, under section 166 of FSMA, is empowered to obtain an independent expert report from a third party (a 'skilled person') about aspects of a regulated firm's activities that have been identified by the FCA as a cause for regulatory concern or where further analysis is required. The report may be used for any of the purposes listed at **33.7** above.

A 'skilled person' is defined in the Glossary to the FCA Handbook as:

> 'a person appointed to make a report required by section 166 (Reports by skilled persons) or section 166A (Appointment of skilled person to collect and update information) of the Act [FSMA] for provision to the appropriate regulator [FCA] and who must be a person:
>
> (a) nominated, approved or appointed by the appropriate regulator; and
>
> (b) appearing to the appropriate regulator to have the skills necessary to make a report on the matter concerned.'

The decision by the FCA to require a report by a skilled person under section 166 of FSMA is normally prompted by a specific requirement for information, analysis of information, assessment of a situation, expert advice or recommendations, or by a decision to seek assurance in relation to a regulatory return. It may be part of a risk mitigation programme applicable to a firm, or the result of an event or development relating or relevant to a firm, prompted by a need for verification of information provided to the FCA or part of the FCA's regular monitoring of a firm.

The decision by the FCA to require the collection or updating of information by a skilled person under section 166A of FSMA will be prompted where the FCA considers that there has been a breach of a requirement by a firm to collect, and keep up to date, information of a description specified in the FCA's rules – for example, under SUP 16 (Reporting requirements), including verification of standing data (SUP 16.10).

The FCA can commission two types of skilled person review, namely: s 166 (Reports by skilled persons); and s 166A (Appointment of skilled person to collect and update information).

The appointment of a skilled person to produce a report under section 166 of FSMA is the tool of supervision most feared by regulated firms. It is resource-intensive in terms of a firm's time, and the allocation of the firm's personnel can often prove very costly for firms who are required, under FCA rules, to bear the costs of the skilled person, and it can lead to referral by the FCA for enforcement action, including redress for consumers who have suffered harm resulting from the firm's activities.

Further detail on skilled persons' reports and when the FCA may use its power under section 166 of FSMA can be found in SUP 5 (Reports by skilled persons) in the FCA Handbook. This provides guidance on the FCA's use of its powers in sections 166 and 166A of FSMA, specifies rules requiring a firm to give assistance to a skilled person and, where a firm is required to appoint a skilled person, sets out certain provisions to be included in the contract with the skilled person.

33.9   CONSUMER CREDIT 'REGULATORY REPORTING'

In order to discharge its functions under FSMA, the FCA requires timely and accurate information about the firms it regulates. Regulated firms are therefore required, under FCA rules, to provide the FCA with substantial amounts of information in the form of 'notifications' and 'regulatory reports' to enable it to meet its responsibilities for monitoring the firm's compliance with requirements imposed by or under FSMA.

Some of this information relates directly to Principle 11 of the FCA's 'Principles for Businesses' (PRIN) in the FCA's Handbook, which requires a regulated firm to deal with its regulator in an open and cooperative way, and to disclose to the FCA appropriately anything relating to the firm of which the FCA would reasonably expect notice. SUP 15 (Notifications to the FCA), among other things, sets out: (1) FCA guidance on the type of event or change in condition which a firm should consider notifying to the FCA; and (2) rules on events and changes in condition that a firm *must* notify to the FCA, both in accordance with Principle 11.

A significant amount of the information to be provided to the FCA by firms (including consumer credit firms) is through 'regulatory reporting'; that is, the submission of regular and timely data-intensive reports (regulatory returns), as set out in SUP 16 (Reporting requirements) in the FCA Handbook. Regulatory reporting is an integral part of the FCA's supervision strategy, and the reporting requirements in SUP 16 form part of its approach to amplifying Principle 11 by setting out in more detail, in rules and guidance, the information that the FCA requires. The reporting requirements supplement the provisions of SUP 2 (Information gathering by the FCA or PRA on its own initiative) and SUP 15 (Notifications to the FCA) and help the FCA monitor firms' compliance with: the Principles governing relationships between firms and their customers; Principle 4 which requires firms to maintain adequate financial resources; and other requirements and standards under the regulatory system.

The regulatory returns, by design, collect the information that the FCA needs to perform what is known as adequate 'baseline monitoring' at a firm-specific and industry level. Baseline monitoring of regulatory returns (BMRR) forms part of the Pillar 2 'Event-driven work' (reactive supervision) of its three-pillar supervision model and involves the FCA reviewing the regulatory data that firms have collated and submitted.

The collected regulatory data is a vital source of information for the FCA, which allows it to identify breaches of its rules and to detect emerging risks, such as notable changes to the financial position of the firm or other signs of strain, including the financial drivers that may result in firms behaving in ways that harm consumers and markets. The data that firms provide therefore must not give a misleading impression of the firm, which means a firm must not: omit a material item; include an immaterial item; or present items in a misleading way (SUP 15.6 (Inaccurate, false or misleading information)).

33.10 REPORTING REQUIREMENTS

SUP 16 (Reporting requirements) is an extensive chapter that runs, at the time of writing, to no less than 416 pages comprising 23 sections and a significant number of annexes. Not all of SUP 16 applies to all firms, and regulated firms should refer to the 'Application and purpose' sections at the start of each SUP 16 section. For present purposes, we are only concerned with firms that carry out credit-related regulated activities (in accordance with section 22 of FSMA and Part 2 or 3A of the Financial Services and Markets Act 2000 (Regulated Activities) Order 2001, SI 2001/544).

The most relevant provisions are set out in the following sections.

33.10.1   General provisions on reporting[1]

SUP 16.3 sets out: the structure of SUP 16; general rules and guidance on the methods of submission of reports; the requirement of timely reporting and, most importantly, the consequences for firms of failure to submit timely reports: 'If a firm does not submit a complete report by the date on which it is due in accordance with the rules in, or referred to in, this chapter [SUP 16] or the provisions of relevant legislation and any prescribed submission procedures, the firm must pay an administrative fee of £250' (SUP 16.3.14), and 'failure to submit a report in accordance with the rules in, or referred to in, this chapter [SUP 16] or the provisions of relevant legislation may also lead to the imposition of a financial penalty and other disciplinary sanctions' (SUP 16.3.14A).

1 SUP 16.3.

33.10.2   Verification of standing data[1]

Standing data comprises the basic information relating to a regulated firm held by the FCA and is displayed on the FCA's website in the publicly available Financial Services Register. Standing data includes the firm's registered name, trading name(s), address details and other matters, set out in full in SUP 16 Annex 16A. SUP 16.10 provides the regulatory framework for a firm to check the accuracy of its standing data, through the relevant section of the FCA website, within 30 business days of its accounting reference date (SUP 16.10.4(1)), and to report any changes to the FCA. If any standing data is incorrect, the firm must submit the corrected standing data to the FCA using the appropriate form set out in SUP 15 Annex 3 and in accordance with SUP 16.10.4A R. The FCA's preferred method of receiving corrections or updates to standing data is by the online forms available on the FCA's website and by using 'Connect', the FCA's online system for notifications and applications.

1 SUP 16.10.

33.10.3   Integrated Regulatory Reporting[1]

Once a firm is authorised, it is a regulatory requirement under SUP 16.12.3 R for the firm to begin reporting information online to the FCA in the form of specified 'data items', at the times and frequencies specified by the FCA in its rules. This requirement is known as 'Integrated Regulatory Reporting' (IRR). Reporting online is carried out via 'GABRIEL' ('Gathering Better Regulatory Information Electronically'), the FCA's online central regulatory reporting system for collecting and storing regulatory data from firms.

At the time of authorisation, an authorised firm must register, for its regulatory reporting, on GABRIEL. Registration enables the firm to access the system, and to identify the returns that the firm is required to submit to the FCA and their corresponding due dates, and it ensures that the firm receives reminders from the FCA about its forthcoming reporting requirements. For more information about GABRIEL, the reader is referred to the FCA's website at www.fca.org.uk/firms/gabriel.

SUP 16.12.3 R sets out the general rules and guidance on reporting requirements for firms and specifies that any firm carrying out any of the activities within each of the regulated activity groups (RAG) set out in column (1) of the table in SUP 16.12.4 R must submit to the FCA the duly completed data items or other items applicable to the firm as set out in column (2) of that table.

SUP 16.12.4 R (Table of applicable rules containing data items, frequency and submission periods) comprises no less than 13 regulated activity groups. RAG 12 is specifically allocated to firms who carry out credit-related regulated activities and lists the data items relating to consumer credit activities as CCR001 to CCR007, collectively known as 'Consumer Credit Returns' (CCRs). When submitting the required data item(s), a firm must use the format set out in SUP 16 Annex 38A (Data items relating to consumer credit activities). Guidance notes on the completion of the data items are set out in SUP 16 Annex 38B.

1 SUP 16.12.

33.10.4   Product Sales Data Reporting[1]

In addition to the reporting requirements under SUP 16.12 (Integrated Regulatory Reporting), credit firms which have Part 4A permission to enter into regulated credit agreements as lenders in respect of high-cost, short-term credit or home credit loan agreements are required to report to the FCA individual 'Product Sales Data' (PSD) on a quarterly basis via GABRIEL. The purpose of collecting this data is to assist the FCA in the ongoing supervision of firms engaged in retail activities and to enable the FCA to gain a wider understanding of market trends in the interests of protecting consumers (SUP 16.11.2(2)).

SUP 16.11 sets out the rules and guidance on consumer credit lending and PSD reporting requirements, and specifies that a firm must submit a PSD report (PSD006) within 20 business days of the end of the four calendar quarters (the reporting period) of each year beginning on 1 January. The PSD report must comply with the provisions set out in part (e) SUP 16 Annex 21R.

More information on PSD reporting is contained on the FCA website at www.fca.org.uk/firms/regulatory-reporting/product-sales-data-reporting.

1 SUP 16.11.

33.10.5   Annual Financial Crime Report

'Full permission' consumer credit firms, subject to the Money Laundering, Terrorist Financing and Transfer of Funds (Information on the Payer) Regulations

2017 (SI 2017/692), are required to file (via GABRIEL) an annual financial crime return (REP-CRIM-Financial Crime Report) with the FCA. Such firms that have reported total revenue of less than £5 million as at their last accounting reference date are excluded from the requirement to submit a report. (Limited permission firms are totally excluded.)

SUP 16.23 sets out the rules, guidance and exclusions on the requirement to submit the annual financial crime report and specifies that a firm must submit the report in the form specified in SUP 16 Annex 42AR within 60 business days of the firm's accounting reference date. Guidance notes for completing the report are located at SUP 16 Annex 42B.

The purpose of SUP 16.23 is to ensure that the FCA receives regular and comprehensive information about a firm's systems and controls in preventing financial crime. The FCA will use the data to assess the nature of financial crime risks within the industry. Affected firms, therefore, need to ensure that suitable internal practices and procedures are in place to capture the required data.

33.10.6 Complaints Reporting

'Limited permission' consumer credit firms (except large not-for-profit debt advice bodies) are required, under the reporting requirements in SUP 16.12, to submit information to the FCA on the number of complaints received in relation to credit-related regulated activities in the format of the data item (CCR007 – key data for credit firms with limited permission) set out in SUP 16 Annex 38A.

'Full permission' consumer credit firms are required, under the 'Dispute Resolution' rules (DISP) in the FCA Handbook, to provide the FCA with a complete report concerning complaints received from eligible complainants, either six-monthly or annually. Six-monthly reporting applies, unless the firm only holds permission to carry on credit-related regulated activities and revenue arising from such activities is £5 million or less a year, in which case annual reporting applies (DISP 1.10.1). The report must be set out in the format in DISP 1 Annex 1R and consumer credit firms are required to complete Part B.

Further information on consumer credit reporting requirements can be found on the FCA website at www.fca.org.uk/firms/regulatory-reporting/consumer-credit-reporting.

Chapter 34

Alternative dispute resolution

34.1 INTRODUCTION AND BACKGROUND

There is a common saying in life that 'You can please some people some of the time, but you cannot please all the people all of the time'. This is particularly true for any business dealing in commercial transactions with consumers, including consumer credit businesses. Despite the best efforts of any consumer credit firm, something within the business will sometimes go wrong and there is always the likelihood that a customer will complain about such matters as: the credit agreement itself; the subject matter of the credit agreement (for example, the goods sold under a conditional sale agreement); or the nature and level of service that is provided by the firm.

Prior to 6 April 2007, consumer credit customers, if dissatisfied with any of their dealings with a firm, relied on the firm's in-house complaints procedure to express their dissatisfaction and to seek redress where appropriate. If that failed, for whatever reason, the next and only step was to challenge the firm in court using the statutory protections provided for in the CCA 1974. Aggrieved customers, however, were reluctant to use the courts on the grounds of risk and cost, and this problem was recognised and seen by Government as a restriction on a consumer's legitimate right of redress.

Against a background of increasing evidence of over-indebtedness, particularly of vulnerable customers, the Secretary of State for Trade and Industry announced in July 2001 a comprehensive review of the CCA 1974. The review involved a process of public consultation with interested parties on the effectiveness of the existing regulation of information disclosure, early settlement, unfair credit transactions, consumer credit licensing, the financial limit above which agreements were not regulated under the CCA 1974 and, notably, consumer redress.

In the review, the CCA 1974 was criticised for: not providing sufficient protection for consumers; restricting rights of redress; and for failing to provide regulators with sufficient powers to tackle improper or unfair conduct by businesses in a flourishing consumer credit market. Government recognised that the CCA 1974 was in need of reform; it needed to reflect the nature of the modern consumer credit market. As a result, in December 2003 the then Department of Trade and Industry (DTI) published a White Paper entitled 'Fair, Clear and Competitive – the Consumer Credit Market in the 21st Century'.

The White Paper stated in its executive summary: 'Although most traders treat consumers fairly there are a few whose practices are unfair. Often it is difficult for consumers to obtain redress and for the regulatory authorities to take effective action to stop a trader continuing these practices'. The reforms outlined in the White Paper aimed, among other things, to address the problem of consumer redress.

The White Paper resulted in a Bill (the Consumer Credit Bill) being formally presented to Parliament on 16 December 2004. The Bill sought to reform, but not replace, the CCA 1974 and included the aim to enhance consumer rights and redress by replacing the 'extortionate credit' test with a new test based on unfairness, and by introducing an Alternative Dispute Resolution ('ADR') scheme to be run by the existing Financial Ombudsman Service ('FOS'). Following the Bill's passage through Parliament, the Consumer Credit Act 2006 was born, receiving Royal Assent on 30 March 2006.

34.2   THE CONSUMER CREDIT ACT 2006 ('THE 2006 ACT') AND THE FINANCIAL OMBUDSMAN SERVICE ('FOS')

The purpose of the 2006 Act was to reform the CCA 1974 to:

- provide for the regulation of all consumer credit and consumer hire agreements, subject to certain exemptions;

- make provision in relation to the licensing of providers of consumer credit and consumer hire and ancillary credit services and the functions and powers of the OFT in relation to licensing;

- enable debtors to challenge unfair relationships with creditors; and

- relevant to this chapter, provide, for the first time, ADR in the form of an Ombudsman scheme administered and operated by FOS (the 'scheme operator'), to hear complaints in relation to businesses licensed under the CCA 1974.

Sections 59, 60 and 61 of the 2006 Act effectively extended the jurisdiction of FOS to hear complaints involving licensed persons under the CCA 1974. The 2006 Act provided for the detailed operation of the new bespoke 'consumer credit jurisdiction' which was intended to 'mirror' the existing 'compulsory jurisdiction' for financial services, determined largely by 'consumer credit rules', made by FOS, subject to approval by, or the consent of, the FSA.

Section 59 inserted a new section 226A into FSMA introducing the new 'consumer credit jurisdiction', which required holders of standard licences under the CCA 1974 to submit to the new jurisdiction of the scheme. Section 29(2) and (2A)(b)(ii) amended section 25 of the CCA 1974 to provide that a contravention by a licensee of any provision relating to the consumer credit jurisdiction may be considered by the OFT in determining that person's fitness to hold a licence.

As a result of new section 226A, from 6 April 2007, FOS comprised three jurisdictions:

(a)   the compulsory jurisdiction ('the CJ'), which covered firms that are required to participate in the FOS scheme in respect of complaints about activities specified by the then FSA and subsequently by the FCA;

(b)   the consumer credit jurisdiction ('the CCJ'), which covered OFT licensees that were required to participate in respect of complaints specified by FOS and arising in the course of consumer credit activities; and

(c)   the voluntary jurisdiction ('the VJ'), which covered financial services activities not included in the CJ or the CCJ. Both regulated firms and unauthorised firms were able to participate in the VJ by contractual agreement with FOS (in accordance with Standard Terms) and are known as 'VJ participants'.

The new ADR scheme came into full operation on 6 April 2007 in relation to all categories of consumer credit standard licence-holders who, as a result, were subject to new detailed 'consumer credit rules' embodied in the FSA's Handbook in the module entitled 'Dispute Resolution: Complaints' ('DISP').

In summary, the provisions of the 2006 Act provided consumers with the option of free access to an ADR scheme (administered and operated by FOS) if they remained dissatisfied with a credit firm's internal dispute resolution service. The DTI hoped that, for both consumers and businesses, the new ADR procedure would provide a quick, efficient and easy resolution of consumer disputes at considerably less cost than court action. The ADR procedure was, and remains, mandatory for all regulated consumer credit businesses.

34.3   FCA REGULATION

34.3.1   Complaint handling and ADR

In preparation for the transfer of consumer credit regulation from the OFT to the FCA on 1 April 2014, article 10, Part 3 of the Financial Services and Markets Act 2000 (Regulated Activities) (Amendment) (No 2) Order 2013[1] effectively abolished the CCJ, bringing, on the date of the transfer of regulation, consumer credit-related activities within the FOS jurisdiction that covers all financial firms regulated by the FCA (i.e., the CJ). Consumer credit consumers still had access to FOS as before, but consumer credit firms (as a result of section 226(2)(b) and (c) of FSMA) were now compulsorily subject to the CJ and to the associated rules and guidance set out in the 'Redress' module in the FCA Handbook under the chapter entitled 'DISP' (Dispute Resolution: Complaints). Some additional obligations were imposed on firms as a result of being subject to the CJ, namely: 'complaint recording' under DISP 1.9; 'complaints reporting' under DISP 1.10; and 'complaints data publication' obligations under DISP 1.10A.

DISP runs, at the time of writing, to 182 pages comprising: 4 Chapters, 2 specialist 'application chapters (DISP App); 1 chapter relating to transitional provisions (DISP TP); and 6 Schedules (DISP Sch). Parliament gave the power to make these rules to the regulator (i.e., the FCA) and to the board of FOS. The four primary DISP chapters are:

- DISP 1 (Treating customers fairly). This contains the primary rules and guidance on how firms, referred to in the rules as 'respondents', should deal promptly and fairly with complaints in respect of business carried on: from establishments in the UK; by certain branches of firms in the EEA; or by certain EEA firms carrying out activities in the United Kingdom under the freedom to provide cross-border services.

- DISP 2 (Jurisdiction of the Financial Ombudsman Service). This sets out rules and guidance on the scope of the CJ and the VJ, which are the Financial Ombudsman Service's two remaining jurisdictions following the abolition of the CCJ on 1 April 2014.

- DISP 3 (Complaint handling procedures of the Financial Ombudsman Service). This sets out: the procedures of FOS for investigating and determining complaints; the basis on which the Ombudsman makes decisions; and the awards that the Ombudsman can make.

- DISP 4 (Standard Terms). This sets out how complaints against VJ participants are dealt with under the VJ.

1 SI 2013/1881.

34.3.2 FCA's supervisory role in relation to complaints handling

The FCA takes an active role in aiming to meet its operational objective to 'secure an appropriate degree of protection for consumers' and, in doing so, the way regulated firms handle complaints is high on its supervisory agenda. The FCA has stated that it is vital that customers know that, if something goes wrong, their complaint will be dealt with in a reasonable way and that they will get a fair outcome. This statement evidences the FCA's strict approach to 'Treating Customers Fairly' ('TCF') in ensuring that regulated firms meet the standards required under Principle 6 of the 'Principles for Businesses' ('PRIN') and meet the desired TCF outcome that 'Consumers do not face unreasonable post-sale barriers imposed by firms to change product, switch provider, submit a claim or make a complaint'.

Under Principle 6 a firm must pay due regard to the interests of its customers and treat them fairly. The FCA expects regulated firms to resolve all complaints they receive properly, in line with the rules and guidance set out in DISP, and, in particular, the FCA expects firms to:

- investigate the complaint competently, diligently and impartially;

- assess fairly, consistently and promptly what the complaint is about, whether it should be upheld; and what action/redress should be taken;

- provide fairly and promptly a clear assessment of the complaint and an offer of redress or remedial action, if appropriate; and

- ensure any offer of redress or remedial action that is accepted is settled promptly.

34.3.3 FCA 'Complaints Thematic Review' (TR14/18)

As part of its forward-looking, pre-emptive market-based supervisory approach in identifying and mitigating risks across multiple firms, the FCA, during 2013/2014, conducted a 'Complaints Thematic Review' (TR14/18)[1] under its three-pillar supervision model. As part of the review, the FCA requested participating firms to carry out complaint handling self-assessments to enable the FCA to better understand how complaints are dealt with in practice, as well as providing their documented policies, processes and management information (MI) for the review. The review focused on whether any barriers existed for firms in handling complaints effectively at any of the five key stages of firms' complaint handling, namely:

(1) identifying a complaint;

(2) recording a complaint;

(3) internal reporting of a complaint;

(4) provision of redress; and

(5) carrying out root cause analysis.

The review identified weaknesses in each of the five key stages of firms' complaint handling (which may affect consumers' experiences and outcomes) and barriers that affect how effective firms are at complaint handling. The FCA's observations, together with the firms' self-assessments and working group discussions, led to the FCA concluding that four main barrier themes existed: (1) the application of FCA rules; (2) cultural barriers; (3) operational barriers; and (4) specific barriers in relation to MI and root cause analysis.

The review concluded in June 2014, and the findings and recommendations were published in an FCA report in November 2014. In the report the FCA stated that:

> 'complaints matter, and how they are dealt with can say much about a firm's culture. Firms should deal with complaints fairly and promptly (using competent staff) and, where appropriate, redress should be provided. Dissatisfied consumers should not find it difficult to complain nor should the procedure be anything other than straightforward.'

In Chapter 4 of the November 2014 report (Next steps), the FCA committed itself, in the light of its findings and participants' recommendations, to carrying out some further research on complaints handling, with a view to developing specific policy proposals.

1 See www.fca.org.uk/publication/thematic-reviews/tr14-18.pdf.

34.3.4 FCA 'Improving Complaints Handling'

The FCA, true to its word, did indeed further consider the Complaints Thematic Review (TR14/18) findings. On 23 July 2015, following a period of consultation, the FCA published a Policy Statement (PS15/19)[1] entitled 'Improving complaints handling, feedback on CP14/30 [Consultation paper – 12 December 2014] and final rules'. In the policy statement the FCA explained: its response to the feedback it received to the consultation; the new rules on complaints handling for financial services firms; and rules limiting the cost of telephone calls which consumers make to firms.

1 See www.fca.org.uk/publication/policy/ps15-19.pdf.

34.3.5 FCA 'Implementing the ADR Directive'

The Alternative Dispute Resolution Directive of 21 May 2013 ('the ADR Directive')[1] aimed to give consumers and traders access to out-of-court schemes to help settle contractual disputes that arise out of the purchase and sale/supply of goods or services. The application of the Directive included financial services, and required the UK Government to ensure that dispute resolution, provided by a qualifying ADR entity, is available for any dispute concerning contractual obligations between a consumer and a business. Member States, including the UK, had until 9 July 2015 to implement the ADR Directive.

Two sets of regulations implemented the ADR Directive in the UK, namely the Alternative Dispute Resolution for Consumer Disputes (Competent Authorities and Information) Regulations 2015, SI 2015/542, and the Alternative Dispute Resolution for Consumer Disputes (Amendment) Regulations 2015, SI 2015/1392. The regulations placed an information requirement on businesses selling to consumers, established competent authorities to certify ADR schemes, and set the standards that ADR scheme applicants must meet in order to achieve certification.

Chapter 5 of the FCA's consultation paper 'Improving complaints handling' (CP14/30) set out the FCA's proposed approach to implementing the ADR Directive. The ADR Directive proposals, contained in chapter 5, and the required changes to the rules were implemented by legal instrument[2] published by the FCA on 24 April 2015, and came into force on 9 July 2015.

1 Directive 2013/11/EU. The full text of the Directive is available at: http://eur-lex.europa.eu/LexUriServ/LexUriServ.do?uri=OJ:L:2013:165:0063:0079:EN:PDF.
2 Alternative Dispute Resolution Directive Instrument 2015. The full text of the instrument is available at: www.handbook.fca.org.uk/instrument/2015/FCA_2015_25.pdf.

34.3.6 Current FCA supervisory tools

'Dear CEO letters' are a supervisory tool that the FCA uses to bring to the attention of Chief Executive Officers of firms, namely regulated businesses, matters of regulatory concern. Thus, the FCA published a 'Dear CEO letter' in September 2017 addressed to firms engaging in consumer credit activities, setting out its concerns about firms' handling of complaints. Whilst it is usual for the letter to be sent directly to the CEO of affected firms, on this occasion the letter was not sent to individual firms, but was instead mentioned in the September 2017 issue of the FCA's regular newsletter, 'Regulation Round-up' and published on the FCA's website.[1]

In the letter, the FCA stated that it recently undertook a review of how consumer credit firms approach and deal with customer complaints and highlighted its concerns relating to:

- the failure of firms to provide appropriate information about their internal complaints handling procedures and to refer complainants to the availability of it;

- the poor quality of final responses from firms about complaints; the FCA found that firms failed to provide clear explanations of factors such as the assessment of the complaint, the decision itself and the reasons why a complaint was rejected;

- the failure of firms to undertake root cause analyses to identify and remedy any recurring or systemic problems, as required by DISP 1.3.3R; and

- firms failing to record and report accurate complaints data.

The FCA concluded the letter by stating:

> 'Actions firms are expected to take now. We expect you to review how your firm identifies, records, and deals with complaints as well as how this is communicated to customers, particularly taking into consideration the above areas. May I also remind you that your firm must be able to evidence its compliance with the applicable regulatory requirements. You do not need to notify us of your review or the outcome of your review. However, in any future contact we have with your firm we may ask for evidence of such compliance, including details of any review you have carried out on your complaints handling arrangements following this letter. Where we find serious failings we shall consider referring such cases to our Enforcement Division for formal action to be taken.'

This statement further evidences the FCA's strict approach to firms' compliance with regulatory requirements and to 'Treating Customers Fairly' in ensuring that regulated firms meet the standards required under Principle 6 of the 'Principles for Businesses' ('PRIN') and meet the desired TCF outcome that consumers do not face unreasonable post-sale barriers imposed by firms to, among other things, making a complaint.

1 At   www.fca.org.uk/publication/correspondence/dear-ceo-letter-consumer-credit-firms-handling-complaints.pdf.

34.4   THE OMBUDSMAN SCHEME PROVIDED BY THE FINANCIAL OMBUDSMAN SERVICE (FOS)

34.4.1   Inception and structure

FOS (the 'scheme operator' under s 225 of FSMA) was set up as a 'free to consumers' independent dispute resolution service under Part XVI of, and Schedule 17 to, FSMA to resolve individual disputes between consumers and financial businesses. It carries out a statutory role on a non-commercial, not-for-profit basis, is a demand-led public service and is a private company limited by guarantee funded by the financial services industry.

FOS has a board consisting of six directors (including the chairman) who are appointed by the FCA; the chairman is appointed by the FCA but with the approval of HM Treasury. The directors appoint the ombudsmen and are required to publish a report annually (annual reviews), as well as minutes of their board meetings. The board members are 'non-executive' public interest directors whose role is to take a strategic overview and ensure that the ombudsman service is properly resourced and able to carry out its work effectively and independently. They are not involved in considering individual complaints.

The rules setting out how FOS (and businesses) should handle complaints are published as part of the FCA's Handbook in the chapter entitled 'Dispute Resolution: Complaints' ('DISP'). DISP 3 (Complaint handling procedures of the Financial Ombudsman Service) specifically sets out: the procedures of FOS for investigating and determining complaints; the basis on which the Ombudsman makes decisions; and the awards that the Ombudsman can make.

34.4.2 Key elements of the service

- Consumers have access to the service only after they have complained to the business first and: the dispute remains unresolved; the business has sent the consumer its final response or a summary resolution communication; or eight weeks have elapsed since the business received the complaint (unless the firm consents to FOS being involved without the firm investigating the complaint first) (DISP 2.8.1R(4)).

- The Ombudsman will attempt to resolve complaints at the earliest possible stage and by whatever means appear to him to be most appropriate, including mediation or investigation (DISP 3.5), and on the basis of what is fair and reasonable in all the circumstances (DISP 3.6).

- The Ombudsman has the power to require the parties to provide information and/or documents necessary to resolve the dispute (s 231 of FSMA and DISP 3.5.8R).

- The Ombudsman's decision is binding on all parties if a complainant accepts the decision. If a complainant does not accept the decision, the decision is not binding on either party (DISP 3.6.6R).

- The Ombudsman has the power to require the business to pay an award (of up to £150,000) or require the business to take steps he/she considers just and appropriate (DISP 3.7).

34.4.3 Funding

FOS receives no Government funding whatsoever. The service (under s 234 of, and Schedule 17 to, FSMA) is funded by regulated firms who are subject to the CJ through a combination of levies and fees paid by them in respect of each case, irrespective of the outcome. The service is entirely free to consumers.

In January each year, FOS consults publicly on its 'plans and budget' for the year ahead – including the amount to be raised through the levy and the level of its case fee. Chapter 5 of the 'Fees manual' ('FEES') in the FCA Handbook sets out the requirement for firms to pay annual fees (through a general levy invoiced and collected by the FCA on behalf of FOS) and case fees (invoiced and collected directly by FOS) in order to fund the operation of FOS.

For further details on FOS, the reader is referred to www.financial-ombudsman.org.uk.

34.4.4   Criticisms of FOS

FOS has been operating for over 16 years, with the last independent review of the service conducted by the Rt Hon Lord Hunt of Wirral MBE. The findings of the review were contained in a report published on 9 April 2008.[1]

The service has been the subject of recent criticism from various sources, including members of the legal profession, the consumer credit industry, consumers and FOS employees and ex-employees. Employees and ex-employees have left significant reviews about the service on 'Glassdoor'.[2] At the time of writing, a total of 353 reviews have been posted, giving the service an average rating of 1.7 out of 5, with the overall average rating steadily declining from 2.7 in early 2016. Research on the reviews appears to show that the decline in the average rating is attributable to recent structural changes within the organisation.

Common criticisms include:

(1)   The scheme is unbalanced in the following respects:

    (a)   If the consumer (the complainant) accepts the decision of the Ombudsman, it is binding and final on the business (the respondent), without any right to appeal, whilst the decision is not binding on the consumer (the complainant) if the consumer rejects the decision.[3]

    (b)   The service is funded by regulated firms which are subject to the CJ, through a combination of levies and fees paid by them in respect of each case, irrespective of the outcome.[4] A respondent is therefore required pay a case fee (currently £550) even if the complaint is dismissed and the respondent has apparently done no wrong.

(2)   Parliament gave the power and duty to the FCA and to the board of the FOS to make the rules ('DISP') applicable to the complainant's cases that FOS handles.[5] The FCA has an operational objective to protect consumers but this is not counterbalanced by any objective, statutory or otherwise, to treat firms fairly.

(3)   FOS is not required to make decisions in accordance with the law. Section 228(2) of FSMA provides that 'a complaint is to be determined by reference to what is, in the opinion of the Ombudsman, fair and reasonable in all the circumstances of the case'. DISP 3.6.4R of the FCA Handbook reflects on this 'fair and reasonable test' and provides: 'In considering what is fair and reasonable in all the circumstances of the case, the Ombudsman will

take into account: (1) relevant: (a) law and regulations; (b) regulators' rules, guidance and standards; (c) codes of practice; and (2) (where appropriate) what he considers to have been good industry practice at the relevant time'. FOS, therefore, can find against the respondent and make a binding award (for payment of up to £150,000), although the respondent has not necessarily committed any wrong in law.

The aforesaid criticisms, amongst others, are contained in a paper 'Restoring the rule of law to financial services compensation – the Defects of the Financial Ombudsman Service and Constructive Proposals for Reform', by Anthony Speaight QC and Peter Hamilton, barristers. This was submitted to HM Treasury in 2011 by way of a response to the Consultation (Cm 8012), 'A new approach to financial regulation: building a stronger system'.[6]

The above criticisms raise the question as to whether is it time to conduct a further independent and comprehensive review of the Financial Ombudsman Service and the principles under which it operates.

1 The Hunt Review 'Opening up, reaching out and aiming high'. The full text of the review is available at www.financial-ombudsman.org.uk/news/Hunt_report.pdf.
2 A website where employees and former employees of companies anonymously review companies and their management.
3 FSMA s 228(5)–(6) and FCA Handbook (DISP 3.6.6R(3)).
4 Ibid., s 234 and Sch 17.
5 Ibid., s226 and Sch17, Pt III.
6 See   www.gov.uk/government/uploads/system/uploads/attachment_data/file/81413/consult_finregresponses_0a.pdf.

Chapter 35

The European Community perspective

35.1 THE ROAD TO EUROPEAN COMMUNITY HARMONISATION

35.1.1 The background

Council Directive 87/102/EEC embodied minimum harmonisation of consumer credit law across the European Community and largely reflected the basic elements of consumer credit law in the United Kingdom. The Directive was amended on two occasions, first by the Directive of 22 February 1990 (90/88/EEC) and then by the Directive of 16 February 1998 (98/7/EEC).

In 1995 the Commission presented a report on the operation of the Directive and undertook a consultation with interested parties. It presented a report in 1996 which disclosed substantial differences between the laws of the Member States in consumer credit law.

In June 2001 the European Commission issued a Discussion Paper for the further amendment of Directive 87/102/EEC. It followed the Commission's conclusion in 1995 (some six years earlier!) that the Directive was no longer sufficiently in step with the situation of the consumer credit market. The Commission ordered a series of studies on a range of subjects: mortgage credit in the EEA; methods of calculation of the APR; harmonisation of cost elements of the APR; the role of intermediaries in the grant of consumer credit; and consequences of non-performance of the credit agreement. The Commission was troubled by the fact that there had been only marginal growth in the grant of credit across the European frontier-free market.

In September 2002 the Commission proposed a Directive aimed at full harmonisation of national legislation. This was rejected by the European Parliament in April 2004. The Commission then submitted an amended proposal enunciating the following guidelines:

(1) re-definition of the Directive's scope so as to adapt it to the new market situation and better tracking of the demarcation line between consumer credit and real estate credit;

(2) new arrangements to take account not only of creditors but also credit intermediaries;

(3) an information framework for the credit grantor to enable him to better appreciate the risks involved in the grant of credit;

(4)   more comprehensive information for consumers and guarantors;

(5)   more equitable sharing of responsibilities between the consumer and 'the professional'; and

(6)   improvement in the processing of payment incidents.

The driving force behind the new Directive is to be found in the Recitals to the Directive of 2008. In summary they state the following:

The *de facto* and *de jure* situation resulting from national differences in some cases leads to distortions of competition among creditors in the Community and creates obstacles in the internal market where Member States have adopted different mandatory provisions more stringent than those provided for in Directive 87/102/EEC. This restricts consumers' ability to make direct use of the gradually increasing availability of cross-border credit. Those distortions and restrictions may in turn have consequences in terms of the demand for goods and services.[1] The development of a more transparent and efficient credit market within the area without internal frontiers is vital in order to promote the development of cross-border activities.[2] Full harmonisation is necessary in order to ensure that all consumers in the Community enjoy a high and equivalent level of protection of their interests and to create a genuine internal market.[3]

In May 2007 the Council of the European Union, by a qualified majority reached, agreement on the Commission's modified proposal for a Directive on credit agreements for consumers to replace the existing Consumer Credit Directive.

The key features of the Council's agreement were the following:

(1)   application: the Directive will not apply to specified exempt consumer credit agreements, to consumer credit agreements secured by a land mortgage or to hire agreements;

(2)   pre-contractual and contractual information: there was to be standard information in the form of pre-contractual information, to enable borrowers to compare different offers;

(3)   right of withdrawal: as a general principle the consumer was to have a period of fourteen calendar days to withdraw from a credit agreement without having to provide a reason;

(4)   early repayment: a debtor should be able to discharge fully or partially his obligations under a credit agreement at any time and be entitled to a reduction in the total cost of credit. Where the agreement is at a fixed rate of interest, the creditor should be entitled to prescribed compensation;

(5)   APR and 'borrowing rate': the APR and the 'borrowing rate' must be stated in advertising information, pre-contractual information and contractual information. In contractual information for overdrafts, the creditor might state either the borrowing rate and charges, or the APR;

(6)   assignment of rights: a consumer must be informed of any assignment of the agreement except where the original creditor, in agreement with the assignee, continues to service the credit.

The Common Position of the Council was reached in September 2007 and amended, in limited respects, by the European Parliament in January 2008. The amended version was accepted by the Commission on 25 February 2008 and approved by the Council on 7 April 2008. The new Directive, Directive 2008/48/EC of the European Parliament and of the Council of 23 April 2008 on credit agreements for consumers and repealing Council Directive 87/102/EEC, was required to be implemented by the Member States by 12 May 2010, two years after its publication in the Official Journal of the European Union.

1 Recital (4).
2 Recital (6).
3 Recital (9).

35.1.2   The Consumer Credit Directive 2008/48/EC

This Directive is a full harmonisation Directive which applies across all EU Member States. It aims to facilitate the emergence of a well-functioning internal market in consumer credit.[1] The Directive's principal provisions are as follows:

(a) It applies to credit agreements with consumers relating to credit of between EUR200 (equivalent to £160) and EUR75,000 (equivalent to £60,260).[2] It does not apply to credit agreements secured by a mortgage or to hire agreements.

(b) Advertising, which indicates an interest rate or the cost of credit, must include prescribed standard information by means of a representative example and includes the annual percentage rate of charge.

(c) In good time before the consumer is bound by a fixed-sum credit agreement or an agreement for overdraft facilities, the creditor or credit intermediary, as appropriate, must supply the consumer with pre-contractual information in the form of the Standard European Consumer Credit Information (SECCI) or the European Consumer Credit Information (ECCI) respectively, as set out in the relevant Annex to the Directive. Prescribed pre-contractual advice and information must be given to the consumer to enable him to compare different offers.

(d) Member States must ensure that credit checks are carried out and determine how the obligation to assess the creditworthiness of the customer is to operate. Creditors and credit intermediaries must supply the consumer with sufficient information and explanations to enable the consumer to assess the suitability of the proposed credit agreement.

(e) Member States must ensure access to databases to creditors of other Member States in order to facilitate cross-border credit.

(f) Prescribed information must be set out in credit agreements and the consumer under a fixed-term credit agreement is entitled to request an amortisation table.

(g)   Where applicable, the consumer must be informed of any change in the borrowing rate.

(h)   A consumer under an overdraft agreement must be kept regularly informed of prescribed particulars.

(i)   A consumer may end a so-called open-end credit agreement free of charge at any time, subject to giving a maximum notice period of one month.

(j)   A consumer has a 14-day period in which to withdraw from a credit agreement without having to state a reason. Where Member States have legislation in place in respect of linked agreements that provide that funds cannot be made available before a specified period, they may allow the withdrawal period to be reduced at the consumer's request. (This does not apply to the UK as it does not have such legislation.)

(k)   A consumer is entitled to repay the credit fully or partially at any time. The creditor is entitled to fair and objectively justified compensation for costs directly linked to early repayment of credit up to 1% of the amount of credit repaid early (or 0.5% if the repayment takes place within 12 months of the end of the credit agreement). Member States may allow lenders to claim further compensation upon proof of greater loss. Any compensation may not exceed an amount of interest the consumer would have paid during the period between early repayment and the termination date.

(l)   The Directive contains a mathematical equation for the calculation of the Annual Percentage Rate of Charge (APR) set out in Part II of Annex I to the Directive. This was subsequently amended by Directive 2011/90/EU.

(m)   A consumer is entitled to raise against an assignee of the agreement any defence he could raise against the assignor. The creditor must notify the consumer of the assignment unless there is no change in the servicer of the agreement.

(n)   Member States must ensure that creditors are supervised by a body or authority which is independent of the financial institutions regulated by it.

(o)   The Directive sets minimum standards for credit intermediaries in respect of the disclosure of their powers and fees.

(p)   Member States must lay down rules on penalties for infringements which must be 'effective, proportionate and dissuasive'.[3]

(q)   Member States must set up out-of-court dispute resolution procedures.

The Directive is a maximum harmonisation Directive which means that Member States may not impose lesser or greater requirements than those set out in the Directive in relation to its subject matter. However, Member States remain free to prescribe their own requirements in relation to areas outside the scope of the Directive.

1 Recital (7).
2 In CCA 1974 Parliament adopted, as it had to, the credit amount of £60,260, but retained, as it was authorised to do, the lower limit of £50 for small agreements. See Art 2(c) of the Directive and CCA 1974, s 17(1).
3 Article 23.

35.1.3   UK law where Directive 2008/48/EC does not apply

Where the Directive directly addresses matters governed by CCA 1974, it sets maximum standards and prescriptions with which UK law must conform and which it may not exceed. This is fully discussed in **Chapter 2**.

In areas not governed by the Directive, UK law in general, and CCA 1974 in particular, continues to govern. These areas include the following:

(a)   consumer hire agreements;

(b)   consumer credit agreements for business purposes where the credit amount does not exceed £25,000. (It is to be noted that the Directive defines 'consumer' as a natural person who, in transactions covered by the Directive, is acting for purposes which are outside his trade, business or profession);

(c)   consumer credit agreements where the credit amount exceeds £60,260;

(d)   consumer credit agreements secured on land;

(e)   exempt agreements under RAO art 60H where the credit amount exceeds £60,260 (exemption relating to high net worth debtors and hirers), under RAO art 60C(3) (exemption relating to business purposes where the credit exceeds £25,000) and under RAO art 60D (exemption relating to the purchase of land for non-residential purposes);

(f)   the hirer's right of early termination under a hire-purchase agreement and the buyer's right of early termination under a conditional sale agreement (s 99 of CCA – so-called 'voluntary termination' or 'VT') as this relates to early termination of the agreement and not to early repayment under Article 16 of the Directive;

(g)   post-contract information requirements including statements and statutory notices;

(h)   regulation of ancillary credit business, except for credit brokerage in so far as credit brokerage is governed by the provisions of the Directive governing credit intermediaries;

(i)   joint and several liability under s 75 of CCA 1974 (as expressly recognised by Recital (9) of the Directive).

35.2   THE MORTGAGES DIRECTIVE

Directive 2014/17/EU on credit agreements for consumers relating to residential immovable property fills the missing link of the control of consumer credit agreements secured by mortgage or otherwise relating to residential immovable property in Member States. *Inter alia*, it introduces the requirements for pre-contractual information and adequate explanations and the obligation to assess the creditworthiness of the consumer. It also imposes certain prudential and supervisory requirements, including for the establishment and supervision of credit intermediaries, appointed representatives and non-credit institutions.

The Directive was implemented in the United Kingdom by the Mortgage Credit Directive Order 2015.[1]

1 SI 2015/910, and see **Chapter 18**.

35.3   CREDIT INSTITUTIONS AND THE EUROPEAN PASSPORT

The Second Banking Directive of 89/646/EEC on credit institutions provided for the co-ordination of laws, regulations and administrative provisions relating to the taking up and pursuit of the business of credit institutions. *Inter alia*, it distinguishes between a 'home Member State' and a 'host Member State'. A home Member State is a Member State in which a credit institution has been authorised in accordance with the Council Directive 77/780/EEC. A host Member State is a Member State in which a credit institution has a branch or in which it provides services.

A home Member State is responsible for the authorisation of credit grantors and a host Member State is obliged to permit the credit institution of a home Member State to operate in its territory. Minimum requirements are laid down for the grant of authorisation of credit institutions in home Member States. The Directive contains a list of activities which are subject to regulation by Member States. These include lending, financial leasing, issuing and administering means of payment, (such as credit cards, travellers' cheques and bankers' drafts), guarantees, money broking and credit reference services.

The Banking Co-ordination (Second Council Directive) Regulations 1992[1] gave effect to the Second Council Directive on the coordination of loans, regulations and administrative provisions relating to the taking up and pursuit of the business of credit institutions (Directive 89/646/EEC). The regulations coined the expression 'UK institution' which means a UK authorised institution or a UK subsidiary. A credit institution is a UK authorised institution if it is incorporated in the United Kingdom, has its principal place of business in the United Kingdom and, in the case of a bank, is authorised by the FCA under Pt IV of the Financial Services and Markets Act 2000 (FSMA) (previously by the Bank of England under the Banking Act or by the Building Societies' Commission under the Building Societies Act).

The regulations established the concept of a 'European authorised institution', which is a European institution or a European subsidiary with equivalent authorisation. As a result of the Directive and the regulations, banks and building societies, and their subsidiaries, are able to enjoy the benefits of holding a so-called 'European passport' which enable them to conduct banking, consumer credit and investment business throughout the European Community.

Before a UK firm can exercise passport rights in another Member State, it must give the FCA notice of intention to establish a branch in the host state, the FCA must have given a consent notice to the host state regulator and the latter must have notified the firm of the applicable provisions or two months must have elapsed since the date on which the FCA gave the consent notice. If the FCA refuses consent the authorised person may refer the matter to the Tribunal set up under that Act.[2]

A firm authorised in another Member State ('the home state') which intends to carry on regulated activities (i.e. governed by FSMA) in the UK ('the host state') must comply with corresponding requirements to those governing UK firms wanting to exercise passport rights in another EEA state.[3]

The Second Council Directive has been replaced by the Banking Directive 2000 (2000/12/EC) and the above Regulations by regulations made under FSMA.[4] Firms in other Member States which wish to operate in the UK are subject to the same approval regime, as spelt out in s 31(1)(b) of, and Schedule 3 to, FSMA.

1 SI 1992/3218.
2 FSMA 2000, ss 31(1)(b) and 37, read with Sch 3, para 19.
3 Ibid., s 31(1)(c) read with Sch 4.
4 Financial Services and Markets Act 2000 (Consequential Amendments and Repeals) Order 2001, SI 2001/3649, which came into force on 1 December 2001.

35.4   AUTHORISATION AND CONSUMER CREDIT EEA FIRMS

The inelegant description of a 'consumer credit EEA firm' refers to an EEA firm which does not have its head office in the UK, falls within para 5(a), (b), or (c) of Schedule 3 to FSMA and carries on, or seeks to carry on, consumer credit, consumer hire or ancillary credit business for which authorisation would ordinarily be required.

Schedule 3, Part II, para 12 provides that, once an EEA firm which is seeking to establish a branch in the United Kingdom in exercise of an EEA right satisfies the establishment conditions, it qualifies for authorisation. The establishment conditions are set out in para 13.

35.5   THE EFFECT OF BREXIT

The various Directives will cease to bind the United Kingdom, and passport rights (see **35.3**) and cross-border authorisation (see **35.4**) will in all probability end, when the United Kingdom exits the European Union in March 2019.

Negotiations currently afoot between the United Kingdom and the European Union may result in compromise solutions on these fronts, although this appears unlikely.

35.6   UNFAIR CONTRACT TERMS

The Directive on Unfair Terms in Consumer Contracts 93/13/EEC aimed to approximate the laws, regulations and administrative provisions of the Member States relating to unfair terms in contracts concluded between a seller or supplier and a consumer where the contract has not been individually negotiated. It thus also extends to standard form credit and hire agreements.

A contractual term will be regarded as unfair if, contrary to the requirement of good faith, it causes a significant imbalance in the parties' rights and obligations to the detriment of the consumer. In the assessment of whether a particular term is unfair, the Directive adopts similar tests to the Guidelines to be found in the Unfair Contracts Terms Act 1977.

The Directive also requires agreements to be drafted in plain, intelligible language. In the event of ambiguity, the provision will be interpreted in favour of the consumer.

The Directive was implemented in the United Kingdom by the Unfair Terms in Consumer Contracts Regulations 1994,[1] which came into force in July 1995 and were replaced by the Unfair Terms in Consumer Contracts Regulations 1999,[2] which came into force in October 1999. These, in turn, were replaced by Consumer Rights Act 2015, Part 2 and Schedules 2, 3 and 4.

1 SI 1994/3159.
2 SI 1999/2083.

35.7   INJUNCTIONS DIRECTIVE

The so-called 'Injunctions Directive', Directive 98/27/EC, was made in May 1998 and provided for qualified bodies in Member States to be empowered to institute injunction proceedings for the protection of consumers' interests and to stop any non-compliance with specified Council Directives. They include Directives relating to misleading advertising, contracts negotiated away from business premises, consumer credit, television broadcasting, package travel and holidays, unfair terms in consumer contracts, timeshare contracts and distance contracts.

The Directive was enacted in the United Kingdom originally by way of the Stop Now Orders (EC Directive) Regulations 2001[1] and now in the form of enforcement orders under Part 8 of the Enterprise Act 2002.

1 SI 2001/1422.

35.8   APPLICABLE LAW AND JURISDICTION

35.8.1   Applicable law

The applicable law in respect of a consumer contract is determined by the Contracts (Applicable Law) Act 1990 which implements the Convention on the Law Applicable to Contractual Obligations (the 'Rome Convention') of 1980. The Convention is an international treaty which displaces the common law conflict of law rules.

Article 3 of the Convention provides that a contract shall be governed by the law chosen by the parties. Article 4(1) provides that, in the absence of a choice of law, the contract should be governed by the law of the country with which it is most closely connected. Article 4(2) presumes this to be the country where the party who is to effect the performance has at the time of the conclusion of the contract, his habitual residence or, in the case of a body corporate or unincorporate, its central administration or, if entered into within the course of that party's trade of profession, the country in which the principal place of business is situated or the performance is to be effected.

Article 5(2) states that, notwithstanding the provisions of Art 3, a choice of law made by the parties shall not have the result of depriving the consumer of the protection afforded to him by the mandatory rules of the law of the country in which he has his habitual residence:

(i)   if in that country the conclusion of the contract was preceded by a specific invitation addressed to him or by advertising, and he had taken in that country all the steps necessary on his part for the conclusion of the contract, or

(ii) if the other party or his agent received the consumer's order in that country.

However, Art 5 does not apply to a contract for the supply of services where the services are to be supplied to the consumer exclusively in a country other than that in which he has his habitual residence.

Where the debtor resides or carries on business in England, he is *prima facie* within the protective provisions of CCA 1974. But such residence is not enough if that is the only point of contact with England. The transaction itself must have some real anchorage in England if CCA 1974 is to apply e.g. the essential steps necessary for the making of the contract were taken in England or the agreement results from advertising, negotiations etc. in England or the credit is to be advanced or repaid in England.[1]

If parties to a consumer credit agreement falling under a jurisdiction other than one under English law, choose English law to govern their contract, they do not thereby contract into the provisions of CCA 1974.

To quote Goode:

> 'The application of the CCA 1974 depends on the spatial reach which Parliament wanted it to have. If the connections with England are considered by the court such as to attract the CCA 1974 it will apply even if the agreement is otherwise governed by a foreign law. Conversely, if the connections with England are considered insufficient to bring the agreement within the Act it will not apply, despite the choice of English law, for the CCA 1974 operates only within its own spatial limitations and is unaffected by conflict of law rules, which can neither reduce not expand its scope, except so far as the CCA 1974 itself otherwise provides.'[2]

The leading illustration of the spatial reach of CCA 1974 is *Office of Fair Trading v Lloyds TSB Bank plc*[3] where the House of Lords held that the liability of a creditor under s 75 of the CCA 1974 extends to credit agreements financing a supply transaction abroad.

Whilst the *lex situs* generally governs contracts relating to immovable property, where a credit agreement was entered into in England to finance timeshare purchasers in Portugal and Spain, *Jarrett v Barclays Bank plc*[4] held that a claim that the vendors had been guilty of misrepresentation and breach of contract against the defendants was justiciable under s 75 of CCA 1974 by reason of the defendants' status as debtors under regulated debtor-creditor-supplier agreements.

The Consumer Credit Directive requires Member States to take the necessary measures to ensure that consumers do not lose the protection granted by it by virtue of the choice of law of a third country as the law applicable to the credit agreement, if the credit agreement has a close link with the territory of one or more Member States.[5]

1 *Goode: Consumer Credit Law and Practice* (LexisNexis Butterworths), IC [49.86].
2 Ibid., EC [49.59]–[49.80].
3 [2007] GCCR 6101, HL.
4 [1999] CGGR 2151, CA.
5 Directive 2008/48/EC, Article 22.4. This is likely to cease to operate after Brexit (see **35.5** above).

35.8.2 Jurisdiction

If the defendant is domiciled in a Member State, the Jurisdiction Rules in the Brussels Convention, (incorporated as Schedule 1 into the Civil Jurisdiction and Judgments Act 1982) apply. In all other cases, the jurisdiction rules or the national laws of the particular country will apply. Under the former, if one or more of the parties domiciled in a Member State has agreed that a court of a Member State shall have jurisdiction to settle any dispute, that court will have jurisdiction. Such jurisdiction is exclusive unless the parties have agreed otherwise.

Brexit will mean[1] the repeal of the European Communities Act 1972 which will cut the strings which tie Regulations of the European Union into the legal order of the United Kingdom, including Brussels I (jurisdiction and judgments), Brussels II, Rome I (law applicable to contractual obligations), Rome II (law applicable to non-contractual obligations) and the Lugano II Convention on jurisdiction and judgments between the EU and Iceland, Norway and Switzerland. Repeal of the 1972 Act will not, technically, affect the Brussels and Rome Conventions, as they were made as international treaties and enacted in the UK by primary legislation.[2] CCA 1974 provides that, for the purposes of the Act, any reference to 'the court' means, in relation to England and Wales, the county court, in relation to Scotland the sheriff court and in relation to Northern Ireland the High Court or the county court. In the absence of a contrary indication in CCA 1974, those courts have exclusive jurisdiction in respect of all actions and applications where specific reference is made to 'the court'. The Civil Procedure Rules provide that a claim may be commenced in any of the county courts, subject to the restrictions set out in the relevant Practice Direction.[3]

1 This paragraph is based on a lecture by Professor Adrian Briggs QC to the Commercial Bar Association, entitled 'Secession from the European Union and Private International Law: The Cloud with a Silver Lining', on 24 January 2017.
2 Civil Jurisdiction and Judgments Act 1982 and Contracts (Applicable Law) Act 1990.
3 CPR, PD 7, para 7.1.

Chapter 36

Concluding reflections

36.1 INTRODUCTION

The future of consumer credit law can be divided into two parts, namely: the established limb based on the foundations of CCA 1974, FSMA and regulations made under those Acts respectively together with rules in the FCA Handbook, notably CONC and MCOB, on the one hand; and the uncertain limb, dependent on the government's ability and willingness to adhere to and implement any EU criteria and requirements following Brexit, especially for the purpose of enabling the cross-border selling, or passporting, of consumer credit facilities, on the other hand.

At the time of writing it is impossible to predict the likely effect of Brexit on the consumer credit sector, especially as the current negotiations and outcome are likely to be dominated by EU political motives, rather than rational considerations such as legal equivalence and mutual economic benefit. This chapter is therefore concerned with reflecting upon aspects of the established limb as described above.

36.2 THE EU HERITAGE

It is worth mentioning that, in the consumer credit sphere, EU law has introduced the following into UK law:

(i)   the criterion of €75,000 (equating to £60,260 at the time the exchange rate was applied) for the purpose of determining when the EU consumer credit regime applies;

(ii)   the Agreements Regulations 2010;

(iii) the right of withdrawal from a credit agreement;

(iv)   pre-contract information requirements under the SECCI, ECCI and ESIS;

(v)   the passporting regime;

(vi)   data protection legislation, notably in relation to cross-border sharing of personal data;

(vii) the Payment Services Regulations;

(viii) statutory unfair contract terms;

(ix)   various consumer rights incorporated in the Consumer Rights Act 2015; and

(x)   cross-border and online dispute resolution for consumer disputes.

36.3   LAWS VERSUS RULES

Much of CCA 1974 and regulations under the Act has been transposed to the FCA Handbook by way of rules. In contrast with rules, which are easily made, unmade and amended, statute and statutory instruments are characterised by a degree of *gravitas* flowing from the procedure employed in their creation so as to give rise to stability, certainty and predictability. In contrast, the FCA Handbook and rules, which are largely principle based, may be appealing in a fast-changing financial world but, by their very nature, are inclined to give rise to uncertainty and to shift the centre of gravity of regulation away from adherence to the law towards compliance with rules. The indispensability of the role of the in-house compliance officer has, as a result, replaced that of the in-house lawyer.

A heavy burden and responsibility is placed on the FCA to strike the right balance in making new rules, which also highlights its invidious role as regulator, rule-maker and enforcer. Ultimately, it functions as judge of both compliance and non-compliance with its rulebook.

36.4   CCA 1974 VERSUS FSMA

The transfer of the consumer credit regime from CCA 1974 to FSMA reflected the transition from the OFT to the FCA, so that much of the original consumer credit legislation now falls within the scope of FSMA. There are certain fundamental aspects that continue to be governed by CCA 1974 and regulations under that Act. They include the meaning of 'credit', different types of credit agreement, entry into credit or hire agreements, pre-contract disclosure, agreements regulations, copy document regulations, matters arising during the currency of a regulated agreement, default and termination including notices in respect of the same and notices of arrears, types of security, judicial control and enforcement including time orders, and unfair relationships.

Whilst the total transposition of consumer credit legislation to FSMA and the FCA is achievable in theory, in practice consolidation of consumer credit law in this way might risk upsetting the remainder of inter-related concepts which were meaningfully knitted together in the original legislation. Already the transfer of the transposed provisions into the RAO and the FCA Handbook has created a dispersal of consumer credit concepts which are not easily linked together.

36.5   MORTGAGES AND GOODS MORTGAGES

Regulated mortgage contracts fall under the mortgages regime, pursuant to the Mortgage Credit Directive Order 2015. The Order took second charge lending out of the scope of the consumer credit regime and brought it into the scope of the mortgages regime. Mortgage lending and administration is now under the supervision of the Prudential Regulation Authority ('PRA') in the case of banks, building societies, credit unions and insurers, and of the FCA in respect of all other firms which do not take deposits.

The Order also implemented governance and control of consumer buy-to-let mortgages by the FCA, requiring such mortgage firms to register with the FCA. With the ever-expanding activity of buy-to-let mortgages and the potential vulnerability of tenants, the FCA's involvement in this area is bound to increase and intensify.

Goods mortgages will replace bills of sale when the Goods Mortgages Bill is enacted as law. The replacement of the outdated Bills of Sales Acts 1878 and 1882 will result in a more usable and up-to-date system of goods mortgages, with less complex documentation, greater consumer protection and an online registration system. It is also likely to release an additional range of goods for the purpose of security for loans which were previously regarded as non-utilisable assets for this purpose.

36.6   THE CULTURE OF REGULATION

The enormous body of rules and regulations that now applies to the consumer credit sector, with attendant consequences for breach, is likely to result in a customer service which, whilst compliant with regulation, is unable to fully address or respond to individual customer needs. The ability of a lender or owner to exercise its discretion by acting 'outside the box', as it were, has been whittled down, if not eliminated. This is likely to result in consumer credit becoming a product of impersonal distant marketing and form-filling.

A further consequence of expanded regulation is the ever-increasing cost of compliance, which ultimately falls on the consumer. Whilst competition in the sector might initially serve to curb rising costs and charges, in due course it is likely to result in lenders merging, as has occurred with corresponding bodies in other sectors of commerce and industry.

36.7   THE NEW DIRECTION

The internet has released lending from the traditional constraints of face-to-face lending. Initially, distance selling took the form of telephone communications and evolved into direct internet lending, online signatures and cryptographic security. It now encompasses peer-to-peer lending and crowdfunding. 'Credit', which is defined as including a cash loan and any other form of financial accommodation, will doubtless in time include lending by way of products of blockchain technology, such as Bitcoins.

Law generally lags behind advances in technology and will need to focus increasingly on, and address, new forms of lending and substitutes for cash. In this respect the FCA's hands-on approach to the financial sector should assist the evolution of financial services law in general and consumer credit law in particular. The governance and control of new technological developments, with laws and rules which apply to them, will require insight and foresight in order to preserve the FCA's three operational objectives of protecting consumers, ensuring market integrity, and promoting effective competition.

Index

[All references are to paragraph number]

A

Accounting
capital allowances, 29.4
dealer lessor, by, 29.1.3
'funding lease', 29.5
generally, 29.1
leasing, 29.3
lessee, by, 29.1.1
lessor, by, 29.1.2
'long funding lease', 29.5
manufacturer, by, 29.1.3
sale and leaseback transactions, and
buyer/lessor, by, 29.2.2
seller/lessee, by, 29.2.1
value added tax
bad debt relief, 29.6.7
charges by credit card companies to
retailers, 29.6.2
credit brokerage, 29.6.4
equipment leasing, 29.6.5
instalment credit finance, 29.6.3
intermediary services, 29.6.4
loans, 29.6.1
taxable services, 29.6.6
Action for damages
enforcement, 25.24
Additional cardholders
generally, 17.4.5
introduction, 17.2
Adequate explanations
pre-contractual disclosure of
information, 8.5
Advance payments
prescribed terms, and, 8.7.3.3
Advertising
'advertisement', 20.1
Advertisement Regulations, 20.1
advertising codes, 20.10
aggressive practices, 20.8.3
'average consumer', 20.8.1
background, 20.1

Advertising – *contd*
breach of provisions, 20.7
'communicate', 20.6.2
Consumer Credit Act 1974, 20.3
credit unions, and, 21.2.2
definitions, 20.1
FCA Handbook
breach of provisions, 20.7
CONC, 20.6.1
definitions, 20.6.2
form and expression, 20.6.4
general requirements, 20.6.3
introduction, 20.2
MCOB, 20.6.1
PERG, 20.6.1
prescribed content, 20.6.5
restricted expressions, 20.6.6
sources, 20.6.1
financial promotion
breach of provisions, 20.7
definition, 20.6.2
prescribed content, 20.6.5
regulatory context, 20.5
Financial Services and Markets Act 2000
financial promotion, 20.5
generally, 20.4
'gift', 20.6.6
'inducement', 20.6.2
'interest free', 20.6.6
introduction, 20.1
'invitation', 20.6.2
MCOB, 20.6.1
misleading action, 20.8.3
misleading omission, 20.8.3
'no deposit', 20.6.6
non-statutory controls, 20.10
offences
introduction, 20.7
Unfair Trading Regulations, 20.8.3
overdrafts, 20.6.6
'product', 20.8.1

Advertising – *contd*
  'public', 20.1
  regulatory landscape, 20.2
  restricted expressions, 20.6.6
  statutory controls
    CCA 1974, 20.3
    FCA Handbook, 20.6
    financial promotion provisions, 20.7
    FSMA 2000, 20.4–20.5
    introduction, 20.2
    other, 20.9
    Unfair Trading Regulations, 20.8
  supply of goods and services on credit,
      and, 15.1
  terminology, 20.1
  unfair commercial practices
    aggressive practices, 20.8.3
    defences, 20.8.3
    generally, 20.8.2
    misleading action, 20.8.3
    misleading omission, 20.8.3
    offences, 20.8.3
    specific practices, 20.8.3
  Unfair Trading Regulations 2008
    aggressive practices, 20.8.3
    'average consumer', 20.8.1
    defences, 20.8.3
    general concepts, 20.8.1
    introduction, 20.2
    misleading action, 20.8.3
    misleading omission, 20.8.3
    offences, 20.8.3
    'product', 20.8.1
    specific practices, 20.8.3
    unfair commercial practices, 20.8.2–
        20.8.3
  'weekly equivalent', 20.6.6
Affinity cards
  And see **Credit cards**
  generally, 17.5.5
Agency
  antecedent negotiations, 14.4.1
  common law, at, 14.1
  Consumer Credit Act 1974, under
    antecedent negotiations, 14.4.1
    contracting out, 14.4.6
    debtor's agent, 14.4.5
    disclosure of business purpose, 14.4.2
    receipt of notices, 14.4.4
    unfair relationships, 14.4.3
  contracting out, 14.4.6
  credit brokers, and
    common law position, 13.6.1
    legislative position, 13.6.2
  disclosure of borrower/hirer business
      purpose, 14.4.2
  estoppel, and, 14.1

Agency – *contd*
  fiduciary relationships, and, 14.1
  Financial Services and Markets Act 2000,
      under, 14.5
  holding out, and, 14.3
  receipt of notices, 14.4.4
  relationship between dealer/retailer and
      finance company, 14.3
  rights of third parties, 14.2
  unfair relationships, 14.4.3
Aggressive practices
  unfair commercial practices, and, 20.8.3
Agreement to aggregate
  generally, 11.9.1
Allocation of payments
  consumer credit agreements, and,
      8.7.3.2
Alternative dispute resolution (ADR)
  background, 34.1
  complaints handling
    generally, 34.3.1
    'Improving Complaints
        Handling', 34.3.4
    supervisory role of FCA, 34.3.2
    'Thematic Review', 34.3.3
  Dear CEO letters, 34.3.6
  FCA regulation
    complaint handling, 34.3.1
    'Complaints Thematic Review',
        34.3.3
    'Implementing the ADR
        Directive', 34.3.5
    'Improving Complaints
        Handling', 34.3.4
    supervisory role, 34.3.2
    supervisory tools, 34.3.6
  Financial Ombudsman Service
    background, 25.22.1
    criticisms, 34.4.4
    elements, 34.4.2
    FCA Handbook, 25.22.2–25.22.3
    funding, 34.4.3
    inception, 34.4.1
    introduction, 34.2
    jurisdiction, 25.22.1–25.22.2
    Regulations 2015, and, 25.22.3
    structure, 34.4.1
  introduction, 34.1
  statutory framework, 34.2
Ancillary credit business
  claims management companies, 16.9
  credit information services
    exclusions, 16.6
    generally, 16.3
  credit reference agencies
    exclusions, 16.6
    generally, 16.5

Ancillary credit business – *contd*
  debt adjusting
    credit information services, 16.3
    exclusions, 16.2.5–16.2.6
    generally, 16.2.1
  debt administration
    credit information services, 16.3
    exclusions, 16.2.5–16.2.6
    generally, 16.2.4
  debt collection
    credit information services, 16.3
    exclusions, 16.2.5–16.2.6
    generally, 16.2.3
  debt counselling
    credit information services, 16.3
    exclusions, 16.2.5–16.2.6
    generally, 16.2.2
  debt management, 16.7
  meaning, 16.1
  provision of credit references
    credit information services, 16.3
    exclusions, 16.6
    generally, 16.4
  unfair relationships, and, 16.8
Annual financial crime
  regulatory reporting, 33.10.5
Annual statements of account
  'agreement to aggregate', 11.9.1
  charges, 11.9.3
  dispensing with, 11.9.6
  errors and omissions, 11.9.4
  fixed-sum credit agreements, 11.2
  formalities, 11.9.2
  joint debtors and hirers, 11.9.5
  running-account credit agreements, 11.3
Antecedent negotiations
  agency, and, 14.4.1
  cancellable agreements, and, 4.5
  credit brokers, and, 13.6.2
Applicable law
  generally, 35.8.1
Appointed representatives
  generally, 30.3
  responsibilities, 30.3.2
Appropriation of payments
  debtor's and hirer's rights, and, 10.12
APR
  calculation, 19.3.1
  CONC rules, 19.2
  credit cards, and, 17.4.3
  historical perspective, 19.2
  MCOB, 19.4
  overview, 19.1
  reflections, 19.5
  statement, 19.3.2
Arrears notices
  'agreement to aggregate', 11.9.1

Arrears notices – *contd*
  charges, 11.9.3
  dispensing with, 11.9.6
  errors and omissions, 11.9.4
  formalities, 11.9.2
  generally, 11.4
  information sheets, 11.8
  joint debtors and hirers, 11.9.5
Assignment
  generally, 7.7
  security, and, 18.2.10
  terms of agreement, and, 9.9
Authorisation
  application procedure, 30.7–30.7.2
  applications, 30.4–30.4.2
  appointed representatives
    generally, 30.3
    responsibilities, 30.3.2
  approach of FCA, 30.6–30.6.3
  'authorised person', 30.2
  business plan, 30.7.1
  definition, 30.1
  EU perspective, and, 35.4
  'exempt person', 30.2
  full permission activities, 30.6.3
  general prohibition, 30.2
  interim arrangements, 30.4.1
  introduction, 30.1
  limited permission activities, 30.6.2
  limited permission credit firms, 30.6.1
  'person', 30.2
  principals
    generally, 30.3
    responsibilities, 30.3.1
  'regulated activity', 30.2
  regulatory business plan, 30.7.1
  responsibilities of a principal, 30.3.1
  responsibilities
    appointed representatives, 30.3.2
    principals, 30.3.1
  threshold conditions, 30.5
  transitional arrangements, 30.4.1
Authorised overdraft agreements
  content, 8.7.6
Authorised persons (AP)
  Code of Practice (APER), 31.5.2
  controlled functions, 31.3
  definition, 30.1
  fitness of candidate, 31.4
  introduction, 31.1
  propriety of candidate, 31.4
  Senior Managers and Certification
    regime, 31.6
  Statements of Principle, 31.5–31.5.1
  statutory framework, 31.2
Automatic decision-taking
  data protection, and, 27.10

'Average consumer'
unfair commercial practices, and, 20.8.1

B

Bank overdrafts
background, 22.5.1
FCA Handbook, 22.5.3
information requirements
entry into current account, 22.5.3.1
significant overdrawing without prior arrangement, 22.5.3.2
regulatory provisions, 22.5.4
statutory provisions, 22.5.2
Banking Code
See **Lending Code**
Bills of sale
discrete consumer credit agreements, 22.3
security
current law, 18.2.5.1
proposed changes, 18.2.5.2
Borrower
meaning, 3.4
Borrower-lender agreements
generally, 4.4.1
relevance of distinction from BLS agreements, 4.4.3
Borrower-lender-supplier agreements
generally, 4.4.2
relevance of distinction from BL agreements, 4.4.3
Borrowing
funding credit and hire facilities, 28.2.3
Brexit
generally, 35.5
British Bankers Association
credit marketing, 21.2.1
Brussels Convention
jurisdiction, 35.8.2
Budget account agreements
common characteristics, 4.7.4.8
general characteristics, 4.7.4.5
generally, 4.7.4.3
Budget account cards
And see **Credit cards**
generally, 17.5.4
Building Societies Association
credit marketing, 21.2.1
Business
ancillary credit business, 16.1
credit brokers, 13.3.1
Business agreements
financing payments connected with death, 6.5.4
Business finance lease
hire agreements, 5.4.5

Buy-to-let finance
consumer mortgage contract, 22.7.3
credit agreement, 22.7.1
mortgage contract, 22.7.2

C

Cancellable agreements
generally, 4.5
linked transactions
exempt transactions, 12.4
legal aspects, 12.3
Cancellation of agreements
debtor's rights, 10.6
generally, 8.7.3.2
Canvassing
conducting business off trade premises, 21.6
Capacity of parties
generally, 3.11
Capital allowances
generally, 29.4
Card protection cover
supply of goods and services on credit, 15.6
Carrying on a business
ancillary credit business, 16.1
Cash settlements
funding credit and hire facilities, 28.2.6.3
CAT standards
credit marketing, 21.11
Charge
And see **Security**
credit balance, over, 18.2.7
generally, 18.2.4
Charge card agreements
characteristics, 4.7.4.8
generally, 4.7.4.6
Charge cards
And see **Credit cards**
generally, 17.5.6
Charges
consumer credit agreements, 8.7.3.2
notices and statements, 11.9.3
Cheque and Credit Clearing Company
fraud, 26.3.1
Cheques
unsolicited credit card cheques, 17.4.1
Children
credit marketing, 21.7
CIFAS
fraud, 26.3.1
Circulars to minors
credit marketing, 21.7
Claims management companies
generally, 16.9

Co-branded cards
And see **Credit cards**
generally, 17.5.7
Codes of practice
advertising, 20.10
credit marketing, 21.9
data protection, 27.12
Complaints
regulatory reporting, 33.10.6
Complaints handling
And see **Alternative dispute resolution**
generally, 34.3.1
'Improving Complaints Handling', 34.3.4
supervisory role of FCA, 34.3.2
'Thematic Review', 34.3.3
Conditional sale agreements
characteristics, 4.7.2.3
features, 4.7.2.2
fixed-sum credit, and, 4.2.3
meaning, 4.7.2.1
overview, 4.7.1
Conduct of business
credit broking, 13.3.2
Conducting business off trade premises
canvassing, 21.6
Confidentiality
data protection
associated records, 27.8
background, 27.1
'breach', 27.3
codes of practice, 27.12
'consent', 27.3
consent clauses, 27.7
'controller', 27.3
data protection principles, 27.4
data subject's rights, 27.11
erasure of personal data, 27.5
EU law, 27.2
freedom of information requests, 27.10
GDPR, 27.2–27.6
introduction, 27.1
lawful processing, 27.4
notification system, 27.9
'personal data', 27.3
'processing', 27.3
processing personal data, 27.4
'processor', 27.3
rectification of inaccurate data, 27.5
registration scheme, 27.9
regulatory framework, 27.2
restriction of processing personal
data, 27.5
security of personal data, 27.4
statutory provisions, 27.1
transfer of personal data, 27.6
electoral register, 27.13.2
Tournier principle, 27.13.1

Connected loan agreements
linked transactions, and, 12.6
Consolidation clause
terms of agreement, and, 9.7
Consumer
meaning, 3.2
Consumer buy-to-let mortgages
generally, 2.6
Consumer credit
'borrower', 3.4
capacity of parties, 3.11
'consumer', 3.2
'consumer credit agreement', 3.5
'consumer hire agreement', 3.9
'credit', 3.1
'credit hire', 3.10
'creditor', 3.3
'debtor', 3.4
EU law, 1.1
'hire', 3.8
'lease', 3.8
'hirer', 3.7
'individual', 3.2
'lender', 3.3
'lessee', 3.7
'lessor', 3.6
'owner', 3.6
regimes, 1.3
'regulated credit agreement', 3.5
relationship issue, as, 1.5
transfer of regime, 1.4
Consumer Credit Act 1974
concluding reflections, 36.1–36.3
interaction with FSMA 2000, 36.4
relationship issue, as, 1.2
Consumer Credit Act 2006
critical reflections, 33.1
Consumer credit agreements
appropriation of payments, 10.12
assignment, 9.9
borrower-lender agreements
generally, 4.4.1
relevance of distinction from BLS
agreements, 4.4.3
borrower-lender-supplier agreements
generally, 4.4.2
relevance of distinction from BL
agreements, 4.4.3
budget account agreements
common characteristics, 4.7.4.8
general characteristics, 4.7.4.5
generally, 4.7.4.3
buy-to-let finance
consumer mortgage contract,
22.7.3
credit agreement, 22.7.1
mortgage contract, 22.7.2

Consumer credit agreements – *contd*
cancellable agreements
  generally, 8.6.7
  introduction, 4.5
cancellation
  general right, 8.6.7
  generally, 10.6
  introduction, 4.5
charge card agreements
  characteristics, 4.7.4.8
  generally, 4.7.4.6
conditional sale agreements
  characteristics, 4.7.2.3
  features, 4.7.2.2
  meaning, 4.7.2.1
  overview, 4.7.1
consolidation clause, 9.7
Consumer Credit Sourcebook
  (CONC), 8.1.1
content
  background, 8.1
  CONC, 8.1.1
  elements, 8.3.2
  FCA Handbook, 8.1.1
  generally, 8.3.1
  legible, 8.3.2
  legislation, 8.1.2
  prescribed form, 8.3.2
  prescribed terms, 8.3.2
  signature, 8.3.2
contracting out, 10.14
copies
  contents, 8.8
  generally, 10.4
credit card agreements, 4.7.1
credit sale agreements
  characteristics, 4.7.2.3
  features, 4.7.2.2
  meaning, 4.7.2.1
credit-token agreements
  characteristics, 4.7.4.8
  generally, 4.7.4.7
  overview, 4.6
creditworthiness assessment, 10.2
debtor-creditor agreements
  generally, 4.4.1
  relevance of distinction from DCS
    agreements, 4.4.3
debtor-creditor-supplier agreements
  generally, 4.4.2
  relevance of distinction from DC
    agreements, 4.4.3
debtor's rights
  appropriation of payments,
    10.12
  cancellation of agreement, 10.6
  contracting out, 10.14

Consumer credit agreements – *contd*
debtor's rights – *contd*
  copies of agreement and
    documents, 10.4
  creditworthiness assessment, 10.2
  disclosure, 10.3
  early settlement, 10.9
  pre-contractual disclosure, 10.1
  protected goods, 10.11
  provision of information, 10.8
  rebate on early settlement, 10.10
  time orders, 10.13
  withdrawal under s 58, 10.7
  withdrawal under s 66A, 10.5
default charges, 9.4.2
default interest, 9.4.1
disclosure
  generally, 10.3
  pre-contractual, 10.1
discrete agreements
  bills of sale loans, 22.3
  buy-to-let finance, 22.7.1–22.7.3
  high-cost short-term credit
    agreements, 22.1.1–22.1.2
  overdrafts on current bank
    accounts, 22.5.1–22.4.4
  P2P agreements, 22.2.1–22.2.3
  residential renovation agreements, 22.6
  student loans, 22.4
early settlement
  generally, 10.9
  rebate, 10.10
elements, 8.2
entire agreement clause, 9.8
excluded agreements
  discretion of FCA, 6.5.5
  financing payments connected with
    death, 6.5.4
  introduction, 6.5
  non-commercial agreements, 6.5.1
  overdraft facilities, 6.5.2
  small credit agreements, 6.5.3
execution, 8.6.1
exempt agreements
  And see **Exempt agreements**
  agreements excluded from CCA 1974,
    Part V, 6.5
  consumer hire agreements, and, 6.4
  distinction from regulated
    agreement, 6.1
  introduction, 6.1
  meaning, 6.2
  overview, 4.1
  types, 6.3
express terms deemed included
  contracts to supply digital
    content, 9.3.2.2

Consumer credit agreements – *contd*
  express terms deemed included – *contd*
    contracts to supply goods, 9.3.2.1
    contracts to supply services, 9.3.2.2
    remedies for breach, 9.3.2.4
    under other Acts, 9.3.2.3
  FCA Handbook, 8.1.1
  fixed-sum loan agreements
    characteristics, 4.7.3.2
    meaning, 4.7.3.1
    overview, 4.7.1
  form and content
    background, 8.1
    Consumer Credit Sourcebook, 8.1.1
    elements, 8.3.2
    FCA Handbook, 8.1.1
    generally, 8.3.1
    legible, 8.3.2
    legislation, 8.1.2
    prescribed form, 8.3.2
    prescribed terms, 8.3.2
    signature, 8.3.2
  generally, 4.1
  high-cost short-term credit agreements
    cost caps, 22.1.2
    generally, 22.1.1
  hire-purchase agreements
    characteristics, 4.7.2.3
    features, 4.7.2.2
    meaning, 4.7.2.1
    overview, 4.7.1
  'implied' terms
    contracts to supply digital
        content, 9.3.2.2
    contracts to supply goods, 9.3.2.1
    contracts to supply services, 9.3.2.2
    remedies for breach, 9.3.2.4
    under other Acts, 9.3.2.3
  'individual', 4.1
  instalment sale agreements
    characteristics, 4.7.2.3
    features, 4.7.2.2
    meaning, 4.7.2.1
  interest on default, 9.4.1
  legibility, 8.3.2
  meaning, 3.5
  modification
    prescribed information, 8.7.5.2
    prescribed terms, 8.7.5.1
  option account agreements
    common characteristics, 4.7.4.8
    general characteristics, 4.7.4.5
    generally, 4.7.4.4
  overdraft facility agreements
    characteristics, 4.7.4.8
    generally, 4.7.4.2
  partly regulated agreements, 6.6

Consumer credit agreements – *contd*
  pawn receipts, and, 4.7.1
  peer-to-peer (P2P) agreements
    definition, 22.2.1
    FCA Handbook, 22.2.3
    operating electronic system as to
        lending, 22.2.2
  pre-contractual disclosure of information
    adequate explanations, and, 8.5, 10.1.2
    Agreements Regulations 1983, 8.4.3
    Agreements Regulations 2010, 8.4.1
    Disclosure Regulations 2004, 8.4.4
    Disclosure Regulations 2010, 8.4.2
    introduction, 8.4
    overview, 8.7.1
    summary of requirements, 8.4.5
  prescribed form, 8.3.2
  prescribed terms
    generally, 8.7.3.1
    introduction, 8.7.2
    overview, 8.3.2
    Regulations 1983, 8.7.3.2
    Regulations 2010, 8.7.3.3
  prescribed terms (Regulations 1983)
    allocation of payments, 8.7.3.2
    cancellation rights, 8.7.3.2
    charges, 8.7.3.2
    early settlement, 8.7.3.2
    financial particulars, 8.7.3.2
    generally, 8.7.3.1
    introduction, 8.7.2
    overview, 8.3.2
    prescribed information, 8.7.3.2
    repayment amounts, 8.7.3.2
    statutory warnings, 8.7.3.2
    total charge for credit, 8.7.3.2
  prescribed terms (Regulations 2010)
    advance payments, 8.7.3.3
    generally, 8.7.3.1
    goods or services, 8.7.3.3
    introduction, 8.7.2
    overview, 8.3.2
    parties, 8.7.3.3
    total charge for credit, 8.7.3.3
  protected goods, 10.11
  provision of information, 10.8
  rebate on early settlement
    calculation, 10.10.2
    entitlement, 10.10.1
    exclusions from calculation, 10.10.3
    statement, 10.10.4
  regulated agreements
    cancellation, 4.5
    meaning, 6.1
    overview, 4.1
  Regulations 1983, under, 9.2.1
  Regulations 2010, under, 9.2.2

Consumer credit agreements – *contd*
  residential renovation agreements, 22.6
  revolving credit agreements
    budget accounts, 4.7.4.3
    characteristics, 4.7.4.8
    charge card agreements, 4.7.4.6
    credit-token agreements, 4.7.4.7
    generally, 4.7.4.1
    option accounts, 4.7.4.4
    overdraft facilities, 4.7.4.2
  running-account agreements
    budget accounts, 4.7.4.3
    characteristics, 4.7.4.8
    charge card agreements, 4.7.4.6
    credit-token agreements, 4.7.4.7
    generally, 4.7.4.1
    option accounts, 4.7.4.4
    overdraft facilities, 4.7.4.2
  secured on land, 8.6.8
  set-off, 9.6
  signature
    generally, 8.6.1
    introduction, 8.3.2
  supply of copies
    definitions, 8.6.5
    executed agreement, 8.6.2
    executed agreement in case of excluded
      agreement, 8.6.4
    unexecuted agreement, 8.6.3
  termination
    customer's rights, 4.7.2.3
  terms
    assignment, 9.9
    consolidation clause, 9.7
    default charges, 9.4.2
    default interest, 9.4.1
    entire agreement clause, 9.8
    generally, 9.2
    included in the contract, which
      are, 9.3.2
    interest on default, 9.4.1
    introduction, 4.7.2.3
    overview, 9.1
    prescribed terms, 8.7.3
    Regulations 1983, under, 9.2.1
    Regulations 2010, under, 9.2.2
    set-off, 9.6
    time of performance, 9.3.1
    unfair contract terms, 9.3.3
    variation clauses, 9.5
  time of performance, 9.3.1
  time orders, 10.13
  total charge for credit, 8.7.3.2
  unfair contract terms
    consumer contracts, 9.3.3.3
    EU perspective, 35.6
    generally, 9.3.3.1

Consumer credit agreements – *contd*
  unfair contract terms – *contd*
    good faith, 9.3.3.4
    non-consumer contracts, 9.3.3.3
    UCTA 1977, 9.3.3.2
    unfairness, 9.3.3.4
  unfair relationships, and, 9.3.3.5
  variation clauses
    generally, 9.5.1
    restrictions in FCA Handbook, 9.5.2
  withdrawal
    generally, 8.6.6
    under s 58, 10.7
    under s 66A, 10.5
Consumer Credit Directive 2008/48/EC
  agreements outside the scope
    form and content, 2.3.2
    general provisions applying, 2.3.3
    principal changes effected, 2.4.2
  agreements within the scope
    form and content, 2.3.1
    general provisions applying, 2.3.3
    principal changes effected, 2.4.1
  application, 2.2–2.3
  background, 35.1.1
  effect on UK law, 35.1.3
  generally, 35.1.2
  principal changes effected by
    agreements outside the scope, 2.4.2
    agreements within the scope, 2.4.1
  principal provisions, 35.1.2
  scope, 2.2
Consumer credit EEA firms
  generally, 35.4
Consumer credit law
  context, 1.1–1.5
  structure, 2.1–2.7
Consumer Credit Trade Association
  credit marketing, 21.2.1
Consumer hire agreements
  appropriation of payments, 10.12
  assignment, 9.9
  business finance lease, 5.4.5
  cancellation rights, 8.7.4.3
  characteristics, 5.3
  consolidation clause, 9.7
  Consumer Credit Sourcebook
    (CONC), 8.1.1
  content
    background, 8.1
    CONC, 8.1.1
    elements, 8.3.2
    FCA Handbook, 8.1.1
    generally, 8.3.1
    legible, 8.3.2
    legislation, 8.1.2
    prescribed form, 8.3.2

Consumer hire agreements – *contd*
content – *contd*
prescribed terms, 8.3.2
signature, 8.3.2
contract hire, 5.4.3
contracting out, 10.14
contracts for the hire of goods
hire of goods other than to
consumers, 5.3.1
hire of goods to consumers, 5.3.1
regulatory reflections, 5.3.4
unique aspects, 5.3.3
copies
contents, 8.8
generally, 10.4
credit brokers, and, 13.1.1
credit hire, 5.4.8
creditworthiness assessment, 10.2
default charges, 9.4.2
default interest, 9.4.1
disclosure
generally, 10.3
pre-contractual, 10.1
early settlement, and, 10.10.5
entire agreement clause, 9.8
equipment lease, 5.5
estimated information, 8.7.4.3
exempt hire agreements
introduction, 6.4
nature of agreement, as to, 6.4.2
nature of hirer, as to, 6.4.4
other exclusions, 6.4.5
supply of essential services, as to,
6.4.3
types, 6.4.1
express terms deemed included
contracts to supply digital
content, 9.3.2.2
contracts to supply goods, 9.3.2.1
contracts to supply services,
9.3.2.2
remedies for breach, 9.3.2.4
under other Acts, 9.3.2.3
FCA Handbook, 8.1.1
finance lease, 5.4.1
financial particulars, 8.7.4.3
form and content
background, 8.1
Consumer Credit Sourcebook, 8.1.1
elements, 8.3.2
FCA Handbook, 8.1.1
generally, 8.3.1
legible, 8.3.2
legislation, 8.1.2
prescribed form, 8.3.2
prescribed terms, 8.3.2
signature, 8.3.2

Consumer hire agreements – *contd*
hirer's rights
appropriation of payments, 10.12
contracting out, 10.14
copies of agreement and
documents, 10.4
creditworthiness assessment, 10.2
disclosure, 10.3
pre-contractual disclosure, 10.1
provision of information, 10.8
time orders, 10.13
'implied' terms
contracts to supply digital
content, 9.3.2.2
contracts to supply goods, 9.3.2.1
contracts to supply services, 9.3.2.2
remedies for breach, 9.3.2.4
under other Acts, 9.3.2.3
interest on default, 9.4.1
lease upgrade, 5.4.7
master lease, 5.4.4
meaning, 5.1
modification
prescribed information, 8.7.5.3
prescribed terms, 8.7.5.1
operating lease, 5.4.2
other payments, 8.7.4.3
overview, 3.9
pre-contractual disclosure, 10.1
pre-contractual information, 8.7.1
prescribed information, 8.7.4.2
prescribed terms
cancellation rights, 8.7.4.3
estimated information, 8.7.4.3
financial particulars, 8.7.4.3
generally, 8.7.4.1
introduction, 8.7.2
other payments, 8.7.4.3
prescribed information, 8.7.4.2
statutory warnings, 8.7.4.3
provision of information, 10.8
rebate on early settlement, and,
10.10.5
Regulations 1983, under, 9.2.1
set-off, 9.6
software lease, 5.4.6
specific agreements
business finance lease, 5.4.5
contract hire, 5.4.3
credit hire, 5.4.8
finance lease, 5.4.1
introduction, 5.4
lease upgrade, 5.4.7
master lease, 5.4.4
operating lease, 5.4.2
software lease, 5.4.6
statutory warnings, 8.7.4.3

Consumer hire agreements – *contd*
  terms
    assignment, 9.9
    consolidation clause, 9.7
    default charges, 9.4.2
    default interest, 9.4.1
    entire agreement clause, 9.8
    generally, 9.2
    included in the contract, which
        are, 9.3.2
    interest on default, 9.4.1
    overview, 9.1
    prescribed terms, 8.7.3
    Regulations 1983, under, 9.2.1
    set-off, 9.6
    time of performance, 9.3.1
    unfair contract terms, 9.3.3
    variation clauses, 9.5
  time of performance, 9.3.1
  time orders, 10.13
  types, 5.2
  unfair contract terms
    consumer contracts, 9.3.3.3
    EU perspective, 35.6
    generally, 9.3.3.1
    good faith, 9.3.3.4
    non-consumer contracts, 9.3.3.3
    UCTA 1977, 9.3.3.2
    unfairness, 9.3.3.4
  unfair relationships, and, 9.3.3.5
  variation clauses
    generally, 9.5.1
    restrictions in FCA Handbook, 9.5.2
Consumer Rights Act 2015
  hire agreements, 5.1
Contract hire
  hire agreements, 5.4.3
Contracting out
  agency, 14.4.6
  debtor's and hirer's rights, 10.14
Contracts for the hire of goods
  And see **Consumer hire agreements**
  hire of goods other than to
      consumers, 5.3.1
  hire of goods to consumers, 5.3.1
  regulatory reflections, 5.3.4
  unique aspects, 5.3.3
Contractual lien
  security, 18.2.11
Contractual set-off
  security, 18.2.6
Copies
  contents, 8.8
  debtor's and hirer's rights, 10.4
Credit
  borrower-lender credit, 4.4
  borrower-lender-supplier credit, 4.4

Credit – *contd*
  debtor-creditor credit, 4.4
  debtor-creditor-supplier credit, 4.4
  fixed-sum credit
    features, 4.2.3
    generally, 4.2.1
    relevance of distinction from running-
        account credit, 4.2.4
  meaning, 3.1
  restricted-use credit, 4.3
  running-account credit
    features, 4.2.2
    generally, 4.2.1
    relevance of distinction from fixed-sum
        credit, 4.2.4
  types, 4.2
  unrestricted-use credit, 4.3
Credit brokers
  activities involving credit broking,
      13.1.1
  agents, as
    common law position, 13.6.1
    legislative position, 13.6.2
  antecedent negotiations, 13.6.2
  'business', 13.3.1
  charges, 13.8
  commission, 13.8
  conduct of business, 13.3.2
  consequences of unauthorised broking
      business, 13.7
  consumer hire agreements, and,
      13.1.1
  credit broking
    business, 13.3.1
    conduct of business, 13.3.2
    definition, 13.1.1
    land agreements, 13.1.3
    operating electronic system as to
        lending, 13.1.2
    unfair business practices, 13.3.3
  credit broking business
    conduct, 13.3.2
    generally, 13.3.1
  credit intermediaries, and
    disclosure of details, 13.11
    generally, 13.1
  debtor-creditor-supplier agreements,
      and, 13.1
  'effecting an introduction', 13.2
  electronic system as to lending, 13.1.2
  fees, 13.8
  fiduciary relationships, and, 13.9
  financial promotions and
      communications, 13.4
  financial services, and, 13.10
  group licences, 13.1
  land agreements, 13.1.3

Credit brokers – *contd*
mortgages, and
generally, 13.10
introduction, 13.1
operating electronic system as to
lending, 13.1.2
other regulated activities, 13.10
regulated mortgage contracts, and, 13.10
remuneration, 13.8
role, 13.1
unauthorised broking business, 13.7
unfair business practices, 13.3.3
unfair relationships, and, 13.5
Credit broking
business
conduct, 13.3.2
generally, 13.3.1
credit information services, 16.3
definition, 13.1.1
land agreements, 13.1.3
operating electronic system as to
lending, 13.1.2
unfair business practices, and, 13.3.3
Credit card agreements
characteristics, 4.7.4.8
generally, 4.7.4.7
introduction, 4.7.1
overview, 4.6
running-account credit, 4.2.1
Credit card cheques
And see **Credit cards**
generally, 17.4.2
Credit cards
additional cardholders
generally, 17.4.5
introduction, 17.2
affinity cards, 17.5.5
APR, 17.4.3
budget account cards, 17.5.4
characterisation of use, 17.2
charge cards, 17.5.6
co-branded cards, 17.5.7
credit card cheques, 17.4.2
creditor liability
generally, 17.2
s 75 CCA 1974, and, 17.4.4
debtor liability, 17.3
debtor's rights
generally, 17.2
s 75 CCA 1974, and, 17.4.4
interchange fees, 17.1
Lending Code, 17.4.5
loss, 17.3
loyalty cards, 17.5.7
misuse, 17.3
option account cards, 17.5.3
parties, 17.1

Credit cards – *contd*
'revolvers', 17.5.1
s 75 CCA 1974 liability
generally, 17.4.4
introduction, 17.2
store cards, 17.5.2
theft, 17.3
total charge for credit, 17.4.3
transaction structure, 17.1
'transactors', 17.5.1
types
affinity cards, 17.5.5
budget account cards, 17.5.4
charge cards, 17.5.6
co-branded cards, 17.5.7
introduction, 17.5
loyalty cards, 17.5.7
option account cards, 17.5.3
store cards, 17.5.2
user, by, 17.5.1
unsolicited cheques, 17.4.1
unsolicited credit-tokens, 17.4.1
user types, 17.5.1
Credit hire
hire agreements, 5.4.8
meaning, 3.10
Credit information services
exclusions, 16.6
generally, 16.3
Credit institutions
European passport, 35.3
Credit intermediaries
And see **Credit brokers**
disclosure of details, 13.11
generally, 13.1
Credit limits
running-account credit, 4.2.2
Credit marketing
canvassing, 21.6
CAT standards, 21.11
circulars to minors, 21.7
codes of practice, 21.9
common law, at, 21.13
conducting business off trade
premises, 21.6
copy of draft credit agreement, 21.5.4
credit reference agency
information, 21.5.1
credit scoring, 21.4
credit unions, 21.2.2
creditworthiness assessment, 21.3.2
crowdfunding, 21.2.4
disclosure of contractual
information, 21.5.3
distance marketing, 21.10.2
distance selling, 21.10.1
entitlement to credit, 21.1

Credit marketing – *contd*
illustrations, 21.5.2
information on credit status, 21.5.1
lending institutions, 21.2.1
loan-based crowdfunding, 21.2.4
minors, and, 21.7
other statutory controls, 21.12
peer-to-peer lending platforms, 21.2.3
Plain English Campaign, 21.11
pre-contractual information
copy of draft credit agreement, 21.5.4
credit reference agency
information, 21.5.1
disclosure of contractual
information, 21.5.3
illustrations, 21.5.2
quotations, 21.5.2
quotations, 21.5.2
responsible lending
creditworthiness assessment, 21.3.2
MCOB, 21.3.3
pre-contractual requirements, 21.3.1
student loans, 21.2.5
Unfair Trading Regulations, 21.12
unsolicited credit-tokens, 21.8
Credit reference agencies
exclusions, 16.6
generally, 16.5
pre-contractual information, 21.5.1
Credit references
provision
credit information services, 16.3
exclusions, 16.6
generally, 16.4
Credit sale agreements
characteristics, 4.7.2.3
features, 4.7.2.2
fixed-sum credit, 4.2.3
meaning, 4.7.2.1
Credit scoring
credit marketing, 21.4
Credit status information
credit marketing, 21.5.1
Credit-token agreements
characteristics, 4.7.4.8
generally, 4.7.4.7
overview, 4.6
Credit-tokens
And see **Credit cards**
generally, 17.1
Credit unions
generally, 21.2.2
Creditor
meaning, 3.3
Creditor liability
generally, 17.4.4
introduction, 17.2

Creditor liability – *contd*
supply of goods and services on
credit, 15.1
Creditworthiness
assessment, 10.2
responsible lending, 21.3.2
Criminal sanctions
civil penalties, and, 26.5.3
defences, 26.5.4
fraud
criminal offences, 26.2.2
extent of problem, 26.1
introduction, 26.1
mortgage frauds, 26.3.1
prevention, 26.3–27.3.3
proceeds of crime, 26.2.2
statutory provisions, 26.2
money laundering, 26.4
offences, 26.5.2
overview, 26.5.1
Crowdfunding
credit marketing, 21.2.4
Crowther Committee
generally, 3.1
hire, 3.8

D

Damages
enforcement, 25.24
Data protection
associated records, 27.8
background, 27.1
'breach', 27.3
codes of practice, 27.12
confidentiality, and
electoral register, 27.13.2
Tournier principle, 27.13.1
'consent', 27.3
consent clauses, 27.7
'controller', 27.3
data protection principles, 27.4
data subject's rights
generally, 27.11
introduction, 27.5
overview, 27.2
erasure of personal data, 27.5
EU law, 27.2
freedom of information requests, 27.10
General Data Protection Regulation
(GDPR)
application, 27.2
content, 27.2
data subject's rights, 27.5
definitions, 27.3
introduction, 27.2
processing personal data, 27.4
transfer of personal data, 27.6

Data protection – *contd*
introduction, 27.1
lawful processing, 27.4
notification system, 27.9
'personal data', 27.3
'processing', 27.3
processing personal data, 27.4
'processor', 27.3
rectification of inaccurate data, 27.5
registration scheme, 27.9
regulatory framework, 27.2
restriction of processing personal
data, 27.5
security of personal data, 27.4
statutory provisions, 27.1
transfer of personal data, 27.6
'Dealer'
definition, 15.1
Dealer agreements
supply of goods and services on
credit, 15.2
Dealer lessor
accounting, 29.1.3
Dear CEO letters
alternative dispute resolution,
34.3.6
Death of debtor or hirer
enforcement, 25.20
Death-related payments, financing of
excluded agreements, and, 6.5.4
Debit cards
generally, 17.6.2
Debt adjusting
credit information services, 16.3
exclusions, 16.2.5–16.2.6
generally, 16.2.1
Debt administration
credit information services, 16.3
exclusions, 16.2.5–16.2.6
generally, 16.2.4
Debt collection
credit information services, 16.3
exclusions, 16.2.5–16.2.6
generally, 16.2.3
Debt counselling
credit information services, 16.3
exclusions, 16.2.5–16.2.6
generally, 16.2.2
Debt management
generally, 16.7
Debtor
meaning, 3.4
Debtor-creditor (DC) agreements
credit unions, and, 21.2.2
generally, 4.4.1
relevance of distinction from DCS
agreements, 4.4.3

Debtor-creditor (DC) credit
generally, 4.4
**Debtor-creditor-supplier (DCS)
agreements**
credit brokers, and, 13.1
generally, 4.4.2
linked transactions, and, 12.1
payment protection insurance, and, 15.5
relevance of distinction from DC
agreements, 4.4.3
supply of goods and services on credit,
and, 15.1
Debtor-creditor-supplier (DCS) credit
generally, 4.4
Debtor liability
credit cards, and, 17.3
Debtor's rights
appropriation of payments, 10.12
cancellation of agreement, 10.6
contracting out, 10.14
copies of agreement and documents, 10.4
creditworthiness assessment, 10.2
disclosure, 10.3
early settlement, 10.9
pre-contractual disclosure, 10.1
protected goods, 10.11
provision of information, 10.8
rebate on early settlement, 10.10
time orders, 10.13
withdrawal, 10.7
**Dedicated Cheque and Plastic Crime Unit
(DCPCU)**
fraud, and, 26.3.1
Default charges
terms of agreement, and, 9.4.2
Default interest
terms of agreement, and, 9.4.1
Default notices
'agreement to aggregate', 11.9.1
charges, 11.9.3
dispensing with, 11.9.6
errors and omissions, 11.9.4
failure to comply with notice
provisions, 25.9
FCA Handbook, 25.3.2
formal notice not required, 25.10
formalities, 11.9.2
generally, 11.5
information sheets, 11.8
joint debtors and hirers, 11.9.5
statutory controls, 25.3.1
sureties, and, 25.5
Delivery of goods
hire-purchase agreements, and, 25.16
Deposits
funding credit and hire facilities,
and, 28.2.2

Discharge of credit agreement
linked transactions, and, 12.3
Disclosure of business purpose
agency, and, 14.4.2
Disclosure of contractual information
generally, 10.3
pre-contractual, 10.1
pre-contractual information, and,
21.5.3
Discrete consumer credit agreements
bills of sale loans, 22.3
high-cost short-term credit agreements
cost caps, 22.1.2
generally, 22.1.1
overdrafts on current bank accounts
background, 22.5.1
FCA Handbook, 22.5.3
regulatory provisions, 22.5.4
statutory provisions, 22.5.2
peer-to-peer (P2P) agreements
definition, 22.2.1
FCA Handbook, 22.2.3
operating electronic system as to
lending, 22.2.2
short-term credit agreements, 22.1.1–
22.1.2
student loans, 22.4
Discretion of FCA
excluded agreements, and, 6.5.5
Dispute resolution
Financial Ombudsman Service
background, 25.22.1
criticisms, 34.4.4
elements, 34.4.2
FCA Handbook, 25.22.2–25.22.3
funding, 34.4.3
inception, 34.4.1
introduction, 34.2
jurisdiction, 25.22.1–25.22.2
Regulations 2015, and, 25.22.3
structure, 34.4.1
Distance contracts
cancellable agreements, 4.5
credit marketing, 21.10.1
financial services, 15.8.2
goods or services, 15.8.1
Distance marketing
credit marketing, 21.10.2
Distress for rent
enforcement, 25.17
Draft credit agreement
pre-contractual information, 21.5.4
**Driver and Vehicle Licensing Agency
(DVLA)**
fraud, 26.3.1
Durable medium
electronic communications, 23.7

E

Early settlement
generally, 10.9
hire agreements, 10.10.5
rebate
calculation, 10.10.2
entitlement, 10.10.1
exclusions from calculation, 10.10.3
statement, 10.10.4
terms of agreement, 8.7.3.2
Electoral registers
use, 27.13.2
Electronic communications
completion, 23.1
distance contracts, 23.3
'durable medium', 23.7
electronic signature
generally, 23.5
introduction, 23.1
entering into regulated agreements
online, 23.1
FCA Handbook, 23.8
online services, 23.6
post-contract information, 23.4
Regulations 2002, 23.2
signature, 23.5
Endowment mortgages
security, 18.2.2
Enforcement
action for damages, 25.24
allocation of business, 25.12
court's additional powers
generally, 25.18
procedure, 25.19
damages, 25.24
death of debtor or hirer, 25.20
default notices
failure to comply with notice
provisions, 25.9
FCA Handbook, 25.3.2
formal notice not required, 25.10
generally, 25.3
statutory controls, 25.3.1
sureties, 25.5
delivery of goods under hire-purchase
agreement, 25.16
distress for rent, 25.17
enforcement orders, 25.13
equitable relief, 25.8
failure to comply with notice
provisions, 25.9
Financial Conduct Authority, by, 25.23
Financial Ombudsman Service
background, 25.22.1
criticisms, 34.4.4
elements, 34.4.2
FCA Handbook, 25.22.2–25.22.3

Enforcement – *contd*
  Financial Ombudsman Service – *contd*
    funding, 34.4.3
    inception, 34.4.1
    introduction, 34.2
    jurisdiction, 25.22.1–25.22.2
    Regulations 2015, and, 25.22.3
    structure, 34.4.1
  financial relief for hirer, 25.15
  formal notice not required, 25.10
  generally, 25.1
  infringement, 25.13
  meaning, 25.1
  mortgages, 25.11
  recovery of possession of goods or
    land, 25.6
  relief from forfeiture, 25.7
  retaking protected goods, 25.7
  sureties, 25.21
  term of the agreement, of, 25.2
  termination notices
    failure to comply with notice
      provisions, 25.9
    generally, 25.4
    sureties, 25.5
  time orders, 25.14
Entire agreement clause
  terms of agreement, 9.8
Equipment lease
  hire agreements, 5.5
Equity
  funding credit and hire facilities, 28.2.1
Errors and omissions
  notices and statements, 11.9.4
Estimated information
  consumer hire agreements, 8.7.4.3
Estoppel
  agency, 14.1
**EU Directive on Consumer Credit
  2008/48/EC**
  critical reflections, 33.1
  generally, 35.1.2
  impact on UK law, 35.1.3
EU perspective
  applicable law, 35.8.1
  authorisation, 35.4
  Brexit, and, 35.5
  Brussels Convention, 35.8.2
  consumer credit EEA firms, 35.4
  Directive
    generally, 35.1.2
    impact on UK law, 35.1.3
  EUropean Passport, 35.3
  generally, 35.1.1
  injunctions, 35.7
  jurisdiction, 35.8.2
  Mortgages Directive, 35.2

EU perspective – *contd*
  Rome Convention, 35.8.1
  unfair contract terms, 35.6
Excluded agreements
  discretion of FCA, 6.5.5
  financing payments connected with
    death, 6.5.4
  introduction, 6.5
  non-commercial agreements, 6.5.1
  overdraft facilities, 6.5.2
  small DCS agreements for restricted-use
    credit, 6.5.3
Exempt agreements
  consumer hire agreements, and
    introduction, 6.4
    nature of agreement, as to, 6.4.2
    nature of hirer, as to, 6.4.4
    other exclusions, 6.4.5
    supply of essential services, as to,
      6.4.3
    types, 6.4.1
  credit unions, and, 21.2.2
  distinction from regulated agreement, 6.1
  generally, 6.2
  introduction, 2.7
  meaning, 6.2
  miscellaneous, 6.3.8
  Mortgages Directive, and, 6.3.7
  nature of the agreement, as to, 6.3.1
  nature of the borrower, as to, 6.3.6–6.3.6.1
  nature of the lender, as to, 6.3.3
  number of repayments to be made, as
    to, 6.3.4–6.3.4.1
  overview, 4.1
  Part V of CCA 1974, from
    discretion of FCA, 6.5.5
    financing payments connected with
      death, 6.5.4
    introduction, 6.5
    non-commercial agreements, 6.5.1
    overdraft facilities, 6.5.2
    small credit agreements, 6.5.3
  purchase of land for non-residential
    purposes, as to, 6.3.2
  total charge for credit, as to, 6.3.5–6.3.5.1
  types, 6.3
**Express terms deemed included in the
  agreement**
  contracts to supply digital content,
    9.3.2.2
  contracts to supply goods, 9.3.2.1
  contracts to supply services, 9.3.2.2
  remedies for breach, 9.3.2.4
  under other Acts, 9.3.2.3
Extended warranties
  supply of goods and services on
    credit, 15.3

F

Fees
credit brokers, 13.8
Fiduciary relationships
agency, 14.1
credit brokers, 13.9
Finance and Leasing Association
credit marketing, 21.2.1
fraud, 26.3.1
Finance lease
hire agreements, 5.4.1
Financial accommodation
meaning, 3.1
Financial communications
credit brokers, 13.4
Financial Conduct Authority (FCA)
alternative dispute resolution
complaint handling, 34.3.1
'Complaints Thematic Review',
34.3.3
'Implementing the ADR
Directive', 34.3.5
'Improving Complaints
Handling', 34.3.4
supervisory role, 34.3.2
supervisory tools, 34.3.6
authorisation
application procedure, 30.7–30.7.2
applications, 30.4–30.4.2
appointed representatives, 30.3
approach of FCA, 30.6–30.6.3
'authorised person', 30.2
business plan, 30.7.1
definition, 30.1
'exempt person', 30.2
full permission activities, 30.6.3
general prohibition, 30.2
interim arrangements, 30.4.1
introduction, 30.1
limited permission activities, 30.6.2
limited permission credit firms, 30.6.1
'person', 30.2
principals, 30.3
'regulated activity', 30.2
regulatory business plan, 30.7.1
responsibilities of a principal, 30.3.1
responsibilities of an appointed
representatives, 30.3.2
threshold conditions, 30.5
transitional arrangements, 30.4.1
authorised persons
Code of Practice (APER), 31.5.2
controlled functions, 31.3
definition, 30.1
fitness of candidate, 31.4
introduction, 31.1
propriety of candidate, 31.4

Financial Conduct Authority (FCA) –
contd
authorised persons – *contd*
Senior Managers and Certification
regime, 31.6
Statements of Principle, 31.5–31.5.1
statutory framework, 31.2
enforcement powers, 25.23
generally, 30.1
permission
applications, 30.4–30.4.2
definition, 30.1
introduction, 30.1
transitional arrangements, 30.4.1
purpose, 30.1
regulatory reporting
annual financial crime report, 33.10.5
complaints reporting, 33.10.6
general provisions, 33.10.1
generally, 33.9
integrated, 33.10.3
product sales data reporting, 33.10.4
requirements, 33.10
'skilled person', 33.8
verification of standing data, 33.10.2
supervision
approach of FCA, 33.4
conduct classification, 33.5
fixed portfolio, 33.5
flexible portfolio firms, 33.5
introduction, 33.1
issues, 33.6
Manual (SUP), 33.3
proactive, 33.6
products, 33.6
reactive, 33.6
statutory framework, 33.2
three pillar model, 33.6
tools, 33.7
transfer of functions from OFT/FSA, 1.4
Financial crime
regulatory reporting, 33.10.5
Financial Fraud Action UK
generally, 26.3.1
Financial Ombudsman Service (FOS)
background, 25.22.1
criticisms, 34.4.4
elements, 34.4.2
FCA Handbook
dispute resolution: complaints, 25.22.4
jurisdiction, 25.22.2
funding, 34.4.3
inception, 34.4.1
introduction, 34.2
jurisdiction
FCA Handbook, 25.22.2
generally, 25.22.1

Financial Ombudsman Service (FOS) –
contd
Regulations 2015, and, 25.22.3
structure, 34.4.1
Financial particulars
consumer credit agreements, and, 8.7.3.2
consumer hire agreements, and, 8.7.4.3
Financial promotion
And see **Advertising**
breach of provisions, 20.7
credit brokers, 13.4
definition, 20.6.2
prescribed content, 20.6.5
regulatory context, 20.5
Financial services
credit brokers, 13.10
distance contracts, 15.8.2
extended warranties, 15.3
Financing credit and hire facilities
borrowing, 28.2.3
cash settlements, 28.2.6.3
deposits, 28.2.2
equity, 28.2.1
government funding, 28.2.6.4
leasing companies, and, 28.2.4
introduction, 28.1
methods, 28.2–29.2.6
refinancing, 28.2.6
securitisation, 28.2.6.1
stock-in-trade, 28.2.5
student loans, 28.2.6.4
swaps, 28.2.6.2
Financing payments connected with death
excluded agreements, 6.5.4
Fixed portfolio
supervision, 33.5
Fixed-sum credit
features, 4.2.3
generally, 4.2.1
relevance of distinction from running-
account credit, 4.2.4
Fixed-sum credit agreements
generally, 4.2.4
relevance of distinction from running-
account credit, 4.2.4
Fixed-sum loan agreements
characteristics, 4.7.3.2
introduction, 4.2.4
meaning, 4.7.3.1
overview, 4.7.1
'Flawed asset' clause
security, and, 18.2.8
Flexible portfolio firms
supervision, 33.5
Form and content of agreements
background, 8.1
Consumer Credit Sourcebook, 8.1.1

Form and content of agreements – *contd*
elements, 8.3.2
FCA Handbook, 8.1.1
generally, 8.3.1
legible, 8.3.2
legislation, 8.1.2
prescribed form, 8.3.2
prescribed terms, 8.3.2
signature, 8.3.2
Fraud
CIFAS, and, 26.3.1
criminal offences, 26.2.2
DVLA, and, 26.3.1
extent of problem, 26.1
Finance and Leasing Association,
and, 26.3.1
Financial Fraud Action UK, and, 26.3.1
HPI Ltd, and, 26.3.1
introduction, 26.1
Joint Fraud Taskforce, and, 26.3.1
mortgage frauds, 26.3.1
prevention
introduction, 26.3
organisations involved, 26.3.1
procedures, 26.3.2
techniques, 26.3.3
proceeds of crime, 26.2.2
statutory provisions, 26.2
Fraud protection cover
supply of goods and services on credit,
and, 15.3
Freedom of information
data protection, and, 27.10
FRS 102
accounting, and, 29.1
Funding credit and hire facilities
borrowing, 28.2.3
cash settlements, 28.2.6.3
deposits, 28.2.2
equity, 28.2.1
government funding, 28.2.6.4
leasing companies, and, 28.2.4
introduction, 28.1
methods, 28.2–29.2.6
refinancing, 28.2.6
securitisation, 28.2.6.1
stock-in-trade, 28.2.5
student loans, 28.2.6.4
swaps, 28.2.6.2
Funding lease
generally, 29.5

G
GAP insurance
supply of goods and services on
credit, 15.4

Goods mortgages
concluding reflections, 36.5
discrete consumer credit agreements,
22.3
generally, 18.2.5.2
Goods or services
And see **Supply of goods or services on
credit**
distance contracts, 15.8.1
Group licences
credit brokers, 13.1
Guaranteed asset protection
supply of goods and services on
credit, 15.4
Guarantees
linked transactions, 12.4
security, 18.2.1

H

High-cost short-term credit agreements
cost caps, 22.1.2
generally, 22.1.1
Hire
meaning, 3.8
Hire agreements
And see **Consumer hire agreements**
contracts for the hire of goods, 5.3
exempt agreements, and
introduction, 6.4
nature of agreement, as to, 6.4.2
nature of hirer, as to, 6.4.4
other exclusions, 6.4.5
supply of essential services, as to,
6.4.3
types, 6.4.1
form and content, 2.3.4
meaning, 5.1
overview, 3.9
specific agreements
business finance lease, 5.4.5
contract hire, 5.4.3
credit hire, 5.4.8
finance lease, 5.4.1
introduction, 5.4
lease upgrade, 5.4.7
master lease, 5.4.4
operating lease, 5.4.2
software lease, 5.4.6
types, 5.2
Hire-purchase agreements
characteristics, 4.7.2.3
features, 4.7.2.2
fixed-sum credit, and, 4.2.3
meaning, 4.7.2.1
overview, 4.7.1
Hirer
meaning, 3.7

Hirer's rights
appropriation of payments, 10.12
contracting out, 10.14
copies of agreement and documents, 10.4
creditworthiness assessment, 10.2
disclosure, 10.3
pre-contractual disclosure, 10.1
provision of information, 10.8
time orders, 10.13
Holding out
agency, and, 14.3
Home credit loan agreements
post-contract information, and, 11.10.3
Home purchase plans
regulated mortgage contracts,
and, 18.2.3.1
Home reversion plans
regulated mortgage contracts,
and, 18.2.3.1
Housing associations
generally, 21.2.6

I

Illustrations
credit marketing, 21.5.2
'Implied' terms
contracts to supply digital content, 9.3.2.2
contracts to supply goods, 9.3.2.1
contracts to supply services, 9.3.2.2
remedies for breach, 9.3.2.4
under other Acts, 9.3.2.3
Indemnities
security, 18.2.1
Independent legal advice
security, 18.3
Individual
meaning, 3.2, 4.1
Information on credit status
credit marketing, 21.5.1
Information sheets
arrears notices, 11.8
default notices, 11.8
Information society services
ancillary credit business, 16.6
Injunctions
EU perspective, 35.7
Insolvency practitioners
ancillary credit business, 16.6
Instalment sale agreements
characteristics, 4.7.2.3
features, 4.7.2.2
meaning, 4.7.2.1
Insurance
linked transactions, and, 12.4
supply of goods and services on credit,
and
card protection cover, 15.6

Insurance – *contd*
supply of goods and services on credit,
and – *contd*
extended warranties, 15.3
generally, 15.4
payment protection, 15.5
Interchange fees
credit card transactions, 17.1
'Interest free'
advertising, and, 20.6.6
Interest on default
terms of agreement, and, 9.4.1
Interest on judgment debts, notice of
'agreement to aggregate', 11.9.1
charges, 11.9.3
dispensing with, 11.9.6
errors and omissions, 11.9.4
formalities, 11.9.2
generally, 11.7
joint debtors and hirers, 11.9.5
Interest-only mortgages
security, 18.2.2
Irresponsible lending
generally, 21.3.1

J

Jurisdiction
generally, 35.8.2

L

Land mortgages
Mortgage Credit Directive, 4.8.1
outside the scope of the Directive, 4.8.3
regulated mortgage contracts, 4.8.2
residential renovation agreements, 4.8.5
security, and, 18.2.2
types of mortgage, 4.8.4
Lease
meaning, 3.8
Lease upgrade
hire agreements, and, 5.4.7
Leasing companies
funding credit and hire facilities,
and, 28.2.4
Legal profession
ancillary credit business, 16.6
Lender
meaning, 3.3
Lending Code
credit cards, 17.4.5
generally, 21.9
Lending institutions
credit marketing, 21.2.1
Lessee
meaning, 3.7
Lessor
meaning, 3.6

Licensing
See **Authorisation**
Liens
security, and, 18.2.11
Linked transactions
cancellable agreements, and
exempt transactions, 12.4
legal aspects, 12.3
debtor-creditor-supplier agreements,
and, 12.1
discharge of credit agreement, and, 12.3
distinction from other connected
agreements, 12.6
duplication of treatment, 12.2
exemptions, 12.4
guarantees, and, 12.4
insurance contracts, and
generally, 12.4
supply of goods and services on
credit, 15.4
legal aspects, 12.3
meaning, 12.1
operation of account, and, 12.4
restricted-use credit agreement, and, 12.1
security, and, 12.1
unfair relationships, and, 12.5
withdrawal from credit agreement,
and, 12.3
Loans secured by land mortgages
Mortgage Credit Directive, 4.8.1
outside the scope of the Directive, 4.8.3
regulated mortgage contracts, 4.8.2
residential renovation agreements, 4.8.5
types of mortgage, 4.8.4
Local authorities
ancillary credit business, 16.6
Long funding lease
generally, 29.5
Loss
credit cards, and, 17.3
Loyalty cards
And see **Credit cards**
generally, 17.5.7

M

Maintenance services
supply of goods and services on credit,
and, 15.7
Master lease
hire agreements, and, 5.4.4
Mechanical breakdown insurance
supply of goods and services on credit,
and, 15.3
Minors
credit marketing, and, 21.7
Misleading actions and omissions
unfair commercial practices, and, 20.8.3

Misuse
credit cards, and, 17.3
Modifying agreements
assignment, 7.7
consumer credit agreements, and
prescribed information, 8.7.5.2
prescribed terms, 8.7.5.1
consumer hire agreements, and
prescribed information, 8.7.5.3
prescribed terms, 8.7.5.1
generally, 7.3
novation, 7.5
practice, in, 7.4
variation, 7.6
Money laundering
generally, 26.4
Mortgage Credit Directive Order 2015
And see **Mortgages Directive**
consumer buy-to-let mortgages, 2.6
form and content of agreements within
the scope, 2.1.4
generally, 2.1.2
introduction, 1.1
residential renovation agreements, 2.5,
4.8.5
Mortgage fraud
generally, 26.3.1
Mortgages
And see **Regulated mortgage contracts**
concluding reflections, 36.5
credit brokers, and
generally, 13.10
introduction, 13.1
definition, 2.1.1
Directive, 35.2
enforcement, and, 25.11
goods mortgages, and, 18.2.5.2
land mortgages
generally, 4.8.1
outside the scope, 4.8.3
regulated mortgage contracts, 4.8.2
residential renovation agreements,
4.8.5
types, 4.8.4
outside the scope of the Directive,
4.8.3
regulated mortgage contracts, 4.8.2
residential renovation agreements,
4.8.5
security, and, 18.2.2
types, 4.8.4
**Mortgages and Home Finance: Conduct
of Business sourcebook (MCOB)**
advertising, 20.6.1
application, 2.1.3
responsible lending, 21.3.3
total charge for credit, 19.4

Mortgages Directive 2014/17/EU
application, 2.1.1
'consumer', 2.1.1
'credit agreement', 2.1.1
excluded mortgage contracts, 2.1.1
generally, 35.2
implementation in UK
generally, 2.1.2
introduction, 1.1
land mortgages, 4.8.1
overview, 1.1
'regulated mortgage contract', 2.1.1
scope, 2.1.1
Multiple agreements
generally, 7.1
practice, in, 7.2

N
Negative pledge clause
security, and, 18.2.8
Negotiable instruments
security, and, 18.2.13
'No deposit'
advertising, and, 20.6.6
Non-commercial agreements
excluded agreements, and, 6.5.1
Non-commercial hire agreements
generally, 5.2
Notice of default sums
'agreement to aggregate', 11.9.1
charges, 11.9.3
dispensing with, 11.9.6
errors and omissions, 11.9.4
formalities, 11.9.2
generally, 11.6
joint debtors and hirers, 11.9.5
Notice of interest on judgment debts
'agreement to aggregate', 11.9.1
charges, 11.9.3
dispensing with, 11.9.6
errors and omissions, 11.9.4
formalities, 11.9.2
generally, 11.7
joint debtors and hirers, 11.9.5
Notice of sums in arrears
'agreement to aggregate', 11.9.1
charges, 11.9.3
dispensing with, 11.9.6
errors and omissions, 11.9.4
formalities, 11.9.2
generally, 11.4
joint debtors and hirers, 11.9.5
Notices
agency, and, 14.4.4
Novation
generally, 7.5

O

Online communications
completion, 23.1
distance contracts, 23.3
'durable medium', 23.7
electronic signature
generally, 23.5
introduction, 23.1
entering into regulated agreements
online, 23.1
FCA Handbook, 23.8
online services, 23.6
post-contract information, 23.4
Regulations 2002, 23.2
signature, 23.5
Operating lease
hire agreements, and, 5.4.2
Operation of account
linked transactions, and, 12.4
Option account agreements
common characteristics, 4.7.4.8
general characteristics, 4.7.4.5
generally, 4.7.4.4
Option account cards
And see **Credit cards**
generally, 17.5.3
Outsourcing
generally, 28.3
Overdraft facilities
advertising, 20.6.6
characteristics, 4.7.4.8
discrete consumer credit agreements
background, 22.5.1
FCA Handbook, 22.5.3
regulatory provisions, 22.5.4
statutory provisions, 22.5.2
excluded agreements, 6.5.2
FCA Handbook
entry into current account, 22.5.3.1
significant overdrawing without prior
arrangement, 22.5.3.2
generally, 4.7.4.2
information requirements
entry into current account, 22.5.3.1
significant overdrawing without prior
arrangement, 22.5.3.2
pawn receipts, 4.7.1
running-account credit, 4.2.1
Owner
meaning, 3.6

P

Partly regulated agreements
generally, 6.6
Passporting
generally, 35.3

Pawn
security, and, 18.2.12
Payday loans
high-cost short-term credit
agreements, 22.1.1–22.1.2
Payment protection insurance (PPI)
generally, 15.5
Payments connected with death
excluded agreements, 6.5.4
Peer-to-peer (P2P) agreements
definition, 22.2.1
FCA Handbook, 22.2.3
operating electronic system as to
lending, 22.2.2
Peer-to-peer (P2P) lending platforms
credit marketing, 21.2.3
Permission
And see **Authorisation**
applications, 30.4–30.4.2
definition, 30.1
introduction, 30.1
transitional arrangements, 30.4.1
Personal loan agreements
fixed-sum loan agreements, 4.7.3.1
Plain English Campaign
credit marketing, 21.11
Pledge
security, 18.2.9
Post-contractual business practices
generally, 11.11
Post-contractual information
'agreement to aggregate', 11.9.1
annual statements
fixed-sum credit agreements, 11.2
running-account credit
agreements, 11.3
background, 11.1
charges, 11.9.3
default notices, 11.5
dispensing with notice, 11.9.6
errors and omissions, 11.9.4
formalities, 11.9.2
home credit loan agreements, 11.10.3
information sheets, 11.8
joint debtors and hirers, 11.9.5
miscellaneous requirements
'agreement to aggregate', 11.9.1
charges, 11.9.3
dispensing with notice, 11.9.6
errors and omissions, 11.9.4
formalities, 11.9.2
joint debtors and hirers, 11.9.5
notice of default sums, 11.6
notice of interest on judgment debts,
11.7
notice of sums in arrears, 11.4
requirements, 11.1

Post-contractual information – *contd*
statements of account
fixed-sum credit agreements, 11.2
running-account credit
agreements, 11.3
store cards agreements, 11.10.1
PPI
generally, 15.5
Pre-contractual disclosure
adequate explanations, and, 8.5, 10.1
Agreements Regulations 1983, 8.4.3
Agreements Regulations 2010, 8.4.1
Disclosure Regulations 2004, 8.4.4
Disclosure Regulations 2010, 8.4.2
introduction, 8.4
overview, 8.7.1
summary of requirements, 8.4.5
Pre-contractual information
copy of draft credit agreement,
21.5.4
credit reference agency
information, 21.5.1
disclosure of contractual
information, 21.5.3
generally, 8.7.1
illustrations, 21.5.2
quotations, 21.5.2
Pre-existing agreements
meaning, 4.4.2
Pre-paid cards
generally, 17.6.1
Prescribed information
consumer credit agreements, 8.7.3.2
consumer hire agreements, 8.7.4.2
Prescribed terms
consumer credit agreements
allocation of payments, 8.7.3.2
cancellation rights, 8.7.3.2
charges, 8.7.3.2
early settlement, 8.7.3.2
financial particulars, 8.7.3.2
generally, 8.7.3.1
introduction, 8.7.2
prescribed information, 8.7.3.2
repayment amounts, 8.7.3.2
statutory warnings, 8.7.3.2
total charge for credit, 8.7.3.2
consumer hire agreements
cancellation rights, 8.7.4.3
estimated information, 8.7.4.3
financial particulars, 8.7.4.3
generally, 8.7.4.1
introduction, 8.7.2
other payments, 8.7.4.3
prescribed information, 8.7.4.2
statutory warnings, 8.7.4.3
introduction, 8.7.2

Principles for Businesses (PRIN)
Treating Customers Fairly, and, 32.3
Proceeds of crime
fraud, 26.2.2
Product sales data
regulatory reporting, 33.10.4
Property insurance
supply of goods and services on
credit, 15.4
Protected goods
debtor's rights, and, 10.11
Provision of credit references
credit information services, 16.3
exclusions, 16.6
generally, 16.4
Provision of information
debtor's and hirer's rights, and, 10.8
'Purpose of the loan test'
generally, 3.2

Q

Quotations
credit marketing, 21.5.2

R

Rebate on early settlement
calculation, 10.10.2
entitlement, 10.10.1
exclusions from calculation, 10.10.3
hire agreements, and, 10.10.5
statement, 10.10.4
Recovery of possession of goods or land
enforcement, 25.6
Regulated credit agreements
And see **Consumer credit agreements**
meaning, 3.5, 5.1
overview, 4.1
Regulated hire agreements
See **Contracts for the hire of goods**
Regulated mortgage contracts
Conduct of Business
Sourcebook, 18.2.3.3
credit brokers, and
generally, 13.10
introduction, 13.1
excluded contracts, 18.2.3.2
generally, 18.2.3.1
individual, 18.2.3.1
meaning, 4.8.2
'related person', 18.2.3.1
Regulated sale and rent back agreement
Conduct of Business
Sourcebook, 18.2.3.3
generally, 18.2.3.1
Regulatory reporting
annual financial crime report, 33.10.5

Regulatory reporting – *contd*
complaints reporting, 33.10.6
general provisions, 33.10.1
generally, 33.9
integrated, 33.10.3
product sales data reporting, 33.10.4
requirements, 33.10
'skilled person', 33.8
verification of standing data, 33.10.2
Relief from forfeiture
enforcement, and, 25.7
Remuneration
credit brokers, and, 13.8
Repayment amounts
consumer credit agreements, 8.7.3.2
Repayment mortgages
security, and, 18.2.2
Representations
cancellable agreements, 4.5
Residential renovation agreements
discrete agreements, 22.6
generally, 4.8.5
introduction, 2.5
Responsible lending
creditworthiness assessment, 21.3.2
MCOB, 21.3.3
pre-contractual requirements, 21.3.1
Restricted-use credit
generally, 4.3
linked transactions, 12.1
Restrictive covenants
dealer agreements, 15.2
Retaking protected goods
enforcement, 25.7
Revolving account credit agreements
budget accounts, 4.7.4.3
characteristics, 4.7.4.8
charge card agreements, 4.7.4.6
credit-token agreements, 4.7.4.7
generally, 4.7.4.1
option accounts, 4.7.4.4
overdraft facilities, 4.7.4.2
Rome Convention
applicable law, 35.8.1
Running-account credit
features, 4.2.2
generally, 4.2.1
relevance of distinction from fixed-sum
credit, 4.2.4
Running-account credit agreements
budget accounts, 4.7.4.3
characteristics, 4.7.4.8
charge card agreements, 4.7.4.6
credit-token agreements, 4.7.4.7
generally, 4.7.4.1
option accounts, 4.7.4.4
overdraft facilities, 4.7.4.2

Running-account credit agreements –
contd
relevance of distinction from fixed-sum
credit, 4.2.4

S
Sale and leaseback transactions
buyer/lessor, by, 29.2.2
seller/lessee, by, 29.2.1
Sale and rent back agreement
Conduct of Business
Sourcebook, 18.2.3.3
generally, 18.2.3.1
Section 75 CCA 1974 liability
generally, 17.4.4
introduction, 17.2
supply of goods and services on credit,
and, 15.1
Securitisation
funding credit and hire facilities,
and, 28.2.6.1
Security
assignment, 18.2.10
bills of sale
current law, 18.2.5.1
proposed changes, 18.2.5.2
charge, 18.2.4
charge over credit balance, 18.2.7
contractual lien, 18.2.11
contractual set-off, 18.2.6
'flawed asset' clause, 18.2.8
form and content
assignment, 18.2.10
bill of sale, 18.2.5.1
charge, 18.2.4
charge over credit balance, 18.2.7
contractual lien, 18.2.11
contractual set-off, 18.2.6
'flawed asset' clause, 18.2.8
goods mortgages, 18.2.5.2
guarantee and indemnity, 18.2.1
home purchase plan, 18.2.3.1, 18.2.3.3
home reversion plan, 18.2.3.1, 18.2.3.3
introduction, 18.2
land mortgage, 18.2.2
mortgage, 18.2.2
negative pledge clause, 18.2.8
negotiable instruments, 18.2.13
pawn, 18.2.12
pledge, 18.2.9
regulated mortgage contract, 18.2.3.1–
18.2.3.3
regulated sale and rent back
contract, 18.2.3.1, 18.2.3.3
rights of surety during life of
security, 18.2.14
general observations, 18.5

Security – *contd*
 goods mortgages, 18.2.5.2
 guarantee, 18.2.1
 home purchase plan
  Conduct of Business
   Sourcebook, 18.2.3.3
  generally, 18.2.3.1
 home reversion plan
  Conduct of Business
   Sourcebook, 18.2.3.3
  generally, 18.2.3.1
 indemnity, 18.2.1
 independent legal advice, 18.3
 land mortgage, 18.2.2
 linked transactions, and, 12.1
 mortgage, 18.2.2
 negative pledge clause, 18.2.8
 negotiable instruments, 18.2.13
 pawn, 18.2.12
 pledge, 18.2.9
 procedural precautions, 18.3
 regulated mortgage contract
  Conduct of Business
   Sourcebook, 18.2.3.3
  excluded contracts, 18.2.3.2
  generally, 18.2.3.1
  individual, 18.2.3.1
  'related person', 18.2.3.1
 regulated sale and rent back contract
  Conduct of Business
   Sourcebook, 18.2.3.3
  generally, 18.2.3.1
 surety's right during life of
  security, 18.2.14
 types, 18.1
 unfair relationships, and, 18.4
Set-off
 security, and, 18.2.6
 terms of agreement, and, 9.6
Short-term credit agreements
 cost caps, 22.1.2
 generally, 22.1.1
Signature of agreements
 generally, 8.6.1
 introduction, 8.3.2
Skilled person
 regulatory reporting, 33.8
Small credit agreements
 excluded agreements, and, 6.5.3
Small hire agreements
 generally, 5.2
Software lease
 hire agreements, and, 5.4.6
Statements of account
 'agreement to aggregate', 11.9.1
 charges, 11.9.3
 dispensing with, 11.9.6

Statements of account – *contd*
 errors and omissions, 11.9.4
 fixed-sum credit agreements, 11.2
 formalities, 11.9.2
 joint debtors and hirers, 11.9.5
 running-account credit agreements, 11.3
Statutory warnings
 consumer credit agreements, 8.7.3.2
 consumer hire agreements, 8.7.4.3
Stock-in-trade
 funding credit and hire facilities, 28.2.5
Store card agreements
 post-contract information, 11.10.1
Store cards
 And see **Credit cards**
 generally, 17.5.2
Student loans
 discrete consumer credit agreements, 22.4
 funding credit and hire facilities, 28.2.6.4
 generally, 21.2.5
Sums in arrears, notice of
 'agreement to aggregate', 11.9.1
 charges, 11.9.3
 dispensing with, 11.9.6
 errors and omissions, 11.9.4
 formalities, 11.9.2
 generally, 11.4
 joint debtors and hirers, 11.9.5
Supervision
 approach of FCA, 33.4
 conduct classification, 33.5
 fixed portfolio, 33.5
 flexible portfolio firms, 33.5
 introduction, 33.1
 issues, 33.6
 Manual (SUP), 33.3
 proactive, 33.6
 products, 33.6
 reactive, 33.6
 statutory framework, 33.2
 three pillar model, 33.6
 tools, 33.7
 Treating Customers Fairly, and, 32.3
Supplier
 definition, 15.1
Supply of goods or services on credit
 card protection cover, 15.6
 creditor liability, 15.1
 'dealer', 15.1
 dealer agreements, 15.2
 distance contracts
  financial services, 15.8.2
  goods or services, 15.8.1
 extended warranties, 15.3
 generally, 15.1
 insurance, 15.4
 maintenance services, 15.7

Supply of goods or services on credit –
contd
payment protection insurance, 15.5
s 75 CCA 1974 liability, 15.1
'supplier', 15.1
third party rights, and, 15.1
timeshare agreements, 15.9
warranties, 15.3
Sureties
enforcement, and, 25.21
Swaps
funding credit and hire facilities,
and, 28.2.6.2

T

Taxation
capital allowances, 29.4
dealer lessor, by, 29.1.3
'funding lease', 29.5
generally, 29.1
leasing, 29.3
lessee, by, 29.1.1
lessor, by, 29.1.2
'long funding lease', 29.5
manufacturer, by, 29.1.3
sale and leaseback transactions, and
buyer/lessor, by, 29.2.2
seller/lessee, by, 29.2.1
value added tax
bad debt relief, 29.6.7
charges by credit card companies to
retailers, 29.6.2
credit brokerage, 29.6.4
equipment leasing, 29.6.5
instalment credit finance, 29.6.3
intermediary services, 29.6.4
loans, 29.6.1
taxable services, 29.6.6
Termination
customer's rights, 4.7.2.3
Termination notices
failure to comply with notice
provisions, 25.9
generally, 25.4
sureties, and, 25.5
Terms deemed included in the agreement
contracts to supply digital content, 9.3.2.2
contracts to supply goods, 9.3.2.1
contracts to supply services, 9.3.2.2
remedies for breach, 9.3.2.4
under other Acts, 9.3.2.3
Terms of agreements
consumer credit agreements
allocation of payments, 8.7.3.2
cancellation rights, 8.7.3.2
charges, 8.7.3.2
early settlement, 8.7.3.2

Terms of agreements – *contd*
consumer credit agreements – *contd*
financial particulars, 8.7.3.2
general, 8.7.3.1
introduction, 8.7.2
prescribed information, 8.7.3.2
prescribed terms, 8.7.3.1
repayment amounts, 8.7.3.2
statutory warnings, 8.7.3.2
consumer hire agreements
cancellation rights, 8.7.4.3
estimated information, 8.7.4.3
financial particulars, 8.7.4.3
general, 8.7.4.1
introduction, 8.7.2
other payments, 8.7.4.3
prescribed information, 8.7.4.2
prescribed terms, 8.7.4.1
statutory warnings, 8.7.4.3
introduction, 8.7.2
Theft
credit cards, and, 17.3
Third party rights
agency, and, 14.2
supply of goods and services on credit,
and, 15.1
Time of performance
terms of agreement, and, 9.3.1
Time orders
debtor's rights, and, 10.13
generally, 25.14
Timeshare agreements
supply of goods and services on credit,
and, 15.9
Total charge for credit
APR
calculation, 19.3.1
historical perspective, 19.2
overview, 19.1
reflections, 19.5
Regulations, 19.3.1–19.3.2
statement, 19.3.2
assumptions for calculation
agreements not secured on land,
19.3.6
agreements secured on land, 19.3.5
calculation, 19.3.1
charges included, 19.3.3
charges not included, 19.3.4
CONC rules, 19.2
credit cards, and, 17.4.3
credit unions, and, 21.2.2
EU Directive, and, 19.2
evolution of regulations, 19.2
MCOB, 19.4
prescribed terms, and, 8.7.3.2
Regulations, 19.2

Total charge for credit – *contd*
  relevance, 19.1
  statement of the APR, 19.3.2
Tournier principle
  confidentiality, 27.13.1
Treating Customers Fairly (TCF)
  approach of FCA, 32.2
  background, 32.1
  conclusion, 32.7
  'culture', 32.5
  current consumer credit market, 32.3
  fair treatment of customers, 32.4
  introduction, 32.1
  management behaviour, 32.5
  management information, 32.6
  objectives of FCA, 32.3
  Principles for Businesses (PRIN), 32.4
  supervision of authorised persons,
    and, 32.3

U
Unauthorised business
  credit broking, 13.7
Unfair contract terms
  consumer contracts, 9.3.3.3
  Consumer Rights Act 2015
    consumer contracts, 9.3.3.3
    generally, 9.3.3.1
    non-consumer contracts, 9.3.3.3
  EU perspective, 35.6
  good faith, 9.3.3.4
  non-consumer contracts, 9.3.3.3
  UCTA 1977, 9.3.3.2
  unfair relationships, 9.3.3.5
  unfairness, 9.3.3.4
Unfair relationships
  agency, and, 14.4.3
  ancillary credit business, 16.8
  application of provisions, 24.2.2
  burden of proof, 24.3
  contract terms, 9.3.3.5
  credit brokers, and, 13.5
  generally, 24.1
  illustrative cases
    generally, 24.2.2
    Plevinv Paragon Personal
      Finance, 24.2.1
  interpretation of provisions, 24.2.2
  linked transactions, 12.5
  reflection on the provisions, 24.4
  security, and, 18.4
  statutory provisions, 24.1

Unfair Trading Regulations 2008
  aggressive practices, 20.8.3
  'average consumer', 20.8.1
  credit marketing, and, 21.12
  defences, 20.8.3
  general concepts, 20.8.1
  introduction, 20.2
  misleading action, 20.8.3
  misleading omission, 20.8.3
  offences, 20.8.3
  'product', 20.8.1
  specific practices, 20.8.3
  unfair commercial practices, 20.8.2–
    20.8.3
Unrestricted-use credit
  generally, 4.3
Unsolicited credit-tokens
  credit marketing, 21.8
  generally, 17.4.1

V
Value added tax
  bad debt relief, 29.6.7
  charges by credit card companies to
    retailers, 29.6.2
  credit brokerage, 29.6.4
  equipment leasing, 29.6.5
  instalment credit finance, 29.6.3
  intermediary services, 29.6.4
  loans, 29.6.1
  taxable services, 29.6.6
Variation clauses
  terms of agreement
    generally, 9.5.1
    restrictions in FCA Handbook,
      9.5.2
Variation of agreements
  generally, 7.6
  terms of agreement, 9.5
Verification of standing data
  regulatory reporting, 33.10.2

W
Warranties
  dealer agreements, 15.2
  supply of goods and services on
    credit, 15.3
Withdrawal
  debtor's rights
    under s 58, 10.7
    under s 66A, 10.5
  linked transactions, 12.3